STUDIES IN THE ENGLISH RENAISSANCE

John T. Shawcross, General Editor

Allegorical Poetics
& the Epic

THE
RENAISSANCE
TRADITION
TO
Paradise Lost

MINDELE ANNE TREIP

THE UNIVERSITY PRESS OF KENTUCKY

Copyright © 1994 by The University Press of Kentucky

Scholarly publisher for the Commonwealth,
serving Bellarmine College, Berea College, Centre
College of Kentucky, Eastern Kentucky University,
The Filson Club, Georgetown College, Kentucky
Historical Society, Kentucky State University,
Morehead State University, Murray State University,
Northern Kentucky University, Transylvania University,
University of Kentucky, University of Louisville,
and Western Kentucky University.

Editorial and Sales Offices: Lexington, Kentucky 40508-4008

Library of Congress Cataloging-in-Publication Data

Treip, Mindele Anne.
    Allegorical poetics and the epic : the Renaissance tradition to
Paradise Lost / Mindele Anne Treip.
        p.   cm.
    Includes bibliographical references and index.
    ISBN 0-8131-1831-X (alk. paper)
    1. Milton, John, 1608–1674. Paradise Lost. 2. English poetry—
Early modern, 1500–1700—History and criticism—Theory, etc.
3. European poetry—Renaissance, 1450–1600—History and criticism—
Theory, etc. 4. Christian poetry, English—History and criticism—
Theory, etc. 5. Epic poetry, English—History and criticism—
Theory, etc. 6. Epic poetry—History and criticism—Theory, etc.
7. Tasso, Torquato, 1544–1595—Influence. 8. Influence (Literary,
artistic, etc.) 9. English poetry—European influences. 10. Bible
in literature. 11. Allegory. I. Title.
PR3562.T73   1993
821'.03209—dc20   92-37472

This book is printed on recycled acid-free paper meeting
the requirements of the American National Standard
for Permanence of Paper for Printed Library Materials.

○

For my husband
and
to the memory of my parents

Contents

PREFACE xi

ACKNOWLEDGEMENTS xvii

PART I. THEORY OF ALLEGORY IN POETRY AND EPIC FROM ANTIQUITY TO THE RENAISSANCE

1. Antiquity to the Middle Ages   3
Late Classical Interpreters and Their Successors   3
Rabbinical Interpretation   7
The Church Fathers and Medieval Allegory   8
The Medieval "Levels"   12
Dante   15

2. Renaissance Theoretical Developments   18
Coluccio Salutati   19
The English Rhetoricians   23

3. The English Mythographers and Their Tradition   28
Bacon   29
Comes and the "Levels"   33
John Harington and His Successors   36

4. "Idea"   42
Philo   43
Boccaccio   44
Sidney   45
Tasso   47

Part II. Theory of the Allegorical Epic from Tasso, Spenser and the Neoclassicals to Milton

5. Tasso: The Practical Problems of the Allegorical Epic   53

"Metafora Continuata"   53
Moral Content: Tasso's "Allegoria"   55
The Resources of "Continued" Allegory   62
The "Lettere Poetiche" and the *Gerusalemme*   65

6. Tasso, the *Discorsi*: Aesthetics of the Allegorical Epic   69

The Mystical Image   70
"Romance" Variety and "Global" Allegory   71
"Truth" and the "Verisimilar"   74

7. Tasso, the Major Tracts: The Poetics of the Allegorical Epic   80

Narrative Unity and Causality in the Mixed Epic   80
The Marvellous-Verisimilar   82
History and Fiction in the Epic   85
History and Allegory: The Late *Giudizio*   88
Tasso: A Retrospect   91

8. Spenser as Allegorical Theorist   95

Spenser and Tasso   96
The "Letter to Raleigh": Schemes of Allegory in *The Faerie Queene*   100

9. Neoclassical Epic Theory: The Debate over Allegory   106

Seventeenth-Century English Theory   106
Addison and Johnson   109
Edward Phillips and John Toland   111
The Late Sixteenth-Century Italian Debates   115

10. Le Bossu on the Epic   119

Allegory as the "Platform" of Truth   121
Unity of Plot via Allegory   124

11. Debts to Renaissance Allegory in *Paradise Lost*   126

Allegorical Matter in *Paradise Lost*   126
The "Levels"   129
Intermittent and Sustained Allegory   131
Allegorical Rhetoric   132
Milton and Spenser   134

12. Allegorical Poetics in *Paradise Lost*   138

Early Indications in Milton's Prose   138
Borrowings from Tasso in *Paradise Lost*   141
Structuring the "Diffuse" Epic: Echoes of Tasso's *Discorsi*   144

13. Allegory and "Idea" in *Paradise Lost*   150

Plot, Subject and "Platform": Justifying God   151
The Problem of the Justice of God   156
"Asserting" Providence   160
"Justifying" through Allegory   162
Allegorical Aesthetics in *Paradise Lost*   165

PART III. "REAL OR ALLEGORIC": REPRESENTATION IN
Paradise Lost

14. Historical Problems in Reading *Paradise Lost*   171

Samuel Johnson   173
Luther and Poetic Fundamentalism   177

15. Scripture and the Figurative Reading of *Paradise Lost*   181

Milton on Allegory   181
Of Christian Doctrine on Interpreting Scripture   182
"Accommodation" in *Of Christian Doctrine*   187

16. Theory of Metaphor in *Paradise Lost*   191

"Accommodation": Raphael's Theory of Discourse   192
Shadows, Similitudes, Dreams: Language as Mediator   200

17. Typology and the Figurative Dimension in *Paradise Lost*   204

"Typological Symbolism" in *Paradise Lost*   205
True "Types" and the Limits of Typological Interpretation   208
Problems in "Typological" Readings of *Paradise Lost*   213
"Typologically" Suggestive Patternings   216
Verbal Echo and Anticipation   219

18. Protestant Homiletics and Allegory in *Paradise Lost*   222

The "Experiential" Approach   222
The Bible, Figuration and *Paradise Lost*: Summary   227

19. "Accommodation" in *Paradise Lost*: The Internal View   231

Milton's Uses of Extra-Canonical Matter   231
Milton's God: Mimesis and Midrash   234

20. Toward an Allegorical Poesis in *Paradise Lost*   239

Realism and Non-Realism: "Probability" to Allegory   239
"Implication" and Simile   243
Emblem and Allegorical Episode   247

21. The "Language of Allegory" and Milton's Allegorical Epic   251

APPENDIX A. Bibliographical Essay on Tasso   257

APPENDIX B. "Idea"   263

APPENDIX C. Tasso and Spenser   267

APPENDIX D. The Literal Level and the "Literal Commentators"   275

APPENDIX E. "Accommodation" and Figuration in *Paradise Lost*   278

APPENDIX F. Typological Criticism   282

NOTES   287

LIST OF WORKS CITED   335

INDEX   350

Preface

This book was originally conceived as a study of the artistic relationship between theme and expressive form in *Paradise Lost*. The perplexing character of so many episodes, scenes, metaphors and other figures in the poem rapidly rendered it impossible to proceed without considering first the implications of allegory in Milton's poem, and the various problems which that concept has raised historically. The difficulties in attempting to deal with such large considerations were in the end productive, even though they deferred the pleasures of engaging in an interpretative study based more extensively on close reading of Milton's poem and less troubled by the problems of theory. Out of the various and often seemingly contradictory views which have been held over the centuries as to the nature of allegory, certain continuities could be seen and certain coherent lines of evolution, and these have themselves become the focus of this study. The present volume thus evolved in the end into a study, of interest in its own right, of the developing traditions in the theory of allegory in poetry and in epic more specifically, up to and including Milton's poem.

However far back we go to study the subject of allegory, similar questions have arisen. To what kind of writing does the term "allegory" most properly apply—to the Bible and religious literature or to didactic secular literature, to literary texts or to criticism of a certain kind (exegesis)? How relevant is the study of allegory within the Bible or of allegorical interpretation of the Bible to the study of literary allegory? Does the understanding of "allegory" within ancient literary texts or the application of allegorical methodologies to the interpretations of ancient literatures correspond in any way to the understanding of allegory in Scripture and its uses in scriptural interpretation? If there is such a correspondence, is that understanding of the same order when applied to both Old and New Testament texts and their interpretation; and how does the act of allegorical interpretation of Scripture relate to intended allegorical figuration within Scripture itself? Further, how does the understanding and application of allegory in all these areas relate to the sophisticated allegorical literature and sophisticated critical allegoresis in medieval and Renaissance times (for our purposes, Italy, France and England)?

The very asking of such questions raises prior uncertainties. There is the initial and very considerable problem of clarifying what kind of intellectual activity or other activity it is that we are dealing with under the blanket term, "allegory." We may ask whether we are dealing primarily with something which is a mode of cognition and investigation, a tool (the three- or fourfold understanding of Scripture, for example); or on the other hand, with a species of writing possessing certain distinctive formal characteristics. If we are dealing primarily with questions of meaning (content), then there seems to be in allegory a dual possibility: of meaning intrinsic, and meaning extrapolated. To make that distinction is in effect to ask the question whether allegorical content or meaning may not be a matter of the exegete's, or the reader's, or even the author's personal construction imposed on the literary text. Yet almost all interpreters traditionally have held the view that the allegorical constructions, their own readings, correspond to some innate, transcendent or otherwise generally accepted truth embodied in the original. An extension of these alternative possibilities is, whether a perceived allegorical content or contents of meaning may correspond to certain clearly defined areas of concern or knowledge particular to some particular historical period, either of the author or of the exegete—or of the reader—and whether literature actually written as allegory necessarily shares those common areas of concern or simultaneity of concerns with those of the exegete. One negative reaction to the above problems (but only in the last century or so) has been to assert that the conscious attribution or incorporation of elaborate secondary meaning to or in a text devalues the literary worth of the artifact. Such a view would have been regarded historically as naive, and it will not be found necessary to engage with this type of argument in the present study.

If—to take the converse possibility to that expressed at the beginning of the preceding paragraph—in dealing with "allegory" we are dealing primarily not with secondary meaning but with the distinctive means of expressing that meaning, we may ask whether literature written as allegory defines itself not according to its latent content but rather by the formal structures, techniques or rhetoric through which it expresses that content. Yet history seems to suggest that allegorical meaning and allegorical method have never really been separable either in critical exegesis or in literary texts, that these two have had a constant tendency to converge. Or indeed, even more remarkably, that allegorical interpretation has often tended to take on the colourings of allegorical literature—just as allegorical literature, conversely, has assumed the function of interpretation. These last possibilities are among those to which we shall find ourselves most frequently returning in the present study—that allegorical critiques tend to accommodate their forms to the formal qualities of the literary texts which they interpret; and that texts with a pronounced allegorical content tend often to structure themselves according to the intellectual patternings devised by the exegetes. But we shall find too that aestheticians and rhetoricians also have made their distinctive and necessary contributions to the character and defining of written allegory.

With regard to allegory formally considered, many questions similarly arise. We may debate whether allegory in literature is to be identified with certain specialized literary techniques or constructs, such as "one-to-one" narrative; or whether the term "allegory" more properly applies to certain literary *genres*; or, on the other hand, whether allegory is to be primarily connected with certain kinds of rhetorical effects. If it is primarily rhetorical in nature, then the inference seems likely that allegory is not a genre at all, but a mode or style which can penetrate many genres. Rhetorical definitions have usually suggested that not only must allegory by definition have a secondary meaning, but that it tends, more ostentatiously, to flaunt the hiddenness of that secondary meaning. How much does the fact of the meaning being tantalizingly hidden or partly veiled contribute to the distinctiveness of allegory—since not all *double* meaning is hidden, sometimes, as in a pun, the second meaning is palpably transparent? For this last reason older rhetoricians have usually proposed more acutely distinguishing marks to identify the presence of allegory in a written text. Their view seems to have been that allegory is not simply equivalent to the gnomic or enigmatic, that it must also possess certain distinctive aesthetic or linguistic characteristics.

In sum, can any one question about allegory be raised without invoking most of the other questions too? To look at even a few of the historical conflicts and debates over allegory is to incline to that view. Yet in that very recognition, and in the realisation that for two and a half thousand years the same questions have arisen in relation to allegorical processes and similar conclusions and practices have evolved, clarification and coherence do emerge. Whether the practices in question be to do with interpretation or with literary composition, whether to do with texts classical or scriptural, Jewish or Christian, whether with biblical exegesis or secular literary criticism, whether they are associated with that great body of English allegorical literature from the medieval period through to the seventeenth century which we recognise as the flowering of allegorical art, or at the other end of the time-scale they are to do with the strategies of romantic and postmodernist literary criticism and literary production, allegory always displays certain features which identify it as an activity of a peculiar universality.

The present study evolved irresistibly into an examination of some of the problems noted above, an examination undertaken, as was said at first, with a view to arriving at a better grasp of the poetics and the aesthetic

processes of *Paradise Lost*. No one scholar could possibly trace a compre-
hensive history of the theory of allegory from classical to Renaissance
times, and this study makes no sort of claim to do so. But even to skim the
surface of this vast subject with a sense of historical sequence is to bring out
significant continuities in theory and application of allegory from ancient
to medieval to Renaissance times, which it is hoped will be helpful to a
spectrum of readers. A broad historical overview also confirms that there
was a long evolution, crystallizing in the late sixteenth century but arising
out of earlier theories of allegory, toward a distinctive theory and practice
of the allegorical epic. I have come to the conclusion that *Paradise Lost*,
recent criticism to the contrary notwithstanding, belongs at the culmina-
tion and not at the tail end of that tradition of epic allegory. Perhaps all
serious epic necessarily participates in allegory in some way. But it will be
the object of this study to demonstrate that Milton's epic belongs in the
allegorical mode in quite specific, recognisable ways. Every stage and
aspect of earlier theory or practice of allegory, interpretative or composi-
tional, which will be touched upon in the present survey, necessarily at
some points a limited one, will be found to throw its own light on how and
in what ways and to what extent *Paradise Lost* may rightly be considered as
an allegorical poem and an allegorical epic.

The main emphasis of this study obviously falls upon Renaissance
theorizing. The abbreviated consideration of classical and other early theo-
ries of allegory, which was all that could be attempted here, nonetheless
helps to set the later Renaissance scene. Renaissance theory of allegory
often presents a superficially confused appearance. An appreciation of
earlier—classical, scriptural and medieval—theories and practices of alle-
gory can help to a better understanding of the development of allegory and
its interpretation at the later periods. A firmer and less confused grasp of
Renaissance theory of allegory and of the allegorical epic (my primary
concerns) may, in turn, help to a better understanding of Milton's poem in
some of its more unusual features, and help us to see Milton's epic in its
totality as a coherent intellectual and artistic structure.

The plan of this study, accordingly, is to survey something of classical,
biblical and medieval origins of the theory of allegory, before taking up in
greater detail Renaissance views on allegory as the language of poetry, as a
unique form of rhetoric, and as the "platform" or "ground-work", the
"Idea", of the epic poem. The views of Spenser and more especially of
Tasso are central to my inquiry. A good deal of the Tasso theoretical
material (as of the Salutati material) included here has not heretofore been
available to the reader in English translation or discussion. The neoclassical
epic context is considered in its turn. Milton's own epic and allegorical
poetics in *Paradise Lost* are then investigated, as are the analogies which
these present to earlier theories and practices of allegory. Lastly, my claims
for adjudging Milton's poem to be an allegorical epic are set in the various

contexts of Milton's Protestantism, his own utterances in his prose and poem bearing on the subject of allegory and allegorical reading, and the practical artistic evidences within *Paradise Lost* itself. These three divisions correspond broadly to the three Parts of this study: theory of allegory in poetry and allegorical exegesis up to and including the earlier Renaissance (Part I); theory of the allegorical epic from Tasso through to Le Bossu, including the theory which we may adduce from within *Paradise Lost* itself (Part II); and Milton's explicit theories on the use of allegory, as expressed in his secular prose and his theological treatise, and also intimated more obliquely in the practices, utterances, or stylistic effects within his epic poem (Part III). A natural extension of this plan would have been to go on (as I had originally hoped) to apply the theories of allegory and the epic traced here to a full analysis of the actual workings of such modes and models in Milton's treatment of *Paradise Lost*. While I have tried in the present study (and elsewhere at greater length) to give some suggestions as to the nature of allegorical processes and devices in Milton's poem, the restrictions of space have not, unfortunately, permitted anything like the full investigation of the practical aspects of Milton's allegorical artistry that they deserve.

Acknowledgements

I am indebted for financial and academic support during the writing of this book to the following institutions: the Calouste Gulbenkian Foundation, which provided a two-year fellowship which I held at Lucy Cavendish College; the Leverhulme Trust, which provided a two-year research award; and the American Association of University Women, who funded a year's fellowship which I held as a visiting scholar in the English department at Harvard University. I am grateful to the latter institution for its academic hospitality, as also to Lucy Cavendish College for its ongoing academic support. I am grateful to the following persons for their generous time and help given in reading certain parts of the manuscript and discussing its problems: Professor Peter M. Dronke, Cambridge University, and Dr. Ilya Gershevitch (retired), Cambridge University, both of whom advised me on the Latin translations; Professor Barbara Lewalski, Harvard University; Professor Marvin Spevack (retired), the University of Munster; and Professor Alastair Fowler, Regius Professor Emeritus, the University of Edinburgh. Dr. Andrew Treip provided thoughtful comments on many problems. I must record particular thanks to Professor John T. Shawcross, the University of Kentucky, and Professor Gordon Teskey, Cornell University, both of whom read the manuscript painstakingly and constructively and were further generous in helping me to follow up inquiries arising from those readings; also to Professor Judith Herz, Concordia University, Montreal, whose ready encouragement meant much at an early and difficult stage of the manuscript. Dr. Daniel Boyarin, the University of California at Berkeley, Dr. Lawrence Rhu, the University of South Carolina, and Gordon Teskey kindly let me see their useful articles while these were still unpublished. On the practical side, I have been greatly assisted by Mrs. Bobbie Coe, without whose skilled computer programming and typing and indefatigable patience this manuscript might have appeared in a much worse state, and by Mrs. Cathy Byfield, who helped me to check the quotations. I owe thanks to my family for their help and forbearance, but particularly, I wish to thank my husband, Cecil Treip, not only for proof-reading the whole manuscript and helping me with other tasks, but for his continuing help, support and encouragement over many years; I am lastingly grateful to him. Finally, I am saddened that two scholars who offered valuable encouragement of my work at an early stage are no longer alive to receive my thanks and gratitude; these are Professor John Douglas Bush, formerly of Harvard University, and Professor Geoffrey Shepherd, formerly of the University of Birmingham.

PART I

Theory of Allegory
in Poetry and Epic from
Antiquity to the Renaissance

ONE

Antiquity to the Middle Ages

Late Classical Interpreters and Their Successors

Certain tensions or oppositions may be perceived to recur throughout the history of allegory. Even though in allegorism no more than in other literary modes can the distinction between "content" and "form" sustain itself for long, one broad opposition which we shall find recurring historically is that between "allegory" conceived as meaning (hidden thought) and allegory defined as a feature of rhetoric, usually a brief rhetorical trope. For Aristotle and Quintilian *allegoria* is a rhetorical figure (sometimes defined as *permutatio* or *inversio*), or a trope which works by saying one thing while meaning another—the ordinary definition in the *Oxford English Dictionary* still.[1] This definition avoids problems by omitting specific reference to the possible length of the figure or the nature of the transposed content or meaning. Sometimes allegory in this view means something like our present understanding of "riddle"; however, *aenigma* in the ancient understanding of allegory is more obscure than "riddle", which is only one form of allegory.[2] But a prevailing degree of obscurity seems to characterize allegory and to distinguish it from irony or sarcasm, which are clearer in intention.

That the quality of obscurity is important to the understanding of the allegorical trope is evident in rhetorical definitions of it from classical times to the Renaissance. It is apparent in the classical connection of allegory with "riddling", or the medieval or Renaissance stress on the "veil" of allegory, the "dark" conceit—all these, as we shall see, both link the figure of *allegoria* to, yet distinguish it from, metaphor. The emphasis on obscurity is also evident in the use of favoured literary devices, as in the European allegorical tradition of enigmatical images or structures such as dreams, dream-visions, disguises, emblems (pictorialized conceits), the bizarre in narrative sequence or other elements, riddling pageant or masque displays, and so forth. A good example is the pageant in the *Divina commedia*

near the end of the *Purgatorio* (cantos 29-31): the "triumph of Beatrice"
unrolls in time, seen as a visual enigma, only partially explained and not
understood, in fact "riddling" the doctrine of the second coming of Christ
expected throughout history.[3] An aesthetic based on enigma or riddle is
also evident behind many modern critical attempts to systematize under-
standing of allegorical methodology, especially in Spenser.[4] More gener-
ally, the classical rhetorical orientation evinces itself in the present critical
tendency to identify allegory with some particular formal technique. This
insistence on allegory as a formal device and riddling trope is, as we shall
later see, confuted by Torquato Tasso, who takes pains to distinguish his
own evolving profounder use of epic allegory from such limited rhetorical
definitions as that of Aristotle—which nonetheless caused him much
unease, given the authority of Aristotle in the sixteenth century.[5]

On the other side stands a tradition from classical into early Christian
times, and evolving from rabbinical into patristic exegesis, which defines
allegory in terms of meaning or meanings ascribed to or discovered in a
text, without (it has been supposed until quite recently) regard to consid-
erations of literary form. In these traditions of exegesis on classical legend,
or for that matter on scriptural text (more often the Old Testament),
allegory is used as a mode of investigative analysis or critical interpreta-
tion. As is well known, such exegesis provided the origins of the science of
literary criticism. The object of the exegete is to discover in a work some
received, unified body of philosophical or religious doctrine. In certain
developments such allegoresis is closely linked to Platonic or Neoplatonic
ethical or religious systems, elsewhere to Stoic thought of a metaphysical-
scientific cast. Such readings use as their "texts" or scriptures classical
myths, notably pre-Homeric or Homeric, often extracted from longer epic
narratives. Several fictive incidents in one poem or from several poems
may be put together, or seen as belonging together, in the interests of
supporting a coherent larger system; alternatively, one convenient episode
may be intensively analysed.[6]

Illustrative of one strand of such early allegoresis is, for example, the
Commentary, according to wider or narrower scientific principles, of Ma-
crobius (A.D. C4-5) on the [*Somnium Scipionis*] *Dream of Scipio*.[7] In the same
vein, exactly, are later works by Renaissance mythographers, such as
Natalis Comes' *Mythologiae* or George Sandys' *Ovid*, with their rich variety
of "natural" (scientific-biological-geographic) as well as ethical readings of
Ovidian, Homeric or other myths. The tradition is best represented in
English, perhaps, by Bacon's innovative work [*De sapientia veterum*] *Of the
Wisdom of the Ancients* (1609). (These works will be considered later.)
Famous "setpieces" of such moralized readings of myths according to
Platonic or later Neoplatonic ethics (often cohabiting with other kinds of
readings, for example cosmological or natural-scientific) may be found in
such early commentaries as that of Porphyry (A.D. *c.* 232-305) on the Cave

of the Nymphs in Homer;[8] again, Fulgentius' (A.D. *c.* 467-532) treatments of seventy-five myths in *Mitologiarum libri tres*;[9] and (picking up the vein) on into the systematic dictionaries of the Renaissance humanist mythographers. In the *Ovide Moralisé*, Christianized readings of myths provide a highly specialized religious development of intermittent exegesis on myth.[10] It has been thought that such classical or Christian readings developed on a Platonic-transcendental model: they reach for truths which may be shadowed by but exist outside of the texts being read.[11] On a more comprehensive philosophical plane, one may cite such later allegorists as the Italian Neoplatonists, Giovanni Boccaccio, Marsilio Ficino and others,[12] who deploy the whole classical pantheon, Platonic myths and pastiches of Platonic treatises in order to project in veiled form entire cosmological and religious thought systems.

While such Renaissance developments in allegoresis reveal an effort to achieve intellectual synthesis and coherence within their allegorical extrapolations, it has too often been assumed (though in certain cases it may be true) that all such treatments of myth show little evidence of sensitivity to the original materials as literature, no great regard for the literary integrity or even for the intellectual coherence of the texts which they employ. Allegorical readings are taken as being concerned with the extraction of certain favoured or received meanings out of the texts, as not seeking to align the extrapolated readings with the coherent narrative line of the original myths—indeed, as flagrantly violating the literal models, and as not having any regard to any formal qualities in the works concerned. They are examples of "imposed" allegory: of meaning or meanings arbitrarily imposed on the unfortunate texts. Their concern is said to be extra-literary and only with the authenticity of the hidden meanings they educe, that being based entirely on the weight of traditional interpretation supporting these. Such alleged disregard of the integrity of the original texts is seen as later perpetuated by a whole line of Renaissance commentaries on vernacular epic, chiefly Ariosto's, the sporadic or episodic nature of which was to cause Tasso much vexation.

There is increasing evidence that the above views represent a radical oversimplification. That early interpreters felt, not without reason, that there were elements *in* their texts which supported their own religious or cosmological interpretations has become clearer. And that their forms of exegesis constantly adapted or invented literary forms and paraliterary linguistic resources analogous to those of the text being interpreted is also becoming apparent. In the same way that the science of biblical interpretation, or of literary interpretation at least until very recently, required that the overall system of meaning educed from the text be governed by conditions and internal correspondences within that text, so early comprehensive literary allegoresis almost perforce developed systems of explanation correspondent with the internal organization of the texts being

studied. Only fairly recently has it been understood how important a
contribution to literary allegory and especially to the later European epic
tradition was made in particular by the allegorical interpreters of Homeric
and Virgilian epic—that is, via their *continuous* expositions of extended
narrative.

As Félix Buffière and Jean Pépin, and, more recently, Robert Lamber-
ton have shown,[13] a mode of analysis which took cognizance of literary
factors in the texts under consideration in actuality developed from earliest
times. The impulse was, certainly, to extrapolate from the old stories, first
Homeric or pre-Homeric, then Virgilian, ethical and religious principles
originally conceived according to ancient thought systems, later developed
on Neoplatonic and Christian lines. But the myths were not necessarily
treated in total isolation from their original literary context. Rather, a
serious effort might be made, for example, to correlate a certain proposed
desirable sequence of ethical development, or a spectrum or hierarchy of
perceived virtues, with the developmental framework of the original nar-
rative. One such early interpreter is Fulgentius, whose *Expositio Vergilianae
continentiae* depicts the twelve Books of the *Aeneid* as a picture of the natural
sequence and growth in wisdom of human life.[14] In the twelfth century
Bernard de Silvestre (Bernardus Silvestris) followed a similar "progress"
pattern and distinctively Neoplatonic ethic and aesthetic in interpreting
the events of the *Aeneid* as an allegory of the moral life of man.[15] Later
follow parallel expositions of Virgil by the Italian humanists, by Boccaccio,
Jodocus Badius and especially Cristoforo Landino;[16] while Coluccio Sa-
lutati performs for both Virgil and the Hercules legends a similar service.[17]

The contents of all of these expositions run in parallel. The myths or
epics are found to portray a steady moral and spiritual development, as
traced in the hero, through phases demarcated by distinct phases of the
narrative, toward a finally achieved "heroic" wisdom and virtue. These
increasingly elaborate allegorical expositions would seem to mark a new
departure and to lay the foundations for a designedly allegorical epic
literature, the spiritual "progresses" of Dante, Tasso, Spenser, Milton.
They do not lift interesting bits out of the original text or indulge in a variety
of interesting but dissociated interpretative forays into the text, but at-
tempt instead to link even disjunct episodes in it and certainly the main
thread of the epic fable with a coherent, complex, ethical developmental
system. Thus the sequence of "interpretation" recreates or transposes the
original literary pattern or structure onto the allegorical critique. In finding
their inspiration in the congruence between the developmental allegory
and the developing narration, these more disciplined interpretations,
however fanciful portions of them may sometimes appear, represent an
advance in the practice of literary allegoresis, one in which interpretation
itself is seen to be acquiring the characteristics of literary narrative. The
foregoing remarks represent a more radical perspective than that which

would see allegorical literature as arising only later, from the "wedding of ancient works (themselves with some allegorical content) and recent [i.e. later] Platonizing allegorical commentary to produce a new kind of deliberately allegorical poetry" in medieval times.[18] In the earliest exegeses on epic, the margin of difference between allegorical interpretation and allegorical literature has already narrowed.

Rabbinical Interpretation

If early Neoplatonist allegorical reading of myth shows more regard for the narrative integrity of the text than has sometimes been thought, it has, again until recently, often been alleged that in their over-concern with extrapolated meanings, transcendental or otherwise, the parallel traditions of early rabbinic and early patristic reading of Scripture did not do so. This view has recently been forcefully challenged by what one might call the New School of biblical-literary criticsm.[19] For the classical or post-classical, the early Christian and the rabbinical traditions of interpretation of their respective scriptures share much common ground. Earlier or medieval rabbinic traditions of Old Testament interpretation (referred to under the general term of *midrash*), like those on their part of the early Fathers who were close in time, or later of Neoplatonist exegetes on epic, were sometimes homiletic in intention, designed to educe a whole religious way of morals, thought and life from the sacred texts.[20] The particular *schemata* which the Jewish exegetes followed, including that of cross-matching texts from different parts of the canon and narratively expanding these into glosses upon each other, or creating multiple, sometimes imaginative commentaries on the texts,[21] were not by them regarded as a wrenching of the text or divergence from it, but on the contrary as a rediscovery or sometimes a reconstruction of the original experiences of faith recorded in Scripture.[22]

Through their various genres or literary forms, midrashic readings provided a philosophic basis for allegorical reading, a way of making the text of Scripture personal, a mode of meaningful appropriation, in intention not dissimilar to certain forms of later Protestant reading.[23] The Bible then as now was understood to be not a homogeneous text but a "self-glossing book" or collection of self-referential texts. By such midrashic methods of commentary, more, not less, order was found in it; as Gerald L. Bruns has said: "As the Rabbis, Augustine, and Luther knew, the Bible, despite its textual heterogeneity, can be read as a self-glossing book. One learns to study it by following the ways in which one portion of the text illuminates another. . . . the parts are made to relate to one another reflexively, with later texts, for example, throwing light on the earlier, even as they themselves always stand in the light of what precedes and follows them. . . . the structure of the Bible [is] a redacted, self-interpreting text."[24] Further, says Bruns, there is "this important exegetical consequence", that "The Bible always addresses itself to the time of interpretation; one cannot understand it except by appropriating it anew. Revelation is never something over and done with. . . . it is ongoing, and its medium is midrash. . . . the task of midrash . . . is always productive of new understanding". "The legendary extravagance [of midrash is a means to ensure that] the text is always *situated*. . . . It is a way of keeping the Bible open to the histories of those who answer its claims".[25] Perhaps in a not dissimilar way, disjunct episodes in Homeric or Virgilian epic could be brought into meaningful approximation by the Neoplatonist exegetes.

Rabbinical interpreters thus seem to have provided early analogues to or sometimes, possibly, premodels for not only Neoplatonizing allegorization on epic but also for important later conceptions of allegory and many specific important types of later Christian biblical interpretation. These latter include a model and method for the thesis of a latent homogeneity across the canon of the Bible (the "analogy of faith", the "Word" amidst all the "letters"); for the reading of typological (messianic) prefiguration in Scripture; and also for certain radical linguistic and narrative methods, characteristic of midrashic readings, in the literary representation of biblical matter. Such allegorical and figurative methods acquire highly distinctive literary characters of their own—something of intense interest to the present line of inquiry. The midrashic protoliterary methods offer close analogues to techniques currently being recognised in seventeenth-century Protestant sermonizing and religious poetry and recognisable also in Milton. While the rabbinical techniques cannot here be discussed in detail, some further comment on them will be found in a later chapter.[26]

The Church Fathers and Medieval Allegory

Out of the vast subject of Neoplatonizing allegory and other forms of allegory in patristic and later medieval Christian usage, one or two pertinent points regarding scriptural allegoresis, insofar as it bears on literary theory of allegory, may be made. Neoplatonizing allegory as practised upon the scriptural text had long been regarded as theologically suspect in the Reformation tradition. It seems to have been historically a widely held view that the writings of Origen in the early third century A.D. (although Origen perhaps never was doubted to have believed in the literal authenticity of the Bible) held a double standard: a plain, or the plain, reading of Scripture would suffice for the populace, while more esoteric, usually Neoplatonic, allegorical constructions were meat for those of profounder understanding. It was of course also feared that allegoresis might in lesser hands not only dislocate the historical solidity of the Hebrew texts or the

Gospels, but also overcomplicate the simplicity of Christian doctrine, or even rationalize it away into philosophical abstractions. All the same, the hellenistic readings of Philo (first century) and Origen were of particular interest to a religious purist such as Milton.[27] One must ask how this could be.

Origen was not, after all, merely an allegorizer, although he was a great innovator in this regard in the Christian tradition, having been one of the original sources of the "triple" reading: literal, allegorical, moral.[28] He had also made great early advances in textual scholarship and in creating a coherent framework of doctrine;[29] having done so, he could scarcely have been neglectful of that content of doctrine. Rather, it is because of his clearer view of doctrine as admixed with other kinds of discourse in the Bible that he could understand some parts of the Bible to be written in different ways from other parts. Origen's views on biblical figuration are earlier but not in kind different from later views, for example, Augustinian theories of poetic aesthetics as founded on biblical discourse, and the views of both Fathers are to be understood as methodologically parallel to the pagan religious-allegorical interpretations of Homer.[30] Origen's famous commentaries on the Song of Songs fastened on exactly that atypical text which early Jewish exegetes had themselves regarded as locking up, or conversely as being the key to, the mysteries of faith—a key to the rest of the Scriptures.[31] His commentaries on this Book became setpieces, emulated and alluded to by generations of later interpreters, in the same way that the Cave of the Nymphs episode in Homer or the descent into the underworld by Aeneas in Virgil became the models or prototypes for similar allegorizations by classical and Renaissance commentators and then by poets. Origen's homilies show a great sensitivity to the range and power of figuration in biblical or other discourse, especially to the power of scriptural figurative language, as in the Song of Songs. (Indeed it was only by relegating this particular Book, as also Revelation, to the fringes of the canon that Reformers, less flexible, were able to deal with the linguistic problems which it raised—they explained it by neglecting it.) In the very consciousness of such Books as that of Solomon as being especially amenable to allegorization, we may see surfacing again an older impulse to link allegorical readings with certain kinds of literary material and features.

For the earlier Fathers the Bible became the single source out of which might be educed a whole Christian-philosophic way of life—thought, conduct, ethical and spiritual rule. But in its later development by the end of the Middle Ages, a new element of scholarship and reserve had penetrated the field of Christian biblical interpretation, as biblical historians such as Beryl Smalley have pointed out. While the interpreters were still concerned to educe a total body of Christian doctrine and ethics from biblical writings, they did this in a newly disciplined spirit, with stricter regard for the history and provenance of the sacred writings, the variations of kind within the sacred texts, the restrictions imposed by the necessity to preserve the coherence of doctrine, the suitability or not of certain types of interpretations (for example, figurative) to certain texts, and a clearer consciousness of what kind of level of interpretation was being applied in each case and its propriety in the context.[32] With all this, either as consequence or cause, came an enhanced sense of the historical solidity of scriptural narrative: the so-called "primacy of the *literal level*",[33] an emphasis which, reinforced, continued into Reformist treatment of Scripture.

With this development comes also a shift in emphasis. We see not that early Jewish or Christian emphasis on a comprehensive or "total" ethical reading of all parts of Scripture such as could sustain the entire round of daily life, nor yet that tendency to total allegorization which is alleged to have developed with Philo and Origen and continued into "fantastic" Kabbalistic or Victorine theories, but a more specific view of figuration. There is a new and heightened sense not just of the differing historical contents of individual Books of the Bible, but of the total sequence of history from the Old Testament to the New. The continuum of physical history embedded in Scripture with its recorded events provides tangible witness to God's grand design and purpose. His progressive unfolding or revealing of His hidden purposes to man throughout human time and scriptural history becomes itself a form of allegory: the literal historical events have meanings beyond themselves.

Predictive figural reading was not invented by the Christian tradition; but as an incarnational religion, Christianity embeds meanings in the sacred texts through the same process that made the Word flesh. God as the author of Scripture has the power to adapt to his purposes not only words but the things themselves signified by the Bible's words. There is a sense now not that an elite *cognoscenti* is discovering hidden correspondences in Scripture; rather, that God is speaking directly to all through his manifest deeds-words. Hence Aquinas: "The author of Holy Writ is God, in whose power it is to signify His meaning not by words only (as man also can do), but also by things themselves".[34] As Charles Singleton puts it, "the sign which is found in things inheres in them objectively. . . . God had put it there. Man . . . discovers it".[35] The sweep of historical events recorded in the Old Testament can reveal to us not only Christ prophetically but God's entire purpose and plan as regards man. Typology, or "figural prophecy" or "phenomenal prophecy" as Erich Auerbach calls it, narrowly considered, lies embraced within the above wider view of figuration—since "figural prophecy relates" specifically "to an interpretation of history",[36] that is, of persons and events in scriptural history. But as with Scripture, so with God's other Book of Nature; the created World, equally, can be read in two ways simultaneously. In the world of nature, as in the concrete events and persons of the Bible, fact and sign or meaning coexist; both are real, both are charged with divine meaning.[37]

The concept of the indivisibility in Scripture of thing from sign, of events and persons in the Bible from their meaning (which is the thing signified, or God's divine plan), puts early and medieval allegorism in a new perspective; equally so with any derived medieval allegorical poetic. Allegations of abstraction in allegory, medieval or other, are not always supportable, for they often depend on associating that term exactly with the most abstract interpretative or literary constructs. One may argue on the contrary that, in a view in which God's deeds are seen as words and his words as deeds, there must be felt to be a peculiar importance attaching to all the literal details of the scriptural, equally of the literary, text. The text is as "real" as God's world around us, and this reality of narrative surface and detail is something that must never be forgotten.[38] The "literal level" holds primacy; and it is this which is to direct interpretation of the allegorical dimension, and not the other way round. Such a view is very distant from the widespread assumption that allegorism inevitably tends toward abstraction and rationalism. Whether we are dealing with the so-called "triple" senses of Origen, Gregory or Ambrose, or the "fourfold" reading popularized by Aquinas, or the twofold theory of Dante,[39] or with any of the many variants and subdivisions of these, it is the "literal level", the details of the narration in the scriptural or literal text, which are to direct further meaning or meanings. Embracing such further meanings, the literal can yet never be lost or dissipated in them. The medieval sense of historical solidity within the allegorical dimension may be compared with the later Renaissance stress on the necessary verisimilar truth or even the historical truth of an epic narration which, even so, may be allegorically directed in its totality. Such an emphasis on the literal level requires that allegorical extrapolations from a text be closely correlated with the narrative structures or other descriptive features in that text. Only with regard to this fact of fundamental importance—the dual and equal nature or juncture of the real and the invisible worlds in earlier scriptural allegorism and in the earlier literary-allegorical aesthetic—can allegorical works such as *Pearl* or the *Divina commedia* be read with the fulness and solidity of meaning in which they were conceived and written. The point of view implied is one which sees either external nature or fictional narrative as the mainsprings of spiritual meaning, yet which never favours "meanings" at the expense of the reality of human nature and the real world, or of the "real" character of the story or scriptural narrative.

Looking ahead, briefly, to the principal subject of this study, a useful comparison may be made here with Milton's *Paradise Lost*. Milton's poem too takes on new dimensions against the above background. As Raphael suggests in Book V in a passage which will later be discussed in detail, the entire physical world may become a kind of allegory of "things invisible to mortal sight"; yet in itself it remains wonderfully "real", and, in Milton's own materialist view, in its very substance is indivisible from spirit. Mil-

ton's like Dante's poem has throughout much of its narrative that histor-
icity and human authenticity of which Auerbach or earlier writers have
spoken, relative to truly "figural" writing or interpretation. Their created
worlds feel real, solid, in the way that what is spoken of in the Bible is real
and solid.[40] But—again like the Bible—the world of these two poems has
something further: both poems have what Singleton describes in the
Commedia as the sense of "this *and* that", rather than any sense of some
allegory of "this for that".[41] Their worlds have the special double nature
that Scripture does. Like the *Divina commedia*, *Paradise Lost* may present us
with a text and aesthetic in which the juncture of narrative form and latent
figurative meaning is indissoluble.

The Medieval "Levels"

Medieval biblical hermeneutics were neither uniform nor simplistic. De-
spite the seemingly fantastic character of some medieval allegoresis (the
Victorine mystics are often cited),[42] biblical scholars find that exegetes
were on the whole sensible and discriminating, and that there were many
understood qualifications as to legitimate material and procedures. As
regards the vexed matter of the "levels", it seems that certainly by the
time of the scholastics a great deal of biblical material, when figurative,
was conceived of as inherently part of the literal level. Some mysterious
figures might have been designedly included in Scripture by God, and
might legitimately be treated as *aenigma* ("mystery" or allegory) because of
their manner of treatment in the original.[43] Other than to such intendedly
figurative expression in Scripture, no figurative interpretation could be
applied to the sacred text—that is to say, not in any context of *doctrine*.
Further meanings extrapolated from the sacred texts could be acceptable
in the context of private meditation or public preaching for moral edifica-
tion; but in respect of theological exegesis, only linguistic and textual or
historical commentary could properly be conducted on the main parts of
the scriptural texts (the "letter"). Yet also belonging to the "literal" level
were certain kinds of metaphor clearly intentional in the original: proph-
ecy, parable, figure of speech, of kinds more perspicuous than allegory.
In such cases the moral values of the text could rightly be construed as
part of its literal significance, and did not constitute a further level or
"tropological value". Many actual histories in Scripture similarly pos-
sessed an innate exemplary value. Job was a classic example, cited by
Beryl Smalley;[44] this text was regularly interpreted as an illustration of the
workings of Providence, and that too was part of its "literal" meaning. All
these distinctions illustrate an awareness by early commentators of dif-
ferent characters of discourse in the sacred text—even though, with the
Bible as with poetry, the close overlap between *exemplum* and a more

hidden tropological (moral-allegorical) meaning could become a source of critical confusion.

The whole question of the three or four "levels" in medieval inter-pretation[45] thus has to be treated with great reserve—not merely because different earlier authorities defined the three or the four senses in dif-ferent ways or in a different order and with differing subsenses, but because it was not always easy to distinguish to what level a particular reading might belong. Thus a high degree of literary sensitivity to the linguistic character of a particular text was needed, if allegorical treatment was not to be misapplied. Different biblical texts or parts of them might be suited to quite different types of reading: rarely, any single text to all. The three- or fourfold reading was applicable to Scripture only as taken *overall*.[46] The Song of Songs and Exodus were treated in a more compli-cated way; but these particular texts had had very long histories of allegorization, through St. Bernard, Origen and rabbinical exegesis.[47] Sophisticated medieval allegoresis required that much discrimination be practised as to quality of language and the immediate context and content of the text, as well as regard paid to context of application. Employing so many reservations and constraints, mainstream medieval exegetes or allegorists cannot be thought to have been either irresponsible or insen-sitive in their readings; and perhaps overall their attitudes were not so far removed from Reformation attitudes to the reading of Scripture as might be supposed. Not only Reformers but schoolmen too believed that their readings were guided strictly and in a scholarly, disciplined manner by "inspiration".[48] It is hardly a new observation that out of scriptural allegorism grew up theory of poetic allegorism or, more recently, the principles of literary criticism, bound by similarly strict procedures and constraints.

These problems and differentiations in biblical interpretation may also tell us something about theory of derived poetic allegory. Medieval and early Renaissance humanists looked to biblical models in writing figurative poetry, and to scriptural-exegetical models in theorizing about poetry.[49] It may be seen that the hierarchy of allegorical "levels" of figuration posited with regard to secular poetry in the Middle Ages runs closely in parallel with the "levels" as construed in scriptural exegesis. In the latter were to be found the two broad divisions, *sensus literalis* (the words or histories in the text) and *sensus spiritualis,* or the secondary sense. The *sensus spir-itualis* (itself sometimes termed, broadly, "allegorical") might include in its wide embrace the more specialized "further" senses: normally, the specifically "allegorical" (restrictedly "typological" or prophetic); the "tro-pological" (moral); and the "anagogic" (not too precise—variously to do with matters of faith). Secular literature and poetry were analyzed analo-gously to this familiar structuring. In poetry was recognised a "literal" sense (the *fable* itself), out of which it was permissible to draw various

historical, etiological, etymological glosses or expressions, just as in scrip-
tural exegesis. Further arising out of the literal were various possible
figurative meanings. These were not the same as those in scriptural analy-
sis but ran in parallel. Conventionally recognised were the "typical" or
generic sense, curiously made correspondent to the typological-prophetic
sense in Scripture (all individual instances mirror one universal subsum-
ing instance); the "moral" sense (the hidden meaning under an Aesop
fable, for example); and the "parabolic", a more widely ranging figurative
application, which might be spiritual, but equally could include, for
instance, the kind of scientific-cosmological application so popular in
Renaissance readings. (Bacon was to use the term "parabolical" as syn-
onymous with figurative poetry.)[50] Aesop's fables provided the standard
model for such secular exegesis, just as the Song of Songs did for the
religious.

But as in the case of scriptural exegesis, the standard secular model did
not fit all cases. Curious anomalies could arise, and acute critics were aware
of the epistemological problems involved. For example, it could be argued
that the fabulous or allegorical element in secular poetry of the Christian
periods or even in pagan poetry, if it expressed an important inner "truth",
could be said to be truer than the fiction—certainly "truer" than any
intended fable which is all literal surface, with no inner meaning. Again,
consider the point (and the parables in Scripture offer a very good instance)
that it is the very element of "falsity" (the fable) which is necessary to
convey a truth at all.[51] Such arguments weighing "verisimilitude" against
"verity" later would be crucial to the Renaissance critical debate on poetry,
and thus find earlier critical precedent founded on biblical interpretation.
Again, depending on the fervency of conviction attaching to the concept of
"poetic truth", there might be surprisingly little difference to be found
between the profane "parabolic" sense and certain looser scriptural *spir-
itualis* senses.

Augustine's theories (developing Origen) on allegory in texts of the
Bible were an important source for the development of secular theory of
poetry. They have been discussed by Jean Pépin and other critics.[52] The
problems identified by Augustine in respect of Scripture are also identified
by him as relating to poetic allegory. His theories are especially relevant to
poems like Dante's or the classical epics, which possess a strong founda-
tion of historical event—that is, a strongly literal level (like the histories in
Scripture) reinforcing the further senses. As with biblical exegesis, the
"levels" in the interpretation of profane poetry, too, did not represent any
schema to be applied exhaustively to every poetic text, nor in equal measure
to each part—as Dante clearly understood.[53] Such observations will be
singularly relevant to the much later Renaissance debates on the allegor-
ical epic.

Dante

Dante's critical theories have been much discussed, and perhaps more internal contradictions of a troublesome kind have been found in them than fundamentally exist.[54] Dante clearly envisages that the principal allegorical emphasis in his *Divina commedia* is on the level of the "moral", as we should understand that term: "the subject of the whole work, considered allegorically [*allegorice sumpti*], is man, through exercise of free will, earning or becoming liable to the rewards or punishments of justice".[55] This moral subject has reference to those "living in *this* life"[56] (by proxy represented by the journey of the single protagonist). Such a prevailingly moral sense does not exclude a shading off into other kinds of secondary meanings, almost incidentally, as Dante suggests in the *Convivio*.[57] But while Dante refers to his work as "polysemous",[58] it is the case that his own view of the *Commedia* as a continuous moral progress works against excessive subdivision of meaning.[59] "Polysemousness" is a theoretical possibility, rather than a working rule at every moment in his poem.

Compatible with this interpretation is Dante's insistence that figurative meaning can arise only naturally and out of the literal aspect of the fable, that to which in his criticism he gives the highest priority and which he alleged to be the principal subject of the *Commedia:* "the subject of the whole work, on the literal level, is the state of the souls after death, in an absolute, not in a restricted sense".[60] Although Dante in many places is at pains to indicate that there is a sustained figurative meaning running throughout his great poem (the epic spiritual journey),[61] he points out that the figurative element, although continuous or pervasive, is not uninterrupted. Indeed, as Singleton suggests, it is the very gaps or intermissions in this continued dark allegory which reinforce our sense of the literal reality of the narrative.[62] As de Bruyne has remarked, lesser poets may easily diverge too far in either of two opposite directions: the materialization of ideas, or the spiritualization of fact (when the fable is seen as a flimsy excuse), so dissolving the close juncture of figurative meaning and "fact" or history (the literal texture of the poetic fable) which in his view characterizes the medieval aesthetic.[63] Dante offers a further illustration of the truth that even at the height of medieval allegorism, "literal" and "figurative" cannot be dissevered; literary form (the narrative) and inner meaning must run together. Such perceptions by one of the greatest writers of figurative fiction, one to whom Milton was indebted, prepare us to recognise that the spirit of Dante's critical poetics—if not all of his inherited scholastic apparatus—will have relevance to *Paradise Lost*, as to other allegorical epics.[64]

In considering the whole subject of allegory in poetry or when interpreting it in the *Commedia*, it does not do, then, to give over-attention to detailed application of the three or the four "levels". Augustine had implied as much, relative to Scripture. Similar conclusions are reached by Dante himself, as his distinguished editors have observed. Allegory may, must, be variable in its applicability: different senses may appear in different texts or in different parts of the same text; sometimes allegory must also intermit (observations, once again, relevant to later allegorical epic compositions). All the same, an allegorical poem has, like the historical texts of Scripture, a concrete base in "facts", in its "literal" fiction. Out of this literal groundwork—the continuing narrative "history"—develops the poem's further figurative dimension of meaning, which also is continuous in the sense that it develops progressively in the fiction. For Dante this figurative aspect is mainly of a monovocal kind; it does not exclude, but neither does it invite or insist on, a spectrum of specific subordinate meanings of specialized kinds. The subject of poetry is "twofold" (like the "two voices" of humanistic theory of poetry, which we shall presently consider). While Dante indicates, and also illustrates, that he understands the "allegory of theologians" understood as the formally subdivided senses, his own comprehensive further sense or second "subject", which is his main concern, may be seen to arise out of the "literal sense" of the *Commedia* in the same way that in Scripture the *sensus spiritualis* or *theoria*, the undivided second sense, arises out of parts of the historical narration.[65]

Such a monovocal theme does not exclude, at intervals, what Rosemond Tuve aptly refers to as the traces of exegesis ever pushing meanings out in mystical directions, comparably to the modes of metaphysical poetry.[66] However, Singleton is surely right in saying that it is this undivided second "subject" which provides the moral continuity of Dante's poem, and that the *Commedia* is not merely a static succession of moralized "states" or separate "allegories", encapsulated in isolated encounters with individuals whom Dante had known in life. Rather it concerns a moral *progress* of one individual in *this* life, the experiencing recipient of all that is encountered or seen being the living soul of the poet himself. It is the continuous aspect or "horizontal movement" of the journey (a figurative dimension entirely in the tradition of earlier allegoresis on epic and of later Renaissance allegorical epic) which is most important to him and to us, inasmuch as it corresponds to the saga of "men's journey, or perfecting" here on earth. The *Commedia* is a reflection of "man's journey to his proper end, not in the life after death, but here in this life", and its allegory is an allegory of moral action, of moral event, a moral perfecting, just as are the subjects of Neoplatonic allegorical exegeses on epic and of Tasso's, Spenser's and Milton's epics. Dante's poem and criticism, together with the medieval view of *theoria*, provide a premodel for the ways in which later Renaissance epic narrative allegory would be written, and the ways in which it was expected that it should be read: one broad (largely moral) "undivided" second theme, not uninterrupted yet a continuum, with occasional further "levels" suggested from time to time—all amidst a sustained sense of the "historical" actuality of the fable. It cannot be sufficiently emphasized how essential is an understanding of this early perspective toward a correct interpretation of later epic or other forms of poetic allegory.

These ideas are implicit in the example which Dante uses in the *Epistle to Can Grande*, the two first verses from Psalm 114 on the theme of Exodus, that text famous among the midrashicists, who found in it always some form of allegory of the spiritual relationship between God and Israel, the journey to God, the progress in life as both exile and release, the finding of the way to freedom. To embody such an allegory, Dante, as Singleton has said, would abandon the abstract allegory of Lady Philosophy which he used in the *Convivio* and return to an allegory "grounded in the flesh . . . grounded in history", an allegory with "an historical Virgil, an historical Beatrice, and an historical Bernard . . . an action which is given, in its first sense, not as a beautiful fiction but as a real, historical event, an event remembered by one who was, as a verse of the poem says, the scribe of it. . . . an allegory . . . bearing within it the reflection of the true way to God in this life"—a journey to perfection which has begun in Reason, in the person of Virgil, and is completed through Faith, in the person of Beatrice.[67]

Milton's epic saga is again close to Dante's in the above ways, and especially in its historicity. The sense conveyed in *Paradise Lost* is of a "real" action recounted, one experienced in vision by the recounter, who is also the Poet-Bard, present by vision and inspiration in a journey which begins with Reason and ends in Faith: a moral and spiritual progress. The parallel mountains at the beginnings of *Inferno* and *Paradiso*, on which Singleton comments, suggest the allegorical nature of the journey: "By a mountain to be ascended the way of a journey is given, upward or downward as it may be, between the two poles of light and darkness".[68] In Milton's tripled mountains, Satan's in Hell, God's Mount in Heaven, Adam's Mount of Eden, there is similarly a Dantesque journey of vertical movement in space, "upward or downward . . . between the two poles of light and darkness", undertaken by a narrator who "visits" all, in parallel to the epic of Adam's fall and rise, his moral and spiritual journey. The great galaxy of classical and Renaissance epics all embrace such themes, similarly enhanced by their allegorical dimension of a journey to perfection, of spiritual progress, through the experiences of Avernus, Inferno, Milton's Hell, Tasso's or Spenser's Woods of Error, to the light of the Celestial City envisaged at their conclusions.

TWO

Renaissance Theoretical Developments

The development of theory of allegory from the early to the later Renaissance shows interestingly divergent or often apparently self-contradictory directions; nonetheless, strong continuities with traditional theory and modes of allegory may also be found.[1] One may observe a sustained effort to define all poetry and the whole language of poetry as in themselves allegory or "translated" (secondary) discourse—since both poetry and allegory share a basis of metaphor. This view is coupled with more professional and technical, if sometimes fragmented, efforts to arrive at more functional definitions of the workings of allegorical rhetoric and narrative methodology in poetry. A scriptural and classical exegetical framework in some ways continues to shape Renaissance interpretation; but distinctive voices emerge amidst the apparent confused pluralism of Renaissance allegorical poetics and exegesis. We may observe that old problems deriving from the explication of scriptural allegory, as articulated by Augustine, Origen or others, resurface in the debates; but increasingly, the concern of Renaissance critics is with and about *poetry*. The analysis of poetry becomes more firmly directed to what one might call the poetics of allegory, or an allegorical poetic. Although older traditions of exegesis as a means to validate poetry as an avenue to truth and to interpret what is already written continue, there is a new or renewed emphasis also on allegory as a means of arriving at a deeper understanding of the poetic process itself. In the sections which follow, we shall trace the development of Renaissance views on allegory both as a method of critical exegesis on prior texts and as a function of rhetorical form or narrative structure within poetry. Then we will begin to address the theory of the allegorical epic, which unites the two avenues of hidden meaning and expressive form, and the beginnings of which (as has already been noted) were substantially present in earlier Neoplatonic expositions of classical epic.

Coluccio Salutati

One of the most remarkable features of Renaissance theory of allegory is the evolution of what amounts almost to a new theory of poetry as allegorical metaphor. Medieval language theory concerning *integumentum* and *involucrum* in poetry (terms meaning literally an outer wrapping or covering, hence coming to imply something concealed, inner meaning, allegory)—theories which had developed, as has been earlier observed, under the supporting analogies of biblical criticism—in the early Renaissance acquire a special focus on poetry as an *art* which makes of them something fresh despite their historical continuities, something linguistically much more sharply defined and marking a transition to a more modern stage in critical theorizing. The early Renaissance critic who most specifically articulated this new kind of poetic or aesthetic was Coluccio Salutati, a near contemporary of Boccaccio. Salutati's vocabulary sometimes echoes the older vocabulary just instanced (similar words, such as "shell" or "rind", as opposed to "kernel" or inner meaning, indeed persist in the remarks on allegory of John Harington and Henry Reynolds, who are later discussed). While Salutati's enthusiasm for poetry as an art of "translated" discourse might suggest some influence from the more exotic medieval concept of *symbolum* (as distinct from "allegory"), his discussions nonetheless are firmly pinned to the word "allegory", with no reference apparently being made to arts of "symbolic" or more mysterious discourse.[2]

In certain of his Letters and in certain chapters of his second, expanded version of his allegorization of the Hercules legends (*De sensibus allegoricis fabularum Herculis*),[3] Salutati follows in the tradition of Boccaccio and earlier critic-allegorists[4] in offering allegorical explanations of poetry as both hiding and revealing truth beneath a feigned exterior. He also follows classically inspired rhetoricians, as later seen in the Renaissance manuals, in defining allegory as a figure which "says one thing while another is understood". However, his descriptions go much beyond conventional definitions of allegory: "This way of speaking is poetical, bearing a false shell in front, within containing a hidden truth. . . . Therefore it is for you to deem that way of speaking as poetical, which, whether through things or through words, means something other than it shows—which way of speaking necessity invented, and usage received and amplified, not only when need requires but also when ornament suggests".[5] Again:

But if something should be found that does not completely fit with either of these [orations of either praise or blame], you will without hesitation pronounce it to be a simple song [*carmen*] and some kind of composition, [but] not a poem nor pertaining to the art of poetry. For even if it should proceed by metrical rules and in imaginative language, do not suppose that everything that is metrically composed is a poem, unless what is bound [metrically] is also an imaginative utterance graced by figures and especially by allegorical language [*alieniloquio:* "speaking other", deriving from the Greek *allos* + *agoria*, "to speak implying other than what is said"]. And by imaginative discourse I mean one that moves imagination and fantasy itself by something that is said whilst another is understood. The remainder of the description touches this point more obviously, when [poetry] is called something that hides truths beneath the mystery, that is, the hiddenness of a narrative.[6]

Salutati, like others of his near contemporaries, compares poetry in respect of its figurative language and hidden truths to Scripture: *all* poetry and *all* Scripture contain a secret sense (even, he says, according to Origen the Creation account in Genesis, which might seem to be absolutely literal). Salutati goes very far here, citing the views of such "total" allegorizers as Servius, Macrobius, Eusebius and Jerome.[7] Speaking generally, he offers the traditional defence of poetry from its detractors through justification by allegory and hidden morality. But what seems distinctive in Salutati's views on allegory and even more remarkable than their sweeping inclusiveness are, first, his technical consideration of the range of structural or figurative elements involved in such a view of allegorical poetry, and second, his refusal to be tied in his definitions of the nature of poetry to conventional ancient classifications according to metre and genre.[8]

As is evident from his statements noted above, Salutati defines poetry as essentially metaphorical discourse and not merely metrical speech. His further argument may be paraphrased as follows. Poetry makes use of various rhetorical figures and other forms of "translated" speech or narrative elements in order to signal another sense than the one on its surface. All of these figurative elements making up a poem implicitly serve the cause of the poet's didactic intention, his controlling Idea. From such a view of the nature and function of poetry as itself "translation", allegory is not to be in any way differentiated. Poetry is metaphorical discourse; all forms of comparison, similitude or allegorical trope also are metaphor; and even those elements in a poem which are not tropes (plot, actions, speeches, *things*) are not to be excepted from the definition of poetry as "translated discourse", inasmuch as these elements too may be used obliquely to convey another sense. Thus, allegorical metaphor (limited to a form of trope in the rhetorical understanding of the term *allegoria*) might from the tenor of Salutati's discussion serve to describe the whole frame of poetic discourse.[9] Poetry and allegory equally are subsumed under the idea and term of *translationes*.[10] This theory of poetry as metaphor or allegorical metaphor, coupled with Salutati's concentration on the related technical and linguistic features, seems quite remarkable for its time, especially given the detail in which he carries his ideas through, and even though he has to fall back on frequent reiteration for want of a more diversified critical vocabulary.

The most central statements setting out the above views occur in the last of the three letters to Samminiato (or San Miniato) and the immediately following letter to Dominici (both around 1405-1406), and in the second chapter of the first Book of the augmented 1405 version of the allegorized *De laboribus Herculis*. In the Letter to Dominici, Salutati makes the suggestive and imaginative statement that poetry, like Scripture, is "bilingual": it is an "art of speaking" which constitutes "a bilingual faculty": "[Poetry] is a certain art of speaking and a bilingual faculty, showing one thing externally but signifying another through an inner sense: always speaking in *figura*, and often binding what it relates in verses". Or, "For what is there in all of divine Scripture that does not have a mystical meaning, whether you consider words or histories or prophecies or precepts of wisdom? All is full of hidden meaning, everything can be brought back to an allegorical meaning. Nothing is in them that is not bilingual, that does not present one thing by the shell [*in cortice*] and intend another inwardly [*intrinsecus*]".[11] The above passages are similar to Dante's idea of poetry as having "two natures", but more specific in that they relate to the *art* of language explicitly.

Elsewhere, similarly to the above statements, Salutati says that poetry speaks in figures, or through "translated" speeches, that is, words in which the original meaning has been altered to another sense ("verbis novatis"): "For since poetry nearly always hides an interior sense, what does the art of poetry do other than what Scripture does? Indeed each of them speaks metaphorically, and in words made new in meaning and 'translated', and implying something wholly different from what they signify".[12] Or he says that poetry is indeed the actual faculty of "translating" speech so that the words signify something else: "This way of speaking is poetic, displaying falsehood on the outer shell but containing hidden truth within. The skill, wisdom or nature of this [art] is called *poesis, poetica* or *poetria*. . . . From this you can easily see that all transferred [*translatis*] meanings or metaphors, schemes, tropes, transpositions and allegories, as well as moral meanings [*tropologias*] and parables, pertain particularly to this faculty".[13] Poetry possesses this marvellous faculty of turning all things into something else (that is, with another sense): "But the other thing which you will find supremely delightful in poets is that wondrous harmonious transmutation, whether of words or objects or even actions, which indeed we see belongs peculiarly to the poet. For all translated speech and metaphors, comparisons and similitudes, and whatever among words or things, speeches or doings, we see being changed into something else, is poetical".[14] It is this transmutation that constitutes poetry's distinctive aspect, and not merely "numbers" or genre.

Now the point about the marvellous power of words in poetry to change or translate or make new ("verbis novatis atque translatis"; *commutatio*) is twofold. First, the process embraces indifferently all kinds of

figures, including technical allegory—metaphors, comparisons, simili-
tudes or other tropes, parables, tropologies, allegories, all equally are
"translations"[15]—the word "translation" serves for both technical allegory
specifically[16] and for metaphor or poetry in general.[17] In this view all forms
of metaphor become allegory, and vice versa. The *commutatio* is not even
confined to figures: things, deeds, exploits, speeches, affairs, as well as
words (figures), qualify for this strange kind of *commutatio* ("tum ver-
borum, tum rerum, tum etiam gestorum . . . quicquid verborum aut re-
rum, orationum et negociorum videmus in aliud commutari poeticum
est").[18] Poetry is like the alchemist's art, but even more miraculous.

This last significant passage may be seen to open the way to a theory of
allegorical plot, character and episode as all qualifying for inclusion with
other forms of allegorical metaphor. (Tasso, certainly, later develops such
ideas.) This "global" view of poetry[19] as total or allegorical metaphor
directed to a double meaning, in which all the poem's elements, whether of
language and figures or plot and fable, form part of an accumulating
process of allegorical intention, is very striking. Salutati repeatedly asserts
that it is the body of poetic narrative and language itself which offers the
means of creating an overall coherence of concealed meaning. Frequently
his own language is such as to imply that there will be a continuous
congruence between the verbal surface of an allegorical poem and its inner
meaning.[20] This property of conveying meaning allegorically may be par-
ticularly suited to poetry (*versibus*), but it is not confined to *verse*; allegory
does not necessarily reject the more diffuse medium of certain prose
writers: "because the art of poetry, I do not say always, but as I said above,
often, binds in verses anything that it relates, nevertheless it does not reject
prose, whether continuous as in Apuleius, or intermittent, as in Marcianus
Capella or Alan of Lille".[21] Given his analogy to allegory in *continuous*
prose, or to continuous allegorical *narration*, the above passage implies that
in Salutati's view a poem, also, may be seen as a single, extended, complex
but coherent allegorical structure, bound together not merely by metre but
rather by its own intricate poetical surface and also (in a narrative poem
such as an epic) by the various ingredients of fable, all these elements
together pointing to the "translated" meaning within.

Salutati's explorations point the way to a practical paradigm of epic
allegory of the kind Tasso would evolve, suggesting how the poet may
weave together the entire linguistic surface of a poem, along with its
narrative substructure, so that "all" in it ("deeds", "figures", "things") will
hang together in one subtle system as forms of "translated" discourse,
together signalling the presence of an underlying Idea or further sense. We
see in Salutati the old concern with the hidden content of allegory (*what* it
says) budding into a more explicit concern with the *how* of allegorical
writing, as seen in not only its rhetorical character but its larger techniques,
structures and medium.

The English Rhetoricians

Interpretations in Renaissance rhetorical dictionaries of *allegoria* as a form of trope (reviving one line of classical thought) find their place in an evolving recognition of allegory not merely as hidden "intendment", but as this accompanied by certain distinctive styles in written discourse. Rhetorical manuals of the late sixteenth century, following ancient or late classical sources, still define allegory as either an enigmatic manner of speaking or as a figure (or figures) working through such effects as enigma, riddle, obscurity, wilful deception and the like. Behind such narrower, more technical concerns, the Renaissance preoccupation with poetry as metaphor and an understanding of allegory as fundamentally related to metaphor may still be seen; for the rhetoricians recognise that *allegoria* is only a more extended form of that same process of "translation" of a word or a thing into a sense other than its literal sense which, as Salutati stressed, is basic to the entire metaphoric process. However, the rhetoricians' emphasis tends to fall on the precise articulation of the particular rhetorical figure and on the quality of the discourse implicated. Normally, therefore, they conceive of *allegoria* as a figure of relative brevity or self-containment; that other Renaissance way of thinking of extended allegorical metaphor as "Idea", "Foreconceit", or very long *"continued* dark conceit", working itself out across an entire poetical narrative, is not within the compass of the ordinary dictionary descriptions.

The concept of allegory as enigmatic secondary discourse or actual riddle had always formed an important element in medieval and earlier Renaissance views of allegory, as well as in ancient formulations. Allegory was something which *hid* the truth (the Delphic riddles are illustrative), whether under arcane figures or more easily construed parables and fables, while at the same time self-consciously "revealing" truth by signalling its presence. Thus Dante had spoken of "the *cloak"* of fables, or (in a defensive formulation common to earlier critics) of the "beautiful fiction [lie]" under which poetry hides its truths.[22] Similarly, for Boccaccio poetry employed the *"veil* of fiction".[23] Yet as Dante had also said, this "veil" or wrapping is so "thin and light" that the reader may "easily pass through [to the truth hidden] behind".[24] But it is perhaps correct to say that for Renaissance writers it is the obscurity itself of the allegorical medium which fascinates. So we have Spenser's *"dim* vele"[25] (and indeed Spenser's ongoing critique in his poetry of Elizabeth and her court gave him good reason to cultivate concealment). Or we have John Harington's reminder that "men of greatest learning and highest wit in the auncient times, did of purpose conceale these deepe mysteries" and "as it were cover them with the vaile of fables and verse for sundrie causes".[26] Or Henry Reynolds' more powerful statement that allegorical poetry is such as to keep "high and Mysticall matters" by "riddles and enigmaticall knotts . . . inviolate".[27]

To look at allegory in the above ways is to see it primarily in terms of a certain aesthetic effect in language marked by a self-conscious obliqueness, and also usually connected with other rhetorically identifiable figures. Henry Peacham and George Puttenham both link *allegoria* with other figures of thought similarly employing indirect or reversed speech, or working (as Puttenham says) through "alteration of sence or intendements", as in, for example, *ironia* and *sarcasmus*, *enigma*, *parimia* (*paroemia*) and other figures.[28] Like these figures, "Aligoria" specifically "sheweth one thing in wordes, and another in sence".[29] However, many of such figures, for example *enigma*, also share with allegory an obscurity which taxes the understanding and which, once resolved, gives delight: a "darcknesse" which is "delectable".[30] The stress on enigma and obscurity can lead in such figures to an exaggeration which verges on bizarreness or absurdity; as in the riddle, ancient or modern, such absurdity then becomes one of the most important ingredients in the allegorical artistry. Spenser's abundantly riddling allegorical techniques capitalize on just such effects, as also do a number of enigmatic emblematic episodes in *Paradise Lost*.[31] Tuve does well to remind us, citing Yeats as example, that riddle is not to be slighted as a device lending an effect of incalculable depth in poetry.[32] Indeed we may go farther than this and say that wherever allegory occurs—even if it is not wrapped up in a conundrum—a self-conscious obliqueness or allusiveness of style, an absurdity in narration, a coy calling of attention to that which it conceals, is likely to be one of its most distinctive effects. It is the tantalizingly enigmatic and the violation of natural probability which beckon us on to probe for hidden significances. Inevitably so: for as Bacon would say, what other sense can we make of certain kinds of seemingly ridiculous fables?

It is noteworthy that nowhere in these or earlier discussions by rhetoricians does allegory seem to be connected with *genre* (although Puttenham does mention some genres, or at least modes, such as the pastoral, as having a concealed intention). Since traditionally a variety of genres of biblical poetry were taken as models for allegorical verse (the pastoral *Song of Songs* was considered to be the epitome of allegorical poetry), this may well indicate an earlier recognition that allegory (whether defined in terms of critically interpreted content, or figures, or manner) can work via many literary forms, whether lyric, narrative or epic, and whether (as Salutati observed) in prose or verse. Our contemporary way in some quarters of defining allegory as a genre is incorrect and a source of confusion.

Even under its restrictedly rhetorical treatment in the manuals, *allegoria* is not confined wholly to the level of style or brief figure of speech. *Allegoria* is classified among the first of a variety of figures relating to *thought*: "*sensable* figures . . . affecting the mynde by alteration of *sence* or intendements".[33] In the rhetoricians' view, *allegoria* shares a common base with metaphor (next to which it is placed in some dictionaries), inasmuch as both figures can be defined in terms of the *translation* of words or speeches from one signification into another: "properly . . . *Allegoria* is when we do speake in sence *translative*, and wrested from the owne signification, neverthelesse applied to another not altogether contrary, but having much cõveniencie with it as before we said of the metaphore".[34] Using the same term as Salutati, Peacham and Puttenham directly bracket metaphor and allegory through "translation" (noting, however, that there must be a necessary degree of congruency or "cõveniencie" between signified and signifier). Both metaphor and allegory share wrested "intendement", and there is no basic distinction to be drawn between the two figures. Perhaps the rhetoricians were also aware, even if they did not cite it, of the older concept of "translation" (as in Salutati's understanding) as covering not only allegorical metaphor but all possible forms of "translated" expression (for example, "things" and "deeds" or plot elements in narrative). Tuve also makes the same kind of point central to her discussion connecting allegory with other characteristic tropes in metaphysical imagery in Elizabethan or seventeenth-century usage, noting that not only is *allegoria* related to the more difficult ("dark") forms of metaphor, such as synecdoche, metonymy, or catachresis (Puttenham places allegory next to these[35]), but that allegory is inseparable from metaphor as such.[36] Two characteristics, however, seem to distinguish the rhetorical figure of *allegoria* from simple metaphor. One seems to be its greater *length*, the other is a certain calculated precision of detail—an authorial central control over the "correspondences", which are not left entirely to the reader's imagination. Yet in view of the post-Romantic insistence on the mechanical rigidity of allegory, it is well worth noticing that for Puttenham an element of free reader-interpretation remains inseparably connected with the figure: "in a full allegorie [the intention] should not be discovered, but *left at large* to the readers judgement and coniecture".[37]

Whereas a metaphor may exist in a single word ("inversion of sence in one single worde"), an allegorical metaphor, as Peacham and Puttenham both point out, is not of "one word", but "many".[38] How many is many? The example which Peacham gives consists of a simple short sentence, two lines of verse from Horace.[39] For Puttenham, the allegorical trope is more extended: a matter of "whole and large speaches".[40] Tuve stresses the need for a certain leisurely amplitude in the allegorical trope; there has to be a "succession" or "series" of closely correspondent details, and it is even possible to have "whole poetic units" acting as "great tropes".[41] And so we arrive at the classic Renaissance definition of *allegoria* as extended metaphor or "continûed metaphor"—Spenser's "continued dark conceit". Or as Peacham says: "An Aligory doeth differ from a Metaphor in this, that in a Metaphor, there is a translatiõ but of one word, but in an Aligory of many: for an Aligory is none other thing, then a contynued Metaphor, for when many translations doe abound together, then is it sayth Cicero, an Aligory".[42] And Puttenham: "properly & in his principall vertue *Allegoria* is when we do speake in sence translative and wrested from the owne signification, neverthelesse applied to another not altogether contrary, but having much cõveniencie with it as before we said of the metaphore. . . . such inversion of sence in one single worde is by the figure *Metaphore* . . . and this manner of inversion extending to whole and large speaches, it maketh the figure *allegorie* to be called a long and perpetuall Metaphore".[43]

But the question must inevitably arise (as indeed it does of metaphor): where does "length" or "extension" in allegory stop? Under certain circumstances we can imagine that an entire narrative or poem could function as a sustained allegorical metaphor. Dante implied as much; Spenser certainly suggests this; and Tasso explicitly develops such a theory. However, for technical reasons the allegorical trope as the rhetoricians conceived it is more self-limiting. This is because the rhetorical figure of allegory, as well as being ample or developed, requires a certain exactness and precision of correspondence between the successive details of "vehicle" and "tenor", signifier and signified, which is not easily achieved in a highly sustained piece of writing. For while the allegorical *intention* may be "dim" or obscure, the *surface* of the allegorical metaphor needs to be lucid, indeed needs to be sharp and plain; otherwise, as Tuve points out, we risk the confusions attendant on double metaphor.[44]

These last features may be recognised in certain kinds of extended allegorical metaphors in both Spenser and Milton. The Houses of Cœlia, Mammon or Busirane in Books I, II and III of *The Faerie Queene;* the episodes in *Paradise Lost* of the Golden Stairs, Hell Bridge, Satan's unwilling serpent transformation and the Dead-Sea Apples in Books III and X; briefer Spenserian allegorical vignettes such as the portraits of Malbecco (Jealousy) or Disdaine (*Faerie Queene*, III.ix-x and VI.viii.22-26); or in *Paradise Lost*, somewhat ambivalently, the "allegories" of Sin and Death—these would fit the outermost measurements of the Renaissance manuals. Such episodes have a certain amplitude, yet compactness and a sharpness of outline; they tend to function as story insets or interludes, semi-autonomous within a larger structure. For these reasons it might be possible for the rhetoricians to include even such extended tropes under the classifiable figure of *allegoria*. Spenser's poem, even more than Milton's, is full of semi-discrete allegorical *personae* (who may, however, acquire linked identities with the protagonists within the rhythm of the poem's total allegorical construction). The concept of compact allegory (or allegories) of this disjunct kind bulks large not only in the sixteenth-century rhetorical manuals but in present-day conceptions of the allegorical mode, whole books of interpretation of *The Faerie Queene* being founded on the principle—not unlike that ascribed often to Dante's *Commedia*—that the poem presents itself as a succession of structurally discrete allegorical images, subcharacter after subcharacter, place after place, all set repetitively within a linking romance narrative of a simplistic, single-dimensioned kind.[45] In *Paradise Lost*, of course, the problem of the presence of semi-autonomous allegorical *personae* has not been so easily resolved.

However, none of the dictionary definitions of allegory fully embrace the concept of poetic "translation" as Dante or Salutati understood this; nor do the rhetorical *schemata* fit Boccaccio's or Sidney's remarks (later to be cited) on "Idea" and allegory. The concept of poetry as bilingual, of allegory as comprising all possible forms of translated speech, of the poem itself as an intricate web of invisible correspondences projecting the Platonic Idea which the writer holds in his mind: all these suggest that the rhetoricians' narrowness of approach, while usefully focusing on language, had always been countered by more generous interpretations of allegory, which more fully took a shaping intention in poetry into account. It may be seen that Tuve, as she explores the implications and limitations of the formal trope of "continued metaphor", shows herself inclined to pass beyond the limiting boundaries of rhetorical definitions and to link *allegoria* not only with certain more specialized forms of metaphor, but also with the entire metaphysical mode, and finally with religious and mystical poetry in their widest character of seeking out transcendental correspondences: "A mystical poem sees all sensible phenomena as metaphor; an allegorical poem is, formally and structurally, metaphor. Both are written in the language of correspondences".[46] Clearly, here is yet another manifestation of the ancient and troublesome dichotomy concerning allegory: form and meaning cannot for long be considered in dissociation.

THREE

The English Mythographers
and Their Tradition

One of the most confusing initial impressions of Renaissance critical alle-
goresis is that the older three- or fourfold framework, as seen in scriptural
exegesis or in the older way of interpreting secular fables, often seems to
persist, yet the levels of meaning extrapolated do not quite fit the older
"senses". We have the impression that Renaissance interpretation is still
layered. But the "levels" as used by Renaissance mythographers are not
those which pertained before, even though many of the older scriptural
disciplined procedures used in defining and clearing the ground, prior to
interpreting an allegorical text, may still be present. Emphases differ; and
in general the Renaissance orientation is more secular. The "moral" (older
"tropological") level is more prominent; a spectrum of interpretations may
be predominantly of a natural-scientific or psychological character; the
older "allegorical" sense (not now predictive of Christ) may embrace a
number of vague, not always even transcendental, planes of relevance,
although sometimes these are still perceived as multiple planes of meaning
surrounding a single text or passage; and the term "allegory" may itself be
a source of confusion, not always signifying a true hidden sense.

Poetic rhetoricians in the Renaissance, as in antiquity, deliberately had
narrowed their definitions of allegory so as to direct attention away from
"levels" of "meaning" and toward defining the formal characteristics of
poetic-allegorical language and constructing a specific allegorical-rhetori-
cal methodology for poetry. In this insistence on *form*, the rhetoricians
made their own contribution to the fluid and sophisticated theory of poetry
as allegorical metaphor which had slowly been growing up in the late
Middle Ages, even though this theory was not yet technically well-geared
to address the problems of poetic allegory in particular genres such as epic.
Similarly, Renaissance mythographers also attempted to clarify allegorical
methodology practised as a critical exposition of literary texts, even while
they seemingly perpetuated a hieratic apparatus of an apparently archaic
and sometimes disordered kind. The best of the mythographers also re-

tained a sense of allegory as a language, the language of poetry and espe-
cially of narrative poetry.

Bacon

Francis Bacon for several reasons offers a convenient starting point for the
study of this next phase. His actual insights into the problems of allegory
and fiction are profound; he has a quite remarkable sense of historical
continuities in these matters, as well as an acute awareness of the radically
different *kinds* of issues being addressed; while his remarks on allegory are
still formulated within the older exegetical conventions and vocabulary, so
providing a convenient bridge from medieval to Renaissance theorizing.
Bacon's allegorical essays in the *De sapientia veterum* themselves extrapolate
largely political meanings or, even more so, that level of meaning, popular
in older Stoic exegesis and again in the Renaissance, which could be
termed "cosmological" or "natural-scientific". His own theories of alle-
gorical poetry, however, successfully avoid the limitations of a "levels"
type of allegorical criticism, or over-concentration on any particular spec-
trum of "meaning" or "meanings".

Bacon's clarity and sharpness of mind is everywhere apparent in his
two essays on allegory: in *The Advancement of Learning* (1605), the passages
on "poesy. . . . Allusive" or "poesy parabolical",[1] and the preface to *De
sapientia veterum* (1609), or *Of the Wisdom of the Ancients*.[2] We may see these
qualities not least in Bacon's consciousness of the difficulties surrounding
the area he is discussing: the "abuses" which allegory has suffered in the
past, coupled with his own conscious opposition to the contemporary
tendency, false in his opinion, to relegate allegory to an archaic position of
mechanical inferiority. It is this largeness of view which makes his observa-
tions particularly useful today, in the wake of the post-Romantic tradition
of devaluation of allegory.

Bacon's sense of historical continuity is best seen in his remarks relat-
ing pre-Homeric to post-Homeric and later allegorizing. Perhaps it is just
because of his use of traditional terms and categories that his arguments
have been misunderstood, as for example by J.E. Spingarn, who wrenches
Bacon's judgements in a direction clearly contrary to that intended by
Bacon himself.[3] Bacon's judgements on allegorism are historically accurate
but not derogatory: "in many the like encounters, I do rather think that the
fable was first, and the exposition devised, than that the moral was first,
and thereupon the fable framed".[4] But such an historical state of develop-
ment in interpretation need not detract from the value or "truth" of the
allegorical exposition, from "the honour of parables in general". Fables
have indeed sometimes been wrenched too far (Chrysippus' readings of
the "oldest poets" as Stoic in thought are given as an example). As a result

of a long tradition of such "old abuse", readers may think that Bacon is "but entertaining [himself] with a toy".[5] Nevertheless, "Parables", as he sometimes calls allegories, or poesy "allusive or parabolical" (in Bacon's succinct formulation, "a narration applied only to express some special purpose or conceit"),[6] were in the first instance—back in the mists of time—devised as avenues to truth. The truths embedded in Homer's fables, deriving perhaps from earlier versions of those same fables, may well have been originally implanted not by Homer but even earlier ("from the very beginning", "designed and meditated from the first, and purposely shadowed out"[7]). The fact that Homer's myths exist in many other and some even older versions is only proof of the authority of their latent meaning, deriving from ancient religions rather than later Greek poetry.[8]

Paradoxically, by "veils and shadows" myths "serve . . . also to clear and throw light" upon the meaning. At first "these were used not as a device for shadowing and concealing the meaning, but as a method of making it understood".[9] In this way, from earliest times, parables participate in the mysteries of religion, sometimes conveying truths almost incommunicable by other means: "to take them away would be almost to interdict all communion between divinity and humanity".[10] "Parables" have not lost that value or function through sometimes being imposed upon a fable instead of originating in it. To come down to the present, men can no more now than then do without these similitudes. Just as in earlier times, "hieroglyphics came before letters, so *parables came before arguments*" (a striking insight), and so "even now if any one wish to let new light on any subject into men's minds . . . he must still go the same way and call in the aid of similitudes".[11] (We are reminded of Bacon's own reliance on metaphors in exposition.) Bacon here explicitly equates allegory or parable with metaphor; both are the stuff of human communication and, implicitly, even more so of poetry.

Thus it is not too much to say that Bacon proposes an allegorical theory of poetry. In stressing the essentially metaphorical nature of allegory, its special effectiveness in communicating difficult concepts, and the inseparableness of "parables" (allegory) from other forms of similitude, Bacon carries on the early humanist tradition as seen, for example, in Salutati, but he does so in a psychologically and scientifically more considered manner. We must also not overlook the fact, remarkable in itself, that Bacon adds to the two ancient principal departments of poetry, "narrative" and "representational" (Aristotle's epic and drama), a third department, poetry "parabolical", which is neither narrative nor mimetic but mystical and figurative. Probably earlier discussions of poetry and Scripture gave him precedent for this. Nonetheless, he appears to differentiate an entirely secular allegorical poetic which locates this kind of poetry within a critical spectrum and yet distinguishes it from other kinds.

In the light of the above crucial point, Bacon's other comments fall into clearer perspective. To a certain extent, the chicken-and-egg argument, still with us, over whether fable or meaning came first is, as he says, not only insoluble but fruitless.[12] What does matter is the metaphorical transparency of fable or parable, the ease with which such poetry lends itself to delivering truths of a religious, moral or even scientific nature. The *kind* of truth delivered may vary; but the marvellous adaptability of fable in general will continue to strike us with amazement. Bacon is conscious of the many ways in which poetical texts can be altered in transmission, of the fact that "Homer's myths" preceded Homer.[13] Yet, as has been observed, even if Homer himself had no specific allegorical intention, is it not possible, since Homer did not himself invent many of his fables, that "such inwardness in his own meaning . . . might have [existed] upon a more original tradition"?[14]

Bacon is not solely concerned with hidden signification. His remarks pass naturally into a recognition that in allegorical fable meaning is not separable from the particular formal structure (Bacon's innate Aristotelianism speaks here). It does not matter much which preceded, fable or secondary meaning; what does matter is the palpable "inwardness" of allegorical narrative ("inwardness", an extraordinarily apt and modern-sounding term, holds for Bacon the further, specialized medieval sense of *involucrum*: allegory).[15] Also notable is the happy congruence which so often may be observed between the details of certain fables and the traditional interpretations put upon, or drawn out of, them. This conformity is too striking to be accidental; to quote in full the passage cited earlier:

For in the first place to let the follies and licence of a few detract from the honour of parables in general is not to be allowed; being indeed a boldness savouring of profanity; seeing that religion delights in such veils and shadows, and to take them away would be almost to interdict all communion between divinity and humanity. But passing that and speaking of human wisdom only, I do certainly for my own part (I freely and candidly confess) incline to this opinion,—that beneath no small number of the fables of the ancient poets there lay from the very beginning a mystery and an allegory. It may be that my reverence for the primitive time carries me too far, but the truth is that in some of these fables, *as well in the very frame and texture of the story as in the propriety of the names* by which the persons that figure in it are distinguished, *I find a conformity and connexion with the thing signified, so close and so evident*, that one cannot help believing such a signification to have been designed and meditated from the first, and purposely shadowed out.[16]

Bacon's stress on the "conformity and connexion" between the "frame and texture of the story" and the "thing signified" moves his arguments onto a literary plane and into an engagement with narrative strategy, in a way which shows sharper perceptions even than Dante's about the "allegorical journey". With great critical objectivity, Bacon adds: "And what if we find here and there a bit of real history underneath, or some things

added only for ornament, or times confounded, or part of one fable trans-
ferred to another and a new allegory introduced? Such things could not but
occur in stories invented . . . by men who both lived in different ages and
had different ends, some being more modern, some more ancient, some
having in their thoughts natural philosophy, others civil affairs".[17] In the
first part of the above statement may be found in embryo some of the most
important theories of the later Renaissance, for instance, Tasso's con-
cerning the relationship between history and fiction in allegorical epic
narration. The general narrative *frame* of the fable must "fit" the meaning,
even if fables have been altered or added to in transmission or composition;
a totally uninterrupted line of secondary meaning is not to be expected;
and there may be some "real history", too, underneath. Even though
Bacon is speaking in a general context of allegorical interpretation and not
of allegorical composition, he is also talking about the nature, the "tex-
ture", of the literary text. The first quotation of the two immediately above
offers a compact description of the long allegorical poems of Dante, Tasso
or Spenser; the second, a recognition of the complexity, technical problems
and limitations involved in constructing a long narrative allegory based
upon "history" or "myth".

Whether or not Bacon was aware of Tasso's almost contemporary
theorizing on allegorical poetry or that of earlier Renaissance humanists is
not clear. But his discussion and vocabulary would suggest that he is in fact
familiar with at least some notable classical and postclassical, as well as
medieval and possibly also some early Christian, sources and theories.
Bacon's significant remarks about the element of the "absurd" as a distin-
guishing feature of allegory is extremely important, occurring as it does at
such a late date:

But there is yet another sign, and one of no small value, that these fables
contain a hidden and involved meaning; which is, that *some of them are so absurd and
stupid upon the face of the narrative taken by itself, that they may be said to give notice from
afar and cry out that there is a parable below.* For a fable that is probable may be thought
to have been composed merely for pleasure, in imitation of history. But when a
story is told which could never have entered any man's head either to conceive or
relate on its own account, we must presume that it had some further reach.[18]

This is far from being the patronizing remark one might at first suppose.
Bacon like Augustine recognises that "absurdity"—that is, flagrant im-
plausibility or else *non sequitur* in description or events—is the very feature
which declares the presence of allegory. (The early Christians had identi-
fied the presence of intended allegory in Scripture and distinguished
figurative discourse from doctrine there by means of this same token of
"absurdity".)[19] There therefore will exist an *underlying* or *allegorical* con-
gruence between the "frame" of the story and its inward meaning; and it

is the absurd element or detail in the story, the departure from what is "probable", which "cries out" to the reader to alert him that "there is a parable below". Spenser's various local strategies of absurdity in allegorical narration at once spring to mind; also, in a larger way, the "fantastic episodes" of classical fiction, allegorized by early critics, or correspondently created by Tasso and Spenser within their more "probable" longer narratives. The evoking of such terms as "absurd" and "probable" itself suggests how neatly Bacon locates himself between early and later theories of "allegorical" as opposed to "historical" narration.

A notable coda to the foregoing brief discussion of Bacon's "parabolical-allusive" theory of poetry is that Bacon tends to steer his argument somewhat away from the "reveal-conceal" paradox stressed by earlier theorists of allegory.[20] He simply notes such a convention, while pointing out its innate and necessary contradiction. Perhaps early overinsistence on arcane and esoteric mysteries, on the "veil" and the "cloak" of allegory, has obscured our own proper understanding of allegorical poetry and minimized its fundamental oneness with other forms of "translated" language, and especially with those forms of metaphor which specialize in the qualities of enigma, riddle or absurdity, to which Bacon so rightly calls attention. It may also be observed that in his brief but cogent critical foray into this field, Bacon has not only touched on but put into historical perspective some of the main recurrent difficulties over allegory. He has readjusted the old "rhetoric-versus-content" argument into one concerning the proper rhetorical identification of allegorical meaning through "absurdity"; he has more or less dealt with the still troublesome question of "imposed" secondary meaning versus inherent meaning by pointing out the inescapable historical intertwinings between fiction, meanings and interpretation; and in his presentation, the "truth-versus-fiction" argument similarly more or less dissolves away. The interpreter is up to a point free, but he will be assisted by both structural correspondences and peculiarities in the fable to identify and construe allegory and to determine where allegory properly underlies the fiction. And Bacon has placed his argument *au fond* on a deep understanding of the metaphorical nature of human discourse—in a modern critical vocabulary which he has anticipated, on the connection yet gap between signifier and "thing signified".

Comes and the "Levels"

The traditional framework of exegesis persists in the work of the Renaissance mythographers, who continue to apply the methods or at least a terminological framework reminiscent of the older three- or fourfold "levels" to the conventional body of allegorized myths, Homeric, Ovidian or other. Their methodology is reminiscent of ancient layered exegesis—although it is often the case that Renaissance mythographical interpretation merely leaves us with an impression of intellectual tidiness, of hierarchical analysis, while its actual contents might appear to resemble those of a litter-bin. A fairer comparison might be to the modern editorial apparatus, in which different *kinds* of problems are clearly distinguished as existing in the text, but without necessarily any interrelationship seen between these different problems, as they are perceived or developed in the editorial annotations. Nonetheless, we may find certain distinctive allegorical emphases in the Renaissance mythographic dictionaries and commentaries.

Bacon, remarkably, was aware that "Homer himself . . . was made a kind of scripture by the later schools of the Grecians".[21] However, the Renaissance exegetes no longer model themselves upon the classical and medieval practice of extrapolating entire systems of theology from the ancient texts. Renaissance applications of the "levels" are usually radically secular in orientation.[22] Basically, Renaissance allegorical interpretation is concerned with certain well-defined general areas such as the natural-cosmological, the moral-psychological and the exemplary (ethical)—with, usually, a nod at the spiritual-theological. Historical or political allegory as such is ill-defined in the mythographers' *schema*, although of course it is present in the literature which they analyse. (Sometimes in the commentaries such senses are termed "allusion".) Supporting these various possible strata of educed meaning, we find an editorial mass of contextual annotations (sources of myths, variants of myths, geographical-historical provenance, "allusion" to historical figures of the past, etc.). It is often the case then, that the rigidly parallel marginal headings which appear in the dictionaries do not straddle all these diverse contents very well. However, when true secondary senses are extrapolated from the literature under analysis, these are most often found to be of the moral-psychological kind, with associated or secondary emphasis on the natural-scientific (including the anthropological) and to a lesser degree on the political-civic. (Bacon is very fond of the latter two kinds of allegory.) On the whole, Renaissance exegetes tend to dissect rather than construct. They often seem to stand away from the literary artifact itself, an impression reinforced by their efforts to recover the external contexts of a text. Their conventional method is to treat Homeric or other myths as detached fragments, so that we sometimes have fragmented readings of fragments. Such highly influential works as the *Mythologiae* (1551) of Natalis Comes [Natalis Conti] or Vicenzo Cartari's *Le imagini de i dei de gli antichi* (1571)[23] may be seen essentially as compilations of editorial annotations, leavened by an element of interpretation; they are the equivalents of the modern critical edition.

Comes divides his annotations into "Génealogie" (etymological); "Mythologie" (usually anthropologically based, but also shading into other interpretations—"what was understood" originally by those reading the myths);[24] and "Allégorie"—this last usually is not a spiritual but a moral-psychological sense, perhaps equivalent to the older "tropological", but often not clearly distinguished from the "sense" referred to under "Mythologie", and like the latter in Comes often having a scientific-cosmological base. Comes' method is first to set all the versions and sources of a myth side by side, to examine their provenance, and after collating the various versions to proceed to an exposition of the myth, each detail being interpreted at several levels or in several ways, according to his own scheme. (An example which he gives is the various meanings of Pan's dress, his appearance, his behaviour, his horns, hooves, skin, each as drawn from the several versions of the myth.)[25] It was understood by this scholarly commentator that in different older interpretations the same detail might carry different secondary meanings; Comes' emphasis is on the anthropological interest inhering in this very diversity. But his predominating interests could be described as biological or psychological, and cosmological. If one is seeking ethical or moralized meanings in Comes, one is apt to feel a little disappointed; the stance is too detached to be deeply ethical; morality is a consequence of biology. Comes' method has analogies to biblical scholarship, where investigation of the text's background becomes a legitimate expansion of the "literal" level, with perhaps an occasional secondary meaning seen as embedded anteriorly in the text. However, out of such expansion there arises only one main avenue of figurative interest for Comes, and that is the natural-scientific application of myths.

Comes' system is imitated by the English translators, editors or annotators of Ovid, as for example George Sandys (1632),[26] and of Ariosto, as for example John Harington (1591). These writers use comparable editorial methods to Comes', although with somewhat individual emphases and more interest in genuine moral allegorizing. Their methods are still loosely reflected in such a late discourse on poetry as that of Henry Reynolds, *Mythomystes* (1632), mentioned earlier. Reynolds' treatise could be described as a loose portfolio of theoretical remarks on and examples of allegory, making use of both the older and the newer mythographic emphases in the matter of the "levels" and of ancient and newer allegorical devices (including etymological allegory), in a rather incoherent mixture. But Reynolds (like Dante on the verses on the theme of Exodus, or Saint Bernard on the Song of Songs)[27] also remembers the older medieval exegetical tradition, as may be seen in his taking a single myth out of which to make a setpiece of layered analysis. It is the pagan tale of Narcissus that Reynolds selects; but his primary emphasis is a spiritualized one. Reynolds' intendedly scholarly and technical yet pseudo-mystical analyses seem to have little in common with Bacon's intelligent critical and scholarly reconstructions of fables, or with the latter's consciousness of the "conformity" (narrative correspondence) between literary texts and allegorical readings of them, and his awareness of the rhetorical character ("absurdity") of allegorical "fables" and, in general, of the methods and purposes of "parabolical" poetry.

The methods of the English annotators were drawn more immediately, perhaps, from the late sixteenth-century Italian editors and allegorizers of Ovid, Ariosto and other old or recent literary texts. Some of those continental scholars had set an example, not always felicitous, of stratified readings which often did superficially at least seem to impose meanings on the text in an arbitrary and fragmented way,[28] one which appears quite opposed to the continuous narrative of classical epics and the "continued" moral-progress allegorizations on these in traditional Neoplatonist exegesis. Particularly when, as in the case of Ariosto, mythographic methods are seriously applied not only to ancient epics but to modern ones written with a professedly allegorical content which is itself partly parody of the methods of earlier epic allegorizers, an impression of naiveté, confusion or unease may result: a problem felt most acutely perhaps by Harington (whose work is next discussed). But an understanding of their more reputable scholarly antecedents in contemporary editorial practices in dictionaries of myth such as that of Comes, as well as of the fact that the late epic allegorizers follow in brief repetitive vignettes established patterns of ethical-psychological interpretation which had been successfully applied in earlier more continuous expositions of epic narration, does something to help us understand the reasons for the popularity and general acceptance of these allegorically annotated editions. The problems which the allegorizers of Ovid or Ariosto betray in their work have to do with the essentially discontinuous but repetitive structures of the romance or quasi-romance narratives which they undertake to explicate, rather than with faults in the art of allegoresis itself.

John Harington and His Successors

Harington is a responsible critic who makes a substantial contribution to English theory of allegory and does his best to avoid the casualness of certain Italian annotators of epic. He carries over into his English edition of Ariosto the tradition of the Italian allegorizers of the *Orlando Furioso*, the elaborately allegorical edition by Pietro de'Franceschi (1584) being in fact the text which Harington used for his own translation.[29] Harington is very much aware of the critical problems inherent in the tradition and material he imports, and is rather burdened by them. No less than three critical prefaces; in addition, ongoing Book-by-Book allegories expressed as individual, layered exegeses set at the end of each Book; marginal annotations embracing a variety of kinds of observations throughout each Book; and a final summary of the main points and directions of all the allegories taken together ("A Briefe and Summarie Allegorie") suggest a conflict either between Harington's various *schemata* or between his received apparatus and his own critical perceptions. Harington's difficulties are created partly by his trying to implant a dictionary method onto a number of quite different approaches to allegory, and further trying, beyond annotating Ariosto's text, to formulate critical-poetical principles and to emphasize a "progress" type of allegory for certain sections of the *Furioso*. He is trying to be both editor and literary critic—perhaps even to formulate an allegorical poetic which can fit the variety within the mixed-genre romance epic. Despite what might at first sight appear to be his incoherent medley of Renaissance and medieval allegorical *schemata*, points of great interest emerge from Harington's remarks. Among later English mythographers, only Henry Reynolds' effort to revive Bacon's theory of "parabolical" or "allusive" poetry (with a Neoplatonic overlay) has comparable critical relevance.[30] While we may sympathize with Reynolds' as with Harington's efforts to break the shackles of the mythographers' quasi-scientific methods and interests, and, in the case of Reynolds, to reintroduce Neoplatonic interpretation of a more spiritual cast ("figurative, typick and symbolick notions"),[31] Reynolds' wildly synoptic though enthusiastic assemblage of every known type of allegoresis from classical to biblical, from the narrowest type of etymological interpretation to the widest theory of figurative poetry, betrays the profound uncertainty in this late period surrounding the whole subject of allegory, with its variety of mingled, rich traditions. Harington, by contrast, seeks to introduce order into confusion.

In Harington's *Ariosto*, some shadow of the old three- or fourfold exegetical apparatus might be thought to be reflected in his tidy marginal divisions of annotations into three or four recurring categories; but, as with other sixteenth-century allegorizers, these compartments do not always give a fair idea of their contents. Harington's immediate predecessors, Italian allegorizers such as Orazio Toscanella,[32] similarly had adopted an apparatus compartmented into linguistic, historical, and "mythological" categories, both theirs and Harington's schemes being very suggestive of that of Comes. In sharp contrast is, later, the individualistic Henry Reynolds who, while ostensibly following an apparently similar four-partite division of "sences" to that of Comes (into categories of "Geographick", "Physick", "Morall", and "Divine"),[33] really cares only for the last. Reynolds' "moral" readings are either perfunctory, or push over the boundaries of the "moral" into the overtly spiritual. Sandys, by contrast, in his *Ovid's Metamorphoses*, annotating but without the marginal divisions along lines closely derived from Comes, reduces the cosmological and expands the geographic and natural-scientific explanations, his own fascination being particularly with "moral" (not to say moralistic) types of reading, and with overtly allegorized treatments of the myths—etymologies, provenance and the like being of merely peripheral interest. Harington, like his successor, Sandys, shows a strong moral or exemplary emphasis, adding a further marginal category (beyond those in Comes' *Mythologiae*) of the "Moral". Thus it seems that beneath the various schemes or frameworks of interpretation, the received opinions of a society, its moral, religious or social presuppositions, its favoured doctrines of classical-ethical and religious belief, its scientific interests, will always manifest themselves, although with individual variations—as Bacon understood.[34] Like other Renaissance commentators, Harington finds his own or the period's characteristic interests within a conventional framework. Yet it is not to be thought that such flexibility generates a contradictory multiplicity of private readings. For, as Harington himself observes (and as he illustrates in offering an "infinite" number of closely similar applications of the Perseus legend), interpretations often may follow a constant general pattern, or run closely in parallel.[35] In his odd emphasis on how *very many* closely similar readings (all spiritual, as he gives them) it would be possible to extract—if it were not so "tedious"—from the Perseus legend (I comment further on this below), Harington may be minimizing this spiritual kind of reading and turning attention away from older allegorical preoccupations toward more contemporaneous areas of interest.

We need not, therefore, be confused when we find that, in his effort to clarify the complex grounds of his exegesis, Harington has set out no less than three separate systems or schemes of allegorical classification. In his "Preface" or "A Briefe Apologie of Poetrie" (the first scheme) he alludes to senses "literall" (or "of an historie"); "Morall" (meaning *exemplary*, the "approving vertuous *actions* and condemning the contrarie"); and "Allegorie" (defined, in the manner of Peacham or Puttenham, as "when one thing is told, and by that another is understood"). The last-named sense is said to be a comprehensive category of figuration, including a "true understanding of naturall Philosophie, or somtimes of politike governement, and now and then of divinitie".[36] Not altogether surprisingly then, the elaborate spritualized apparatus with which Harington graces (and then dismisses) the Perseus legend[37] does not altogether fit the hermeneutical hierarchy previously announced. It recalls rather Dante's setpiece on two verses on Exodus in the *Convivio*, or Saint Bernard's commentaries on the *Song of Songs*, and the general tradition of the medieval *quatre sens*. In this setpiece of Harington's, we observe that the "moral" sense as proposed by himself is indeed a *figurative* sense and not a merely "exemplary" one (which is Harington's ordinary interpretation of the term "Morall", using it as a noun), and that all the variations including the so-called "naturall" sense have more than a touch of "divinitie". No wonder then that the pragmatic Harington finds this Perseus showpiece a little "tedious". He has shown that he can "do the older thing", but he is perhaps not very interested in it. This kind of allegorizing—the *Ovide Moralisé*—is out of date.

To understand what Harington intends, we may look at the briefer

notice or "An Advertisement to the Reader" (the second scheme), where
he gives a four-part division rather more in line with Renaissance diction-
ary practice,[38] and which represents the scheme he himself follows in his
marginal annotations to Ariosto's text and also in the individual commen-
taries appended at the end of each Book. Here the division is into "Morall",
"Historie", "Allegorie" and "Allusion". The second and fourth categories
affect a nod at Renaissance scholarship of the Comes sort, but of which
there is little to be found in the English Ariosto. It is the first or sometimes
the third of the above "senses" in which Harington is most interested.
Although throughout his text he points out numerous "examples" of
virtues and other qualities, his own "Allegories" on the other hand repre-
sent true figurative readings and are always of a moral-ethical-psychologi-
cal kind. They follow a standard Aristotelian-Platonic psychology, the
reason-passion model so familiar in Renaissance literature, perhaps occa-
sionally diverging into the classical and Christian *schemata* of virtues and
vices characteristic of earlier periods of allegory. Harington's so-called
"Morall" marginal annotation, it must be stressed, does not (and he wishes
it to be understood that it does not) represent any true figurative "level" at
all; in this shallowness or transparency the "Morall" reading, an exemplary
reading, is quite unlike the designedly moral or ethical *allegory* which he
gives for the Perseus legend.[39]

It is necessary to comment on Harington's repeated efforts to clarify
the foregoing highly important distinction between "allegory", some-
times then popularly conceived of as didactic *exemplum,* and "Allegorie"
understood as true ethical figuration.[40] The distinction is a difficult one,
because exemplifications of virtues and vices can so easily shade into
schematic allegorical constructs in earlier literature. The distinction per-
haps is forced upon him by the highly episodic and variegated nature of
Ariosto's fable, in which numerous loosely associated incidents and char-
acters cannot easily be fitted into any coherent scheme of continuous
secondary meaning. Many discrete episodes or persons in the adventures
may only stand as rather obvious illustrations or sub-illustrations of
various types or shades of personal behaviour: types of love, courtesy and
so on, seen in various contexts and connections. We can see the same
problem arising in *The Faerie Queene,* and in the "Letter to Raleigh"
Spenser makes a similar distinction between "ensample" (as in the "im-
age" of Arthur, "a brave knight") and proper allegory.[41] In *The Faerie
Queene* as in the *Orlando Furioso* many isolated character-vignettes merely
illustrate various *types* of ethical behaviour, rather than allegorically "figure
forth" or "shadow" the inner aspects or problems to do with virtues or
vices, as do some other characters (for example, the three female personae
of Elizabeth). Exemplary instances in Spenser are all the bad kinds of lovers
and friends in Book IV. But the ethical *continuum* of the "continued dark
conceit" going on beneath the surface of Spenser's plot in more covert

ways greatly expands the meaningfulness of the other, directly moral
dimension.

It is everywhere plain from Harington's discussions, descriptions and
glosses that exemplary writing (a "moral fable" which is not even a parable)
is what he intends by the term for that "level" or "sense" which he
designates as "Morall". In his "Briefe Apologie" and in the concluding
"Briefe and Summarie Allegorie" (the third scheme, stressing example)
Harington speaks of Ariosto's poem as particularly illustrative of conduct.
It has to do with love and war, with men virtuous and bad, with types of
lovers or kings, examples of courtesy and arms, and so forth. In the "Briefe
and Summarie Allegorie" he acknowledges that these "sundry examples
both of men and women" form a substantial part of Ariosto's fable. The
"Briefe and Summarie Allegorie" itself comprises a mixture of comments
on this and that kind of conduct, interspersed with more serious allegoriza-
tions in which the episodes are not read literally. Again, the Book-by-Book
explications of characters in Harington's edition, as of Rogero in Book XXII,
reveal mainly illustrations of moral conduct: for example, Rogero is said to
be "the verie Idea and perfect example of a true Knight". ("Idea" here is
partly used in the Platonic sense of "pattern": a conception which for
different reasons, as we shall see, can verge upon allegory.) But it is
apparent that the moral-ethical explications given under Harington's "Al-
legorie" are of a quite different nature, showing more secret correspon-
dences to the narrative.[42]

There is some residual confusion in Harington's use of the term
"moral", since the "moral" sensus as a truly secondary sense was formerly
included in the hierarchy of meanings within the older fourfold allegorical
apparatus. The reason for the inclusion of this name in Harington's scheme
would appear to be twofold: the fact that the "exemplary" does concern
moral meaning, and the fact also that (as has been remarked) the exem-
plary can sometimes shade over into allegorical schemata of virtues or vices
(for example, if the individual exemplary character is presented in conjunc-
tion with other cognate characters so that all together form parts of some
whole virtue). The distinction which Harington makes between "Morall"
(frankly exemplary) and "Allegorical" (usually covert psychological-ethical
figuration) raises technical questions of importance for the entire Renais-
sance debate on allegory, and even more so for the modern understanding
of that debate. This apart, the fact that Harington distinguishes so sharply
between the two kinds of possible "moral" value in a fable, one direct, the
other figured, is surely very helpful to us in a consideration not only of
Spenser but of Paradise Lost. It informs us that in no way is the exemplary
value of Milton's story lessened—its value as Samuel Johnson saw it, as a
cautionary tale—if we are further led to find complementary and perhaps
more complex ethical or spiritual depths in certain parts of the same story.
The two kinds of "moral" meanings are not mutually exclusive. It is notable

too that Harington is among those critics (like Tasso) who are struggling to articulate a new poetic—an allegorical poetic—which will fit the particularly protean nature of the new vernacular romance epic and which will also, as Harington says, be relevant to the "sweete statelinesse" of "Heroicall Poesie".[43]

Other aspects of Harington's allegorical analyses also prove helpful in a consideration of the allegorical epic. He believes, with Comes, that there is a certain groundwork of objective truth in most myths—if only in the sense that these myths emanated from specific places and peoples and perhaps contain traces of historical civilizations and persons. Yet in fable is also universal truth, hidden, but as appropriate to "us" as to "them": "the Allegorie of some things that are meerely fabulous, yet have an allegoricall sence, which every bodie at the first shew cannot perceive".[44] Harington shares the Renaissance perception that truth may be approached from contrary directions: through facts and scholarship at the literal or historical level, and also through the imagination, that is, through the figurative or allegorical. Thus in Ariosto's epic, "truth" is to be found even in, or equally in, the "fabulous bits".

Harington's value as a critic of allegory and epic resides perhaps especially in his ultimate clearing of the mind. Out of his three superficially ill-matching *schemata*, there emerges an apprehension that an epic fable is an inclusive genre which may contain very different strata of fictional and allegorical representation. Certain of an epic's ingredients may be literally or fictively "true"; it may have an exemplary value in its basic plot, its "typical" characters and incidents; and it may have deeper significances over a wide range of important concerns, perhaps ethical predominantly— these often being contained particularly in the parts which are sometimes derided as ridiculous or "meerely fabulous". Perhaps to this blunt-seeming yet intelligent interpreter too, the ancient importance of "absurdity" in allegorical fable was still apparent. However, in his preoccupation with always disengaging several different layers of meaning, sometimes in a fragmented way, from poetic fable, Harington finds himself in difficulties over reconciling an inherited, rather rigid scholarly and analytical apparatus with his consciousness that the nature of poetic discourse and of myth is textured and variable. Following the methods practised by the mythographical dictionaries and the Italian annotators, Harington did also help to perpetuate that view of allegorical epic as "episodic" (containing straight fictions, sometimes overtly didactic, intermingled with discrete "allegories") which has confusingly persisted to the present day, but which had never represented the true thrust of the early Homeric and Virgilian traditions of exegesis, nor the practice of the greatest writers of allegorical epic fiction.

FOUR

"Idea"

Other apprehensions of allegory in the Renaissance developed in directions better suited than those of the mythographers to the consideration of allegorical poetry as a specialized art of communication, as well as a purveyor of hidden truths. Such views had already been theoretically initiated by Dante and other medieval critics when they affirmed that the reading of a text may be seen as falling into two broad divisions, rather than always a hierarchy of meanings. These two divisions were the *sensus literalis* and the *sensus spiritualis*, the *sensus spiritualis* being a single, embracing and fluid secondary figurative dimension, which was more easily conformable to the vagaries of a long narrative poem. Similarly, an important view of allegory in the early Renaissance had defined *all poetry* as having "two natures" or speaking with "two voices", or, as we have seen in the case of Salutati, as in all its elements taken together constituting a form of "translated" discourse. One aspect of poetry lay in its external dress or show, the fictional fable which is delightful, while the other lay in its more inward nature, its hidden meaning. The latter was often expressed in terms of an anterior controlling "Idea": that is, allegory in the specific sense of a hidden, abstract conception or didactic intention. Although Renaissance discussions within this tradition of "Idea" could take less or more cognizance of poetry as an allegorical *language*, discussion tended in the end to lead back to the unavoidable fact that communication of hidden (or indeed any) meaning is inseparable from its external dress, from *discourse:* that poetry has to do with language, and that poetic narrative has to do with temporal or other formal structures. Thus discussions of secular literary allegoresis in the Renaissance had increasingly to come to grips with the problems of the "how"—with problems of narrative and language in the literary allegorical text, especially the epic.

It is via the familiar Renaissance concept of "Idea" that we must initially explore the developing Renaissance allegorical poetic. This concept of "Idea", so familiar in the Renaissance (later confusingly equated with the more modern term, "Ideal Imitation", which overlaps but has a different range of meanings), then as now was seldom fully understood.[1] Various interpretations could attach to the term. For instance, given the truism that poetry for the period possessed a moral or instructive purpose, it could be felt that such a purpose was sufficiently served simply by projecting generalized or idealized representations of external nature or of man's moral nature.[2] The concept of "Ideal Imitation" in this sense may date back to Aristotle's emphasis on "general nature", the representative man, or to Plato's doctrine of ethical "Ideas", seen now as embodied in ethically ideal characters. Different kinds of efforts were made to interpret "Idea" in Aristotelian terms of unity of artistic purpose, the *telos* of a unified plot, for example. With all of these views we are not primarily here concerned—although the Platonic doctrine of "Ideas" as essences has some relevance to the nature of allegory as considered in the present study.[3] The above formal views concerning "Idea" as "Ideal Imitation" indeed existed in the Renaissance or later, and are certainly perpetuated in our own critical understanding; but although such ideas were involved with Renaissance criticism, they do not account for what was then generally understood by "poetic teaching", "Imitation of the Ideal" or "Allegory" (in the period the three concepts may often be found linked and the terms interchangeable). Beneath its sometimes platitudinous surfaces, the thrust of Renaissance critical language could be specific and searching. It moves toward the expression of not merely a didactic theory of poetry as embodied in Platonic examples of ideal actions and conduct, but toward a theory of hidden and figured didactic content expressible via a unique kind of metaphor: toward defining the essence of the poetical art as itself allegory, rendering visible the abstract Idea. Late in the Renaissance, technical discussions of poetic allegory as "translated" expression would crystallize into a specific theory of the allegorical epic (and, of course, there was good foundation for such theory in the earlier traditions of continuous allegorical exposition of epic myth). But as we have seen, earlier phases of Renaissance literary criticism did not distinguish between allegory in the epic and that in other kinds of poetry, but spoke generally in terms pertaining to all poetry—for the good reason that allegorical language, since it was equated with poetry itself, was not divisible by genres.

Philo

The sources of Renaissance allegorical theories relating to "Idea" go back at least as far as Philo, the hellenizing allegorist of the beginning of the Christian era.[4] In Book I.lvi on the Fall, Philo says: "Now these are no mythical fictions . . . but modes of making ideas visible, bidding us resort to allegorical interpretation guided in our renderings by what lies beneath the surface". Again, in Book I.iv-v on the Creation:

Like a good craftsman [who] begins to build the city of stones and timber, keeping his eye upon his pattern and making the visible and tangible objects correspond in each case to the incorporeal ideas. Just such must be our thoughts about God. . . . He conceived beforehand the model of its parts, and . . . out of these He constituted and brought to completion a world discernible only by the mind, and then, with that for a pattern, the world which our senses can perceive. As, then, the city which was fashioned beforehand within the mind of the architect held no place in the outer world, but had been engraved in the soul of the artificer as by a seal; even so the universe that consisted of ideas would have no other location than the Divine Reason, which was the Author of this ordered frame.

Philo, in his conviction that God's concern in the Old Testament is to "make ideas visible", might appear in the readings which he offers on Genesis to pass abruptly from one to another quite different allegory on the same verses, without concern as to whether or not these fragmented readings cohere, or without regard for the integrity of the total narrative of the original. This is probably a misunderstanding of his methods. In the light of midrashic reading, earlier discussed, Philo's technique may appear as less capricious, since in that tradition it was thought that all diverse interpretations of a passage of Scripture could only return the reader to the infinite plenitude but unalterable identity of the sacred text. Each reading in its own way is expressive of the particular text's anterior and unchanging content; although the rainbow of associated readings can sometimes create a new literary texture of its own, in the exposition. More simply perceived, Philo's theory of allegory as an anterior didactic concept standing behind the divine narrative text seems to have become absorbed into the Renaissance theory of allegorical poetry and epic. Some of Philo's specific allegories on Genesis (for example Adam and Eve as Mind and Sense, and the Serpent as Pleasure) were also an influence on *Paradise Lost*, although that subject cannot be taken up in the present study.

Boccaccio

Boccaccio initiates one of the most significant Renaissance treatments of the art of poetry, expressing with Platonic reverberations and in what seems to be the new vocabulary (despite his relatively early date, just after Dante and contemporary with Salutati) a view of reality and art which takes the outer dress of poetry, its language and fictive details, as "shadows" or reflections, signs or figures of a further reality which preexists the poem as a higher "Idea" or transcendental truth. Behind any poem there stands an anterior concept which uses the visible materials of the poem as its artistic clay. Like the potter's guiding hand, this Idea provides the shaping "Form" in the poem, realizing itself in the flesh or dress, the fable or medium of language. This seems to be Boccaccio's essential point in his critique of poetry in the *De genealogia deorum gentilium*, Book XIV, apart from his predictable defence of poesy against "lying" and immorality: "fiction [*fabula*, poetic myth] is *a form of discourse, which, under the guise of invention, illustrates or proves an idea*".[5] Boccaccio's conception is similar to Philo's, but more precise. Poetic fiction not only illustrates an *idea* (Philo says "makes visible"), it seems to do so through some natural internal correspondence between the preexistent idea and the poetic fiction, this presumably to be achieved through some particular qualities or forms of speech or perhaps of narrative structures—since "fiction" is a *"form of discourse"*. The particular emphases are interesting in Boccaccio's compact statement. The "Idea" may either be *illustrated* (exemplified perhaps) in the "fiction", or it may be "proved" (as in an argument); to "prove" implies that the "Idea" being expressed is not merely exemplary, nor some idealized "pattern" of conduct, but an abstract intellectual concept. However, this "Idea" departs from logic in that it is carried by a special *"form of discourse"* (the "invention", or the poetic fable). That would suggest that some degree exists of internal connectedness between the anterior idea and the form of discourse carrying the concept, that *form* and *idea* run together. Further, the Idea is conveyed *indirectly*: it exists under a "guise" (allegorical disguise) or "veil" of invention, the fable itself: "If, then, sense [meaning] is revealed from under the veil of fiction, the composition of fiction is not idle nonsense". Albeit so briefly, Boccaccio suggests a comprehensive description of allegory. The value he affords to allegory in secular poetry links it also with Scripture: "what the poet calls fable or fiction our theologians have named figure".[6] Poetic allegory has a comparable basis in truth to that form of predictive metaphor which theologians find in the Bible.

Sidney

Philip Sidney in *An Apology for Poetry* (1595) seems to be attempting to formulate a theory of poetic art and act which follows along the Neoplatonic lines of Boccaccio, although curiously, Sidney's theory is less specifically addressed to the problems of *discourse*. The poet through his "foreconceit" is in a manner of speaking in direct touch with that higher or "second Nature" which all poetry aspires to portray. The Platonic Idea preexists in the poet's as in the Divine Maker's Mind: "give right honour to the heavenly Maker of that maker, who having made man to His own likeness, set him beyond and over all the works of that second nature".[7] The Idea precedes the poem, and the poem endeavours "substantially" to realise it—to realise it in the flesh. Sidney praises the fertility of the poet's art and invention without too closely involving himself in the practical questions of how this higher mimesis is to be executed. However, his language is charged with significant innuendo: poetry "*delivers* forth", "*figures* forth", and "worketh *substantially*"; it fleshes out and makes manifest, through figure, the Idea or Platonic pattern: "any understanding knoweth the skill of the artificer standeth in that *Idea* or fore-conceit of the work, and not in the work itself. And that the poet hath that *Idea* is manifest, by delivering them forth in such excellency as he hath imagined them. Which delivering forth also is not wholly imaginative, . . . but so far substantially it worketh, not only to make a Cyrus . . . but to bestow a Cyrus upon the world to make many Cyruses".[8] The sense of reality, concreteness, livingness, is strong in Sidney's language. Here is no remote transcendentalism by which the veil of fiction is stripped away to reveal the abstract truth standing on its own; this "Idea" is born, delivered, *substantially*. Its impact is emotional, immediate, enthralling.

Sidney's language at the end of the passage above suggests the exemplary or idealized example mode; the Platonic *pattern* of a Cyrus will inspire many would-be Cyruses to emulation. His language may also be thought to invoke the notion of "Idea" as formal design. But there can be no doubt that Sidney is also thinking of "Idea" or "fore-conceit" in terms of allegory, since he specifically uses the term in its traditional association with Aesop: "though [the poet] recount things not true, yet . . . he lieth not . . . think I none so simple would say that Aesop lied in the tales of his beasts; for who thinks that Aesop writ it for actually true [?] . . . What child is there that, coming to a play, and seeing *Thebes* written in great letters upon an old door, doth believe that it is Thebes? . . . [these] things [are] not affirmatively but allegorically and figuratively written".[9] There is of course a distinction to be drawn between fabling as in a theatre and actual allegorical poetry; however, it is apparent that in the lines quoted above Sidney is thinking of other genres as well as the dramatic. By "Idea" Sidney in fact implies all three modes—aesthetic design, moral example ("a Cyrus"), and certainly, figure or allegory.

There is no doubt that Sidney's own descriptive method in the revised *Arcadia* increasingly embodies an allegorical form of metaphor—that is to say, the descriptions pass beyond what might be called "exemplary" or even "symbolical". His descriptions of persons or scenes are charged with emblematic nuances suggesting specific ethical-psychological concepts relevant to the problems and characters of the protagonists. These nuances are of so pointed a kind as in effect to constitute forms of allegorical correspondence.[10] In his Introduction to Sidney's *Apology* Geoffrey Shepherd considers that the Elizabethan poet or artist thought of the poetic "image" as an emblem; he thought not so much in terms of the "neo-Platonists' flashing recognition of a Platonic Idea" or an "intuitional image", but in terms of a "complex Idea" of the kind intended by Locke, involving a good deal of conceptual thinking. Images of this latter kind involve abstract analysis, "trains and groupings of concepts",[11] something, in short, resembling the compressed allegorical image or the allegorical emblem. It is no accident that in Kalander's House in Book I, chapter 3, of the revised *Arcadia* we directly confront such trains of images visually represented as pictures.[12] And of course Sidney's entire romance offers a model of the traditional epic-allegorical education in the formation of virtue, which has fled from men's sight in the absent person of "Urania".[13] There is one place in the *Apology* which in fact suggests that Sidney may well be thinking of allegory in the epic, or in his epic prose-romance: namely, when (in the same paragraph citing allegory quoted above) he speaks of readers as "looking but for fiction" in Poesy, but finding further that they "use the narration but as an *imaginative ground-plot* of a *profitable invention*".[14] An extended didactic figure operating *pari passu* with plot would thus seem to be in Sidney's mind here. It is interesting to speculate as to why Sidney is relatively so guarded in his allusions to allegory in poetry, when his whole discussion seems to be grounded on that concept.

Tasso

Torquato Tasso, whose theories will be considered in greater detail in the next three chapters, and later in connection with Milton,[15] in the "Allegoria" to his *Gerusalemme liberata* moves the Sidney argument one step further along (if we may reverse chronology).[16] He unhesitatingly and repeatedly gives to the artist's anterior or ulterior Idea or design, the didactic and aesthetic "fore-conceit" according to which the epic poet shapes his poem as God does his Creation, the actual name of allegory. Paradoxically, the term "Imitation" in Tasso's use becomes detached from any association with a higher Nature or transcendental reality (as in Sidney's use) and is reduced instead to the lively representation of external reality; it becomes the mere external "dress" or outward show, "representation" in its most literal sense. In this radical revision of conventional terminology, "Imitation" presents only the surface, while didactic allegory is the conception behind. "Allegory" (that is, the poem's "Idea") then corresponds to the "soul" of the heroic poem, while "Imitation" is only the body: "Heroical Poetry, as a living creature, wherein two natures are conjoined, is compounded of Imitation and Allegory: with the one she allureth unto her the minds and ears of men, and marvellously delighteth them; with the other, either in virtue or knowledge, she instructeth them. And as the heroically written Imitation of another is nothing else but the pattern and image of human action; so the Allegory of an Heroical Poem is none other than the glass and figure of Human Life". "Imitation" offers an external reflection and exemplary model ("pattern and image") of human life; but allegory offers a "glass and figure", in St. Paul's sense of seeing in a mirror darkly, a premonition of higher truths which cannot be revealed plainly:

> But Imitation regardeth the actions of man subjected to the outward senses, and about them being principally employed, seeketh to represent them with effectual and expressive phrases, such as lively set before our corporeal eyes the things represented. It doth not consider the customs, affections, or discourses of the mind, as they be inward, but only as they come forth thence, and being manifested in words, in deeds, or working, do accompany the action. On the other side, Allegory respecteth the passions, the opinions and customs, not only as they do appear, but principally in their being hidden and inward; and more obscurely doth express them with notes, as a man may say, mystical, such as only the understanders of the nature of things can fully comprehend.[17]

Thus Tasso, while adopting a Neoplatonic language and aesthetic in many ways predictive of or analogous to Sidney's, is actually reversing the terminology, as used by Sidney, in the interest of a more precise poetic. Poetry secretly "allures" and "delights"; with obscure "notes . . . mystical" it "instructs" in a higher truth. The fable is the corporeal image which makes the Idea visible, setting before the senses things, words, deeds or actions; but it is the inner Allegory which not only "instructs" but appeals to the mind, conveying in some more universal way the internal essences of human experience. (As indicated in the above quotation, for Tasso such essences are of a distinctly ethical-psychological nature.)

As Tasso goes on to analyse his subject further, we shall see that not only is he discussing epic and allegory in epic, but he is taking into account different *kinds* of theme or subject in allegorical epic. He considers not only the allegorical epic of the contemplative life such as Dante wrote, but as well the epic of heroic enterprise, of civil life and personal ethical development within a society. This is a significant distinction:

> it may be said, that the Life of Man is [also] contemplative, and to work simply with the understanding, forasmuch as this life doth seem much to participate of heaven, and as it were changed from humanity, to become angelical. Of the life of the contemplative man, the Comedy of Dante and the Odyssey, are, as it were, in every part thereof a figure; but the civil life is seen to be shadowed throughout the Iliad and Æneid also, although in this there be rather set out a mixture of action and contemplation. But since the contemplative man is solitary, and the man of action liveth in civil company, thence it cometh that Dante and Ulysses, in their departure from Calypso, are feigned not to be accompanied of the army, or of a multitude of soldiers, but to depart alone; whereas Agamemnon and Achilles are described, the one general of the Grecian army, the other leader of many troops of Myrmidons. And Æneas is seen to be accompanied when he fighteth, or doth other civil acts; but when he goeth to hell and the Elysian fields, he leaves his followers, accompanied only with his most faithful friend Achates.[18]

The epic of the solely contemplative life is not to be Tasso's heroic action (although the *Gerusalemme* contains a few such pointedly solitary, "contemplative" episodes, as does *Paradise Lost*). However, in both sorts of epic, allegory works "hidden" and with "notes mystical", such as only "the understanders of the nature of things" can comprehend.

It may be observed that in both Sidney and Tasso a characteristic syndrome of closely associated words and concepts clusters around their Neoplatonic and allegorical view of art. Words like "Idea", "glass", "figure", "figure forth", "shadow" and also "image" and "imagined" constantly appear, recognisable echoes of allegorical vocabulary from Saint Paul onward. Both critics also see the poet as a Maker, emulating the divine Artificer who realises his conceptions, his Idea(s), in his living creation and (as biblical exegetes had said) in the external world through the persons, deeds and events of the Bible, all of which act as His "words". In such a view, scriptural-typological figuration parallels the figuration with which secular poetry also may invest the living world in the imagination. But in neither case does the scriptural view of typology or the parallel Renaissance view of allegorical figure in poetry reduce the living world to any pallid shadow, despite the Neoplatonic aesthetic affiliations of the Renaissance outlook. The medieval bond between figure and the real literal level, reinforced by scriptural traditions of exegesis, remains strong. And so when in *Paradise Lost* we shall find Milton playing with similar language and conceptions, we will be aware that even in his "real" epic of scriptural history we are still in the presence of a certain sustained tradition of allegorical discourse in poetry and in epic. As we shall see, Milton consciously brings to the fore similar conceptions to those of Sidney or Tasso concerning the relation of higher realities to poetic discourse, and he similarly engages with the problems of finding the right form and shape, style and language to mirror his own "great Argument" or his Idea, the guiding conception behind his poem.

PART II

Theory of the Allegorical Epic from Tasso, Spenser and the Neoclassicals to Milton

Tasso: The Practical Problems of the Allegorical Epic

It is apparent that Tasso—the most significant theorist and practitioner of allegorical epic in the Italian Renaissance, whose criticism will be considered in greater detail from this point[1]—passed through a difficult evolution of thought, partly reflecting some of the divided conceptions of allegory in the Renaissance or earlier, and during which his own conception of allegory underwent a progressive broadening. Cognizant of purely rhetorical definitions of allegory in the classical oratorical tradition, he became dissatisfied with their restrictiveness. In a letter of 1576 (No. 79), explaining the progress of his *Gerusalemme liberata* and his evolving allegorical conception of it, and in the *Discorsi del poema eroico* (published in 1594 in revised form, expanding the earlier *Discorsi dell'arte poetica* of 1587, and so incorporating some of Tasso's maturer views on allegorical poetics), Tasso takes up some of the above difficulties.

"Metafora Continuata"

In Letter 79 he says flatly that the kind of allegory which he is interested in formulating is not the same as the classically defined rhetorical figure. He goes on to cite Aristotle's passing mention of the figure in the *Poetics* ("Aristotle says something or other about allegory in the *Poetics*"), gives a short one-line example of rhetorical *allegoria* similar to Peacham's, and dismisses it with the remark that this kind of "metafora continuata" is not at all what he, Tasso, has in mind in constructing the *Gerusalemme*.[2] In the *Discorsi del poema eroico*, Book V, during a substantial interpolated discussion of ancient and medieval allegorizing in which he shows himself familiar with both the formalist definitions of the classical rhetoricians and also with that other early tradition of continuous moral allegorization on Homer, Tasso exhibits awareness of epic allegoresis and allegorical writing from earliest classical times to Porphyry, Proclus and Plutarch and cites the comparatively recent model of Dante as an example of total allegory. He puzzles for a while over whether by *aenigma* Aristotle may not have intended allegory in the profounder sense that those writers and Tasso understand it. But at last he leaves this tantalizing speculation and dismisses the rhetorical figure of *aenigma* (or riddle) as, though venerable, inadequate to be identified with serious allegory. The only kind of allegory which is worthwhile is that which carries a moral value. Possibly Aristotle, because he did not know the term "allegory", was in fact thinking of its substance under some other name.[3] (Elsewhere, Tasso infers that it is not impossible that some discussion of allegory now lost to us existed in the two "missing" books of the *Poetics*.)[4]

Whatever the case, Tasso considers that the use and figure of allegory are of peculiar importance to the epic, lending grandeur as well as import: "Allegory has rightly been said to resemble night and darkness; it is therefore to be used in mysteries and in poems full of mystery like the heroic".[5] "Mysteries" of course means concealed truths. Although in the *Discorsi del poema eroico* Tasso relegates the question of allegory to the sections on rhetoric and style, his ample discussion there actually is such as to maximize it and emphasise its philosophical importance in the epic. He is in fact under more general theoretical umbrellas in these *Discorsi* also discussing many other kinds of problems peculiar to the allegorical epic.

Yet after all, the very point which Tasso was trying most centrally to make about allegory—that it must have a serious conceptual and didactic basis—can be recognised, as his argument develops in the letters associated with the late period of composition of the *Gerusalemme* and is finally summarized in the poem's "Allegoria" itself, to be adequately conveyed by that very rhetorical formula which Tasso had been at first inclined to reject. Tasso's entire poem could be seen (as Spenser, perhaps aided by Tasso, saw his own) as a "continued dark conceit", as "metafora continuata", once Tasso has ceased to allow the rhetorical definition of the figure of allegory to dominate his thinking and instead has related the principle of extended metaphor more largely to the poem's ongoing moral-didactic purpose and progress. The conception of an entire poem as extended allegorical metaphor, or the sustained correspondence of a primary narrative and poetic structure with a secondary sense, will oblige him not only to conduct a fruitful examination of the technical nature of the ongoing artistic correlations, but also to consider fully the didactic character of the poem's intentions: that is to say, the significance of that foreconceit or Idea at the heart of poetic composition, and which Tasso in his "Allegoria" to the *Gerusalemme* dared to call the soul of the long epic poem, consciously allowing didactic allegory to usurp the traditional pride of place accorded by Aristotle to plot or "imitation" in the representational sense. It will take Tasso almost his entire critical career to arrive at a satisfactory resolution of these problems concerning "metafora continuata."

The consequent problems for his reader are considerable; and something must therefore first be said about the organization of the present discussion of Tasso's critical theories and the use of Tasso materials. Broadly speaking, the three topics relating to allegory in Tasso's criticism with which we are in this study most concerned might be summarized as follows. First is moral allegory in the epic (its nature, means of expression, as for example in the management of the characters, and its content); this topic he discusses in some degree throughout the works here cited, but most specifically in the "Allegoria" to the *Gerusalemme*. Second is the techniques and structuring of the long allegorical epic poem ("Plot" versus "Episode" allegory in particular), which he discusses most specifically in the *Lettere*, but also collaterally in the "Allegoria" and, without so directly invoking the term "allegory", in the *Discorsi del poema eroico* and a number of shorter prose writings. The third topic we might in a general way define as problems relating to the poetics and aesthetics of the epic poem and the place of allegory within those. These problems are glanced at briefly in the "Allegoria", but treated more systematically in both sets of *Discorsi* (the second set incorporates any relevant observations in the first), and discussed most sweepingly in the late *Giudizio*, the *Apologia* and certain shorter tracts. My analysis will proceed in approximately the order just given; but reference back and forth to Tasso's various documents and the interlacing threads in his developing discussions will be unavoidable, and indeed will more accurately reflect the hesitant evolution of Tasso's thinking on the subject of epic allegory.

Moral Content: Tasso's "Allegoria"

What then is the precise content of this all-important Idea or allegory which lies behind the epic poem in especial? Although Tasso tends in public utterances to screen his sources, the allegorical matter which he proposed for his epic was far from being original with himself. Such matter had formed the familiar staple of centuries of moral commentary on first the classical and then the modern epics, from late classical commentators like Porphyry to Renaissance allegorizers of ancient epic or myth such as Landino and Salutati and the modern commentators on Dante and Ariosto.[6] The tradition in question, not now so well critically acknowledged as it used to be, cultivates as its principal value the concept of "Heroic Virtue"—or as the period sometimes put it, an "heroical degree of virtue"—seen objectified in the moral hero, who stands in opposition to the classical type of the physically strong or crafty hero.[7] The concept of heroic virtue (Aeneas persevering, Hercules suffering and stellified) concerned itself not so much with an already achieved virtue made manifest in invincible exploits as, more instructively, with the pragmatic process of the acquisition and consolidation of a fixed and unshakeable (hence "heroi-cal") degree of virtue. This would be achieved by means of the trial of the moral hero, his testing through adversities, his experience of failure and defeat and his consequent gain in self-knowledge; equally, through his constant exercise and practice in making moral choices, so that his initial good disposition or will toward virtuous action at last becomes totally fixed and formed, operating on both an intellectual basis (the cognitive under-standing of the good) and on an intuitive, almost reflexive basis (instant conviction and implementation of the right course of action). Such para-digms are to be discerned in Spenser's Knights, or indeed, in part, in Milton's failed hero Adam, who after the Fall develops in both moral character and clear understanding. Christian writers supplement such theories of rationally informed and developing good conduct with an understanding of even the moral hero's need for assistance through heav-enly grace. An unfailing point of intersection is found at which the highest and almost superhuman degree of moral effort in man still unavails in the face of inalienable human weakness; however, such effort finds its failings made good by the ultimate support of divine grace. Thus the Christian ethical writer is less proud of man's unaided moral effort than the classical moralist or Stoic might be. Whether in literary exegeses on classical epics or in the literary epics of the Renaissance modelled in general outline upon those, such patterns may be seen—the emphasis on the hero's personal development usually also being set within some social or civic context pertaining to him.

The theories outlined above rest on a conventional foundation of Aristotelian and Platonic ethical psychology, combined in varying degrees with Christian ethics and doctrines. They hinge on such well-tried Aristo-telian or Platonic concepts as a reason-versus-passions antithesis in the structure of the soul, with the need for the moral aspirant to cultivate a guiding principle of wisdom in his actions and choices (Platonic *sophrosyne* or temperance-wisdom, understanding enlightening good behaviour; and Aristotelian *phronesis*, prudence, a sense of that mean applicable in any given set of circumstances[8]). These ideals will later be reflected in the Spenserian or Miltonic ideals of "Temperance" seen as a balance in conduct in all the moral spheres.

Such ethical-allegorical matter, whether in Renaissance moralized commentary on epic or in written epic, does not exclude the values of the intellectual or contemplative life. But the Renaissance emphasis tradi-tionally is more on the active, effortful moral life of man in his social context (Tasso's model) than on his mystically contemplative or retired life (com-monly considered to be Dante's model). The hero's personal moral devel-opment is presented within his social or civic context (as is again the case with both Spenser's and Milton's moral heroes). This type of ethical-psychological allegoresis on epic, with its distinctive undermeanings, lent itself well, as has earlier been noted, to the tradition of written epic, since there is a profound congruence between the developmental aspect implicit in the allegory of the growth of man's moral nature or the slow formation of his virtue, and the long time-scale (usually a lifetime) of the traditional epic quest, journey, voyage or pilgrimage, with the gradual growth in stature of the epic hero throughout. A conquest over odds involving much self-sacrifice and hardship, a victory of a magnitude verging on the super-human, this is the objective of both the classical epic hero and the later moral-allegorical epic hero—though realised on different planes. The narrative patterns of traditional epic thus can be continually reworked in later moral epic, following along established lines of exegesis.

Tasso's conception of the formation of moral virtue in the epic hero follows along well established lines, although he found certain problems in reconciling the prolonged developmental allegory implicit in the foregoing theories with other views and models of allegory; he also experienced difficulties in that he felt it necessary to square his own views with re-spected bodies of ethical theory, ancient and modern (and indeed to reconcile both Plato and Aristotle in his own theories). In his more public critical utterances such as the *Discorsi del poema eroico* and even late works such as the *Giudizio*, Tasso at first tends to describe the conceptual centre of the heroic poem in wide and on the whole unrestrictive terms. In those treatises the "allegory", "idea", "purpose", or "end" of the poem seems in some undefined way to address whatever broad, instructive purpose the poet has in view, his object in writing, or some unparticularized complex of ethical, moral, spiritual and theological ideas of a general or universal relevance. We may remind ourselves that by established convention alle-gory had never been restricted to any specific set of ideas but, strictly speaking, as a cognitive mode was intended to help clarify various possible areas of intellectual or conceptual relevance at a number of different "levels". As to this, Tasso is quite aware.[9]

But in other works Tasso's ideas on allegory are much more sharply defined. That poetry should "teach" was of course a Renaissance cliché. For Sidney its function and purpose remain somewhat vaguely defined: the end of poetry is to "teach and delight", the second by its lively outward representations of external nature, the first through its imaginings of a "higher" or "second"[10] nature. Perhaps these imagings involve the Pla-tonic shapes of ideal virtues as represented in idealized characters (al-though the revised *Arcadia* throws any too simplistic view of Sidney's ethical characterizations into question). Tasso in the *Discorsi del poema eroico* begins with similar general formulations; but the area of relevance he seeks for poetry and the epic is quickly fined down. Thus near the beginning of that treatise we are told that the aim of heroic poetry is that of "giving profit through delight"; or, that it has the "purpose of moving the mind to wonder [the characteristic epic effect] and thus being useful". However, such profit is at once qualified by Tasso as directed to the moral and active life of man: "Poetry, then, is an imitation of human actions, fashioned *to teach us how to live*".[11]

In the "Allegoria" we were told more specifically that the allegory of the *Gerusalemme* concerns the internal and ethical life of man: "Allegory respecteth the passions, the opinions and customs . . . principally in their being [essence] hidden and inward". In Letter 79, a significant document, there is a sharper hint: Tasso's particular allegory has to do with "the mind" or it is "written in the book of the mind"[12]—it is psychologically grounded; there is a suggestion of an intellectual *schema*. The exact details of this allegory are spelled out in the ensuing parts of the "Allegoria"; it is evident enough that they derive, via Neoplatonic intermediaries, from Aristotle's scheme in *The Nicomachean Ethics* (Book VII.1), and even more from Plato's paradigm in *The Republic*, Book IV. Tasso staunchly set himself the task of amalgamating these two authorities with the views of Renaissance commentators upon them, so as to produce an unassailable scheme of moral virtue.[13]

Such a resolve is indicated in Tasso's Letters. What Tasso has written is a new mixture of Plato and Aristotle. In Letter 76: "You will see treated, and considered and reconsidered many times, a large part of moral philosophy, sometimes Platonic, sometimes Aristotelian [*peripatetica*], and always concerning the science of the soul". From another letter (79) of the same period: "The moral doctrine I have made use of in the allegory is all his [Plato's], but [interpreted] in such a way as to be amalgamated with Aristotle's: and I have striven to join up the one and the other truth in such a way that a compatibility between the opinions may result. . . . I would suppose that in combining Plato with Aristotle I am making a new synthesis".[14] Certain elements in Tasso's plan are, however, more strongly reminiscent of Plato. Tasso cites the *peripeteia* of the *Gerusalemme*, the return of Rinaldo to Godfrey's aid, as especially Platonic; and his view of Rinaldo's role in this matter and elsewhere links it closely with the Platonic idea of the activating role of anger or "spirit".[15] But the allegory overall is as much "peripatetic" as Platonic because, like the philosophy of both these ancients, Tasso's scheme is psychological in essence and, as Tasso spells out more fully in the allegorical preface itself, concerned primarily with the interrelation and coordination of functions or powers in the soul.

A pertinent point is that Tasso's ethical characterizations are concerned not with virtues shown in their perfected shapes (as Sidney's characters and sometimes Spenser's have been taken to be) but with the *process of acquisition* of virtue (a character's slow progress toward "Heroic Virtue"). The precise scheme of the "Allegoria", which is now set out below,[16] makes the "perfecting" aspect plain. Tasso begins by analysing the nature of man: "Allegory, which, as the Life of Man is compound [*doppia*],[17] so it represents to us, sometime the figure of the one, sometime the figure of the other. Yet because that commonly by Man, we understand this compound [*composto*] of the body, soul, or mind, Man's Life is said to be that which of such compound is proper, in the operations whereof every part thereof concurs, and by working gets that perfection, of the which by her nature she is capable". The key phrase in a sentence which follows soon after is "many together ['molti insieme'] and to one end working". The integrated powers of mind and body in the well-ordered soul are comparable to the obedience and cooperation of the various ranks or groups in the well-regulated state (here as elsewhere are echoes of *The Republic*, Book IV): "Moreover, the operation of the understanding speculative, which is the working of one only power, is commodiously figured unto us by the action of one alone; but the operation political, which proceedeth together from the other powers of the mind, which are as citizens united in one commonwealth, cannot so commodiously be shadowed of action wherein many together and to one end working do not concur".

It is on the basis of this central analogy to an army that the complex psychological allegory of the *Gerusalemme* is constructed, in which a multiplicity of characters and the whole of the plot in its main and subordinate parts are all seen as integrally correspondent—in just the way that Tasso will describe in his Letters—to man's mental and bodily faculties and to the processes of inner psychic integration (or conversely disorder). The central portion of the Allegory now follows:

The army compounded of divers princes, and of other Christian soldiers, signifieth Man, compounded of soul and body, and of a soul not simple, but divided into many and diverse powers. Jerusalem the strong city placed in a rough and hilly country, whereunto as to the last end are directed all the enterprises of the faithful army, doth here signify the civil happiness which may come to a Christian Man (as hereafter shall be declared) which is a good very difficult to attain unto, and situated upon the top of the alpine and wearisome hill of Virtue; and unto this are turned, as unto the last mark, all the actions of the Politic Man. Godfrey, which of all the assembly is chosen chieftain, stands for Understanding, and particularly for that understanding, which considereth not the things necessary, but the mutable and which may diversely happen, and those by the will of God. And of princes he is chosen Captain of this enterprise, because Understanding is of God, and of nature made lord over the other virtues of the soul and body, and commands these, one with civil power, the other with royal command. Rinaldo, Tancredi, and the other princes are in lieu of the other powers of the Soul, and the Body here becomes notified by the soldiers less noble. And because that, through the imperfection of human nature and by the deceits of his enemy, Man attains not this felicity without many inward difficulties, and without finding by the way many outward impediments, all these are noted unto us by poetical figures.

Thus we have expressed one kind of allegory, that carried by the main plot, and such "outward impediments" to the main epic purpose as are

suggested by rebellion and separation may be seen to correspond with the
historical ("verisimilar") part of Tasso's fiction. But "inward impediments"
also exist, and are themselves of a double kind. He continues:

coming to the inward impediments, love, which maketh Tancredi and the other
worthies to dote, and disjoins them from Godfrey, and the disdain which enticeth
Rinaldo from the enterprise, do signify the conflict and rebellion which the con-
cupiscent and ireful powers do make with the reasonable. The devils which do
consult to hinder the conquest of Jerusalem are both a figure and a thing figured,
and do here represent the very same evils which do oppose themselves against our
civil happiness, so that it may not be to us a ladder of Christian blessedness. The
two magicians, Ismen and Armida, servants of the devil, which endeavour to
remove the Christians from making war, are two devilish temptations which do lay
snares for two Powers of the Soul, from whence all other sins do proceed. Ismen
doth signify that temptation which seeketh to deceive with false belief the virtue, as
a man may call it, opinative: Armida is that temptation which layeth siege to the
power of our desires: so from that proceed the Errors of Opinion; from this, those of
the Appetite. The enchantments of Ismen in the wood, deceiving with illusions,
signify no other thing than the falsity of the reasons and persuasions which are
engendered in the wood; that is, in the variety and multitude of opinions and
discourses of men. . . . The fire, the whirlwind, the darkness, the monsters, and
other feigned semblances, are the deceiving allurements which do show us honest
travails and honourable danger under the shape of evil. The flowers, the fountains,
the rivers, the musical instruments, the nymphs, are the deceitful enticements,
which do here set down before us the pleasures and delights of the Sense, under
the show of good.

"Inward impediments" resulting in intellectual confusion, or, on the other
hand, in false desires thus correspond, respectively, to the different super-
natural episodes in Tasso's fiction, or to the magician Ismen and the
seductive enchantress Armida respectively. The double-pronged narrative
method of showing "outward impediments" to virtue, carried by the
verisimilar plot, and two basic inward impediments, carried by the super-
natural episodes, comprise Tasso's unique allegorical method in the plot.

   Having at this point also given consideration to further details of the
story which are susceptible of a specifically religious construction, distin-
guishing a kind of Christian marvel from devilish prodigies, Tasso now
reverts to the historical ethical allegory in the verisimilar part of the plot,
continuing with a more specific interpretation of the chief parts played
by "Understanding" and "Ire" and showing how these two faculties are
reflected in the two main roles and energies of the two principal charac-
ters, under *"the veil* of their actions" (Tasso uses the familiar Renaissance
metaphor):

Godfrey and Rinaldo being two persons which in our poem do hold the
principal place, it cannot be but pleasing to the reader that I . . . do particularly lay

open the allegorical sense, which under the veil of their actions, lie hidden. Godfrey, which holdeth the principal place in this story, is no other in the allegory but the Understanding. . . . And . . . because in the powers more noble the less noble are contained: therefore Rinaldo, which in Action is in the second degree of honour, ought also to be placed in the Allegory in the answerable degree. But what this power of the mind, holding the second degree of dignity, is, shall be now manifested. The Ireful Virtue is that, which amongst all the powers of the mind, is less estranged from the nobility of the soul, insomuch that Plato, doubting, seeketh whether it differeth from reason or no. And such is it in the mind, as the chieftain in an assembly of soldiers: for as of these the office is to obey their princes, which do give directions and commandments to fight against their enemies: so is it the duty of the ireful, warlike, and sovereign part of the mind, to be armed with reason against concupiscence, and with that vehemency and fierceness which is proper unto it, to resist and drive away whatsoever impediment to felicity. But when it doth not obey reason, but suffers itself to be carried of her own violence, it falleth out, that it fighteth not against concupiscence but by concupiscence, like a dog that biteth, not the thieves, but the cattle committed to his keeping. This violent, fierce, and unbridled fury . . . is . . . principally signified by Rinaldo. . . . Wherein, whilst fighting against Gernando, he did pass the bounds of civil revenge, and whilst he served Armida may be noted unto us anger not governed by reason: whilst he disenchanteth the wood, entereth the city, breaketh the enemy's array, anger directed by reason. His return and reconciliation to Godfrey noteth obedience, causing the ireful power to yield to the reasonable. . . . as the reasonable part ought not . . . to exclude the ireful from actions, nor usurp the offices thereof, for this unsurpation should be against nature and justice, but it ought to make her her companion and handmaid, so ought not Godfrey to attempt the adventure of the wood himself, thereby arrogating to himself the other offices belonging to Rinaldo. Less skill should then be showed, and less regard had to the profit which the poet, as subjected to the policy, ought to have for his aim, if it had been feigned, that by Godfrey only all was wrought which was necessary for the conquering of Jerusalem.

In the above psychological allegory, Tasso makes several important points. Godfrey represents the intellect or power of understanding: but not this faculty seen in either its more philosophical or its more mystical aspects (such as would, as Tasso has previously said, be better "shadowed" allegorically by a solitary journey like Dante's, or like Aeneas' descent into hell), but the understanding regarded in its more pragmatic aspects, its concern with the "diverse" and "mutable" circumstances of life, such as are shadowed by the "civil company" of men. That is, man's reason is thus figured inasmuch as it relates to the active moral arena, where it is perforce associated with other faculties of mind and body ("many together").

Constituted by God and nature sovereign lord over the other powers ("virtues") of soul and body, just as Godfrey in the history is called upon by a higher power to assume leadership over the fragmented and disunited confederation of princes, the intellect ought to reign supreme. But in the rebellion made upon it by the lesser powers and especially by its second-in-chief, the faculty of ire (Rinaldo), which ought to be its principal support, the intellect, true though its (Godfrey's) perceptions of duty and the right courses of action may continue to be, is found to be rendered powerless. The truth of this psychology is reflected in Godfrey's singularly inert role in the poem—he being a supervisory and admonitory figure, the active roles all being played by others; the idea is specifically founded in the theory from which Tasso is drawing, which holds, as he puts it above, that the higher ("more noble") powers of mind contain the lower ("less noble") within them. That is to say, man's reason acts through and by the means of his lesser faculties, they being the active agents of the directing power. It is on these grounds that, as Tasso explains in the "Allegoria" quoted above, he has allowed Rinaldo to perform the major action of the poem, the disenchantment of the wood; it would not be suitable for Godfrey to arrogate to himself the principal active adventures.[18] The unsuccessfully subordinated role of Tancredi (who is presumably the "concupiscent" power, in contrast to Rinaldo's "ireful" role in the soul) may be reflected in the tragic outcome of Tancredi's love-story, as opposed to Rinaldo's more successful amorous adventure. For Tancredi's pursuit of Clorinda alienates him irremediably from the crusaders in spirit if not in act; the emotions, uncontrolled by reason, must inevitably lead the individual to moral disaster. When, however, ireful and concupiscent powers together with bodily strength or righteous anger are united under Reason, success in the epic project and also spiritual perfection follow: "Finally, to come to the conclusion, the Army wherein Rinaldo and the other worthies by the grace of God and advice of Man, are returned and obedient to their Chieftain, signifieth Man brought again into the state of natural justice and heavenly obedience: where the superior powers do command, as they ought, and the inferior do obey, as they should. Then the wood is easily disenchanted, the city vanquished, the enemy's army discomfited; that is, all external impediments being easily overcome, man attaineth the politic happiness".

The Resources of "Continued" Allegory

Through what resources of plot structure or poetic language may such developmental allegorical-moral themes as those projected in Tasso's "Allegoria" best be projected in an epic poem? This question can be answered by returning to the old definition of allegory as "continued metaphor"[19] and considering what kinds of "continuity" may in practical terms be involved.

Three different kinds of answers suggest themselves and were explored by Tasso during various phases of his career—not without much wavering, apparent self-contradiction and circling round the arguments, in his efforts to come to terms with certain entrenched Renaissance critical positions while at the same time struggling to articulate his own distinctive ideas. These are, first, the notion that continued allegory in epic may express itself first and foremost through the main plot-line and the psychological relationships between the main characters—a radical view explored most thoroughly in the "Allegoria" to the *Gerusalemme*, as has just been seen, but also implied in many of Tasso's Letters. Second, that allegory may operate also in a narratively less sustained fashion through special episodes which stand somewhat apart from, but are not thematically disconnected from, the main plot, these episodes being usually of a "fabulous" or "marvellous" kind. (This argument was in fact incorporated into the "Allegoria", but it is more to the fore, with its attendant problems, in the Letters, where Tasso is trying to rationalize the use of *both* kinds of allegory.) And third (a later view), that allegory, or the poet's didactic Idea, the universal truth which he is concerned to express, inasmuch as it is an informing purpose and pervasive conception in the poem, may express itself in an embracing way via any or all of the poem's varied ingredients: its wider dispositions, its varied elements of plot, its words and rhetorical resources of language—in short, through any and all of those aspects of the poem which are the product of the poet's own invention (are "translated" metaphor, as Salutati had said).

The principal places where Tasso works out these interrelated problems are in certain of the "Lettere poetiche" of 1575-77 (not only those letters dealing with *meraviglie* in the *Gerusalemme*, as seen in supernatural episode, but also those dealing with the evolution of main-plot allegory, as distinct from episode allegory); in the actual "Allegoria" to the *Gerusalemme* (1581), as seen above, where he not only gives a synopsis of his theories of epic allegory, but also outlines the content of the poem's allegory and provides a working model in the shape of a psychological-moral exegesis on his own poem, hinting in passing at how to fuse historical with romance allegory; in rather more general terms, in the *Discorsi del poema eroico*, which also engages with the question of history and fictive truth in epic; and finally, with increasing clarity and conviction, in the *Giudizio sovra la Gerusalemme* (written 1595 and published posthumously). Certain briefer, less weighty tracts in the decade of approximately 1580 to 1590 which also touch on or highlight these matters will be drawn into the discussion as seems relevant. It will clarify Tasso's never easy discussions if we begin with the first of the three "solutions" explored by him, looking once more at the "Allegoria", and leaving discussion of the less coherent Letters of five years earlier to follow.

It was perhaps in his working out of the practical problems attaching to the concept of a single, sustained line of allegory, expressing itself through developments in the main plot and involving all the principal characters of a poem and their actions, that Tasso made his most distinctive contribution to the theory of the allegorical epic.[20] The continuance of such allegorical plots from the earliest example of the *Psychomachia* by Prudentius (C4-5 A.D.)[21] to Bunyan's several allegorical novels late in the seventeenth century indicates that extensive "continued" narrative allegory was in practice a long-established convention. Yet it is this kind of ongoing or developmental plot metaphor which has been least well understood, even in Spenser's epic and certainly in Milton's. Tasso was the most important and perhaps the first critic to prescribe not only exactly how this form of allegory might be projected into the main plot, but also how it could be linked with the more conventional "fabulous episodes" of Renaissance or classical epic. The two kinds of allegory (main plot and episode) are not necessarily incompatible; in his later criticism Tasso will advance elaborate aesthetic arguments which can reconcile the two. But even in his early critical explanation of his allegorical scheme in the *Gerusalemme* one may see that he plainly viewed the two kinds of allegory as complementary— the convex and concave aspects, so to speak, or the active and passive demonstrations of a single, embracing didactic theme. So in the "Allegoria" Tasso explains that the fantastic episodes of Ismen's Wood or Armida's Garden show the two broad types of "intellectual" and sensual "errors" to which the ireful and concupiscent powers in the soul can become subject, whereas the story of the First Crusade, the verisimilar-seeming main-plot allegory, by showing the basic psychology of the mind and the first causes of such vulnerabilities—namely, the initial separation of those two lesser powers of the soul, ire and the passions (the two principal knights) from their guide, Reason, represented by Godfrey—demonstrates how such errors may initially be set in train. After Tasso, Spenser and then Milton will use main-plot allegory and supernatural episode (allegorical interlude) in this same interlocking way: the former experientially, to project aspects of their moral-didactic Idea under the guise or disguise of real life; the latter more emblematically, to intellectualize and examine the Idea's implications via overt allegories. (Spenser's allegorical "Houses", the "allegorical core of each Book", as C.S. Lewis called them,[22] offer examples in that the allegorical-psychic states depicted therein, although more static, correspond closely to the moral experiences and relationships rendered in a more superficially verisimilar allegorical mode by the actions of the main characters in the plot.)

Tasso's achievement in the "Allegoria" of theoretically correlating two quite different modes of allegorical fiction within a single complex but coherent epic plot represents a crucial contribution to allegorical poetics in the epic. For this reason I would make the point that Michael Murrin's suggestive interpretation of Tasso's Wood, which he sees as thematic (reiterative) allegory, so constituting the "continued" element in Tasso's allegory,[23] does not adequately put Tasso's case. Tasso's view is "radical" in the broadest sense, in that it explores and correlates both kinds of "continued" metaphor in epic: the one in the main verisimilar plot, the other in fantastic episodes. Nor are the latter simply reiterative (as Murrin suggests of the Wood); rather, as between themselves they are psychologically discriminating. Armida's enchantments represent sensual or concupiscent weakness, Ismen's are intellectual errors; both sorts of *meraviglie* cooperate with the more verisimilar allegory in the main plot. It is in this context that, in Letter 84, Tasso's resistance to his correspondent's (Luca Scalabrino's) evident criticism of the allegorical role of Rinaldo or the "concupiscent power" in the soul (Scalabrino has been citing an ethical treatise by Flaminio Nobili), and Tasso's allusion to the Landino-Virgil tradition of continuous moral exposition of epic, assume particular importance.[24]

The "Lettere Poetiche" and the *Gerusalemme*

Although many of the same issues are discussed in general terms throughout Tasso's critical works as well as in the specific context of allegory in certain other specialized treatises, Tasso's Letters are of special interest both because they delineate the Platonic-Aristotelian ethical foundation of the particular allegory which Tasso used in the *Gerusalemme*, and because they take up in detail the particular problems of applying such allegory to a very extended storyline.[25]

In the Letters, Tasso is seen struggling to formulate a coherent, sustained ethical allegory which will almost completely correspond to the main lines of his verisimilar plot and which can include all the main characters and main incidents, yet can still embrace allegorical episodes written in a fantastic vein. To assert this view he must resist the conventional argument of the period that epic allegory is to be restricted to a few marvellous or supernatural episodes—which argument may explain why he seems to oscillate between praising his own episodes of this sort, and praising main-plot allegory. Equally, he must resist the converse, equally erroneous supposition that absolutely *everything* in an epic fiction must be allegorical. In any "continued" allegory there must remain a few mundane plot links which have no secondary sense. All these new discoveries he finds intensely exciting. Especially in Letter 76 he asserts that there is allegory in the *whole* of his poem, not only in isolated parts; there is *nothing* in all of the poem, that is to say, no *principal* person nor action, which does not contain "marvellous mysteries". All the parts and personages are tied together among themselves, and all conform with the "literal sense" or story, and at the same time they accord with Tasso's own (allegorical) poetical principles.[26] The "Allegoria" to the *Gerusalemme* does in fact fulfil these sweeping claims, all the principal and even the secondary characters being linked with Godfrey in the comprehensive Reason-Passion allegory outlined above, which pivots on the theme of separation, dispersal and consequent loss of purpose among the participants in the First Crusade, and in which even the most ordinary, unsupernatural actions and seemingly trifling events and characters nearly all do fall into place in the allegory. The precursors of this type of total allegory in earlier epic commentary and its classical-ethical sources have been discussed earlier. Tasso's various adjustments to the poem, adding to or subtracting from the plot in order to make it conform, are noted by himself in his Letters.

In other Letters, Tasso tries to anticipate and meet possible objections to and problems involved in such a sweeping hypothesis as that an entire epic may constitute a continued allegory. For example, in Letter 79 he notes that [extended] allegory may be found throughout certain Books of Homer and Virgil, although not in their whole works. But it is not necessary that the allegory should correspond to every single particular in the literal story; citing Ficino (the source is Augustine), he says that some gratuitous material necessarily has to be added for the sake of the order and connection of the parts.[27] In Letter 84, far from accepting the views of Scalabrino and his cited source, Flaminio Nobili, that the ethical allegory in an epic poem could or should relate specifically to the fabulous parts,[28] Tasso shows himself reluctant to abandon his own idea of one continuous, embracing allegory running in parallel with the main plot. He could cite, he says, various opinions in support of his own view from current scientific treatises on virtue (such as that of Massimo Tirio), as well as from the standard interpretative methods employed by the commentators on the non-fabulous parts of Homer and Virgil. (This is a significant reference to the tradition of Landino and other epic allegorizers.) Tasso cannot see why the allegory should not go into rather more detail ("particolareggiare l'allegoria") than Nobili would appear to favour, or why he should not bring allegory (cercar, "to seek for") into the non-fabulous parts too.[29] Tasso would regret abandoning his ideas, because it seems to him that his own Rinaldo particularly well expressed the concupiscent power of the soul.[30] In certain other Letters, No. 56, for example, Tasso discusses various adjustments and alterations he had made to the plot for the sake of improving the allegory (as in Canto 15, where he wished to remove "the battle of the monster" because it resisted allegorization).[31] We may remember also Tasso's pleasure in his new allegorical device of the Fountain of Mirth with the maidens bathing in it in Canto XV, stanzas 55-66, lifted wholesale by Spenser, along with the famous passages describing Armida's garden, bower and amorous play with Rinaldo in the next canto (Canto XVI, stanzas 9-20), for Book II of The Faerie Queene.[32]

However, at other times and in other Letters or even in the same Letters Tasso speaks in ways which suggest that he is also thinking of allegory in terms of conventional "marvellous episode". Thus in Letter 48, he speaks of the maraviglioso (a favourite term), and of those "wonderful parts" of his fable ("quelle parti mirabili") which are so particularly well suited to the allegory; or again of miracles, that is, marvels ("i miracoli miei del bosco").[33] But again, in Letter 56 he speaks of the problem of tightening up the allegory, which can actually be impeded by unrestrained fantasy; he agrees that it may be better to reduce some of the element of the fantastic in the fiction.[34] Yet throughout such remarks there is no indication that he is not still thinking as well of a sustained and coherent allegorical meaning, rather than just old-fashioned isolated allegories presented in disjunct episodes. Nowhere does he imply that sporadic allegory or disconnected episode (after the manner, say, of Ariosto in the House of Logestilla interlude) is acceptable; indeed he is emphatic that it is not.[35] The "Allegoria" which Tasso eventually proposed for the *Gerusalemme* demonstrates that he has in fact successfully interleaved or interwoven the marvellous elements into the main didactic plot and allegory.

In the earlier Books of the *Discorsi del poema eroico*, as we shall see, Tasso, when dealing with the interrelation of plot, history and fiction, couches his discussion of the use of the marvellous in more general terms, without attempting directly to promote a critical theory of allegory. He justifies marvels by reference to a realigned concept of "verisimilitude" (understood by him as in certain contexts equivalent to inner truth, as opposed to outward realism), and with a certain inconsistency or perhaps deviousness he introduces rather sweeping ideas on allegory into the final three Books dealing with particulars of language and rhetoric. Only in his final comments on the subject of epic allegory in the late *Giudizio sovra la Gerusalemme* (1595, published 1666) was Tasso able, it would seem, satisfactorily to resolve that troublesome critical problem of the relation of marvellous episode to main-plot allegory. There, resuming the earlier discussion in the *Discorsi del poema eroico*, Book II, about the place and quantity of true history appropriate in the epic (as distinguished from that verisimilar kind of fictive history which in the Letters and the "Allegoria" he has already shown can carry allegory), he will firmly take up the position that allegory begins wherever the literal sense (true history) stops:[36] by which we are to understand that allegory can inhere not only in isolated marvellous episodes—although in such places notably—but also in any of those parts of a poem which pass beyond the immediate confines of historical fact and are in some way the product of the poet's own imagination.

No conception can be more crucial than that of Tasso just outlined for a correct understanding of Milton's artistic methods in *Paradise Lost*. Milton's treatment of his poetic matter must be reassessed in the light of the Italian tradition of a mixed representational and non-representational art, the two modes combined in the interest of didactic allegory. Milton, like Spenser before him, has made use of Tasso's method of a narrative treatment containing in fact a *double* allegorical articulation. A unifying "Idea" or didactic theme expresses itself not only through conspicuously allegorical marvellous "episodes" (the supernatural episodes concerning Sin and Death and Satan, and others), but also in an allied way through allegorical shadowings within the main story-line. That is to say, all those parts which represent the poet's personal and fictive elaborations or expansions of his received historical material are open to allegorization, in complementary strands of verisimilar and non-verisimilar fiction, both embedded in the framework of a "real" or "historical" narrative which yet retains its own literal identity and authority. Such a method ideally fitted the late Renaissance epic as Tasso knew it, characteristically a fusion of the ongoing narrative of heroic enterprise, with romance-supernatural episodes freely interspersed. By an ingenious adaptation, the strategy would prove ideal also for Milton's complex biblical-humanist materials and his own purposes.

SIX

Tasso, the *Discorsi:*
Aesthetics of the Allegorical Epic

We may now begin to address that third and more elusive conception of Tasso, suggested in the last section of the preceding chapter, in which the entire poem seems to become one comprehensive allegorical metaphor for all that the poet has to say. Tasso's position here must be approached via his more philosophical statements on art. It was earlier observed that Tasso, while endeavouring to resolve the critical problems involved in the construction of the *Gerusalemme liberata* and to tighten up its whole intellectual scheme, had located the allegory of that poem in a rather distinctive body of psychological-moral thought and had associated it with certain rather sharply defined narrative strategies. But in other mainly later writings he shows an impulse to widen the entire philosophic and aesthetic basis of his discussion of allegory in quite radical ways. In these writings his discussions of allegorically oriented art quickly and inevitably become involved with fundamental Renaissance critical issues concerning poetic "Imitation" and the nature of artistic representation: issues concerning "Verisimilitude" or the nature of "truth" in poetry, the relation of historical truth and outward realism to other or higher forms of "truth", and so on. In such discussions it may sometimes appear that Tasso is not discussing allegory at all, when in fact his premises are entirely relevant to that subject, even though it may be difficult always to find specific statements citing allegory. Tasso's constantly self-encircling methods of exposition do not make matters easier. But we may turn to some revealing passages in the *Discorsi del poema eroico* and the later *Giudizio,* as well as to some shorter tracts, for an intimation of the directions in which his thoughts on allegory were moving in the later stages of his critical career, his views as they developed deepening and broadening the more practical expositions in the "Lettere poetiche" and the "Allegoria".

The Mystical Image

In the "Allegoria" Tasso had briefly indicated the ethical scope and impor-
tance of the allegorical Idea of the epic poem: "the Allegory of an Heroical
poem is none other than the *glass and figure of Human Life*" ("figure" means
an allegorical metaphor).[1] In the principal later treatises, the poet's control-
ling didactic Idea is universalized, passing beyond specific moral-psycho-
logical matter to reach out in directions both mystical and intuitive and also
deeply personal. In one of the most eloquent passages in the *Discorsi del
poema eroico*, Tasso alleges that the universal Truth to which the poet directs
the reader partakes of the nature of the eternal itself. Inspired perhaps by
the mystical Dionysius the pseudo-Areopagite (who is referred to through-
out the *Giudizio*), Tasso gives a fervent account of the kind of truth at which
allegory darkly hints. The truth held in the poet's mind is solemn and
profound; divine, it is yet essentially his own intuition and creation. Like
the divine Creator, the poet conceives images and "commands them to
be", commanding them to take form, to be *born* in his poem, shaping his
artistic creation according to anterior truths perceived by himself before the
poem came into being. By his "perfecting" and his mystical "signs", the
truths realised in concrete visible shapes in the poem, the poet acts as a
mediator between God and man. Anticipating Sidney, Tasso writes: "[The
poet] is a maker of images in the fashion of a speaking painter, and in that is
like the divine theologian who forms images and commands them to be.
. . . occult theology . . . is contained in signs and has the power to perfect.
. . . Now to lead to the contemplation of divine things and thus awaken the
mind with images, as the mystical theologian and the poet do, is a far
nobler work than to instruct by demonstration, the function of the scho-
lastic theologian."[2]

The poet's domain thus passes not only beyond that of the historian
but also beyond that of the philosopher or theologian. In his act of *creating*
images which "awaken the mind" to a vivid response to truth and so are
able to "perfect", the poet resembles the mystical (rather than the scholas-
tic) theologian, or God himself: "just so, I judge, the great poet (who is
called divine for no other reason than that as he resembles the supreme
Artificer in his workings he comes to participate in his divinity) can form a
poem".[3] The poem reveals and realises the poet's Idea in the same way
that God's creation answers His own prior conceptions and mysterious
purposes. The created "world" of both is imbued with meaning; the
"signs" imaged by the poet have the power to awaken to truth. As in the
earlier medieval view the visible world of nature and the events in Scrip-
ture were both filled with meanings which could be discerned by reading
allegorically, so the poet's living images (born, "formed", not flat *schemata*
of virtues) beckon the reader onward to the fulness of those truths which
allegory here can only darkly intimate, revealing and concealing with its

mystical signs. In a significant later statement in the *Giudizio*: "This is the aim of allegories, through which, as they unveil themselves in the eternal light of heaven, the shadows of figures must all come to an end, and be perpetually illuminated".[4] And, in the *Discorsi del poema eroico*, Tasso asserts that such allegories, clad in night and mysteries here in this world, are the especial gift of the heroic poem: "Allegory has rightly been said to resemble night and darkness; it is therefore to be used in mysteries and in poems full of mystery like the heroic".[5] Tasso's mystical fervour in the above two passages and his stress on obscurity ("night and darkness") might suggest that at such moments, and even though he is still writing specifically in the context of narrative allegory, his language is being illuminated by those more mysterious concepts of "symbol" or "enigma" which, while so intimately related to allegory, yet seem to carry the most profound of allegories up onto a plane in which their reverberations finally elude the most determined explicator.[6]

"Romance" Variety and "Global" Allegory

It would seem that after writing the *Gerusalemme*, with its precise ethical allegory, Tasso felt the need to formulate a more capacious allegorical po-etic which might define those poetic modes suited to such a moving and ex-alted conception of heroic poetry as expressed in the last passage quoted, or as might be appropriate to all poetry. In something approximating to the older view that all poetry is "translation", a language of allegory in which one thing is said but another intended, *everything* that lies within the poet's artistic control eventually seems to become, in Tasso's intuition, a means of giving substance to those sublime truths which the poet figures behind the shadows of real world. Poetry in all its elements speaks the language of allegory. Whereas Sidney never actually defined the means by which poetry was to execute its higher mimesis, Tasso throughout his critical works offers a variety of hints, which, put together, appear to constitute something approximating to Salutati's view of poetry as "global" alle-gorical artifact, or total allegorical metaphor.[7] We may draw some of these hints together, turning to certain of Tasso's minor tracts and once again to statements in the *Discorsi del poema eroico* in order to trace the deepening of his thought.

The simplest form of allegory is that projected through ideal exam-ple—in one sense not "translated" discourse at all. The "exemplary", as was earlier noted, was nevertheless accepted by the Renaissance as one part of the allegorical apparatus. It is only the younger Tasso and not the mature critic who stresses this kind of allegory. We may find for instance in the appended Allegory added in 1583 to his early epic *Il Rinaldo* (1562), a somewhat simplistic exemplary allegory with a slightly Neoplatonic idealistic colouring, interpreting that poem's action (a very ordinary "love and war" romance) as illustrating what has been summarized by Danilo L. Aguzzi as "the progress of an individual toward the acquisition of the moral habit under the impulse of his love for a beautiful and virtuous woman".[8] The poem and its hero and its subordinate actions serve as moral examples in the sense of offering illustrations of virtuous conduct in love, or perhaps of the problems in love, rather in the manner of much of Harington's Italian-inspired commentary on Ariosto. Tasso's introductory comments are as follows: "In Rinaldo . . . may be seen, how rivalry is a great stimulus stirring the magnanimous soul to virtuous action. In [his] being in love with Clarice . . . is seen, how easily we are ignited in the flames of Love, which, once ignited, then make us behave virtuously, in order to please the beloved object".[9] The moral *intention* of the above is apparent; but it can be observed that the "allegory" here is not well distinguished from the examples in the story itself of the powerful effects of love and hence its power for good.

In his two sets of Discourses on the epic poem, Tasso again speaks of heroic poetry as offering exemplary images of virtue, or rather of the different virtues, or of these virtues at their highest pitch: "[Heroic poetry] paints in their souls forms of courage, temperance, prudence, justice, faith, piety, religion, and every other virtue that may be acquired by long practice or infused by divine grace".[10] However, his discussion now is set in a more distinctly Platonic aesthetic context which alters the emphasis: "virtue" is now subdivided into *various* virtues (or essences), with their individual exemplars. Tasso's further stress in the two sets of *Discorsi* on the *acquisition* of virtue "by practice" (in complement to its infusion "by grace") also suggests the much more complex psychological allegory of nascent virtue worked out in connection with the *Gerusalemme*. There, as we have seen, his methods became overtly allegorical, and the literary means stressed were the interleaved use of main-plot allegory (in the principal narrative) and "episode" allegory (in the interspersed, recurring "marvellous" or supernatural episodes). These two types of allegory were found to connect with each other, dramatically and psychologically, via the cohering, overall, allegorical "Idea". Or in Tasso's words in the more generalized discussions to which we shall presently turn, the two plot elements are linked through a specialized principle of "verisimilitude" (the underlying truth running through the poem), rather than through mere "necessity" (external plausibility of events and "probable" causation).

Still considering matters of narrative, we may observe that Tasso in the *Discorsi del poema eroico* suggests that narrative organization and disposition in their widest senses may themselves become the means of projecting the unity of didactic purpose in the poem, or its *telos* (Tasso's adaptation of the Aristotelian concept of formally unified plot). Thus a romantic diversity of incident, "the variety of the poem" and "the number and novelty of the things seen", for example the obstacles which Aeneas encounters in his travels, "of many kinds, almost of many natures", may be made coherent by "the unity of the fable"—that is, through the underlying goal of the story, in this case Aeneas' final historical objective of founding Rome, which is a figure for the perfecting of man through suffering and perseverance. "The principle on which the means depend is one and the end to which they are directed is one". The two great classical epics "appropriately direct all things to a single end".[11]

While the test of the kind of unity which Tasso conceives is expressed in the conventional terms that nothing must be superfluous and that nothing can be removed without damage to the whole fabric of the plot, it soon emerges that it is not Aristotle, the critic of the *Poetics*, but the moral philosopher, Tasso, speaking through him, whom we hear: "the poem that contains *so great a variety of matters* none the less should be one, one in form and soul; and all these things should be so combined that each concerns the other, corresponds to the other, and so depends on the other *necessarily or verisimilarly* that removing any one part or changing its place would destroy the whole".[12] The specific allusion once more to connection of parts via necessity *or verisimilitude* (in Tasso's special understanding of the word) indicates that the above remarks represent more than a simple defence of digressive episode or romance "variety" in epic. By turning the language of neoclassical formalism back on itself, the statement constitutes a defence of non-realistic narrative in didactic-allegorical art. At this point in his Discourses Tasso is coming to the defence especially of marvellous episode, on the grounds that it relates in a broad way to the anterior didactic Idea or purpose of the poem. "Relevance" need not only be through Aristotelian causality ("necessity"); other kinds of connections, correspondences, dependences, between parts also are possible "verisimilarly" (in terms of underlying truth). Thus the classical and neoclassical dictum that a plot should be so constructed that "removing any one part or changing its place would destroy the whole" takes on implications beyond those of formal unity of design.[13]

Such a free yet meaningful use of narrative structure as Tasso implies above is filled with artistic potential. We might briefly draw one kind of analogy from *Paradise Lost*. Milton—like all great narrative poets—fully realised how a free use of narrative structure in the poem could contribute to its shaping, purpose and ideas. In *Paradise Lost*, in response to the inner "verisimilitude" of the poet's initially formulated plan, or Milton's "Justification" of God, rather than bowing to a mere narrative "necessity" or literal sequence in events, Milton has Fall announce Fall, rebellion foretell further rebellion. But at the same time and by a counter-movement the poem proceeds *from* darkness *to* light (Hell to Heaven and Eden, Books I-II to III-IV), and Creation (Book VII) *follows* destruction (Books V-VI), these dispositions intimating how Restoration must follow the actual Fall and destruction graphically shown in Books IX, X, XI and XII. These are not overtly allegorical structurings; however, they take their place within a larger view of poetry and narrative structure as total allegorical metaphor. Milton, like Tasso, will additionally deploy his anterior "Idea" in more intricate allegorical ways—through fantastic narrative episode connected to the plot by "verisimilitude" (inner truth), as well as through a form of allegorical shadowing in the main plot.

Language too has its unique value and place in Tasso's "global" view of the allegorical art of poetry. In the *Discorsi del poema eroico*, Book II, Tasso had spoken of the mystical "images" or "signs" (*imagini*) by which the poet communicates a perfecting truth.[14] By "images" he means perhaps in the broadest sense all that the poet makes us see and conceive—those mystical or allegorical "signs" by which events, persons or descriptions, as in the Bible, acquire a charged or higher value over and above their historical or narrative senses. Images (symbolic images), then, also form part of the allegorical expression. And lastly, so do *words*. The linguistic surface itself of the poem can become (as it certainly does in Spenser and Milton and in Tasso's poem) a tissue or system of significant correspondences, all signalling a higher meaning. "Words follow concepts": need this insight from the fifth Book apply only to proper elocution and appropriate diction?[15] In the *Giudizio*, at any rate, Tasso clearly suggests a conception of poetic language (as indeed of all poetry) as in essence allegory, in terms reminiscent of Salutati's cited earlier. The words on the poem's surface build into an invisible edifice of latent meaning: "Therefore . . . the words which are dispersed over the surface have to be understood inwardly; and in this manner, above the foundations of the fable, there may appropriately, by means of the allegory, be erected an intellectual structure, one of the mind, as I might call it".[16]

The difficult and delicate perceptions sketched above coalesce in the significant passage from the *Discorsi del poema eroico*, Book III, previously cited. There, having discussed the epic poem's interconnected variety of parts, Tasso compared it to "the world that contains in its womb so many diverse things [and yet] is one, its form and essence one . . . just so. . . . the poem that contains so great a variety of matters no less should be one, one in form and soul".[17] Like God's world which is in "form and essence one", the epic poem with all that it contains must be "one in form and soul" both. Body and thought, dress and Platonic Idea, concrete particulars and allegory, mesh in an indivisible perfection of transcendental thought given palpable and visible form. The "mystical image" is the epic poem itself.

"Truth" and the "Verisimilar"

We shall next follow the evolution of Tasso's arguments as he tries to establish a theoretical aesthetic or philosophical basis for the allegorical relationship envisaged by the poet between his historical and his more inventive or fabulous materials. For Tasso, as for all other critics of the period, the crucial issues revolve around the sixteenth-century Neo-Aristotelian and counter-Aristotelian arguments over the vexed question of realism in representation. The problem for the epic poet is how he may correlate his historical with his fabulous or his invented materials, in the interests of the particular kind of "ideal" moral purpose which he envisages, "truth" (in the one view) or (in another view) "unity" of plot, the Aristotelian *telos*, at which the epic genre aims. For Tasso, as for his contemporaries, the nub of the matter is that age-old question: what constitutes "truth"? Tasso progressively moves away from even a liberal Aristotelianism such as Lodovico Castelvetro's to a more flexible view of fictive representation. Poetic "truth" can accommodate both "real" and highly imaginative forms of mimesis.

Since Tasso in the two major sets of *Discorsi* deals with allegory indirectly, for the most part treating the subject inferentially and within the context of his discussion of general aesthetic principles or principles of narrative structure (except for the great burst of praise for mystical figures and allegory in Book V of the later set), it is easy to suppose that the concept of allegory is incidental to his main body of theory there, or at any rate confined to those writings directly associated with the *Gerusalemme* (the Letters, the "Allegoria", and the late *Giudizio*). In fact, there is little in the better known treatises which does not contain at the very least the potential for allegory.[18] Further, a whole spectrum of incidental tracts prove to be relevant to the same question. It should be kept in mind that the *Discorsi*, subjected to revision almost immediately on publication in their earlier form in 1587, in composition coincide with Tasso's most intense period of idealist Neoplatonizing criticism, reflected in his minor tracts and theorizing on allegory during almost the entire decade from 1575-85. It thus is almost as if Tasso were conducting a single argument on a double level: the more public one framed in general terms to do with "verisimilitude" and didactic truth in the epic, the other a more technical and personal argument geared to defining specific allegorical narrative techniques suited to an epic such as the *Gerusalemme*, with its precise ethical-psychological content. Perhaps Tasso did not himself for a time realise that it was one and the same argument that he was conducting. Or perhaps, since the subject of allegory was such a critically embattled one, historically surrounded by difficulties, he deliberately took refuge in the generalities of the two sets of *Discorsi*, which were a more formal statement addressed to a wider public. Tasso himself vacillated much and it is likely that he took long to clarify the subject in his own mind. Only at a late stage in his criticism do the various associated problems seem to resolve themselves for him in a frankly and fully allegorical theory of poetry and the epic, one on which he is then content to take a public stand in the *Giudizio*.

We may therefore discern a coherent, if not in terms of publication dates chronologically consistent, development in Tasso's thinking, leading him from his first dissatisfaction with the restrictive and conventional understanding of "allegory" (still a problem for him in the *Discorsi del poema eroico*) as a brief rhetorical figure; through an exploration in general terms, in the same treatise and its earlier version, of the aim of poetry as a Platonic reaching after a higher truth and of the poetic art as itself the visible rendering of that truth (suggesting an allegorical underlay to this his public view on epic); through the rather technical discussions of around 1575 in the Letters of the problems of accommodating his own epic narrative to a specific allegorical theme, and thence to the fully worked out statement and allegorical *schema* in the "Allegoria" of 1581; to, finally, the realisation that in a more generous understanding of allegory he has to hand the very concept which can enable him to translate his exalted view of the function of poetry and epic into a working theory of allegorical narration, one in which there can be a satisfactory reconciliation between the conflicting claims of history and fidelity to outward nature and those of deeper kinds of truth in poetry. In this process of evolution the two sets of *Discorsi*, constantly in process of revision, full of insights too cautiously expressed, his best known yet not his ultimate critical statements, although written subsequently seem as if they lag behind the insights into allegory discernible in the actual allegorical modifications to the *Gerusalemme* and the various prose statements on allegory attaching to it. It is as if the treatises never quite caught up with Tasso's critical *aperçus* concerning the poem.

We may recall that in the "Allegoria" Tasso had identified the directing conception behind the heroic poem specifically with didactic allegory. Using the analogy of the living creature, man, allegory became as it were the mind or soul of the epic poem, leaving "imitation" as the less valuable outward body or dress. Given that Aristotle had defined plot, the actual representation of literal events, as the soul both of tragedy and the epic poem, Tasso's stance represented a radical reversal of the conventional and offers a measure of the distance his poetic was in fact moving away from Aristotelian orthodoxy.[19] For Tasso at this juncture, Imitation regards only those "actions of man subjected to the outward senses", it "lively set[s] before our corporeal eyes the things represented", showing not the inward but the outward manifestations of life "in words, in deeds, or working". Allegory on the other hand has a deeper significance: it is "the glass and figure of Human Life", that is, of the interior life; it considers the "customs, affections, or discourses of the mind" and "the passions, the opinions and customs, *not only as they do appear, but principally in their being hidden and inward*". Allegory does all this, which Imitation cannot perform. Thus Allegory is addressed to an élite, to the few "understanders of the nature of things".[20]

Such remarks offer a clear rationale for an allegorical "foreconceit", but they do leave Tasso in a certain difficulty over that more delightful aspect of poetry, its outward imitation of nature, now relegated to an inferior status. We can in fact in the Letters of 1575-76 observe Tasso twisting on the prongs of the dilemma which he has characteristically created for himself. His comments frequently betray an uneasiness over whether he has maintained a satisfactory balance between correct "Imitation" and the preoccupations of interior truth as sought through allegory.[21] Hence in other writings the problem seems to be attacked from just the opposite direction. Allegory is mentioned slightly, and "Imitation", rehabilitated, takes over allegory's function of interiority or anteriority, in a similar way to that in which Sidney uses the term and the concept of Imitation. Tasso's ability to turn terms inside out is notable. He is not alone in this in the period, and one must read behind and through this distracting habit to perceive his genuine development as he tests his thoughts and slowly shifts his positions within the vocabulary of established critical discourse.

What is it that, through poetic "Imitation" understood in the new way, the poet seeks to imitate? Truth, of course: but not outward appearances, historical or literal facts, but rather "a kind of truth"—a kind which Tasso increasingly identifies with his own concept of "verisimilitude", thus cunningly separating this "kind of truth" from that other "truth" which is mere outward fidelity of representation. In the following *Discorso* on the poetic criticism of Francesco Patricio, or Patrizi (1585), we hear that Aristotelian principles applied in poetry can only be true if understood "in a [certain] way", for the reason that poetry is concerned with "truth" only in the sense of "verisimilitude" (in Tasso's own use of that term): "the principles of Aristotle. . . . are also *true in that way* in which principles can be true *in an art which teaches us verisimilitude*; for poetics [or the art of poetry] is not an art in which one learns how to distinguish the true from the false, as in dialectic, but from it we learn how to imitate [the truth]".[22] Exasperating though this word-twisting may seem, Tasso's defence of the imaginative in art shines through the irksome restraints imposed by the period's compulsory Neo-Aristotelianism. Milton—or Milton critics—have had an analogous problem with the restrictiveness imposed by Christian historicism in reading *Paradise Lost*. It is relevant to point out how, in its echo of the last line of Tasso quoted above (or perhaps both poets echo a common tradition), Milton's famous distinction in *Of Education* between poetry and dialectic locates his own art also within the kind of persuasiveness pertaining to the imagination and not to the literal or logical.

In the *Discorsi del poema eroico*, Tasso speaks more plainly; Imitation is by its nature linked not with the kind of truth involved in recording outward particulars, but with a deeper verisimilitude.[23] That higher Truth which the poet seeks is the truth of universals, or Ideas. In a bold statement in a dialogue embedded within his *Apologia* (1585), Tasso says: "*For[estiero]* Thus the poet does not spoil the truth, but he seeks it in a perfect form, imagining in place of the truth of particulars that of universals, which are Ideas. *Segr[etario]* This we are to believe concerning the divine philosophers [theologians]. *For[estiero]* And of poets equally, who in their consideration of ideas are philosophers".[24] To depict only objective or external truth in poetry would be, forsooth, to "spoil truth". The poet's representation (so runs the parallel argument also in *Discorsi del poema eroico*, Book III) constitutes an ideal or heightened version of reality; he "consider[s] things not as they were but as they ought to have been, with regard rather to the universal than to the truth of particulars".[25] For "if Lucan is not a poet, it is because he binds himself to the truth of particulars with little regard to the universal".[26]

In one aspect it could appear that many of these statements are compatible with Aristotle's views in the *Poetics* concerning "ideal" or "representative" mimesis. Poetry represents not true historical facts but probable actions, and not specific individuals but man's general or universal nature. And in fact much of the early argument in the *Discorsi* is indeed addressed to the duty of poetry to portray the "probable" or the "credible", as against the merely false or fantastic.[27] But under the aegis of a liberal Aristotelianism, Tasso is progressively removing his poetic farther and farther away from Aristotelian poetics.[28] Even the statement immediately above that poetry "considers things . . . *as they ought to have been*" has more in common with Sidney's type of ideal didacticism than it does with Aristotle's theory of general nature. In the end Tasso goes well beyond the Platonic position most familiar to English readers as represented in Sidney's ideal "shapes of virtue". This evolution becomes more apparent in the late *Giudizio*, where Tasso again asserts, with regard to the "false parts", those for example which the poet may have added to true history, geography or personages (and, with history kept to a minimum, there are a great many of such possible "false parts"), that these too, since they may carry a hidden sense or allegorical meaning, constitute a legitimate form of imitation.[29] Thus we have come full circle from the "Allegoria", where "Imitation" stood in opposition to the higher principle of "Allegory". Now Imitation has subsumed allegory. So we arrive by a different route at the same view of the artistic process: poetry is to be understood in terms of an allegorical-didactic theory of art, in which all poetic representation (barring a minimum of historical fact) participates in the universal truth of an allegorical-verisimilar. Expressed in general terms though the foregoing statements are, the linking of "Imitation" with an "idea" drawn from "philosophy" (that is, an abstract conception) must imply a theory of secondary signification of a conceptual kind in poetry.

Since in Tasso's words "perchance the whole action does not need to be true, but it must leave its appropriate part to the verisimilar, which is proper to the poem",[30] we may inquire what kinds of "invention", then, are suited to this versimilar part? What sort of fiction is suited to carry the "universals", "ideas" or "allegory" which constitute that "verisimilar" "proper" to the epic poem? It will become increasingly apparent that Tasso's answer to this question would be, almost everything that lies within the province of the poet's imagination. Not only "marvellous Episode" or romantic digression, but all feigning, whether of the Aristotelian "apparent-probable" kind, or the Sidneyan moral-ideal type, or the frankly fabulous—all the invented materials in the poem, whether less or more realistic in mode, less or more naturalistic and convincing, everything that the poet himself introduces, whether borrowed or his own, by way of amplification of his historically grounded narrative, all may be pressed into service in the cause of such an epic verisimilar. (Thinking of Tasso's, Spenser's and Milton's epic poems, we shall not forget the rich vein also offered by metaphor and similitudes.) In this view of art the poet's invention is liberated. There can be no aspect or element in the epic poet's feigning which may not be pressed into the service of such truth of a higher order. This intuition lies at the heart of Tasso's poetic, and it offers the key to his interpretation of the Christian historical-didactic epic and the problems of marrying it with the romantic-fantastic epic. To that topic we may now turn.

SEVEN

Tasso, the Major Tracts:
The Poetics of the Allegorical Epic

In this chapter we shall explore the final stages of Tasso's increasingly confident formulation of an allegorical epic poetic based upon his own preferred concept of the "verisimilar". There are three practical contexts. The first has to do with *plot* and the old question of narrative unity in the epic, considered against the twinned problems of "diversity" or multiple actions, and "necessity" or causality in narrative sequence. This is a question rendered acute by Tasso's need to defend interpolated episode in romance epic against the strictures of Italian neoclassicism, with its emphasis on single plot-line. The second context, very central for Tasso, concerns the place of the "marvellous" and in particular of the "marvellous-verisimilar" in epic. And the third concerns the place of history (and "true religion", as a part of history) in the verisimilar and didactic epic. All three questions are closely interconnected. We shall again be considering Tasso's three major tracts, along with a number of related shorter writings.

Narrative Unity and Causality in the Mixed Epic

To take up the first context, plot unity and causality. Aristotelian neoclassical criticism demanded a formidable unity of action in the epic as in the dramatic poem, as part of its overall realism or probability of effect. The epic poem like the tragic must have a beginning, middle and end; that end must follow inexorably from the line of events in the middle, these having been set in motion by the nature of the beginning. In Tasso's view the principle of the unifying "verisimilar", or that ideal truth which the poem seeks to convey, becomes the equivalent of Aristotle's unity of action, inasmuch as it provides a centre of reference for all the poem's elements. However we may term it, the "end" (*telos*), "principle", "Idea" or "Allegory", this ideal truth is the intellectual centre which gives coherence to all the poem's diverse parts. As has been seen from the arguments already cited from the *Discorsi del poema eroico* and other treatises, the inclusion of quite unrelated incidents in modern Renaissance epics as in classical can be justified on such grounds. "Fantastic episode" similarly can be justified in terms of some deeper connection with an underlying allegory or didactic theme, as Tasso's discussion of the "marvels" in the *Gerusalemme* demonstrated. The problem of causality or logical narrative sequence, or in Tasso's words "the connection of parts", becomes particularly interesting in this context, and it is best illustrated in connection with the arguments concerning "Episodes". Aristotelian theory of plot requires above all a certain inevitability in events: consequences must spring from causes, however trivial or overlooked these may have been. In Aristotle's ideal plot, as in nature, nothing is without a cause. Or to use Tasso's interesting formulation, "in nature there are no episodes" (uncausal happenings).[1] Such a requirement is awkward for the romance-allegorical epic with its great variety of incident, multiple actions, and interpolated episode often in quite different mode. Appeals to the unifying ideal truth of the "verisimilar" are again the key to Tasso's defence of the mixed epic.

The connection between incidents or between episodes and main plot may be, Tasso said, according to "necessity" (natural causality), but equally via the "verisimilar", that is, through the dominant truth or idea which the poem is "imitating".[2] In this way even with many "episodes" a poem may not suffer the fault of being "episodic" (one cannot but admire Tasso's ingenuity in turning words inside out).[3] One of the most philosophical statements of this position occurs in Tasso's *Delle differenze poetiche* of 1587, where Tasso argues that verisimilitude implies a looser or at any rate a different connection of parts than that which is required by necessity. Art cannot have the "necessary" arrangements of nature, in which all the parts have a fixed order and interdependency; but it can have its own kind of connectedness of disparate parts, through its "verisimilar" unity. Tasso in this treatise says: "And since nature performs nothing in all the universe 'episodically', [the universe] which is so vast and adorned with all kinds of species and with all beauties, art also would like to demonstrate its riches and ornaments, and bring all the parts of the poem into, as it were, a fixed order and give to each part its necessary place and dependency; but not being able to attain such perfection, it sometimes does in a verisimilar way that which it is not able to do via necessity".[4]

Such statements represent a new and daring assertion of the artistic validity of romance epic in the context of a near stifling Italian neo-classicism. Richness and ornament, the diversity of species and beauties, will be introduced on the basis of their deeper relevance, their allegorical truths, rather than causally. To achieve this, the modern poet like his ancestor needs "daring and licence in feigning".[5] He may have to defy Aristotle (while appearing to follow him in a more subtle way), and defy nature also, not to speak of defying the sixteenth-century critics. In one of his Letters (87), Tasso had already explained that "I believed at one time that in the epic poem the unity of many [actions in one] was more perfect than that of the single [action]. . . . This I believe more firmly than ever, that it is more or less impossible these days to make a poem which will please, with an action concerning a single knight [i.e. protagonist]: and so I still believe, having woven here [in the *Gerusalemme*] *a unified action of the many in one*".[6]

More forcefully still, in his reply of the same period to Castelvetro (written around 1576, published only in 1875), Tasso denies that the materials of "history" and poetry can ever be the same. The poet must challenge nature:[7] "the imitation required of poetry . . . can be called a rivalry of the poet with the arrangements of fortune or with the course of mundane affairs".[8] We may compare Tasso's surprisingly forthright defence of historical unveracity (whether in sequence or sequel of poetic events, or in other matters) in the *Discorsi del poema eroico*: "the poet should first of all consider whether some event in the material he is going to handle *would be more marvellous or verisimilar if it had happened otherwise*. . . . And with all such events, that is with all that might be better if they had happened differently, he may *without regard to truth or history change and rechange them at will*, arrange and rearrange . . . as he thinks best, mingling the true and the fictitious".[9]

Tasso's passages above on the "connection of parts", or the construction of a fable according to the principle of interior "verisimilitude" rather than natural sequence or historical fact, are particularly valuable as critical background to *Paradise Lost*, for perhaps no aspect of the poem has disturbed critics more than the apparently arbitrary intrusion into the main action of what an earlier period would at once have recognised as supernatural "Episodes" carrying a relevant interior truth (as when, for example, Sin opens the Gates of Hell to Satan). Milton's defence of this as of certain other less or more fantastic instances in his poem where he defies causality or the ordinary "course of mundane affairs", himself rivalling "the arrangements of fortune" and rearranging certain events "without regard to truth or history", would like Tasso's undoubtedly have been framed with regard to the deeper truth of the allegorical-verisimilar over external nature, as well as with regard to the need to interleave in an epic the two kinds of action, probable and fantastic, with their different kinds of verisimilitude or truth. It is almost certain that Milton was influenced by the Italian debates and especially by Tasso's theories on non-verisimilar truth in epic.

The Marvellous-Verisimilar

Tasso increasingly associates "verisimilitude" in poetry with an active principle of the "marvellous"—the second "practical context" noted at the beginning of this chapter. Earlier, as we saw, the marvellous was associated with occasional allegories ("marvellous mysteries", usually found in "Episodes"). Tasso progressively widens the range of meanings of the term "the marvellous", until in the late *Giudizio* it comes to mean, more or less, a complex form of continuous allegory. (The double narrative basis for such continued allegory he has already worked out in the "Allegoria" to the *Gerusalemme* and the associated Letters.) Such a conclusion is already implicit in Tasso's handling of the discussion of epic wonder and marvels in the two sets of *Discorsi*, especially the later set. The distinctive characteristic of epic there is "to afford its own delight with its own effect—which is perhaps to move wonder";[10] this comes about through the use of striking, unusual, unexpected or amazing incident, as well as through the lofty style itself. Through the impact of wonder the mind becomes more receptive to higher (didactic-allegorical) truth.[11] While in the epic context such wonder may be inspired simply by high heroic incident or "great and eventful actions",[12] Tasso's epic practice and theory specify also that epic wonder is most fruitfully inspired by miracles or "prodigies", that is, by fantastic or supernatural episodes and events outside of natural probability. In the *Discorsi del poema eroico* Tasso focuses on the significant potential of "prodigies" for carrying the allegorical truth implicit in his own version of "verisimilitude". He comes to formulate a special concept for the sort of truth carried by this type of incident, and conjointly for the sort of incident itself: the concept of the "marvellous-verisimilar". This is one of the most important concepts in Tasso's epic poetic, capable of reconciling the most extreme contradictions and diversities of the mixed epic. The "marvellous-verisimilar" comes to be the very hallmark of the didactic epic.

The *how* of achieving the wonderful literary marriage of opposites implicit in the "marvellous-verisimilar" requires detailed thought. In practical terms, Tasso is concerned that the fantastic or supernatural parts of an epic poem should not be thought of or treated as separable from any other parts which are concerned with "truth". Interpolated supernatural episodes, for example, need not in his view stand apart from the serious main action and they are not put in merely for relief or entertainment; rather, they participate in the serious truth of the poem in an integral way. All these views are summed up in one of the most important sections in Book II of the *Discorsi del poema eroico*:

But now let us pursue our argument as to how the verisimilar may be combined with the marvellous. . . . The verisimilar and the marvellous are very different in nature . . . different almost to the point of being antithetical; yet both are necessary in a poem, though to join them takes the art of an excellent poet. And while many have done this well enough before now, *no one, to my knowledge, teaches us how to do it*. In fact, some men of the greatest learning, perceiving the incompatibility of the

two, have judged that the verisimilar part of the poem is not marvellous and the
marvellous part is not verisimilar, and argued that, since both are necessary,
sometimes the verisimilar is to be sought, sometimes the marvellous, in such a way
that each may be tempered by the other without yielding to it. But I do not approve
this view, *nor do I grant that any part of the poem need not be verisimilar.* And this is my
reason: poetry unquestionably is nothing but imitation; imitation cannot be sepa-
rated from the verisimilar . . . no part of poetry, consequently, can be without the
verisimilar; in short, the verisimilar is not one of the conditions required in poetry
for greater beauty and ornament, but proper and intrinsic to its essence. . . . Still,
though I hold the epic poet to a perpetual obligation to preserve verisimilitude, I do
not therefore deprive him of the other part, the marvellous. Rather I judge that *one
same action can be marvellous and verisimilar, and I think there are many ways to join the
two discordant qualities.*[13]

Thus the romantically diverse actions of the late sixteenth-century type
of epic poem may acquire a "unity" as deep as that of any Aristotelian
model: namely, that of an underlying didactic meaning, the unity of "that
Idea which is the poet's domain". In this connection we may look not only
at such directly allegorical personifications as are to be found in Ariosto,
Spenser, or *Paradise Lost,* but also at the various *miracoli* in the *Gerusalemme*
(all integral to the plot): the supernatural enchantments of Armida and
Ismen, Armida's magic palace, the Wood itself—in Tasso a recurring fig-
ure for intellectual error,[14] as it is in Spenser. In *Paradise Lost,* as illustra-
tions of Tasso's marvellous-verisimilar containing an inner truth, we may
look not only to the negative "marvels" enacted by the fallen angels in Hell
or to Satan's symbolic animal transformations, but to many other divinely
inspired "wonders" which unite the epic marvellous with the "truth of the
verisimilar". But the "truth" expressed by all such marvels is not different
in kind but only in means, Tasso would argue, from the "truths" expressed
by less surprising fictions.

Tasso is careful to stress that no poem should be excessively full of
"prodigies".[15] Yet the intensity of his concern with the didactic and alle-
gorical value of the marvellous can be seen not only in his staunch defences
in the *Discorsi del poema eroico* of the *maravigliosa* (exemplified also in his
own *Gerusalemme liberata*), but even more so in the late *Giudizio* where,
discussing his revisions to the earlier form of the poem made in the retitled
and reworked *Gerusalemme conquistata,* he asserts that he has made his
poem *more* allegorical or marvellous and in consequence *more* true, "con-
forming myself in many particulars to histories; and I added allegory to
history . . . leaving no part in the poem to [mere] vanity, filling each one of
them, even the smallest and least obvious, with hidden and mysterious
senses".[16] He has indeed "sought the marvellous through the excess of
truth". This paradoxical phrase, repeated elsewhere in the *Giudizio,*[17]
means, we may suppose, just its opposite: the poet has "sought the height
[excess] of truth through the heightening of the marvellous", that is,

through prodigies or marvels, which have this special capacity for deeper allegorical meaning.

It would be interesting to know more precisely what Tasso has in mind when he says in both the *Discorsi del poema eroico* and in his *Risposta . . . Al . . . Lombardelli* (1586) that the marvellous and the verisimilar may not only coexist in one action but may be joined *in a variety of ways* ("there are many ways to join the two discordant qualities").[18] His general point undoubtedly is that allegorical truth (the truth of the "verisimilar") may be carried by both prodigies or supernatural events and by more plausible fictions; both in their special ways are "marvellous". One problem which may be involved, though perhaps not centrally, is the place of Christian miracles in the epic poem. Can these also be used to convey an allegorical type of truth, since to the believer they are literally true? ("Credible", though not "probable", they carry more conviction than the "miracles" wrought by devils or certainly by pagan deities.)[19] Tasso allows that Christian miracles may be impressive and marvellous, and he does employ and interpret them allegorically, or at least symbolically, in the *Gerusalemme*. But there they do not carry the weight of the poem's allegorical meaning; the diabolical enchantments, involved with the moral allegory, are much more central. Echoes of this same problem are to be found in Milton. Milton's language in *Paradise Lost* is such as to draw attention to the Tassonic distinction: God's miracles, for example the act of Creation, are "true" (in the sense Abraham Cowley will give to the literal truth of "Christian miracles") without being allegorical. (This in fact is so only sometimes: since God also sets out the Golden Ladder and Golden Scales in Books III and IV of *Paradise Lost,* and these spectacles are clearly figural or allegorical.) However, by conjoining the "marvellous" and the "verisimilar" in *various* ways, Tasso may be thinking more of the correct fusion of historical and allegorical narrative in the epic. This point we shall discuss in the section which now follows.

History and Fiction in the Epic

The last and most important of the three previously noted questions is possibly the most basic of all for the epic practitioner: the relation of "history" (historical materials) to "truth". This question is of peculiar importance to Tasso, as it is to Milton, since under "history" is included religion, comprising both scriptural history and dogma. How is the poet not to "spoil" this inviolable truth? The problem is explored very precisely by Tasso in some lengthy and valuable passages in, notably, the *Discorsi del poema eroico* and the *Giudizio*. His earlier tracts and those of the mid-1580s had begun to clear the theoretical grounds involved; the Letters and "Allegoria" connected with the *Gerusalemme* had worked out the nature of the ethical-allegorical Idea and the related problems of structuring and plot; now the later writings proceed with increasing conviction toward a firm theoretical statement of an allegorical poetic which is compatible with "true religion and history".

In passages already cited from the earlier *Estratti dalla Poetica di Lodovico Castelvetro* and the *Risposta . . . Al . . . Lombardelli*, we noted Tasso's efforts to preserve a degree of flexibility in the use of historical materials in the epic poem, and to permit the "rearrangement" of fortune and the adaptation of fact and event so as to preserve a certain degree of imaginative flexibility— and so more "truth". Countering such extreme propositions as that of Castelvetro that the best poetry is that which is most like history,[20] Tasso speaks with greater decisiveness and less circumlocution than usual. In the *Risposta* he had made the points that, although poetry and history are both concerned with truth (here he means fact), and although such truth is a necessary foundation for all poems, poetry differs from history in respect of *imitation* and in that the poet must add something to the truth. "Poetry is not merely a retailing of historical facts",[21] since "all poems have some foundation of truth, some more and some less, according as they partici-pate more or less in perfection. We must nevertheless note that just as the whole structure is not the foundation, so perchance the whole action does not need to be true, but it must leave its part to the verisimilar, which is proper to the poem".[22]

This statement, in its stress on a form of truth beyond the historical so much more specific than the conventional Renaissance contrast between history and poetic fabling, is further particularized in the *Discorsi del poema eroico*. There Tasso reiterates the view that since Homer epics have been and should continue to be based on history: "in my judgement much better that the argument be taken from history, as it would not be if it were wholly invented. . . . truth provides a more suitable basis for the heroic poet".[23] The kind of history referred to is specifically moral and patriotic: "epic illustriousness is based on lofty military valour and the magnanimous resolve to die, on piety, religion, and deeds alight with these virtues, proper to epic but less fitting to tragedy". Also: "The poet should also consider the glory of his country, the origin of cities and illustrious fam-ilies, the beginnings of kingdoms and empires, as Virgil above all others did".[24] Epic is also concerned with love, insofar as love is "not merely a passion . . . but a highly noble habit of the will. . . . Hence we may regard actions performed for the sake of love as beyond all others heroic".[25] But the best of all plots is an "action of the utmost nobility", such as "the coming of Aeneas to Italy: the subject in itself is great and illustrious . . . since it gave rise to the Roman empire".[26] All these subjects increase credibility, since "great and eventful actions cannot be unknown". But the epic profits by *"the authority of history"*, rather than attempting to convey factual history itself.[27]

Under history Tasso includes religion: "the argument of the best epic should be based on history. But history involves a religion either false or true". True religion obviously is best: "The argument of the epic poem should be drawn, then, from true history and a religion that is not false".[28] In a statement which reverberates in Milton's prose, Tasso declares: "Besides, I do not know why anyone who wishes to form the idea of a perfect knight should deny him the commendation of piety and religion. That is why I would put Charlemagne or Arthur as epic persons far ahead of Theseus or Jason. Finally, since the poet's great concern should be with improving men, he will kindle the souls of our knights much more with the example of the faithful than with that of infidels. . . . For identical reasons Christian victories over the infidel nowadays supply a most welcome and noble argument for poetizing".[29] In this passage Tasso has summarized the century's ideal and his own of the Christian didactic-historical epic— an ideal which passed on to Spenser and, ingeniously reinterpreted, to Milton.

It is important to observe how cunningly Tasso, having so clearly earmarked Christian history as the proper argument of epic, then goes on to restrict and qualify the historical element. How much of actual histories should the poet use? The answer is, not too much, if he is to leave space for his own invention and the more important truths of the verisimilar and the marvellous-verisimilar:

the poet, when it comes to this material of ours, must first of all consider quantity; for in taking up a matter to handle, he necessarily takes up together with it some quantity. Let him then be careful not to take so large a quantity that, when he proceeds to weave the fable, if he wishes to insert many episodes and adorn things . . . the poem grows to unbecoming and immoderate size. . . . Such matters [as the Civil War between Caesar and Pompey or the Second African War], vast in themselves, could fill the entire space allowed to epic magnitude, leaving no room at all for the poet's invention and ingenuity.[30]

For similar reasons, the historical matter which the poet chooses should be neither too recent nor too familiar, but instead of a "convenient remoteness from memory"; and it should not be too detailed in its historical descriptions of people's customs and ceremonies, since overparticularity would restrict the poet's own inventiveness: "Between modern and ancient times, let him choose those of a convenient remoteness from memory, as a painter sets his picture not too close to our eyes, nor yet so far away that it cannot be recognized".[31] Again: "Modern stories offer a great advantage and convenience in this matter of custom and usage, but almost entirely remove the freedom to invent and imitate, which is essential to poets, particularly epic poets. . . . the present or the recent past should not be the subject of a heroic poem. . . . the deeds of contemporaries or men of

recent memory may be [better] handled by orators". In accordance with
Aristotle we should prefer "narratives of things neither too new nor too old
. . . we distrust things that are too remote . . . but on the other hand we
seem still to feel those that are too recent".[32] It is the appearance of history,
"the semblance of truth", that the poet chiefly emulates: "the poet *seeks to
persuade us that what he treats deserves belief and credit*; he makes an effort to
gain such belief and credit through the authority of history and renowned
names".[33] Such a line of reasoning had led Tasso to choose the sufficiently
remote but historically still important twelfth-century First Crusade as his
matter. Equally, Milton could apply the principle to the remote and scanty
material, yet of even more immediate importance, in Genesis 1-3.

Further, in religious history certain matters are best avoided, specifi-
cally, "the most sacred"—those parts of the Bible, evidently, to do with
doctrine: "histories and other writings may be sacred or not sacred, and
among the sacred some have more and some have less authority. Eccle-
siastical and spiritual writings command greater authority. . . . The poet
had better not touch histories of the first type; they may be left in their pure
and simple truth, since with them discovery takes no effort and invention
seems hardly permitted".[34] The extremely important distinction made
here between the more and the less authoritative in sacred matter, and
between what should be left as "pure and simple truth" and what may be
elaborated through fictive invention, throws light on one of the most
difficult aspects of Milton's handling of his scriptural subject. Milton is in
fact bolder than his Catholic predecessor; he undertakes to deal with
doctrinal matters among his "sacred" material; but he nevertheless, as we
shall see, maintains a clear distinction in his own style and treatment
between matters in sacred writings which have greater and those which
have lesser doctrinal importance, and between what is authentic scriptural
event and what is his own invention or synthesis.

History and Allegory: The Late *Giudizio*

The *Giudizio* continues the argument about history before reintroducing
the question of allegory. In the *Risposta* to Lombardelli, Tasso has said that
the whole of a poetic action need not be true, although the foundation
should be. The *Giudizio* tells us even more exactly than the *Discorsi del poema
eroico*, Book II, *where* factual history can be most usefully incorporated:
specifically, at the beginning and end of a poem (thus leaving the middle
parts free for invention).[35] Of these two places, "truth" in the beginning is
especially needful (the principle which Tasso had followed in his own
poem). To explain: "As to what concerns the mixing of the true with the
false, my opinion is, that the true ought to have the principal [*maggior*] part,
thus so, because the beginning, which sets in train the whole, must be true;

[equally], so, the truth of the ending, towards which everything is directed: and where the beginning, and the end of the narration [are] true, the false may be easily hidden in the middle parts, and be interposed, and inserted with episodes".[36] In the middle parts, we may deduce, that other kind of truth-in-falsehood (fabling) may be "hidden" (perhaps under the veil of plausible fiction); "interposed" (as in digressive actions); or "inserted" (as in fabulous episodes). Thus these middle parts may be elaborated by both the allegorical heightening of the true and the introduction of the fabulous.

However, in the *Giudizio* the emphasis is not quite so much as it is in the Letters and the *Discorsi del poema eroico* on prodigies and marvellous episodes, rather it falls on fictive plausibility: "the *aspect* of truth" or "the *image* of history". The entire train of argument suggests that in this "image of history" Tasso seeks and finds the vehicle for his own version of "verisimilar" truth: "if the true things had been narrated by me in a historical way, I should not merit any praise as a poet; but having treated them in a poetic manner, and having sought the marvelous through the excess of truth, in those things in which I have most completely preserved the image of history and as it were the aspect of truth, I have merited the greatest praise for admirable poetic artistry".[37] To sustain "the image of history" and "the aspect of truth" in the larger part of his poem, and so to promote the truth of the verisimilar (didactic allegory), would come to be Milton's aim also.

Thus Tasso is able to argue that in the reformed *Gerusalemme* he has made his poem simultaneously *more* historical and yet, by means of allegory, also *more* "true". Now all the false parts, even the slightest, are seen as filled with allegorical meanings (this is a more extreme statement even than those made in the Letters). Episodes, and the narrative parts of the story, contribute in equal measure:

As we have already said, with the authority of St. Augustine in the *City of God*, that that which is of significance cannot be false or vain: whence allegory, by means of the hidden senses of the things signified, can defend the poet from frivolity [*vanità*] and from falsity similarly. For this reason, in revising my story, I sought to make it more similar to the truth than it was before, regulating myself in many things according to histories, and I added allegory to history—in such a way that, as in the world and in the nature of things there is no space left for a vacuum, so in the poem there is no part left to frivolity—filling every one of them, even the tiniest, and least obvious, with hidden and mysterious meanings; and besides in the Episodes, and in certain parts of the story, I sought to infuse marvels with an excess of truth, which to perform appears to me the proper office of the poet and the poetical art.[38]

It may be seen that in the *Giudizio* "allegory" or related terms have been reintroduced to stand in place of more general terms such as "verisi-

militude", or the "truth of the universals", or the "Ideas", as used in the
more discreetly worded *Discorsi del poema eroico*. Tasso intends by either
set of terms the same thing: that special further truth which can most
satisfactorily be conveyed by the fictive or the imaginative, of whatever
variety. And allegory, or this inner truth, can begin, he tells us, wherever
factual history in the poem leaves off. In a totally committing statement
Tasso makes it plain (given that for him, factual "history" is to be brief
and confined mainly to the beginning and end of the epic) that the bulk of
even the most historical-seeming epic must be infused with allegory. The
epic as a genre becomes the allegorical epic: "I use allegory most in those
parts of my poem in which I have departed farthest from history, esteem-
ing that where the literal sense stops the allegorical and the other senses
must substitute for it; nevertheless I have taken care not to use any al-
legory which might seem inappropriate in the figure and appearance".[39]
The "figure" which he then goes on to rehearse is that which constitutes
the full "Allegoria" to the *Gerusalemme*—the main central body of the
narrative and its inner psychological action are Tasso's continued dark
conceit.

Thus Tasso has finally united his earliest defences of the marvellous
as conveyed especially via *miracoli* or "prodigies" or supernatural epi-
sodes—although he had never, in connection with the composition of
the *Gerusalemme*, abandoned his intuition that the *entire* poem and *all* its
parts and persons could carry "marvellous mysteries"—with his more
general arguments for a "kind of truth", the truth of the universals or
Ideas, as expressed especially in the two *Discorsi*, and with his further
arguments for allegorical truths conveyed under the plausible "image of
history", as put in the late *Giudizio*. Putting together all of the above
arguments relating to allegory over the main part of Tasso's career, we
see that he has progressively argued his way to a position which defines
the epic poem as a narrative which preserves an external skeleton of
history and the semblance or "air" of history overall, and which thus
has behind it the authority of history and religion, while it yet maintains
a flexibility and freedom of invention which may be deployed in a di-
versity of ways in the service of allegorical or higher truth. Especially
through his central perception that allegory, or the truth of the verisim-
ilar, may take over wherever literal history stops, Tasso frees the epic
poem from the shackles of a narrow historicity. All those parts of the
poem which are the product of the poet's own free imagination, ampli-
fication or invention, as much so those parts cast in the seeming image
of history as those which strike with epic wonder through their fantastic
marvels or their very opposition to the mode of history, all may become
the vehicle of that inner truth which the poet is chiefly concerned to
convey.

Tasso: A Retrospect

A summary of the development of Tasso's ideas on allegory, as discussed in the last three chapters, is now indicated. In the foregoing sections we have traced the development of Tasso's ideas on epic mimesis (understood as essentially allegorical), as they move away from rhetorical interpretations of allegory to "Imitation" of an "Idea", loosely defined but clarifying as something beyond an aesthetic concept of decorum or an ideal of genre-model (for example, the unity-in-variety of the mixed romance epic form). Then, working through the commonplace notion of exemplary characters, we have seen Tasso's conception progress to a much more original view of the Christian epic, in which the "Soul" is its conceptual allegory, its didactic purpose or Idea. Imitation here becomes the mere outward "dress" of the fiction-making process; terms such as "imitation" or "idea" are replaced by the term "allegory" as a leading concept. Concurrently, we have seen Tasso arrive at a particular formulation of the complex structuring of the mixed allegorical-historical epic. We saw in his writing a persistent drive (not always expressed with chronological consistency, but intensifying in the decade concerned with the completion and publishing of the *Gerusalemme*), toward an allegorical-epic poetic, the hinge of which lies in his special concepts of poetic "verisimilitude" and the "marvellous-verisimilar". These are principles which provide the unifying bonds, in an epic, between history, fictive-verisimilar expansion of history (which can carry allegory), and the truth-in-fiction expressible via the marvellous (as in fantastic episode).

The term "Idea", used in the *Discorsi del poema eroico* but not there directly coupled with allegory or with continuous didactic allegory (although it clearly had that potential), increasingly elsewhere in his writings is identified with allegory, or indeed displaced by the latter term in Tasso's mind, as he works himself out of his original terminological problems over inadequate existing definitions of "allegory" and out of his cinquecento doubts over its permissible use in a Christian poem—an historically recurrent debate. The *Discorsi del poema eroico* offers a more general, public kind of statement on the allegorical epic, one more aware of controversial criticism and less willing to court it, one which tries to express Tasso's ideas perhaps in more guardedly general terms. This treatise expresses much less of the direct, evolving excitement of Tasso's critical discoveries as he actually worked on his poem, and as recorded in his Letters. However, the treatise offers valuable specific instructions on how to combine "true" history with "verisimilar" (fictive but potentially allegorically loaded) "histories"; and it offers some penetrating general discussions of the relationship of the "marvellous" to "truth".

It is evident that, as Tasso becomes more involved with a deeper conception of allegory, seen both as a unifying artistic principle and as the concealed, directing intellectual intention in epic, he is also inevitably obliged to come to terms with increasingly pressing practical questions of narrative structuring and form—with the problem of unifying diverse modes of fiction and diverse narrative and poetic devices in an epic through their common linking themes ("Idea" now to be understood in the sense of hidden content). In the *Discorsi del poema eroico* and still later treatises such as the *Giudizio*, Tasso indicated the necessary balance (indeed a disbalance) to be observed between historical fact and the fictive-verisimilar expansion of history in the epic; he indicated the nature of the moral epic ideal hero (epic shows "shapes of virtue"); he defended variety. Much of all this could suggest didactic epic conceived of simply as exemplary moral action. However, the *Discorsi del poema eroico* and later treatises further stressed the importance of the *phantastike* (the "marvellous") as not merely productive of epic "wonder" but as a means to inner truth. But it is in the special interplay indicated in Tasso's critical remarks in the Letters (between fantastic episode and main-plot allegory) and in the "Allegoria" to the *Gerusalemme* (on extended allegory in the main parts of the plot, with allegorical episode as complement) that his matured views on epic allegory as a deeply expressive means and also a cohering structural principle in epic can be fully recognised. Such integration is to be reasserted more boldly in his last major critical treatise.

In the above working documents, two areas of intellectually expressive allegory relating to plot are seen to be acting in conjunction. The main plot offers a more "continued" dark conceit, "Episode" is its more intermittent but thematically coherent counterpart. In Tasso's analysis in the "Allegoria" of the relationship between Godfrey (Reason; the leader) and the knights (Rinaldo and Tancredi: ire and passion), powerful in their cause when united, weak and ineffective when dispersed, Tasso suggests the first kind of "continued allegory", that is, in the main plot itself, although not in every single action of it. This main-plot allegory is psychologically based and runs deeper than the merely exemplary value of the surface plausible incidents, such as the Crusaders' objective of taking Jerusalem, or Rinaldo's loss of personal purpose through sensual indulgence. The allegorical roles of Ismen (errors of opinion: intellectual delusion) and Armida (sensual desire) in together weakening or blinding the rational faculty of mind, complete Tasso's analysis of the "internal impediments" to consolidated virtue and firm moral purpose, the magicians' activities frequently being expressed through magical "Episode". Coupled with the "outward obstacles" to virtue in the shape of the physical hazards of the crusaders' quest, the whole poem offers a complex paradigm of the progress of the fallible but perfectible soul toward an heroic virtue, tested and improved through external and inward adversity, through failure, self-examination and experience, and also strengthened by grace and revelation, exemplified in Peter the Hermit's and Godfrey's visions and in the angelic messengers.

As the Letters and the "Allegoria" record (as Tasso evolves theory and imaginative invention simultaneously during the composition of the *Gerusalemme*), the second or complementary kind of significant epic allegory lies in fantastic Episode devised in the supernatural and not in the verisimilar mode. In the *Gerusalemme* this mode is only *apparently* digressive, and probably reiterative more than genuinely intermittent. This kind of fiction, stressing *meraviglie*, is a potent means of imaginatively expressing moral truths and is particularly fitted (as in the extended description of Rinaldo as thrall in Armida's palace, or of the knights repeatedly wandering in their dark wood) to record subtly the varying moods and psychological complexions, the hesitations and repeated lapses, of the mental journey to self-understanding and fit action. (And incidentally, only such an approach in reading makes sense, and very good sense, of Armida's final self-subjugation to Rinaldo and reacceptance by him, *after* she is defeated by his sword: all passions are fit, in their due and subordinated place.)

Thus the whole of the *Gerusalemme*'s action taken in all its parts together comprises Tasso's "*continued* dark conceit", illustrating his express conviction that the "verisimilar" (understood as ethical truth) may be of "many kinds", and that what he sometimes called "Episodes" (the supernatural, or digressive adventures) may be connected with the main thread of the plot by other means than "necessity" (natural causal connection between events). Tasso's "continued dark conceit", of such intricate narrative structuring, makes of his poem something far beyond a simple exemplary action or series of *exempla* of moral virtue or virtues, and also something beyond a verisimilar historical narrative interspersed with didactic allegories.

Tasso's views have never been well understood, and they were out of accord with other continental and English neoclassical critical theories in his own and the following century. Much Italian neoclassical theory in the late sixteenth century and English theory especially in the mid-seventeenth century was such as to lay a primary emphasis on outward verisimilitude or realism in the epic. Narrowly Aristotelian interpretations of epic structure and purpose, the efforts to make the epic read more, not less, like pure history, and more simplistic interpretations of epic-moral intention (characters demonstrating what Tasso in the *Discorsi del poema eroico* had referred to as the "perfect *shapes* of virtue"), often seem to dominate criticism on epic poetics, while Tasso's careful development of the theory of epic allegory, the relationship of such allegory to and its differences from allegory understood as rhetorical trope, also its difference from aesthetic or formal interpretations of "Idea", and further, the practical applications of such poetics to the structuring of a long and complex narrative based on history, all these contributions are seemingly ignored or distorted, even though Tasso's theories were far from unknown in the seventeenth century. Although there were enlightened and important exceptions to this neglect—one of them being Milton—the concept of poetic allegory after Tasso in the northern European tradition tends once again either to become narrowed to rhetorical trope, that is, to figures of speech, or to be equated with interspersed "fable" (artistically suspect if of extended length), or else to be confusingly identified with moral *exemplum*. Thus, for the major English epic poets of the Renaissance and later the old problem remained—yet now with Tasso's prescriptions and example to help—once more to redeem from the bondage of literalistic theories of art the marvellous, the freer flights of the imagination.

EIGHT

Spenser as Allegorical Theorist

Before turning to neoclassical developments, we may look at Spenser's statements on epic allegory. Spenser's theories on allegory are included at this point, rather than earlier in the general section on Renaissance allegory, because the direct line of influence, Tasso-Spenser-Milton, is such an important one; to consider the views of the two English epic artists next to Tasso's helps to reveal their affinities and, frequently, their indebtedness. Some of Spenser's views on allegory may seem on the face of it more archaic than Tasso's. But in point of fact, each phase of Spenser's poetical art and theory is preceded by almost a decade by a comparable phase in Tasso's; and Spenser's theory of epic allegory is better attuned to Renaissance advances and to Tasso's ideas than might at first appear.

Spenser offers an interesting glimpse of a practising poet caught at a confusingly complex moment of transition in literary theory, and in something of a time-gap between northern and southern European cultures. The image of the medieval allegorist is that which until recently was most commonly held up to Spenser. One view of the allegorical patterning of *The Faerie Queene*, as explored by Tuve among others, relates it to medieval theoretical developments deriving from Aristotle: namely, the classifications of the virtues and vices into schemes and sub-schemes, allegorically represented by, or "opened out" into, a number of major characters and innumerable lesser sub-characters—the "shapes" of virtues or vices, infinitely graduated or subdivided.[1] Another view, promoted by C.S. Lewis, detected medieval didactic-allegorical pageant as constituting the true allegorical "cores" of Spenser's cantos, such cores being surrounded by other multiple episodes of pure romance fantasy.[2] The foregoing represent only two among many elements of Spenserian allegory. Substantial traces of more advanced Renaissance rhetorical and mythographical thinking on allegory also can be detected in Spenser's various theoretical pronouncements on allegory, as well as in the internal practices of *The Faerie Queene*; while the influence of Tasso and the tradition of "continued" moral meta-

phor in the epic is basic to Spenser's poem, although it is to some extent
overshadowed by the surface complications of his narrative and the variety
of contributory allegorical devices which he introduces.

Spenser and Tasso

Our contemporary unawareness of the extent of Tasso's influence on
Spenser hinges on inadequate assumptions concerning the availability of
late sixteenth-century Italian critical texts and poetry to Spenser—es-
pecially Tasso's influential works. It is to be remembered that Haring-
ton's English translation of Ariosto, the author whom Spenser wished to
"overgo", with its copious moralized glosses, prefaces and appendices on
allegorical interpretation, some of a quite modern cast, was published in
1591, still within the period of composition of the *Faerie Queene*. Many of
Harington's glosses were themselves taken from earlier Italian commen-
taries on or editions of the *Furioso*, such as those of Fornari or Bononome, in
which Spenser could have read Ariosto "allegorized" in the Italian orig-
inals. Such formal exegetical apparatuses as those of Harington, Fornari,
Bononome, embodied important contemporary theories of allegory and
poetry.[3] As has been earlier observed, the content of Harington's various
allegories, although they are episodic (given his original, necessarily so),
usually follows a standard Renaissance pattern of ethical commentary, as
for instance in his constant use of the same basic Reason-Passion allegory
concerning the dispersal and separation of the mental faculties and their
ultimate reintegration, and the progress through human error toward
consolidation of moral virtue. If Spenser's scheme of virtues and subvir-
tues and its chivalric framework owes something to medieval theory and
literary practice, it is certainly the Renaissance epic allegorizers who pro-
vide the psychodynamics of Spenser's six-times repeated progression
toward "virtuous discipline" in his six Books of *The Faerie Queene*.[4]

A Reason-Passions type of allegory, projected via fragmented charac-
ters, as patchily but recurrently given by Harington in his annotations on
the *Orlando Furioso*, was, as we saw, worked out very systematically in the
"Allegoria" of Tasso, published with the first authorized Italian edition of
the *Gerusalemme* as early as 1581 (although not in English translation until
Fairfax, 1600). The "Allegoria", together with those of Tasso's Letters
written during the 1570s when the *Gerusalemme* was being composed, some
relating specifically to the "Allegoria", and published as early as 1587, con-
stitute Tasso's most explicit documents on epic-allegorical theory. These
documents were available or potentially available to Spenser by the above
mentioned dates (if not earlier through private circulation)—which means
that they were available or potentially available during all or part of the
period of his composition of *The Faerie Queene*, and certainly in time to

modify his first plans.[5] There is no doubt whatsoever as to the strength of impact of Tasso's poem itself upon the *The Faerie Queene* from Book II onward; and while the more general theorizing about the Christian, historical and marvellous epic in Tasso's *Discorsi del poema eroico* (in substance published much earlier in the *Discorsi dell'arte poetica*) may or may not have come within Spenser's ken, as may or may not the published Letters, it is hard to see how the *Gerusalemme*'s allegorical preface, introducing the first full Italian edition of 1581 and included in most later editions, could have failed to do so; or why, if Spenser took so much from Tasso's actual poem for his own Book II and onward in *The Faerie Queene*, Tasso's allegorical plan for the *Gerusalemme* should not equally have impressed itself on Spenser's mind, struggling as he was to impose an order on his unruly poem. In any case, Spenser's "Letter to Raleigh" clearly cites Tasso's two epics as models of allegorical theory of epic applied to contemporary practice.[6]

Similarly (since there is evidence that a collection of Tasso's prose had been seen by at least one Englishman by 1593),[7] some of Tasso's Letters published in 1587 and relating to the allegorical evolution of his poem cannot be completely excluded from the orbit of Spenser's knowledge during the period of composition of *The Faerie Queene*.[8] But it is the *Gerusalemme* in particular, with its extended fictive dark conceit and its key explaining how to interpret the poem, a practical working document, poem and gloss together illustrating how fantastic-allegorical episode could interplay in meaning with a more continued moral allegory expressed through the main action, that represents an allegorical schematology available to Spenser and one which could not but have been of interest to him. All the main materials relating to Tasso's new conception of his poem were in print and, we must assume, some at least were known to Spenser well before he completed his first three Books of *The Faerie Queene* or began the second three Books. A brief account of Tasso's influence in England between 1580 and 1600, a collation of the relative dates of Tasso's and Spenser's writings, and some indication of the direct or possible influences of Tasso's poem and prose writings on Spenser's poem and theory are given separately in Appendix C.

If we look now at the internal evidence of Spenser's poem, it could be thought that he has grafted onto a main narrative-allegorical scheme several lesser parallel schemes, plus a variety of subordinate allegorical structures. The larger, a cohering strategy, lies in the relationship of the six knights, seen as six Virtues, to Arthur, and in Arthur's share, increasingly less as the knights mature, in their adventures. His is the total achieved virtue or perfection within each of the other Virtues against which the progress toward their separate Virtue by each of the six Knights is measured. They represent different Virtues, but the same moral progress may be seen within each Virtue or character toward psychic balance, gain in confidence and self-understanding. This is the principal psychological scheme. One could say that this scheme conforms to the Renaissance developmental model in allegorical epic (or earlier in epic exegesis), as exemplified in and discussed by Tasso, and that Spenser's poem simply exhibits a multiplication by six times of the traditional "moral progress" of the epic moral hero, with Arthur seen as a kind of superego to each knight.

Within that broad scheme (the larger strategy within each Book, and through repetition and via Arthur linking all six Books) lie a multiplicity of subordinate allegorical structures: some on the medieval pattern, others more "modern". For instance, Books III and IV exhibit several kinds of heroines or "loves" as the "unfolding" of that virtue (or "opening out", to use Tuve's term); the undivided virtue itself is implicitly summed up, perhaps, in Queen Elizabeth. But in Book II Guyon stands in relation to Cymochles and Pyrochles, sensual torpor and anger, exactly as in Tasso's Platonic-psychological paradigm Godfrey stands to Tancredi and Rinaldo. (Reason is above passion and ire: that is, Cymochles and Pyrochles are not *vices*, but innate faculties of the soul, of Guyon's soul, seen in exorbitant disbalance.) Each of Spenser's other Books exhibits analogously some form of psychic disbalance within the main protagonist. We may perceive that the chivalric love-relationship of each pair of knights and ladies is, in every instance, initially flawed psychologically. Redcrosse's "eye of reason" is "with rage yblent" (I.ii.5); and it is not for nothing that Scudamour suffers hammering migraines in the House of Care (Jealousy: IV.v), since the name of "Amoret" or "Amoretta" signifies in Italian "flirtatious". (Spenser puns a good deal on names and their etymologies; but this feature as applied to *foreign* etymologies has not been as widely noticed as it might be.) Thus the theme of psychic disintegration and reintegration, foundation of each and all achieved Virtues, is sketched out repeatedly in the various lovers' separations and reunions; while the "unfolding" of Loves in Books III to IV proves to be a secondary pattern imposed on the repetitive underlying psychological scheme of the poem. (Guyon's lack of a partner constitutes an interesting narrative exception, but the same psychological theme of *temperantia*, balance, continues within the single protagonist's adventures in Book II.) Such ongoing narrative ethical-psychological allegory thus is much alike in all six Books. Spenser explicitly stresses this continuity, not only by linking characters from Book to Book, but in such statements as that of Calidore at the opening of Book VI (i.6), that he now begins to "tread" again the same "endlesse trace" just completed by Artegall, the protagonist of the preceding Book. The moral journey "withouten guyde, / Or good direction", six times repeated in Spenser's poem, represents the foundation of his allegorical plan and a direct parallel to the psychological models of Tasso or Harington, or of earlier epic allegorists in the Landino tradition of commentary on Virgil.

Intermixed into such larger parallel narrative schemes in Spenser's poem, the "continued dark conceit" seen in mirror multiplication and constituting the more "verisimilar" aspect of his allegorical fiction, are, again, numerous detached *exemplum* allegories on the earlier Renaissance epic model, which serve the same purpose as do Ariosto's minor *exemplum* characters (explicated by Harington as "types" of love, courtesy, and so forth, and their opposites). Examples in Spenser are Malbecco/Hellenore (III.ix-x), or Blandina/Turpine (VI.iii, v, vi): personified, minor, always unenigmatic representatives of virtues and vices, who do not represent true allegories of the "continued metaphor" kind. Old-fashioned, too, might seem to be Spenser's "straight" allegorical personifications and allegorical Houses—C.S. Lewis' "cores", or straight didactic inset allegories on the medieval pattern, such as Cœlia's House, the House of Alma, the Temple of Isis, and all their opposite numbers. These might seem like intermissions in the plot. But most of Spenser's central and seemingly disjunct fantastic or supernatural allegories, such as the Man of Despaire and Orgoglio's Cave of Despair (I.ix; vii), the Cave of Mammon (II.vii) and Acrasia's Bower (II.vi, xii; this latter appropriated from *Gerusalemme*, Book XV), the Wood of Error (I.i), or the Wandering Isles (II.xii)—to take some negative cases—are used by Spenser much more in Tasso's thematically continuous way than in Ariosto's episodic and discrete way. These "marvels", like Tasso's Wood, are usually reiterative versions of each other; like the Wood, they have a deepening psychological meaning within each Book (or even sometimes as between Books) and, as in the instances just cited, usually an inverse relationship (intensifying failure) with the sought-for Virtue. Thus such "episodes" in Spenser are not static allegorical setpieces, as C.S. Lewis would have it, but essential parts of the moral narrative, running thematically in parallel with each other and with the dynamics of the main developmental progress in each Book, the poem's "continued dark conceit". It may be added that the principal inward obstructions to the pursued Virtue, Spenser's Archimago and Duessa/Acrasia, bear a remarkable resemblance to Tasso's Ismen and Armida. Each pair represents the *inner* errors born of delusion (perceived outwardly as illusions) on the one hand, and sensual weakness on the other. The main outlines of Spenser's dark conceit thus closely concur with Tasso's.

And finally, allegorical narrative designs and more static devices in *The Faerie Queene* are reinforced by a pervasive network in language, metaphor, simile, of oblique allusion and intimation (often ironic, punning, gnomic or "absurd"), self-echoing and self-referential, which identifies Spenser's total poem as not merely a model of recognisable allegorical rhetoric but as something equivalent to the early Renaissance view of all poetry as itself allegory—allegorical throughout its poetic texture as well as in its didactic core, all expressive of a central Idea. The internal character of Spenser's allegorical poem thus suggests that it is by no means the kind of picturesque, freely improvised hotch-potch for which it used to be taken. Although overcomplicated, perhaps, in respect of their overlapping schemes, the various kinds of allegory in *The Faerie Queene* all have their appointed place within the total ongoing narrative conceit. Almost all of Spenser's major allegorical constructs and "episode" allegories find parallels in Renaissance allegorical theory and practice. Medieval literary models of allegory are not lacking in *The Faerie Queene*; but on balance, the dominant model is the psychological-moral progress of the newer Italian epic or of epic exegesis in the Virgilian tradition, to the support of which subschemes, older medieval *schemata* and literary forms, and allegorical linguistic features all are cunningly allied.[9]

The "Letter to Raleigh": Schemes of Allegory in *The Faerie Queene*

The Faerie Queene is thus, by its own internal evidence, substantially indebted to the psychological model of extended narrative allegory, as seen in Renaissance epic practice and theory. It is especially indebted to Tasso, although sharing something of other Renaissance theories of allegorical rhetoric and method. Such indebtedness is borne out pretty well by Spenser's cryptic theoretical statements in the "Letter to Raleigh", the Proem to Book III and a few other scattered references.[10] Although the 1579-80 Spenser-Harvey correspondence had suggested Ariosto as romance-epic model for *The Faerie Queene*,[11] it must be stressed again that the sixteenth-century Ariosto was nonetheless the Ariosto of the Italian allegorizers and of Harington, late emulators of the tradition of Landino's Virgil or the allegorizers of Homer—recorders of the painful progress of the moral hero toward moral perfection, to heroic virtue or a virtue more heroic than the martial virtues held up in the classical epics. Spenser's allusion in the first stanza of the proem to Book I ("Fierce warres and faithfull loves shall *moralize* my song") puts *The Faerie Queene* directly into that same tradition of Renaissance moral exegesis on epic narrative. The same arguments which in late cinquecento criticism raged over whether Dante's *Commedia* could rightly be called an epic apply to Spenser's also; both are so, in that special sense of showing the continued moral progress of the protagonist, allegorically represented. It is to be noted that in the 1589 "Letter to Raleigh" (perhaps Spenser's conscious parallel to Tasso's exposition of his own poem in 1581) Spenser cites Ariosto only briefly, but Tasso at greater length, coupling Tasso with Virgil and Homer as models— just as these three poets together, Homer, Virgil and Tasso, become the chief models for Milton in what Milton was to term the "diffuse" (long and mixed) epic. It is rather striking that Spenser, poet of Faerieland, in the "Letter to Raleigh" puts himself and his poem into the tradition of classical or European "antique Poets *historicall*":[12] as if he had in mind the *Discorsi del poema eroico*, with its long discussion of the correct (that is, mainly fictive) treatment of history in an epic. As would the younger Milton, Spenser looks into early English idealized "history" and to Arthur for the hero of a national epic—Arthur who, strikingly, was also one of Tasso's two recommended hero-models in both the *Discorsi del'arte poetica* and *Discorsi del poema eroico*.

Spenser's description of his epic in fact suggests not the kind of historical epic illustrated by, for example, Luis de Camões' *Os Lusiadas*, but rather the mixed historical and fabulous, allegorically loaded kind of epic which Virgil and Homer were taken to have written and which Tasso had sketched out in his Letters and the "Allegoria" to the *Gerusalemme*. As Spenser sees it, Homer's two epics respectively and then Virgil's and Tasso's epics within themselves illustrate on the one hand the private and on the other hand the public virtues. In Spenser's own scheme similarly are illustrated not simply different "shapes" of virtue but different *contexts* of virtue: private and public, or "Ethice" and "Politice" (civic), to use Spenser's terms. In Virgil the two schemes are seen by earlier allegorizers and by Spenser as conflated into a single but naturally self-dividing epic plot: Aeneas illustrates the private and public man in, respectively, his actions before and after Latium. Thus while Homer had one hero in two different kinds of epic (the *Iliad* showed the "politice" or national cause, the *Odyssey* a contemplative or solitary journey), and Virgil had one hero in a single epic, progressing from the personal to the public context within the different phases of the *Aeneid*, Tasso (reversing Ariosto's procedure of joining up both contexts in a single epic hero and single action) is seen by Spenser as "dissever[ing]" them again, dividing private ("Ethice") and public ("Politice") virtue between his Rinaldo (of the earlier epic) and Godfredo (of the *Gerusalemme*). Analogously, in Spenser's original scheme of twelve plus twelve Books, Arthur as questing prince and Arthur as achieved king, we hear a direct echo of Landino's treatment of the *Aeneid*, in which Virgil's six Books on Aeneas' wanderings and failures illustrated the formation of virtue, while the other six, concerning Aeneas at Latium, showed the irresistible progress of achieved heroic virtue.[13] (Although Spenser's Arthur in another sense is from the beginning perfected virtue, his surrogate knights are still "in progress", seeking their own ultimate perfection as epitomized in his own.) Spenser, over-ambitious to say the least, seems to have intended to double the Virgilian-Landino twelve-Book scheme.

While the possibly fictitious, or more probably fictional, report by Lodowick Bryskett of 1606 (allegedly reporting an earlier "conversation" with Spenser of around 1582), giving Spenser's plan for a poem in which would be assigned "to every vertue, a Knight to be the patron and defender of the same", and "whose actions and feates" would "express" the "operations of that vertue", while its opposing "vices & unruly appetites" would be "beatē downe & overcome"[14], might suggest a static, triumphant

display of various virtues[15] rather than a unified developmental treatment
showing a maturation in virtues, what Spenser in his 1589 Letter outlines is
not a static series of such displays but some scheme effecting a "pleasing
Analysis" of the *education* of a noble person "in vertuous and gentle disci-
pline", represented through an "historicall fiction" and a sequential action.
(A primary sense of "discipline" in Spenser's time, according to the *Oxford
English Dictionary*, is "*training* . . . to proper conduct and action by instruct-
ing and exercising".) I take it therefore that when Spenser speaks of his
"*continued* Allegory, or darke conceit" (the last word of which phrase ety-
mologically signifies "idea" or "concept"), he means exactly what Tasso
meant: a predominant moral Idea to be expressed darkly, "clowdily en-
wrapped in Allegoricall devises" (which could or would include the devel-
opmental narrative itself), and extending right across his poem. The overt
"instruction" is given in the few genuinely static didactic interludes; the
"exercise" of virtue lies in all the other adventures, allegorically read. The
failures and lapses of the six knights and their slowness in consolidating
each his Virtue are more important almost than their successes (easy, at
first, in their lesser trials)—just as Aeneas' lapses or Odysseus' mistaken
journeys or Adam's failure, but subsequent progress of each toward the
achieving of virtue, constitutes the body of those moralized epic actions.
Therein lies the interest of these epics, rather than in any facile illustration
of an already achieved virtue—or of unfallen perfection. Thus we have the
meaning of Spenser's "generall end" of his poem, didactic in purpose,
formative and progressive: "to *fashion* a gentleman or noble person in
vertuous and gentle discipline", which is allegorically "the whole *inten-
tion*" or "generall end" of his conceit (the complete Idea of his work), and
which he has from his opening lines identified with the poem's allegory or
its dark conceit.

One example of the perfecting process which Spenser cites in the
Letter is the "hard Enchauntments" and "long sorrow" suffered by Scuda-
mour. Such painful psychological progress to virtue would seem to be the
meat or kernel of Spenser's enterprise, the epic's "intendment", its main-
plot allegory reenacted in Scudamour and many other times; to which
there stand contrasted, as he says, a series of incidental actions ("adven-
tures" or "Accidents" "intermedled") which are not the main design. ("Ac-
cidents" mean narrative intrusions.) Such "accidents" are most often
psychologically relevant to the story at large, and so Spenser's words about
casual accidents meddled in would seem to be an instance of his capacity
for deliberate obfuscation concerning some of the more intimate parts of
his allegory. Spenser mentions Florimell's captivity in Neptune's cave and
Britomart's love—incidents which hardly seem irrelevant to the main
design. (Hellenore's "lasciviousness", on the other hand, is more in the
exemplum tradition and is genuinely "accidental".) Like Tasso's repeated
magic enchantments in his Wood, such episodes, through parallel alle-

gorical incidents, often do deepen and expand the implications of the main actions. At any rate, we can see in the two different kinds of actions indicated by Spenser some understanding of the double narrative technique which Tasso had earlier outlined: the counterpoint of episodic allegory, accidents only seemingly "intermedled", with main-plot continued allegory.

Spenser's further remarks in the Letter, which represents a mature if overpacked statement of purpose, may be intended to show his awareness of various contemporary avenues or approaches to the knotty subject of allegory. "As Aristotle hath devised" and "Aristotle and the rest" probably are more accurately to be referred to the Landino-Tasso tradition of critical exegesis on the epic, stressing a moral progress, than to some, to this day unlocated, Aristotelian-based schematic classification of all the virtues. (In any case, for Aristotle in the *Ethics*, II.4, "Virtue", initially a "disposition", is the acquisition by practice or "repeated performance" of the habit of virtue.) Tasso's letters indicated that he hoped to fuse Aristotle's ethics with Plato's. Bryskett's "Dialogue" indicates the same conflation of philosophies, "easily" taught by the "late Italian" philosophers (he cites Giraldi Cintio and also Pigna, one of whose ethical treatises was allegorized by Tasso). Bryskett draws the same distinction as did Tasso between "contemplative" and "practicke" felicity, stressing the latter ("the Ethicke Part of Morall Philosophie"), and he attributes a specialist knowledge of this entire context to "Mr. Spenser". Whether the Dialogue is fictitious or not, the locating of Spenser in it and the attribution to him of current fashionable Platonic-Aristotelian epic models is suggestive of the contemporaneousness of Spenser's thinking on epic.[16] However, even if the Bryskett account represents an authentic recollection, it still corresponds, in its emphasis on Ariosto, to an earlier stage in the development of Spenser's thought. Tasso's poem, theories and letters on allegory, published throughout the same decade, if coming to Spenser's attention during the few years after 1581, would have given a new impetus to and foundation for Spenser's critical plan and actual construction of his poem. It is Tasso whom in *The Faerie Queene* Spenser cites—cites three times in explicit contexts and by name—rather than the earlier generation of Italian poets or critics instanced by Bryskett. And when Milton chooses one of Spenser's allegories for citation in *Areopagitica*, it is one which relates to the Virgilian-Landino-Tasso and thence the Spenser tradition: Guyon's visit to the Cave of Mammon, a parallel to Aeneas' visit to the underworld, both illustrating the ultimate trial of heroic virtue, trained and prepared, yet humanly fallible.[17]

Apart from the references to plot allegory and to main-epic allegorizers ("Aristotle and the rest"), the bits of the "Letter to Raleigh" which are most familiar to us are probably those invoking that other traditional idiom of poetic allegory understood as rhetorical figure: "translation" of sense,

coupled with obscurity, and sometimes passing into enigma—hence
Spenser's associated words "darke", "clowdily enwrapped", "veil" and
"shadow". Such words are as much part of the Renaissance idiom relating
to allegorical aesthetics as they were of the classical. A more difficult
statement is the reference to the Faerie Queene herself as meaning "glory
in [Spenser's] *generall intention*", but in the "particular" intention the per-
son of the Sovereign. This terminology may well relate to the first two of
the older secular *quatre-sens*, outlined in my first chapter:[18] the "literal"
sense (which corresponds to Spenser's "particular"), and the "typical" or
generalized sense (Spenser's "generall" end or intention). There is equally
something to do, one may suspect, with the "levels" of allegory as more
loosely redefined in the later Renaissance. Renaissance exegetes had
shifted the balance of their interpretations to more mundane or secular
areas, tending to favour historical-geographical, cosmological, anthropo-
logical and moral interpretations over theological and freely "spiritual"
interpretations. But, as we saw earlier, Renaissance interpreters did not
work within a fixed three- or fourfold parallel scheme reflecting a rigid
world view, despite the illusion sometimes conveyed of hieratic readings,
but instead turned sometimes to one kind of interpretation, sometimes to
another—as Spenser does. Spenser's "particular" sense relates to a real
historical level ("allusion", in Harington's term): that is, it implies histor-
ical reference to the real queen (or perhaps to other factual matter in
Spenser's political allegory, such as the allusions in later Books to Sir
Walter Raleigh or Lord Grey, who are not instanced in the Letter). Spen-
ser's "generall" intention then would become equivalent to Harington's
"Allegorie", a compendium of moral-spiritual senses or a comprehensive,
variable higher level, one more universal than "allusion", exemplary
"Moral" or mere "example", or even Harington's "Morall" would imply. In
this larger sense Gloriana, or Glory, is the allegorical reward of Arthur or
the Magnanimous/Magnificent man, and she is the ultimate object of every
Virtue's quest.[19] There are of course still other more specific Renaissance
levels of allegory clearly apparent in the body of Spenser's poem: cosmic
and geographical relevances, or the Renaissance "physical" level (as with
Florimell/Marinell in Books III-V: earth/sea); and there are, as well, spir-
itual-anagogic referents, as at the ending of Book I. Thus there is a strong
admixture of the newer with perhaps some of the older fashions in Spen-
ser's way of thinking about the "levels" of allegory.

Spenser also seems to distinguish between universal versus particular
(or historical) *levels* of meaning, as offering one kind of scheme of allegor-
ical exegesis, as contrasted with another kind of allegoresis (Neoplatonic
perhaps, and which is not quite the same as the "levels") in which different
aspects of one historical person may, like Elizabeth's, be "expressed"
(unfolded) under several different persons or shapes, in the Letter indi-
cated as different *fictional* women: Gloriana, Belphebe (and, he might be

tacitly adding, regal Britomart who, unlike Belphebe, does not embody personal or "particular" allusions to the Queen, but rather represents her public role and destiny). In the proem to Book III (stanza 3) Spenser seems to be suggesting this different kind of "pleasing Analysis" of virtue, the kind under which he said in the Letter he "otherwise *shadow*[s]" Elizabeth: something in which the aspects or Virtues of the Queen are expressed allegorically under many "colourd showes".[20] Spenser rather elaborately contrasts this Platonic ideality (realized, he says in the preceding stanza, in the living person of the Queen) with the humbler outward copying of even a Zeuxis or Praxiteles.[21] (*Ut pictura poesis*, and vice versa, is a commonplace *topos* of Renaissance literary theory as well as pictorial art, and it is a sophistication in Spenser to allude to it here.) This strain of allegorizing may reflect medieval allegorical *schemata* of the kind Tuve has discussed, or it may also bear a relation to Renaissance Neoplatonic aesthetic theories of ideal representation (aggregation of beauties) in art.

Spenser shows as well critical awareness of the tradition of *exemplum* allegory, and perhaps of its overlap with other kinds of Platonic allegory concerning Forms or Essences. Like the "antique Poets historicall", he has "*ensampled*" in Arthur "the image of a brave knight" perfected in all the virtues; just as the individual Forms are modelled in the individual knights. In the same way, Tasso, Virgil and Homer have, Spenser says, "ensampled" in their heroes patterns of conduct in both the public and private (ethical) departments of life. Tasso had made similar observations in his "Allegoria" and in the *Discorsi del poema eroico*.[22] (Yet where does direct moral example shade into "clowdily enwrapped" allegory? That question always faces the reader of *The Faerie Queene*. Presumably such deepening occurs when the "dissevering" or fractionating of characters, among other allegorical devices, takes place.) Spenser speaks again of "ensamples" of virtue in *The Faerie Queene*, Book III (proem, stanza 1).

In sum, then, Spenser shows himself as a compendium of both all available recent and some older literary theories and forms of allegory. Yet the main narrative structures of his allegorical epic place him firmly in the more modern traditions of epic and epic commentary, as do his aesthetics and hermeneutics. Recognition of Spenser as an advanced theorist of allegory in Renaissance modes is important, and it puts Milton's tacit allegorical dialogue with Spenser into a correct and more contemporaneous perspective.

NINE

Neoclassical Epic Theory:
The Debate over Allegory

Much of late *cinquecento* criticism on the epic had turned on Aristotle and the debates between stricter and more generous interpretations of "unity" in plot, history versus romance, and other issues. One of the main defences of romance episode, multiple plot, or fantasy was that these could most effectively embody allegorical "truth". Tasso had effected a form of compromise between the linear historical epic and a revitalised treatment of romance-interpolated epic by joining both in the new thematic or allegorical unity of the "marvellous-verisimilar". Although it is often supposed that a total shift in taste or some gap supervened between even late sixteenth-century epic poetics and the emergent neoclassical norm, such is not the case. The earlier debates merely continued under new guise, with more polarization, and slightly different lines of defence constructed for the protection of the imaginative, allegorical and fantastic in art. Milton's epic, like Tasso's, marks a novel and important effort to achieve a compromise aesthetic of contemporary relevance. The tradition of criticism on epic now to be examined (largely English, with one important exception) will be discussed not in chronological order but rather in an order designed to display the divergent attitudes to epic art which reached to the period of *Paradise Lost* and helped to direct Milton's choices between alternative models for epic and to shape his own epic poetics.

Seventeenth-Century English Theory

English criticism on the epic in the half century and especially the decade preceding Milton on the whole adopted a narrowly neoclassical interpretation of "Aristotle and the rest" (the Italian commentators). Such strict late seventeenth-century tenets developed subsequently into the fuller statements of the eighteenth-century critics, who partly followed suit. The strictures of Cowley or his near contemporaries, Charles de St. Évremond and Thomas Rymer,[1] on allegory and fables, even it would seem on the use of any imaginative element in religious poetry or epic, their devaluation of Spenser, their advocacy of "plain truth", Christian doctrines and straight historical (preferably biblical) material, as well as their substitution of "Christian miracles" for Tasso's kind of "marvels" or the "marvellous"— all register the change of temper in the later English period.

In the essays on epic of Sir William Davenant (1650), Thomas Hobbes (1650), or Cowley (1656), traces of more general epic prescriptions similar to those expressed in Tasso's *Discorsi del poema eroico* may be detected,[2] but the tenor is far removed from Tasso's emphasis on the truth of the imagination—although Hobbes, so often thought of as a denigrator of the imagination, is less illiberal than some of his contemporaries. The mid-seventeenth century's denigration of Spenser's "extraordinary Dreams" and allegories[3] is extended back to Tasso's "errors"[4] and even to the imputed errors of the ancients, to Homer and Virgil (Hobbes here issuing a solitary caveat).[5] What Cowley and Davenant wish is that there should be no "Episodes" of the kind which Tasso and Spenser allegorically modelled on such incidents in Virgil as Aeneas' descent into the underworld, or in Homer as the transformation of Odysseus' mariners—incidents probably originally, and increasingly in later exegesis, invested with allegorical values. The English critics' objections to the fantastic or marvellous relate as much to their own exaggeratedly Aristotelian insistence on single plot-line (no "Episodes") as to their objection to imaginative fantasy. (Of the three contemporary critics, only Hobbes, again, defends Fancy—in moderation.)[6] The "Christian poet . . . little needs the aid of Invention"[7] or the marvellous, since he has "the true *Miracles* of *Christ,* or of his *Prophets* and *Apostles*" at his service.[8] The Christian poet can indeed even dispense with the traditional epic Invocation, since the latter is an unchristian—certainly an unprotestant—device. (Davenant used no invocations in *Gondibert*.)[9]

Such narrowly Christian attitudes to art[10] are matched by narrowly neoclassical literary norms, reflected in the assumption that the best epic most closely approximates to the pattern of a tragedy. Tasso had certainly incorporated the subjects of heroic or alternatively tragic love into the *Gerusalemme;* but Davenant goes further and in his heroical-tragical epic of love and ambition introduces a "five-Act" structure.[11] Equally narrow is the English emphasis on true *scriptural* histories concerning historical individuals as proper argument for epic.[12] It is also made quite clear that any concept of "poetic truth" relates only to fictive invention of a *probable* or *possible* kind, and not at all to Tasso's wider idea of the allegorical "verisimilar", or his further ulterior truth of the "marvellous-verisimilar". For Hobbes, "as truth is the bound of Historical, so the Resemblance of truth is the utmost limit of Poeticall Liberty".[13] Thus when Davenant speaks of "mend[ing] the intrigues of Fortune by . . . probable fictions"[14] (an echo of Tasso), he does not in fact mean what Tasso had meant in saying that "episodes" could be connected to the main plot by other means than "necessity" or Aristotelian causality. What all these early neoclassical critics of the 1650s have in mind, as Hobbes succinctly puts it, is that an epic should be a fictive-exemplary demonstration: not unsweetened didacticism, but *"the manners of men . . . , manners presented, not dictated"*.[15] Or as Davenant says, "truth operative, and . . . alive" rather than "Truth narrative and past" (a concession to the standard notion that poetry is not unvarnished history).[16] It is likely too that when Cowley speaks of Poesie's "bright and delightful *Idœa's*" and "the *Idea* that I conceive [of the Christian epic poem]", he is thinking simply of invention in the first instance ("many noble and fertile Arguments")[17] and of decorum of genre in the second. He does not mean what Tasso and others meant by "Idea", namely, an underlying intellectual conception in the epic, its *hidden* text.

The neoclassical model of the plausible fiction, an exemplary or literal demonstration of moral and Christian truths, convincingly amplified with fictive detail and set in a framework of Christian-historical fact and constructed on a unilateral plot-line closely approximating to tragedy, is certainly that which has been held to be closest to *Paradise Lost*.[18] But such an assumption does not satisfactorily account for the allegorical mode in overt instances and episodes and also in the subtexture of Milton's poem. Nor is it what Milton intended by the "Idea" which he claimed as standing behind his own poem and echoing God's:[19] his didactic plan for justification of God's Providence. Milton's poem frequently "asserts" (to use his own word) Christian truth or morals—as, apparently, it should not, according to Hobbes ("manners *presented, not dictated*").[20] On the other hand, not only does *Paradise Lost* have an invocation (indeed, four), but in many other respects it bypasses the early English neoclassical theories and reverts to earlier models and even to the "errors" of the Ancients. *Paradise Lost* includes many incidents which much more than in Homer and Virgil do (Hobbes' terms) "exceed . . . the *possibility* of nature" or show an "exorbitancy of the fiction".[21] The neoclassical model also does not account for the pervasive and almost self-advertising presence in *Paradise Lost* of both Spenser and Tasso with all their lamentable "errors", a presence felt not only in simile or verbal reminiscence but in poetic incident and narrative, or in rhetorical devices of more exotic kinds, including the allegorical. Neoclassical efforts to refine the epic may have influenced Milton's final choice, treatment and dressing of his subject in certain aspects or parts. But the kind of Christian-historical, literal epic which Cowley and Davenant strove with such conspicuous unsuccess to write is not Milton's model. Had it been so, Milton's epic might have been as dull as the impeccably correct efforts of Cowley's *Davideis* or Giangiorgio Trissino's *Italia liberata dai Goti*.

Addison and Johnson

It is small wonder that later generations of English neoclassical critics, notably Joseph Addison and Samuel Johnson, were disappointed in the failure of *Paradise Lost*—a poem which had never been designed to do so— to live up to the tight neoclassical norms proposed by two earlier genera- tions of English critics. Eighteenth-century criticisms of *Paradise Lost* in some respects closely parallel the strictures on "incorrect" epic by English writers of the 1650s to 1670s; although perhaps the eighteenth-century writers are less religiously doctrinaire (save for Johnson), and their concern with questions of style is more pragmatic and allows a little more to the freedom of the imagination. The later critics draw their arguments from many quarters, old as well as new, not all of which can be canvassed here. But we may see that, as in the middle seventeenth century, eighteenth- century arguments continue to fix on the question of "Episode" (which is to say, unity of plot) and on the issue of verisimilitude, which is fairly strictly construed as narrative probability or possibility. On both the foregoing counts, unity of plot and literal verisimilitude, digressive episodes of the traditional epic kind employing the supernatural or fantastic seem to be ruled out. The later neoclassicists concern themselves with the issue of poetic conviction understood principally as it relates to the manners of men. (In Johnson "conviction" is also conflated with the degree of Chris- tian truth in poetry.) An entangled issue is that of the epic "marvellous" (perhaps only in Johnson is this tied down absolutely to Christian mira- cles). The eighteenth-century critics tend to see the "marvellous" more as an aesthetic quality, and the new word is "sublimity".

There is one important exception to the foregoing generalizations. In late neoclassical criticism there does resurface the important notion (lack- ing in Davenant, Hobbes, or Rymer and unclear in Cowley, but specific in René Le Bossu, who is later discussed, and Addison) that epic is distin- guished by having an intellectual concept lying behind it, an Idea which can be expressed either as exemplary Moral (which does not mean merely idealized characters), or more specifically as allegory. Indeed one may wonder if such a conception had ever wholly disappeared. John Hughes, for instance, takes as an accepted principle that an epic poem may have a "cover'd moral", a "tacit Parallel" or an underlying Idea intentionally oblique; but he distinguishes this kind of allegory from a second sort which attaches specifically to "fictitious Persons or Beings" (personifications) and lies "without the Bounds of Probability or Nature". Hughes actually admits the effectiveness of the wild imaginativeness of the second sort of allegory (a "License peculiar to itself") in Spenser and in Milton both, and he is glad to see the recent revival of the allegorical mode in Addison.[22] Brief rhetori- cal "allegories" of the second sort are never rejected as such in epic by the eighteenth century—except perhaps by Johnson writing on Milton. Occasionally the eighteenth century finds itself in a particular quandary over Milton's "allegories", since these blur the boundaries between realistic plot and rhetorical figures of speech: yet Milton's "allegories" do possess par excellence the quality of sublimity (in fact, of the "marvellous") so highly esteemed by the period.[23] Again, eighteenth-century critics do not so much as those of the seventeenth century concern themselves over the question of Christian history as the best material for epic—indeed Johnson finds that such a subject poses difficulties—as with the general problem of preserving a prevailing realism in epic narrative.[24] Throughout their arguments, the ghosts of Tasso's or other sixteenth-century *dicta* on epic can still be glimpsed.

Addison, the most lastingly and in some ways perversely influential critic of Milton, does allow *Paradise Lost* as an Epic to possess an allegory or hidden meaning. He does not explain this meaning, but it is striking to see that he seems to take it for granted: "besides *the hidden Meaning of an Epic Allegory, the plain literal Sense* ought to appear *probable*".[25] Thus while the surface texture of the action should be entirely realistic across the entire narrative, it would seem to be accessory to a further, hidden signification. Milton's "interwoven" allegories of Sin and Death and the "*Lymbo of Vanity*"[26] and other passages in Books II and X are of another order and raise different problems for Addison. While "astonishing" or "wonderful", they are faulty, not because they are allegorical but because they become entangled with the action, although they are not "credible" or "Probable" themselves.[27] In themselves fine or even inspired, such allegories do not belong in an epic—not even though they conform with the need for the Marvellous: "Such Allegories rather savour of the Spirit of *Spencer* and *Ariosto*, than of *Homer* and *Virgil*".[28] Allegories—that is, personifications— should really as in Homer or Virgil be confined to rhetorical tropes ("short Expressions"), and they should not assume active parts in the action.[29] (This is of course an untrue picture of the classical epics.) In this curiously ambivalent response to Milton's allegorical episodes, or in such a statement as that the epic poet ought to "relate such Circumstances, as may produce in the Reader *at the same time* both Belief and Astonishment" (be both "Probable" and "wonderful"),[30] one perhaps hears echoes of earlier Italian sixteenth-century arguments concerning historicity versus romance. But Addison's approach to epic art is fundamentally historical and rhetorical. Tasso's view that the verisimilar and the marvellous in narrative *can* be conjoined (by means of allegorical truth) is not what Addison intends by the conjunction of Belief and Astonishment in an Epic action.

Dr. Johnson (whose comments on Milton will be considered again in a later chapter)[31] in some ways follows an almost harder line than that of the mid-seventeenth century, despite his admiration for Milton's sublimity and power of "invention". Milton's Christian subject, according to Johnson, is wrongly taken; theology is too sacred for the "licentiousness of fiction". Milton was wrong too in employing allegorical figures like Sin and Death, who break the action by entering into it; these figures therefore do not constitute true epic "episodes". For Johnson "Episodes" are merely episodes, to be restricted to actions narrated retrospectively (in this, as we shall see, he is following Le Bossu in the letter but departing from him in spirit). However, at other times the "probable" and the "marvellous" do coincide in *Paradise Lost*, namely, in the substance of ordinary scriptural history and Christian miracles. (Tasso, by contrast, had allowed for Christian miracles without abandoning his active preference for other kinds of supernatural or fantastic *meraviglie* conveying allegorical truths.)

Where a true line of descent from Tasso's arguments may be traced in Johnson's account is in the latter's rather perplexed allusion in the "Life" of Milton to Le Bossu's prescription about a necessary "Moral" standing behind the epic poem. Milton alone among epic poets, evidently, had followed along the lines advocated by Le Bossu in framing a "Moral" *antecedently* to the poem, and modelling the subsequent action accordingly. (Since Johnson does not remark on the fact that the publication of *Paradise Lost* shortly preceded Le Bossu's treatise on the epic poem of 1675, the assumption may be that Le Bossu's or similar ideas were familiar before publication of his work.) Milton's epic moral is "essential and intrinsick" (integral), rather than "incidental and consequent". But Johnson chooses to interpret this Miltonic "moral" simply as the narrative's didactic, surface *exemplum*. The purpose of the plot of *Paradise Lost* is to show "the necessity of obedience to the Divine Law" through displaying the consequences of disobedience. This is what Johnson means in saying that Milton's epic displays "the reasonableness of religion". In this way the "probable" surface of Milton's fiction is made to coincide with its antecedent Moral (in such a view not really hidden at all), and both coincide with Johnson's fundamentalist beliefs. Nonetheless, it may well be in Johnson's reference to Le Bossu, the most famous neoclassical theorist on the epic, that we find the key to the neoclassical dilemma, continuing into the present day, over Milton's mixed mode: how it was that Milton's epic could be at one and the same time so "refined" and yet so seemingly anachronistic. Le Bossu's important treatise will be examined in greater detail after consideration first of two critics more intimately associated with Milton, and a retrospective glance at the late sixteenth-century critical tradition from which I believe Le Bossu to have emerged.

Edward Phillips and John Toland

Le Bossu with Edward Phillips, their works both published in 1675, attest to the living continuance of a Tassonic type of critical tradition concerning allegorical epic near to the date of composition of *Paradise Lost*. (Such a continuance is witnessed, for example, in that the famous French editor and translator, Jean Baudouin, translated Tasso's *Discorsi del poema eroico* into French as late as 1638.) Milton's use of the Italian critics and of Tasso, whom he of course also knew at first hand, therefore is far from anachronistic. His preference for this tradition over the more fashionable contemporary tradition represented by Corneille, Boileau and Racine represents a deliberate choosing, from among the various neoclassical avenues of criticism developing from the late sixteenth century, of that vein of poetic theory which could afford him the greatest range of artistic expressiveness, as well as the firmest practical guidance in the structuring of a complex epic poem—all these, combined with a firm view of the epic as purveyor of serious truth in covert as well as overt modes.

Phillips' remarks on epic in his *Theatrum Poetarum* are extremely important in that, published so soon after his uncle's major poem and death, they must inevitably bear on *Paradise Lost* and probably embody something of Milton's own conception of his epic. Phillips' views offer a corrective to the literalist views on epic expressed by English critics of a generation earlier and a bridge to the later eighteenth-century views. Phillips in general admired Italian models in poetry as well as Spenser, and his writings echo both Milton's own theoretical statements in his prose and probably also Tasso directly.[32] We may quote Phillips' remarks on epic allegory:

it is not a mere historical relation spiced over with a little slight fiction, [nor] now and then a personated virtue or vice rising out of the ground and uttering a speech, which makes a heroic poem, but it must be rather a brief, obscure, or remote tradition, but of some remarkable piece of story, in which the poet hath an ample field to enlarge by feigning of probable circumstances. In which and in proper allegory, invention (the well management whereof is indeed no other than decorum) principally consisteth, and wherein there is a kind of truth even in the midst of fiction. For whatever is pertinently said by way of allegory is morally though not historically true, and circumstances the more they have of verisimility the more they keep up the reputation of the poet, whose business it is to deliver feigned things as like to truth as may be.[33]

This capsule description of epic, syntactically overcompressed, reads like a redaction of some authority, either Tasso in the *Discorsi del poema eroico*, or Tasso filtered through some later authority. Le Bossu's formulations seem just too late for Phillips; yet, as will be seen, the two critics are writing within a similar framework. In Phillips we see received epic-allegorical theory of the late sixteenth century in its moderate extension into the later seventeenth. Phillips' use of Tasso or other earlier critics is modulated by a neoclassical emphasis on decorum and the need not to strain the reader's belief too far. But the core of what Tasso wrote seems to be present: the distinction between "proper allegory" (Tasso's "soul" of the epic poem) and "probable circumstances" (Tasso's "Imitation" or outward dress of the poem); the insistence that epic through allegory may carry "a kind of truth even in the midst of fiction", that a fiction may be "morally though not historically true" (we may compare Tasso's special use of the principle of the "verisimilar"); and as well, the more general prescription about historical epic being something quite distinct from "a mere historical relation spiced over with a little slight fiction".

That the epic "must be rather a brief, obscure, or remote tradition, but of some remarkable piece of story, in which the poet hath an ample field to enlarge by feigning" is a straight echo of *Discorsi del poema eroico*, Book II. Phillips, like Tasso, says that the verisimilar expansion of the "brief" history should itself be credible: "not too much exceeding . . . what is possible or likely"; the poet requires "*probable* circumstances" not "positively contradictory to the truth of history".[34] But there is no indication in Phillips' account that he feels any tension between probable circumstance and allegorical episode, of the kind that might strain credulity and such as Johnson later objected to. Phillips takes the presence of allegory in the epic for granted, and seems not to feel any need to be defensive. The one element stressed by Tasso which is not directly named in Phillips' formulation is the allegorical epic's quality of the "marvellous" or "marvellous-verisimilar". This omission, if it is one, remains something of a puzzle, since allegorical episode is certainly prominent enough in *Paradise Lost*, and "marvels" (under other names) are valued by other critics contemporary with Phillips. But Phillips may just be taking the presence of marvels for granted, since he speaks presently of deities as natural in epic.

As regards the "proper allegory" which is to accompany the poet's verisimilar expansion of a brief history, I believe that by "proper" Phillips may in part imply "true to genre": distinctive. (He had already invoked a concept of "decorum" in connection with "invention" and "allegory".) The word "proper" as used of allegory could of course only mean "appropriate",[35] or signify a mere tactful restraint, a rhetorical decorum. But if Phillips did intend that allegory should be understood only in such bland senses, then we are hard put to it to understand what his evaluation may have been of the many bizarre episodes in his uncle's probably circumstanced "remarkable piece of story", however amply enlarged with "verisimility" of detail. "Marvels" would not be excluded under such an interpretation of allegory—within limits. Although he does not define the character or structure of Milton's own allegory, Phillips might have been likely to interpret it in the conventional period terms of an ongoing concealed signification underlying the narrative or running in parallel with it. (John Toland, a near contemporary of Phillips, certainly was in no doubt as to the narrative character of Milton's "peculiar allegory or Moral".) For Phillips, heroic allegory such as Milton's is ethical (it has moral truth), but it is not something so simplistic as Johnson's exemplary "Moral" or narrative *demonstration* of "obedience" and "disobedience". Allegory is a "truth even in the midst of fiction"—there is an innuendo of something shadowed, of the "veil of fiction". Allegory is also to be distinguished from Addison's rhetorical tropes or allegories. It is quite clear that Phillips' entire description of allegory (as, probably, he understood it in *Paradise Lost*) implies something more fundamental than mere rhetorical trope.

John Toland's "Life of Milton",[36] appearing as the preface to the 1698 collected edition of Milton's prose, presents an even stronger view of the allegorical *epos* than does Phillips. Toland offers three important specific additions to Phillips' description. Toland links the inspiration for *Paradise Lost* directly to Tasso (via Milton's talks with Manso, Tasso's patron); he stresses that epic in general and Milton's in particular possess "som peculiar Allegory or Moral", comparing Milton's poem in this respect with Tasso's *Gerusalemme* and specifically citing Tasso's "Allegoria" or his prefixed "Explication"; and he interprets the specific content of Milton's allegory. According to Toland the allegory has to do with the "different Effects of Liberty and Tyranny"; he links this theme with Milton's well-known statement of purpose at the end of *Of Reformation Touching Church-Discipline*.[37] The Allegory or Moral involved is also more particular than some "general representation of Passions and Affections, Virtues and Vices"—although an epic may include these as well. How the allegory is to be manifested artistically, Toland does not say: perhaps that is not the biographer's province. In any case, Le Bossu's treatise had some twenty years earlier already spelled out the means, and his prescriptions were well known. Toland's identification of *Paradise Lost* with Tasso's writings and principles concerning the allegorical epic, with the Manso-Milton critical discussions, and most notably, with Tasso's prose allegory for the *Gerusalemme*, constitutes a formidable claim for the direct poetical and critical descent of Milton's theories from Tasso. Toland's remarks from the "Life" must now be quoted more fully.

The first reference comes half way through the Life: "I don't question but it was from *Manso's* Conversation and their Discourses about *Tasso*, that he first form'd his design of writing an Epic Poem, tho he was not so soon determin'd about the Subject". Toland resumes this thread near the close of his account:

An Epic Poem is not a bare History delightfully related in harmonious Numbers, and artfully dispos'd; but it always contains, besides a general representation of Passions and Affections, Virtues and Vices, som peculiar Allegory or Moral. *Homer* therfore, according to *Dionysius Halicarnassæus*, expresses strength of Body in his *Iliad* by the Wars of the *Greecs* and *Trojans*, but particularly by the valiant Deeds of *Achilles*: and in his *Odysseus* he describes generosity of Mind by the Adventures and Wandrings of *Ulysses* in his return from *Troy*. Thus *Torquato Tasso* has prefixt an Explication to his *Gierusalemme Liberata*: Nor was *Milton* behind any body in the choice or dignity of his Instruction; for to display the different Effects of

Liberty and Tyranny, is the chief design of his *Paradise Lost*. This in the conclusion of his second Book of *Reformation*, publish'd in [16]41, he tells us was his Intention at that time; and he afterwards made this promise good.

Milton does in fact at the close of *Of Reformation* ambiguously link his future epic poem with a celebration of the "end to all earthly *Tyrannies*". However, Toland's words, "the *different* Effects of Liberty and Tyranny", potentially widen Milton's purpose from a specifically political allegory of Liberty to include related ethical or other themes (for example that of domestic liberty; of free will); while Toland's reference to "som *peculiar* Allegory" beyond the "general representation of Passions and Affections, Virtues and Vices", raises Milton's final allegory above the level of a mere didactic exemplum.

The Late Sixteenth-Century Italian Debates

Tasso's contemporaries, Jacopo Mazzoni and Lodovico Castelvetro, have been reserved for brief retrospective mention until now. In that earlier debate between historicity and romance fantasy or allegory in epic we can see a direct foreshadowing of the similar divergences a century later between, on the one part, Cowley, Davenant or Hobbes and, on the other, the more liberal Toland, Phillips and Le Bossu—as, in lesser degree, between Johnson and Addison, or John Hughes and Richard Hurd, still later. But to look back to the late sixteenth-century Italians after reading their English seventeenth- and eighteenth-century critical counterparts is to realize at once how much more sophisticated were those continental debates on Aristotle and the epic. The Italian criticism, as later perpetuated in such enlightened views as those of Phillips or Toland, or, in the French tradition, of Le Bossu (rather than Boileau), gives evidence of a lively background of vigorous and liberal critical theory concerning the semi-allegorical epic, a still present tradition from which Milton could draw, while also feeling free to adapt and innovate.

Tasso stand in the middle of a triangular debate, mediating between the historicism of Castelvetro (who was in fact less strict about history in the epic than were Cowley, Davenant or Johnson) and the permissive warmth of imaginative fantasy approved by Mazzoni in his defence of Dante.[38] It may be significant that in *Of Education*[39] Milton names these three not in chronological order of their major writings on epic but in exactly that triangular juxtaposition—Castelvetro, Tasso, Mazzoni, with Tasso in the middle. To the present writer, it appears that the three great Italian critics and even the historically-minded Castelvetro do not so much adopt incompatible stances as fall into positions veering to right, left or centre of a shared common awareness of epic poetry as *imaginative fiction*, and as also having a serious intellectual intent. None of these writers attempts to tailor epic (or tragedy) to any Procrustean shape; although their vocabulary is overacademic, and despite their endless hairsplitting over Aristotelian subcategories, they do not dogmatize over the exact content of epic. Their aim is to formulate an appropriate poetic and aesthetic. Their basic concerns are seen to be with the fundamental question of the meaning of poetic "conviction" and the aesthetic problems of structuring a complex and imaginatively various epic action. A brief look at each of Tasso's academic colleagues may help us to understand how Tasso's median position on the epic effected a compromise between incipient neoclassical realism or historicism on the one hand, and free fantasy (which could be put into the service of allegory) on the other—a compromise which carried forward into the next century and could still be of use to Milton. It is precisely because all these Italian critics, although fully cognizant of the serious function of poetry, were *au fond* not religious dogmatists that Milton (also not a dogmatist), even though working from a different religious background, could still measure and devise his poem against their tradition.

While Tasso, rebutting Castelvetro, stressed that the materials of history and poetry are definitely not the same and that a poem represents a "rivalry by the poet . . . with the arrangements of fortune",[40] Castelvetro, writing from an indubitably realistic vantage point, had in fact said no more than that "the matter of poetry should be like the matter of history and resemble it, but it ought not to be the same".[41] That is to say, Castelvetro's stress is on verisimilitude as we ourselves would understand that term in fiction. By contrast, Tasso is constantly trying not only to argue for historical-fictive verisimilitude, but also to "join" verisimilitude with the "marvellous" or with allegorical truth in "various ways". Although Castelvetro's sections on the "Impossible and the Incredible" and on the "Improbable" in epic (part of a discussion of "Faults")[42] can seem tiresomely mechanical and hair-splitting, he is nevertheless able to admit, looking at Homer, that the impossible and the incredible are "made tolerable" and are to be excused in Homer:[43] better an improbable good poem than a probable bad one.

Similarly, "Episodes" (or "Digressions"), although said to be "injurious" or "otiose" if they do not forward the plot,[44] nonetheless, if they are "appropriate", may enlighten obscure bearings in the plot.[45] (Here Castelvetro is thinking of retrospective or prospective narrations, especially in tragedy; this restricted view enlightens Johnson's later limitation of the term "Episode" in epic to narrative flashbacks.)[46] But for Castelvetro, Episodes may include gods, demons, visions, miracles and supernatural interventions[47]—a large enough licence to the imaginative powers. Elsewhere Castelvetro censures but half admires the "audacious" episodes of Virgil, as in having Aeneas descend to the underworld—more daring than anything in Homer.[48] Allegory is not mentioned, but it cannot be assumed to be excluded under the foregoing stipulations, nor under Castelvetro's discussions of the marvellous.[49] Despite the neoclassical tending toward single plot-line ("links in a chain"),[50] something is yet to be allowed to narrative digressions: *one* such digression, says Castelvetro, may be admissible. Such a digression may be admitted if the questionable part can be withdrawn without damage to the whole fabric of the plot (improbable episodes are made "tolerable" if not "integral" to the main line of action).[51] Or they may be excused in great poets if they are "cloak[ed]" by "the mantle of other excellences".[52]

Castelvetro's neoclassical refinement of epic structure retains a considerable degree of imaginative permissiveness. It also bears a certain relationship to the neoclassical side of Milton. Milton's material does in the main lines "resemble" that of history; and his most ostentatiously supernatural Episodes (Sin and Death, or Chaos, for example), although more than "one" and extended, could in a certain sense (or all but that of Sin at the Gates of Hell) be withdrawn without actually destroying the linear continuity of the main action. Castelvetro had suggested that "Episodes" or "Digressions", though to be severely restricted in number, might enlighten obscure bearings in the plot. Milton in fact deploys such Episodes with even more deliberate intent than Castelvetro envisages. To understand that darker aspect of Milton's artistry, his allegorical subtext, we would have to look at Tasso's serious arguments for the "marvellous-verisimilar" as a means to truth through allegory, or to analogies in Mazzoni's defence of the "phantastic" over the "icastic" type of poetry, or to Le Bossu's defence of multiple Episodes as "chains of metaphors".[53]

Redefining "credibility" in the same way that Tasso did the "verisimilar" (that is, as inner truth, and on the grounds that all poetry shares in the representation of that which is either not literally true or else is false or impossible), Mazzoni arrives at the theory of the "credible marvelous":[54] poetry is a mixture of truth and meaningful falsehood.[55] This premise then becomes his definition of both poetry and epic plot.[56] All of us know that truth can be stranger than fiction:[57] "Dante's voyage . . . being both impossible and marvelous, is nevertheless made credible through allegorical treatment".[58] Dante's is a "poesia phantastica";[59] the best poetry is perhaps always "phantastic" rather than "icastic imitation",[60] working by "sensible images" or "perceptible means in representing the thing of which [the poet] speaks"[61]—that is, through the power of the imagination as an image-making faculty. We may hear in Milton's well-known definition of poetry in *Of Education* a certain echo of this view: the first two terms of Milton's formula, "simple, sensuous and passionate", equate with Mazzoni's "sensible image".[62] Such a view of the imagination is also germane to Tasso's conception of the "mystical image".

It may be seen, then, that Tasso incorporates something of the best from the arguments of both his contemporaries. The modern epic must have a stronger main plot-line than, say Ariosto's; the main action must have a prevailing verisimilitude; but such a surface is designed to give only the *appearance* of history. And an audacity of imaginative invention even beyond this level of surface realism may be consciously fostered, so as to convey truth through allegory. But where Castelvetro went only so far as to say that "digressions" were allowable if they provided background for the main plot, Tasso, like Mazzoni and like Milton later, overrides that boundary, mixing "fiction" with "truth" in more radical ways. Over this point critics of Milton from the eighteenth century to the present have continued to quibble—just as the influential Mazzoni-Tasso line of argument, of so great importance to the imaginative poet, represented in its own time an embattled critical position.

TEN

Le Bossu on the Epic

In this chapter we shall consider in rather more detail that vein of late seventeenth-century criticism on the epic which most clearly seems to perpetuate the valuable and imaginative compromise in epic art effected by Tasso. The more liberal side of the continental neoclassical critical tradition is summed up *par excellence* in the influential treatise of Le Bossu, *Traité du Poëme Épique* (1675), which unequivocally supports a view of the epic as allegory notable at that date.[1] Famous enough in the eighteenth century to be parodied by Pope, taken by Johnson as a yardstick by which to measure *Paradise Lost*, and in some of its definitions of epic very close to those of Milton's two biographers, Toland and Phillips, the views and values represented in Le Bossu's pragmatic and sensible adaptation of the Aristotelian position on epic can hardly have been totally unknown in the European critical context during the genesis and period of composition of *Paradise Lost*. There may well have been corresponding critical discussions or writings in the Italian academic circles known to Milton two or three decades earlier; and although the modern editor of Le Bossu seems to suggest that this important work appeared, written by an anonymous monk, as if out of nowhere, such is never the case with critical ideas. The continuous chain of ideas from Tasso's *Discorsi del poema eroico* (1594), to Baudouin's French translation of the Tasso work (1638), to Le Bossu's treatise (1675), is itself sufficient to establish a plausible continuity, one which places Milton in a meaningful contemporaneous critical tradition to do with allegorical poetics and the epic.

Le Bossu seems to have bypassed the vexatious philosophical disputes of earlier Italian discourses on the epic. Entirely avoiding contentious or doctrinaire issues in a way that Tasso could not, Le Bossu managed (as Tasso somehow also contrived to do) to adapt and mediate between rising neoclassical tastes for historicity and artistic restraint on the one hand, and on the other hand the better instincts toward imaginative richness and poetic flexibility and versatility in epic structuring, with the freedom of the poet to convey what he centrally wishes to say by the means he finds most suitable, the ancients once more being cited as precedent for artistic licence. In pragmatic, lucid and precise terms, Le Bossu deals with, among other issues, that of fictiveness and truth and the different shapes which these may take in epic; the artistic problems involved in structuring a long and complex narrative embracing different species of narrations, and the related question of sustaining thematic unity over a long narrative space (that is, maintaining a coherence of intellectual purpose as well as unity of "action"); and the question of achieving a striking style or epic impact. We must pass over the last, and also over the finer points in his brilliant analysis of the relation between fictiveness and truth,[2] remarking only how, in lucid expositions which can be readily understood in their practical bearings, the points often being supported by analogies from Aristotle's own examples (rather than always by Aristotle's theoretical positions), Le Bossu explores the various kinds of difficulties posed to the epic writer by the concept of poetic "probability". He interprets "probability" generously, sometimes as a truth in the midst of improbable fiction, at other times as fiction with an "air" of reality, showing how the differing sorts of fiction may be kept in play without interfering with each other or with the reader's sense of integrity in the narration. His liberal position in these matters is closer to Tasso's than to Castelvetro's; Toland and Phillips may well owe something to Le Bossu as well as to Tasso. Le Bossu is also materially assisted by the fact that he sees epic and tragic structures and proprieties as much more clearly differentiated from each other than did many neoclassical critics.[3]

A brief synopsis of some important points in the *Traité* now follows. It is worth noting beforehand that in the first few pages of his very modern-sounding analysis, Le Bossu nonetheless frames his discourse by analogy to traditional allegory as found in the ancients, in Old Testament typology and in Aesop. He notes that epic poets are not wont to give express "notice" of their concealed allegory, but rather tend to begin their story with an allusion to their "Action". All the same, Le Bossu assumes the existence in every epic of a "conceal'd . . . piece of *Morality*", one which is left in "Allegorical and Figurative Obscurity". He defines an epic action with its hidden content thus: "it is *Universal*, it is *Imitated*, it is *Feign'd*, and it contains *Allegorically, a Moral Truth*", a truth veiled and concealed under an "Action . . . really feign'd and invented by the Author, [which] . . . yet will seem to be taken out of some very ancient *History* and *Fable*".[4] Le Bossu begins his discourse with these axioms, whereas Tasso only worked up to such ideas after many efforts. But the correspondences with Tasso's views are evident.

Allegory as the "Platform" of Truth

It will be useful to define certain of Le Bossu's principal terms, since they are employed in different senses from the usages of the Italian writers of the sixteenth century. Le Bossu's usages are also not identical with parallel terminology as understood by the eighteenth-century critics. By "Fable" (in the singular) Le Bossu usually means the fictive plot itself, conceived in a particular and special sense. Epic "Fable" not only is not simple "fiction", it is not even exemplary history. Rather, "Fable" is closely tied to an underlying "Ground-work", *"Platform"* or hidden theme which is expressed through but is not synonymous with the "action",[5] and which is closely associated with a didactic intention (often concealed) termed the "Allegory", or sometimes the "Moral". Epic "fable" in this sense (exactly the sense that we ascribe to Aesop's fables or stories)[6] thus is "a Discourse invented to form Men's Morals by Instructions disguis'd under the Allegories of an Action".[7] We are to note particularly that " 'the *Epick Poem* is a *Fable*; that is, not the *Rehearsal* of the *Action* of some one *Hero*, in order to form Mens Manners by his Example; but [rather] . . . a *feign'd Action* . . . made choice of, after the *Platform* of the Action . . . is laid' ".[8]

An invented epic discourse or Fable, then, is equivalent to a *disguised* allegorical action. Such a Fable is composed of "two Things. . . . The one is *Truth*, which serves as a Foundation to it; and the other is *Fiction*, which Allegorically disguises this *Truth*, and gives it the *Form of a Fable*".[9] The "fiction", then, is not the essence of the "fable", but merely its dress. Elsewhere: "The *Truth* lies conceal'd; and is that piece of *Morality* the Poet would teach us. . . . The *Fiction* is the Action or the Words, whereby these Instructions are veil'd".[10] Or again: "the most essential part of the *Fable*, and that which must indispensibly serve for its Foundation, is the *Truth* signified".[11] This "Truth" being a concealed truth, or truth allegorically disguised, the epic Fable is thus synonymous with the allegorical epic. It can be seen that Johnson in his "Life" of Milton adopted that part of the foregoing proposition concerning an anterior truth in epic, but not that part assuming such a truth hidden under an allegorical disguise.

"Truth" for Le Bossu means prevailingly a moral truth. The action of an Epic Fable, seemingly historical, is actually feigned[12] and is chosen for its appropriateness to the author's anterior or ulterior intention: "The first thing we are to begin with for Composing a *Fable*, is to chuse the Instruction, and the point of Morality, which is to serve as its Foundation, according to the Design and End we propose to our selves".[13] The definition of an "Epic" or narrative "Discourse" in verse proceeds from the foregoing, the definition being repeated with variations several times in a formula generally reminiscent of Tasso's openings in the two sets of *Discorsi:* "The EPOPEA is a Discourse invented by Art, to form the Manners by such Instructions as are disguis'd under the Allegories of some one important Action, which is related in Verse, after a probable, diverting, and surprizing Manner".[14] "Surprizing" here signifies epic wonder, equivalent to Tasso's "marvellous" or to neoclassical "sublimity". The term "Allegories" (plural) in this context refers not to the actual hidden content but to the dissemblingly fictive outward dresses of the underlying truth or "Platform"[15] of the Action. The poet's concealed intellectual purpose or "Idea" falls in with the traditional sense of that term in allegorical poetics: "nothing can be more effectual thereto [to making the 'Precepts' of an Epic Fable memorable], than proposing one single *Idea*, and collecting all things so well together, that so they may be present to our Minds all at once, the *Poets* have reduc'd all to one single Action, under one and the same Design".[16] A unified action parallels a unified allegorical design, purpose or "Idea".

That this Idea in the epic is to be indirectly presented makes it clear that for Le Bossu—as he himself said in an earlier quoted passage—allegory signifies meaning "disguised" under a fiction, and not just an exemplary "Moral" as in the Johnsonian understanding. Such allegory may perhaps be expressed with the help of various characteristic devices, personified figures and so forth, but there are more basic poetical means also which concern the narrations themselves: "an Allegory [or Fable] is nothing else but a Series and Chain of Metaphors linked together".[17] Like so many of Le Bossu's statements, this is extremely enlightening. His constant stress on epic fable as itself allegory in the fuller sense is historically very important, in view of the post-romantic dogma that the seventeenth century saw "the death of allegory"—Milton somehow being anachronistic in his persistent use of the mode. Allegorical literature was not dead in the seventeenth century. It was simply, as it always has been in every epoch, redefined—as a special, more specific form of metaphor, epic plot with Episodes constituting a linked chain of such metaphors.

On the other hand, by "*exemplary* Fables" (specifically contrasted with *Fable*, in the singular), by Le Bossu closely identified with supernatural "machines", Le Bossu intends something more like what Castelvetro and Tasso had meant by "digressions" or "Episodes" (fantastic *meraviglie*), or what Addison too intended by "Allegories" (in the plural). Exemplary Fables are not excluded from nor are they irrelevant to the principal "Design"; but they have to be kept distinct and at distance from the main narrative plot-line. (This is exactly what Milton does in *Paradise Lost*.) Unlike "true Episodes" or subordinate links in the main causal chain of events—Le Bossu uses "Episode" in the same sense as Dr Johnson[18]— these other "Fables" are an "intermixed" kind or "species" and not subdivisions of the main plot ("sub-fables"); they "should be so disengaged from the Action of the Poem, that one may subtract them from it, without destroying the Action".[19] This is a crucial distinction, and one that can be seen to explain the difference between Milton's usually contingent uses of "allegories" as a kind of independent second plot-line (Sin and Death; the angelic machinery, frequently) and Tasso's or Spenser's more direct uses of large allegorical episodes within their main plot-lines.

Le Bossu's net for imaginative admissibility of Exemplary Fables is cast wide. He points to the Ancients' free uses of "Mysteries and Allegories. . . . Truth . . . mask'd under . . . ingenious Inventions. . . . *Fables,* or *Sayings*", these often being treated under "the Umbrages [shadows] of . . . Allegorical Expressions" and concerning not only *"Divinity"* but *"Physiology"*.[20] In the usage of modern epic poets, he continues, these concerns have developed a superadded emphasis on "Morality", and they are often presented under the guise of supernatural *"Machines"*: gods, oracles, dreams, "extraordinary *Inspirations"*, miraculous interventions, or metamorphoses.[21] Nonetheless, such interpolations are perhaps to be used less often and with more narrative discretion in the present age and taste, which is more "regular" than that of "other times".[22] It is undoubtedly this kind of tact which made Le Bossu's quite traditional ideas on epic so palatable to the "modern age." In appreciating the potential of all of the above types of fantastic fictions as useful moral-allegorical devices, Le Bossu shows a deep understanding of the allegorical process. His remark that, "among the Gods, there are some *Good,* some *Bad,* and some between both; and . . . of our very Passions we may make so many *Allegorical Deities"*,[23] throws much light on Milton's treatment of certain figures such as Sin and Death, and indeed affords a singularly modern and psychological approach to the reading of the ancient epics. Le Bossu, it should be noted, by "Allegorical Deities" does not here implicate the Christian God.

Various categories of fabulous "machines" can exist in epic, each drawing upon its own kind of credence from the reader. Certain of these kinds of Fables may rest only upon "Divine Probability":[24] pagan gods or the Christian God and miracles once persuaded or now persuade men because of the reader-audience's own beliefs. Such incidents, in the way already indicated, should stand "disengaged" from the "Action". Such in fact is the case with much of the angelic or supernatural "machinery" in *Paradise Lost* in the very limited sphere of influence given it over human events—the temptation by Satan being treated in a quite different, realistic mode, and not as supernatural. (In *Paradise Lost* God's actions, although treated sometimes, in the way Le Bossu describes, as manifestations of divine power, are self-limiting and similarly stand apart from the main human and moral action of the Temptation and Fall.)

Failing this first kind of credibility, supernatural incidents should be "grounded upon human Probability",[25] that is, given a show of external plausibility (many of Satan's activities, such as his mining activities in Heaven or Hell, are a case in point). But a third recourse is that such elements be made to contain pleasurably recognisable allegorical truths: "in these Fables [the poet has] given . . . all the Pleasure that can be reap'd from *Moral Truths*, so pleasantly disguised under these Miraculous *Allego-ries*. Tis by this Means that he has reduced these *Machines* to Truth and a Poetical Probability".[26] Fables (in the plural), Allegories (also in the plural), or "Machines" are, then, the terms applied to particular artistic manifesta-tions of the underlying allegorical "Idea". In Le Bossu's scheme "Poetical Probability" becomes something not unlike Tasso's special "verisimili-tude" or his joining of the "marvellous" with the "verisimilar". In this crucial concept Le Bossu, like Tasso, meets the neoclassical insistence on "probability" with an unanswerable insight into the irreducible difference between "historical" and "poetical" truths—or indeed, between history and serious poetry. His "Poetical Probability" becomes the "poetical truth" of eighteenth- and nineteenth-century critical theory.

Unity of Plot via Allegory

Le Bossu's differentiation between the two kinds of epic material, "true" or "proper" "episodes" or the interconnecting segments of the main plot, and "Fables", "Fictions", "Allegories" or "Machines" standing "disengaged" from the main action—both kinds of material however falling under the governing "Design" or "Ground-work", that is, under the epic's general "Moral" or "Allegory", also sometimes termed its "Fable"— is largely analogous to Tasso's double narrative-allegorical scheme ex-pounded in his "Allegoria". The same distinction is also crucial to a correct understanding of Milton's two-pronged narrative method in *Paradise Lost*. That poem too depends upon a continuous epic action with a plausible surface, punctuated by marvellous or supernatural episodes, such as Sin and Death or others, which are seemingly unrelated (and indeed could be narratively disengaged), but which in reality fall under the governing didactic design of the poem and are closely linked psychologically and thematically with the main actors and actions. Only in one instance, Sin opening the gates of Hell to Satan, does Milton allow any of his "allegorical Fables" to obtrude directly upon the central action—and this particular event holds in itself a complex of allegories at different levels including the theological. Its very unusualness in standing not disengaged from the verisimilar action but engaged with it is an indication of its central impor-tance. Neither this nor the other allegorical "Fables" or *meraviglie* in *Paradise Lost*, standing methodologically in contrast to Milton's "probable" or "veri-similar" "history", Satan's seduction of man, lack for "poetical truth" or correspondence to his characters' "very Passions".

Le Bossu's critique on epic is distinguished, among certain neoclassical efforts in the opposite direction, by his refusal to tailor epic structure to the narrow requirements of a play watched on a stage. His view of epic is much more generous. Similarly, while certain central parts of Milton's action may indeed be watched almost as if on a stage, there is far too much supernatural incident and "fabling" in *Paradise Lost* which does not fall into this narrow class, and in which we must look for significances of more universal, hidden kinds. Le Bossu's comment on Virgil is apposite; it is surprisingly modern in its stress on the theme of *imperium* as central to Virgil's story and allegory, yet absolutely traditional in its understanding of epic allegory as basically "Moral" and universal—a fiction which can be read simply by some, yet also holds something more:

After all, it may be said, that not only ev'ry individual person finds his story [in an epic fiction], and meets with his satisfaction in this Practice: But likewise Men of Learning see more solid Truths therein, than any the Vulgar can meet with; and more certain than those of History which the Poet disregards. The more learned they are, the less will they expect these Historical Truths in a Poem, which is not designed for that, but for things more Mysterious. The Truths, they look for there, are Moral and Allegorical Truths. The *Æneid* was never writ to tell us the Story of *Dido*, but to inform us under this Name of the Spirit and Conduct of that State which she founded, and of the Original and Consequences of its differences with *Rome*.[27]

We shall return to this statement and its peculiar appositeness to *Paradise Lost* in a later chapter.

ELEVEN

Debts to Renaissance Allegory
in *Paradise Lost*

The moment has come to gather together the threads of the preceding
historical discussions of theories of allegory, and to try to determine,
beyond the brief indications already given, how far such Renaissance or
earlier conceptions of allegory in critical exegesis, in poetry, and especially
concerning epic subject and structure, affected and helped to shape
Milton's practice. It does not seem necessary to argue the question of
whether Milton did employ allegory in *Paradise Lost*, or whether his use of
such a mode was a conscious use. Allegory is not only a conscious but a
self-conscious artistic mode in his as in other allegorical epics, deliberately
obtruding itself on the attention. The problem has always been not to
demonstrate the presence of allegory but to account for its conspicuous-
ness in Milton's poem, and to arrive at an adequate understanding of its
relationship to the poem at large. But first it will be as well to remind our-
selves just how large is the quantity of deliberate allegory in *Paradise Lost*.

Allegorical Matter in *Paradise Lost*

By any reckoning, one fifth to one quarter of Milton's approximately ten
and a half thousand lines in his twelve Books are rendered in modes which
are either overtly allegorical (such as Sin and Death in Books II and X,
Chaos' court in Book II, the Limbo of Fools in Book III, Satan's transforma-
tion in Book X); or which contain devices and apparatus recognisable in
older poetic-allegorical methodology (for example, emblems, such as the
Golden Stairs and Golden Scales in Books III and IV, prophetic dreams,
such as Eve's in Book V, or visions, such as Adam's, recounted or experi-
enced, in Books VIII and XII); or which represent passages of pure fantasy,
meraviglie, supernatural actions not coated with "verisimility" but conspic-
uously otherwise (such as the raising of Pandemonium, or Satan's rapid
metamorphoses in Books II, IV and IX). Almost all of these occur within the

first ten Books: that is, they are closely associated with the fallen angelic and imminently fallen human action. Even if one were to take as straight literal representation most of the unfallen angelic "machinery" (in which, however, shadows of covert meaning clearly lurk), and also take as straight representation the bulk of the central verisimilar action of the human Fall (in which, again, elements of psychological allegory may be detected in the way certain aspects of the relationship between the two principal characters are presented); even if one were to discount also the depiction of Hell (which most, however, have agreed is not literal but psychological representation), and were to discount, as well, certain aspects of Eden (which also has its moral geography, the inverse of that of Hell); or even if one were to except from an allegorical count not only the "divine Miracle" of the Creation in Book VII but also the entire War in Heaven, which occupies two whole Books (and which, however, Raphael himself declares is a form of continued dark conceit); we must yet acknowledge a further margin of equivocal forms of mimesis beyond the instances cited above, of "realistic" narrative which at times unexpectedly transgresses "probability", and which vastly increases any count of the quantity of allegorically oriented discourse in the poem.

Such equivocal representation may be seen in larger scale in the episodes depicting the Son's golden Compasses in the scene of the Creation in Book VII, or in certain details of His victory in Book VI; also in the grotesque throwing of hills during the heavenly War in Book VI; again, in Abdiel's symbolic "victory" over Satan, ineffectual in any literal sense; or, in the sequel to the Fall, in the angels' action of pushing the axis of the Earth out of alignment. These and other similar features of Milton's story quite clearly carry secondary meanings and contain elements which involve a quite different plane of fictiveness from what could possibly be deemed literally credible "Christian miracles" (credible to believers)— since neither Milton nor any fellow-Protestant, any more than Raphael, could have believed that all of the events concerned happened in those exact ways. So that including covert as well as overt allegorical incident in various guises throughout *Paradise Lost*, we might well conclude that quantification is not possible: perhaps the bulk, even, of *Paradise Lost* exposes itself to secondary interpretation. And this is without taking into account Milton's "accommodated" descriptions of the Throne of God, or God's physical appearances in the Garden, or His conversations with the Son—all screened from too literal an understanding by constant paradoxical juxtapositions of the seemingly anthropomorphic with grammatical, syntactical or still obscurer forms of allegorical metaphor which ultimately pass beyond the logical. Such a quantity in *Paradise Lost* of direct allegory or semi-allegory or near-allegory in verbal device, or of allegorical figuration in the broadest senses, cannot be dismissed as the outworn vestiges of an archaic mode. Either all of the above scenes and devices belong within some total artistic conception which Milton entertained of his poem as a special kind of poetry and epic, or else *Paradise Lost* is a very bad poem and *epos* indeed.

We therefore need to establish what kind of relationship Milton envisaged between the above oblique kinds of artistic materials and the actual intentions of his only partly "exemplary" fiction, intentions given notice of at its outset by himself. The pervasive presence of allegory in *Paradise Lost* acquires a rationale when Milton's actual practices in *Paradise Lost* and his allusions in his middle-period prose to Renaissance epic-allegorical theorists are laid alongside the practices of his immediate predecessors in the allegorical epic, the tradition of the epic allegorizers, and the carefully worded statements of Renaissance rhetoricians or other earlier theorists of allegory and epic allegory. That is, *Paradise Lost* must be considered in relation to the critical tradition from which it grew.

As I have suggested, it is probable that the theories on allegorical poetry and epic outlined in my earlier chapters continued to form a very important part of seventeenth-century critical theory. As was also indicated at the beginning of this study, the line of thinking on allegory extends back unbroken not only to medieval literary practice and theory and to religious exegesis in both the Jewish and Christian traditions, but to ancient or late classical exegesis on Homeric or Virgilian or other mythic materials, subsequently reflected in later European readings of classical or modern epic. Each vein of allegory earlier discussed has something to reveal about the allegorical artistry of *Paradise Lost* and how that complex poem coheres. Thus, having considered all these avenues, we are able, when we come to sixteenth- and seventeenth-century theory of the epic, to see more clearly how Milton, while exploiting certain older traditions of allegory, also aligns himself with more modern ones, drawing upon recent writers who had already adapted the ancient modes of allegorical exegesis and rhetorical allegory to the technical requirements and problems of the long allegorical epic. In the remaining chapters of this second Part of my study I shall first give some indications of how those earlier theories and modes of allegory in poetry or in the interpretation of myth (reviewed briefly) relate to Miltonic strategies and intentions in *Paradise Lost*. I shall then take up some of Milton's own statements in his prose and his poetry linking him with the long tradition of allegorized epic. I shall next discuss his indebtedness especially to the allegorical theory and practice of Tasso, of Spenser, and, it would seem, to that complex body of theory on the epic probably preexisting and then codified in Le Bossu's *Traité*. Finally, I shall consider Milton's own view of his epic "Moral" or "Fable"—his shadowed allegorical purpose—as expressed in *Paradise Lost* itself.

The "Levels"

The relevance to *Paradise Lost* of certain specific forms of imaginative application of Scripture to the private life of the believer (apart from strict typological reading), deriving originally from early patristic or rabbinical practice and later to be emphasized in certain Protestant uses, will be discussed in the third and last Part of this study.[1] We may here speak more generally of earlier scriptural or scripturally based traditions of allegorical interpretation. Of all that Milton might have taken from the long avenues of biblical exegesis, Jewish and Christian, one of the most important for his own fiction-making process was the sense of the need, in an allegorized fiction as much as in direct interpretation of Scripture, strongly to sustain the truth of the "literal level". Drawing its resonances from the unchanging solidity of the Word in its historical aspects in Scripture, there was transferred into the mainstream of western secular critical theory a consistent emphasis on historicity or plausibility not only in the literary representation of the externals of an epic action but, in a certain sense, in any secondary allegorical reading of such an action. That is to say, the literal integrity of the main narrative line of the fiction must not be violated in allegorical interpretation, any more than in allegorical composition.

These emphases may be seen reflected in *Paradise Lost* in the plausibility of its external fiction, especially in its human aspects, despite the poem's "Foundation" or "Platform" of "disguised" truth. Allegorical implications might legitimately interweave in and out of Milton's reworking of the Genesis account; but Adam's and Eve's story, and Satan's, must always maintain historicity in their main outlines as derived from the scriptural narration, and must sustain credibility in the sequence of probable causation or links between events, as well as in the particulars of the human psychology and actions. Even Dante's allegorical pilgrimage through his three supernatural regions was constructed around a core of such verisimilar action, or actions, and of naturally developing human responses and growth in understanding. But it was recognised in earlier periods, and understood by Milton, that allegory or allegorical reading when carefully controlled and directed need offer no contradiction to the truth of the literal level. The two kinds of truth may support each other. That the Bible throughout its historical narrations in the Old Testament could also "speak in deeds", prefiguratively, of the New (as apart from merely using occasional deliberately allegorical figures) validated the figurative reading of historical epic. And indeed, for an earlier literary aesthetic "all poetry is allegory", speaking with "two voices", the one its "literal fiction", the other a "translated" language. The epic fable of *Paradise Lost* also has two voices, a sustained double language, in many of its components, including much of its plausible surface. But no more than in the Old Testament does this doubleness invalidate its literal history.

There is not space here to speak in any detail of the medieval three- or fourfold levels of interpretation in relation to Milton's poem, although there are certainly some instances suggestive of such a layered structuring in *Paradise Lost* (just as there are reminiscences of older allegorical literary models, for example, in the psychomachia of Milton's War in Heaven). That particular stratified way of reading, along well understood lines, certain parables, passages in Scripture, or myths from ancient literature, for the purpose of moral, theological and spiritual edification, had by the Renaissance acquired new vitality as a method of analysis in poetry of strata of meaning perceived in largely secular terms.[2] Whether the Dantesque or Thomistic three- or fourfold levels of analysis, namely, literal, allegorical (that is, strictly typological), moral, and anagogic or spiritual (to do with faith), or, on the other hand, the more loosely applied multiple analyses of Renaissance mythographers, stressing variously levels of meaning "literal" (the actual myth or fable), "physical" (geographical-cosmological) and "moral" or psychological, with a background of historical "allusion" and occasionally a more vaguely designated "allegorie" (sometimes a portfolio term, sometimes designating a spiritual sense), are of greater relevance to *Paradise Lost* is difficult to say. There are certainly moments in Milton's epic, as in Spenser's, of cosmological allegory, as seen for example in the warring legions of atoms in Milton's Chaos. The "moral" level, as registered by the inner development of Adam and Eve, displayed in allegorical as well as exemplary mode, is of course a continuum in *Paradise Lost*, as it is in *The Faerie Queene*. Yet from neither Milton nor Spenser can an element of purely theological allegory be excluded. This includes true typological meanings, which may infrequently be found in *Paradise Lost*, and "anagogic" or more widely spiritual secondary senses, also occasionally to be discerned. Examples of the latter include the second coming of the Messiah, foreshadowed in the particular way in which the divine termination of the War in Heaven is presented in Book VI; Abdiel's solitary triumph of faith in his single-handed "victory" over Satan in Book VI; and Sin's and Death's freezing breath in Book X, resembling the freezing wind from the sails of Lucifer's wings in Dante's *Inferno* (canto xxxiv, lines 46-52). Both winds petrify created matter, and Milton's freezing wind is clearly the allegorical inverse of the infusing breath of life of the Spirit, which was seen at the Creation in the opening lines of Book I. Further examples of pure theological allegory in Milton's poem are found in Sin, Death, and at times in Satan himself, including the idea, recently proposed, that the latter two figures embody the Augustinian and Miltonic view of evil as negation, as non-existence.[3] Similarly, in *Paradise Lost* the self-redefining emblem of the Tree of Knowledge (Books IV and IX), the *scala*/Golden Ladder (Book III), the *scala*/Tree of Life, which is the Son (Book IV), seemingly mutates through a number of recognisable older "levels": literal, moral, anagogic, and allegorical. Yet elements in Books I to

II and V to VI may suggest that Milton was also capable of projecting topical political relevances as one part of his total allegory, in more contemporary Renaissance fashion.

Intermittent and Sustained Allegory

Such glimpses of older allegorical conventions in *Paradise Lost* as the "levels" of allegory, for the most part fleetingly seen, although fascinating are somewhat peripheral to the main concerns of this study, except insofar as they indicate that Milton's epic conforms to Renaissance emphases in stressing the "moral level" as the *continuum* of its narrative dark conceit. Of more direct interest are those Renaissance understandings of allegory in the epic as, in various ways, a structuring concept. As in Tasso or Spenser, both intermittent and sustained allegory may be seen to act in conjunction in the narrative fable of *Paradise Lost*, along with varieties of *exemplum* allegory. Detailed illustration of these matters would be the subject for a separate study. Here we are only able to indicate the historical and contemporary models with which Milton's epic aligns itself.

Much of earlier Renaissance allegoresis on epic and allegorical composition in epic is by nature episodic and concerned with vignettes. Collected under the scantiest of "actions", such as Rogero's quest in the *Orlando Furioso*, such episodes constituted the main matter of widely diversified romance epics. Similarly, a string of allegorical interpretations constituted the bulk of the apparatus in Harington's critical annotations on Ariosto, or Sandys' on Ovid. Tasso had disliked "intermittent" or freestanding allegories, especially of the wilder kinds indulged in by certain Italian commentators. Yet what stands out of great value from Harington's schemes of analysis and of great importance for understanding later literary practice of allegory in Spenser or Milton, is Harington's clear differentiation between the kinds of episodes (whether or not intermittent) which stand simply as *examples* of moral behaviour and those which carry a more hidden ethical or further significance, at whatever "level".[4] In Ariosto's numerous characters, or Tasso's Christian and pagan knights, or Spenser's great spectrum of subcharacters from all walks of life, or Milton's fallen angels in Council or heavenly archangels, we may easily discern different *types* of bad or good human characters, drawn from life. But these characterizations are to be distinguished from the allegorical treatments of the same or other characters at different times, conducted in more oblique modes—as we may observe in, say, the obscurer implications of Satan's encounter with the Old Anarch Chaos, as opposed to Satan's literal exemplifications of hatred and revenge in this and other scenes, or in the way in which Adam and Eve (each a "real" character) also possess personalities and engage in actions suggesting that they are complementary and sometimes disunited aspects of a single psychic whole. These latter instances constitute a more indirect form of allegory than *exemplum*.

Although intermittent allegory occurs and is important in *Paradise Lost*, of more central importance to Milton's epic is the humanist conception of a sustained moral allegory underlying an entire epic action. Such exegesis was early conducted by Landino and his predecessors and followers as continuous exposition of the whole plot of the *Aeneid*, interpreted as the hero's moral development against all temptations and odds, or a continuous learning process. This approach, as espoused by Landino, was quite different from the construing of the external action of Virgil's epic by other early critics (and some later) as deepening into allegory only at a few supernatural points, such as the deific interventions in the action, or Aeneas' visit to the underworld. A reading of epic as continuous allegorical progress is theoretically set out in Tasso's allegorical explanation of the *Gerusalemme*, and practically exemplified in that poem's actual oblique demonstrations of psychic disintegration and reintegration, presented under a new, more "historical" surface. Such a developmental interpretation of the physical action is also seen in Spenser's "dark conceit", which exhibits a sustained action or inner moral progress within each principal virtue or character, repeated with "endlesse trace"[5] in each knightly quest. This inner development in Spenser's Redcrosse or Guyon is not very different from what we perceive in Tasso's Rinaldo—or in Milton's Adam. In all we may witness the painful development of the moral hero through failure and error toward self-knowledge and a more seasoned virtue, toward a moral virtue first striven for by human effort, then strengthened through experience, and finally "infused by grace". Milton shares the earlier humanist ideal of the *moral* epic hero, "more heroic" than the pagan warrior, and he shares in that earlier effort to formulate as object of emulation an Heroic Virtue which is also Christian, retrieving its deepest successes out of humiliation and defeat. What has been difficult for many critics of *Paradise Lost* to apprehend is that whatever deep convictions Milton may have held concerning the literal truth of the principal incidents of his Genesis story, such beliefs are still totally compatible with his further personal amplification of the biblical account in the direction not only of *exemplum* allegory or exemplary Moral (the "lesson of disobedience and obedience"), but also in the direction of a more abstract and complex allegorical "Idea". The "literal level" in *Paradise Lost* retains its indestructible autonomy—as it always does in convincing allegory.

Allegorical Rhetoric

Renaissance conceptions of allegorical rhetoric also affect Milton's art. We may refer to some observations made in earlier parts of this discussion.[6]

On the one side stood a body of late Renaissance theory concerning epic-allegorical narrative, developing out of earlier interpretative readings and designed to ensure, in exegesis as in allegorical composition, that allegorical meaning should match the fable, should not do violence to the form of the narrative. Hence the growth in Landino, in Tasso, or in Spenser of the idea of *continuous* exposition: a long, *continued* dark conceit matching a continuous narrative. On the other side were the rhetoricians. The notable attempts of Salutati and his medieval and patristic predecessors to formulate an allegoric aesthetic which included the whole stuff of the language of poetry were impressively sweeping, but remained vague concerning the distinctive aesthetic qualities of allegorical discourse, although these had been recognised as early as by Quintilian in his *Institutio*. Earlier Renaissance theoreticians, other than hinting at the obscurity of allegory ("dark", "dim", "veiled", etc.), often had little to say about the precise linguistic characteristics of hidden discourse. But later Renaissance rhetoricians of a more formal cast, reviving one line of classical thought, drew attention once more to *allegoria* as a distinctive *trope*—one not merely having a different "intendment" from what it professed, but actually artistically designed to mislead. "To reveal and conceal", or to "veil" (that is, *lightly* screen) with allegory, is in fact to hint conspicuously while conspicuously concealing. That which is so ostentatiously hidden must necessarily call attention to its own hidden presence—otherwise hidden meaning might remain forever hidden. Whereas Boccaccio's or Salutati's arguments that "all poetry is allegory" designed to "prove" an "Idea" rested on some wide analogy between allegory and metaphor (both are forms of *translatio*), rhetoricians like Peacham or Puttenham tried more specifically to distinguish between *allegoria* and its sister tropes of metaphor, irony, enigma and others. All of these tropes on the surface say one thing but "intend" another; however, allegory is closer than the others to enigma, or perhaps to riddle, in that it is *consciously* misleading. Allegorical metaphor possesses a certain naughtiness: it is "duplicitous", it "dissimulates".[7] The fictive surface of an allegorical trope often has an ostentatious absurdity, incongruity, or whatever, which frustrates and allures and the solution of which challenges the intellect and is pleasurable and satisfying, like the solving of a riddle. This token of the "absurd" in identifying allegory was, as we saw, present also in the early Christian tradition—a continuity, perhaps, from the Greek allegorical tradition. Bacon, as a scholar aware of both these diverse traditions of allegory, had alluded to such a quality of absurdity as something self-evidently and fundamentally to do with allegory: some fables are so "absurd" that any imbecile must recognise that such stories must mean something other than what on the face of them they seem to say.[8]

Seeming "irrelevance", "absurdity", riddle, grotesqueness, bizarre or unexpected shift in mode (devices analogous to but accentuating romance capriciousness), are the signals by which allegory has always disclosed its hidden presence. Spenser by such means constantly alerts the reader to moments of particular allegorical significance in *The Faerie Queene*. By such devices similarly we can recognise the presence of hidden meanings in *Paradise Lost*. The very features which the eighteenth century found most grotesque and inappropriate in *Paradise Lost*, the grinning personification of Death or the disgusting personification of Sin, the more disgusting because her emotional relationships are so "real", or elsewhere in the poem the bizarre or unexplained intrusions of the Paradise of Fools, the Golden Ladder, the Golden Scales, are those features which, by the repulsion or exasperation which they cause the reader, inform him that at these places he must pause and think, must search for relevances. To be at once alerted by such absurdity or incongruity is a reading trick to be learned in reading Milton as in Spenser. In *Paradise Lost* even the more plausible supernatural machinations are not without such moments of literal narrative "absurdity". The personification of Sin "lets Satan out" of Hell in Book II; Uriel or Gabriel are inexplicably shortsighted or tardy at moments of crisis in Books III and IV; and so on. Milton's gloss on the Uriel episode as a kind of overt allegory on the efficacy of hypocrisy does not quite compensate for the severe break in narrative plausibility, since Uriel's behaviour up to that point—he, "The sharpest sighted Spirit of all in Heav'n" (III.691)—has been in accordance with a strict credibility. We may suspect that Milton is deliberately, for some reason, undermining his own angelic machinery. So that critics search in vain for "plausible" explanations of such breaks in Milton's verisimilar narrative, or mistakenly censure him for failing to conform to a mode of narrative realism to which such incidents were never intended to conform. Here or there in *Paradise Lost* critics perforce acknowledge certain brief or disjunct episodes of deliberate allegory. But to do so is still not to address the underlying problem which the mere presence of such obtrusively allegorical incidents, or else Milton's sudden switches from realism to some form of allegory, raise about the nature of Milton's fiction. In the later part of this study a number of such troublesome episodes or elements in *Paradise Lost* will be further cited, and the need will be pointed out to improve our understanding of their function in the poem and to revise our expectations of the nature of Milton's fiction-making. Full investigation, however, would again be matter for a separate and detailed study, conducted on the lines of a critical-allegorical reading of *Paradise Lost*.

Milton and Spenser

The preceding brief retrospect on various Renaissance views on allegory may conveniently lead us to a final comparison of Spenser's allegorical artistry with Milton's, before we return to our main line of enquiry concerning allegorical "Idea" in Renaissance epic and in *Paradise Lost*. In the mid-eighteenth century, Bishop Hurd probably correctly assessed the situation when he said that Milton restricted his taste for chivalry and romance in an age becoming less sympathetic to the "Gothic". Milton "dropped the tales" which had entranced him in his youthful reading, the fables of Faerieland in *The Faerie Queene*, but "he still kept to the allegories of Spenser"—meaning, probably, such fantastic elements as Spenser's allegorical Houses and monstrous personifications, among other devices.[9] That Milton did retain something of Spenser's "allegories" in an age so different in taste is an index to the importance which allegory still held for him in his conception of the didactic epic. I cannot therefore agree with the view recently expressed by John M. Steadman that while the moral crises in Tasso or Spenser resemble those in Milton's epics, Milton differs *fundamentally* in depicting "the temptation crisis literally".[10] This may be true of *Paradise Regained*; it is not true of *Paradise Lost*, which uses the methods of literal representation together with those of allegory—as Tasso did himself. While the main lines of Milton's plot are certainly more literal than Spenser's, Milton did also retain not only Spenser's "allegories" (in Hurd's sense), but also a wide range of other effects from Spenser's allegorical apparatus, and a host of specifically allegorical devices: emblems, icons, dream-visions, allegorical landscapes, metamorphoses, as well as the Spenserian allegorical personifications and allegorical "Houses"—each of which would require, like Milton's handling of main-plot allegory and allegorical Episode, separate and detailed treatment to be properly illustrated. Although Milton's uses of these Spenserian devices are kept more in the background than is the case in *The Faerie Queene*, such allegorical methodology in *Paradise Lost* is no less loaded with covert meaning.

But perhaps Milton's most eloquent debt to Spenser lies in the verbal texture of his rhetoric—that most elusive debt to define. For the constantly self-reflexive, self-echoing texture of Milton's allusively allegorical language in *Paradise Lost* is singularly like that of *The Faerie Queene*, constantly nudging what lies buried in the peripheries back to the centre of consciousness. And frequently Milton's allusive style carries echoes of Spenser's allegorical conceptions and motifs, as well as of his methodology. In these respects, Milton's mimesis conducts a kind of dialogue with Spenser's, redefining its proper issues through its tacit Spenserian dimension. Spenser's text is that through which we read *Paradise Lost*—the more so, because it was also the text through which Milton read and wrote his own poem. Such conscious evocation in *Paradise Lost* of Spenserian linguistic resources, as well as direct echo of *The Faerie Queene* and overt imitation of Spenserian allegorical devices, constitute Milton's true debt to Spenser as both moral teacher and supreme writer of didactic fiction. Milton's way of using reminiscences of Spenserian language, motif and device as a whole distinct dimension of allegorical innuendo in *Paradise Lost* constitutes a masterly and master's tribute to another, an acknowledgement of kindred spirits, moral aims, poetic.[11]

Two examples may be cited of Spenserian verbal-allegorical methods in enactment in *Paradise Lost*. One is the "Error" motif, which in *Paradise Lost* constitutes a direct imitation of Spenser. (An associated motif is that of the "divided paths", emblem of wavering choices, which I have discussed in greater detail elsewhere.)[12] Another instance is Milton's development of the motif of "Death", which offers a close analogy to Spenser's methods. In both instances, overt allegory becomes in each poem merely the ultimate exteriorization of a subterranean current of ongoing reiterative allusion which, throughout, has been steadily shaping itself into overt allegory—a double form of secondary discourse in Milton's case, inasmuch as the Spenserian echo is part of the game. We may illustrate further, beginning with the motif of "Death".

One of the first words which we encounter in *Paradise Lost* is "Death". The biological fact and conception of Death expands dialectically to become Raphael's warning about Death, hard for Adam to understand (VII.545-47); further expands to become the verbal sentence of Death imposed on Adam in Book X (48-50, 206-10); still later it becomes Adam's anxious speculations about the nature of death and inherited death (X.770-820). Death becomes literally exemplified (or almost does) in narrative incident in the War in Heaven, and is shown with fulness in other, human wars which do kill (XI.637-82); it becomes the historically presented, hideous pageant of all possible manners of dying in Book XI (466-99); it becomes allegorically personified in the allegorical figure of Death in Book II, more mysterious there, and in Book X, his figure embodying the full horror, uncertainty and inevitability of all that we have seen or thought about Death. But the *enigma* of that particular allegorical personification lies in its curious, emphasized, narrative and verbal connections with the person of Adam, as revealed by the latter's words, acts, and situations in Books VIII, X and elsewhere. And the word itself, "death", echoes throughout the poem, through Adam's appalling vision, through the angel's or God's terse declarations and Adam's speech, just as it echoes back in figure of speech in the scene describing the engendering of Death by Sin: "I fled, and cry'd out *Death*; / Hell . . . sigh'd / From all her Caves, and back resounded *Death*" (II.787-89).[13] This way of expanding from bare word to fictive depiction to allegorical figure is an intensely Spenserian mode of development, one here and elsewhere imitated by Milton in his ongoing linguistic dialogue with his better teacher.

We can see the artistic process at work once more in Milton's treatment of that primal Spenserian theme of "error", the Dark Wood, emblem of moral straying, first intimated and then emblematized in the first few stanzas of *The Faerie Queene*, and recreated in so many later phrases, figures and scenes. Taking the process in reverse this time, we find that the "scaly fould" of Milton's allegorical figure of Error-Sin in Book II, drawn from Spenser's serpent brood of Error in his Book I (canto I, stanzas 14-16), are recreated in Satan's "rising foulds" in Book IX, which resemble "a surging *Maze*" (498-99). Thus the serpent's folds themselves become a *selva*, like Spenser's dark Wood, misleading "th' *amaz'd* Night-wanderer", who here is Eve (IX.640). Similarly the byways of "error" are inversely remembered in the innocently *"mazie error"* of Eden's brooks (IV.239), just as they are, more ambiguously, in Eve's "Dissheveld . . . wanton ringlets wav'd" (IV.306). This theme of "error", first rendered allegorically in *Paradise Lost*, then rendered descriptively, takes clearer intellectual shape when we read of Satan's fictively-literal wanderings *"Alone, and without guide"* in Chaos (II.975)—apparently a direct echo of Spenser's Calidore's words in Book VI (i.6). (Chaos himself is the allegorical epitome of Confusion, straying, error.) Similarly when we read of the fallen angels wandering in *"confus'd* march forlorn" in Hell (II.615), their "wandering" paralleled by their intellectual straying "in wandring *mazes* lost" of debate (II.561), the figure of "error" appears yet again. The straying of the fallen angels relates also to the poet's fears lest out of presumption he fall upon "th' *Aleian* Field . . . / Erroneous* there *to wander* and forlorne" (VII. 19-20); and of course this last wandering forecasts fallen Adam's and Eve's futurity of *"wandring* steps and slow" (XII.648). "Error" in its more intellectual aspects is also recorded in the mention of men's erroneous readings of pagan myths (of Mulciber: "thus they relate, / *Erring* . . .", I.746-47), and in the listing of all the false opinions and philosophical errors held by men since time immemorial, immortalized in the allegorical Limbo, which is filled with examples of "painful Superstition and blind Zeal" (III.452) and opinions, like their owners, blown "transverse" (III.488). So the word or theme of "error", which began in the full allegorical episode of Sin in Book II, holding all, subsequently fragments and diverges through the verbal tapestry of the entire poem, reappearing as direct allegory from time to time.

The above are but very brief illustrations of workings common to many of Milton's allegorical themes, each of which could and should be explored in depth. They are themes which dilate and condense, weave in and out of our field of vision, interlace in a manner reminiscent of Spenser's, *re-membering* Spenser, although kept more in the background, more strictly controlled in Milton's more neoclassically unified epic. Yet the very obliqueness of the Spenserian dimension in *Paradise Lost* tacitly leaves a margin expressive of the differences between the two poets, indicating Milton's need to set out, within a more severely historical Christian framework, aesthetic modes of epic and allegorical truth moderated to the pressures of a colder neoclassical imaginative clime, one constantly threatening to damp the intended wing.

TWELVE

Allegorical Poetics in *Paradise Lost*

Early Indications in Milton's Prose

There should be little need to demonstrate Milton's familiarity with the Renaissance theorists and practitioners of allegory in poetry and epic whose views and applied practices have been outlined in the foregoing pages. Such familiarity, especially with the Italians and notably with Tasso, is unambiguously indicated in Milton's own fragmentarily sketched poetic in his prose writings of the early 1640s.[1] Such familiarity is also seen in his parallel ambitions to those of the ancients and moderns to achieve a great poem, probably in the "Epick form" and professedly didactic ("doctrinal and exemplary to a Nation"),[2] which would vie with Virgil's, Homer's or Tasso's. Tasso is the only modern epic poet to be named.[3] Milton's familiarity with the continental critical tradition is seen specifically in his looking principally to the three greatest critics of the late Italian Renaissance, "*Castelvetro, Tasso, Mazzoni*", in whose debates Milton seeks guidance as to the best "laws . . . of a true *Epic* Poem".[4] It is of particular significance that in this context Milton speaks, in *The Reason of Church-Government urg'd against Prelaty*, of the "diffuse" rather than the "long" epic poem, which would be the logical opposite to the "brief" epic poem on the model of Job.[5] This is a crucial distinction, one which has not been enough noted in Milton studies, and which suggests some looser and more intricate structure in epic than the straight neoclassical historical-narrative model—Milton's will be a poem more like the ancient epics, or like Tasso's. It will be an epic perhaps more closely structured than the relaxed romance epics of Spenser and Ariosto, but it may share something of the flavour of those.[6] Hence we find Milton wondering "whether the rules of *Aristotle* herein [on plot unity] are strictly to be kept, or nature to be follow'd, which in them that know art, and use judgement is no transgression, but an inriching of art".[7] This comment on "nature" being an "inriching of art", coupled with Milton's unusual use of the word "diffuse", suggests that he may even at this early stage be inclining towards the kind of compromise envisaged by Tasso between "rules" (historical causality and verisimilitude) and "nature" (as in the romance-epic).

Milton's deep and sustained commitment to the view that poetry and epic are inherently ideational, universal and didactic—that they must *teach*, teach specific things—equally aligns him with the tradition of allegory, such "teaching" in poetry, as we have seen, being historically inseparable from an allegorical poetic. Milton's important discussions are set out in considerable detail in the Preface to Book II of *The Reason of Church-Government*, in a passage whose familiarity may blunt recognition of its critical importance. It is given in reduced form below, with indications in square brackets of its correspondences with late Renaissance theory:

[Poetical] abilities . . . of power beyond the office of a pulpit, to inbreed . . . the seeds of vertu, and publick civility, to allay the perturbations of the mind, . . . to celebrate . . . Gods Almightinesse, and what he works, and what he suffers to be wrought with high providence [the last part describes the subject of *Paradise Lost*] . . . to sing the victorious agonies of Martyrs and Saints, the deeds and triumphs of just and pious Nations doing valiantly through faith [echoes here of *Discorsi del poema eroico*, Book I]. . . . whatsoever in religion is holy and sublime, in vertu amiable, or grave, whatsoever hath passion [the tragic effect] or admiration [the epic effect] in all the changes of that which is call'd fortune from without, or the wily suttleties and refluxes of mans thoughts from within [echoes here of Tasso's psychological "Allegoria"]. . . . Teaching over the whole book of sanctity and vertu. . . . with eloquent and gracefull inticements to the love and practice of justice, temperance and fortitude, instructing and bettering the Nation at all opportunities, that the call of wisdom and vertu may be heard every where.[8]

Milton also in *The Reason of Church-Government* envisages a new theatre of moral didacticism, a form of teaching which is to operate "not only in Pulpits, but after another persuasive method . . . in Theaters, porches, or what other place . . ."[9] (we may compare his own attempt at reforming the theatre's function in *Comus: A Masque*). Although a little earlier in the Preface to Book II Milton had used the word "exemplary", giving no specific hint of allegory, the formulation in the passage quoted above, "fortune from *without*, or the wily suttleties and refluxes of mans thoughts from *within*", corresponds well not only with the "Dramatick constitutions" of Sophocles and Euripides, which Milton cites, but equally with the double facets of Tasso's "Allegoria", Armida and Ismen, the external and internal impediments to virtue, as well as with Spenser's parallel psychological-allegorical constructs, Duessa and Archimago (themselves borrowed from Tasso). Of outer and inner obstacles, it is the internal which are in Renaissance epic most appropriately allegorized. (By contrast, in *Samson Agonistes*, a pure tragedy, the "changes of . . . fortune" and "refluxes of . . . thoughts" are both presented more in dramatic terms.) There is no reason to think (whatever allowances we may or may not have to make for a degree of rhetorical overstatement in the prose of the early 1640s)[10] that Milton ever abandoned either these earlier expressed views regarding epic form and purpose or his original interest in the Italian critics and poets. In his discussion of epic at the beginning of *Paradise Lost*, Book IX, we can almost hear him picking up the same words at the very point he had left off his discussion in the treatise on *Church-Government* some twenty years before. Then: "[if] there be nothing advers in our climat, or the fate of this age".[11] And now, in the poem: "unless an age too late, or cold / Climat, or Years damp my intended wing" (IX.44-45).[12]

As to Milton's specific interest in allegorical modes and genres, it is a not uncharacteristic omission in him to fail to discuss these or any other poetic modes or issues in much theoretical detail. Milton almost uniquely among the great English epic poets has no long critical discourses. His readers are obliged to proceed by inference, and one of the best ways of following his train of thought lies in taking close note of the characteristics of those particular critics and models whom he deigns to mention by name. All those models whom Milton cites in his prose in any connection with epic (Virgil, Homer, Spenser, Tasso, Ariosto) directly or indirectly fall within an allegorical epic tradition. It should not be necessary, either, to point to Milton's early experimentation, recorded in the Trinity Manuscript, with a completely allegorical type of drama—notably in his outlines for an allegorical masque-drama or allegorical tragedy on the themes of "Adam unparadiz'd" or, alternatively, "Paradise Lost", both with allegorical personifications, including those in the "mask of all the evills of this life & world".[13] Such an allegorical pageant evokes, perhaps, Walter Benjamin's conception of baroque allegorical death dramas of a phantasmagoric kind.[14] This early inspiration Milton later realized in the pageant of violence, illness and death presented almost as if "on stage" to Adam by Michael in Book XI. Nor need we refer to Milton's success in the highly allegorical masque form in *Comus*. Nor to his citing of one of Spenser's most complicated allegories, Guyon in the cave of Mammon, in the course of professing his own admiration for Spenser's allegorical poem as the most *effective* form of moral teaching ("a better teacher then *Scotus* or *Aquinas*").[15] The specific political-allegorical dimensions of Milton's long poems, in the seventeenth century taken for granted, are now once again well recognised in both his mature epic and his late tragedy. Despite the absence of technical discussions by Milton on the subject, there are as well continuing allusions to allegorical modes of discourse throughout Milton's poetry (as there are in his prose, for that matter): from "Il Penseroso", where "more is meant then meets the ear" (line 120); to "Lycidas", where he exercises the poet's right to moralize and censure while speaking through the pastoral veil; to *Comus*, whose arcane meanings and allegorical apparatus have yet to be fully fathomed. The recurring allusions, in those sections of *Paradise Lost* most particularly concerned with problems of narration, to enigmatical "shadows" and "types" and to "accommodated" narration[16] are only the poetical articulations of Milton's persisting preoccupation with allegory.[17] The pervasive presence of allegorical conceptions, constructs, modes and expressions throughout so much of *Paradise Lost* and indeed others of Milton's works needs to be acknowledged and fully accounted for. It is in the continuity and links of his own poetic with earlier and especially the late Italian traditions that we shall find the needful explanations.

Borrowings from Tasso in *Paradise Lost*

It was primarily Tasso's work (directly, and as developed in the succeeding century) which supplied the theory as well as in large part the practical model which enabled Milton to correlate an historical type of narrative, a biblical narrative history, with an allegorical fiction displaying a moral Idea. Such an assertion would not have surprised Milton's contemporaries, and such was assumed to be the case by his closest biographer. Tasso afforded Milton the key to the problem of how to shape his epic structure around a "Moral" or anterior Idea, and how to accommodate the epic's form to the historical necessities of what Milton finally hit upon as the supreme "historical" subject: the archetypal human history, far exceeding the documentary records of ancient Israel from the Old Testament, or British-Roman material in what Milton termed "our own ancient stories". We will proceed from instances of direct emulation of Tasso's poem by Milton in his own epic, to debts of critical theory.

Merely the extent of Tasso's poetical influence in every genre and on every aspect of Milton's art, including *Paradise Lost*, makes it impossible to believe that Milton could have left the Italian critical theories behind him after the prose of the middle-1640s.[18] Milton's poetry throughout his life bears witness to Tasso's influence translated into Miltonic practice. This we can see, beginning with Milton's early poem to "Mansus", a kind of self-dedication to the art, in which Milton expresses his admiration for his venerable poetic forebear. Giovanni Battista Manso, Marquis of Villa, was Tasso's protector, and he must have communicated many details about the great Italian poet's life, work and critical thinking to the young poetic aspirant when Milton visited Manso in Naples in 1638.[19] As Toland suggested, Manso may indeed have imbued Milton with the idea of writing an epic comparable to Tasso's.[20] Milton's total oeuvre approximates closely at every stage to Tasso's (much more so than to Virgil's). In both Tasso and Milton we see the development from early pastoral drama, to mature *rime* or sonnets, to the major achievement of a great humane and religious epic, with a final more austerely religious poem (in Tasso, his revised

Gerusalemme conquistata) recasting the theme of the first epic. Each has a "Creation" poem; for Tasso, it is *Le sette giornate del Mondo Creato;* in *Paradise Lost* extensive Creation matter is incorporated into Books III, IV, VII, and VIII. *Paradise Lost,* like the *Gerusalemme,* Canto IV, also incorporates into its main action a Satanic revenge theme; and a tragic love interest is strong in both epics. And finally, the oeuvre of both poets is consummated in a late heroic tragedy, Tasso's *Il Re Torrismondo* being matched by *Samson Agonistes.* There is also the enormous influence, now well recognised, of Tasso's highly distinctive versification, with its nobility of diction and its stately and difficult syntax enhanced by metrical and other forms of *asprezza,* on the versification of Milton's sonnets and *Paradise Lost.*[21] Tasso chiselled out the grand style which Milton too found "answerable" to a grand design.

There is an almost incalculable quantity of direct echo of the *Gerusalemme liberata* in *Paradise Lost,* from innumerable verbal details, through extended similes, to much larger descriptive sequences. Milton like Spenser *absorbed* Tasso, although not always with the same emotional or moral overtones as in the original. Only a few examples of similes borrowed or copied by Milton are these: the descending Satan and the alighting Archangel like a radiant stripling angel or a Phoenix (*Paradise Lost* III.636-44, V.270-76; *Gerusalemme* I.13-15, of Gabriel); the devils dispersed (*Paradise Lost* I.514-22; *Gerusalemme* IV.18-19); Satan's giant stature like Atlas, or Typhoeus, or a comet burning (*Paradise Lost* IV.985-88, I.199, II.706ff.; *Gerusalemme* II.91, VI.23, VII.52-53 of Argantes; IV.6, 7, 8 of Pluto); Aetna and the geography of Hell (*Paradise Lost* I.230ff.; *Gerusalemme* IV.8); Satan in serpent folds (*Paradise Lost* IX.495-503), taken from the serpent guarding Armida's garden (*Gerusalemme* XV.48); the swarming serpent masses (*Paradise Lost* X.519ff.; *Gerusalemme* IV.4-5). There are many, many other similar telling echoes.

Examples of larger descriptive sequences borrowed from Tasso are these: the fallen angels in the dreadful environs of Hell and the diabolical trumpet (*Paradise Lost* I.61ff., 314-15, 531-43; II.405, 514-20; *Gerusalemme* IV.2, 3, 9, 10); the revengeful personalities and motives of Satan and his cohorts and of Pluto (*Paradise Lost,* e.g. I.637 through 662, II.345-76, etc.; *Gerusalemme* IV.1, 9-17); Satan's rousing address to his troops and the Council in Pandemonium (*Paradise Lost* I.315ff., II.11ff.) and Pluto's address and Council (*Gerusalemme* IV.9 ff.); contrasting character types in Satan's lieutenants, Moloc and Belial, seen in Hell (*Paradise Lost* II.43-120 ff.) and the similar contrasting personalities and rôles of the pagan envoys Argantes and Aletes (*Gerusalemme* II.58-59 ff.); the topography of the Garden of Eden (*Paradise Lost* IV.222-68) and Armida's garden (*Gerusalemme* XVI.8-13—the latter lifted bodily, with much more from this canto, by Spenser); the two contrasted heavenly messengers, Raphael and Michael (*Paradise Lost* V.247ff. and XI.203ff.), and Gabriel and Michael sent down to

Godfrey (*Gerusalemme* I.11-17 and XVIII.92-96). In both poems the earlier of these angelic visits carries a humane message, the later represents a visionary and celestial moment.

These are only a random few out of the vast number of direct and major borrowings from Tasso or close recastings of his poem in *Paradise Lost*, the sheer quantity and still less the importance of which have even now not begun to be fully apprehended.[22] Even if the Italian of Tasso's poem were more generally accessible to Milton's modern readers, it would be virtually impossible exactly to disentangle all Milton's borrowings, so embedded are Tasso's phrases, lines, comparisons and situations in the texture of *Paradise Lost*, and coming as they do through the filter of Fairfax's translation of Tasso and Spenser's equally extensive borrowings often of the same materials.[23] And of course, the borrowings also pass through the refracting lens of Milton's humanist and Reformist imagination—as may be seen in the case of the garden of Armida in Canto XVI of the *Gerusalemme*, which is translated into Eve's blameless bower in *Paradise Lost*, Book IV. (Tasso makes Armida's garden bad; Spenser splits it into a bad garden in *The Faerie Queene*, Book II, canto xii, and a parallel good one in Book IV, canto x; Milton makes the same bower first good in Book IV, later sullied in Book IX.)

Within *Paradise Lost* itself we can see many epic and narrative structurings similar to those prescribed by Tasso in his *Discorsi* and used by him in the *Gerusalemme*. We may see *Paradise Lost*, like the *Gerusalemme*, as an epic embracing love and war, or perhaps a tragedy of love set within a chivalric action.[24] Both poems employ such striking devices as the Heavenly Father looking down and (within the bounds of man's free will) directing the action from above; we may note the striking parallel near the opening of *Paradise Lost*, Book III (56-59 ff.), with *Gerusalemme* (I.7-8) or similar scenes showing God the Father looking down from above the stars at his Creation. A Heavenly Messenger is in each poem *twice* sent down by the Father, in such a way as to commence and conclude the full epic action. This framing of the epic action between two heavenly embassages markedly different in temper is a parallel almost more striking than the resemblances in content between Raphael's lecture to Adam in Book V (404 ff.) and that of Tasso's own "gentile Spirito", speaking to the poet in the prose dialogue entitled *Il Messaggiero* (1582).[25] Milton like Tasso in his epic assigns different archangels to the two separate embassages, giving Michael a higher celestial rôle than Raphael. As in Tasso, it is the archangel Michael who near the end of the poem grants a celestial vision to the human protagonist, whereas Milton's Raphael earlier, as does earlier in the *Gerusalemme* Tasso's Gabriel (I.11 ff.), brings exhortation and warning; at both epic endings the second archangel is shown not as affable but as martial. In the *Gerusalemme* (XVIII.92-96) Godfrey is granted a vision of the angels fighting overhead unseen on his side, and they are compared, allusively, to those at Dothan (from 2 Kings 6.13-18); this is a simile Milton picks up, now with specific reference to Dothan, in his memorable description of Michael's "heav'nly Bands" at the close of Book XI (208-220). Thus the vision at the close of *Paradise Lost* of the "bright array" of armed Cherubim expelling the humans, and the Gate of Paradise "with dreadful Faces throngd and fierie Armes" (XII.627-28; 644), is mediated by the preceding conception of warrior angels who are somehow at the same time protectors—an inspiration provided by Tasso's lines.

Just as Tasso stressed epic wonder and marvels, *meraviglia* and *meraviglie*,[26] so in *Paradise Lost* there is constant verbal stress on epic "wonder": "wonder, but delight", at the true miracle of the Creation (VIII.11),[27] not dissimilar to Cowley's advocacy of "Christian miracles". Such wonder is ironically contrasted with Satan's specious technological "wonders".[28] In *Paradise Lost* we find in Adam the traditional Renaissance formulation of the epic hero as a balanced ethical personality compounded of "contemplation . . . and valour" (IV.297)[29]—a hero who, however, initially lacks that experience of outer trial and his own inner weakness which distinguishes the ultimately more heroic hero (IX.13-15), described by Tasso too as succeeding through "long practice" and "infused by divine grace".[30] Although Milton did not in his few remarks concerning his future epic in the prose of the 1640s suggest the kind of allegory formally outlined by Tasso, he does in fact use as the basis of his psychological action in the main part of his epic a Reason-Passion-Fancy *schema* closely resembling Tasso's in the "Allegoria", one used also by Spenser as the *continuum* of the moral action in each Book of *The Faerie Queene*. In *Paradise Lost* this scheme corresponds closely to the mental paradigm of Reason-Will-Fancy-Passions outlined theoretically by Adam in Book V (100ff.), and thereafter exemplified in the plot or shadowed in various muted metaphorical or allegorical ways throughout Milton's narrative. The detailed applications by Milton of this important Tassonic mode and matter of psychological allegory in *Paradise Lost* merit fuller consideration than they have as yet received from critics.

Structuring the "Diffuse" Epic: Echoes of Tasso's *Discorsi*

We may now turn to more specific questions of epic poetics. Tasso's assistance to Milton with the practicalities of structuring what Milton rather carefully termed the "diffuse epic" (the didactic mixed-genre epic, containing an admixture of romance elements and allegory, along with true or feigned "history", and preserving a strong central heroic plot-line) goes far beyond Tasso's useful generalization that the factual historical matter in an epic should be kept brief, remote in time and unfamiliar in *mores*, so as both to remove the possibility of any inadvertent errors in historical detail and to leave, as Phillips said, ample scope for feigning in the fictive-historical parts.[31] No such better subject could be found for Milton's purpose than the enigmatic second and third chapters of Genesis. They constituted the ultimate, archetypal piece of history, yet for Milton's purposes also the most practical. The Creation and Fall of Man represent a "true" story, yet one so cursory and so full of unanswered questions that it leaves the entire background and foreground open to be imaginatively sketched in. The brief Genesis account provided a canvas which Milton could paint elaborately and verisimilarly, a skeleton of history which he could flesh out with his own Idea concerning the nature of man's destiny.

It is apparent that Milton had Tasso specifically in mind throughout the important discussion of poetry and epic in *The Reason of Church-Government*, because the echoes of Tasso there are so explicit and striking. Even if Tasso is to some extent voicing broad commonplaces of his period, it is his voicings of them which we hear echoed in Milton's treatise, and which continue to resonate into the discussions of poetry and epic within *Paradise Lost*.[32] Thus, as to the nature and character of the best epic hero, Milton ponders in *The Reason of Church-Government*, whether "as *Tasso* gave to a Prince of *Italy* his chois whether he would command him to write of *Godfreys* expedition against the infidels . . . or *Charlemain* against the Lombards; . . . [so Milton might] present the like offer in our own ancient stories". So too Milton might consider what "K.[ing] or Knight before the conquest [Arthur, as Milton at one stage seriously contemplated] might be chosen in whom to lay the *pattern of a Christian Heroe*".[33] Tasso had said virtually the same, also citing Charlemagne and Arthur: "I do not know why anyone who wishes to form *the idea of a perfect knight* should deny him *the commendation of piety and religion*. . . . I would put Charlemagne or Arthur as epic persons far ahead of Theseus or Jason".[34] Milton echoes the Tassonic formulation concerning "the idea of a perfect knight" again in *An Apology [for] Smectymnuus* (among other places): the poet, like his own epic hero, should be a "*patterne* of the best and honourablest things".[35] Again, Tasso's remarks about "kindl[ing] the souls of our knights much more with the example of the faithful than with that of infidels", and that "epic illustriousness is based [not only] on lofty military valour and the magnanimous resolve to die, [but also] on piety, religion, and deeds alight with these virtues, proper to epic",[36] surely find specific echoes in *The Reason of Church-Government* and in *Of Reformation*, as well as in the values expressed in the Invocation to Book IX of *Paradise Lost*.[37]

A further, crucial parallel is this. Discussing "the argument of the epic poem [which is to] be drawn . . . from true history and a religion that is not false", Tasso had distinguished between two sorts of sacred material: "histories and other writings may be sacred or not sacred, and among the sacred some have more and some have less authority. . . . The poet had better not touch histories of the first type"—that is, those writings which

Tasso had termed "ecclesiastical and spiritual".[38] These statements accord with Milton's differing treatments of material fictively amplified from Genesis, and material taken directly from the Gospels, as used in Books XI and XII of *Paradise Lost*. The account of Jesus' life and ministry at the end of Milton's poem is treated in what amounts to verse paraphrase; no "feigning" is to be found there. The actual events and most of the words of key doctrinal passages in Genesis 2 and 3 also are preserved more or less intact in various places in Books I-X of *Paradise Lost*—as if to maintain their doctrinal element in its purity. The Old Testament, although containing the important doctrines of the Creation and Original Sin, was not in the Christian view considered to be throughout its entirety in the same category of sacredness as the Gospels. Parts of the Old Testament Milton regards as historical, yet susceptible to typological figuration or other kinds of allegorization;[39] while the enigmatic brevity of Genesis, like certain other biblical stories, seems to invite fictive amplifications with moral or spiritual undertones. Milton, bolder than Tasso, does use "ecclesiastical or spiritual" material (to wit, doctrinal passages from both Old and New Testaments); but he uses it in such a way as to distance it from his own fiction, thus maintaining Tasso's distinction.

It is an historical curiosity that, given all he took from Tasso's directives on the Christian epic, Milton as a Protestant could nonetheless set his projected epic apart as being the only "Christian" effort among all that "the greatest and choycest wits of *Athens, Rome, or modern Italy*, and those Hebrews of old" had achieved.[40] Notwithstanding this anti-Romish gesture, the entire context and content of that important discussion of the "diffuse" epic in *The Reason of Church-Government* could not more clearly acknowledge Milton's debt to Tasso. Milton names Tasso twice, placing him next to Homer and Virgil; he alludes to and echoes the *Discorsi del poema eroico;* and even in this same context includes a literary-biographical anecdote about *Tasso* ("As *Tasso* gave to a Prince of *Italy* his chois . . ."). I have already indicated the various circumstantial evidence suggesting that Milton knew Tasso's critical theories, and not only in this instance. Not only the two sets of *Discorsi*, but Tasso's Letters and "Allegoria", as well as other dialogues and discourses exploring the practical implications for epic of "continued allegory", were long since published and famous. The "Allegoria" was itself included in the English translation of Fairfax's *Jerusalem Delivered*, with which Milton was directly familiar and from which he borrowed many memorable metaphors, lines and phrases. Inevitably, Tasso's writings would have been among those critical documents discussed publicly in academies or privately with Manso when Milton visited Italy.

Whatever the truth of the historical connections between Milton and Tasso, it is apparent that in *Paradise Lost* Milton, with the assurance which can come only from the confidence that someone else has already solved the logistical problems, follows that complex set of interrelated formulae connecting history, the romance-fabulous and allegory which we can glean from Tasso's laborious critical writings and his comments on his own experiments with allegory while composing the *Gerusalemme*. In the Letters and a number of short prose treatises, Tasso showed how it was possible to reconcile within the outline of a scanty but complete historical plot various heterogeneous or even seemingly contradictory kinds of fictive materials, shaping them all into a coherent epic-allegorical structure and bringing all the diverse parts into a thematic unity through the focus of the underlying Idea. This conception was expressed in the famous passage from the *Discorsi del poema eroico*, earlier cited, which has been said to contain the "potential" for allegory.[41] The passage clearly must have that potential, given the distinction which it draws between "necessity" (probability) and "verisimilitude" (inner truth, or allegory, in Tasso's developed understanding). That passage may now be quoted in full: "Yet the poem that contains so great a variety of matters none the less should be one, one in form and soul; and all these things should be so combined that each concerns the other, corresponds to the other, *and so depends on the other necessarily or verisimilarly* that removing any one part or changing its place would destroy the whole. And if that is true, the art of composing a poem resembles the plan [*ragione:* rational scheme, law, or proportion] of the universe, which is composed of contraries, as that of music is".[42] This passage has sometimes been loosely read as simply a justification of romance variety in epic. It is more than that. Tasso's description here of an epic poem of mixed form, containing both romance-allegorical elements ("verisimilarly" connected) and causal plot ("necessary" dependencies), hence resembling a composition of contraries in music or a *harmony* of unlike parts, none of which is expendable but rather all combining in a planned unity of form (a narrative structure from which nothing can be removed) and of thought (intellectual "plan" and "proportion": the Idea), analogously to the divine order and design in the variegated universe, offers a novel and striking conception which provides an aesthetic rationale for Milton's own mixed or "diffuse" epic mode.

To turn to technical details, Tasso had prescribed the use of a not too recent, brief piece of history, but one of Christian and heroic significance. In the fictive amplification of such material there remains "ample room for feigning". Thus the main plot itself may be made to carry an allegory, through the plausible but not strictly historical superadded detail (which forms in fact the bulk of Tasso's story, as of Milton's). However, as Tasso added in his Letters, not every last detail need fit the allegory: "nuts and bolts" are needed in any narrative. Such narrative allegory is quite distinct from any moral values merely exemplified in the actions and characters of the protagonists. And the marvellous, embodied in the fantastic or supernatural parts or "Episodes", can also be meaningfully stitched into the main allegorical Idea underlying the narrative, showing through its magical character the elusive inner psychological obstacles to virtue, hidden adversaries more potent than any encountered externally.

The above "rules" are those by which we may measure Milton's "true epic poem". In the many-dimensioned action of *Paradise Lost*, also, we see the brief piece of true scriptural history, giving away almost nothing as to character or motive in any of the protagonists; the fictive-verisimilar expansion, on the surface largely realistic and plausible, "explaining" the Fall in religious terms, and perhaps "demonstrating" morality, but also more covertly suggesting certain hidden internal impediments to virtue in the disharmony between man and woman, which reflects the disorders within each soul; and the cryptic allegorical episodes, fantastic or supernatural, in ulterior ways playing meaningfully against the main narrative line and themes. In *Paradise Lost* Satan, offering temptations both sensuous and intellectual, not unlike Tasso's Armida and Ismen, bridges both or indeed several levels, being seen now in a wholly realistic light, now ambiguously, now producing "enchantments". Satan's overt participation in allegorical episodes and his many metamorphoses are *more* fantastic even than Tasso's or Spenser's, although some of his transformations draw an authority of a kind from the serpent disguise in Genesis. On the other hand, whereas in Tasso's plot magical episodes directly affect the principal action, in *Paradise Lost* a greater degree of neoclassical restraint may be perceived as to matters of "fables", "allegories" and "machines", as was to be advocated by Le Bossu. Milton pushes overt allegory more into the background of his plot, and he keeps his verisimilar action well in the foreground, so that not only are the connections between the two strands more obscure but the presence of allegory in the verisimilar main plot is also more hidden. Thus Milton to a degree aligns his theoretical model of epic with contemporary neoclassicism, while yet drawing heavily from the late sixteenth-century Italian model.

Le Bossu advocated several methods of making "machines" more "credible", and we may notice that whereas Tasso makes no effort to rationalize the storm raised in the Woods by demons or the enchantments of Armida's palace, many of Satan's most fantastic activities are given a plausible veneer. Thus, his journey through the warring elements of Chaos, "with difficulty and labour hard" (II.1021), his journey through the solar universe, his well-timed magical reincarnations in Eden, his engineering works in Pandemonium and his private arms race are all conducted with such an air of verisimilitude, such a wealth of detail analogous to our own experience of arduous adventure, voyages of discovery, or the familiar processes of industry and war, that the reader tends to forget that all this is not "real". He may forget, that is, until he is drawn up short by the spectacle of Satan "suitably shrunken, enlarged, or otherwise transformed", then "freez[ing] into emblematic fixity",[43] or by the extraordinary appearances on the scene through "connatural force" (X.246) of Sin and Death. Or again, the reader may be left baffled by some unexplained, seemingly unrelated emblem, seen usually by Satan—interestingly, never by Adam or Eve—such as the Golden Stairs, God's Golden Scales,[44] or the Limbo. Or he may be left in a state of suspended understanding by one of those numerous enigmatic or disturbing comparisons or similes in which the poem abounds, as in the likening of Eden's garden to dubious classical paradises in Book IV (268-85). Certain other similes, comparisons which verge on the "marvellous", such as those describing Satan's multiple metamorphoses into (or only *as if* into?) various animals when approaching Paradise in Book IV (401-8), or the devils described as diminished (or only *as if* diminished?) into elves or pygmies (I.779-90), seem with almost deliberate provocativeness to blur the philosophical boundaries between "truth" and "fiction" (difficult enough to define in the Italian critical tradition). Thus in *Paradise Lost* the overt allegory, the marvels, can become even more "mysterious", more elusive, than in Tasso. In these similes, which hang suspended between real incident and metaphor, we may sometimes see traces of Spenserian evasiveness. But Milton's evasive blurring of the boundaries between allegory and metaphor may in part also represent his own neoclassical modulation of both Spenser and Tasso. Is there an allegorical content in the instances cited above, or is there not? The doubt in the one kind of case helps to screen Milton's intentions elsewhere in other, disconcertingly overt uses of allegory in other places.

All such extraordinary allegorical events and tropes Milton has set into the "brief history" of Genesis, the "letter" of which is yet also faithfully followed and kept carefully apart from the poet's verisimilar expansions of Scripture and the interspersed *meraviglie*. Milton achieves this integrity by attaching to the more strictly biblical materials markedly different modes of poetic discourse, such as the "plain" speech of his paraphrases of the Bible, or the still barer sinews of doctrine or theological argument, or the quasi-Gospel narration of Michael's accounts in the final Books. Such instances permit of no philosophical blurring as to the nature of "truth". Tasso not dissimilarly had made use of "plain truth" in the heavenly exhortations by the Archangels introduced into his epic. Thus, although Milton cited Spenser's epic as his "original", we may come to feel that much of Spenser's influence on *Paradise Lost* lies beneath the verbal surface, while the actual shape of Milton's epic has been directed much more by Tasso. Milton's epic incorporates a more striking mixture even than Tasso's of historicity with romance allegory. Milton's epic harks back to the advanced late sixteenth-century continental model of the allegorical epic disguised as true history—the Tassonic epic with a Moral or Idea expressing itself via the plausible fiction, and also through fantastic fictive modes, though in Milton's case the latter are more discreetly managed.

THIRTEEN

Allegory and "Idea" in *Paradise Lost*

The shared fundamental conception of a hidden Idea underlying the epic narrative is that which links Milton most surely with the humanist tradition of allegorical epic. From Boccaccio to Sidney and Tasso to Milton, through the Italian, French and into the English neoclassical traditions, the argument or assumption continued that epic (or indeed all poetry) expresses some anterior Idea, an abstract intellectual concept which is more than simply the poem's preconceived aesthetic design or its surface "moral". The conviction continued that such an intention or master plan was, as Tasso had said, the soul of the epic ("Imitation" of external reality being merely the outward dress of the Idea), and that such an Idea, communicated by means of certain shadowed or enigmatic or else fantastic modes of expression, modes either rhetorical or narrative, was synonymous with epic allegory properly understood. In the humanist tradition such an Idea essentially concerned, as Tasso said, the moral life of Man. That Milton did understand "Idea" in this abstract sense, exactly analogously to Le Bossu's notion of the epic as built on the "Platform" or "Foundation" "of the truth signified",[1] as well as in various other Platonic senses such as that of "forms" or "essences", has been clearly established by Irene Samuel from Milton's various uses of the word, "idea", in his prose and verse, of which the most important are his usages in *Of Education* and *Of Christian Doctrine*.[2]

We may look back at some comparable uses of "Idea" in Milton's epic predecessors. Du Bartas (or his translator, Joshua Sylvester) similarly employs "idea" in the sense of divine "plan" in his *Divine Weeks:* "It may be also, that he meditated / The Worlds *Idea*, yer it was Created".[3] Tasso also does so, more philosophically, in famous passages in his two most important treatises, the *Giudizio* and the *Discorsi del poema eroico*. In the first he compares his Crusaders' goal of attaining the earthly Jerusalem (allegorically the quest for perfection) to *"the idea of that celestial Jerusalem"*,[4] and in the second, he compares the poet to "a maker of images in the fashion of a speaking painter [that is, a painter who conveys an abstract idea in his painting], and in that is like the divine theologian who forms images and commands them to be. . . . the poet is almost the same as the theologian and the dialectician".[5] The partial likening of the poet to "the divine theologian", or again to "the theologian and the dialectician", suggests that the epic poet's speaking image carries a specific intellectual argument or even a mystical content; it is what Tasso elsewhere terms "the mystical image" which can "perfect".

In *Paradise Lost* Milton, just as du Bartas and Tasso had, validates the abstract centre to his own poem (his "great Argument")[6] by analogy with that Divine Idea which realized itself not only in the finished artifact of the Creation but in the providential meaning with which that Creation was invested. The crucial sentence is to be found in *Of Christian Doctrine:* "For the *foreknowledge of God* is nothing but the *wisdom of God, under another name, or that idea of every thing, which he had in his mind* . . . before he decreed anything".[7] God's "foreknowledge" refers to divine history, and not just to the physical Creation at its inception. When therefore in *Paradise Lost* (VII.556-57) God looks at the Creation and sees it, "how good, how faire, / Answering his *great Idea*", he implicitly sees it not only aesthetically, in its pristine beauty and physical fairness, a masterpiece of design, but as intellectually meaningful—invested with the hidden, providential significance for the future race of man which he has built into it. Similarly the poet, regarding his own handiwork.

Plot, Subject and "Platform": Justifying God

We must now consider what may be the exact nature of that crucial Idea which, as I have suggested, underlies Milton's allegorical epic. The presence of an underlying allegorical conception need in no way be restrictive to the comprehensiveness of Milton's poem, any more than it is narrowing to his artistry. Allegory in his epic cooperates with elements of factual "history" and with plain and many other special forms of discourse. Further, whether allegory is narrow or large, restrictive or liberating, depends on the range of its expressive artistry and on the universality of the Idea conceived. Milton's Idea, his oblique intention, that which I take to be at the core of his poem, is broad in scope. It lies without doubt in the "Justification" of the ways of God which the poet himself sets out as the poem's *raison d'être*, taking pains to outline its ensuing development, in broad and in its parts, at the very beginning of his poem. The first thirty-five or forty lines of *Paradise Lost* compactly outline the scope of Milton's material and state in overt terms his intellectual conception underlying *Paradise Lost*—a conception which will subsequently be developed in covert terms also.

The continental tradition is helpful here, in showing that we have to distinguish Milton's purpose, "Idea" or allegory (the "Ground-work" or "Platform" of his action, in the slightly later terminology of Le Bossu), from both his "Subject" (strictly, the Fall of Man) and his "Action" (the revenge of Satan upon Man). (Milton's phrase, "this great Argument", hints at his abstract conception, even though the word "Argument" traditionally has oratorical connotations too.)[8] In the same way that Le Bossu identified the psychological mainspring of the "Action" or plot of the *Odyssey* as the revenge which Odysseus takes upon the suitors,[9] Milton identifies the mainspring of his own action as Satan's revenge: "Th' infernal Serpent; hee it was, whose guile / Stirrd up with Envy and Revenge, deceiv'd / The Mother of Mankinde" (I.34-36). This is the kernel of Milton's action or *plot*, as he himself presents it, originating in a faithfully recorded very brief piece of history, swift and inevitable in its development and denouement. The facts of this history—its beginning, middle and end—"happened"; but the details which flesh it out did not necessarily happen, or not in the way Milton presents them as having happened. So we can distinguish the revenge "action" from the "fable" or fictive aspect of Milton's poem. Milton can then manipulate the fictive part for further purposes, in exemplary and also in more oblique didactic fashion, besides using the fiction verisimilarly to create a general air of plausibility in the events leading up to the Fall.

The action of the plot of *Paradise Lost*, then, is only a very thin line within its fictive development. The actual subject-matter (in the sense that we would ourselves give to that term), again, is not completely synonymous with the fictive amplification of the plot, that is, with the reconstructed Genesis Fall story. So much also is indicated in Milton's "preface" or his first "Invocation" ("invocation" being a term not used by Milton himself). His actual *subject-matter* is there described as falling into three parts, swelling over and around, or in time behind and forward from, the fictive-verisimilar, expanded Fall story. Milton's preface says (I.1-6) that his poem will include in its scope the origins of human history, that is, human fallen history, starting with the "Fruit / Of that Forbidd'n Tree", but the ensuing allusions to Moses and the engendering Spirit (lines 6-8; 19-22) carry us both forward to God's promise to Man and backward to the antecedent Creation (lines 9-10), so preparing us for Book VII which shows the creation of the Universe, and Books XI-XII which record the promise of Jesus to mankind. The poem will also include all the pangs of "mortal" life as we know it, "Death" and "woe" and "loss"—"loss of *Eden*" becoming in line three the inherited loss of all that we love, life included, "*our* woe". It will include failure and error (not yet in *Paradise Lost* termed "sin"), both of which are to become permanent features of human life—"Mans *First* Disobedience" implying an unending succession of acts of disobedience embracing all possible forms of future errant behaviour.[10] And Milton's subject-matter will cover a time-span running not just over the day of the

Fall embraced by the neoclassical plot-line, nor even over those actions in Heaven which directly lead up to it (presented retrospectively in two "true Episodes", as defined by Le Bossu or Johnson). Rather, the subject-matter will stretch out over the whole of recorded time: "*till* one greater Man / Restore us" (lines 4-5). Milton's "subject" in its large sense stops there: it looks past Adam, past Moses, "great" men, up to and as far as but not (within the terms of the fiction) directly at Christ in His rôle of Redeemer and act of Redemption. The historical life of Jesus is given toward the end of Book XII in a simple summary account in unembellished style reminiscent of the Gospels—as if to make the point that this "true history" stands away from the main fictive part of the poem. And the life of Jesus has not yet taken place, of course, although his mission is foreshadowed in certain details of the poem.

Milton's larger "subject" also is not, in any simple sense, purely doctrinally instructive or exemplary. This is a common misunderstanding, for even the theology in the poem is itself projected (and even in the Heavenly pronouncements) in a variety of non-obvious, oblique ways, as well as through plain statement. The true subject is humanly huge: man's total life, which includes but is not confined to theological beliefs and religious commitments. This largeness is in accord with the traditional encyclopaedic emphasis in epic and with the characteristic emphases of Renaissance epic allegory, which tend to stress the ethical and humane aspects of man's life, set within an acknowledged framework of religion. What Milton's *subject* for heroic song concerns most immediately, to be conveyed through both the rich poetic texture of the background and through the narrative foreground, as also through more shadowed allegorical discourse, is what Tasso expressed as the proper concern of heroical poetry: the whole *"Life of Man"*.[11] Or as Milton otherwise put it in *Areopagitica*, "the state of man *as [it] now is"*—imperfect, full of potential, fallible, rich.[12] Mythical allusions, simile, verbal reminiscence and other forms of quiet intimation in the poetic subtext, along with the more self-conscious devices of literary allegory such as personification and emblem, can converge with verisimilar narrative and shadowed secondary narrative in the complex mimesis which can best render such a huge variety of considerations. And it is because of the coherent poetic network of subdued secondary associations plus overt allegory, holding together, across the vast expanses of the poem's time scale and plot, such diverse considerations and various levels of experience as Milton undertakes to project, that we can speak of Milton's total enterprise as *allegorical:* allegorical in artistry as well as in purpose. The history of allegory shows that allegorical form and Idea run together, and that successful allegory in poetry rapidly becomes total or "global" metaphor.

In Milton's vast subject, not only the external dress or circumstances of man's life are to be included (Tasso's materials of "Imitation"). Examples of these in *Paradise Lost* are the kinds of recognisably seventeenth-century public circumstances of politics and war in Books I-II, linking with human history as shown in Books XI-XII; or the kinds of domestic circumstances, archetypally rendered, shown in Books IV, V, VIII, IX and X. More particularly, Milton like Tasso will concern himself also with the passional and mental or inner bearings of man's life. Whereas Imitation "lively set[s] before our corporeal eyes the things represented", Allegory is "the glass and figure of Human Life" (mystical figure, showing the viewer to himself, the phrase evoking St. Paul's *aenigma* or allegory). Allegory "respecteth the passions, the opinions and customs . . . principally in their being [essence] hidden and inward; and more obscurely doth express them with notes . . . mystical".[13] Milton in *The Reason of Church-Government* similarly had indicated his own fascination with the hidden aspects of man's nature, the "wily suttleties and refluxes of mans thoughts from within", material suited equally to tragedy or epic, and which after some experimentation with other forms, he worked up into epic form. Such psychological material in tragedy does not require the use of allegory, but epic is more amenable to allegorical treatment.

In the second part of his invocatory preface to *Paradise Lost* (and now *intention* begins to shape itself as something beyond both plot and subject matter), Milton probes the motives for an act which bears all the earmarks of perversity: "say first *what cause* / Mov'd our Grand Parents in that happy State, / . . . *to fall off* . . . / *For one restraint*, Lords of the World besides?" (28-32). As the poem develops, this initial question will expand into a wide-ranging examination of the sources and nature and workings of "perversity", or evil. (In *Of Christian Doctrine* evil is defined as "*deviation* [*obliquitas*]": a falling off, as it were, "from the line of right".)[14] In *Paradise Lost* such "deviation" or "perversity", understood by Milton as a turning back, backsliding, a "falling off", is to be explored in the individual human mind in Adam and Eve, in human history, in Satan's and the angels' rebellion, and in the cosmic frame. (The actual word "perverse" will recur in various grammatical forms many times, including instances in Books II.625, 1030; VI.562, 706; IX.405; XI.701). Frequently also the same idea is signified by the use of other words physically (and symbolically) indicating deviance, such as "transverse", "awry", "[a]thwart" (as in Books III.488 and X.703, 1075). Deviation is, equally, explored via individual descriptive amplifications which sometimes verge on the allegorical, or in the kinds of chains of metaphorical episodes which Le Bossu cited as carrying allegory; an example is seen in the pushing askew of the Earth's axis in Book X, which is the culmination of a whole series of earlier images in the poem suggesting reversion to primal physical disorder. Also, in harmony with Le Bossu's prescription, deviation is shown in the direct "Allegories" taking the form of magical supernatural "Episodes" or "Machines". The problem of perversity or "deviance", the apparent reversal of the goodness and fairness of

God's first creative "Idea", first suggested in the opening lines of the poem, will thus become a leading part of Milton's allegorical Idea.

So we see three stages or phases, expressed sequentially in Milton's preface and the ensuing lines, and developing into a more formal statement of intellectual design. There is the initial mention of the primal act of disobedience under Satan's revengeful influence, and its direct consequences: that is the plot or the "action". There is the whole material of fallen and to us highly familiar human life adumbrated, "death" and "woe" and "loss", which will be dramatically represented or poetically or allegorically intimated in endless ways—man's life and history seen as set within the divine frame, from "the Beginning" and "till" its end, dimly foreseen in time. And there is the poet's own intellectual inquiry into the origins, causes and ultimate *meaning* of error, deviation, or evil, in man's mind and in nature—that almost incredulous question, "what cause"? What cause could have moved man, so blessed, "to fall off . . . / *For one restraint*, Lords of the World besides?" (I.30-32). It is in his own form of answer to this question, worked out over the whole course of the poem, that we must seek Milton's allegorical purpose or hidden Plan. The rapid transition in the Invocation itself from searching question to rather pat answer (*"Th' infernal Serpent; hee it was"*, I.34), setting aside the thought of Adam's blame, as it were, displacing it all onto one external cause, starts the plot rolling but it provides an unsatisfactory answer to that first incredulous question. The whole poem must provide the answer, at every level of relevance. The first verse paragraph setting out the scope of Milton's Plan concludes (at lines 25 to 26) with a terse statement of epic intention: the poet will first "assert", then he will "justifie", Providence (otherwise defined as "the wayes of God to men")—two approaches, evidently not the same. We are left to conjecture just what these two different terms may mean; the methods of their artistic realization in the poem are left unexplained.

That the humane as well as the theological justification of Providence ("justify the ways of God as perceived by *men*"), and so the justification of the existence of evil, is Milton's broad poetic and intellectual design throughout *Paradise Lost,* his Idea in fact, can hardly be doubted, in view of the carefully differentiated, two-pronged declaration concluding his preface. Many critics have of course felt in a general sort of way that Milton's "Justification" is his main purpose.[15] But the sense in which I read Milton's Idea is specific: namely, as equal to the poem's underlying allegory, as Le Bossu or Tasso understood that term. The theme of Providence concludes the opening Invocation and prefaces the commencement of the action. It also concludes the poem's last lines—Providence embracing the whole poem, as it does men's lives. The assistance which Milton invokes to his great Argument is that of Urania, "Sister" to Wisdom ("Wisdom" being another way of speaking of God's Providence), and iconographically

closely associated with Providence in both *Paradise Lost* and earlier visual
and literary traditions.[16] Milton's immediate problem is to "justify" this
Providence, to show all its labyrinthine workings as good in the human
and immediate context, as well as at the distant end of time. This is a task
which cannot adequately be fulfilled by any merely exemplary demonstra-
tion, any short-term didactic lesson on the disadvantages of disobedience
and the advantages of obedience, or even by the longer-term promise of
Christian reward. The Johnsonian religious message on its own leaves too
many human questions unanswered. Justifying God's methods to men
(not the same as God's Justification of man through Christ) involves a
slower and deeper process of mental and emotional conviction, artistically
best expressed in shadowed "notes mystical" rather than in direct ways.
The reader (like the protagonists) must be persuaded of God's beneficence
not only in the future life but in this life; the "justifying" of God's actions in
ways which humans can accept rationally must precede in temporal time
(and in the poem does precede) the Justification of man *by* God. It cannot be
the task of the present study to do more than suggest the allegorized
workings of Milton's hidden ways to his readers. But the theory of the
allegorical epic can lead us toward establishing, through background,
context and internal evidence, the presence of an allegorical "Ground-
work" and poetic in *Paradise Lost*; it can help us to excavate the infrastruc-
ture of that poetic and Plan, laying bare their general outlines as embedded
in the narrative, descriptions and language, and exposing the problematics
involved. To the last (the problems involved for the poet in justifying God's
Providence) we may now briefly turn.

The Problem of the Justice of God

In this section we shall consider several abstract themes and problems
which interlace in the intellectual fabric of *Paradise Lost* as parts of Milton's
general design of justifying God's ways, and which individually are sub-
jected to poetic-allegorical development in various of the modes illustrated
earlier. Here, however, we shall consider these themes or problems in their
abstract character.

Milton's task of justifying God's ways is made more difficult by the
Calvinist contention that God's Will is separable from his Reason in his
treatment of man, and that original sin stands as a "prior decree". The
Calvinist stance is tantamount to a belief that God's Wisdom is equivalent
simply to his foreknowledge and therefore to his intention or will that man
shall fall, a few to be redeemed and others not. Milton disputes this view in
Paradise Lost, in the heavenly colloquies in Books III and X, in *Areopagitica*,
and in *Of Christian Doctrine* at length (Book I, chapters iii-iv). One of his
most crucial statements pertaining to the issue of free will is the following,

in which, as in *Paradise Lost*, he refuses to equate God's prescience with his naked will or prior decree, making God's foreknowledge instead coequal and simultaneous with His grand design of a beneficent Providence: "That the will of God is the first cause of all things is not intended to be denied, but his prescience and wisdom must not be separated from his will, *much less considered as subsequent to the latter* in point of time".[17] Put another way (in a passage cited earlier): "the foreknowledge of God is nothing but the wisdom of God, under another name, or that idea of every thing, which he had in his mind . . . before he decreed anything".[18] God's Providence stands anterior to any of his decrees. His disposal of things follows his Wisdom, not the other way round; and his Wisdom coincides with "*that idea of every thing,* which he had in his mind . . . *before* he decreed anything". Like Milton's poem, God's Creation and subsequent disposal of events answers to his foreconceit, to "his great Idea".

For Milton it follows that to "justify" God's ways must be bound up with convincing the reader (represented in Adam) not only of the ultimate goodness of God, in the face of apparent universal deviance, but even further, of the present goodness of Providence, which acts not *in despite* of the freedom of man's aberrant will, but indeed expresses itself *through* that very freedom. Man is not a puppet in the hands of a capricious Deity who hands out rewards or penalties at random. Justifying God's ways is thus inextricably bound up with the necessity to convince the reader not only that man's will is integrally free, but that such freedom can continue even after the Fall to operate in man's better interests. This conviction of the continuing freedom of man's will forms one of the cornerstones of the poem's intellectual design, and it is inextricably bound up with the poem's defence of God's ways. This conviction stands behind *Paradise Lost* as a major part of its anterior conception, in the same way that the Deity's intellectual plan and good providential design stand anterior to His Creation, stand behind the "new created World / . . . how good, how faire, / *Answering* his *great Idea*" (VII.554-57). It is no accident that Milton echoes this phrase when later discussing his own epic intention and style—a form or style which will be "answerable" to his "higher Argument" (IX.20,42). The parallel phrase at the end of the poet's opening peroration in Book I, analogously, expressed the wish that he might rise "to the highth of this *great Argument*" concerning "Eternal Providence" (I.24-25). "Idea" for God becomes "Argument" for the poet, each realized in a creative design. As the informing Idea in both cases, each intellectual design is a form of allegory. God uses "deeds as words" or uses history prefiguratively and providentially to unfold his meaning; men and the poet have to use words and the image of a plot.

It must be stressed again—Milton himself draws the distinction—that to *justify* Providence, humanly speaking, in the poem ("justifie [to men] the wayes of God") is not at all the same thing as merely to *assert* it (to "assert

Eternal Providence"). Indeed, contrary modes are implied. Dogmatic "assertion" might involve theological arguments and philosophical demonstrations in attempted proofs of itself—if, indeed, "proofs" are required at all; but to "justify" for Milton implies other means, since, as is evident in the well-known passage in *Of Education,* Milton *opposes* the means and effects of poetry to the operations of logic and dialectic.[19] To "justify" (*in poetry* taking the word as standing in opposition to "assert") means to persuade and *convince,* emotionally as well as rationally. God's *assertion* in Book III (117-18) that "if I foreknew, / Foreknowledge had no influence on thir fault" remains an assertion. It asserts man's active responsibility for his own bad choices and bad deeds, yet seems to take the first origin of these out of his own hands, and so remains bewildering ontologically to everybody, in the plot as well as in the hard nut of doctrine. (Hence Satan's and Adam's bewilderment over God's ways in Books I [637-42] and X [743-52] is genuine; God has "concealed" His true powers from Satan and allowed Satan to think himself powerful; He has created Adam man without Adam's knowledge or wish; they did not know beforehand the rules of the game they are made to play.) What justice or sense can there be in creating man so that he is able to will his own fall, in then exposing him to temptation, and finally in punishing him and his descendants forever with *more* sin, all for an original sin the proclivity to which or at least the capability of which (according to what God seems to say in the speech which opens the action of Book III) was ingrained in the very nature which God himself created? These questions lie at the core of the poem, asked by the protagonists again and again, and unsatisfactorily answered by Raphael's injunctions to "take heed", "beware", "stand fast" (VIII.635-40), or not completely answered for that matter even by Michael's "hope no higher" and his specifically religious instructions (XII.575-85). Not even the highly exemplary demonstrations of much wrongdoing and a few good deeds in the "historical" accounts or visions given by either archangel in Books V to VI or XI to XII can, I think, wholly allay such human doubts.

How then is Milton's defence of Providence and the apparent harshness of the ways of God to man to be made good, in the face of his story's tragic outcome, the bleakly unexplained facts of Genesis, and the painful intellectual questioning within the poem in despite of its Christian moral? Adam may stand well "instructed" by divine "prediction" at the end of Book XII (557, 553); but a great deal has had to come to pass in the human context before this compliance, this point at which faith takes over, can be reached. Something more constructive must arise out of the poem's long, bad human experience than the flat exemplificatory *lesson* of disobedience, punishment and repentance which Dr. Johnson drew from a poem which, if really as he had presented it, would today remain largely unread. There must be something a little more supportive for Adam as he wanders out into human history, and more "answerable" to the reader, if that negative undertow of fallen human experience so prominent in *Paradise Lost* is to find its place in the beneficent scheme of things alleged to exist, and if the poem's doubts and questions about the conditions and the very nature and meaning of human existence are to be resolved.

Milton's entire enterprise of justifying Providence is, therefore, inextricably tied up with the whole question of God's justice to man in this life. I would suggest that the *present* justification of that justice becomes Milton's leading conception in *Paradise Lost,* and that this conception lies at the root of the poem's intellectual design, just as it forms the foundation of the poem's theological assertions. It is the pivotal question on which all the other ethical issues of the poem must depend. And it is bound up, as I have already indicated, with Milton's own conviction of the liberty of the will as a gift, a gift held perpetually for good as well as for evil, never wholly lost, or if lost, then by more than a little part restored. There can be little doubt that by "justifie *the wayes of God to men*", Milton means exactly that: to justify God's behaviour to men, as reflected in the conditions of man's existence on earth. The poet has to make it be seen and felt (even beyond the divine proofs and revelatory assertions of dogma) that God is reasonable and fair in His present dealings with men, and to persuade of this in humanly comprehensible terms. God has to be *seen* to be fair, in the same way that one would understand another human being to be fair. And God is fair, because he has made Man lastingly free.

These questions are raised and answered in these exact terms in *Of Christian Doctrine.* God's "reason" or his "reasonableness" is correspondent to his creation of "men and angels *reasonable beings,* and therefore *free agents*"; to think otherwise is "unworthy of God" and leaves "the very name of liberty . . . altogether abolished as an unmeaning sound".[20] Nor is liberty unreasonably abolished with the Fall: "When . . . God determined to restore mankind, he also without doubt decreed *that the liberty of will which they had lost should be at least partially regained, which was but reasonable*".[21] Similarly in the poem. The "reasonableness"—sometimes not immediately obvious—of God's dealings with men and of the "terms" on which he created them (Adam's unpleasantly legalistic word at X.751, "Thy terms too hard") is not only *asserted,* as at the poem's opening and again in the various often paradoxical divine pronouncements in Books III and X, not only debated and discussed in logical human terms in Books II, IV, V and X by the fallen angels, Satan, Raphael and Adam, not only presented dramatically, but further still, the idea of God's reasonableness, his fairness, as manifested in his gift of free will with its attendant obligations on man and the difficult privilege of self-responsibility and self-correction, is absorbed into the very poetic texture, language and allegorical constructs of the poem—since Milton knows well that although logic is more fine and subtle, poetry is more sensuous and moving to the passions. The specific allegorical development of this one motif of "free

will", or "choice", may be traced out in the poem in multiple ways and
patterns,[22] similar to those earlier illustrated in association with the themes
of "Error" or "Death".

In a very large variety of structural and aesthetic ways the poem
comes to enact its large providential justificatory design, becoming its
own total metaphor or one vast allegorical "intendment". Particularly
through constant self-reversals in statement, narrative sequence, situa-
tion, cosmic setting, incident or description, as well as through other
shadowed devices in number and kind too numerous and detailed to
enumerate here, the poem (as well as assertively stating) hints, shows,
figures forth, or otherwise leads us to feel how God's plan for the creation
is continually to reverse that first perverse "falling off" and to turn evil
back to good—good apprehended in human terms, as well as promised
through divine redemption. It has often been observed that the poem's
texture constantly prognosticates Fall. But the opposite is equally true; its
texture also constantly prognosticates recovery. Justification of God's jus-
tice implies a continuous process of reversals throughout time, the con-
stant bringing of good out of deviance or evil. This grand reciprocal
pattern, translating abstract conception into poetic design, forms the main
platform of Milton's providential Idea, his "Moral", Allegory or Ground-
work, on which hang all the related themes of the poem and the main
design itself of the poem.

"Asserting" Providence

The "assertion" of God's justice through statement and counter-statement
provides an intellectual framework which itself takes on the character of a
structural patterning of Milton's Idea. Dogma, often "asserted" paradox-
ically by God and at first perceived as incomprehensible or hostile by the
protagonists, punctuates the poem at crucial intervals. It supplies a tran-
scendent statement of the providential design, asseverating the enact-
ments of a beneficent Providence which surprisingly and marvellously
always operates by turning evil into good in the here and now as well as in
the future resolution of history, thus constantly reversing human or cosmic
"deviation". God asserts; Satan (or man) perverts; good is again reas-
serted. The reciprocal assertions by God of man's guilt and by the Son
of man's salvation—balancing counter-assertions, rhetorically counter-
pointed—form one such self-reversing sequence near the beginning of
Book III. Another such sequence concerning reversal and counter-reversal,
deviation and righting, is illustrated in a chain of statements beginning
with Raphael's remarks on the divine Wisdom in Book VII, which empha-
size how the good of creation came originally out of the destruction of the
war in Heaven:

> to him
> Glorie and praise, whose wisdom had ordaind
> *Good out of evil to create,* in stead
> Of Spirits maligne a better Race to bring
> Into thir vacant room.
>   VII.186-90

The providential design had early been recognised by Satan, who sees his destined rôle in a constant attempt to subvert it:

> If then his Providence
> *Out of our evil seek to bring forth good,*
> Our labour must be *to pervert* that end,
> *And out of good still to find means of evil.*
>   I.162-65

In Books IX-X the protagonists, Satan, Eve and Adam, are at first genuinely confused over the apparently inextricable mixing of good and evil, the one unattainable without the other.[23] But in Book XII Adam at last perceives the grand design of God in its full amplitude:

> O goodness infinite, goodness immense!
> That all this *good of evil shall produce,*
> *And evil turn to good;* more wonderful
> Then that which by creation first brought forth
> Light out of darkness!
>   XII.469-73

The rhetorical reversals of Satan's and Adam's lines pattern the underlying reversals of which they speak ("evil . . . to . . . good"; "good . . . to . . . evil"; "good of evil"; "evil turn to good"). Finally, nearer the end of the poem we have Adam's private application of the divine process of reversal and renewal to the personal conduct of his own life:

> ever to observe
> His providence . . . *with good*
> *Still overcoming evil,* and by small
> Accomplishing great things, by things deemd weak
> *Subverting* worldly strong.
>   XII.563-68

"Assert", "pervert", "subvert": the rhyming words across the whole poem also rhetorically pattern the Idea (recalling such Spenserian word-chains as the "impair-repair" sequence in Book I of *The Faerie Queene*). But each of Milton's carefully aligned statements above carries a slightly different value. The first lines quoted refer to God's providential plan in its unknowable and inexhaustible plenitude. The second lines refer to Satan's attempted evil *perversion* of God's good (evil in its metaphysical origins, coming always out of the materials of good, as is shown graphically in Satan's evil constructions being built out of the crude materials underlying Heaven's floor in Book VI.472-91). A third passage (not quoted), Adam's soliloquy in Book X, in a maze of paradoxes on the theme of how "inexplicable / [God's] Justice seems" (754-55), displays the intellectual confusions attendant on the human attempt to understand the inseparability of good and evil in human life. The fourth passage quoted affords a religious statement of the Felix Culpa, which brings to pass the Redemption—a divine conjunction of evil and good. And the last passage, the speech by Adam in Book XII, in the short part quoted relates to the moral conduct of daily life in a world where man must for the foreseeable future continue to err, yet is continually to be found achieving the betterment of that fallible condition, thus in small measure contributing to the grand paradoxical and redemptive design.

"Justifying" through Allegory

The vast assertions sketched above of a rationally beneficent and humanely just Providence, which constitute the dogmatic foundation of the poem and its intellectual skeleton, constitute at the same time the framework for that "Idea" (the Justification of God's ways) which holds Milton's poem together, providing a *point d'appui* for every one of the poem's numerous subordinate interdependent themes. The paradoxical assertions and counter-assertions serve as the key to the poem's largest narrative or structural patternings, which themselves incorporate and reenact the "reversals" of the providential design (as in light after darkness, in Book III after Books I-II; creation after destruction, in Book VII following the War in Books V-VI). But in the human minutiae of living and for the human protagonists in *Paradise Lost*, who are also the reader, neither the grand assertions nor grand narrative design can entirely suffice. The kinds of human questions raised in the poem concerning the justness of God in making the conditions of life with which we all are faced demand human answers, and not merely one grand ultimate solution at the end of history. Not even the sweeping reversals of the divine process, as recorded in Book XII in the stories from the Old Testament of repeated historical falls, with repeated if isolated renewals (stories themselves foretold in the earlier satanic activities in the poem's self-echoing fabric), however aesthetically or religiously satisfying these patterned reversals may be, could ultimately convince the reader of the satisfactoriness of death, and woe, and loss of Eden. Are we to see *Paradise Lost* as, after all, a tragedy? If not, some human transition toward acceptance must be made, and made probably not only consciously but unconsciously—in the way of poetry, simply, sensuously and passionately—through images, some "mystical", through descriptive details, and through the evocative power of words. In accordance with the broad self-reversing patterns in the poem, good must be *felt* to come out of evil at every major crisis within the narrative, and be seen to do so in the present human state and condition, as well as in the long-term divine scheme.

But since rationally optimistic assertions run so against the dark grain of the Genesis account, run against all the evidence of human history displayed in Books XI-XII, against the doctrine of original sin and the facts of despoliation, deviancy, loss and death which are all foreshadowed, displayed and magnified throughout the poem, a powerful burden is placed on the artistry of *Paradise Lost* simultaneously to *justify* and *persuade* that, on the other part, present good does come out of so much present evil. For if God is to be *justified* in men's eyes, then the plaintive human voices of the fallen world must be heard, and that question must be convincingly answered which Job, Adam and every man at some time has asked, "why was I born?" "Did I request thee, Maker, from my Clay / To mould me Man . . .? / . . . unable to performe / Thy terms too hard" (X.743-51). And without that persuasive justifying of God—namely, Milton's discursive fictive expansion and personal rereading of the historical Genesis story, in the light of an optimistic free-will philosophy of moral endeavour perfected by grace, one which is pleasing to a "reasonable" God—Milton's enterprise would remain an *assertion:* dogma, supported perhaps by example, but unlikely to be transformed into a story of universal emotional conviction.

It is in performing the above tasks of quiet persuasion that the allegorical aspects of Milton's artistry manifest their success. Shadowed discourse and hidden intimations, enigmatic figures or structures, whose meaning unfolds across the total poem, paralleling in poetic space the slow processes in time of the growth of emotional conviction, are ideally suited to convey those many murmurs of human plaints and problems posed, and correspondingly of human consolations rendered and humane resolutions achieved, which through so many secret channels converge like the rivulets of Eden into a powerful underground current flowing strongly through the poem and carrying the reader, along with Adam and Eve, toward acceptance. "Allegory respecteth the passions, the opinions and customs, . . . principally in their being hidden and inward", Tasso had said; it may "more obscurely . . . express them with notes, as a man may say, mystical, such as only the understanders of the nature of things can fully comprehend".[24] Allegory in *Paradise Lost* is able to discover and express obscurely the hidden and inward, the mental or passional, bearings of the events recorded. It can with notes mystical intimate to the thoughtful reader how the faculties of man's mind may be realigned and the passions redirected; it may suggest how human life, as Adam and Eve have bequeathed it to their posterity, continues to be good and hopeful, and capable of renewing itself morally. However often it is proved deviant from good, human life, like the providential design itself, is capable of reversing its deviancies and turning loss and failure into further gain. That awful vision of the World groaning on, "To good malignant, to bad men benigne" (XII.538), held up to Adam at the periphery of the poem, is not something which he could have carried unrelieved into his exile. Such a dark vision, even though cheered by the divine promise of redemption, still requires the countervailing persuasion, born from reiterated evidence within the action and verbal tissue of the poem, that good may continue to come out of evil in the daily round and in one man's span. The conclusion impressed by dogma or dramatic outcome is borne in upon us more powerfully still by the thousand filaments of metaphor, passing into allegorically suggestive artistry and language.

Into such a hopeful proposition as that of his human justification of God, the Idea governing *Paradise Lost*, Milton can incorporate all the traditional humanist and Christian epic matter concerning *Heroic Virtue:* the thesis (following Aristotle) that "virtue" implies a gradual process of formation, is an *acquired* habit born of practice, one strengthened through error and testing and (in the Christian-humanist formulation) only finally "infused by grace". Adam surely is the hero-in-the-making of *Paradise Lost*, and not its failed hero as Dryden alleged; the failed hero, if anyone, is Satan. Like Samson, Adam is "more Heroic" (to use the words of Milton's third Invocation, in Book IX.14) *because* of his suffering and failure; unlike Satan, whose resolve, recorded in Book I (94 ff.), is never to change, Adam allows himself to change. His ethical and moral development within the body of the poem becomes a maturer statement of the true warfaring virtue praised in *Areopagitica*—no longer, with the slightly brash, youthful overconfidence of an Eve in Book IX, sallying out to find her adversary, but more soberly confronting evil in the new knowledge that, as Eve's allegorical dream had intimated in Book V, the enemy lies within.

Within such a moral and spiritual framework. Milton can emphasize those particular humanist themes and persuasions, by no means alien to the entire Protestant tradition, which he made peculiarly his own. Notably, these are his convictions that even fallen man continues to possess a *will free* to determine his own *choices*—if sometimes for bad, then on further occasions for better; the belief also, fundamental to *Paradise Lost* no less than to *Areopagitica*, that man as a moral creature can learn only through *experience*, however superb his innate intellectual equipment may be, and that such experience necessarily (as Spenser emphasized in the old allegorical figure of the *selva*) involves *error*; also the countervailing belief that man may be guided through that all too familiar dark Wood by the leading virtue of "true *temperance*", mediator and guide in all things.[25] It is on such a foundation of strengthened ethical understanding that Adam is able finally to embrace the Christian virtues opened out in Book XII; without this foundation, his declared obedience at the end of the poem would not be a matter of free choice of the best, as Abdiel put it in Book VI (174-81), nor would it be any pleasure to God (III.107), but it would be the mere puppet-like submission to authority repudiated in both the early and late Miltonic view.[26] But these Miltonic themes are far more effective when adumbrated, as they are in the poem, in poetic and indirect ways than they would be if expressed only as direct exemplificatory lessons, moving though the dramatic development of these ideas also is. Milton's poetic rendering of each of these special themes (those picked out above by italics, and other related Miltonic themes and motifs) need to be fully explored in the context of his epic-allegorical methodology and allegorical artistry.

Allegorical Aesthetics in *Paradise Lost*

A clearer understanding of the latent content and the complex aesthetics of Milton's epic undertaking might obviate many of the difficulties which have so often been felt in reading *Paradise Lost*, particularly as regards its mixing of overtly allegorical with verisimilar modes. Allegorical "Episode", for instance, is only one manifestation of epic allegory understood in the broader sense, that is, as a specific cohering Idea with a counterpoint of narrative or metaphorical or linguistic structures patterning the underlying theme over an entire poem. In *Paradise Lost* the epic Idea, allegorical because anterior, abstract and largely shadowed, holds the poem together at all its different levels of brief history, exemplary fiction, verisimilar fiction with allegorical colourings, intricate poetic subtexture of intimation, allusion and ambiguous simile, and flagrantly allegorical episodes involving emblems, personifications, or the like. Toward the execution of an idea of such huge importance as that informing *Paradise Lost*, the justification of God's ways to men—which is to say, the justification of the human condition—all modes of discourse may converge. For if the "Spirit and Conduct of [Dido's] State" and "the Original and Consequences of its differences with *Rome*" could be for Le Bossu the hypothesized allegorical subject of Virgil's epic,[27] why not the human state of man, and its relations and differences with God, of Milton's? Le Bossu's remarks on Virgil seem strangely apt: many will read *Paradise Lost*, or the *Aeneid*, for its story; but learned men will recognise in both something more.

To read the poem in such a way would be, at the very least, a way of reading it entirely at one with the way epic had been understood before and still was understood in Milton's period. It is epic allegory (using the term in its specific sixteenth- and seventeenth-century sense of a prior intellectual intention governing the whole design) which artistically controls the whole complex of forms, modes and devices in Milton's diffuse epic. The Idea, or in Milton's formulation his Justification of God, balances the poem's humane thesis and oblique modes against the stark assertions of scriptural history and bald doctrine, or the "exemplary" demonstrations of sin and punishment. Such ideational allegory in traditional manner constantly signals its presence in *Paradise Lost* through the self-consciously rhetorical effects of allegory understood as rhetorical trope: enigma, surprise, dissonance, reaching into the bizarre and the "absurd"—traditional aesthetic effects of the allegorical trope. Always catching at us by these means are the filaments of the Idea, residual in the cobweb of verbal iterations traced across the poem, threads leading us through their development into larger enigmatic images or other shadowed structures, and thence always back to that Idea or complex of themes at the core, themes dramatized concurrently in the main narrative. Always such themes will be found to collect into a pattern around the matrix of Milton's "great Idea", *answering* that Idea, in the loaded and various style which Milton sought and found.

In a certain sense it does not matter how many closely interrelated motifs or themes may be perceived within that vast controlling providential Idea—and here we might usefully remember Harington's conception of "like infinite Allegories" unfolding themselves along a common axis. Nor does it matter how many variations of shadowed aesthetic development different readers may find in their different readings of *Paradise Lost,* or whether Milton wove such complexities of design always with calculation or sometimes intuitively. All such variations and thematic developments seem to spin somewhere out of that one magnetic matrix, the questioning and then the justifying of Providence, the questioning of the meaning of life and belief—Milton's personal exegesis on the cryptic second and third chapters of Genesis. The articulation of such a conception, with its subordinate motifs and patterns held in place like the lines of force of the magnet, is so extensive and on the whole so precise and controlled in *Paradise Lost,* in the main so deliberate (though often veiled) throughout the poem, that such terms as "poetic intention" or "archetypal imagery" or even "symbolism" (in the Romantic sense) become inadequate to describe it. "Symbol" in the more explicit medieval sense of the term may perhaps evoke a few of those special moments in *Paradise Lost* when rhetorical trope lifts onto the plane of what is ultimately inexpressible in words. But the medieval understanding of *symbolum,* as was noted earlier, itself stressed the close association of this latter trope or concept with "allegory".[28] "Typology", traditionally only one narrow division of the *quatre-sens,* also, as I shall later suggest, as a figurative mode is insufficiently comprehensive to describe Milton's aesthetics. His poetic procedures can be properly identified and analysed only within the traditional language and terminology of poetic and epic allegory, a language with which Milton was entirely familiar.

Allegory, as the Renaissance understood it in epic and poetry and as it developed out of scriptural and literary exegesis, provides a mode of shadowed discourse which constructs out of veiled hints and enigmas a tangible witness to the pervasive presence of an anterior or controlling Idea. In its use, distinctive content and distinctive literary expression march together, as they had always done in traditional epic-allegorical composition or tended to do in the more sophisticated forms of scriptural exegesis or critical exegesis on epic. In that interplay of abstract content with expressive form Milton's allegory, like all allegory, defines itself, giving renewed support to the belief, once commonplace, that epic and allegory in classical and Renaissance practice are inseparable.

PART III

"Real or Allegoric": Representation in *Paradise Lost*

FOURTEEN

Historical Problems in Reading
Paradise Lost

In the preceding two Parts of this study, Milton's allegorical "Idea" and allegorical artistry in *Paradise Lost* have been set and measured against earlier traditions of critical commentary on allegory and of allegory in written epic stretching from medieval or earlier commentators to the eighteenth century. In this last Part, I shall attempt to measure Milton's understanding of epic allegory against Protestant contexts of interpretation of Scripture in Milton's time, and more specifically, against Milton's own statements bearing on the subject of allegory in his prose and his indirect statements within his epic poem. These discussions cannot take place without prior consideration of some of the problems which have beset critics in the reading of *Paradise Lost*. Restrictive critical attitudes derive partly from an earlier short-lived spell of neoclassical criticism in England which was hostile to imaginative fantasy in poetry, especially epic, and most of all in religious poetry or epic; partly from a misunderstanding of certain Protestant views concerning the proper reading of Scripture, and the inappropriate application of narrow views on this matter to the reading of *Paradise Lost*; and partly from a misunderstanding of Milton's own statements on the interpretation of Scripture in *Of Christian Doctrine*, with consequent further misunderstanding of the applicability (or inapplicability) of such statements to his epic constructs in *Paradise Lost*. Following these discussions will be my own reassessment of the diverse quality or qualities of figurative representation and discourse, passing into allegory, in *Paradise Lost*, and of the place of allegorical discourse and artistry within the total poem. These assessments will be drawn from the actual evidential circumstances of Milton's poem.

An unlikely perspective on these issues is provided by Satan in Book IV of *Paradise Regained*. There Satan tells Jesus that he foresees a Kingdom predicted for Him: "A Kingdom they portend thee, but what Kingdom, / Real or Allegoric I discern not" (389-90). Satan uses the term "allegoric" here partly in a general sense of "figurative" or metaphorical, partly (with unconscious or ironic allusion to the Old Testament tradition of messianic prophecy) in the older theological sense of "typical" (typological). That is, an earthly kingdom is seen as a "type" or prophecy of the reign of Christ. Satan does not know if the kingdom promised to Jesus via the prophecies foretells an earthly power or adumbrates some less literal kind of reign (as we but not he know, a spiritual kingdom). However, for Satan the second sense, whatever it "portends", does not have much significance. He uses "allegoric" reductively, almost with a sneer. Christ's Kingdom is "eternal *sure*, as without end, / Without beginning" (IV.391-92). It is foretold by the "Starry Rubric" (IV.393)—by fortune-telling or astrology. There is more than a hint that something which has neither end *nor* beginning is, in plainer words, a fiction—*not* "real", a mere figure of speech.

What is most intriguing about Satan's statement is its either/or aspect. If the kingdom is "real" it cannot be figurative, and if it is figurative then it cannot be "real"; the two have to be mutually exclusive. Yet in traditional scriptural multi-layered reading and certainly in typological reading such was not the case. The historical or "literal" level of truth remained always perceived in the background, and in typology directly present. Type and antitype both are historically real, while both also participate in a kind of mutual correspondence: type adumbrates antitype and is imbued with the future meaning, antitype encompasses and fulfils what is already past. Both are "real" *and* simultaneously "allegoric". It is hardly surprising that Satan fails to understand these higher matters. The problem is rather why so many readers have seemed to experience an analogous difficulty to Satan's. Milton's poem has to be read as *either* real *or* allegorical, but it cannot be read in both ways—not when read as a Protestant or indeed the ultimate Protestant epic. The notion of oblique meanings or allegory in *Paradise Lost* arouses old antagonisms; one may not read the whole poem or substantial parts of it in allegorical or even in more general figurative ways and still have the poem retain its scriptural authenticity. "Real" and "allegoric" are indeed mutually incompatible. Those who hold such views might find support in Milton's placing of the sole occurrence in his poetry of the actual term, "allegory", in Satan's mouth. Others who do not hold such views might think that just possibly Satan's own narrow literal-mindedness is being ironically exposed to question in Milton's lines.

The attitude of mind which Satan betrays is one that has dogged Milton criticism from the late seventeenth century to the present. To put the matter in the bluntest terms, it is an attitude founded on the assumption, largely unexamined, that Milton identifies himself with a certain kind of Puritan fundamentalism and that the artistry of his poem therefore reflects a certain deliberate narrowness of imaginative approach. The substance of *Paradise Lost* is a literal or literalistically expanded account of biblical happenings considered by Milton to be historically true and without further dimensions.[1] It is an account freely enlarged by doctrine also perceived as without problem or paradox "true", and embellished with religious sentiments plainly expressed and pleasing or not pleasing according as the individual reader's religious attachments may happen to agree with them or not. The aesthetic which Milton adopts *necessarily* is a corresponding one of historical literalism: realism in description, plausibility in psychology and characterization, a strict dramatic probability in plotting, with, additionally, a severe curtailment of metaphor, especially in respect of the kind of metaphor which harbours any ongoing secondary or hidden meaning. (One dissenting reaction to this vew has been that which asserts the existence of a prevailing, strictly typological, form of figuration in the poem; this view will be discussed in a later chapter.)

Unfortunately (so the view paraphrased above has also sometimes run), *Paradise Lost* does not succeed very well in sustaining its own self-confessed decorum. In too many respects the poem is very badly adapted to its intended purposes. Classical epic conventions (for example the supernatural machinery) are clumsily imposed by the poet on recalcitrant Christian materials; the dramatic mode espoused is intermingled with crudely expressed doctrine and far too much religious polemic and statement (this is the anti-Christian but still literalist response); and altogether incompatible elements, as with the abstract allegories of Sin and Death, are tastelessly intruded upon the decorum of the "real". Metaphor (as in the epic similes) frequently runs away with itself (a somewhat older view), while at other times an excess of realism mars the representation of the immaterial, as in the descriptions of God or of the War in Heaven. There are even moments when, apparently, Milton has not had the wit to keep the details of his own "real" story straight. Altogether, there is not an artistic balance kept in the poem, and Milton's artistic judgement is thrown into question. There has always been an underlying current in all such criticism which tends to suggest that a religious poem in the kind of area Milton attempts is impossible of success. The Miltonic enterprise is self-defeating.

Samuel Johnson

Some of the most formidable expressions of the attitudes expressed above (and doubtless one of their original and most damaging sources) are to be recognised in Johnson's "Lives" of Waller and Milton. (Similar views were apparent in slightly earlier Milton criticism, such as Addison's and Bentley's.[2]) It would seem that Johnson put into his "Life" of the lesser poet criticisms of Milton's chosen type of poetry even more stringent than he could bring himself to express in the "Life" of the greater. A redaction of the relevant passages in the "Life" of Waller follows. Johnson begins with the famous dictum that "poetical devotion cannot often please. The doc-trines of *Religion may indeed be defended in a didactick poem* . . . [by] the happy power of arguing in verse. . . . [But] Contemplative piety, or the inter-course between God and the human soul, cannot be poetical. . . . The essence of poetry is invention; such invention as, by producing something unexpected, surprises and delights. The topicks of devotion are few, and being few are universally known . . . they can be made no more. . . . *religion must be shewn as it is.* . . . Omnipotence cannot be exalted; Infinity cannot be amplified; Perfection cannot be improved". As to style, Johnson continues, the limitations which a religious content imposes on the poet must be absolute: "Of sentiments purely religious, it will be found that the most simple expression is the most sublime. . . . All that pious verse can do is to help the memory and delight the ear, and for these purposes it may be very useful; but it supplies nothing to the mind. The ideas of Christian Theology are too simple for eloquence, *too sacred for fiction*, and too ma-jestick for ornament; *to recommend them by tropes and figures* is to magnify by a concave mirror the sidereal hemisphere".[3]

The determining phrases of this argument, as italicized above, are those which assert that a religious subject is by its very nature inimical to poetry and to poetical invention, tropes and figures. It says some-thing about Johnson's honesty as a critic that, bringing such preconcep-tions as the above to Milton's poetry,[4] he could still find so much to admire in *Paradise Lost*, even those imaginative powers of invention (including the "justly censured" "mythological allusions", and similes expanded "beyond the dimensions which the occasion required") which he had specifically abolished from the proper domain of religious poetry in the "Life" of Waller. Nevertheless, the essence of Johnson's argument remains the same in both essays. Milton is seen as placed in an awkward position, caught between "religious reverence" and the "*licentiousness* of fiction". (It is interesting how "poetic licence" becomes, in a sacred context, "poetic licentiousness".) The summary which follows below indicates Johnson's position, although it gives an inadequate idea of his personal ambivalence toward Milton's poem and his frequent more fa-vourable criticisms upon it.

The materials of *Paradise Lost* are real; its forms, modes and styles therefore are required to be in keeping. "The substance of [Milton's] narrative is truth", including the doctrines of the Christian religion and the true "history of a miracle, of Creation and Redemption", the "two parts of a vulgar epick poem", the "*probable* and the *marvellous*", herein being one and the same: "the probable therefore is marvellous, and the marvellous is probable". In keeping with the poem's substance and decorum of truth are its convincing characterizations (at least of the fallen beings), its Aristo-telian unity of plot, its pure religious sentiments, put into even Satan's mouth, and (Johnson is forced to concede) Milton's uniquely imaginative expansion of the biblical subject. Strictly speaking, imaginative invention ought not to have been introduced into a religious poem, yet Milton contrives to succeed where others fail; his poem impresses the mind without giving offence.

Johnson's references to the "probable" and the "marvellous" as coinciding in Christian miracles in Milton's epic reveals a familiarity with the Italian neoclassical debates on the proper character of epic and with the French tradition of Le Bossu (whose scheme he follows in other particulars). In restricting the "marvellous" element in epic to Christian miracles, Johnson tacitly aligns himself with the position of Castelvetro and other strict historicists and Christian dogmatists on the nature of epic, as opposed to the more liberal positions concerning imagination and truth espoused by Mazzoni and Tasso. The issue of course concerns the place not only of fantasy but of the imagination itself in religious epic, and the definition of "truth" in poetry—whether the criteria of history and theology should be applied to literary invention.

Even in a Milton, the element of the overtly fantastic, Tasso's *meraviglie*, is inadmissible—Johnson's argument so continues. The allegorical personifications, especially, in *Paradise Lost* are misconceived and in bad taste; they should not have been allowed to impinge upon the real actions and persons. "Milton's allegory of Sin and Death is undoubtedly faulty"; it is "unskilful"; when the personifications enter into the real action, "the allegory is broken". (That is to say, such allegories should be presented only as ornamental tropes.) Johnson does not allow that the allegorical interludes in Milton's poem (romance fantastic Episodes after the Italian mixed-epic model as employed by Tasso and Spenser) are true epic "episodes". He recognises only one interpretation of "episode" (where Le Bossu gave two related forms):[5] that, after the classical model, involving retrospective narration, or else "prophetick account". Thus there are only two valid "episodes" in the whole of Milton's poem: Raphael's account of the War in Heaven and Michael's vision of futurity. And even the first of these is misconceived. In the War in Heaven, or in other representations of "the operation of immaterial agents", the "confusion of spirit and matter" (Milton's peculiar failing) "fills [the narration] with *incongruity*". Incongruity (in fact one of the signals of allegory) is strongly repudiated by Johnson. As regards the problem of representing angelic beings the answer is simple: "immateriality" had much better have been kept "out of sight". The entire convention of gods and angelic messengers in epic from Virgil to Tasso, supernatural "machinery" thought by Le Bossu to be of so much efficacy in delineating the passions, should, according to Johnson, have been dropped from Milton's poem. How much else of *Paradise Lost* would have been better omitted? The eighteenth century's and Johnson's strictures suggest a stripped-down "ideal" version of the poem curiously resembling one of Milton's original dramatic sketches for *Paradise Lost*,

"Adam Unparadiz'd", a composition in which the allegorical personifications were to have been kept firmly in their places (having only a choric function), in which plot would have been limited strictly to the events in the Garden, from which most of the poetical embellishment would have been omitted, and which would have borne little resemblance to the many-dimensioned epic which Milton did write.

As to the purpose of *Paradise Lost*, for Johnson it admits of no doubt. Milton's "moral" (Johnson borrows Le Bossu's, Toland's and Phillips' earlier term, but uses it in a sense denuded of allegory) is, exactly, "to shew the reasonableness of religion, and the necessity of obedience to the Divine Law". In observing that the poem indeed has a distinct and antecedent moral, and that Milton alone among epic poets, following Le Bossu's prescription,[6] found this moral first and framed the action afterwards (that is to say, the moral is not "incidental" but "essential and intrinsick"), Johnson was making a singularly important historical observation. Milton's epic was written because the poet had something to say, and that something, the intention according to which the poet is working, precedes the actual fable in his mind, is distinct from the fable, and is that according to which the entire fable is shaped. Yet, having made this important critical observation and with some acuteness located its origin in Le Bossu, Johnson proceeds to interpret Milton's moral simplistically. Milton's purpose to "vindicate the ways of God to man" is tantamount to constructing an exemplary *lesson* in "religion" and "obedience". Any personal comment which Milton might have felt impelled to make on the human condition and destiny, any individual colouring in his interpretation of God's ways, any embracing human relevance in his fictively expanded story, or any further figurative truth ("a kind of truth in the midst of fiction", as Phillips had put it, describing "proper allegory")[7] is neither to be desired nor found. The action carries a moral only in the sense that we now (or the Renaissance sometimes did) give to that term, namely of offering an *exemplum*: the fate of Adam and Eve may serve as an awful warning to us all. The poem works through its literal examples of disobedience, contrasted with its converse examples of obedience, or of repentance followed by obedience. These are religious lessons; of human relevance in any non-specifically doctrinal sense, there is little if any: "the want of human interest is always felt". The "lessons of morality or precepts of prudence occur seldom"; since the *Paradise Lost* "admits no human manners till the Fall, it can give little assistance to human conduct". It will be necessary to examine more closely the reasons which could have led Dr. Johnson to such surprising conclusions about a poem which many would regard as deeply engaged with the traditional concerns of and as following in the broadest European traditions of moral and moralized Christian epic.

Luther and Poetic Fundamentalism

It is not difficult to see that Johnson's strictures, although expressed in terms of the literary proprieties and decorums proper to the Christian epic, are not in their underlying preconceptions literary at all. The fundamentalist attitude, if it may be so termed, to religious poetry which Johnson betrays has its roots in an extreme strictness of position—in the main a Protestant development, but one which had surfaced also in late sixteenth-century Counter-Reformation attitudes—regarding the reading and interpretation of Scripture and the legitimate uses of its material. This view is reflected in (among other Protestant sources)[8] such statements as the following of Luther. It is not permissible, says Luther, to

twist all the words of divine promise and declaration, just as it pleases [Erasmus], by discovering a figure of speech in them. . . . Let this be our sentiment: that *no implication or figure is to be allowed to exist in any passage of Scriptures*. . . . We should adhere everywhere to the simple, pure and natural meaning of the words, according to the rules of grammar and the habits of speech which God has given unto men. . . . *The Word of God must be taken in its plain meaning*, as the words stand. . . . *the words must be understood according to their literal meaning*.[9]

Of course Luther in this statement is adopting an extreme position in the course of his rebuttal of Erasmian rationalism, and his use of the term "literal" can be very equivocal. The issue of "literal" understanding of the Bible by Luther or other Reformers is complex. A degree of figuration was traditionally recognised as legitimately included within the "literal level" if employed intentionally by the original writers—so that in fact almost any degree of figuration in Scripture, even allegory, could theoretically be swept away under this carpet. Conversely, to read "according to the spirit" could itself imply a certain form of anti-literalism, and Luther could be breathtakingly inconsistent, attacking "mystical senses" *and* "the letter" as *equally* "carnal and literal": "*The law of the letter* is whatever is written in letters, said in words, conceived in thoughts, the tropological, allegorical, anagogical or whatever other mystical sense. . . . All of these are carnal and literal when the letter has sway and the spirit is absent".[10] Nevertheless, such sentences as those italicized in the prior passage quoted above betray or rather flaunt a very considerable degree of anti-figurative bias. A straight "literal" reading is what Luther evidently would advocate, in his famous desire to read and understand Scripture "only by that spirit in which Scripture was written".[11]

The reasons for such severe Protestant restrictiveness were twofold: a disquiet lest, through figurative interpretation, the historical value of the Bible be lessened, and an anxiety lest, through the reading of Scripture with any latitude, basic Christian doctrines be impugned. The rationalist, it was argued, could always take refuge in figurative interpretation from any doctrine or passage in the Bible which he found unpalatable.[12] The disquiet expressed by Luther invites extension from Scripture itself to religious poetry, especially any closely based on Scripture: men must seek the literal meaning only—no implications or figures anywhere—just as Dr. Johnson later said. Allegory especially (historically suspect since the intellectualism of Origen and the East had been thought to have infected the Western Church) comes into disrepute. Along with allegory so also may almost every other kind of poetic figuration: myth, allusion, simile, fantasy or romance elements, almost the very process of poetic invention itself— all come under suspicion when introduced into religious literature. The rejection of so many forms and modes which had been accepted in medieval and earlier Renaissance religious writing is remarkable, and it would seem in the early English neoclassical context to have been a rejection virtually complete. Only exemplary religious narrative, doctrine, and historical record in religious verse evidently are to be exempt from the cultural revolution being promoted not only by radical Protestant enthusiasts but also (it is sometimes forgotten) by their Counter-Reformation counterparts.

The kind of aesthetic which could thus be extrapolated from such opinions as Luther's on the reading of Scripture finds a striking parallel in the new spirit of historicism and realism growing up in literature from the later sixteenth century on the Continent to the later seventeenth century in England. The phenomena now cited are familiar items in literary history. In the drama is to be seen an interpretation of the "unities" tighter even than Aristotle's—that is, an intensified effort to meet external criteria of realism in theatrical representation, matched in such writers as Racine by a heightened degree of psychological realism. In the field of narrative poetry a new tide of historical or geographical epics, such as Camões' *Lusiadas*, Trissino's *Italia liberata dai Goti*, or Tasso's *Gerusalemme liberata* (which in its historical aspect also qualifies for inclusion), displaces the old-fashioned, more diversified romance-epic of Ariosto, Matteo Boiardo, or Spenser. Less widely perceived, perhaps, is the corresponding new and rigorous emphasis, earlier noted in Cowley, Davenant and other English writers, on the Christian epic as the direct vehicle of Christian truths: Christian doctrines, Christian theme or subject, Christian *history*, the Christian hero— all these are by many writers and critics preferred to the moral, spiritual or mystical truths expressible through metaphor, myths and allegory in such imaginative works as the spiritual epic journey of Dante or the moralized epic quest of Spenser. The definition of "truth", as we have seen in Italian criticism, is in this period itself under pressure. History and fact plus revealed truth, also regarded as fact, everywhere in the period might seem to supercede more imaginative means and modes of apprehending reality.

Fact and history together appear to hold the reign over imagination and language.

The aesthetic spirit of mid-seventeenth-century England is well represented by the verdicts on epic of Cowley (writing during the high period of the Puritan ascendancy) and his immediate successors. The following may be added to the extracts quoted earlier from Cowley's Preface to his *Poems*:

> When I consider . . . how many other bright and magnificent subjects . . . the *Holy Scripture* affords and *proffers*, as it were, to *Poesie* . . . It is not without grief and indignation that I behold that *Divine Science* employing all her inexhaustable riches of *Wit* and *Eloquence* . . . at best on the confused antiquated *Dreams* of senseless *Fables* and *Metamorphoses*. . . . Are the obsolete threadbare tales of *Thebes* and *Troy* half so stored with great, heroical, and supernatural actions . . . as the wars of *Joshua*, of the *Judges*, of *David*, and divers others? Can all the *Transformations* of the *Gods* give such copious hints to flourish and expatiate on as the true *Miracles* of *Christ*, or of his *Prophets* and *Apostles*?[13]

The equivalent spirit of French neoclassicism was carried to London by the influential Saint-Évremond: "Truth was not the inclination of the first ages. . . . [In] all their discourses . . . there was nothing to be seen but fictions, allegories, and similitudes. . . . The genius of our age is quite the opposite to this spirit of fables and *false mysteries*. We love *plain truth;* good sense has gained ground upon the illusions of fancy, and nothing satisfies us nowadays but solid reason".[14]

One observes with a certain fascination how easily in the language of the above statement there is established the equation of fiction, allegories, similes and fables, with *lies*: "fables and *false* mysteries". Fancy fosters illusions, and mysteries (allegories) promulgate falsehood; both fables and allegories (like metaphor itself, or the fictive imagination) stand in opposition to the poetry of sense, solid reason and *plain truth*. "Plain truth" may suggest a religious bias, as much as an historical one. That corollary soon slips in, when "allegory" and "mystical meaning" become synonymous with religious superstition (or popery) in the forthright declaration of Thomas Rymer: "it was the vice of those Times *to affect superstitiously* the *Allegory;* and nothing would then be currant [*sic*] without a mystical meaning. We must blame the *Italians* for debauching great *Spencer's* judgment". The fault was Ariosto's: "Spencer . . . suffer'd himself to be misled by *Ariosto*; with whom blindly rambling on *marvellous* Adventures, he makes no Conscience of *probability*. All is fanciful and chimerical . . . without any foundation in truth".[15] The voice of staunch Protestantism speaks, to make *conscience* of Probability and *debauched superstition* of allegory and the traditional epic marvellous. Even metaphor and similitude, according to Saint-Évremond, are now incompatible with *truth* and therefore with good poetry.

   The almost unconscious slippage in the language especially of Rymer
between religious and literary connotations betrays how unthinkingly and
narrowly the assumptions appropriate to the one context, religion, could
sometimes be transferred to the other context, literature. It has been
assumed, and perhaps it was also assumed by many of Milton's contempo-
raries, that Milton as the most notable late Protestant poet must or ought
naturally to have followed the new trend toward unvarnished truth. Yet
the rearguard action which had been fought in defence of the imaginative,
the fantastic and especially the "marvellous-verisimilar" in poetry and epic
by such important Christian poets and critics as Tasso, Sidney and Spenser
remained profoundly important to Milton, affecting the way in which he
interpreted and modified the new aesthetic of history, realism and "plain
truth".

FIFTEEN

Scripture and the Figurative Reading of *Paradise Lost*

Milton on Allegory

Milton not only did not repudiate allegory, he not infrequently mentions the term in a positive way and makes use of it in his prose writings, including his theological treatise. In Milton's poems the word "allegory" (apart from its sole use in *Paradise Regained* IV.389-90) is not found as such, although the concept is certainly present. The related words "type" and "shadow" occur a number of times, the first being used more strictly to render the predictive level of Christian meaning inherent in certain parts of the Old Testament, the second in a looser way. Instances in *Paradise Lost* of the first kind of sense are, "*Tophet* . . . the Type of Hell" (I.404-5); "by *types* / And *shadowes*" XII.232-33); and "From *shadowie Types* to Truth, from Flesh to Spirit" (XII.303). "Shadow" (later discussed) occurs among other instances in Books V.575, VI.655, VIII.311, IX.12 and XII.233. It is used in a variety of non-theological senses, ranging from physical shadow or reflection to allegorical personification (as of Death), and also in a number of contexts vaguely in between. When Milton intends "type" in the theological sense, he tends to use that word alone (or sometimes in conjunction with "shadow", which then means "dim"); its reiterated use in the context of the prophecy of Jesus' Kingdom in Book XII is illustrative. On the other hand, "shadow" on its own does not necessarily denote "type". Both words, but especially "shadow", are of course common Renaissance terms for any kind of allegorical figure. We may compare Spenser on his Gloriana in the "Letter to Raleigh", "I doe otherwise *shadow* her", and George Sandys in his moralized translation of Ovid, "Typhon *is the type of Ambition*".[1]

Milton's uses of the term or concept of allegory in his prose are intentionally more specific. There are several important instances in *Of Christian Doctrine* itself. In Book I, chapter x, Milton observes that "God himself, *in an allegorical fiction*, Ezek.xxiii.4 represents himself as having espoused two wives, Aholah and Aholibah; a mode of speaking [*in para-*

bola] which he would by no means have employed, especially at such
length, even in a parable . . . if the practice which it implied [divorce] had
been intrinsically dishonorable or shameful".[2] Milton here uses the Latin
term *parabola*, one of the older terms for allegory; the Columbia edition
accurately translates as "allegory", because the figure in Ezekiel xxiii.4 and
following is too enigmatic to be equated with parable in the ordinary
understanding. Allegory, then, has an honourable status; God would not
have employed such a mode of speaking if He had thought the practice of
divorce dishonourable. It is surely significant of Milton's opinions on the
subject of allegory that he allows himself to introduce the topic into a
treatise on Christian doctrine, and all the more so in relation to God. In his
secular prose also Milton affords to allegory (naming the term) a significant
and honourable place, associating it most specifically with interpretative
reading of the Old Testament. Some instances are given in my notes.[3]

Two other occurrences in *Of Christian Doctrine*, Book I, chapters ii and
xxx, where Milton speaks of "both in the literal and figurative descriptions
of God" in the Bible ("semper vel describi vel adumbrari") or of "literal and
figurative expressions" in the Bible ("locutionis propriæ et figuratæ dis-
tinctio")[4] in terms which are certainly synonymous with forms of allegory,
will be discussed presently. In another instance in the *Christian Doctrine*,
Book I, chapter iv, arguing the important subject of predestination, Milton,
using the specific term "allegory", says that "if an argument of any weight
in the discussion of so controverted a subject can be derived from alle-
gorical and metaphorical expressions" ("si metaphoris et allegoriis in re
tam controversa nitendum est")—the subject in question concerns the
Book of Life, as mentioned in the Bible—he will make use of these, and he
goes on to cite several instances of allegory in Scripture. At the end of the
same chapter, as we earlier noted, he cites Homer and a pronouncement
on free will by Jupiter (that is, a myth or allegory) as his final word against
those who "impugn the justice of God".[5]

Satan, then, in *Paradise Regained* may be dismissive of allegory; but
Milton in his theological treatise treats the subject with respect, if also with
a certain degree of care. We will next pursue the matter further by looking
at those comments in *Of Christian Doctrine* which directly take up the
question of figurative language in and the figurative interpretation of
Scripture, to consider how these may bear on Milton's own language in
Paradise Lost.

Of Christian Doctrine on Interpreting Scripture

It has been suggested in recent criticism that there exist various kinds of
specific (not necessarily negative) correspondences in literature of Milton's
period and especially in *Paradise Lost* between Protestant views on the strict

interpretation of Scripture and the appropriate limitations on imaginative creation imposed by a biblical subject. There may, for example, be a significant association between Milton's individual use of certain qualities of metaphorical language in *Paradise Lost* and what has recently come to be termed "Protestant poetics". A more rigorous view, drawing from Milton's remarks in the *Christian Doctrine* on "accommodation" in Scripture, in effect revives the Johnsonian view of a necessary literalism in religious verse: a necessary bareness of metaphor in *Paradise Lost* may, it is recently alleged, be found to be mediated only or largely by a "typological" cast of figuration.[6] However, the search for a distinctive Protestant aesthetic is not a simple one, nor is it in the case of Milton quickly concluded. It is easy to oversimplify or misunderstand Milton's complex purposes and achievement in *Paradise Lost*, and indeed to misunderstand his actual theological assumptions and their proper area of application, as first defined by himself in his prose and subsequently applied in his poetry. All the more reason why we should look very closely at what Milton has to say in both places on the subject of metaphor and scriptural interpretation, and at how his statements may relate to his own theories and practices in artistic representation. Milton nowhere makes specific theoretical pronouncements on the subject of figuration, although much can be inferred from the tenor of his compact remarks in *Of Christian Doctrine*, *The Reason of Church-Government*, the preface to *Samson Agonistes*, and from the nature of the opening and later Invocations in *Paradise Lost* and Raphael's discourses in Books V to VIII (including the latter's remarks on the problems of narrating scriptural event)—and also, we should perhaps add, from Edward Phillips' derivatively Miltonic statement on epic, at which we have already looked.

It is necessary to read the *Christian Doctrine* with great care, because certain statements there have regularly been made the basis for an anti-figurative interpretation of Milton's aesthetic in *Paradise Lost*. Certain of Milton's utterances in the *Christian Doctrine* are in fact remarkably elusive for so plain and logically argued a text, and literary critics have repeatedly looked at the same few sentences in isolation and out of context, seeing in them what is not at all certainly present and failing to see some of what is present, taken in the light of other statements in the same chapter or other chapters of the treatise. Critics have not given the same attention to overall consistency between statements in various places in Milton's treatise, or to coherence or tone, which they would as a matter of course bring to bear on any of his poems, and which Milton as a trained exegete himself specifically brings to bear in his own arguments concerning the reading of Scripture. This entire area of Milton commentary is one in which there has been an anxiety to display Milton's theology as more favourably orthodox than it used to be thought, and in which it is extremely easy to distort the careful balance maintained in the *Christian Doctrine* between reforming

Puritanism on the one hand and Milton's independence of religious judge-
ment on the other.

   Like others of his contemporaries, Milton interprets Scripture accord-
ing to a stringent set of scholarly and editorial principles which dictate that
never shall a single verse be read out of context, or without being tested
against all the other verses on the same matter elsewhere in Scripture, or
other than according to the overall coherence and consistency of doctrine
throughout the Bible. He requires that interpretation shall preserve a keen
awareness of the facts that there exist quite different levels and modes of
discourse within the Bible; that the canon of authority is not uniform as
between the various Books; and that Gospel truths are often spoken amidst
other different kinds of utterance, or amidst factual matters carrying less
weight. The relevant statements are in *Of Christian Doctrine*, Book I, chapter
xxx, the paragraph beginning: "The requisites for the public interpretation
of Scripture. . . ." Milton's specific points are, that in exegesis regard
should be paid to linguistic and textual scholarship; to context, and com-
parison of texts; to consistency of doctrine throughout the Bible ("the
analogy of faith"); and that "care" should be taken "in distinguishing
between literal and figurative expressions" ["locutionis propriæ et figur-
atæ distinctio"]. He does not suggest that figurative expressions do not
exist or are to be ignored in the Bible, he says merely that they may not be
used *to prove points of faith*. Milton also notes that not all parts of the Bible
are "of equal authority", and that the uncanonical Books must not be
"adduced as evidence in matters of faith".[7] (He himself makes substantial
use of uncanonical matter in non-doctrinal contexts, as for example in the
inventions concerning Raphael in Book V of *Paradise Lost*, and also in a
number of similes, as I later note.) Most of what Milton says above suggests
a regulated flexibility in respect of doctrinal interpretation; but none of his
"rules" imply any narrowness in respect of fictive or partly fictive *artistic*
representation, a matter which is never raised even by implication in the
Christian Doctrine. In fact, what Milton says in the two quotations cited
above clearly declares that there are at times valid avenues of figurative
application within Scripture itself (when the text is non-doctrinal); why not
then in comparable areas in scriptural poetry, if we are to look for analogies
between the reading of Scripture and the writing of scriptural poetry?
Milton's stance of carefully regulated regard to context and careful balance
between strictness in certain respects and figurative latitude in others, as
formulated in the *Christian Doctrine*, will be found equally to be the key
to the aesthetic of *Paradise Lost*.

   There is no doubt that Milton is very rigorous in certain respects about
the interpretation of Scripture. But he brings informed judgement and
considerable flexibility to bear, and he is certainly no literalist, even though
he prides himself on taking every one of his doctrines straight from Holy
Writ. If he sometimes appears to be echoing Luther, Calvin or other

authorities, this is because he writes in broad accordance with most of the basic Reformed positions (although not without important reservations on key issues).[8] His broad orthodoxy is evident in, for example, the familiar Protestant assertions that Scripture must be the sole rule of faith, is to be interpreted by each according to his individual conscience and judgement, guided by the "Spirit"; further, that Scripture is pure and "simple", offering "the clearest light . . . sufficient for its own explanation, *especially in matters of faith and holiness*", and that it is "plain and perspicuous *in all things necessary to salvation*".[9] Here are the familiar Protestant stresses on the straightforwardness, sufficiency and inviolability of Scripture *in matters of faith* or those things necessary to salvation: that is, in respect of *doctrine*. But of course not even the canonical Books, although equally inspired throughout, consist solely of doctrine.[10] It is specifically in the context of doctrine that Milton makes his well-known remarks about not subjecting Scripture to "intricate metaphysical comments", "useless technicalities" and "empty distinctions".[11] His first Book of the *Christian Doctrine* is, after all, expressly concerned with doctrine—that is, with those points of faith which are to be elicited from Scripture and are to be believed[12]—rather than with any of the other ways or aspects in which we may understand or apply certain other parts of the Bible. We must bear in mind the limitation so precisely expressed in Milton's statements above. Milton's remarks do not refer to every part of Scripture, but only to those parts needed to determine points of faith and which concern salvation. Scripture is "plain", and probably scriptural poetry ought to be plain too—*in those statements pertaining to doctrine, faith and salvation.*

The second statement which Milton makes, equally important for the purposes of our inquiry, is that "No passage of Scripture is to be interpreted *in more than one sense*".[13] This is the familiar Protestant doctrine of *"one sense to one place"*: the figurative, in its place, is not excluded. Equally, nowhere does Milton say or even hint that this sole sense must always or necessarily be the *literal* sense.[14] What his statement means is that on any given occasion we have to decide whether the appropriate sense is a literal sense or some other (figurative) sense. The solitary exception to this rule against double reading occurs in the Old Testament, where the "sense is sometimes a compound of the historical and typical" ("saepe est compositus ex historia et typo").[15] Milton in this instance simply notes the possibility that certain passages of the Old Testament, according to an older, traditional Christian practice and one still accepted by Protestants, may be read simultaneously as historical and also prefigurative of Christ (as the examples adduced, Hosea xi.1 and Matthew ii.15, indicate).

Milton does not, as far as I can see, in the *Christian Doctrine* or elsewhere lay much if any stress on typological figuration understood in a large sense as a form of *metaphor*. He thinks of the "typical" sense in terms of direct prophecy. Although in the treatise he says that "every thing advanced in the New Testament" can be "proved by citations from the Old",[16] when he uses the term "type" there it relates strictly to Christ, and it is always in a denudedly plain, historical sense, as if he were determined to press the point that the prefigurative sense is part and parcel of the historical. The uses of "type" in Milton's secular prose correspond;[17] and the same is true of the scant uses of "type" in *Paradise Lost*. The contrast, then, between Milton's mentions in his theological tract of allegorical *metaphor* in the Bible, understood in a larger, non-typological sense, and what he there or elsewhere defines or uses as plain typological *prediction*, is marked. We shall find that this contrast is borne out in the different kinds of language adopted in *Paradise Lost*.

What implications for his epic aesthetic may we draw from Milton's discussions on the interpretation of Scripture? Milton doubtless believed in the historical reality or literal truth of large parts of the Bible (the specific exceptions he makes being the uncanonical Books, which sometimes contain admixture of "some things fabulous, low, trifling, and contrary to true religion and wisdom").[18] But this does not mean that nowhere in the attested Books does he not recognise passages which are purely figurative or even explicitly allegorical—as we have already noted. Indeed, Milton's simple mention of the necessity to distinguish between "literal and figurative" expressions in the Bible assumes the existence of metaphor or allegory. The Bible does contain metaphors and figures (apart from any "typical" senses), and an indication of the true importance which Milton attaches to these is surely given when he notes that "God himself" in the Bible speaks of Himself "in an allegorical fiction" (*in parabola*).[19] Here alone, one might think, is warrant enough, if we are seeking correspondences between the *Christian Doctrine* and Milton's aesthetic, for the use of "allegorical fictions" or other forms of oblique metaphor (or any metaphor) in religious poetry or biblical epic.

Apart from these special places where God speaks of Himself in an allegorical way, there exist, as biblical scholars have always recognised, many other passages in the Bible which contain figuration; and "care" must always be taken in "distinguishing between literal and figurative expressions" ("locutionis propriæ et figuratæ distinctio"),[20] so that each may be construed in its proper context. It is not to be expected that in a treatise *on* doctrine larger considerations as to the uses of such figure or metaphor in the Bible and their further applications in other kinds of writing would be appropriately introduced; however, if a poetic for *Paradise Lost* is to be extrapolated from Milton's views on scriptural interpretation in *Of Christian Doctrine*, then his statements cited above are some of the important places to begin.

Relative to the degree of figuration allowed by Milton in understanding the Bible, we have also to note that the problem of figurative interpretation is not to be disposed of by the convenient explanation that a degree of figuration had always been regarded as a legitimate part of the "literal sense" of the Bible.[21] Milton makes no effort to sweep away figuration in Scripture under this convenient carpet. His emphasis on figurative discourse in the Bible is too explicit, and his words about God using allegorical fictions are too suggestive, to give grounds for doubting either his interest in or the value he places on such elements of language in the Bible.

What Milton is saying in the *Christian Doctrine*, it seems to me, in sum is this. There exist in separate places in the Bible diverse strata of "truth": the frankly fabling or false, or at least historically unreliable, as in the uncanonical Books (materials which he is not, however, by any means averse to using in *Paradise Lost*); the unambiguously literal, plain facts or statements containing doctrines (or history), which must be preserved pure and intact;[22] and areas of writing variously in between, in which truths of more oblique kinds may be communicated through figure, metaphor, parable, and also allegory. Milton's second and third categories of discourse, the literal and the figurative, may conflate in special instances in the historical "types" of the Old Testament predictive of Christ. We are not meant to conduct *simultaneous* interpretation elsewhere. But equally we need to preserve a discriminating consciousness that there do exist these different levels and modes of discourse in different passages throughout much of the Bible, and we need to be aware of the differing values and uses attaching to each. In such a judicious balance lies the key, I believe, to any poetic which Milton would have extrapolated from his own theological premises. The Bible is various and contains diverse levels of truth, diverse degrees of literalism or figurativeness in speaking to us; so by analogy must scripturally inspired poetry be adjusted to a variety of occasions, modes of discourse and kinds of "truth", account being taken in each instance of the nature of the statement or utterance being made, its sources and their degree of authority, and its correct application and use in the particular context in the poem.

"Accommodation" in *Of Christian Doctrine*

To turn now to the much-discussed lines in Milton's treatise concerning the representation of God in Scripture: the so-called theory of "accommodation" in *Of Christian Doctrine* I.ii.[23] The passage in question has more often than otherwise been cited in support of Milton's allegedly "literalist" position on the "representation" of God in Scripture and poetry. In fact, the issue and the passages in question are much more complex than such a position would allow. Milton's lines on accommodated understanding are certainly very suggestive; but they can be made, and historically have been made by Milton critics, to support either of two opposed positions. The one critical view, an earlier view, is that which takes Milton's lines as actually sanctioning figurative reading of Scripture (hence metaphor in *Paradise Lost*)—"accommodation" in this interpretation meaning the use of a particular form of God-directed metaphor to convey that which lies beyond understanding; while the other, opposite and more widespread view is that which construes "accommodation" as advocating a stringent literalism in reading the descriptions of God in Scripture (and, by extension, artistic representations of Him)—"accommodation" in this understanding meaning that the reader is to narrow his conception of God to the level of the anthropomorphic depictions often found in the Bible, which are allegedly intended there to be taken at face value. The truth is that Milton seems to be trying to keep both points of view in play simultaneously. We can achieve a true perspective on his "accommodation" passage only by recognizing its internal balances, which become more evident when it is read in the context of all those other passages in the *Christian Doctrine* concerning figurative language in Scripture, and especially that one about God referring to Himself in "an allegorical fiction".[24]

The gist of Milton's argument in the "accommodation" passage runs as follows. God is depicted in the Bible (not only in the "literal" but equally in the patently figurative passages) not as He "really is" at all, but as our limited understandings can best comprehend Him, that is to say, under forms which we can relate to our own persons, natures and lives. To be "safe", we had best not probe too far into the mysteries which manifestly must lie behind these accommodated descriptions, but instead take them on their own terms. Notwithstanding, we must retain a lively consciousness that the descriptions *are* accommodated; that is, we are to understand that the anthropomorphic depictions (even while we accept them) do not really correspond to God as He is at all, but are *analogies* found for more spiritual truths. Milton's words in the Columbia edition translation are these:

> When we speak of knowing God, it must be understood with reference to the imperfect comprehension of man; for to know God as he really is, far transcends the powers of man's thoughts, much more of his perception. . . . God therefore has made as full a revelation of himself as our minds can conceive, or the weakness of our nature can bear. . . .
>
> Our safest way is to form in our minds such a conception of God, as shall correspond with his own delineation and representation of himself in the sacred writings. For granting that *both in the literal and figurative descriptions of God* ["talem semper vel describi vel adumbrari"], *he is exhibited not as he really is,* but in such a manner as may be within the scope of our comprehensions, yet we ought to entertain such a conception of him, as he, in condescending to accommodate himself to our capacities ["ipse se ad captum accommodans nostrum"], has shown that he desires we should conceive. For it is on this very account that he has lowered himself to our level, lest in our flights above the reach of human understanding,

and beyond the written word of Scripture, we should be tempted to indulge in vague cogitations and subtleties.[25]

It is hardly surprising that critics have not been at one about this passage, since it can appear in such varying lights. Milton's tone is guarded, neutral, exploratory, to the point at moments of seeming to hedge. "Our *safest way*", "*we ought* to entertain", "*granting* . . . he is exhibited": we may hardly construe these phrases as the language of certitude. Here and in associated passages we may sense Milton's sense that he is dealing with a difficult issue on which, perhaps, not too much should be concluded or even thought—that the interpretation of this knot of doctrine is awkward. One cannot however suppose that Milton is merely equivocating on such an important matter. It is more as if he is struggling to reconcile two paradoxical yet both valid points of view, trying to bring both into some genuine correlation—or perhaps, to move on to a third, more qualified stance than either. Small wonder, therefore, if James Holly Hanford could draw from this passage a Neoplatonic theory of "Ideal" artistic representation, while a critic such as H.R. MacCallum does the opposite and connects the same passage with Protestant moves towards literalism in the reading of Scripture and the writing of religious poetry.[26]

Despite his comments to the effect that God has revealed Himself in a way that our limited minds and weak nature can bear, and that He has lowered His depiction of Himself to our human level—both of which would appear to recommend a literal or anthropomorphic conception of Him—Milton immediately goes on specifically to confute any form of anthropomorphism,[27] and to recommend that we "conceive of him, not with reference to human passions, that is, after the manner of men". Milton then sends us back once again to Scripture for God's own descriptions of Himself—which, in those places where they turn out to be "literal", are to be accepted as appropriate although not as simply human. In the end, what Milton seems to be trying to arrive at is that we should understand God or the nature of God, *insofar as He* (in His descriptions of Himself or elsewhere) *has been pleased to impart what needs concern our salvation:* "*such knowledge of the Deity as was necessary for the salvation of man*, he has himself of his goodness been pleased to reveal abundantly". Again: "those have acquired the truest apprehension of the nature of God who submit their understandings to his word". By which "word", then, we are perhaps meant to understand "Word", or *doctrine.* Thus in the end Milton, unwilling to commit himself, returns us in a circle to that same equivocal point from which he started: "In arguing thus, we *do not say that God is in fashion like unto man* in all his parts and members, but that *as far as we are concerned to know*, he is of that form which he attributes to himself in the sacred writings". But which form is that? Quite simply, our level of understand-

ing is such that we are to know, and not know, from what is written in
Scripture; to entertain a conception, yet not entertain it, or entertain it in a
limited manner, or entertain it with a further reference, perhaps with
reference to those saving doctrines which are our true concern. "As far as
we are concerned to know" implies a resistance to fruitlessly speculative
readings of the Bible; but it is not a recommendation to a purely literal kind
of reading.

The matter rests, then, on the innate ambiguity of the word "accom-
modation". Does it mean accommodation *upward*, or *downward*? God,
certainly, makes an act of condescension toward limited human com-
prehension; but do not men, also, have to make a large reciprocal act of
accommodation in understanding that God is more than the descriptions
of Him show, even while accepting those? "Not as he really is" remains the
telling phrase in Milton's passage. God is not as He is shown in *either* "the
literal" *or* the "figurative descriptions" of Him (or "both" . . . "and", as in
the Columbia translation, which really amounts to the same thing). Extra-
literal meaning exists in *both* cases, and not just in those particular in-
stances in Scripture in which metaphor (or allegory) is so pointed as overtly
to steer us away from literalism. We are to see God in *both* ways, literally
and non-literally, Milton's passage implies—insofar as we may envisage
Him at all, or understand Him apart from His doctrines—just as the
language of Milton's own passage "accommodates" two contradictory
perspectives.[28] And that would suggest a surprisingly radical rather than a
conservative aesthetic or poetic—one in which literalism or a certain kind
of fidelity to the Bible is held at a narrow point of balance with a sense of
mystery and the reality of the non-literal in the representation of God in
Scripture. Just as in Milton's own prose analysis two contrasting modes of
understanding God hang poised, fused in opposing statements, so in
religious poetry, we may suppose, two contrasting ways of representing
and understanding divine "reality" might be reconciled—perhaps bal-
anced as between carefully juxtaposed, contrasting kinds of description, or
even, sometimes, Milton's words almost seem to imply, accommodated
within the same description. All of the foregoing passages from the *Chris-
tian Doctrine* concern the representation of God in the Bible, which is a
particularly sensitive case. All the more might one imagine, then, that in
wider uses of scriptural materials in poetry no lesser a degree of latitude
concerning figurative writing and understanding is admissible.

SIXTEEN

Theory of Metaphor
in *Paradise Lost*

The questions which arise over the principle of "accommodation" in *Of Christian Doctrine* necessarily carry over into *Paradise Lost*. Two observations are to be made at the outset. First, I believe that the too close identification of the "accommodation" question, as it is raised in *Of Christian Doctrine* or potentially in *Paradise Lost*, with Neoplatonism has been the cause of profound and unnecessary confusion.[1] Neoplatonism is, historically, linked with an Idealist aesthetic or poetic the literary expressions and expositions of which from Tasso to Sidney or even later were of importance to Milton. Occasionally, as we have seen in Tasso and briefly in Milton, such an aesthetic could take on overtones verging on the mystical. But this is not to say, either, that Milton could not discriminate as to the kinds of contexts to which he applied such mystical poetics.

Even more obviously, Milton would not have felt bound, in accepting certain highly traditional views of Neoplatonic colouring about the poet's role and about poetic function, thereby to subscribe to the full body of Platonic thought—especially within a scriptural poem. The symbolic and expressive potential of Neoplatonic aesthetics mattered to him; we know that Neoplatonic ethical theory had been of peculiar importance to him in his earlier writings, as for example in *Comus*, and was still important in *Paradise Lost*; also that, as Irene Samuel has pointed out,[2] Plato had profoundly influenced Milton in two other important areas, namely, his views on the methods and function of education and, more specifically, on the didactic end of poetry. But Milton's mature thought also held major differences from Plato and Plato's successors. Platonic-based metaphysics asserts the unreality of the phenomenal world, while Milton's distinctive metaphysic is strongly opposed to this view, joining forces with his Christian and Protestant feeling, so forcefully projected in *Paradise Lost*, that God's created world, like that ancient one described in the Bible, is substantial and real—even though both may at times also afford mystical or other kinds of hidden adumbrations. Milton's poetic representation in

Paradise Lost, infused with a sense of the literal reality, the active presence of the world of Genesis, but not itself therefore always or simply literal, shows just the same degree of difference from a fully mystical Neoplatonic art as does his distinctive Christian form of materialism from the shadowier Platonic world-view. Milton's world and poetry are (like Scripture) *both* convincingly "real" *and* often also "allegoric", they are both figurative and literally true—even though (to echo Milton's words on Scripture) care must be taken to distinguish when the poem may be speaking mainly with one kind of voice and when with the other.

"Accommodation": Raphael's Theory of Discourse

The second observation is, that I do not think that valid inferences about Milton's poetic art can be made exclusively by extrapolation from his theories on exegesis in *Of Christian Doctrine* (that is, from doctrinal commentary of the strictest kind)—significant though certain of such correlations may sometimes be—without supporting evidences of intention or practice from within the poem. Therefore Hanford's theory about Milton's view of poetry in *Paradise Lost* as an "accommodated" art of figurative representation stands not so much, I believe, on the basis of the passages in *Of Christian Doctrine*, Book I, chapter ii, alone,[3] as by virtue of the apparently deliberate echo and amplification of those passages in Book V, lines 563-76 of *Paradise Lost*. I refer to the well-known lines in which Raphael makes an act of condescension to the limited understandings of his human audience in Eden, a narrative "accommodation" comparable to that which Milton says God makes to man in the Bible. Raphael says that he will recount for Adam's benefit the story of the angels' rebellion in Heaven by making use of a sort of fictive *analogy* to the "real"; he will tell the event *as if* it had been a human war, and in this way what is spiritual and beyond man's apprehension will become recognisable, accessible, and morally useful. I begin with the lines toward the end of the passage:

>   what surmounts the reach
> Of human sense, I shall delineat so,
> By lik'ning spiritual to corporeal forms,
> As may express them best.

This might seem at first sight to be a straightforward act of heavenly accommodation *down* to man's capacities; we are to take Raphael's impending account in a fairly straightforward way as a useful metaphor or "likeness", but without exploring too far into the nature of the thing signified. His narrative is "real"; or it is real enough for us, and we need not worry about the matter any further.[4] Yet this passage and its immediate contexts are full of expressed doubts and palpable difficulties which act to undermine any such complacent acceptance. For one thing, Raphael displays a seemingly Puritan reticence about the "lawfulness" of using any kind of figure at all, even analogy, in connection with heavenly matters: "how last unfould / The secrets of another World, *perhaps / Not lawful to reveal?*" This speculation on the dangers of metaphor is answered by himself; it would appear that a *dispensation* exists in this instance: "yet for thy good / *This is dispenc't*" ("dispenc't" is a technical word indicating exemption from a religious obligation or restriction). Raphael goes on to say that it will after all be legitimate to use a metaphor, figure, or whatever, in the same way that a preacher might, that is, for purposes of a moral or spiritual lesson to man—"for thy *good*". (Raphael's account is not to be exegesis, not interpretation of doctrine; the case would be more dubious, one presumes, if revealing "the secrets of another World" meant in any way that Raphael was through metaphor engaging with points of doctrine.) The fiction of the heavenly War is admissible in what is clearly a homiletic moral context; this the "application" which Raphael draws at the end of his talk with Adam (VIII. 633-37), stressing passional control as well as obedience, confirms.

Further, Raphael shows himself exceedingly conscious of the inadequacy involved in his act of approximate figuration—the degree to which "sign" falls short of the thing "signified". Yet his very stress on the mysteriousness of the thing figured enforces acknowledgement of the potency of sign, its necessity, if his account is to convey anything meaningful at all:

> how shall I relate
> To human sense th' invisible exploits
> Of warring Spirits . . . how last unfould
> The secrets of another World . . . ?
> . . . yet . . . *what surmounts the reach*
> *Of human sense, I shall delineat so,*
> By lik'ning spiritual to corporeal forms,
> *As may express them best.*

The expressible may, must, be used to "express" the inexpressible. Is this really "accommodation" only in the literalistic downward sense often imputed to Milton's remarks on the self-representation of God in Scripture? Or do not Raphael's teasingly doubtful remarks also imply "accommodation" in the more subtle upward sense, in which the reader makes a conscious effort to recognise (to borrow the words of the *Christian Doctrine*) that the thing represented both is and is not shown "as [it] really is"?

There is an air of indecisiveness and difficulty suffused over the Raphael passage which at once recalls the tone of suppressed questioning, the curious reserve, in the parallel passage in the *Christian Doctrine*. It seems to me that Raphael's statement is no less open-ended than that in the *Christian Doctrine*; if anything it is more so, since the problem as Raphael raises it here is not confined to the specific and unique matter of the depiction of God, but concerns the much more general issue of the fictive rendering of any scriptural event, even something so enigmatically alluded to in the Bible as the fall of Lucifer, "son of the morning", in Isaiah xiv. Furthermore, comparing the verse passage with the prose passage in *Of Christian Doctrine*, we observe that the thought in the former moves not away from speculation toward apparent suppression of doubts but in the reverse direction, toward an awakening of speculation. Raphael's initial matter-of-factness about "lik'ning spiritual to corporeal forms" gives way to increased uncertainty as to how he or Adam (a proxy for the reader) is to understand the impending narration, or indeed to understand the entire problem of figuration in scripturally based fictions. The hesitating, probing tone throughout ("how shall I relate . . . / how . . . unfould."); the central ambiguity of "as *may* express them best" (exactly what mode of discourse does "express" imply? and why not *"will* express"?); the pervading air of "mysteries" ("high matter", "secrets")—all these work against any superficial assumption that Raphael's account is going to present a simple analogy. So many shifts in tone and stance seem to nudge us in the direction of oblique signification, hidden meanings—in effect, toward some form of allegory.

To confirm our feelings of unease, there comes finally Raphael's famous and disturbing afterthought at the end of the passage, which conspires against the earlier parts to undermine confidence and maximize the opening uncertainties which had apparently been laid to rest: *"though what if Earth . . ."* Lest we should have been inclined to pass over Raphael's hesitations as mere gestures toward narrative propriety (or even a lame excuse on Milton's part for awkward management of this part of his fiction), lest we fail to attend to all those hints about *mysteries*, Raphael's concluding words so abruptly thrown out seem to leave a vast question mark hanging not only over his own narration but over the entire poem: "though what if Earth / Be but the shaddow of Heav'n, and things therein / Each to other like, more then on Earth is thought?" The implication of these last lines would seem to be, "may" not this mode of narration about to be employed by Raphael also "express" some further deep meaning, contain some truth beyond its superficial analogy? (Otherwise, what is the point of surmising some closer, more hidden correspondence between Heaven and its "shaddow", its metaphor, Earth; why introduce the remark at all?) Raphael had already said that the "War" could not adequately correspond to the heavenly realities it represents. Now the words with which he concludes the preface to his long impending narration seem to open up unlimited vistas, suggesting that, yes, something of unusual significance *can* be communicated by figure—by Raphael's particularly long "continued dark conceit". His interjection with its abrupt "though" acts as if to undercut all that Raphael had previously said about the inadequacy of metaphor.

Whatever else they may mean, these last lines effectively preclude our taking the passage in the way that some have taken the "accommodation" passage in the *Christian Doctrine*—that is, as a disincentive to figurative speculation.[5] The passage is exactly the reverse. "Earth / . . . the shaddow of Heav'n" raises every conceivable kind of question, while the slippery syntax prevents us from reaching a conclusion on any. Does "therein" refer to Heaven (as grammatically it should), or does it refer to Earth, or to both places? Does "Each to other like" stand as an elliptical contraction for "each [*thing* in Heaven is] like to [the corresponding] other [thing on Earth]"— which is a surprising way round to put things—or does the blurred syntax vaguely imply some mutual symbolic reciprocal shadowing between the two spheres ("each" is "like" the "other" and vice versa)? Raphael's statement had been about to conclude with the proposition that events on Earth could shadow those in Heaven; but that Heaven may copy Earth, or that each may copy the other, is a quite different and, as I said, a strange and surprising thought. (Unless of course Raphael is hinting that details in *his* fictive account of the heavenly War will correspond in some significant manner to human situations on Earth; the heavenly War then becomes not analogy but direct allegory.)

A conventional Platonic outlook would rest content with the unilateral assumption that it is Earth or the phenomenal world which offers a faint shadow of the higher. That is not, it seems, the sense whch is being conveyed by Raphael's last three lines. The total effect, indecipherable, is to intertwine heavenly and earthly realities in some intensely inseparable way, more substantial than the phrase "Earth the shaddow of Heav'n" taken on its own might imply. It is impossible to say with certainty what the lines do or do not mean, do or do not include or exclude. Certainly they cannot be pinned down to any literalist understanding of "accommodation"; neither to typology (*all* things in Heaven evoking *all* things on Earth is far too sweeping, and has nothing to do with Christological prophecy). And although superficially the memorable phrase, "Earth the shaddow of Heav'n", could appear to be invoking Platonic philosophical thought, there are, as we see, problems in making too direct an equation. We may experience the same difficulty that we feel in connection with Raphael's earlier exposition of the great Chain of Being in Book V, in the "body up to spirit work" lines (469ff.), a passage which has significant links with that we have just been discussing. Body in the earlier passage is too "spiritous", spirit too substantial, to fit in easily with the Platonic or Neoplatonic ladder of love and beauty, and Raphael in the earlier passage is reduced to a form of verbal equivocation, rendered in the hesitant and ambivalent speculation, that men may, in the course of time, "wing'd ascend / Ethereal, as wee," (lines 498-99).

On the other hand, a late Neoplatonic *aesthetic* may well be in question, such as was evolved by Plotinus and Porphyry or Origen, and (via Marius Victorinus) passed on to Augustine and Proclus, thence with resonances from the medieval Victorine mystics, through Pico to the Renaissance—a tradition of which Lamberton, among other scholars, has traced the earlier lines of descent.[6] Is Raphael trying, for example, to hint at something like the older Victorine system of universal correspondences, a hermetic system which pushed allegorism toward a mystical extreme, one in which all in the real world, heavens and earth, man's body itself, as well as the real events recorded in Scripture, are simultaneously a book of mystic symbols to be read spiritually?

The continuing existence of the Victorine tradition or something very like it into the late Renaissance is apparent in the commentaries on the *Orlando Furioso* by Simone Fornari, whose allegorical interpretations of that poem were a principal source for Harington's, and are in themselves of great interest.[7] Fornari ascribes his theory of allegory to "St. John" (the Evangelist), a figure introduced into Canto XXXIV.54 of the *Furioso*, in an episode continuing through Cantos XXXIV-XXXV. John later, with Astolfo visiting the Moon, there demonstrates living allegories, so to speak, including that of the "lost wits" in Canto XXXIV.82ff., which Milton imitated in Book III (lines 444ff.) of *Paradise Lost*—John's demonstrations prefacing a more elaborate allegory of poetic fame beginning in Canto XXXIV.87 and running through to Canto XXXV.30. As Fornari develops his exposition in some technical detail, more immediate sources than "St. John" would seem to be in question. A suggestively similar discussion of allegory to both Fornari's and Raphael's is to be found in Origen's famous commentary on the Song of Songs, quoted first now, with the Fornari passage following: "So, as we said at the beginning, all the things in the visible category can be related to the invisible, the corporeal to the incorporeal, and the manifest to those that are hidden; so that the creation of the world itself, fashioned in this wise as it is, can be understood through the divine wisdom, which from actual things and copies teaches us things unseen by means of those that are seen, and carries us over from earthly things to heavenly".[8]

The visible world becomes in Origen an analogy, or a metaphor, for the invisible; "things and copies" on earth serve to "teach" about heavenly "things unseen". Fornari develops Origen's type of theory of a "didactic" universe in more elaborate detail. He (drawing directly from Pico) observes with some explicitness how the structure of the universe on the one hand, and exegesis and poetry on the other, provide vocabularies for each other:

For that reason it was the opinion of Anaxagorus and approved by the Pithagorians and the Platonists that there are three worlds: one supercelestial, otherwise called intellectual; another next to this and called by him celestial; the third sublunary, and it is this one which we inhabit; they join also the fourth and they hold that it is the body of man. In all these four worlds the said Anaxagorus says that total correspondence exists and that no thing is found which does not have its similitude in the other three. But those things which are in the inferior worlds are also in the superior, although there of greater note and condition than in the lower. As, for example, in the human body heat is found, in the earth the element of fire, in the heavens the sun, and in the superworldly country the seraphic intellect. For which reason St. John said to Astolfo [35. 18. 3]: *'Every effect which occurs in Earth is in Heaven, but in different appearance'. Hence it comes that all heavenly things appear as imitations of earthly things: from this principle again proceeds the learning of every allegorical sense.* For this reason *these worlds, bound together in a binding chain, lend common words and appelations* [sic] *one to the other as nature does.* Because of such things, *for him who makes allegorical verses and for that other who explicates them, it is necessary to know the nature of the said worlds and what thing of one world corresponds to and what thing can be compared to the specific thing of another world.*[9]

Fornari's statement is remarkable not only for its verbal similarities to Origen's (which may be a source for both Fornari and Pico), but also for the extraordinary resonances which the passage finds in Raphael's speech in *Paradise Lost*. We see, for example, in Fornari the same strange apparently *inverted* "imitation" of things on Earth by things in Heaven (the seeming opposite of a Platonic scheme) which we find in Raphael's lines (V.572-76) quoted earlier. Further, somewhat in the way Origen turned the theory of universal correspondences to the function of "teaching", Fornari has gone on to connect the same theory with both allegorical explications and allegorical verses—just as Raphael, too, uses the theory of earthly and heavenly correspondences to validate a theory of allegorical teaching (in verse) in his forthcoming account to Adam. Fornari's paraphrase of Ariosto is taken from a specific statement on allegory in the *Furioso* itself (XXXV.18), a passage which Milton would have read for himself. I give the passage in Harington's translation:

> Know first (said he) there cannot wag a straw,
>   Below on earth, but that the signe is here:
> And each small act, doth correspondence draw,
>   Although in other shew it doth appeare:
> That aged man, that running erst you saw,
>   And never baits, nor resteth all the yeare,
> To worke the like effects above is bound,
> As time doth worke below, upon the ground.[10]

Milton as we know read Ariosto in Harington's allegorized edition;[11] also, without doubt, in an original language edition. In all probability any Italian edition which Milton read, and certainly Harington's edition in English of the *Furioso*, contained allegorical annotations and expository material. The two Cantos from Ariosto, XXXIV and XXXV, themselves contain very elaborate and long allegories, much the larger one (of which the stanza quoted above is a small part) being that concerned with that subject most dear to Milton's heart, poetic fame.[12] It is Milton's use of satirical allegory that is usually cited as deriving from Ariosto (as in Book III in Milton's "Paradise of Fools" episode). But at least as important to Milton would seem to have been the larger Ariostian allegory of poetic fame (of which the instance of the "lost wits" is a negative illustration); and it is this larger allegory which embraces within itself "St. John's" theory of heavenly correspondences and allegory in "act" and "signe" (deeds and language). This larger Ariostian allegory, with its statement on the theory of earthly and heavenly correspondences, comprises the main material of Cantos XXXIV-XXXV—cantos which, as we can see, may thus have impressed themselves on Milton's mind through at least three contexts of significance to himself: the theme of poetic fame (initiated in Ariosto's Canto XXXIV, stanza 73, a theme which is Milton's central preoccupation in the personal passages of the *Reason of Church-Government*); satirical allegory on false or fleeting "wits" (as emulated in *Paradise Lost*, Book III.444ff., and as cited in the *Reason of Church-Government*, where the satirical stanza 80 of the *Furioso* is quoted); and the theory of didactic poetic allegory (as explained by "St. John", and as similarly expressed in Raphael's important aside). The same theory of universal allegory which was expressed and illustrated in Ariosto's stanzas reached Milton also in the more elaborated forms expounded in Harington's commentaries or in those of some of Harington's sources, Italian allegorizers such as Fornari. These are theories which seemingly have ultimate origins in older well established allegorizers such as Origen (with whom also Milton was directly familiar). Thus an elaborate chain of circumstances connects Milton with a whole tradition of hermetic allegory based on essential or universal correspondences: correspondences enacted via "deed and word". The further explicit connections by Origen and, more elaborately, by Fornari, of the theory of universal correspondences with "teaching" and with *written* allegorical commentary and allegorical poetry gives further credence to the possibility that Milton is indeed using Raphael to promote a critical theory of didactic allegorical poetry or secondary discourse in, and in relation to, the verse narrative of *Paradise Lost*.

If so, Milton's attempt is well disguised. The Raphael passage is so constructed that we cannot conclude anything definitely from it. The whole passage becomes a supposition, a wild surmise: "what if . . . ?" All the same, we cannot but feel a weight of pregnant implication pressing in upon us; meaning *is* present, far *"more then on Earth is thought"*. The likelihood remains that the "shadowing" of which Raphael speaks represents a cautious move on Milton's part (cautious, because it might be perceived as religiously radical), and sheltering under Raphael's wing, toward a theory of poetic or literary allegorism. Given its highly respectable sources in such writers as Augustine,[13] the application of theory of allegory to a poetic narrative-fictive context such as Milton's would not have been inconsistent either with the preservation of pure scriptural truth or with Protestant proprieties concerning the reading and exposition of Scripture, as Milton himself saw the case—that is, provided due care and attention were given to the use of such a mode in proper contexts. To liken "spiritual to corporeal forms", and to "express" what otherwise lies beyond "the reach / Of human sense" by means of metaphorical likeness to something sensible, remain entirely accurate descriptions of the allegorical process, whether as represented in traditional hermeneutics or in earlier secular allegorical exegesis and literature. Raphael's harping on "secrets", arcane mysteries and "shadows" itself betrays the characteristic idiom and thought processes of traditional allegorism. To "speake one thing and thinke another", or to intend "another meaning, then the proper signifycation doth expresse", or to speak via a "translation" or "metaphor" (Raphael's words provide close paraphrases of all of these formulations)—all these are among the oldest rhetorical descriptions of allegory, constantly revived in Renaissance dictionaries.[14] But the word "shadow" provides what may be the most explicit key in Raphael's statement to the language of literary allegory. "Shadow", as was said at the outset of this chapter, is itself in the Renaissance a general term for allegorical figure—not necessarily only Platonic and not necessarily typological in implication.[15]

The question which Raphael's prefatory words leaves so pregnantly hanging in the air is this: if everything on earth may be but a "shaddow of Heav'n" (that is, may through figuration signify higher or spiritual realities), and if Raphael's own narration itself stands as a prime example of this process, what is the corresponding status of Milton's poem? May not it too comprise a mode of discourse which in at least part of its intricate fabric is designed to convey shadowed truths? The more one reflects on Raphael's remarks, and bearing in mind their striking similarity to earlier statements on allegory such as Origen's, Ariosto's and Fornari's, the more impossible it becomes to say with certainty that Raphael has not been inferring a mode of narrative allegory for his impending account, and implicitly for *Paradise Lost* a poetics of allegory. All the more might we suppose this to be so, since Raphael is here specifically engaging with the very question historically so pertinent to the Christian epic, the relationship between figurative analogy and "truth". It must be remembered that Raphael is not in his impending narration concerning himself with any kind of theological or doctrinal commentary, or with anything that might be termed direct interpretation of Scripture. Rather, he is in the immediate context (the heavenly War) engaged in a reworking of an obscure small portion of Old Testament narrative, the fall of Lucifer, into a long *fictive* discourse, one representing a highly personal expansion (as Raphael himself indicates) of a certain scriptural event, and which is to be used for a different kind of purpose, for moral edification. And since, as everybody knows, Raphael's supposed fiction is not his own but Milton's (almost one third of the poem), we may be forgiven if we suppose that Milton through Raphael may be making a necessary point about his own poem.

This probability seems the more likely, since elsewhere we find Milton as narrator so closely identifying himself with the words of Raphael as narrator in Book V. We may observe, for example, how Raphael's phrase about the difficulty of recording the fall of the angels, "Sad task and hard" (V.564), is echoed by Milton later in his own preliminary to the human fall: "Sad task" (IX.13). If we follow out this connection, Raphael's account of the angels' fall becomes an intentional parable for, or an allegory of, the impending human fall. It becomes increasingly difficult therefore not to connect the Raphael passage, and through it the narrative mode of a substantial part of Milton's poem, with the whole, long, continuing tradition of biblical and, derivatively, of poetic allegorism. In my own view as well as that of others, neither Milton nor any other great writer of imaginative religious literature (Protestant included) ever did or ever could wholly abandon that tradition—since, as Tuve, that illuminating critic, reminds us,[16] and as the early writers cited in previous chapters demonstrate, the entire basis of allegory is inseparably linked with the basis of poetry itself, that is to say, with metaphor, of which allegory is only one special form. Raphael stands as exemplar of the one mode of discourse in the poem—figurative, metaphoric, allegorical, however we like to view it, the human mode of "likenesses", correspondences and analogies; Michael by contrast exemplifies that other, complementary mode, the plain factual style appropriate to divine history and to doctrine.[17]

Shadows, Similitudes, Dreams: Language as Mediator

In the preceding section and chapter we have discussed Milton's theological views on the interpretation of Scripture and their bearing on figuration in *Paradise Lost*, and what degree of connection may obtain between Raphael's statements on heavenly "accommodation" and Milton's on scriptural "accommodation" in *Of Christian Doctrine*. In the next chapter we shall be discussing theories of typological figuration and their bearing (or otherwise) on the poetics of *Paradise Lost*. As a bridge between these two discussions, I wish to consider, without for the moment imposing a distinction between scripturally based and non-scripturally based metaphorical processes, what further evidence we may find in *Paradise Lost* of Milton's interest in probing the philosophical boundaries of figuration. It has been argued with some force recently that Milton distrusted the imagination or image-making faculty, or at any rate, that he compressed his own image-making into an orthodox typological mould. Attention to his actual language shows neither allegation to be true, and that Milton does not make the kind of rigid distinction between areas of metaphor that has been wished upon him by some of his critics, but rather, with good historical precedent in older secular and theological aestheticians, considers all aspects of the image-making faculty as interconnected and valid. We may focus this question through a further consideration of Milton's uses of the word "shadow" and associated terms.

It is impossible not to be struck, once one has become alerted to it, by the fascination which Milton evinces with *shadows* and related semblances in the poem ("shadow", "reflection", "image", also "dream" and "vision"), or by the verbal play he makes with these phenomena, in exploring their connectedness with sign and similitude. It is as if he is continually probing that mysterious barrier, sometimes so delicately slight, sometimes so opaque, which separates "shadow" from concrete reality, image or reflection from original, metaphor or similitude from object of comparison, "representation" from "truth". Milton shows a specific concern with the function and role of language in these instances, with the potency of figure to encompass two kinds of truth simultaneously, and with the power of sign and symbol not merely to designate but to participate in the realities which they adumbrate.

It would require more detailed study than the present context permits fully to explore this dimension in *Paradise Lost*, and the way Milton's imagined scenes constantly invoke the questions, which is "reality", which the "image" or the "shadow"? What is the relation of sign or similitude to the thing signified? When do too many shadows darken, when enlighten?[18] When are images and resemblances real, when illusory? Thus, newly created Eve's reflection in a pool offers her a "smooth watry *image*" (IV.480), one which is fallacious, even though she herself takes it as real. God has presently to lead her "where *no shadow* staies / Thy coming" (IV.470-71), that is, to Adam's more substantial presence. But in contradistinction to the foregoing examples, the word "image" in *Paradise Lost* more often implies some degree of co-identity with an original, hence of substantiality—as when Milton describes how in Adam's and Eve's faces "The *image* of thir glorious Maker shon" (IV.292; similarly, V.95). Again, the Son is "The radiant *image* of [God's] Glory" (III.63). The divine spark, man's rational soul, shines out of his intelligent countenance, reflecting God in a lesser but analogous way to that in which Christ substantially reflects God's image. By contrast, Satan offers only the empty "*Idol* of Majestie Divine" (VI.101).

Let us look at "dreams", another kind of "image" or "shadow" of reality. Adam, having been created during a kind of waking dream and then brought into Eden, imagined that he was still dreaming—yet he awoke to find "Before mine Eyes all real" in Paradise, exactly "as the *dream* /

Had *lively shadowd*" (VIII.310-11). This "dream shadow" was "lively" ("living", as well as "vivid") and proved to be wholly "real"; yet Adam's language also carried unmistakeable connotations of prefiguration, "shadowed" in that sense.[19] Eve's dream on the other hand, recounted earlier in Book V, *is* a dream, and it is quite opposite to Adam's. She awoke to find that her tempting flight to the skies had been "but a dream" (V.93), and a most misleading one, like the moon at night "*Shadowie* set[ting] off" only "the face of things" (V.43)—showing superficies, not essences. Yet Eve's dream was "true" in a quite different, in a prefigurative and allegorical sense. Had she been able to discern the case, that dream had held a true foreshadowing of the inner actualities of her temptation and the outer ones of her fall, which come to pass later, in Book IX. Which kind of "truth" is more "true", then: the literal-prefigurative, or the figurative-prefigurative— or does each validate the other? Is straight "allegory" (of which Eve's dream represents one recognisable form, the dream-vision) any less true, less valid, than the other (Adam's) kind of dream prefiguration—since each dream comes to be realised in fact? Or, perhaps, does the one merely represent a lower, human level of the other's higher, divinely foreshadowed, truth?

We might with advantage explore what seem evidently to be the most purely physical uses of "shadow" in *Paradise Lost*. In Book III the Sun, all light, can cast no shadows onto its own clear surface, so that physical sight, as represented in Uriel, is perfect there. Yet the situation is so contrived as to show us that the false external resemblance assumed by Satan can obscure perceptions of a deeper order. Which then is more "real", perception or perceptiveness: eyesight or insight? During the War in Heaven, mountains come "shadowing" over the plains of Heaven; do they cast a "real" shadow, in an episode which is palpably a metaphor for something else; or does this almost excessive touch of the "literal" here, as elsewhere in the War episode, press us invertedly toward some act of "accommodated" or figurative understanding? Throughout all such episodes and instances there often seems to be an uncanny, almost wilful blurring between image, reflection, shadow, dream and those *things* imaged, reflected, dreamed of or "shadowed". "Shadows" acquire a paradoxical intensity—an indication that we may be in the presence of such "shadows" understood in the deeper senses of metaphor, *parabola* or sign.[20] And in the almost mystical concreteness of relation between "sign" and "thing signified", as Ernst Gombrich has said, "Who can always tell where the one begins and the other ends"?[21] For Earth is indeed the "shaddow of Heav'n" in Milton's poem in some very remarkable ways. Eden's fourfold rivers and central Fountain mirror in solid substance the mystical geography of Heaven in Book III (344-64); these "solid" outlines in Milton's Garden, through that which they shadow, surely serve to remind us also of the more impalpable landscapes of the enduring Paradise and that "paradise within". So that other "things", as well, in Milton's "real" poetic world may serve as mysterious shadows, in ways more covert than Raphael cares too openly to admit.[22]

An astonishing expression of Milton's perception in *Paradise Lost* of the close relationship between allegory, adumbration, or metaphor ("likeness", to use Raphael's word) and divine realities is seen in Milton's reference to the "begott'n" Son as "Divine *Similitude*" (III.384). "Similitude" is a word which as well as meaning *resemblance* carries inescapable period and present-day connotations of *metaphor*, or even, earlier, of something akin to symbol. The Son, that is to say, is not merely a resemblance or reflection of the Highest but a visible image of or a living metaphor for the Divine. He renders invisible Deity visible, "translates" God into what may be seen by human eye, makes us see what God is "like". (All these innuendoes are also embedded in the Invocation to light at the beginning of Book III.) The Son as "Divine *Similitude*", similarly to "Man in our *image*, Man / In our *similitude*" (VII.519-20), but in manner more "conspicuous" (III.385), displays and in a deeper sense *is* that which he mirrors.[23] Milton's choice in these instances of such words as *image, similitude*, inevitably draws in the context of poetry. The poet himself strives to "express" the Son (how "May I *express* thee", III.3) through metaphors of light (III.6-8) which do not offer simple comparisons but suggest a participation in the divine essence. As the Son both "expresses" and participates in the divine nature, so poetic metaphor likens to and also shares in the reality which it adumbrates. The Son in being Himself a "Similitude" would appear to validate figuration in human language.[24]

We may conclude with an analogous instance, bearing on the connections between human metaphor and divine truth, which occurs both in Milton's prose and in *Paradise Lost*. Milton in *The Reason of Church-Government* and in certain passages of *Paradise Lost* presents the roles of the poet, the angels and Christ as in parallel, all being forms of "interpretation"—a word which refers to *language* as well as to intercession. For example: the poet is to be "an *interpreter* & relater of the best and sagest things"; Uriel is "Interpreter through highest Heav'n" of God's "authentic will" (III.656-57); Raphael is "Divine Interpreter" (VII.72)—this ties in directly with Raphael's doctrine of accommodated language; and finally, we see the Son "interpret" for man in the penultimate Book of *Paradise Lost* (XI.33), in a very curious passage, probably figural in some unusual way, which has been recently discussed by Sanford Budick.[25] Milton in these passages thus seems to be choosing and using words in such a way as to show the underlying connectedness between various kinds and contexts of metaphor and higher or divine truths. Human language and poetry—shadow, figure, allegory and all forms of metaphor—all mirror the divine act or acts of accommodation or mediation and have a share in metaphysical realities.

SEVENTEEN

Typology and the Figurative Dimension in *Paradise Lost*

Many readers of Milton have not found it easy to interpret *Paradise Lost* along the lines of any such widely embracing theories of metaphor and allegorical poetics as those suggested in the foregoing chapters. One may surmise that readers have been inhibited by historical preconceptions, recently given a new twist, concerning the necessity for literal truth and a literalist aesthetic in religious poetry and notably in a scriptural epic such as *Paradise Lost*. Contemporary Milton criticism therefore seems to be in something of an irreconcileable divide. On the one hand we have seen a huge development, dating from the 1950s, of secularly addressed studies which approach *Paradise Lost* via image, rhetoric and metaphorical structures, exploring the poem's meaning with increasing awareness of it as a work filled with the most intricate systems of oblique correspondences, the most delicate resonances in language, verbal echoes and allusions, structural and narrative resonances too, a poem which is a kind of gigantic metaphor or web of metaphors for all that it has to say, and which is anything but simplistic or literalistic in its forms of mimesis. It almost seems as if many in this group of critics feel able to discuss *Paradise Lost* as poetry and in these rich ways only by avoiding explicit engagement with the poem's doctrinal commitments, or, occasionally, by challenging them. On the other part, and as a later development from a different group of dogmatically oriented critiques of the postwar decades, we have seen several schools of interpretation which approach the problem of metaphor and oblique allusion in *Paradise Lost* from the reverse direction. Taking cognizance of recent claims for a more rigorous Protestant orthodoxy of belief and a correspondingly strict poetic in Milton's work, the group of critics in question have either sought to define Milton's aesthetic within the sphere of "Protestant poetics" or, somewhat more narrowly, within the sphere of "typological symbolism", in which the wide-ranging metaphorical richness of *Paradise Lost* is seen as largely funnelled into predictive patterns of futurity and recollection, based upon traditional typological readings of the Old Testament.

"Typological Symbolism" in *Paradise Lost*

My present concern is with the last vein of criticism mentioned above, the effort of which has been to interpret figuration in *Paradise Lost* almost entirely within the context of "types" understood in a Christian pre-figurative sense. Not helped by the vexatious "accommodation" theory in *Of Christian Doctrine*, which has usually been seen not as potentially an imaginatively liberating doctrine but as one constraining to a narrow literalism in artistic representation, some of the most influential Milton critics of the last twenty or thirty years have turned toward theories of "typological symbolism", as perhaps a way out of the difficulties they may have felt in reconciling Milton the Reformation poet with Milton the imaginative artist. "Typological" reading of *Paradise Lost* has evidently been felt to be more legitimate than secular modes of interpreting Miltonic metaphor, perhaps because the typological, the second of the older scriptural "levels" of meaning (or "allegory" in the technical theological sense), and that most unambiguously asserting the concurrent reality of the historical and any further sense, is the one kind of *double* reading cited by Milton as admissible in connection with the interpretation of the Old Testament. (It is not, however, the only kind of figurative language which Milton finds in the Old Testament.)

The precise contexts of "typological" reading of the Bible delimited by Milton in *Of Christian Doctrine* (I.xxx), where he stresses that the Old Testament, only, "sometimes" offers readings which are a "compound of the historical and typical" (prophetic-Christological) senses, have been discussed earlier.[1] Also noted earlier was the much broader recognition of the existence in the Bible of various other types of figurative metaphor, including allegory, expressed by Milton in other places in the *Christian Doctrine* or in his other prose writings, or inferred by him in the "one sense to one place" rule and in his exposition of "accommodation" in *Of Christian Doctrine* (I.xxx and I.ii). The last group of critics mentioned have not, as far as can be seen, attempted to exploit the full imaginative potential latent in these discussions by Milton but have instead afforded us a variety of loose interpretative extensions of the typological conception, *viz.*, that certain characters or events in the Old Testament *sometimes* offer anticipations of Christ, his rôle and his Church in the New dispensation (which is what Milton says), and also (what Milton does *not* specify in *Of Christian Doctrine*, although it is an otherwise common conception) of the converse, that the New Testament events in their accomplished "antitypes" meta-

phorically glance back at and complete the adumbrations offered by the
Old. Various fluid extensions of this theory of "typological symbolism"
(not without some historical precedent) have been elaborated to embrace
as much as possible of Milton's highly allusive art in *Paradise Lost*.

The very effort to fit so much of the figurative innuendo in Milton's
epic under the orthodox umbrella of "typological symbolism" would itself
seem to hint at that persistent critical unease which historically has sought
to find in "literal" truth (since "typological" metaphors are also "literally"
true) a self-justifying basis for interpreting the art and content of Milton's
scriptural epic. The approach represented in "typological symbolism" has
been welcomed as one which legitimizes disputed areas of metaphorical
exploration and figurative invention in Milton's poem. Consequently, we
have been sent on, in some readings of *Paradise Lost*, from strict historical
"types" and "prophecies" of the person and functions of Christ (what
Milton in Book XII.291 calls "shadowie expiations weak") to larger and
larger and more and more personal extrapolations into so-called "typologi-
cal" schemes of metaphor or other figures. These Yeatsian gyres have
sometimes been made to embrace almost any kind of phasal movement in
the poem and almost all forms of anticipation, recapitulation, reiteration,
echo or allusion.These techniques have been applied not only to criticism
of poems such as *Lycidas* or certain of Milton's sonnets which would appear
to lend themselves through their content to typological interpretation, but
also to *Paradise Regained*—although it is in the latter poem that Milton's use
of typology is most limited, bare, historical and exact, and linked specifical-
ly with Old Testament messianic prediction—as well as to Milton's early
minor poems and *Samson Agonistes* and *Paradise Lost*.

It would not be possible here to survey the entire range of typologically
based Milton criticism, much of which, especially in the earlier studies, has
been very valuable.[2] Nor is it possible or necessary to enter here into the
theological background to typological reading, as seen in Protestant bibli-
cal commentaries or in more formal theological writings. This work and its
application to a range of seventeenth-century literature has been well per-
formed by such scholars as Barbara Kiefer Lewalski and, with a somewhat
different orientation, Georgia B. Christopher. These critics have analyzed
the ways in which expanded forms of biblical typological reading became,
especially as applied in the more private types of religious verse or devo-
tion, "a means for probing and exploring the personal spiritual life with
profundity and complexity".[3] Something of such patterning may indeed
be present in *Paradise Lost*, in contexts which I later note; and some
indication of the way in which typologically oriented schemes or pattern-
ings may become the frame through which the religious writer or preacher
can project himself and his own experiences into those of the Bible are
included in my discussions in the next chapter.[4] However, Milton criticism

latterly has seemed in some danger of being swamped by this mode of figurative reading, to the exclusion of other valid figurative modes.

One of the most searching efforts to read *Paradise Lost* itself along typological lines has been that of William Madsen. Madsen says, after discussing Raphael's lines on "Earth the shaddow of Heav'n" in Book V: "It is my contention that . . . Milton is using 'shadow' here not in its Platonic or Neoplatonic sense but in its familiar Christian sense of 'foreshadowing' or 'adumbration', and that the symbolism of *Paradise Lost* is typological rather than Platonic".[5] Madsen also speaks more generally of wide patterns of anticipation and recapitulation running throughout the poem, all of them composed on loosely typological analogy. We may compare *The Cambridge History of the Bible* on Reformist exegesis: "According to this mode of exegesis the history of the Old Testament becomes as it were a symphony in which a theme is developed with variations, never with exact repetition, but with recognizable adaptations . . . leading up to an ultimate resolution".[6] But as I have already said, it is hard to see why so widely suggestive a phrase as "Earth the shaddow of Heav'n", echoing, if anything, traditional formulations of allegory, is to be attached exclusively to the Christian doctrine of Old Testament historical types; or why every premonition of futurity and recollection of the past in Milton's poem need be drawn under the typological umbrella.[7]

While typological criticism has struck some important veins in Milton's poetry and has helped us to see Milton the Reformation and Christian poet as a poet and not merely as a dogmatician, I would suggest that this way of reading, so illuminating in the context of the seventeenth-century Protestant devotional meditation or the private lyric such as George Herbert's, may be less appropriate to an epic which is a public and more inclusive mode, and that such readings can be exaggerated when applied to *Paradise Lost*. Milton does employ "types" in *Paradise Lost*, but, with his customary precision, within rather strictly defined limits clearly evident within the poem itself, and applied in accordance with his remarks on the subject in *Of Christian Doctrine*. He occasionally uses straight typological prophecy; he also constructs looser repetitive patternings in event, imagery and description, especially those relating to Fall and Restoration, which may suggest typological analogues (although it is not clear that he himself would have thought of these patterns in such a way). But I am inclined to think that Milton rather carefully avoids the most extreme applications of such systems in *Paradise Lost*, partly because he is something of a precisian and unusually sensitive to Old Testament historical proprieties (in this case the Edenic-Hebraic setting of Genesis and *Paradise Lost*), partly because such systems carried to extremes can have a *converse* effect to the historical fidelity sometimes imputed as justifying their use, and may move us instead in the direction of abstraction and over-intellectualization.[8]

Thus, we shall note that there are certain contexts in *Paradise Lost* where Milton declines to invoke typological or indeed any form of symbolism, in the interests of preserving the "literal" texture or quality of the events or experiences which he records. Equally, Milton frequently does make use of certain forms of spiritual or moral figuration and poetic allusiveness which, while they may sometimes be reminiscent of those recurrent or phasal patternings which characterize certain forms of typology, are not necessarily best understood within that framework. Typology is not geared to the conveying of ethical, social, or cosmological considerations; it is geared to dogmatic or else devotional considerations. It is allegory which, traditionally and as used by the Church Fathers, serves moral considerations. To insist that all of the symbolism in *Paradise Lost* is typological is to insist that all metaphor in the poem and thus the poem's entire content is directed solely by doctrine or prayer; and this simply is not the case. The poem's epic scope includes many other dimensions and departments of human life, thought and conduct—things magnificently of both divine and human use, as Milton put it in *Of Education*[9]—some of them more readily expressible through metaphor or allegorical figure than doctrine and prayer may be, or expressible through other forms of figuration than the typological. Doctrine is an essential part of Milton's poem, but it is perhaps more often rendered in *Paradise Lost* "plainly and perspicuously" than through figure of any kind; while prayer also is represented in a direct form in the poem, usually under distinctively parabiblical dress or biblical paraphrase, as of the Psalms. Even when matters of faith are touched upon in *Paradise Lost*, as they sometimes are through a respectfully oblique penumbra of figure, these instances are not always to be described as "typological", but are probably better explained through different kinds of scriptural decorums.

True "Types" and the Limits of Typological Interpretation

An earlier chapter has alluded to Milton's mentions of "types" in *Of Christian Doctrine* and in *Paradise Lost*.[10] We may return to that topic now. Traditionally, and by definition, typology is historically based, prophetic and Christocentric. It relates specifically to certain central facts about Christ's life, the Christian mediation, His Church and His new dispensation. Jean Daniélou discusses several varying strains of patristic typology, all of them founded on the messianic typology of the Old Testament prophets. He distinguishes between two main patristic avenues of typological application, the one eschatological (or directed to Christ's person and life), the other sacramental (or relating the types to the history of the Church), with a third and later Alexandrine development which related historical "types" to the interior life of the Christian. All of these are to be distinguished from the use of moral allegory, which was also employed by the Church Fathers, especially those in the Alexandrine tradition of Philo. However, Daniélou says, the "fundamental types", that is, the principal Old Testament figures, themes or events which are read prophetically, are universal, few in number and always the same: the sacrifice of Isaac, the marriage of Isaac, the Exodus, the crossing of the Red Sea, the figures of Moses and Joshua.[11]

Milton's uses of typology follow these traditional patterns, with emphasis on the two earlier forms of typology (the eschatological more than the sacramental). And certainly one can recognise in the types employed in *Paradise Lost* the principal Old Testament figures or themes noted above. Milton defines Christ's three rôles as prophet, priest and "King", in their sometimes double (that is, their outward and inward) aspects, with great explicitness in a special chapter (I.xv) of the *Christian Doctrine*.[12] In that chapter, Milton's references to "types" of Christ are plainly historical—the historical Old Testament characters always predict the historical Christ. Orthodox typology, as Helen Gardner has said, is doubly historical, in its "belief in the historical actuality of both the type and its realization".[13] Milton evidently wishes to keep such distinctions in plain view in *Paradise Lost* when he several times (notably in Michael's speeches in Book XII) directly connects "types and shadows" with specific Old Testament historical personalities in their predictions of Christ. Moses, for example, is a "figure" of Christ:

> to God is no access
> Without Mediator, whose high Office now
> *Moses in figure beares, to introduce*
> One greater, *of whose day he shall foretell.*
> (239-42)[14]

Such specialized uses of "figure" (the above is one of only two uses of this word in *Paradise Lost*), employing the main Old Testament personalities, are always brought back by Michael (or Milton) to the person, sacrifice or rôles of Christ: "religious Rites / Of sacrifice, informing them, *by types / And shadowes,* of that destind Seed" (231-33). Further in the same speech:

> Law can discover sin, but not remove,
> Save by *those shadowie expiations* weak,
> The Bloud of Bulls and Goats . . .
> Some bloud more precious must be paid for Man.
> (290-93)

And:

> Up to a better Cov'nant, disciplind
> *From shadowie Types* to Truth . . .

From imposition of strict Laws, to free
Acceptance of large Grace.
(302-5)

In the passages above, then, we see much more specific uses of "shadow" and "figure" (to signify Christological prefiguration) than it is possible, for example, to infer from "Earth . . . *the shaddow* of Heav'n" or, for that matter, from "Sin and *her shadow* Death" (IX.12)—where the words have quite different ranges of allusion from the lines quoted from Book XII. It is therefore entirely appropriate that it should be Michael, purveyor of divine truths and divine Promise in the poem and himself a deliberate exemplar of plainness in narration, who should expound this doctrine of plain and plainly narrated historical "types" in *Paradise Lost* ("Henceforth *what is to com* I will *relate . . .*", XII.11), while it is left to Raphael, the more sympathetically human of the two archangels, to speak via metaphors, "likeness" and allegory, through earthly "shadows", and in more oblique imaginative ways. The poem embraces both modes, Raphael's and Michael's, the first balanced against or perhaps narratively held within the second. The amply metaphorical and allegorical mode, centrally placed, subsumes the larger part of the poem with its human concerns. The divine mode, direct, historical, occasionally typological (although in such a straightforward way as often hardly to seem like figure at all), closes up and completes the poem in the final Books.[15]

Let us further consider the evidence for and against Milton's alleged uses of the more extended forms of typology. Another observable limitation on Milton's use of "types" may be this. Neither in the *Christian Doctrine* nor in *Paradise Lost* does he seem to allow for any figurative development or application of the concept of "antitypes". Nowhere does he say in his theological treatise or suggest in his poem that elements in the New Testament may be read in a "compound" (doubly referential) sense, in the way that the Old Testament may be read. The Old Testament prefigures the New sometimes, in its own literal facts, events and persons; but the New Testament neither acts through its own characters as further prefiguration of the Christian hope, nor is it, apparently, to be freely read as a backward retrospect on the Old. The New Dispensation certainly *perfects* the Old, and everything in the Old has led up to it; and the types of the Old Testament are of course implicitly realised in the perfect "antitype" of Christ. But what I mean is, that Milton does not seem to read New Testament history and event with quite the freedom of symbolic reference, within a general typological framework, that is sometimes applied by other Reformation writers. Thus while we once or twice find retrospective as well as prospective typological allusions in *Paradise Lost*, (for example, "blest *Marie*, second *Eve*", V.387), what we do not seem to find in the poem is that any of the accounts of the Nativity or of Jesus' life or ministry, as narrated in Book XII, are allowed to take on symbolic charges of recollection or resumption from the poem's earlier "historical" events, whether those be taken from Genesis, or are fictive-heavenly. (A true retrospect occurs if anywhere in *Paradise Regained*, where poem and protagonist, point by point in the argument, step by step in the setting, narration and images, echo but reverse the events entailed in the loss of Paradise by Adam; but it is not at all clear that this significant technique can be construed as "typological".) It would seem that Milton prefers that form of typology, based on Old Testament messianic prediction, which "implies a doctrine of progress" or the "non-recurrence" of "historical events", and in which the terms of type and antitype "were not reversible".[16]

In their conspicuous plainness, the late sections of *Paradise Lost* concerning New Testament events operate aesthetically in a fashion totally different from that of the evocative late descriptions of human (that is, Old Testament) history in Books XI-XII, the events from Tubal Cain to the Giants and the Flood, which do subsume and echo in closely detailed ways many of the earlier events concerning Satan which were recounted at greater length in Books I to II, IV, and IX to X. Examples of such *metaphorical* resumption are the foundry of Tubal Cain (XI.564 ff.), which recalls the technology of Hell and Pandemonium (I.700ff.); "th' obdurat King" and his drowned host (Pharaoh: XII.205-14), recalling Satan's ravaged "*Memphian* Chivalrie" (I.304-11); the Giants of Book XI (lines 642 and 688), who recollect "Typhon" and "Atlas", associated with Satan in Books I (lines 195-200) and IV (line 987); the tower of Babel ("the work Confusion nam'd", XII.62), which echoes the noisy court of Chaos in Book II (951-67); Noah's "horned floud" (XI.829-35), which dislocates the Mountain of Eden and echoes the disruption of the Garden in Book X (particularly lines 664-71); and so on. Satan, or his activities as reflected in men, can hardly be considered as a focus of typological figuration. Even in such instances, it may be noticed, these multiple patterns of repeated Fall and deviation, countered by the single prospect of the "one just Man" (XI.818) recurring periodically to reconcile God to man, are confined specifically within those epochs of human history embraced by the Books of the Old Testament (although inevitably with reverberations extending into present human history, as suggested in the rather advanced technology of Hell and of the warfare in Heaven). By contrast, those elements in the poem dealing with Christian history, facts and truths do not seem subject to the same kind of imaginative extension. Prophecy and resumption, the correlation of "type" and "antitype" within event, seem in *Paradise Lost* to stop with the advent of Christ. The New Testament histories occurring at the end of the poem are, instead, told simply and nakedly, with the flatness of ultimate truth—no resonances. It would seem that in the free light at the summit of the ladder of Christian history we no longer need look backward or down at the shadowy steps and stages below, nor see through figures as in a glass darkly.

Milton's disinclination to extend the theory of "types" and "figures" too far into wider areas of symbolism is paralleled, it seems to me, in his known tendency, increasing in his later poems, to avoid any of the more serious forms of Renaissance euhemerism. The retrospective (or as the period supposed, prospective) identification of the heroes of classical myth with Old or New Testament figures was one manifestation of the tendency to see human history as running in repetitive cycles or predictive phases up to Christ. Such euhemeristic identification was not in itself necessarily reductive, and it is not as used by Milton necessarily negative. However, instead of the Christ who in the "Nativity Ode" is young Hercules or "mighty *Pan*" (lines 227-28; 89), in *Paradise Lost* we more often find negative identifications of certain Old Testament figures with those in classical myths. Satan is linked with Typhon, Atlas and Briareos; the fallen angels with various pagan idols ("Devils to adore for Deities", I.373); or occasionally, Adam and Eve are connected with classical figures of dubious provenance or seen at doubtful moments of their lives. Adam is like *"Herculean Samson . . . /* Shorn of his strength" (IX.1060-62); Eve is compared with *"Eurynome,* the wide- / Encroaching *Eve,* perhaps", mate of the "Serpent" (X.580-82), or with jealous *"Rhea"* (IV.279). The comparisons of Eve with Ceres and Proserpina in Book IV (lines 268-72) are more poignant, and some have seen Christian echoes in them; but the weight in Milton's treatment in this instance falls more on human loss and deviation than on salvation. And we are always conscious that all such stories are *"fables"*, like Mulciber's fall (I.740-41). These classical similes certainly do not incorporate true types, they do not record past literal events; they may be revelatory of what will come to pass in the *poem,* but they are not prophecies of Christ. In such cases Greek myths blend into Old Testament historical personages and events in the poem with more complex kinds of relevances than the typological or strictly prefigurative can afford. The myths relate to man almost wholly in his human, fallible or fallen nature (hence his pagan affinities), and not to man in his redemptive potential. Such myths are not used by Milton disparagingly, as is sometimes said. Rather, they become the basis for a variety of explorations of man, his nature and failings, his society and its errors, his history and beliefs— many useful considerations, but not centrally, I think, to do with Christ's place in the providential scheme, although our awareness of man's continuing need of redemption is kept continually in the background.

The above distinctions and qualifications in Milton's uses of "types" must be stressed, because any too exclusively typological a theory of symbolism in the interpretation of *Paradise Lost* has a narrowing and distorting effect, in that it inhibits us from reading the poem in wider ways than the doctrinal. Doctrine is a vital dimension of *Paradise Lost*, but it is not the only dimension. Typology, even in its more extended imaginative patternings and applications, is simply too specialized a framework to be made to contain the entire metaphoric content and symbolic structuring of Milton's poem. Traditionally a limited compartment within the undivided second sense (*theoria*, or the *sensus spiritualis*) in formal older scriptural exegesis, typology is inadequately adjusted to carrying the full weight of implication, human as well as spiritual, with which events, images and depictions in *Paradise Lost* are charged, or to embracing the full variety of resonance and oblique allusion in the poem.

"Typological symbolism" is not, for instance, well equipped to explore allusively the vagaries of man's moral and psychological nature. The concept of "Error" in *Paradise Lost*, to take an example earlier discussed, is explored not as simple disobedience to the word of God, but as a prior rational and volitional *failure*, "sin" in Miltonic terms comprising all the possible forms of deviant actions flowing from rational misunderstanding or imaginative delusion, arising (as by token) from "the force of that *fallacious* Fruit" (IX.1046). The "fallacious Fruit" is in effect man's own inner capacity to fail, to be "By *fallacy* surpriz'd" (*Paradise Regained*, I.155). Man in his rational, moral and psychological nature, as well as in his spiritual nature, with all the varieties of potential failure implicit in those natures, is richly investigated in *Paradise Lost* through metaphor and other forms of figuration; but these are far from being necessarily or always typologically directed. Nor can typological symbolism convey the more contemporaneous and personal colourings of Milton's story, or its political, social and topical nuances; yet man as an individual and social being, man as an historical, political and domestic being, also is earnestly explored in *Paradise Lost*. It seems probable that not even in devotional and spiritual contexts is the poem's impact carried mainly through forms of typological figuration (prophetic and resumptive structures). Recent investigation into "Protestant poetics" and related subtleties of language, as reflected in *Paradise Lost*, or into the wide variety of biblical genre models followed by Milton and influencing *Paradise Lost*, or into midrashic linguistic analogies, would suggest quite otherwise. "Allegory", if we could overcome some of the historical distrust and misunderstanding of that important concept, might be a more suitable term generally to embrace the multiple planes of allusion in *Paradise Lost*—and it might simplify any religious or conceptual difficulties involved to recall that "allegory" in one wide original understanding embraced within its inclusive or undivided "second sense" (*theoria*, or the *sensus spiritualis*) the typological dimension, located as one element only within a much wider framework of interrelated planes of meaning.

Problems in "Typological" Readings of *Paradise Lost*

One kind of difficulty which arises in attempting any comprehensively "typological" reading of the symbolism of *Paradise Lost* is that the poem's true typological relationships in time and history tend to become blurred, if interpretatively conflated with looser kinds of figurative constructions in the poem. This at once becomes apparent in the poem when we look at any instances of Christocentric allusion which might seem to pass beyond flat typological prediction or retrospection. Direct typological prophecy does, as has been said, exist in *Paradise Lost*: as when the archangel *"Haile /* Bestowd" on Eve, as "Long after to blest *Marie, second Eve"* (V.385-87); or in Michael's mention of Old Testament blood sacrifices as "shadowie expiations weak" and similar statements in Michael's last discourse. Again, in a standard antitype formulation, Christ is mentioned as "Our second *Adam"* (XI.383); more often, in an almost factual way, He is spoken of as mankind's "second stock" or "second sours" (XII.7, 13), or as standing "in *Adams* room" (III.285). Of course, the central *fact* of Christ as second Adam, of man redeeming man, is kept in view from the poem's opening to its close—from "Of *Mans* First Disobedience . . . till *one greater Man /* Restore us" (I.1-5) to the "paradise within thee" promised in Book XII (587); it is kept in view, indeed, beyond the poem's end, as signalled in "Recoverd Paradise *to all mankind, / By one mans* firm obedience fully tri'd" (*Paradise Regained,* I.3-4). In these last italicized phrases explicit typological *prediction* is apparent; but if they have a retrospective cast, they yet remain totally within the strict framework of fact, event and history, with little figurative penumbra.

On the other hand, if we try to extend the structure of type and antitype to the more hidden reminders of Christ which sometimes surface in the poem, we run into difficulties. For instance, Adam's "On mee, mee onely . . . / all the blame lights due" (X.832-33), and still more so, Eve's "On mee, . . . / Mee mee onely just object of his ire" (X.935-36), verbally recollect the self-sacrificial iterations of Christ in Book III of the poem: "Behold mee then, mee for him, life for life / I offer" (236-37). There might seem to be in these instances the wider kind of co-identity and reciprocal interchange which is said to characterize expanded antitype-type relationships: since Adam and Eve antedate Christ historically, their actions and speeches anticipate His sacrifice, and what were their words have become His, His theirs. (Satan's similarly worded self-sacrificial utterance in Book II, lines 827-28, does of course make it rather awkward to sustain any inference of "typological" connection in the "Mee's" of Books III and X.) But the analogy is in any case not exact. Since the relationship in *poetic time* is deliberately reversed in Milton's poem, Adam and Eve speaking seven Books after Christ, they cannot well stand as "types" anticipatory of Him; in the poem itself they can only echo *His* already declared offer earlier in the narrative, made indeed *before* their Fall. Furthermore, when we come to the actual account of the Crucifixion as told by Michael in Book XII, in the barest minimum of words and in a simple narration following closely the earlier Gospel accounts and narrative style, we have no sense whatsoever of any hearkening back to or incorporating of the sacrificial words of Adam or Eve uttered earlier. Man may echo Christ; Christ *echoes* none but Himself or God. The oxymorons and antitheses of Michael's scanty tropes, "so he dies, / But soon revives", and "Thy ransom paid, which Man from death redeems, / His death for Man" (XII.419-20, 424-25), remember for us not Adam's and Eve's but Christ's own or God's words earlier: "Though now to Death I yeild, and am his due / All that of me can die" (III.245-46) and "Giving to death, and dying to redeeme" (III.299). In all these passages Christ becomes not so much the prophesied *fulfilment* of Adam and Eve as *their model* for the Christian life of love and self-sacrifice.[17] Adam and Eve here, standing for the reader, for everyman, enter as it were unwittingly into the spirit of Christ's sacrifice, in the way that a later Christian would draw the lesson of the Passion to himself. But their words in these passages, whether recollective or prospective, have nothing whatsoever to do with any status as true "types".

Similarly, the Abdiel episodes in Books V-VI might more properly be said to constitute a "lively shadow" or living allegory of Christian faith and devotion than any form of typological prefiguration. Milton's Abdiel (a figure scarcely mentioned in the Old Testament—and certainly no historical "type"), like Adam or Eve antedates Christ in biblical chronology but not, in the chosen time-scheme of the poem, the Son. In his isolation, loyalty and faith, he functions not so much as any prefigurative "type" of Christ, but rather as a model for the subsequent Christian life, as exemplified in Christ Himself. Again, there is an effect of blurring of time, or timelessness, which is not characteristic of strict predictive typology and does not fit into any historical pattern. Christ as Himself the "one just Man" is later in the poem again predicted in the true historical type of Enoch (XI.664-71); but Abdiel not only is not historical, he is manifestly a poetic invention, within an episode the fictive aspect of which has already been stipulated by its semi-fictive narrator, Raphael.[18] Something is lost in attempting to make all episodes in *Paradise Lost* which may be suggestive of the good Christian life fit into some universal pattern of "typological symbolism" stretching across Milton's entire poem. We lose sight of the personal and individual characters of the various episodes or allusions, of their specific contextual colourings, their differences from each other and their variety of uses and applications. The point is not that the above episodes do not carry a centrally Christian content, for of course they do. For Milton as for other Christians not only Genesis but much else in the Old Testament carried Christian meanings. The point is rather that by trying to see these reiterative episodes and speeches exclusively within a framework of typological, that is, doctrinal allusion, or even of devotional allusion, we distort the poem's metaphorical structure. We not only miss other important relevances which such allusions may contain, but we may fail to perceive the true artistic

interrelationship of all these echoing narrative configurations to other
forms of implication, allusion, echo or cross-reference within the poem.
We may fail to see that many such instances of Christian suggestiveness
belong within some much more comprehensive aesthetic pattern of figur-
ation and oblique allusion that Milton is trying to work across his entire
poem.

"Typologically" Suggestive Patternings

An even more curious dislocation of the expected historical biblical align-
ments occurs if we attempt to bring into "typological" correlation such
episodes as those, for example, linking the Satanic party and actions (as in
Books I.670-709; VI.205ff.) with the succession of dubious Old Testament
historical personages and events strikingly echoing them in Books XI-XII
(for example, at XI.556-73; 638-64). When we encounter the later events or
personalities, we may experience something of that shock of recognition
which is one of the features of relationship between antitype and type—
"we have been here before, seen all this before, it is being realised again
in time". Something of the cyclical or phasal feeling said to characterize
New Testament typology or a certain Christian view of history may also
seem to be present. But the conventional forward and backward connec-
tion in concrete historical time between Old and New Testaments, the
prophecy and its fulfilment, both within history, these are not present.
Instead of Old Testament predicting New, we have in the passages cited
above even "older" (heavenly) events prognosticating Jewish history, or
elsewhere, events early in the Old Testament predicting events in later
Books (as in the successive scenes portrayed in Books XI-XII of *Paradise
Lost*). Yet all is without any sense of resolution.[19] Even if we wished to
believe that Milton regarded all the events which he records in the War in
Heaven and its immediate sequel as "literal", it is hard to see how his
large mythic expansions of Lucifer's fall, still less the obviously fictive
amplifications of Satan's career which Milton constructs in Hell, Pan-
demonium and Chaos, even though they are antecedent in poetic time
and, in a sense, in scriptural time to the human histories from the Old
Testament recorded in the two final Books of *Paradise Lost*, can be said
typologically to predict the latter. Satan's actions *foreshadow* the actions of
fallen humanity, certainly; the events in Hell become predictive moral
metaphors; but they contain no direct reference to the Christian dispensa-
tion and its central protagonist, and no resolution whatsoever. These
recurrent forward reflections from Hell, Pandemonium, Chaos (even
from Satanic heavenly prehistory) into human history (Old Testament,
Elizabethan, our own) have the widest of spiritual and moral implica-
tions; but their weight falls not on prefiguration through "types" (even in

a morally inverted sense), but on the endless emptiness of a negative and unredeemed human destiny. The immediate thrust of these episodes is toward probing and characterizing the springs of continued human deviation, perversity and failure; and any critical insistence on continuous "typological" interpretation deflects Milton's emphasis from the kind of self-examination to which these or other recollective configurations are meant to direct the reader. Such reiterative events and episodes are concerned with the moral foundations of the Christian life, not with its completed structure or final end. The Christian life and Christian doctrine are sufficiently embodied, often in the most direct form, in *Paradise Lost* as not to require co-option of every suggestive nuance, inflection and echo in the poem.

Let us take a more complex set of reiterations, often cited as evidence of a "typological" connection (because they have a predictive character). These are the recurrent "Fall" episodes or motifs, little and great, echoing back and forth across the poem, from its dramatic opening ("Him the Almighty Power / *Hurld* headlong . . . down / To bottomless perdition", I.44-47); to the projection of Satan's actual fall into Greek myth, in Mulciber's fall ("From Morn / To Noon he *fell*, from Noon to dewy Eve", I.742-43); to the poet's expressed fear of himself falling ("Least . . . / on th' *Aleian* Field I *fall*", VII.17-19); to Adam's and Eve's actual Fall in Book IX (there was also Eve's premonitory flight and fall earlier); to the pair's symbolic descent or "fall" from Paradise ("*down* the Cliff . . . / To the *subjected* Plaine", XII.639-40). Here we have fall after fall, reverberating through time and space in the poem. But in what way, if we think about it, can the semi-fictive representation of fall, its poetico-mythic projection into the dreamlike, summer's day-long fall of Mulciber onto Greek Lemnos (so specific and so beautiful); our "grand parents' " real enough fall; and every man's feared fall, including the poet's; be said to be mutually related through any theory of types? In this pattern of reiterated Falls through time, history and myth, not only is the predictive content entirely negative, but the prophecy-resolution character which forms the essential nexus of the type-antitype relation is conspicuously absent. We have only the endless succession and repetition of falls.

Perhaps it is possible to see in such patterns something of that continuing reapplication of biblical, or quasi-biblical, event to the individual Christian awareness, upon which a certain kind of extended "typological" construction has been said to base itself[20]—although, as will presently be noted, there have been other ways of defining and describing such a phenomenon. "Patterns of Christian history" may also be distantly present behind these schemes, perhaps of the sort implicit in the more intellectualized New Testament kind of typology, as distinct from the earlier more historical typology found in the Old Testament. (The later kind is that which sees divine events, or even sometimes, as in the Miltonic "fall"

passages, the antitheses of those, as embedded within history and there-
fore constantly recurring—"the beginning and end of history are within
history"; while the earlier kind is that which implies a "doctrine of prog-
ress" of a more linear, historical sort.[21]) Yet we are always to remember
that true typology has its roots in the historical *actuality* of both type and
antitype, whereas much of the predictive-recollective "event" recounted in
Paradise Lost is of a manifestly unhistorical kind; that Milton's preferred
uses of typology are of the literally historical, Old Testament kind, imply-
ing a goal and "doctrine of progress" (like his own ladder leading "From
shadowie Types to Truth", "Up to a better Cov'nant" in Book XII.303, 302);
and that his own conception of the doctrine of types, as expressed in the
Christian Doctrine, was of a limited and profoundly concrete kind. What
Milton may be trying to express through such cyclical reiterations and
echoes as those described above, therefore, may not be fully interpretable
within even the widest understandings of typology.

We must ask ourselves the following questions. Do all those various
Fall episodes speak only with one voice, in unison, to tell us in wearisome
iteration what we already know, that man has fallen and inevitably must
always do so; or, over and above this persistent theme, does not each
individual episode also have something special to say, speaking in a kind
of counterpoint as well as in chorus? For example, may not Mulciber's fall
"From Morn / to Noon . . . to dewy Eve, / A Summers day" (I.742-43)
prospectively delineate the exact tragic space of Adam's and Eve's final
summer's day in Eden, thus directing our attention forward to the par-
ticular and, it may be, meaningful time-sequence of events in that tragic
twenty-four hours—which, like Mulciber's, also ends with a descent-fall at
evening? Or Eve's Fall dream in Book IV, is this too no more than another
chord in the endless Fall chorus, in the pattern of true falls and false ascents
reversing the Christian scheme behind the poem, and which will itself in
turn be reversed; or has that dream something more particular to tell us,
directing us through the details of its presentation forward to the fit of
human *hybris* in the separation scene which precedes Eve's fall and is in
part its cause? Eve's dream in Book IV can only be called a "type" of her
actual fall by draining the term of all Christological reference—or by falling
back on a different and looser use of the term, one which in fact implies
allegory. In any case, the importance of the dream episode lies not in its
prognosticating character as such, but in its analytical moral content. It tells
us obliquely but exactly the how, why and wherefore of the way that future
fall will come about—and might, with greater insight, have been averted.
We may thus question any poetic which attempts to constrict our reading
of all such meaningful recollective and prospective instances into one
narrow vein of dogma, while neglecting the human grounds of the actions
or events delineated in the poem.

Verbal Echo and Anticipation

There is also a much larger dimension of *Paradise Lost* in which anticipation or recollection is conveyed not so much through direct foreshadowing or recapitulation embodied in substantial episodes or characters as by fleeting allusion or echo, often caught up within a single word. The question might arise whether such resonances, which penetrate the texture of the entire poem, portentously building up our expectation and apprehension of the outcome, do not also form part of some extended scheme of typological symbolism. The Fall poem within itself seems at every point to contain and predict its own known outcome, in a fashion not dissimilar to that in which every seemingly casual remark or detail in a Greek tragedy may be seen by the reader as suffused with a tragic and ironic future relevance. We may note a few of the many familiar instances of this kind in *Paradise Lost*. Eve's unconsciously straying "*wanton* ringlets wav'd" (IV.306), or the unfallen nature in Eden which innocently "*Wantond* as in her prime" (V.295), seem to adumbrate the deadly "*wanton* wreath" (his invitation to indulgence) curled by the Serpent (IX.517), or to contain the seeds of the "*wantonly repaid*" glances shot by Eve at her fallen partner (IX.1015). And both unfallen and fallen "wantoning" in Eden are further seen to have been already adumbrated in the "*wanton* rites" of "alienated *Judah*" mentioned as early as Book I (lines 414, 457), or (in a reversed perspective) to *be* adumbrating the "*wanton* dress" and behaviour of Eve's historical daughters, described toward the end of the poem (XI.583). A curious pattern of interchange takes place in the above instances between paradisal prototype, fallen human archetype, and historical Old Testament exemplar: between unfallen analogue and fallen realities. Yet the pattern is morally reversed, displaced from Christ, without end or resolution, moving always into always unfinished history.

Again, the "liquid *Lapse* of murmuring Streams" in Eden (VIII.263) seems to foretell man's impending "original *lapse*" (XII.83); or, in another important set of recurring motifs, the "*mazie* error" of the wandering streams in the Garden (IV.239) prefigures the "surging *Maze*" of the Serpent's folds (IX.499)—a visible maze which, symbolically miming the snares of Satan's burnished rhetoric, will lead Eve (like "th' amaz'd Night-wanderer" soon to be "swallowd up and lost", IX.640, 642) into a bewildering, Spenserian "Error's train", a serpentine maze. And all of those mazes surely recall the "wandring *mazes*" of disputation in which the debating angels in Book II also find themselves "lost" (561), or foretell the comparable circles of "reasonings, though through *Mazes*" (X.830), in which Adam finds himself caught after his fall. The word "wandering", traced through the poem, creates similar significant chains of verbal repercussions. Paradisal prototype; fallen archetype; historical human figures or similar "types" (using the word in its most ordinary sense)—it could be supposed that in these cross-associations there again exists something of that patterning peculiarly attributed to typological symbolism of the later, cyclical, New Testament kind, which sees "the beginning and end of history [as] within history". Yet the instances above do not suggest any ending. Nor are all such murmurs of the future in the poem negative; some seem to look not only toward Fall but beyond it, to Restoration—as perhaps might be sensed in Adam's request to Eve to help him "to *reform* / Yon flourie Arbors" (IV.625-26), a bold choice of word on Milton's part, if a pun. (If the metaphor of over-luxuriance in the garden of Eden adumbrates human deviancy, then its pruning must imply, in the bringing back to orderliness, its "reform-ation".)

In the above or other vast, loose reiterations, predictions and complementarities of Fall and Restoration, a Christian patterning does clearly begin to emerge, one which forms a main emotional matrix of the poem. Yet we may continue to debate whether such patterns spreading out through the poem do not display salient differences from traditional forms of typological symbolism, even in the loosest understandings of that concept. Apart from the facts that such anticipations and recapitulations are more often imaginative-mythic than historical, that they are often negative in content and involve few true Old Testament types or figures, we see, as for example in the "wanton", "lapse", "maze" and "error" sequences, that the polarity of feeling is in most cases *reversed*; innocent unselfconsciousness becomes luxuriousness, "error" in its etymological sense of unrestricted freedom is transformed into being "lost". This is the converse of what we should expect of the true typological relation, in which type is normally fulfilled, not reversed, by its antitype. Therefore we need to ask ourselves, once again, what purposes these echo chains serve in the poem. We may doubt that they merely play a prognosticatory set of variations on the endless theme of human lapse, confusion, error and deviation; and we may wonder instead whether each one of these minuscule verbal anticipations or recollections does not speak also with its own distinctive voice, directing our attention to some particular aspect of fallible or fallen experience—sexual or intellectual, theological or moral, or to do with the natural world. We may suppose that these parallel but varied instances exist not only in their past-future relationships, or in their historical bearings, but also present themselves to our vision in their particular, *present* characters and significances. The instances detailed represent only a very few of the many, many self-echoes, recollections and anticipations in *Paradise Lost*, all of which eventually melt into a vast system of internal correspondences which becomes the poem's entire metaphoric structure, becomes the poem with all it has to say, as the two motifs of "Error" and "Death" examined in an earlier chapter illustrated. The totality of such correspondences in *Paradise Lost* is too vast and too intricate to be contained under any one simple dogmatic label. If an aesthetic label is to be applied, it would be more appropriate to invoke the concept of continuous allegory, expressing itself through a multitude of verbal resources, as well as through the larger narrative contours outlined in my earlier chapters.

Typological prediction undoubtedly exists in *Paradise Lost*, and perhaps to a degree paratypological schemes also. But the view which I would propose is that such schemes are best seen as part of a more comprehensive figurative organization, one geared not only to prospection and retrospection, but also to introspection in a wide variety of modes and keys. I venture to suggest that the briefer and larger typologically suggestive recollections or predictions considered in the previous two sections, along with the strict typological prophecies themselves in the poem, all form parts of the poem's total figurative patterning and purpose, embracing many planes: moral and spiritual, devotional, social and political, and extending occasionally into areas of the metaphysical and theological too. That pattern and purpose are so designed as constantly to express themselves via a poetic of covert allusion and hidden intimation, of which recollection and anticipation, including typological predictive forms, are only one aspect among other aspects. Such a pattern and purpose, while not in Milton's usage systematic in quite the formal way of some early allegory, may perhaps be most readily understood by analogy with older systems of allegorism based on or modelled after Scripture, systems which historically embraced true typological intimation, along with other forms of shadowed truths, in a multi-layered system of allegorical interpretation (by no means always *simultaneous* interpretation), and which in their more respectable uses strove always to preserve a strong sense of the "literal level"—literal truth, literal events, real personalities—much as Milton is trying to do in his own poem. Such exegesis when performed on Scripture could legitimately in certain contexts employ the methods of fictive amplification and metaphorical invention, or in non-scriptural contexts could make use of the resources of figurative language and allegory, in parallel to those found within Scripture itself. Standing in conscious parallel with the scriptural systems, systems of secular literary allegorism, such as those involved in Renaissance theories of layered meaning in poetic texts (texts which, however, also sustained a fictive "verisimilar"), afford an analogous avenue to understanding Milton's purposes. The literary theories of how to weave such complex patterns of oblique signification into a continuous exposition (a secondary narration), and their assimilation into written epic as "continued metaphor", have already been discussed. We may view *Paradise Lost* from all these interrelated allegorical perspectives.

EIGHTEEN

Protestant Homiletics and Allegory in *Paradise Lost*

The "Experiential" Approach

In this chapter we will consider the relationship of recognised contempo-
raneous Protestant modes of reading the Bible, in non-doctrinal contexts,
to Milton's allegorical enterprise in *Paradise Lost*. There are in certain
Protestant or earlier traditions of scriptural interpretation continuing ele-
ments which go much further than typology toward explaining what
Milton's art is sometimes trying to accomplish. These elements involve the
use of Old Testament "types" in a manner which bears some superficial
resemblance to orthodox typology, but is best considered as a separate
kind of practice. Such aspects relate more broadly to *homiletics*; and it seems
strange that there has not been more general recognition that a didactic
epic such as Milton's may have more in common with certain forms of
preaching[1] than it does with that area of biblical study devoted strictly to
the exposition of Christian doctrine—although correlations of a kind exist
here too, as may be seen in Milton's radical representation of God. *Paradise
Lost* has a careful foundation of Christian doctrine, but its purpose is not
the same as that of the *Christian Doctrine*. The poem is freer than the treatise
to express itself in a large variety of ways. Milton's epic shares its broader
purposes less with the theologian's than with the Protestant preacher's
way of reading, understanding and writing about the Bible on those
occasions when he is *not* concerned specifically with the winnowing and
sifting of doctrine, but instead with the multitude of purposes concerning
edification, moral instruction, comfort and hope which comprise his more
everyday staple. These are the recognisable purposes of Milton's epic also:
to enlighten and instruct fallible man, to comfort and offer hope, and, in
the moral sphere, to lead him to the kind of self-understanding and
acceptance of individual responsibility which alone can provide a founda-
tion for restoration (whether understood in divine or human terms), and so
justify God's ways. In such at once humane, moral and spiritual inten-

tions, *Paradise Lost* shares with Spenser's and a long line of Renaissance epics a humanist and Christian purpose: the fashioning of the individual in "vertuous and gentle discipline", the training of him to see both with the "eye of reason" and the "eye of faith".

Roland Bainton in *The Cambridge History of the Bible*[2] directs attention to the fact that the Reformers' way of reading the Bible and Luther's own way in fact allowed for a very considerable degree of imaginative and figurative latitude in preacherly contexts. Over and above the searching out of the prophetic sense or any direct "forward reference to Christ" in the Old Testament, comprising "allegory of a sort", or "not exactly allegory" but typology—for Luther legitimate, since an integral part of the literal sense—what the Reformers further did was to abandon the "wooden schematization" of the older allegorical three- or fourfold structure for a more personal but still figurative way of reading. When using certain kinds of scriptural material, personal applications of a very free-ranging kind might be made, "interpretations plastic, fluid, and profound". Yet this "disrupt[ion]" of the "traditional mode of exegesis" and "advance in the art and science of exegesis" over the medieval was nonetheless one "more in the form than the substance". What resulted was still a form of allegory, in fact. There are several reasons why the Protestant mode of reading did not represent a substantial break with the older allegorical tradition: "the Middle Ages [had] agreed that the literal was the primary sense and that allegory was not to be used in disputation [to establish doctrine]. *Luther never ceased to use it for edification nor could he reject it utterly*, since it had been employed by the Apostle Paul. . . . Since *the tropological* [the old moral sense] brings out the implications of a passage for conduct and *the anagogical* for consolation, *they could never be ruled out in preaching*".

One distinctive way in which Luther and other leading Protestant divines read and understood the Bible (New Testament as well as Old) was, as they phrased it, by putting themselves into "that Spirit in which the Scriptures were written". In a doctrinal context this meant not erratic personal inspiration but, in part, a disciplined, discriminating and patient endeavour to read with due regard for consistency of doctrine throughout the scriptural texts. But to read according to the Spirit had also sometimes a different connotation, not dogmatic. It could in certain contexts imply the commentators' "sinking themselves" into the biblical accounts "experientially"—that is, in a highly imaginative or semi-fictive way. In this "experiential approach" (a kind of personal meditation on scriptural topics akin to older practices of meditation), the writer wrote and described scriptural events "sometimes with more acuteness of feeling than the record itself relates". A certain "warming of the heart enabl[ed] the hearer or the reader to see, feel, participate, and believe in that which God once spoke".

This experiential reading could produce quite diverse approaches to the same passage, although the diversities were not perceived as contradictions:

Luther was quite clear that this approach would not issue in a multiplicity of interpretations because the Spirit is one. Yet it is instructive for us to see how three men [Luther, Calvin, Castellio], all sinking themselves experientially into the Scriptures [in their reading of the Joseph story], could find in the same account valid yet variant elements consonant with the faith and experience which they brought to the passage. . . . Luther's attention focused upon Joseph in prison under false accusation. . . . Calvin centred on God's overruling Providence. The brothers. . . . unwittingly and unwillingly . . . were the instruments of providence to their own ultimate salvation. . . . But Castellio, the prophet of religious liberty, fastened upon Reuben's device for saving his brother from murder. . . . For the first commentator the point was the anguish of the forsaken, for the second the providence of God, and for the third the iniquity of persecution. All three interpretations are valid. Each writer laid hold of a genuine aspect of the scriptural account. The point here is simply that the experiential approach can itself lead to diversity, though not necessarily to contradiction.[3]

It may be seen from the above account that the "levels" at which these three interpretations move are indeed quite diverse. They range from the sufferings of the isolated faithful, a devotional aspect, to questions of Providence and faith, explored not so much in their dogmatic aspects as in their personal relevance, and range still again to civic matters such as the right to religious liberty of conscience. All of these applications can fall loosely under the umbrella of "allegory" in some of its traditional formulations, but not all of them can assimilate so readily to even the more extended forms of "typology" (although the anxiety of the Reformers to identify such readings as typological may well indicate the Reformation unease over the use of image and figure). In such applications the emphasis and to some extent the content is displaced from the figure of Christ onto the individual personal experiences and social contexts of the Christian reader.

I would suggest that the foregoing descriptions take us some way toward explaining the nature of many of the imaginative processes in *Paradise Lost*. Very considerable parts of Milton's narrative, of the more plausible kind displaying the "appearance" or "air of history", as for instance the extended Garden episodes, with their highly authentic descriptions of human domestic activities and human conversations, represent an "inspired" amplification of parts of the Bible somewhat along the lines of the three Reformers cited above. (Admixtures of other kinds of "plausible" material concerning Satan or the angels are also used by Milton in inventive ways.) The scenes in question are not intended to constitute any new or further revelation, one rendered in greater detail than the original revelation, so to speak; such a notion would have been abhorrent to Milton. And they are certainly not intended to function as interpretations of scriptural doctrine. Neither do they fit into that desire to find ever more old or new "types" in Scripture, which was one feature of earlier Christian and some later Protestant traditions. I would prefer to link such Miltonic expansions to that new Reformation mode akin to meditation which is described in *The Cambridge History of the Bible*, and to interpret such scenes in *Paradise Lost* under the umbrella of an inclusive conception of allegorism. The scenes represent an imaginative, semi-fictive entering into the quality and texture of the invoked biblical experience, as was the case with the three Calvinist theologians who expanded the Joseph story, projecting what it was like "to be there", what the characters might have thought, felt, done, how they behaved and occupied themselves—an imaginative entering into another historical world, conducted in order to draw out of the scanty biblical record something personal and important to the writer, something which is in his view an authentic if latent part of the original's meaning, and which he considers to be of universal relevance.

Through such an approach, Milton's poetry can be seen to retain its base of literal scriptural truth, while at the same time there is room left for a variety of "applications"—I am not speaking of simultaneous readings— of the sort which any sermon-writer might make, some of these obvious, others more oblique or hidden. Every reader of the Bible, the Reformers would have considered, is entitled to make his own approach to the Bible in this "experiential" way (with due reservations concerning the use of specific passages involving doctrine). So also every reader of *Paradise Lost* may legitimately feel entitled to do with the poem—if he does not lose sight of the fundamentals of Milton's faith "perspicuously" expressed in distinctive passages within the poem, or of the truth to Milton of the "historical" elements of his story. Thus if Christopher Hill finds in *Paradise Lost* an allegory of the spiritual failure of the English Revolution,[4] that too may be a valid way of reading the poem. (Hill was not the first to offer a political interpretation of *Paradise Lost*; Toland preceded him by three centuries.) Other oblique slantings than the political may also obtain in Milton's narration, more apparent perhaps to another kind of reader. Each interpretation may be valid, each lays hold of a genuine aspect of Milton's account. The proviso must always be, of course, that there exists concrete evidence in the shaping details of Milton's verisimilar narration to show that he has rendered its meaning capable of being bent in such directions. However, a certain distinction is to be maintained between the lifelike or "inspired" amplifications of biblical event presently under discussion, which seem to be several degrees closer to "history", and the also present, very considerable spectrum of recognisable fictions, fables and allegories (biblically inspired or other) in *Paradise Lost* which, while serving similar purposes of conveying through allegorical "shadows" a variety of interior or ulterior meanings, are frankly fictive at one level while conveying inner truths at another.

Protestant sermonizing may assist us, therefore, to understand what critics historically have had difficulty with: how it is that, through employing fictive or semifigurative modes in recreating certain biblical stories, Milton's poem may express something personal, yet not impugn either the historicity of the biblical records or the doctrines they were believed to contain. The literal basis of Genesis (and other canonical accounts, when used) is firmly preserved in Milton's epic, along with the pure "kernel" of truth (doctrine) inside the "shell" of the fictive-verisimilar expansion. A vivid analogy may be found in the way in which Luther described the Word (the Gospel, Christ) as lying wrapped in the straw of the manger, that is, in the surrounding scriptural narration. Not everything, Luther said, in the scriptural accounts is "Gospel truth" in the doctrinal sense, even though all the events described may have really happened. But while the Word is the most valuable, the straw of the manger can afford its nourishment too.[5]

In a parallel way, when Milton comes to those particular places in Genesis which have afforded important points of doctrine, he takes pains neither to allegorize nor "apply" (amplify in a personal interpretative way), but to stay conspicuously close to the original. Instances are his treatment of the accounts of the Creation and the Judgement on Adam and Eve (Genesis 1 to 3), both of which accounts, it had always been considered, were particularly unsuited to allegorization, since the one contains our only record of the origins of the world and the other the basis of the doctrine of original sin.[6] In the first instance Milton's version is in places expanded, but it is without latent innuendo, other than to convey a generalized impression of the great richness, fertility and essential goodness of God's works. His narration of the Judgement, by contrast, is conspicuously bare and close to the original, except for a few passages of necessary narrative infill. But we may observe in both cases the scrupulous and quite remarkable way in which the poet takes pains either to stay within the exact words and phrasings of the scriptural accounts or to keep coming back to them. Repeatedly and pointedly he circles back, in the Creation or Six Days' Work account (VII.216-640), to the style, phrasings and words of the Old Testament, reverting to them at least fifteen times, three times at length, and with great emphasis on the biblical words concerning the Prohibition (lines 542-44). Similarly, in the Judgement scene in Book X Milton quotes the Bible at least seven times, taking whole paragraphs from Genesis almost verbatim, including that of the questioning of Adam by God (lines 116-23), the sentence pronounced on Adam and Eve (lines 193-208), and the curse on the Serpent (lines 175-81). In such circlings back from his own wide rich sweep to the plain words of Genesis, so different in flavour, tone and diction from the "grand style" of *Paradise Lost*, it is as if Milton were serving notice that he does not equate his own writings with Scripture; that (he is reminding the reader in these places) he does recognise and preserve a distinction between the Word of God and his own words—even though *at other times* he may write in personal ways, amplifying Scripture in meaningful directions only latent within the original, but which nonetheless are felt by him to be deeply in accord with the "spirit" and proper uses of the original.

The Bible, Figuration and *Paradise Lost:* Summary

In the preceding three chapters discussing the relationship between shadowed discourse in the Bible and in conventional Protestant readings of Scripture, and analogous modes in Milton's poem, we noted the more liberal types of reading and "applications" of scriptural narrative made use of in Protestant preaching, and the close connection of *Paradise Lost* with these practices in some of its purposes and structures. In Chapter 15 we noted numerous further delicate proprieties and discriminations in the understanding of Scripture, or its literary reconstruction in literature, flowing from the Milton's cognizance as a Protestant exegete of the many different levels of discourse in the Bible and their appropriate uses. Milton saw clearly that quite diverse kinds of language and therefore different kinds of "truth" coexist in the scriptural narratives. For purposes of establishing *doctrine*, this awareness is of *negative* importance: what might be said or read metaphorically or even allegorically in Scripture needs to be kept distinct and apart from what is said literally, historically and doctrinally. But both kinds of discourse are there, and neither is to be forgotten; although figurative expressions are to be understood or made use of in a different way from the literal.

We further argued earlier as follows. There is or is latent within the Bible (and so by analogy in the language of *Paradise Lost*) a whole spectrum of discourses. We find in Scripture a gradation ranging from the plainest truths, to fictive moral or spiritual histories such as parable, through to the patently figurative and allegorical, all useful in different ways. Although the "spirit" informing all these elements in the language of the Bible is one, it is also various. The foundations of the Bible are the elements of historical event, fact and divine utterance comprising the doctrines of the faith, which must be taken exactly as given and the fountain kept pure. So are doctrine and divine utterance preserved pure in *Paradise Lost*. Literal truth subsists in both texts in more complex conjunctions also. There are those particularly delicate instances in the Bible, as for example God's anthropomorphic depictions of himself (a literalism rather carefully reproduced in *Paradise Lost*), where some extraordinary balance, some form of apprehension suspended between the literalistic and the figurative, has to be sustained through an "accommodated" understanding. Milton's equivocal views on "accommodation" in Scripture, expressed both in *Of Christian*

Doctrine and in his poem via Raphael as narrator, were discussed in the first two of the three preceding chapters of my text, and his views were seen to open the way to a complex interplay of plain and figurative narration in the representation of God, as also in other areas of *Paradise Lost*.

On the question of "typology", it was noted that there are true "types" to be read in the Old Testament and in Milton's poem in those special places, prophetic of Christ, where a "compound" of the literal and the figurative senses is admissible. In a looser understanding of typology, certain interpreters have discerned in the Bible (although such are nowhere indicated in *Of Christian Doctrine*) various recapitulations and intimations linking scriptural event, place or person into wide-ranging patterns of type and antitype. While such wider patterns of typological prefiguration are not uncommon in certain late patristic and Protestant forms of reading Scripture, considerable difficulty arises in attempting to read comparable typological relationships into the many recapitulative patterns of imagery in *Paradise Lost*. It was felt that Milton's own use of any such evocative and reiterative patternings, often hingeing on thematic words with chains of verbal echoes and resonances, is much more comprehensive in its range of reference to the entire content of man's inner and outer life, within its Christian setting, than any purely doctrinally based conception such as "typology" or "typological symbolism" could imply. Such patterns in Milton's poem form part of the broader figurative and aesthetic shaping of his poem.

Where such patterns involve Old Testament histories, their immediate purposes may again be compared to Milton's or other "preacherly" amplifications of that considerable dimension of literal narrative and fact in the Bible which does not contain doctrine, but which may still be usefully applied in moral or spiritual directions relating to aspects of the individual's personal life or his social or other contexts. Obviously, in his tract specifically on doctrine Milton would not have been in the business of describing such enlarged uses of scriptural material. But the method of secondary "application" of Scripture is validated by the "one sense to one place" rule in the *Christian Doctrine*, it is embedded in Protestant homiletics, and it is continually evident in Milton's own techniques of poetic amplification. An important parallel to semi-fictive or imaginative invention in Protestant preaching practice may also lie in Milton's rather distinctive uses (to be considered presently) of apocryphal matter, traditionally employed in Christian "Wisdom" literature, though never for doctrine. Apocryphal narrative was by courtesy considered as remaining in varying degrees within the imaginative penumbra of the "literal" level, while in fact employing recognisably fictive methods. The air of solidity which apocryphal material lends to Milton's narrative reinforces that sense of presence occasionally imparted by Milton's situational and verbal plays on "dream", "image", "reflection" and especially "shadow", which can act so as to suggest not the "shadowy" but instead a substantial reality. The uncertainty resulting from the strange suspension between figurative and literal which we sometimes find in the poem acts to alert us to the "parabolic" or allegorical intention behind such uses of language.

There also exist in Scripture, as Milton notes in *Of Christian Doctrine*, not only manifest figures of speech and metaphors but frank fictions, fables and allegories. We may think not only of the apocryphal Books, recognisably fabulous yet useful, but, in the canon, of more authoritative elements, such as the Parables of the Gospels, the mystical Books of the Bible, and, here and there, those metaphors and "allegorical fictions" which, as Milton specifically observes, God himself does not disdain to use of Himself. It was sometimes argued by exegetes that all of these figurative elements—as it was later argued of loose forms of typology—formed part of the "literal" meaning of Scripture, in the sense that they had been uttered by the same one author of revelation. Milton himself makes no effort to sweep away figurative discourse in the Bible under any such convenient carpet, and he has no inhibitions about unashamedly using figurative discourse in his biblical epic. As can be seen from his references in *Of Christian Doctrine* and other prose works, he finds such figuration in Scripture valid and valuable in its own right. Analogously to Scripture, Milton in his poem makes use of the frankly fabling or fictional: apocryphal matter, classical myths, brief metaphors, longer "allegorical fictions" such as those concerning Sin and Death, and besides, a whole spectrum of virtually unclassifiable metaphorical or allegorical correspondences, allusions and intimations. All fall into place within a poem which may offer an almost perfectly complete biblical analogue in terms of diverse strata of discourse, diverse gradations of truth and figuration, all of them accommodated within the strict bare framework of Christian history and dogma. It has perhaps been more usual for critics to look for biblical genre models in *Paradise Lost* than for any such comprehensive model of stratified biblical discourse.

To read *Paradise Lost* with a consciousness of the presence of many diverse strata of "truth" and fiction in the poem, diverse levels of language and figuration, including but not confined to the typological, just as exist in the Bible also, is to preserve a discriminating appreciation analogous to Milton's own of the resources inherent in both scriptural and poetico-scriptural language and invention. It is to understand, in a way that the eighteenth century did not but the seventeenth and sixteenth centuries still did, that diverse forms of non-literal "truth" in scripturally inspired inventions or in scripturally based fiction or poetry could coexist with purity of doctrine and with no vitiation of the historical basis of the Bible. We may therefore read Milton's poem without uncomfortable feelings that Milton the poet may be in some way in conflict with Milton the believer. We may find in *Paradise Lost* an authentic Protestant aesthetic such as we would expect Milton to have tried to formulate, as part of his self-imposed mission as leading poet and celebrator of the Reformation.

Doctrine and the Christian reading of Genesis form the intellectual framework and the underlying narrative skeleton in *Paradise Lost*. But to appreciate the totality of intention which lies behind the complex and varied structures of biblically analogous discourse in Milton's poem, with their intricate strategies of oblique allusion, means to read not only with attention to doctrinal statement or to example, but to read the poem also with responsiveness to its many layers of suggestive linguistic detail. Such reading involves disentangling the poem's complex web of inner meanings according to something like the exegete's own tests of internal cohesion and correspondence between details, plus overall consistency of thought, and with a further constant sensitivity on the reader's part to the nature of the language being used in different contexts.

Obviously, fully to characterize the strategies of language, figuration and allegory involved in Milton's poem also requires that we pass beyond biblical exegesis and biblical linguistic models, and that we set *Paradise Lost* in its immediate literary traditions too. Measuring his practices against those of his acknowledged predecessors and models in epic and epic poetics, it is extremely interesting to observe that Milton's more flexible interpretation of Scripture in certain non-doctrinal, homiletic or homiletically analogous contexts finds a direct parallel in the way in which Tasso or other writers of Christian epic in the Renaissance made use of the historical convention. History in epic meant an exact but bare framework of fact, to be filled in, in the main, with poetic amplification of a "verisimilar" kind. As Tasso said, epic had the authority of history coupled with the freedom of poetic invention. The epic convention which the Renaissance inherited and developed involved the use of poetic invention to make space for the more hidden kind of truths which could be conveyed through "proper allegory"—since, as Phillips said, "whatever is pertinently said by way of allegory is morally though not historically true". Milton's or other contemporary Protestant views on the free imaginative use of Scripture, within the limitations of doctrine, run closely in parallel with Renaissance epic theory on the necessary close interplay between external historical truth and inner, allegorically presented truths, both being held in balance within the framework of a unified narrative.

NINETEEN

"Accommodation" in *Paradise Lost:* The Internal View

In the foregoing chapters the questions raised concerning poetic represen-
tation and "truth" in poetry and the nature of mimesis in *Paradise Lost* have
been considered against a background of theoretical considerations relat-
ing to Protestant modes of scriptural interpretation, to Milton's own views
on scriptural exegesis and his theory of metaphor implicit in *Paradise Lost*,
and to Renaissance theory of epic, and allegory in the epic. The basic
question underlying my discussions has been this: was *Paradise Lost* really
intended by Milton to be, as some have supposed, a direct literal rendering
of reality, that is to say, of Old and New Testament historical events,
persons, facts and doctrines; or did Milton employ some more complex,
more oblique form of mimesis, better described under a wider aesthetic
such as the allegorical mode of figuration might imply? We may now return
to this basic question to explore it more from inside the poem, and to
consider how an internal view of the poem as artifact may match with what
has been deduced about its aesthetic largely from external and theoretical
contexts.

Milton's Uses of Extra-Canonical Matter

We have noted various strategies by which *Paradise Lost* sustains scriptural
accuracy and verisimilitude within its larger fiction. In some very conspic-
uous ways, however, the poem does seem to over-insist on the literal truth
or reality of the fictive things which it describes.[1] Quite apart from its
verisimilitude of character or plot in their main lines, or the pervasive sense
of *presence* in place (a strange effect, since the "realities" of despair in Hell or
delights in Eden are much more internal experiences than external fea-
tures), the manner in which Milton's narration is presented seems itself to
connive at the Johnsonian misconception—at the "literalist fallacy". The
Bardic voice in the Invocations, for example, repeatedly puts the poet in

the position of one who was physical witness to or one who actually took part in the events described—"he was there", like his own Muse. The poet identifies himself not only imaginatively but almost physically with his *dramatis personae*; he too is "detaind" in Hell, "re-visit[s]" the light of Heaven, has "venture[d] down / The dark descent" and strives to "rea-scend, / Though hard and rare" (III.13-21), in personal journeys as arduous as those of Satan in the previous Book, which they closely echo. The poet participates vicariously not only in the scenes in Eden but, through Urania (who is either the Christian Muse or, once at least, seemingly, in Book I.17-23, the Holy Spirit itself), in the events of the Creation and the events in Hell and Heaven. She is to "Instruct" him—for she too *was there*, "Thou from the first / Wast present". It is her "Voice divine" that he is "following" in Book VII (lines 2-15), as she "leads" or "guides" him into "the Heav'n of Heav'ns" and "down" again. What could be more authentic than events learned from Urania, or possibly from the Holy Spirit itself? This would seem to be the ultimate in "inspired" reading of Scripture, or the writing of religious poetry most literally "according to the spirit".[2] Small wonder then that certain critics have taken Milton's claims to inspiration as literal and have supposed that he is placing his own story on a par with the kind of revelation afforded to Moses (whom Milton cites, in Book I, lines 6-10, as his own poetic-prophetic predecessor). The corollary to such a view unfor-tunately tends to be that if Milton did think of himself as inspired in this literal way, then every detail in his descriptions must somehow also be felt by him as true and real.

As if the Holy Spirit were not sufficient authority, Milton further lines himself up in *Paradise Lost* behind a whole series of biblical narrators of imposing status: Moses, he "who first taught the chosen Seed / In the Beginning how the Heav'ns and Earth / Rose out of *Chaos*", these lines (I.8-10) glancing both at Milton's didactic purpose and his own subsequent retelling of the creation story; then Raphael, who authenticates the middle two and a half Books by recounting them himself, in Milton's place; and lastly Michael, who narrates the final two Books, again standing in for Milton. There is in fact not very much of the story which does not travel with impeccable scriptural certification. With so many scriptural au-thorities to vouch for it, who can fail to be convinced of the "truth" of Milton's narration? Yet although Moses is historical enough, Raphael certainly is not. He is virtually an extra-biblical character, in Scripture scarcely more particularized than Abdiel, and, like two other principal angelic characters in *Paradise Lost*, Uriel and Gabriel, built up almost entirely out of what Milton called "fables" in the uncanonical Books,[3] or from a medley of those and Jewish cabbalistic traditions.[4]

We may, then, ask why the poem insists in this way on the authenticity of its often manifestly fictive characters and events. Does Milton really wish to deceive us, is he defensively hedging his fiction round with pseudo-fact—or is he attempting to persuade us indirectly of another kind of "truth" inhering in these convincing fictions? The word "connive" as I earlier used it seems appropriate; for where Milton does use real scriptural history, he does so with a plain brevity implying respect for the original, a wish not to tamper with it, whereas when he is treating quasi-scriptural or pseudo-scriptural history he becomes much more expansive and intimate, using the manner of one personally familiar with the scriptural events, so that the reader must surely become convinced of their reality. Even the seventeenth-century reader, more aware than ourselves of scholarly discriminations in the interpretation of different elements in the Bible, might have felt that a principal effect of Milton's way of using such characters and episodes was to enhance the poem's pervasive atmosphere of historicity. On their surface the features just noted would certainly seem to reinforce the poem's apparent claims to literal authenticity and total realism.

To understand Milton's purposes, we have to turn back to Reformation traditions concerning the use of the Apocrypha, which may be read for "'example of life and instruction of manners', but not used to establish doctrine".[5] Behind Milton's use of some of the fascinating episodes from the fifteen uncanonical Books, there lie centuries of homiletic use of this dubiously scriptural material for edification and "wisdom", that is, for application to man's secular and moral life. It seems, then, that Milton is using apocryphal characters and events in a double way: actually to *remove* certain parts of his story from literalism (since the Apocrypha are well known not to be literally "true" in the way that the rest of Scripture is true); and on the other hand, through their vivid and familiar detail to do the opposite, to enhance the poem's air of real presence. Similarly with the meal in Eden. Milton's use of apocryphal matter in both of the Garden scenes in Books IV and IX, in such similes as those about Tobit in Books IV and V, or in depicting the figures of Raphael, Uriel or Gabriel, lends solidity to the poem. Milton thus achieves an air of historical-biblical respectability, in the same way that Tasso liked to give his epic the "air of history". At the same time, since the reader well knows such events not to be literally true, he is impelled to seek different reasons for their inclusion. All these episodes and characters are of course there, as the instructed reader recognises, to make moral-allegorical points. The meal in Eden illustrates Milton's theory of the integral connection between spirit and matter. Uriel's and Gabriel's behaviour in Book IV illustrates the truth that moral rectitude without actual previous experience of evil finds men ill-prepared to cope with it. The simile concerning Tobit and Asmodeus (IV.166-71) carries complex, contradictory suggestions: the outrageous smell of Satan's evil introduced into Eden, set against the promise of the ultimate expunging of evil. And so on.

Any strictly literalist reading of Milton's characters and events is thus

bound to break down, since such "plausible" narrations or descriptions as
those just cited and many others like them regularly refuse to behave with
due decorum and consistent verisimilitude. Instead, Milton's descriptions
offer continual aberrations from realism, verisimilitude, and even finally
from the most elementary kinds of plausibility. Let us look briefly at the
question of character. On the one hand the protagonists in certain parts of
Paradise Lost are characterized with admirable dramatic plausibility and
psychological acumen. We need scarcely detail Satan's jealous motives for
revenge, his manipulation of personalities in the military Council in Hell,
his exploitation of the particular weakness of character in Eve, the tenacity
and enterprise with which he pursues his ends. Or again, the human
quarrel and attendant circumstances, convincing because in themselves so
trivial, yet leading so unerringly up to the disaster. Also remarkable is the
depiction of the fatal complementarity of weaknesses between the two
human protagonists. Yet the behaviour of the unfallen angels, for exam-
ple, who behave like very real people for the most part, is not always
plausible but quite the reverse, as will be noted presently. Similarly, there
is a problem over those "characters" in the poem who are not real people at
all but abstractions, such as Sin and Death and the Old Anarch, Chaos.
And there has certainly been a problem over Milton's God.

Milton's God: Mimesis and Midrash

Milton's God is the character in *Paradise Lost* who is most open to the
charges of a literalism in representation which becomes oppressive, te-
dious or inappropriate, however truthful to Scripture it may be thought to
be. He is, as John Donne also complained of God, too harshly "literal" a
Deity.[6] Objections have been registered in equal measure to God's appar-
ent game of cat-and-mouse with the main characters, His patronizing
manner, His legalism, His "lack of charity", His wrathfulness and seeming
cruelty, His derision of His enemies (that hollow laughter in Heaven), His
apparent indifference to men, even His all-seeing Eye.[7] Milton in bringing
out these characteristics is of course conforming to an Old Testament
decorum and to one understanding of the principle of "accommodation".
But by stressing such aspects of the Deity, those harsh features of His
dealings with men which are prominent in the Old Testament, Milton
finds the opportunity by counter-suggestion to make the point that it is
exactly these aspects which the New Covenant had been specifically in-
stituted to soften, providing Faith as against Law, Mercy as against Justice,
humility as against power—all of which other, complementary aspects of
the Godhead are dramatized in *Paradise Lost* in the second Person of the
Trinity, who is seen in constant reciprocal interaction with the first Person,
and indeed sometimes as indistinguishable from God.

Thus the presentation of God as a "character" in *Paradise Lost* is something of an illusion from the start. We are given a number of other things in place of character, all of them highly abstract forms of representation, and three of which can be noted here. We have, first, *doctrine*, delivered straight from God's mouth, "plain and perspicuous" and conveying "all things necessary to salvation". Doctrine is presented with absolute straightforwardness in Books III and X—no glosses, no metaphors, no dramatization, only occasionally a form of trope (antimetabole) which engages in verbal repetitions with reversals of phrase, as in God's speech in Book III (lines 168 ff.), a feature found also in Adam's and Eve's hymns of praise, as in Book IV (lines 720-35), and which may have its origins in the language of the Psalms. We have, second, a ritualized representation, through the dialogues between the Father and the Son with their liturgical rhythms, of the dual nature of the Godhead: Old Testament Justice and New Testament Love and Mercy in perpetual and paradoxical reciprocation.[8] In Milton's descriptive images of both God and the Son as Light, we often have embedded further subtle theological distinctions concerning the nature of that relationship. And a third resource, something more elusive and interesting still, involves a poetic decorum which seems to be entirely Milton's own invention, a further adaptation from his particular view of the theory of "accommodation", and one which is figurative in the highest degree. This decorum also may be said to constitute a form of allegory, since under the seeming appearance of one thing we discern something else, a rarefied truth.

In this decorum, Milton seems deliberately to exaggerate the "literal" and anthropomorphic in his descriptions of God (following the device by which God "accommodates" Himself to men in Scripture), to such an extent that the literalism undermines itself. Thus he creates the opportunity (taking up the hints expressed in *Of Christian Doctrine*) to intimate the recondite truths involved in our vivid simultaneous apprehension of God both as a literal figure, as He seems to be described in Scripture, and, at the same time, our apprehension that this is how He really cannot be.[9] On the one hand, then, there are the various conversations, instructions or complaints which God holds, issues or makes, all of which in their tone are reminiscent of many Old Testament passages and are seemingly designed to portray God in the same human way—often an antipathetic or hostile way—in which He often portrays Himself in Scripture, that is to say, in the form in which men may most easily understand Him. We have an anthropomorphic God who speaks, argues, casts blame, who could not counter Moses' strong complaints (as Herbert said in "Decay"), a God who is angry, legalistic, rigorous. Milton in short emphasizes the Hebraic aspects of the scriptural God, just as is the case in the Old Testament itself and in much Hebrew commentary. Yet, on the other hand, this God, in His discourses in *Paradise Lost* may, paradoxically, be seen to circumvent and

subvert that same ordinary language ascribed to Him, so as to convey
something transcendent.

On the more obvious plane, Milton softens the harsher delineations of
God with mysterious touches—not only by describing God as embedded
in Light, as in the Invocation to Book III (1-5), or as not Person but "vision"
or "Presence" (VIII.356; 314), but also in his curious blurring of identities as
between the Father and the Son. Thus, in the Judgement scene enacted in
the Garden in Book X, the *Son* "descended", but it is the "voice of *God*"
"*heard . . . walking*" (X.90-98). "Heard walking" is in itself a sufficiently
extraordinary phrase. Radical compressions of divine time as measured
against human time hold a similar surprise. Satan takes a large space of
Book III to reach Eden—from his first alighting on the shell of the World,
over three hundred lines (III.418-742); Raphael takes ten lines (V.266-76);
the Son (or God), half a line (X.90)—the space that it takes to say that for
God, "Time counts not" (X.91). Such details seem designed to hint at the
transcendence of God in His dual nature and inscrutable purposes and to
suggest figuratively His abstract or even theological attributes—just as in
scriptural "accommodated" descriptions we are aware of a figurative di-
mension beyond the anthropomorphic. Much of Milton's presentation of
Heavenly events is again comprehensible only in these terms. For exam-
ple, the description of the ending of the Heavenly War, with the Son
accompanied by an army of *saints* visible *first* to the eyes of the faithful
(VI.767-74), is tantamount to an evocation of the triumph of faith over its
enemies (the Saints see "with the eye of faith").

Rabbinical exegesis also can offer some striking insights into what
Milton is trying to achieve in his representation of God. The radical
linguistic methods of midrashic readings, recently explored in some nota-
ble articles in English by Hebrew scholars and literary critics, have been
shown to create literary artifacts in their own right. Since the Bible within
itself offered explicit models of literary allegory—figures, parables, prov-
erbs, riddles or enigmas—rabbinical interpreters could follow suit (as did
the Christian practitioners of allegorical poetics). They not only could
devise similar allegorical or figurative structures, the *mashal* or short fa-
ble,[10] for example, or a string of such (sometimes very enigmatic), but even
more obliquely, through stringing together single biblical verses from
different parts of the canon they could create a new meaningful form of
narrative, a new and personal amplification and explication of the Old
Testament. Yet always in such writings we are led back *from* the Word *to*
the Word; we have never left Scripture behind.[11] Whether or not such
paraliterary interpretations as applied to the Old Testament constitute
forms of allegory in the stricter sense has been disputed by biblical schol-
ars. That they constitute forms of obliquely figurative literary activity
closely related to allegory can hardly be denied. Such "rabbinics" can
generate multivalent, equivocal or ambivalent readings, often, like the

Protestant homiletic expansions of Scripture earlier cited, personal to the writer's period or context. Yet however various, these interpretations are still felt by the exegete to inhere within and not to come from outside the text. Such readings can even generate a paradoxical argument out of a single scriptural text. An instance is the theme of the honeymoon/alienation of Judah with God and from God, created in certain midrashic expositions of the Song of Songs.[12] In another quarter, it could be argued that Philo's multiple, abruptly divergent allegorical readings of the same text, for example the serpent of Genesis 3 (and, Philo appends, the "snake-fighter", an animal not in Genesis),[13] offer a close parallel to the rabbinical practices, just as the multiple interpretations offered by Harington of the Perseus legend similarly offer a close analogue. Philo's exposition or in this instance Harington's do not correspond to the conventional layered three- or fourfold analysis of older allegoresis, but like structuralist readings represent an infinity of interpretations radiating along a unitary axis. Perhaps Philo and Harington, too, felt that such unlimited refractions of readings from a single text or myth corresponded to something always inherently in the originals, to the infinite luminescence of meaning in these unchanging writings or myths.

It would be interesting to explore Milton's uses of scriptural texts or other linguistic elements in *Paradise Lost* in order to discover whether any of the foregoing theologically directed manipulations of language by the rabbinical expositors are similarly employed by him. In one unusual aspect of his language Milton would certainly appear to follow or write in parallel with the midrashicists. One of the most remarkable of all figural linguistic resources adopted by Milton in his efforts to convey God's mysterious side lies in his cultivation of highly sophisticated mechanisms not only in scene description or narration or the use of "time" (as in examples cited above), but also in grammar and syntax, when simulating God's utterances. Grammar and syntax themselves are, as in the midrashic writings, specifically deployed so as to create some sense of the immanent presence and care of a physically absent Deity—since through Israel's exile or Man's Fall He has removed Himself from the earth.[14] This last feature is particularly striking in the final two, metaphorically denuded books of *Paradise Lost*, in which some very strange forms of quasi-allegorical figure of a doctrinal character are to be found, as in the descriptions and metaphors in the Intercession scene (XI.1-44).[15] We see comparable effects in certain grammatical forms of speech employed by God throughout the poem—those in which different tenses or different agreements of person are collapsed or conflated. Thus when God switches person-verb agreement and switches back again in His compressed, "*I am who fill* / Infinitude" (VII.168-69) (*I* becomes *who*, singular, which becomes *fill*, ambivalently first or third person), we perceive that Milton is actually recreating that "dimentionless" (XI.17) attribute of the Divine which is also more elaborately simulated in the later

Intercession scene. (Beyond this, Milton is also, in the "I am", literally translating the Hebrew name of God.)

All such resources of figuration in scripturally inspired imaginative writing or commentary must fall within a spectrum of figuration which it would be meaningless to dissociate from allegorical figure. In such writing as Milton's, or in the rabbinical writings—fables, dialogues, or other more recondite linguistic modes—new literary-allegorical forms are constantly being created out of the biblical text, or indeed out of the theological apprehensions of the commentators and writers themselves, in their readings of the biblical text.[16] The self-conscious literariness of the figurative devices in question, and the fact that abstract conceptions form their second term, are the key to their common bond with serious allegorical fictive strategies. Milton's God, therefore, has been badly misunderstood by those whom Browne in an inspired phrase called "the literal commentators". It is not God but Milton's commentators who have been too literal. Milton's God is one of his most radically allegorical constructs, one which does not emanate directly from the tradition of epic allegory but seems to augment that and to enter a new dimension of scriptural quasi-allegorical poetics.

TWENTY

Toward an Allegorical Poesis
in *Paradise Lost*

Realism and Non-Realism: "Probability" to Allegory

In *Paradise Lost* plot and description as well as character can present contradictory swings between extreme realism and unrealism, the latter carried sometimes to acute implausibility. Incongruous details appear in the most "realistic" passages. For example, there are Milton's seeming difficulties in the handling of the supernatural epic machinery in Heaven and Eden, raising such questions as why the angels deputed to guard the approaches to the Garden in Book IV prove so remarkably inefficient about their duties, especially after such a parade of military efficiency as is shown there (lines 776-90), or why Uriel's warning and the subsequent angelic search party so conspicuously prove the truth of the maxim, "too little and too late", finding Satan only *after* he has begun to suborn Eve. Again, one may wonder (realistically) why the angels fail to expel or are prevented from expelling the Enemy from the Garden, and why they do not at once take Satan prisoner (they halt him but never arrest him). We might coin a Johnsonian dictum: "From supernatural Beings, one might have expected something more". (What Johnson actually did say was that it would have been much better to leave out the angels altogether, in order to prevent such embarrassments.) At the opposite extreme, the question arises how it is that one lowly Angel can overthrow the mightiest champion of Hell (Abdiel in VI.189-98). All these instances are in varying degrees improbable, the guardian angels being made to appear dull-witted and slow or limited in the one case, and Abdiel excessively superhuman in the other—an error Tasso had specifically cautioned against when defining heroic actions.[1]

The War in Heaven, for which there have been offered a dozen different critical explanations, seems an aggravated case of the opposite fault, implausibility arising from an excess of verisimilitude. This War is too much like a human war. In its final stages it is so exaggeratedly literal, with cannons, cannon-balls, fuses, angels mown down in their thousands, attack and counterattack, the final hand-to-hand struggle with conventional weapons abandoned and degenerating at the last into what appears as a surpassingly vulgar brawl, with mountains thrown about, that finally it becomes increasingly difficult to see the War as anything but futile and ludicrous: a kind of Homeric parody in contemporary Elizabethan dress. Of course Raphael had warned that the War was not to be taken literally— but then why make it so literal? In any case, God Himself appears to regard the whole event not only as a foregone conclusion but as something of a joke ("thou . . . / Laugh'st at thir vain designes and tumults vain", (V.735-37). It seems too much to believe that Milton alone among his cast of characters can take this War seriously.

Our clue is in the changing tone. From being earlier "convinced" by the swift and dignified march and preparations of the two parties of angels (VI.61-86, for example), we seem to have been almost deliberately led to a state of disbelief by the end of the heavenly War. We must therefore deduce that these episodes have some quite different kind of rationale. The supernatural machinery is placed there by Milton in the way that Le Bossu had hinted it could be used when he said that "of our very Passions we may make so many *Allegorical Deities*".[2] It is there largely to reflect the *human* situation, predicaments, inadequacies, hazards, inner resources. (Note that the heavenly laughter at the War closely echoes that at the *human* confusion in the building of Babel: "Ridiculous"; "great laughter was in Heav'n": XII.62,59). The final incongruities of the War offer the very signal of allegorical "absurdity" which sends the reader off in search of some other kind of meaning—just as is the case with so many of the bizarre details in the allegorically loaded descriptions of the fights of Spenser's knights. Something (we are being signalled) stands behind this crude weight of armies, armour and warriors in Milton's War; these are "accommodated" descriptions which neither the warring angels, nor Adam, nor the reader at first quite understand—although God may. The lightning and absolutely non-literal conclusion of the War makes the point effectively. But what exactly that non-literal meaning may be remains to be discovered.

At the other extreme end of the probability scale, what kind of verisimilitude in plotting makes the entire issue of the human drama hinge on Satan's exit from Hell through the intervention of a non-existent person, Sin, and through actions which seem wholly capricious and arbitrary, measured against the verisimilar plot? The poet ascribes this act, like others in the poem, to God's controlling Providence (see, for example, God's remark at III.85-86). But because of the concreteness with which the Sin episode is handled—the "Key" to Hell's Gates, the "key-hole", the "wards . . . Bolt and Bar", the "redounding smoak and ruddy flame" at the threshold (II.871, 876-77, 889), and so forth—two troublesome effects, well recognised, arise. On the one hand dramatic credibilities become strained; on the other, moral issues become confused. God may appear as cruel and capricious, or else He may seem to be manipulating the entire action and all the cast of characters, like puppets. A sort of predestinarian slander arises: if Providence takes such a specific hand in human affairs, have the actors in this plot ever had any genuine choices concerning their destinies? This kind of criticism of God or of *Paradise Lost*, or both, usually with a predictably anti-religious and anti-Miltonic bias, was prominent in criticism of the 1950s.

We may reasonably look instead for a non-literal rationale for such troublesome episodes. By his radical switch in narrative mode and through the sheer irrationality of the obtruded details in the personification allegory, Milton must be making a different kind of point. In shifting to a totally different plane of representation, one not dramatic and not concerned with either consistency of "character" or probability, he is universalizing, and so bringing an awkward philosophical difficulty out into the open. He is testing against the sharp edge of experience (the lifelikeness of the human drama) doctrines which elsewhere in the poem, as in Books III or X, are asserted only dogmatically and baldly—especially the doctrine of man's free will and moral responsibility, that God made man "Sufficient to have stood, though *free* to fall" (III.99). But *did* He, the Sin-Death allegory asks? The expressed *doctrine* in Book III is "plain and perspicuous" to the point of bluntness; yet it is also paradoxical and puzzling—like the allegory. For sometimes (as when Sin, with God's forbearance, lets Satan out of Hell) it seems as if men do not have free will, as if the Fates (or God) are unfairly stacking the odds against them. Or it may even sometimes seem, in a form of psychological determinism, that Adam's own endowed character is conspiring against him, or Satan's similarly against him. This is a view sometimes expressed by the characters themselves, for Adam complains in Book X, lines 743-52, of having been created too weak to withstand temptation, while Satan's constant complaint—or boast (as in Books I.96 and IV.79-82)—is that he *cannot* change. Whether man indeed has free will is an issue germane to the entire poem; it is the central idea, almost, in Milton's thought. It is a problem the investigation of which continues throughout *Paradise Lost*: was Eve in reality simply ensnared by superior guile and external circumstances, and did she really have no other choice; was Adam in truth the victim of other, equally difficult circumstances, the victim of his not unworthy love for Eve?

The allegorical adumbration of this problem in the Sin episode in Book II is one of many seeds early planted in our minds that the problem of free will is not a straightforward one, and that complex new aspects of it are forever arising. The *problem* is real enough—even if the figure of Sin is not. Thus it is far more than a figure of speech that makes Sin open the gates *out* of Hell as well as, later, construct the path back *into* Hell. The later allegory is easily understood; but the former allegory, as Milton presents it, and despite its familiar allusion to James 1.15 (saying in effect that Satan through his desire for Sin brings evil into the world and that the issue of Sin is Death), masks a difficulty which is much less readily explained, the release of evil into the world by a God who is supposed to be good. Sin pointedly says in Book II (lines 774-75) that the powerful Key to the Gates had been given over into her charge—by, it is to be presumed, God's order; and God in Books III and X is perfectly aware of Satan's or Sin's and Death's depredations. The difficulties arising through Sin's vivid presence and too literal actions, then, are part of the wider philosophical difficulties with which the poem is engaged.[3]

We have previously considered the rationale in historical theory and practice of the "mixed" epic for such intrusions of allegorical persons or episodes into the poem, and the eighteenth-century unease, still persisting, inspired by their sometimes bizarre development in Milton's use. Not only are characters like Sin and the Old Anarch Chaos given personalities and allowed to participate in the action, they are made more disturbing still by the way in which Satan, an almost wholly "real" figure, is drawn into active confrontation or dialogue with them. Rather than suppose that Milton has badly "mixed his modes",[4] a more prudent reaction would be to wait and see whether the change of key does not begin to make sense later; whether it does not form a temporary dissonance which is eventually absorbed into the total fabric of the poem's unfolded meaning—whether, for example, Satan's seeming impercipience in addressing the allegorical (and therefore non-existent) characters, or certain oddities in the actions and appearances of these latter, may not have something indirect to tell us about the characters who matter most in the poem. In short, we would do better to await with patience the unfolding of the ulterior meanings and thematic connections which, historically, allegory in epic was understood to carry. In the instance of Sin and Satan, Spenser's bad allegorical characters and their interaction with the human knights might also provide a good point of entry into the problematic episode, one not dissimilar to that offered by another aspect of the biblical allegory in James 1, that conveyed by verses 13-14. Both Spenser and these two biblical verses suggest that no person is ever tempted save by himself; none can blame God or any external cause. Sin's Key is everyone's key.

Quite apart from the pointedly disruptive allegorical episodes, many kinds and levels of realism and non-realism coexist everywhere in *Paradise Lost*, and the reader is consciously or unconsciously accommodating from one to another all the time. With Satan, for example, we easily switch from one kind of response, to the dramatically plausible, tormented, alienated hero of Books I-II, to the quite different level of imaginative response involved in accepting Satan's miraculous, or diabolical, tricks and inventions in Hell (Pandæmonium seems to arise half through engineering, half through conjuration), or his "magical" reappearance there in Book X, or his various disguises and transformations in the intervening Books. But even these magical tricks (like those of Homer's gods) represent something different again, fictively speaking, from the almost pure fantasy of the similes near the end of Book I describing the fallen angels as if reduced to bees, pygmies and fairies (lines 668-88). Yet we can accept these "transformations" too, although in a somewhat different way, more by a form of poetically suspended disbelief. The *actual* diminishing of the angels is mediated by the fact that it seems to have occurred in simile.[5]

There is further confusion in the strangely mixed modes of Satan's science-fiction journey across Chaos, so convincing in its sensation of physical difficulty amidst appalling violence, so unnaturalistic in the allegorical character of the episode, with its partly metaphysical and ontological, partly scientific, partly moral emphases (all three emphases correspond to recognised "levels" in Renaissance dictionary definitions of allegory). When Satan once enters the created World, we may contrast the cinematographic realism of his wonderful perspectived plunge in Book III, down through the reaches of the solar system, with the extraordinary sense of brightness in the Sun at the halfway point, an effect contrived through mainly mystical metaphor and alchemical allusion rather than through realism. Again, there is a quite different kind of unrealism, an "ideal reality", in the description of the Garden—Poussin, one might say, in place of the baroque foreshortenings of Space or the *chiaroscuro* of Hell. In these scenes we move from mixed modes in narration (verisimilar, allegorical) to mixtures of realism and non-realism in painterly styles or in effects conveyed in words. Even within the single episode of the War, as was noted, the mode is shifting all the while, from recognisable models of military activity to what verges on the impossible and ultimately on the transcendent. As readers, we go along with such changes and assimilate them as somehow parts of the poem's complex perspectives. But occasionally the reader is pulled up short by some particularly surprising anomaly; and that is his cue to begin to wonder what has been going on beneath the surfaces of the descriptions or narrations all the while.

"Implication" and Simile

Another important feature which we come to recognise as characteristic of the poem's peculiar forms of representation is the following. Even where the descriptions contain nothing overtly bizarre or incongruous, even where the decorum of verisimilitude seems to be most strictly maintained (as in the depictions of Adam and Eve), it is often the case that much of the detail given does not seem to correspond exactly to the occasions, circumstances, personages, which have evoked it. Certain details seem to lie *athwart* the narration, or even in feeling to clash with it. This artistic habit in *Paradise Lost* is so confirmed that we may speak of it as a conscious technique. We might call it a technique of *implication,* in which in a subterranean way descriptions or narrations often seem to be alluding to something elsewhere in the poem than that moment with which they are engaged. Certain details in a simile, certain mythical allusions, certain particulars in a scene, instead of fitting the situation which they are supposedly amplifying seem to allude to some other time, place, scene, often quite disparate. They may point to events in the past or in the future, either within the poem's own world or in the world quite outside of the poem, or they may evoke something different, inappropriate and disturbing to the poem's present situation.

Many readers and critics have been struck by this almost uncanny aspect of *Paradise Lost* and the strange dissonances which it creates. But few have recognised in this technique of implication one of the most characteristic features of Spenser's highly allusive and oblique art, or indeed a practice universally present in allegorical language. For one of the most basic definitions of allegory is that it "says one thing but intends another"—a description of function which links it closely with *ironia.* Milton's ironical descriptions, like Spenser's, often seem to say one thing while they intend another. They are looking somewhere else than the place on which our eyes happen to be fixed; they seem to want to tell us something that we need to know and which concerns the present moment, but which does not quite fit into the present field of vision. It is a quite mistaken effort to try to separate oblique allusion of this deliberate kind from other varieties of allegorical language and covert allusion, or from that nonexistent thing called "pure allegory".[6] The allegorical mentality is a manner of orientation. It involves acquiring the habit of double vision, of hearing "two voices" or being "bilingual", and it works through a whole spectrum of oblique devices involving displacement of meaning, of various kinds and in matters large and small.

The undercurrent of further relevance involved in Milton's enigmatic allusions is most often found to relate to the human present, reaching back from the ideal prelapsarian and supernatural worlds with which we are ostensibly concerned in the poem to something more immediate. To begin with the slightest of such ripples, we find that even (or particularly) in indirect comparisons or mythic allusions made in connection with Satan the time-scales and distance-scales are pointedly *human:* "Nine times the Space *that measures Day and Night / To mortal men*" (I.50-51); "As farr remov'd from God and light of Heav'n / *As from the Center thrice to th' utmost Pole*" (I.73-74). Of Mulciber, a surrogate for Satan, we hear that:

> *from Morn*
> *To Noon he fell, from Noon to dewy Eve,*

> *A Summers day;* and with *the setting* Sun
> Dropd from the Zenith like a falling Starr,
> On *Lemnos* th' *Ægæan* Ile.
>   (I.742-46)

The italicized details have been said to "anchor" these supernatural descriptions in the natural world. But "mortal men" are almost too conspicuously present—by name, in fact. Space-Time, Day-Night, Earth's Centre and her Pole, Summer, Morn-Noon-Eve, the vantage point of Earth (looking up at Mulciber seen like a falling star), the human dimensions and perspectives as well as the precision of time and place, day, night and season, force connections in our minds with all the human contexts and places elsewhere in the poem. As was earlier noted, the allusions in the passage describing Mulciber's fall are such as much later to link it in our minds with the long noon to midday to twilight sequence of Adam's and Eve's final "Summers day" in Eden, and with *their* "setting Sun". More immediately, of course, the Mulciber description also brings in Satan's fall, not merely through direct recapitulation but also through the references to Lemnos (a *volcanic* isle, recalling the appearance of Hell at I.230-37) and to Mulciber (or Hephaestus, recalling the smelting of ore for Pandæmonium at I.700-711). But the final covert equation which establishes itself (Lemnos:Eden:Hell) is still humanly oriented, so that it is hard to know which is the more ironically poignant: to find Greek islands and seas and summery days identified with Hell, or to find the subterranean veins of fire in Hell associated with Eden.

To move to explicit similes, when Milton first describes the Garden it is through that famous series of negative comparisons (IV.268-85) relating Eden to human or mythic-historical places not simply beautiful, although they are so, but riddled with fallen human passions. Thus Eden becomes "that faire field / Of *Enna*" where Proserpina was ravished; or "that sweet Grove / Of *Daphne* by *Orontes*" (a notorious pleasure garden at Antioch, by the river Orontes); or "that *Nyseian* Ile" where "*Ammon*" or "*Libyan Jove*" hid illegitimate Bacchus from "*Rhea's* eye"; or lastly, "Mount *Amara*" . . . / A whole dayes journey high", the remote place "where *Abassin* Kings thir issue Guard". The last is an intriguing vignette, extraordinarily placed in connection with Eden, since the Abyssinian kings were said to have shut up their numerous progeny, fifty princes at a time immured in the luxurious pleasure-gardens and palaces of Amara, in order to avoid sedition. Thus Amara is identified as a beautiful prison containing a potential threat of sedition—an innuendo which must spill over into Eden, which is here compared to it. (Pandora and her box offer a similar, more obviously damaging comparison, which Milton later uses in connection with Eve in Book IV.714-16). Or rather, Eden *is* and *is not* like these places. The comparisons constitute double negatives: negative in content, and negative in that the similes are made to stand away from (as well as tacitly relate to) Eden. Eden is *not* like Enna, *nor* like Daphne's grove, *nor* like the Nyseian Isle, *nor* like Amara, but incomparably beyond these (more beautiful? or also more violent, notorious, illicit, seditious?). If Eden is not like these places, what purpose do the similes serve (as Bentley asked some time since)? The answer is that they force our attention away from paradisal beauty to a world that has since become deeply fallen, making us see Eden as if veiled and disfigured by that fallen world. Eden, in short, becomes *now*; the negative anticipations have undermined it before it has even begun to exist in our imagination. Bentley did not like these particular or other negative comparisons,[7] for the very good reason that the fallen world is altogether too much present in them. But such persistent and powerful indirect charges of negative implication must surely have been intentional; spun in chains, such metaphors move toward a form of allegory.

We will notice further that Milton models his Enna series of similes in structure, form and moral content on a similar set of negative comparisons in Spenser's allegorical gardens of Acrasia in *The Faerie Queene* (II.xii.52)— rather than borrowing from Spenser's garden of Adonis in Book III, which might have seemed more appropriate. In this stanza Spenser cites a number of lovely mythical locations, beginning with "*Rhodope*, on which the Nimphe, that bore / A gyaunt babe, her selfe for griefe did kill", and proceeding through other classical places of beauty or pleasure, in the main connected with devastating sexual passions, to finish, like Milton, with a direct reference to Eden: "Or *Eden* selfe, if ought with *Eden* mote compaire". In Spenser such allusions bear emphatically on the whole context of sexual indulgence developed in the Acrasia episode in Canto xii. Through echoes of this stanza, Milton has imported into his poem the Spenserian situation and content of allegorical implication connected with Acrasia's Bower, and somehow linked them with his own Eden. Thus the Spenserian reminiscences themselves constitute an additional dimension of allegorical suggestiveness in *Paradise Lost*. In Book IV they bring in with tactful obliqueness, but precision, strong hints as to the nature of the flaws which lie at the heart of Eden.

One could continue to find many illustrations of oblique human allusiveness in Milton's supernatural or ideal worlds, for such allusion to experiences paradoxically rich and flawed, beautiful and terrifying, penetrates Milton's entire poem. Such allusiveness is present in the *deliberate* similes, such as those four negative metaphors concerning Eden, or the Eve-Proserpina comparisons, or the series relating Satan to trading ships plundering the riches of the Eastern Indies (II.636-43 and IV.159-67). It is present, by a heightened form of *implication*, in word, phrase, or casual comparison. It is present also in larger descriptive contexts, the landscapes for instance. There can be little doubt that the wild geography of Hell with its fierce extremes comes ultimately to stand for Satan's turbulent state of mind and internal conflicts—just as the harmonious balances of Eden's landscapes in Book IV (236-63), contrasts pleasing because never exaggerated, become the analogue for unfallen Adam's and Eve's temperate ("tempered") dispositions. (The gardens afford another Spenserian echo, this time taken from the descriptions of the tempered landscapes in the gardens at the Temple of Venus, *Faerie Queene* IV.x.24.) Through such cosmic renderings and vast intimations, through charged simile, through evocations of the Spenserian dimension of allegory in landscape or other description, or through the individual allusive word, phrase or comparison, Milton's poem does not simply move toward its Fall climax, or move in a straight line out of a supernatural and ideal world into the mundane, or out of a remote past into the present. Rather, we come to feel that the human present with its various colourings, dark and light, has been embedded in the fiction from its very beginnings. In *Paradise Lost* Milton would seem to be writing not only about original Eden, but quite as much about the only world we can actively know—which is to say, our own. Only through the obliquer decorum of allegory could he have achieved, with propriety, such a double vision.

Emblem and Allegorical Episode

If such a weight of human implication is to be felt pressing in upon us through the surfaces of Milton's language and descriptions, there is relevance of a sharper kind to be gleaned from the enigmatic emblems or symbolic episodes which, along with the personification allegories, punctuate the narrative from time to time. Often it cannot be understood why these mysterious emblems and episodes should break into the poem just where they do, or what bearing they can have on their immediate contexts. The emblems and episodes are peculiarly opaque, displaying that baffling inappropriateness or displacement from their true context which characterizes the allegorical trope. They also exhibit that disingenuous Spenserian trait of being "explained away" by the poet. One example is the Golden Stairs (III.501 ff.) which Satan finds immediately after landing "On the bare outside of this World" (III.74). It is not apparent why it should be *Satan*, coming as intruder and assassin, who is vouchsafed such a splendid vision, nor why it should be shown just here; the rather weak alternative explanations offered by the poet at lines 523-25 lack conviction and only enhance the singularity of the manifestation. A similar case is the impressive, inscrutable emblem of the Golden Scales, which the Almighty hangs out at the end of Book IV (lines 995 ff.). Gabriel's partial reading of the significance of the emblem (at IV.1011-13) is his personal interpretation only, and it must leave us dissatisfied, for there remains too much in the emblem and the whole scene which still lacks explanation.[8] So too with the more bizarrely intrusive serpent transformation which unexpectedly over-takes Satan near the end of Book X (lines 504 ff.), just in his moment of glory; Milton interrupts the action for a long passage in order to describe a grotesquely reenacted Fall and proliferated, compulsive eatings of ashen apples. These condensed allegorical emblems or emblematic episodes hide their complex meanings and disturb by their sudden intrusion, as well as by their extraordinary shifts in mode from the ongoing realism of the "heroic" narrative. These particular scenes in fact form part of a much larger structure of imagery relating significantly to that leading theme and problem of free will—free choice and volition, which are so central to Milton's thinking and to *Paradise Lost*. Their true importance may be measured exactly by their disproportionate scale and development, com-pared with the relatively trivial actions which appear to call them up in the immediate context. With the more expanded allegories of Chaos, Sin and Death, these emblematic incidents fall into what Le Bossu identified as exemplary "Fables", linked chains of metaphors which help to project the epic's disguised allegorical "Moral", under its verisimilar action.[9]

It is only after long gaps in his understanding, comparable to the laborious learning experience undergone by the poem's protagonists, that the reader comes to grasp the full emotional, psychological or moral values attaching to such emblems as those instanced above. In such delayed responses we may again note a Spenserian technique: the allegorical education of the reader proceeding in slow parallel with the moral educa-tion of the protagonists. It is through the reader's long experience of the multiple verbal links, situational echoes and acrostic connectors, all of which work across the whole poem and act as catalysts, that the latent connections between rarefied, abstract or covert allegorical figures and devices and the life-situations upon which they provide a coded commen-tary finally unfold. Some allegorical figures, more than others, may retain their mystery long after an initial reading of the poem is completed. "Mystery", "enigma" or "riddle"—a penumbra of "darkness" sometimes never completely lifted—as we saw, constituted one of the defining marks of allegory, according to the Renaissance rhetoricians whose theories were reviewed in earlier chapters. The *enigmatic* in Milton's allegorical figures, emblems and episodes is the pointer to their acute relevance in the poem. It is the ostentatiously irrelevant detail or component which itself provides the admonitory, alerting signal to the presence of allegory in *Paradise Lost*—just as it does in Spenser and earlier allegorists.

Those most overtly allegorical episodes in the poem, in which Sin and Death (also the figure of Chaos), together with Satan, act out what con-stitutes almost an overplot to the main narrative, therefore also fall into place in the overall allegorical design of *Paradise Lost*. We may see them as the most externalized or stylized expressions of all the hidden innuendo in the poem. Despite their alien appearance and alien mode, or indeed because of these, the scenes with Sin and Death crystallize out those obscure relevances which the reader so often feels pressing upon him through the echoing verbal intimations, the innuendo-filled descriptions, the proleptic similes with deliberately displaced detail, the intrusive, enigmatic emblems. All share in some degree that same quality of "irrelevance", whether it be only slight incongruity or on the other hand bizarre displacement or intrusion, which links them into a coherent aesthetic scheme. What we have in the Sin-Death episodes is merely an intensification of oblique allusion or symbolic figure into declared allegory—marked by the exaggerated change of tone and pace, the shift in mode and perspective, which suddenly throws into focus and exposes the counter-directions in which the poem has from the start been driving.

A further comment may be made on the personification allegories. It was noted earlier that "shadow" in the period's use and in Milton's was often a synonym for literary allegory. Death is called more than once in the poem a "Shadow" (II.669, X.264), or the "shadow" or "Shade" of Sin (IX.12, X.249). A shadow of course follows the person who casts it. But the word further acts as a multiple pun. It is traditional to allegorical language that a "shadow" obscures and yet reveals; just as in the external world a shadow both casts a shade and also throws a silhouetted image, so an allegorical shadow (to borrow the language of Bacon and other rhetoricians) "conceals" while it also "reveals". Sin and Death on numerous occasions "shadow" or grotesquely mime the Holy Trinity, in ways that have more than a suggestion of inverted theological allegory. But beyond such parodies as those in Book II (lines 727-870), Sin and Death are also, less obviously, inseparable shadows of the human creatures, even though they are never seen directly together with Adam and Eve but rather, by displacement, are matched with Satan. Not unlike Tasso's magical persons, Ismen and Armida, who, to use Tasso's words, "layeth siege" respectively to the male and female powers of the soul (the intellect or "virtue . . . opinative" and "the power of our desires", the senses),[10] or like Spenser's Archimago and Duessa, these monstrous male and female creations of Milton's imagining seem to parody and warp all that is natural and good in their human counterparts. The actions of the allegorical personages mime or "shadow" those of Adam and Eve in many significant contexts, even to verbal echoings, reflecting as in a magnifying and distorting mirror all the secret flaws and crooked lines in the human psychology, and displaying love, family affection, natural desires, even spaciousness of spirit, corrupted into infatuation, bondage, unnatural lust, greed and *hybris*.

Paradise Lost is in its most important aspect a scenario for human choices. But more important, more complex and elusive than the mere demonstration of choices good or bad, right or wrong, is the searching out of all the hidden difficulties, internal more than external, which hinder right choices and moral judgements. Such internal obstacles may lie in the lack of self-recognition, the unconscious or suppressed motive, the half conscious self-deception or wilful twisting of understanding, the secret wishful or wilful self-indulgence, the lack of internal discipline—all those secret lets and hindrances which (quite apart from contingent external circumstances) surround and impede right human decisions, and which only long experience and arduously acquired "prudence" (in the Aristotelian sense) can teach to control or forestall. It is in conveying these more equivocal aspects of human conduct that the personification allegories play such a crucial part, rendering bizarrely visible that darker side which we otherwise only dimly sense in the human personalities—aspects which, being human, the protagonists, like ourselves, would prefer not to know about. Again, it is likely to be small situational or verbal echoes in the fantastic allegorical characters and episodes that tie these bearings to the human characters and into the themes of the main plot—just as was the case with verbal details in the emblematic episodes or deliberately nuanced similes. Yet because the supernatural, allegorical or "shadowing" episodes are displaced and often widely separated in narrative space from their correlative human situations, and because they also contain easily recognisable theological allegories with more general bearings on the plot, it is easy to ignore the troublesome, more intimate connections with Adam and Eve. The element of allegory, however, consistently warns us not to do so, through intractable enigma refusing to be ignored.

TWENTY-ONE

The "Language of Allegory" and Milton's Allegorical Epic

We may conclude with the question with which the final Part of this study began: the problem of "realism" and "literal" representation in *Paradise Lost*, versus the fictive, figurative and allegorical. We have now to ask whether the two modes need necessarily be regarded as incompatible or out of harmony with each other. Rather than suppose that Milton, the most precise and conscious of artists, is being repeatedly and unwittingly inept in the management of his fiction, that he introduces all manner of inappropriate elements, small and large, into it, that he cannot control his own plot or characterizations or their impact upon us, or that in relapsing into "archaic" literary modes he has transgressed his own professed decorums concerning the interpretation of Scripture, would it not be more logical to assume that Milton knows what he is about, that he is not merely blundering from one level of representation to another in the poem, and that he may, even more than has commonly been imagined, be manipulating our responses with extraordinary skill? We can then reach a conclusion which at least has the advantage of showing *Paradise Lost* as consistent in its aesthetic. We can acknowledge that the main bulk of the poem (all that is fictive and the poet's own invention) is in a significant degree and a variety of ways covert in implication, or allegorical, without being one whit less "real" in its "historical" component; that the poem is in fact written in a consistently figurative mode, with nuance, metaphor and symbol passing more explicitly into allegory—a system of oblique figuration of a fluctuating intensity, but one that is enclosed within an external framework of historical realism, and marked throughout large parts of the narrative by a persuasive "air of history".

It is relevant to observe that the lengthening and shortening of the allegorical focus, or the alternation between "pure" allegory and "straightforward" verisimilar narration (which may indeed be filled with allegorical innuendo), is itself one of the distinguishing features of Spenserian allegorical composition, being one form of the well-recognised romance struc-

tural device of *entrelacement*. *Entrelacement*, in the sense that Tuve defined it
in medieval romance, is to be understood as the use of "irrelevant" epi-
sodes which thematically further the progress of the main character, al-
though they may appear to leave him behind.[1] This was a device which
Spenser brilliantly adapted, and one which Tasso also adopted and ex-
tended in his own way, through the interpolation of fantastic episodes into
his "historical" plot. Milton's plot is in its main outlines more historical,
linear and Aristotelian, his treatment overall more "verisimilar" than Spen-
ser's, and allegory in *Paradise Lost* more often is mediated through meta-
phor, simile, allusion, intimation, or echo than through overt allegorical
devices, which occur in Spenser with greater frequency than in Milton.
Nevertheless, conspicuously allegorical elements do occur in substantial
number in Milton's epic, and no explanation of his artistic processes can be
adequate which does not find room for these elements within his larger
intentions and scheme. As in an archaeological underlay, the hidden
contours of an earlier epoch of allegorical epic project through the surface
outlines of Milton's more historical and modern epic, giving signs of a
whole subterranean construction. Personified allegorical overplot, the
main plot itself, sometimes, in certain allegorical shadowings, interpolated
emblematic or symbolic episodes, all these, along with the pervasive
dimension of oblique and passing allusion, the technique of "implication",
supply that detached intellectual commentary on the "real" action which
characterizes traditional allegorical narrative. We instantly recognise such
an interplay as characteristic of the Spenserian enterprise: the event, the
façade of lifelike "action", alternating with the oblique allegorical commen-
tary on it conveyed through a multitude of devious devices. Centuries of
traditions of scriptural exegesis in allegorical or quasi-allegorical modes
also helped to shape Milton's figurative art in other, specialized ways. But
Milton could not well have neglected or rejected the imaginative resources
available to him also from so long and distinguished a literary tradition as
the Renaissance allegorical epic offered, given his own deep commitment
to both emulate and outdo the best in classical and modern epics. He
necessarily also shaped the undermeanings of *Paradise Lost* and developed
their fictive expressions in the light of his own rich experience of Renais-
sance didactic-allegorical epic theory and practice and of Renaissance
rhetorical theories of allegory in poetry.

    The final question therefore to be asked is whether, by setting *Paradise
Lost* against a background of allegorical theory and practice in the epic, as
well as against a background of allegorical exegesis on Scripture and on
earlier epic narrative, and against other Renaissance traditions of alle-
gorical rhetoric in poetry, we do not achieve a much more coherent and
integrated view of Milton's poem, enabling us to see it as a coherently
sustained artistic and intellectual structure, speaking with "two voices"
but to one purpose:[2] to express that complex Idea or Justification of God's

ways and of man's destiny which Milton cited as his principal design in writing *Paradise Lost*. *Paradise Lost* may wear the external dress of reality; but its soul, like that of Tasso's epic, lies in its didactic allegory. Milton's own contemporaries were not in any doubt about this. They took it for granted that a mixture of verisimilar action ("probable circumstances") with "proper allegory" was in the nature of the epic genre, and they even ventured (glancing more than once at Tasso) to define the "peculiar [personal] Allegory or Moral" intended by Milton's "instruction" or "design" in *Paradise Lost*.[3] Our own conclusion too may be that *Paradise Lost* speaks in the structures, forms, and language of allegory, in order to express those things which Milton has to say and which lie beyond the poem's sharply defined content of doctrine and its framework of scriptural history.

As has been stressed before in this study, there need have been no conflict felt by Milton between the factual authenticity of Genesis and that Idea or complex of ideas which he undertakes to expound through expanding the scriptural story. It was entirely in accord with standard Protestant homiletics that Milton should engage in this way with a scriptural narrative. Protestant preachers like Luther often had engaged in a "kind of allegory", or personal expansion of narrative elements in Scripture. Milton's scriptural narrative similarly shows a remarkable capacity to act as figurative expansion of the Bible, to be imbued with the meanings which the author personally drew out of the scriptural record for the edification, comfort and hope of man. These meanings Milton was able to "apply" to the universal situation of man, in the light of his own personal convictions, and through amplification of the original narrative in particular directions, yet always within the limits of the restrictions and proprieties imposed by the decorums of scriptural interpretation which he had himself closely considered in *Of Christian Doctrine*. For Milton, the homiletic convention in treating Scripture found reinforcement in analogous literary views on the correct "rules" and practice of the late allegorical epic. "History" could and should be "brief" in an epic poem, so that imaginative invention not only of a verisimilar kind but of an allegorical kind could take over, wherever the history stops.[4]

Tasso has been proposed in this study as the principal synthesizer and disseminator of the theory of the mixed historical-allegorical epic and the chief arbitrator on its decorums. He drew together for his own period the diverse strands of current and earlier opinions on the long epic and, against the background of the extensive classical and Renaissance Neoplatonic traditions of ethical-allegorical exegesis on epic, he formulated a flexible, coherent body of theory and praxis of the mixed epic. His conception of the allegorical epic as a genre in which history and Christian truths could marry with the different sort of truth conveyed by the "marvellous-verisimilar"—that is, the truth of allegory, the truth of the imagination—remained influential long into the seventeenth century. When we read Milton's literary allusions in his autobiographical prose with care, it is quite apparent that he was consciously planning and measuring his own epic against the entire background of the late sixteenth-century Italian critical debates concerning the proper character of the heroic poem, and that he was relating all the problems he would have to sift out concerning the right subject, the right hero, the right style and decorum, to their highly sophisticated arguments. What *were* the best "laws . . . of a true *Epic* poem . . . to observe"? In the "Italian Commentaries of Castelvetro, Tasso, Mazzoni", but especially of Tasso, as well as through the creative examples of Tasso and his great imitator, Spenser, Milton seems to have found very many of the needful answers. Tasso's model, especially, enabled Milton to correlate an historical type of narrative with an allegorical fiction displaying a moral Idea. In Tasso's commentaries Milton found the key to the practical problems of how to shape his epic structure around such a "Moral" or anterior Idea, and how to accommodate the epic's form to the historical necessities of what Milton finally hit upon as the supreme "historical" subject for his project: the archetypal human history of Genesis, far exceeding in importance the documentary records of ancient Israel with which he earlier had dallied, or British-Roman material "in our own ancient stories."

Tasso's special formula, historically a compromise solution, of the mixed-genre epic, part history, part "romance", but didactically unified throughout in the light of the poet's particular Idea which was the epic poem's "platform", as Le Bossu later put it, was to remain in Milton's mind over the twenty years' gestation of *Paradise Lost*, helping him to bridge the gap between the older styles of Renaissance allegorical epic and the new historical styles in epic. Retaining a subtle dialogue of echo, acknowledgement and qualification with each of Tasso and Spenser, Milton devised a mixed allegorical-historical epic of a more suitably contemporary kind, a version of his own, namely, an epic based on *scriptural* history and *scriptural* truth, fused with imaginatively perceived and allegorically rendered truths. This would be a poem whose poetic "laws" would not only be adjusted to the literary decorums peculiar to the mixed epic (or the "diffuse" epic as Milton called it), but could also be "accommodated" to those scriptural proprieties to which Milton as an accomplished theologian was particularly sensitive. Thus Milton would achieve a poetic doubly validated, in his epic both "real" and "allegoric". It would seem to be the case that neither has the complete character of his poetic intentions yet been fully recognised nor, as yet, has any full study of this poetic as realised within his poem been attempted.

A concluding word may be said about the language of allegory in *Paradise Lost*. I have argued that allegorical discourse, while not the only mode of discourse in the poem, is nonetheless that mode which occupies a central place in Milton's epic and affords a poetic control over the largest part of his poem, knitting many disparate and some incongruous elements of language, description and style into a purposeful thematic unity. Allegory offers an intended rich counterpoint to the plain modes of scriptural-historical narration and dogmatic pronouncement which are, so to speak, the skeleton of discourse in the poem. Milton's Idea, fleshed out by the fictively enacted imitation of external reality, in a verisimilar fiction which is itself allegorically coloured at times, an Idea projected also through oblique or enigmatic or emblematic allegorical devices and verbal suggestions in many other dimensions, works to "justify", explain, and render humanly comprehensible and humanly acceptable the assertions of dogma, under the apparent inscrutability or hostility of Providence.

Milton's allegorical language, rhetoric, and strategies have multiple sources, as has been suggested in my earlier chapters. Earlier models of secular or scriptural exegesis, Renaissance theories of allegorical rhetoric or theory of all poetry as allegory, Protestant hermeneutics and sermonizing, to a limited degree modes of typologically directed readings of Scripture, as well as the humanist tradition of continuous moral-allegorical exposition of classical epic or of "continued metaphor" in written epic, all these provide analogies to or conspicuous sources for allegorical discourse in *Paradise Lost*. Still other modes of shadowed theological innuendo in the language of *Paradise Lost* have recently come to be explored, under the umbrella title of "Protestant poetics". One less well recognised but cognate variant of this element of language in the poem—one of the products of Milton's effort to convey some apprehension of God other than as He is shown in His literal self-presentation in the Bible—seems to relate to certain still earlier, specialized practices in medieval rabbinical exegesis on the Word. *Midrash* gave rise to certain highly abstract and oblique varieties of verbal mimesis designed to convey, through the barest rudiments of language, grammar and syntax, some sense of God's mysterious attributes and His relationships with men. This dimension in language, successfully reconstructed in *Paradise Lost* as part of Milton's radical interpretation of the doctrine of "accommodation", may indeed constitute one of his most novel contributions to figural poetics. The presence of so many related modes and uses of shadowed language in *Paradise Lost* may confirm our perception, stressed at the beginning of this study, that all the various modes of figural discourse, including the mode and devices of epic allegory, are special developments of metaphor, not wholly separable from each other and certainly not mutually exclusive.

The above remarks on special varieties of Christian or midrashic figural language as cultivated by Milton open slightly different perspectives from those which have been the concern of the main parts of this study. There I have tried to relate *Paradise Lost* more specifically to Renaissance theories of allegory in poetry and in the epic. Those are the most immediate theoretical contexts on which Milton drew in devising his poem and, in my view, the immediate contexts within which *Paradise Lost* most needs to be explored at the present time. The present study has tried to offer a broad outline of such theory, of the ways in which it evolved from earlier times, and of the relation to it in which Milton, his Protestant tradition, and his poem stand.

APPENDIX A

Bibliographical Essay on Tasso

In the first part of this Appendix, I attempt to indicate some of the historical problems in Tasso criticism in respect of his allegorical intentions and their realisation. The status of the "Allegoria" to the *Gerusalemme liberata* is of course involved in this question. Also involved is the question of the relationship between the earlier and later versions of Tasso's major treatise on the epic poem, which I briefly discuss. Subsequently I indicate some of the most relevant studies on Tasso in English and a few in Italian, with particular reference, again, to their views on the question of allegory. In the second part I give a few annotations on certain of the Tasso editions and works which I have used.

I.   Most Tasso scholars do not now subscribe to the nineteenth-century critical view (not shared by Tasso's contemporaries) that his "Allegoria" was merely an afterthought to his poem, written under the pressures of the Counter-Reformation. This earlier view relies heavily on certain of Tasso's remarks in his Letters, particularly the opening of his Letter (no. 79) of June 15, 1576, to Scipione Gonzaga, in which he says that he had had no idea of allegory when he began his poem, but that it recommended itself to him in mid-composition, partly because of the strictness of the times (see *Lettere*, vol. 1, p. 186). Nonetheless, this letter goes on to give a long and informed discussion of allegory as a workable structure for the epic, explaining why Tasso had not been able from his earlier critical reading and understanding to take allegory in the epic seriously, but why after deeper thought he can now do so. I have discussed this letter in my chapter 5, section "The Lettere Poetiche".

     For discussion of his views on the epic, I have not used Tasso's *Discorsi dell'arte poetica*, but (with a few comparisons to this earlier treatise) work instead from the revised *Discorsi del poema eroico*, as the maturer expression of Tasso's aesthetics. For an analysis of the compositional relationships between the two sets of Discourses, the reader may refer to Annabel

Patterson's discussion in "Tasso and Neoplatonism". Patterson finds that
in each of the six Books of the *Discorsi del poema eroico* (including the newly
added Book I and expansions of the old Books I and III of the *Discorsi
dell'arte poetica*) Tasso has reworked his ideas of epic form and purpose
along Neoplatonic aesthetic lines more congenial to allegorizing. Danilo
Aguzzi (p. 515) thinks that in the *Discorsi dell'arte poetica* "discussion of
allegory is almost totally absent"; however, he notes the allegorical rele-
vance of some of the more general statements, standing in parallel, in the
two sets of Discourses, concerning "Imitation", "Verisimilitude", or "His-
tory", and the use of the "fantastic" in epic (see pp. 523-24 and nn.). It
would seem, perhaps because they were written *post hoc*, that the revised
Discorsi more accurately reflect the character of the allegorical poetics
worked out during the actual writing of the *Gerusalemme* and summarized
in its "Allegoria". An allegorical potential for the Neoplatonic aesthetic
worked out more explicitly in Tasso's later *Discorsi* and other writings is not
absent from the earlier *Discorsi*, and many of the important passages
overlap between the two texts. Lawrence L. Rhu (see below) also has noted
that the earlier *Discorsi* contain passages with a Neoplatonic-allegorical
potential.

Although both versions of Tasso's *Discorsi* were published late, their
material belongs with the decade 1575–85. Interestingly enough, Tasso's
epic of the *Rinaldo* also, in 1583, acquired in print an allegorical preface,
some twenty years after its first publication (though the preface was
composed much earlier). Thus the period from 1575–76 (Tasso's "Poetical
Letters") to 1583–86 or later, embracing most of the major and minor critical
texts of Tasso which I discuss, shows an extraordinary outburst of diverse
writings by Tasso on various aspects to do with allegory. This supports
Aguzzi's thesis that allegory, although not of the sort used by Ariosto or
Trissino, was entirely serious in Tasso and central to his developing poetic,
that "the evolution of Tasso's critical thought presents a remarkable co-
herence" (p.523), and that such thought did not simply emerge as a *post-hoc*
justification of Tasso's epic under the pressures of Neo-Aristotelianism
and the Counter-Reformation. There has been more willingness of late to
accept the internal evidence of Tasso's own poetical and critical writings on
this important question. For citations of some critical debate on this matter,
see especially the notes to Aguzzi's sections on Tasso, pp. 504-37, and
Michael Murrin's discussions in *The Allegorical Epic*.

Rhu (see below) in two useful articles effectively helps to counteract
modern assumptions that Tasso's "Allegoria" was imposed on his poem
only *post hoc*. (On the allegorical relevance of a few of Tasso's changes to his
poem see also Murrin, *The Allegorical Epic*, p. 95.) Rhu establishes that
Tasso's actual *cuts* to the *Gerusalemme*, as well as his additions of allegorical
episodes as cited by himself in his "Lettere poetiche", artistically enhance
the process of allegorization; pieces of characterization and incident incom-

patible with the allegory are removed. The Francesco Osanna and Scipione Gonzaga edition of the *Gerusalemme Liberata* (1584) in an Appendix gives the excised stanzas. However, Murrin in *The Allegorical Epic*, p. 90, says that because of the complex chronological intertwining of revisions in various drafts of Tasso's manuscripts, the actual situation is more confused than Osanna's Appendix suggests. Murrin (*The Allegorical Epic*, p. 233, n. 5) cites Angelo Solerti's critical apparatus in vol. 1, pp. 93-130, of his three-volume edition of the *Gerusalemme* (1895-96) as still the most crucial discussion of Tasso's text and revisions. For a substantial discussion of the dates at which Tasso did or did not introduce certain allegorical episodes into the *Gerusalemme* and some of the cuts which he made, also a table listing the chronology of some of the Letters developing Tasso's theory of allegory, see Murrin, *The Allegorical Epic*, especially pp. 89-105.

Of Rhu's two articles, "From Aristotle to Allegory" and "Tasso's First Discourse on the Art of Poetry as a Guide to the *Gerusalemme liberata*", the first measures Tasso's evolving poetic and practice from Aristotelian to allegorical between 1575 and 1581 against only his original position as seen in the earlier *Discorsi*. However, as the later *Discorsi* (rewritten from 1587 and published 1594) are themselves markedly less Aristotelian than the earlier, this comparison gives an incomplete idea of the continuing and ultimate real extent of Tasso's shift in view. Nonetheless, Rhu detects a potential for allegory in the famous "unity-in-variety" passage in its very first articulation (see especially pp. 35-37 of the *Discorsi dell'arte poetica*, edited by Poma). This passage is further reworked in *Discorsi del poema eroico*, Book III, pp. 77-79. Rhu in his investigations in his second article into Tasso's theory of poetry usefully makes the point that Tasso's well known uncertainty and lack of artistic self-confidence, as betrayed in his letters especially, render the argument for a serious purpose and progress toward allegory during the course of the composition of the *Gerusalemme* just as probable as the reverse theory, despite the hesitations, retractations and even opportunism which the poet expresses from time to time. Rhu's investigations into Tasso's poetic are to continue in a forthcoming larger study.

Two recent Italian critics who take seriously Tasso's moral-ethical "Allegoria" as a statement of his poetic are Luigi Derla, "Sull'Allegoria della 'Gerusalemme Liberata' ", and Lucia Olini, "Dalle direzioni di lettura alla revisione del testo: Tasso tra *Allegoria del Poema* e *Giudizio*". Olini, citing W.J. Kennedy in "The Problem of Allegory in Tasso's *Gerusalemme Liberata*", stresses that Tasso's type of allegory in the *Gerusalemme* is primarily "moral" and not "figural"—"figural" allegory being characteristic, rather, of the revised *Gerusalemme conquistata*. (Kennedy's study is, in fact, almost wholly *anti*-allegorical; see his p. 47: "The only kind of allegory that operates to any degree [in the *Gerusalemme*] is oblique and problematic moral exemplification".) Aguzzi's study cites criticism on Tasso and allegory (largely negative) in English and Italian studies before 1959. B.T. Sozzi's study, "La Poetica del Tasso", offers an historical account of Tasso's critical writings without direct reference to their allegorical development.

The relevant studies in English of Tasso by the three principal critics (apart from Rhu) who have, to the date of completion of this study, seriously engaged with Tasso's criticism may be summarized as follows. Aguzzi's work focuses on moral allegory in Tasso's prose criticism and his epic; Murrin in *The Allegorical Epic*, on the Renaissance sources of the Neoplatonic ethical allegory formulated for the *Gerusalemme*, and on the consequent thematic patterning of the poem, as well as on the progress of Tasso's developing thoughts on the "Allegory" to the poem as recorded in the Letters of 1575–76; while Bernard Weinberg engages more generally with Tasso's aesthetics and poetics in his prose writings, in relation to other contemporary Italian debates on poetry. Invaluable though it is for its source material, the organization of Weinberg's study by "Debates" (that is, according to different Renaissance controversies), as well as its large historical sweep, preclude any systematic discussion of the evolution of Tasso's own thinking on allegory. The strictly chronological arrangement of material in Aguzzi's work also does not permit the latter to analyse the erratic evolution of Tasso's thinking on allegory, and Aguzzi's treatment of Tasso's texts, other than the *Lettere*, the *Discorsi del poema eroico* and the *Giudizio*, is patchy. Murrin's later, carefully researched book with chronological tables successfully dips into the theoretical problems involved for Tasso at the point of composition of the *Gerusalemme* and in connection with Tasso's Letters.

Kennedy's briefer article on Tasso's "Allegoria" has been noted above. A more recent study by Robert L. Montgomery, chapter 5 in *The Reader's Eye: Studies in Didactic Literary Theory from Dante to Tasso*, based entirely on Tasso's two sets of *Discorsi* and his statements on history (only) in the *Giudizio*, makes no reference to any of Tasso's many statements about allegory and presents Tasso solely as a proponent of historical and didactic epic (in opposition to Mazzoni). Two further, very recent short studies explicitly or implicitly accept the existence of specific allegories in Tasso's epic and suggest an underpinning in his critical theory, as expressed in the "Allegoria" and the later *Discorsi*. In chapter 4, "Tasso: Romance, Epic, and Christian Epic", of his book, *Poets Historical: Dynastic Epic in the Renaissance*, Andrew Fichter argues the existence of an Augustinian "allegory of Christian salvation" (p. 132) in the *Gerusalemme*; Fichter also argues (p. 124) that "Tasso's purpose in the *Discorsi* is not to counterpose romance and epic as antithetical literary forms but to argue their identity, to draw romance into the shadow of epic"—an interpretation which I would support. Fichter does not engage with structural or artistic questions raised by the poem's allegorical character, as neither does Richard Helgerson in his essay, "Tasso on Spenser: Or the Politics of Chivalric Romance" (which he has kindly let me see in manuscript). This essay assumes a dominant political purpose (perhaps an allegory) in Tasso's poem. Both of these studies cast useful light on Tasso's critical purposes and poem, but I would suggest that the focus of both is too narrow, in that neither study acknowledges the anteriority (and perhaps primacy) of the *moral* foundation of Tasso's poem, and of its allegory as "the glass and figure of Human Life".

An earlier, biographically oriented book on Tasso by C.P. Brand, *Torquato Tasso: A Study of the Poet and his Contribution to English Literature*, echoing earlier Italian criticism is dismissive of allegory as a serious mode in the *Gerusalemme*. Brand's had been for long the only full-length study of Tasso in English; till recently there has been little else to direct English appreciation of Tasso's relationship to the allegorical epic, to Spenser, and to Milton. Judith A. Kates' book on *Tasso and Milton: The Problem of Christian Epic* does not discuss the subject of allegory at all—although she considers "interior" (moral) values to run in parallel in Tasso's, Spenser's and Milton's epics.

It is hoped that the present study may be of assistance, especially to English readers, in interpreting Tasso's maturing theories on allegory and epic across a wide range of his prose during the period from roughly 1575 to 1595, and in setting Tasso's theories into closer relationship with the English allegorical and epic traditions. However, more work is needed in this area of basic importance to the study not only of Tasso but of Spenser and Milton and the development of the theory of the sixteenth- and seventeeth-century English epic.

II.   Tasso's works have had to be read in a variety of different editions, there being no complete collected edition, while individual "collections" of his prose works are often incomplete, as well as overlapping. I have indicated in my notes and Bibliography the various specific editions of works of Tasso which I have used or quoted from. Additionally, I give below a few annotations on points of bibliographical interest or unusual arrangement in some of the collected editions and editions of individual works of Tasso cited, especially those in Mauro's.

La Gerusalemme Liberata, edited by Scipione Gonzaga, published by Francesco Osanna (1584). Appendix gives stanzas excised by Tasso.
Gerusalemme liberata: Poema eroico di Torquato Tasso (1581), edited by Angelo Solerti et al., 1895–96. Vol. 1, pp. 93-130, contains Solerti's discussion of Tasso's revisions to the *Gerusalemme*.
Jerusalem Delivered: a Poem (1600), translated by Edward Fairfax, edited by Henry Morley, 1890. Contains Fairfax's English translation of Tasso's "Allegoria" (completed May, 1576; published 1581.) It is placed at the end of the volume (pp. 436-43 in Morley), instead of at the beginning as in the Italian and Fairfax originals.

Le Lettere, edited by Cesare Guasti. 5 vols., 1857. Includes in vol. 1 the "Lettere poetiche" of 1575–76.

Le Opere, edited by Giuseppe Mauro. 12 vols. 1722–42. This beautiful edition reprints much collateral material, including contemporary debates with Tasso and the texts of some of the tracts answered by him. For a complete list of the works of Tasso which I have cited from this edition, see my Bibliography. The volumes specified below include the following works of Tasso:

> Vol. 1 (1722). *Il Goffredo, ovvero la Gerusalemme liberata* (1581). This is prefaced (6 pp., unnumbered) by the "Allegoria del Poema" (written *c.* 1576). Vol. 1 contains similar, shorter prose allegories to each canto, by Francesco Birago and Guido Casoni.

> Vol. 3 (1735). *Discorso sopra il Parere fatto dal Signor Francesco Patricio in difesa di Lodovico Ariosto* (1585).

> Vol. 4 (1735).

> *Del Giudizio sovra la Gerusalemme di Torquato Tasso, da lui medesimo riformata, libri due* [written 1592-95; published 1666].

> "Allegoria del *Rinaldo*". This *Allegoria*, first written in a letter of 1562, was included in all editions of *Il Rinaldo* from 1583, along with individual allegories to each canto. Mauro appends this allegory to his text of *Il Rinaldo* (the text also is in vol. 4).

> Vol. 7 (1737).

> *Il Ficino, ovvero dell'Arte. Dialogo* (written *c.* 1592–93). The dialogue is between two speakers, "Ficino" and "Landino", indicating the Neoplatonic basis of Tasso's aesthetic.

> *Il Messaggiero. Dialogo* (1582, unauthorized edition). A sketch of Tasso's angelology, which Milton's resembles in some respects.

> *Il Porzio, ovvero delle Virtù. Dialogo* (1666).

> *Il Manso, ovvero dell'Amicizia. Dialogo* (1586). The dedicatee is the Manso of Milton's poem.

> Vol. 8 (1738). *Della Virtù Eroica e della Carità. Discorso* (1579; published 1583).

> Vol. 10 (1739). *Lettere Poetiche . . . particolarmente in materia della Gerusalemme Liberata* (1587). The Poetical Letters were early known under this title.

> Vol. 12 (1742). "Allegoria del Poema" (to *Gerusalemme liberata*, 1581). The "Allegoria" (composed *c.* 1576), which also appears in Mauro's vol. 1 prefacing the poem's first edition of 1581, in vol. 12 stands alone. Mauro evidently included it again in the miscellaneous prose of his final volume, in recognition of the "Allegoria's" critical importance.

Le Prose Diverse, ed. Cesare Guasti. 2 vols. 1875. Vol. 1 includes the following, not in Mauro's edition:

> *Estratti dalla Poetica di Lodovico Castelvetro* (c. 1576; published 1875). This treatise appeared first as notations made upon extracts from Tasso's copy of Castelvetro's *Poetica* (1570 edition).

> *Delle differenze poetiche per risposta al Signor Orazio Ariosto* (1587).

Risposta Del S. Torq. Tasso, Al Discorso Del Sig. Oratio Lombardelli. 1586. This short tract apparently is not reprinted in any of the later collected editions of Tasso's prose, but is cited by Weinberg from the original edition. See the Bibliography to *A History of Literary Criticism in the Italian Renaissance*, p. 1153.

APPENDIX B

"Idea"

I. The problem of "Idea" or "Ideal Imitation" in Renaissance theory and its connection with conceptions of allegory is complicated. Values enter from both the ethics and poetics or aesthetics of Plato and Aristotle, and from medieval and Renaissance Neoplatonic developments from either source. Annabel Patterson, in "Tasso and Neoplatonism" (pp. 110-16), discussing Tasso's two main treatises on the epic poem and also two of his dialogues, *Il Messaggiero* and *Il Ficino*, suggests that Renaissance art theory, including Tasso's, embroiders on the Platonic notion of "Pattern" or "Idea" in ways which stand somewhat in tension. These are, the Platonic "exemplary forms" or the "Idea" conceived as transcendental absolute, versus "the artificial proportion of . . . things" (Ficino), the structural plan of a work, or more elaborately, an intellectual design in poetry seen in analogy to that in the divine creative mind. Either interpretation can impinge on allegory. Patterson develops mainly the aesthetic implications of the above categories for Tasso's ideas on genre, or alternatively for an aesthetic process which is analogous to eighteenth-century "idealization" in art: "gleanings of perfection" are gathered into one exemplary character, as in Tasso's "l'idea d'un perfetto Cavaliero" (see *Discorsi del poema eroico*, Book II, ed. Poma, p. 98; also in *Discorsi dell'arte Poetica, Opere*; the Italian is as given by Patterson, p. 125, nn. 30 and 31, and is taken from the edition of Niccolò Capurro, 1821–32). Either one character subsumes all the virtues, like Virgil's Aeneas, or different virtues are represented in different characters, as in Homer. Thomas Greene writes in a similarly Platonic vein, impinging on both the Platonic categories above: "Tasso used a form of Ficino's system to pattern his fable" (*The Descent from Heaven: A Study in Epic Continuity*, p. 213). That is, Tasso's knights illustrate a Platonic ladder of loves ascending from wealth to God, his women a variety of loves and probably a ladder of values in love.

Analogies may be perceived to Milton. In *Paradise Lost* Mammon, Belial, Eve and Adam, Abdiel, illustrate a ladder of loves; "perfect shapes" of various virtues may be perceived in various of the archangels; whereas in the Son in *Paradise Regained* they are all gathered into one: he "of good, wise, just, the perfet *shape*" (III.11). (See n. 2 to my chap. 13.) Similarly, in *The Faerie Queene* Arthur, in Toscanella's type of interpretation (see William Nelson, *The Poetry of Edmund Spenser*, p. 121), subsumes all the virtues individually illustrated in the six knights. In Milton's *Comus* the Lady "visibly" sees the "unblemish't *form* of Chastity" (lines 214-15), and "immortal *shapes*" also inhabit the Attendant Spirit's mansion (line 2). Again, Satan abashed sees in Eve "Vertue *in her shape* how lovly" (*Paradise Lost* IV.848). All these instances invoke the Platonic Forms or essences. I cite these examples in order to indicate Milton's specific verbal acknowledgements of one kind of Renaissance understanding of "Idea" in poetry, that is, as exemplary form. It is not that kind of "Idea" in *Paradise Lost* with which the present study is primarily concerned, but the first kind mentioned above by Patterson, the more abstract intellectual plan standing behind the poem, as it does in the divine mind.

II.   The scholar who has most often and deeply, to the profit of others in the field, discussed problems relating to the concept of "Idea" in the Renaissance and their connections with Milton is John M. Steadman. His latest view, expressed in *The Wall of Paradise* (pp. 41, 46, italics mine), is that Milton adopts like or from Tasso an *aesthetic* interpretation of "Idea" as the organizing of plot and incident in accordance with a *formal* structuring (this ordering is then equivalent to the "Idea" announced in Milton's epic): "Milton . . . achieve[d] the formal structure or 'idea' of the epic that Tasso had regarded as primary"; "The plot of *Paradise Lost* is simultaneously the imitation of an action and the imitation of a divine idea; the *design of its plot* is the image of a providential design". The word "formal" and the statement seem to imply that the narrative design of *Paradise Lost*, in its unfolding sequence of connected actions, imitates the unified, aesthetically ordered design of the divine physical creation. Steadman's statements evidently do not imply any similarity between abstract intellectual intention (allegory) in Milton's poem and the hidden divine providential intention. This however is the understanding of "Idea" that is central to my own interpretation.

On "allegory", a concept of which Steadman is distrustful relative to *Paradise Lost*, his treatment is so involved with wider conceptions of "Idea" as aesthetic form that I cannot well separate the two in his discussion. But it is necessary to address the issues here, since I have to record a measure of disagreement with Steadman's interpretations. He notes, for instance, that there is a distinction to be made between *exemplum* seen as a particular instance, and the concept of example as subsumed in the universal or involving a generalizing process in *art* (thus in epic the "aggregation" of heroic qualities into one individual may verge upon allegory of a kind).

Nevertheless, Steadman concludes that the "modes [involved] tended to overlap in practice", and that the methods of *exemplum* and "Ideal Imitation" or allegory are so closely associated as to be effectively indistinguishable. He himself recently tends increasingly toward the interpretation of Renaissance "Ideal Imitation" as *exemplum*, and of Renaissance "allegory" as not far off the exemplary. I have argued, following early critics such as Harington, against such assimilation between *exemplum* and allegory.

For Steadman's discussions, see *The Lamb and the Elephant*, especially chap. 5, "Image and Idea: Imitation and Allegory", pp. 106-45, and chap. 4, "The Garment of Doctrine: Imitation and Allegory", pp. 71-105. The information in Steadman's Foreword, Preface and especially his footnotes is particularly useful. See: pp. xiv, xxiv, xxvi (on various aspects or applications of "Idea" and allegory and their evident inseparability; on the intellectual content of allegory); p. xxiv ("The verbal and the visual icon . . . as the vehicle of a universal idea"); p. xxvi (varieties of Renaissance emblematic and allegorical expressive modes tending to overlap in practice); pp. xxxix-lxi, nn.3 and 4 (*exemplum* and allegory; fabulous allegory, *exemplum* and imitation are all closely associated); pp. 96-97, n.1 ("Idea" and "Ideal" in Renaissance criticism are not well distinguished); pp. 100-102, n.6 (Harington and allegory); p. 102, n.10 (criticism on Dante's allegory); pp. 103-4, n.18 (Johnson and neoclassical antipathy to allegory); pp. 169-72, n.4 (in the Renaissance "Idea" often equals "Beauty" or an aesthetic ideal), similarly pp. 172-73, n.6 (also on the different senses of "Idea"); pp. 175-77, n.13 ("Imitation", "Ideal" and verisimilitude in the Renaissance); pp. 200-202, n.1 and pp. 140-42, n.2 (Boccaccio on poetic fiction as allegory, versus Castelvetro); pp. 200-202, n.1 (Boccaccio, Sidney, and others on poetry, verisimilitude and allegory). Tasso is discussed in this and others of Steadman's works chiefly in relation to the *Discorsi del poema eroico* and as a proponent of "idealized example" (see e.g. *The Lamb and the Elephant*, pp. 138-40). In the wealth of disparate comments by Steadman cited above, distinctions actually made by some Renaissance writers, as in the case of Harington concerning *exemplum*, do sometimes seem to get lost.

Steadman's earlier interpretation of Milton in *Milton's Epic Characters: Image and Idol*, as in his *Milton and the Renaissance Hero*, shows a plainer inclination to construe Miltonic "imitation" or "Idea" (hence Miltonic "allegory") as exemplary, rather than in any deeper sense conveying a secondary meaning. In *The Wall of Paradise* Steadman argues more strongly still that *Paradise Lost* is verisimilar fiction, didactic *exemplum* or "literal presentation" (p. 62) of a "moral crisis", and that Milton "restrict[s] . . . allegorical presentation in the interests of verisimilitude and probability" (pp. 33-34). While this may be quantitatively true in respect of the more overt episode or personification allegories in *Paradise Lost*, it does not take account of ongoing, more submerged kinds of Miltonic allegory and their thematic interconnectedness in the poem.

Given these views, Steadman has not, I think, been able entirely satisfactorily to explain the marked presence of Renaissance allegorical methodology or of the mixed epic mode in *Paradise Lost*, acutely conscious though he is of both. See *The Wall of Paradise*, p. 62, n.8, where he calls attention to several "patently allegorical elements in *Paradise Lost* besides "the relationship between Adam and Eve" and other "symbolic techniques underlying his representational modes". Such statements as the above, admitting to the existence of a variety of modes of allegory in *Paradise Lost*, or those in *The Lamb and the Elephant*, e.g., p. 96 and pp. xxiv, xxxv, do not consort easily with Steadman's reservations cited above. Finally, in *The Wall of Paradise* (p. 62), Steadman carries his reservations about allegory to the conclusion that the epic theme of *Paradise Lost* is almost entirely "verisimilar" in the manner of Job: "Milton follows the precedent of Job in depicting spiritual ordeals through literal presentation". Again: Milton, in contrast to Tasso, "having chosen a subject based on spiritual combat, could imitate the temptation crisis literally, without having to resort to allegorical methods". Behind Steadman's argument is apparently the notion, expressed by him elsewhere, that Milton might legitimately follow Renaissance allegorical *styles* or poetic *modes*, while yet moving away from the *matter* of allegory. But in allegory mode and matter are inseparable—as I have argued. I have also argued that Milton's two-pronged method is to try to bring literal (historical) truth into alignment with other forms of truth in epic representation.

On the subjects of Idea, Imitation and allegory in Milton, see more traditional statements in Steadman's earlier article, "Allegory and Verisimilitude in *Paradise Lost*: The Problem of the 'Impossible Credible'". On the subject of "epic wonder" and allegory, see similarly "Miracle and the Epic Marvellous in *Paradise Lost*", and pp. 105-19 in *Epic and Tragic Structure*. On Steadman's arguments in respect of "Idea" and "allegory" in *Paradise Lost*, see further my notes 8 and 15 to chap. 13.

APPENDIX C

Tasso and Spenser

I. Tasso in England

J.C. Smith, in his "Introduction" to *Spenser's Faerie Queene*, vol.1, pp. x-xi, comments on the speed with which Spenser assimilated Tasso's poem during the early composition of his own. He notes that in Book I of *The Faerie Queene* there is only one "doubtful" echo of *Gerusalemme liberata* (at I.vii.31); but "undoubted imitations begin to appear in II.v, vi, vii, viii, and II.xii blazes with spoils from the Garden of Armida". The most amazing of these, as is well recognised, are Phaedria's song and Spenser's description of the Fountain with naked maidens bathing in it, extended passages taken almost intact from Tasso. For a transcript of the Italian passages in *Gerusalemme liberata* XV.55-62 (this is the fountain in Armida's garden, referred to by Tasso in Letter 56), with parallel passages in English from *The Faerie Queene* II.xii.60-68, see Kates, *Tasso and Milton*, Appendix, pp. 165-170. Other Tasso-Spenser parallels were noted as early as 1610 by William Drummond of Hawthornden, who wrote in his copy of *The Faerie Queene* (of VI.ix.20): "all . . . Tassos". See Alastair Fowler's and Michael Leslie's article in *TLS*, "Drummond's Copy of *The Faerie Queene*", pp. 821-22; the authors note that Drummond had read the *Gerusalemme* in three languages *besides*, evidently, the Italian, knew the Tasso edition of Ferrara (1583-87), and by 1610 owned Tasso's *Opere*. Drummond annotated, among others, the Spenser borrowings at *Faerie Queene* VI.ix.17-32 (from *Gerusalemme* VII.11 and 17, the Erminia rustic interlude, transposed by Spenser to his Pastorella-Melibœ episode), and again at Book VI.ix.24, 25, 26, 31 and 32 (quoting from *Gerusalemme* VII.12, 13, 14, 15, 16); also at *Faerie Queene* VI.xii.15 (Pastorella's rose-mark, taken from *Il Rinaldo* XI.88-90).

For further detailed evidence as to the early high reputation of Tasso's poetry and prose in Elizabethan England and until late in the nineteenth century (including some remarks on his impact on Spenser and Milton), a list of imitations of Tasso's verse by English poets, and indications of early familiarity with Tasso's prose writings, see the edition of Fairfax's Tasso by Kathleen M. Lea and T.M. Gang, Introduction, pt. III, "Tasso's Reputation in England", pp. 25-34, and pt. IV, "Fairfax's Reputation", pp. 35-44. See also Mario Praz, "Tasso in England", in *The Flaming Heart*. Tasso's early reputation in England and his connections with Spenser are discussed also by Alberto Castelli in *La Gerusalemme Liberata nella Inghilterra di Spenser* and (pp. 28-38) by Brand in *Torquato Tasso*.

A few only of the many striking details recorded by Lea and Gang are as follows. A Latin version of parts of the *Gerusalemme* by Scipio Gentili was dedicated to Sir Philip Sidney in 1584; Queen Elizabeth memorized passages from Tasso; up to the end of the eighteenth century, there were several new or reprint editions of Fairfax's Tasso, as well as some new translations (Fairfax's edition was in its own time a big scholarly production collating several Italian texts); a play called "Tasso's Melancholy" (a theme already legendary) was listed in the repertory of the Admiral's Men, along with a play entitled, "2 Godfrey of Bulloigne", in 1594; Thomas Kyd translated a minor Tasso tract in 1588; John Eliot as early as 1593 records his familiarity with edition[s] seen at Ferrara of Tasso's *Works*, which included, besides "divers . . . verses", a comedy and a tragedy and some prose dialogues and discourses (see Lea and Gang, eds., p. 28). We may add, that the first five Cantos of Tasso's poem were translated into English well before Fairfax (by "R.C." [Richard Carew], 1594); Cowley probably used passages from the *Gerusalemme* (unacknowledged) in his *Davideis* (see Brand, p. 250); Dryden (like Milton and Spenser) rated Tasso next to Virgil (see Brand, p. 256). There are as well an astonishing number of imitations of and borrowings from Tasso continuing unabated through the seventeenth century until the nineteenth century. For an indication of Milton's own prolific echoes of the *Gerusalemme*, see my chap. 12, sect. "Borrowings from Tasso in *Paradise Lost*", and n. 22.

Many of the above dates as cited by Lea and Gang fall well within the later period of composition of *The Faerie Queene*. But the main fact to be noted is that Tasso's poem (then probably known as *Il Goffredo*, or *Godfrey*), with its accompanying critical allegory, was known in England in its original Italian from probably soon after the appearance of the first Italian edition in 1581. The other indications of Tasso's fame in England merely support this certainty, as does Spenser's use of the *Gerusalemme* so early in *The Faerie Queene* as Book II. Thus Spenser had ample opportunity to assimilate Tasso's poem and critical ideas into his own work.

We must also take into account the numerous indications of the seriousness with which Tasso was regarded in England as critical authority and poetic model in Spenser's period and up to Milton's time. Lea and Gang point out that Abraham Fraunce uses Tasso for *exempla* (unacknowledged in the first edition) eighty-four times in his *Arcadian Rhetorike* (1588); and that Harington in the critical "Apologie" to his *Orlando Furioso* (1591) gives his own version of a stanza from *Gerusalemme liberata* (I.3). We may observe, with Lea and Gang (p. 26), that Spenser himself refers to Tasso's *Aminta* in *The Faerie Queene* III.vi.45 ("Me seemes I see *Amintas* wretched fate"), and in the "Letter to Raleigh" shows that he is "aware of [Tasso's] allegorical interpretation of Rinaldo's ethical, and Godfredo's political significance". The editors do not specify *which* Rinaldo of Tasso; I take the allusion to be more probably to the Rinaldo of the earlier epic poem, to whom and to whose creator there may be a direct reference in *The Faerie Queene* (IV.iii.45: "*Rinaldo . . .* / Described by that famous Tuscane penne"), rather than to the Rinaldo of the *Gerusalemme* and the separate allegory of that poem, or to Ariosto's Rinaldo in *Orlando Furioso*. Spenser in the "Letter" thus would be drawing a contrast between Tasso's *two* epics with their separate heroes; he is pointing to the "dissevering" of one complete hero into two parts, one part for each epic—namely, Rinaldo, the "Ethice" part, hero of the earlier epic, and Godfredo, the "Politice" part, hero of the later epic. Tasso's two poems Spenser then compares with those two of Homer, who also had written two different epics to illustrate the two different aspects, while Virgil (Ariosto similarly later) had joined the two aspects up in a single hero, Aeneas. (If Spenser had in fact been thinking of the Rinaldo of the *Gerusalemme*, then his understanding of that poem's allegory would not match with that expressed by Tasso in his critical exposition.)

Henry Reynolds, despite his own preference for mystical allegory, commends "the grave and learned" Tasso in his "*Sette giorni . . .* and his *Gierusalem liberata*, so farre as an excellent pile of meerely Morall Philosophy may deserve" (*Mythomystes*, p. 7). We may again note with Lea and Gang, or rather more specifically than they do, that Sir William Davenant used Tasso's *Discorsi* (1594) in his own "Preface" to *Gondibert* (1650); that Abraham Cowley also used Tasso—without acknowledgement—in the "Preface" to his *Poems* (1656); and that Dryden's heroic plays were modelled, in conformity with Tasso's epic prescriptions and poem, around the twin themes of "love and war". And so on, into the eighteenth century and Pope, who again ranked Tasso as "the greatest epic poet of Italy" (see Brand, p. 260). Only for a few generations (Cowley's to Addison's), observe Lea and Gang (pp. 31-32), was Tasso's reputation as poet or critic at all dimmed; by 1762, with Bishop Hurd's *Letters on Chivalry and Romance*, the tide had turned back again. Since Tasso's importance has in this century once again been eclipsed outside of his own country, it is necessary to draw attention to the evidence of the continuing esteem in which he was held in England as poet and critic from the late sixteenth until the nineteenth century.

II. Tasso and Spenser

The opinions of the *Spenser Variorum* critics concerning the lack of Tasso's influence upon Spenser seem, with one important exception, to be out of date. For example, W.L. Renwick, *Edmund Spenser: An Essay on Renaissance Poetry*, p. 54 (cited also in "Plan and Conduct of *The Faerie Queene*", *Spenser Variorum*, vol. 1, pp. 359-62), feels that since Spenser's "scheme is as early as 1580" (from the evidence of the Harvey correspondence), Tasso's influence came too late to influence Spenser's allegorical scheme in any constructive way. Renwick, like R. Neil Dodge and other early editors, believes Aristotle's scheme of the virtues to have been the source of Spenser's allegorical design. But surely there is no reason to think that Spenser's design was fully formed as early as 1580, or that it was never modified in train of composition? At the least, any plan could not have been fully established in Spenser's mind so long before the "Letter to Raleigh" of 1589. In contrast to the scholars just named, Merritt Y. Hughes, *Virgil and Spenser*, pp. 399-406 (cited also in *Spenser Variorum*, vol. 1, pp. 357-59), opposes the view that the allegorical epic tradition of Tasso and earlier epic exegetes is not important to Spenser. Hughes cites Landino as "prince of Virgilian allegorists" and formative on Spenser's poem—as Landino also was, via intermediaries, on Tasso's: "In the allegorical interpretation of the *Aeneid* by the Neo-Platonic writers of the Renaissance we have the key to the allegory of *The Fairie Queene* [that is, a psychological progress]".

Hughes draws parallels between Spenser's plan and Tasso's design in the *Discorsi del poema eroico* (Book I, p. 5) to show all the "forms of courage, temperance, prudence, justice, faith, piety, religion, and every other virtue that may be acquired by long practice or infused by divine grace". Tasso had expressed the same ideas even earlier in the *Discorsi dell'arte poetica* (see the ed. of Poma, p. 12), where he selected Aeneas, Achilles, Ulysses, as the forms or "excellences" of piety, fortitude, prudence. In this statement the virtues are shown as allegorically distributed among separate characters. Tasso also alludes in the same passage to another type of presentation: "indeed in some of these [characters] one discovers the sum of all these virtues" ("anzi pure in alcuni di questi il cumulo di tutte queste virtù"). However, this idea of showing simple examples or, alternatively, aggregation of virtues (one critical view of the relationship between the six knights of *The Faerie Queene* and Arthur) had already been qualified by Tasso as early as his brief, developmental-style allegory to the 1583 edition of the *Rinaldo* (on which, see Appendix A, pt. II, and my chapter 6, nn. 8 and 9). Similarly, in other passages in both sets of *Discorsi*, as in subsequent critical essays of the early 1580s, Tasso wrote in favour of a theory of developmental moral metaphor in epic plot. Thus Hughes is essentially correct in looking to the tradition of allegorical epic commentary preceding Tasso and by inference to Tasso for the sources of Spenser's plan. Both authors employ a dynamic psychological allegory which is far removed from the static medieval *schema* of virtues and vices, derived from Aristotle via medieval interpreters, which Renwick and Dodge find in *The Faerie Queene*. Hughes' views have not gained the recognition which they deserve.

The record of the close interleaving of Tasso's and Spenser's dates of composition and publication, set out below, points toward a positive view of Tasso's strong critical influence on Spenser. I have listed those dates bearing significantly on the *Gerusalemme* and *The Faerie Queene*. However, a close relationship also persists throughout the two poets' careers. Tasso is roughly ten years ahead of Spenser at every point and in every genre. We may compare, in pastoral, Tasso's *Aminta* (performed 1573; printed 1580-81) and Spenser's *Shepheardes Calender* (1579); their two major "diffuse" heroic epics (Tasso's, 1581, and Spenser's, 1590, 1596); in the sonnet genre, Tasso's *Rime* (published in part, 1567; then 1581-82, unauthorized; 1584-86, 1591, 1593) and Spenser's *Amoretti* (1595); the late religious works, Tasso's *Sette Giornate* (completed 1594; published in part 1600; 1607) and Spenser's *Mutabilitie Cantos* (1609) and the two last of his *Fowre Hymnes* (1596). The two main periods of composition of the *The Faerie Queene* (1580s; 1590-96) seem to be separated by a critical reshaping, as indicated in the "Letter to Raleigh" (1589), in which a new and rather sophisticated critical awareness, possibly due in part to Tasso, manifests itself. So also before, in the mid-1570s, had come the second phase of composition of the *Gerusalemme liberata*, with the insertion of allegorical episodes and new theorizing, as recorded in Tasso's Letters of that period. As can be seen from the Spenser-Harvey correspondence, the manuscript of *The Faerie Queene* and knowledge of Spenser's plans were circulated prior to publication of the poem (see *Spenser Variorum*, vol. 2, p. 230, n. to *FQ* II.iv, stanza 35). Tasso's unfinished poem seems to have circulated even more widely, in manuscript or print, as is evinced by the first incomplete pirated editions of the epic under the title of *Il Goffredo*. The table of dates given below is illustrative of the intertwining of the publications, dates and poetic aims of the two poets. On the interconnections of Tasso's "Poetical Letters" of 1575-76 with his evolving theory of allegory, and the compositional innovations or adaptations of the *Gerusalemme liberata* in the interests of a sharpened allegory, see: my Appendix A, pt. I; chap. 5, sect. "The 'Lettere poetiche'"; Murrin, *The Allegorical Epic*, pp. 87-105; and Rhu, "From Aristotle to Allegory". (Rhu's discussions, despite his reservations, do point in such a direction.) For the purposes of the present argument supporting a positive view of Tasso's critical influence on Spenser, the key facts are the publication of Tasso's epic poem, his "Allegoria" to it and his "Poetical Letters", together with the first version of the major *Discorsi*, all well before Spenser's "Letter to Raleigh". The

Gerusalemme and its "Allegory" were certainly known in England in the 1580s; the critical letters, published 1587, possibly known soon after— particularly we may think so, since these Letters were included in an early edition of Tasso's famous *Discorsi*.

III. Table of Tasso-Spenser Dates

1560s   "Historical" parts of *Gerusalemme* composed.

1562   Publication of *Il Rinaldo* of Tasso (contains some allegorical episodes).

1564-66   Composition of Tasso's early *Discorsi dell'arte poetica e del poema eroico* (more historical in orientation than as later revised).

1567-70   Tasso had given Academy lectures on allegory.

1570s   Second phase of composition of *Gerusalemme*; insertion of more allegorical episodes, and defence of allegory as a plan for the epic in Tasso's Letters to Scipione Gonzaga.

1575-76   Tasso's Letters to Scipione Gonzaga and others discussing allegory; some published in 1587 (see below).

1575-80   Composition of Tasso's *Discorsi del poema eroico*.

1576   Tasso's Letter 76 to Luca Scalabrino suggests that the prose "Allegoria" has been completed.

1579   Publication of pirated version of part of *Gerusalemme*.

1579-80   *Faerie Queene* begun; a "parcel" of manuscript sent to Gabriel Harvey by 1580; Spenser-Harvey letters published.

1580   Letter of 1580 from Harvey to Spenser, alluding to Spenser's hope to "overgo" Ariosto, but alleging in fact little resemblance between Spenser's "Elvish Queene" and the *Orlando Furioso*. (*The Complete Poetical Works of Spenser*, ed. R.E. Neil Dodge, Appendix.III, p. 773.)

        Publication of 16 cantos (not all complete) of *Gerusalemme* as *Il Goffredo* (unauthorized), at Mantua.

1581   Publication of first complete edition of *Il Goffredo, ovvero la Gerusalemme liberata*, containing Tasso's comprehensive "Allegoria".

1582-85   Publication of a number of editions of the *Gerusalemme*.

1582 [?]   Lodowick Bryskett's "fictitious" account of Spenser's plan, pub-
           lished in 1606, but dated by J.J. Jusserand as much earlier:
           "apparently composed during the earliest period of Spenser's
           stay in Ireland" (see "Spenser's 'twelve private morall vertues as
           Aristotle hath devised' ", p. 379. Bryskett's tract is most probably
           an exercise in the genre of the didactic Dialogue, appropriating as
           speakers the personae of notables; if a genuine account, it reflects
           earlier critical views held by Spenser. Piccolomini and Giraldi
           Cintio are cited by Bryskett as interpreters of the "Ethick part of
           Morall Philosophie" concerning "active or practicke felicitie",
           both Aristotelian and Platonic, in which "M. *Spenser*" is "very
           well read" (pp. 22-25). Cintio had also written in defence of Arios-
           tian romance (1550s), and had corresponded on the epic with
           Bernardo Tasso, Tasso's father. An extended ethical allegory, not
           necessarily of a developmental kind, is suggested by Bryskett as
           being Spenser's concern.

1583   Publication of Tasso's prose "Allegory" to the *Rinaldo* (from Tasso
           letter of 1562).

           Edition of *Il Rinaldo* with the "Allegoria". (This epic is later
           alluded to in Spenser's "Letter to Raleigh").

1584   *Gerusalemme* published at Mantua (Osanna-Gonzaga edition),
           with excised passages given in Appendix.

1580s   Spenser's speedy assimilation of Tasso in *Faerie Queene*, Book II.
           The whole of the *Gerusalemme* evidently is known to Spenser,
           since Armida's Gardens come late, in Canto XIV of Tasso. Fur-
           ther direct references to Tasso occur in *Faerie Queene*, III and IV.

1585   Publication of Tasso's *Apologia . . . Con alcune altre Opere* (Ferrara);
           this edition includes Tasso Discourses and Dialogues and some
           letters.

1585-87   Several collected editions appear in Italy of Tasso's works in verse
           and prose, including his criticism and "Poetical Letters".

1586   Publication of Tasso's *Risposta . . . Al . . . Lombardelli* (Ferrara),
           foundation document for Tasso's allegorical poetics. (There are
           different degrees of "Truth" or the "proper verisimilar" for each
           genre; and the marvellous and verisimilar may be conjoined in
           various ways in the epic.)

1587   Publication (apparently unauthorized) of Tasso's *Discorsi del Sig-
           nor Torquato Tasso. Dell'Arte Poetica, Et In particolare del Poema
           Heroico* (Venice). Note well: this edition of the *Discorsi* was
           printed together with Tasso's "Poetical Letters" relating to the

composition of *Gerusalemme*. This edition is cited in Weinberg's Bibliography, vol. 2, p. 1152.

Publication of *Delle differenze poetiche*. (On Episodes: poetic "verisimilitude"—in Tasso's special use of the term—implies a looser connection of parts in poetry than exists in nature, which knows only strict causality.)

Publication of Tasso's "Lettere poetiche", together with the *Discorsi dell'arte poetica* (see above). Why too late, then (see Renwick, my Appendix C, pt. II), for Spenser's matured scheme as expressed in the "Letter to Raleigh"?

1589   Spenser's "Letter to Raleigh" shows specific awareness of Tasso's two epics (*Rinaldo* and *Gerusalemme*) and of the Homeric-Virgilian tradition of continous ethical-psychological allegoresis. It represents a full plan, like Tasso's grafted onto an older conception, and evidently a new plateau gained in Spenser's critical thinking about allegory. Reference to "Aristotle *and the rest*" indicates awareness of cinquecento Neo-Aristotelian criticism and of the Tasso-Mazzoni-Castelvetro type of debates. Note well: Spenser's reference to Ariosto here is much briefer than that to Tasso; Ariosto is said to show a hero composed of all the virtues, but Tasso, like Virgil and Homer (in the hands of the allegorizers), effects an allegorical fragmentation of a single character into two heroes.

1590   Publication of *Faerie Queene*, Books I-III; a strong influence of Tasso seen from Book II onward.

1593   John Eliot records that he has seen at Ferrara "3 Toomes" of Tasso's poetical and prose works (including "divers Dialogues and discourses in Prose". Tasso's works by now are widely known in England; edition or editions seen may have included some of Tasso's critical prose and letters, and certainly, long since, the "Allegoria" to the *Gerusalemme*.

1594   Tasso's *Discorsi del poema eroico* (development of *Discorsi dell'arte poetica*) is at last published. Contains discussions on epic structure; verisimilitude; history and fiction; marvels; and significant discussions of allegory in the expanded final Books.

1596   Publication of *Faerie Queene*, Books IV-VI.

1610   Drummond of Hawthornden annotates Spenser's extensive borrowings from *Gerusalemme*.

APPENDIX D

The Literal Level and the "Literal Commentators"

Volumes, past and present, have been written on the "literal sense", its relation to figurative meanings in the Bible and its importance to the Christian and Protestant traditions. We may cite as examples of contemporary views, Edgar de Bruyne, chapter "La Théorie de l'Allégorisme" in *Études d'Esthétique Médiévale*, vol. 2, pp. 311-12; and Beryl Smalley, "The Bible in the Medieval Schools", chapter VI.3 in vol. 2 of *The Cambridge History of the Bible*; also Smalley's book, *The Study of the Bible in the Middle Ages*, chapters I.1 and V.2. Both writers make the point that in the earlier medieval tradition (as later under the Reformation), intentionally figurative writing in the Bible could be regarded as a legitimate extension of the "literal" meaning: that is, the "literal" was seen as an *inclusive* sense. Even in the extrapolation of various moral or mystical senses by an individual exponent of Scripture, a strong emphasis persisted on retaining a basic awareness of the literal level of meaning. These traditions carried over into secular literature.

Rosemond Tuve, in *Images and Themes in Five Poems by Milton*, pp. 158-60, makes the very important point that earlier secular allegory, analogously to the scriptural variety, always retained a strong sense of the "reality of the first term" (italics in the quotation are mine):

Metaphor, allegory, and symbolism are linked in respect to the nature of their relationship to the real. . . . In its greatest days, an essential element in the definition of allegory, which rhetoricians call briefly a metaphor continued, was the reality of the first term. In typology or strict allegory, this could be understood as the literal historical reality of the types. . . . When allegory is secularized, and when myths are allegorized. . . . The first term's historical and literal reality consists in its being a true account of every man's innumerable encounters with unregenerate natural man as he meets him in himself. . . . But allegory is not any series of little metaphors; it contains many such within *a* metaphor, which is "continued". . . . *The simultaneous presentation of the two modes of reality is the real excitement of allegory.*

An illuminating analysis also is that of Helen Gardner in her chapter, "The Historical Sense", in *The Business of Criticism*, especially pp. 136-41. The substance of her argument is that in religious writing of any imaginative kind, such as Donne's sermons (also some of his exegetical essays), the literal and figurative senses in a given passage are constantly playing against and into each other, almost with the force of a pun or conceit. The stress on the historical realities embodied in a text or verse of the Bible is the very factor which infuses life into any secondary spiritual sense found, so that the two levels are mutually reinforcing and inseparable. Hence the peculiar power of Donne's writing. It could certainly be said of *Paradise Lost* that Milton's treatment of his material is such that the pervading sense of literal reality (relative to places, presences, even the person of God) is the very factor which gives intensity to the shadowy, more oblique relevances present at many moments of his poetic narrative.

Donne gives the literal sense equal weight with other figurative interpretations of the Bible, including that of the "types". We find a good illustration of his views in the following passage on Psalm 38.4, taken from Donne's "Sermon No. 3 Preached at Lincolns Inne"; see *The Sermons of John Donne*, edited by George R. Potter and Evelyn M. Simpson, vol. 2, p. 97: "all these things are *literally* spoken of *David; By application, of us; and by figure*, of Christ. *Historically, David; morally*, we; *Typically*, Christ is the subject of this text". While other late Protestant writers display greater reticence about simultaneous interpretation in theological exposition (although not necessarily in homiletics or other forms of non-doctrinal writing), Donne, as Barbara Lewalski notes in *Protestant Poetics*, pp. 136-39, is aware of and employs the earlier multi-levelled as well as the newer Protestant typologically oriented avenues of scriptural exegesis.

On the whole, Donne's interpretations are framed, verbally at least, within Protestant conventions. Some remarkable passages from Donne's *Sermons* exhibit the subtleties of his discriminations concerning the "literal" sense (always paramount) and the further senses. In the first passage he says: "there is no necessity of that *spirituall wantonnesse* of finding more then necessary senses; for, the more *lights* there are, the more *shadows* are also cast by those many lights. . . . when you have the *necessary sense*, that is the meaning of the holy Ghost in that place, you have senses enow". ("Sermon No. 17, Preached at Saint Pauls", in *Sermons*, vol. 3, p. 353). "Shadow" as used by Donne above is a pun, meaning both "figures and allegories" and, negatively, "obscurities". Donne might here appear to be opposed to allegorical figures, asserting that there is, in opposition to shadows or figures, *one* "necessary" (literal) sense only. But all he is saying is that there must be only one sense in any one place; *that* is the "necessary", the appropriate, sense. Elsewhere Donne's emphasis clarifies, and it is not anti-figurative. The "necessary" sense is, as it had always been, that which is paramount in any one place. Intentional figuration in Scripture falls under the literal sense, but it remains figuration; we are to interpret according to the author's underlying intention (that is, not literalistically): "The literall sense is alwayes to be preserved; but the literall sense is not alwayes to be discerned. . . . *the literall sense of every place, is the principall intention of the Holy Ghost, in that place:* And his principall intention in many places, is to expresse things by allegories, by figures; so that in many places of Scripture, a figurative sense is the literall sense". ("Sermon No. 2, Preached at S. Pauls", in *Sermons*, vol. 6, p. 62; italics mine.) Looked at in the full context, this passage makes it quite clear that Donne is here engaging specifically in a *defence* of figurative reading, from which "allegories" are not excluded.

Similarly, consider the passage from the 19th "Devotion", where Donne employs striking paradoxes (God is a "literal God") in an effort to *oppose* pure literalism in interpretation:

My *God*, my *God*, Thou art a *direct God*, may I not say, a *literall God*, a *God* that wouldest bee understood *literally*, and according to the *plaine sense* of all that thou saiest? But thou art also . . . a *figurative*, a *metaphoricall God* too: A *God* in whose words there is such a height of *figures*, such *voyages*, such *peregrinations* to fetch remote and precious *metaphors*, such *extentions*, such *spreadings*, such *Curtaines* of *Allegories* . . . so *retired* and so *reserved expressions*. . . . The *stile* of thy *works*, the *phrase* of thine *Actions*, is *Metaphoricall*. The *institution* of thy whole *worship* in the *old Law*, was a continuall *Allegory; types* & *figures* overspread all; and *figures* flowed into *figures*, and powred themselves out into *farther figures; Circumcision* carried a *figure* of *Baptisme*, & *Baptisme* carries a *figure* of that *purity*, which we shall have in *perfection* in the *new Jerusalem*. Neither didst thou *speake*, and *worke* in this *language*, onely in the time of thy *Prophets*; but since thou spokest in thy *Son*, it is so too. How often, how much more often doth thy *Sonne* call himselfe a *way*, and a *light*, and a *gate*, and a *Vine*, and *bread*, than the *Sonne of God*, or of *Man*? How much oftner doth he exhibit a *Metaphoricall Christ*, than a *reall*, a *literall*?

From *John Donne: Devotions Upon Emergent Occasions*, edited by Anthony Raspa, pp. 99-100. Barbara Lewalski cites part of the above passage in the course of her discussion of Donne's typological use of figuration, in "Typological Symbolism and the 'Progress of the Soul' in Seventeenth-Century Literature", *Literary Uses of Typology from the Late Middle Ages to the Present*, edited by Earl Miner, p. 85. It might be possible to present the above or previously quoted passages as illustrating Donne's ambivalence about figures—his being caught between his poetry and his Puritanism, so to speak. Much better, however, like Gardner, to see Donne's stress on both the literal sense and the close dependence of any figurative sense upon the literal as essential to his unique literary power, part of his strong "metaphysical" style.

APPENDIX E

"Accommodation" and Figuration in *Paradise Lost*

The doctrine of "accommodation", discussed by Milton in *Of Christian Doctrine*, Book I, chap. ii, has been made the rationale for quite contradictory interpretations of Milton's use of figurative language in *Paradise Lost*. It will be useful to preface some examples of these with a trained theologian's exposition of the topic and its relevance to Milton's poem. Roland Frye explains in *God, Man and Satan* that in "the great mainstream of Christian interpretation", which was the tradition of the great Reformers also, and with the help of the "accommodation" theory repeatedly used, though not invented by, the great Reformers, symbols (i.e., representations) in Scripture are, as Calvin says in *The Institutes of the Christian Religion*, understood in such a way as to show us not "what God is in himself, but what he is to us". Nonetheless, such depictions are not "mere" symbols conveying "an abstract conception of God". Rather, Frye says, "the Christian system of symbols . . . is based largely on *the analogy* of personality. God, though in his essence beyond human comprehension, is to be dealt with as a person, rather than as an abstraction or an absolute". Further: "To the great Reformers, the exposition of Scripture was a *literary* analysis, and when they emphasized the level of the *litera* they were not calling for mechanical concentration on what the modern fundamentalist means by literalism" (italics as in Frye's text). They were speaking rather with a kind of verbal "transfiguration", or "falsification at one level for the sake of truth at another" (here Frye cites John Knox in *On the Meaning of Christ*). The Reformers were speaking in a mode which could be compared to the older "parabolical" meaning as adduced, for example, by Aquinas. Thus "the arm of the Lord" conveys to Aquinas not "the literal sense . . . that God has such a bodily member, but that he has what such a bodily member indicates, namely active power". Similarly (Frye is here speaking of Genesis as a whole): "the central conception . . . is of an existential truth, a truth relevant to man's present condition and his ultimate redemption. *The truth of the Genesis accounts is a figurative truth; that is, it is both figurative and true*". It is, Frye adds, "This conception, which will dominate our treatment . . . of *Paradise Lost*". (Quotations are from Frye's Introd., pp. 11, 10, 12, 13, 8, 12 and 15; italics, except as otherwise indicated, are mine.)

Frye's conception of a rendering of Genesis "both figurative and true" offers an insight into the special case of the representation of God in *Paradise Lost*. God there appears sometimes as literal and personal to a degree which has distressed readers; yet, as has been argued in the present study (see my chap. 15, sect. " 'Accommodation' in *Of Christian Doctrine*"), perhaps this personalization is deliberate, in that semi-symbolic way of which Frye speaks, one "based largely on *the analogy* of personality". As was noted, we may often see that Milton is emphasizing a conception of God both as He shows Himself to us in the Bible (apparently in human form), and yet often also with mysteriously suggestive hints as to "what he is to us" in respect of His powers, and in matters of faith and grace. Milton's art thus becomes not daringly anthropomorphic, as it has been supposed, in any literalistic sense, but daring rather in its radical Protestant reworking of traditional multi-layered reading. Very recent criticism of *Paradise Lost* has in fact moved in this direction and away from either literalistic or narrowly "typological" readings.

It is fascinating to find in Thomas Browne a contemporaneous and recognisably Protestant statement which confidently uses the "accommodation" doctrine, in a similar phrasing to Milton's, in order to endorse a special kind of figurative reading of the Bible: "I cannot dream that there should be at the last day any such Judiciall proceeding, or calling to the Barre, as indeed the Scripture seemes to imply, and the literall commentators doe conceive: for unspeakable mysteries in the Scriptures are often delivered in a vulgar and illustrative way, and being written unto man, *are delivered, not as they truely are, but as they may bee understood*; wherein, notwithstanding the different interpretations according to [the] different capacities, [they] may stand firme with our devotion, nor bee any way prejudiciall to each single edification". (*Religio Medici*, 1643, in *The Works of Sir Thomas Browne*, edited by Geoffrey Keynes, vol. 1, p. 56; italics mine.) Browne, whose work was enormously popular in Protestant Europe, thus firmly resists the "literall commentators".

Criticism of *Paradise Lost* earlier in the present century supported a more freely figurative interpretation of Milton's "accommodation" doctrine than has been current lately. We may cite James Holly Hanford's influential view expressed in *A Milton Handbook*, pp. 190-91. Hanford saw Milton's discussion of the scriptural representation of God in *Of Christian Doctrine* as lending itself to a Neoplatonic, figurative and anti-literalistic theory of art in *Paradise Lost*. In the relevant passage in *Of Christian Doctrine*, Hanford says, "much light is thrown on the degree of literalness with which the poet took the concrete details of *Paradise Lost* (whether these details were strictly Biblical or not). . . . When Milton undertook to write the epic of the Fall . . . he must have taken satisfaction in the thought that the original word itself was but accommodated truth. . . . He, too [like Moses], had heard the voice of God and was no less than his predecessor the author of divine fictions. His own poetic elaboration of the Biblical story might, therefore, claim a place beside the imagery of Scripture itself as a shadow of reality". Nonetheless, "imagination . . . must only supplement—not contradict—the Biblical data, and it must conform to the framework of a body of reasoned doctrine". A distinction, that is, must be maintained between what Milton viewed as matters of faith and what as proceeding from the imagination. This position accords with my own understanding of the aesthetic of *Paradise Lost*. However, as was earlier noted, Hanford's important statement on "accommodation" in *Paradise Lost* may somewhat exaggerate the poem's directly Neoplatonic correlations.

Mary Ann Radzinowicz in *Toward Samson Agonistes*, pp. 308-9, summarizes the current critical position concerning Milton's vexed "accommodation" question as divided between (1) the "Platonist-humanists" (2) the "scripturalist-typologists" and (3) the "eclectics" (herself of the last group). That is, she believes that Milton in *Paradise Lost* makes use of *both* the method of Neoplatonic "correspondences" (as exemplified by Raphael) *and* the method of "typologies" (as outlined by Michael). The two narrators stand for the two contrasted and complementary types of discourse within the poem, human and divine.

H.R. MacCallum ("Milton and Figurative Interpretation of the Bible") has been among those critics who interpret Milton's remarks on "accommodation" in *Of Christian Doctrine* in an almost wholly anti-figurative way. A literalist interpretation of these remarks is directed by him toward a literalistic reading of Milton's poem and a reductive view of Milton's theory of the imagination:

Milton's [accommodation] theory prevents the extrapolation of metaphysical or mystical theories from the concrete imagery of the Bible. . . . Milton reveals throughout his life, and most intensely in his late works, a belief that the order and coherence sought by the symbol-making imagination are dangerous and liable to enslave man and force the spirit. Reacting against those forms of religious speculation which delight in veiled mysteries, mysteries partially hidden by the very symbols through which they are bodied forth, Milton held that Scripture is plain and perspicuous in all things necessary to salvation and that its revelation is adapted to the mind as physical light to the eye. (Pp. 412-13.)

Few, perhaps, would wholly agree with the above remarks on Milton's view of scriptural language, or with the further claims that Milton consequently "desire[d] to limit the authority of metaphor and . . . distrust[ed] . . . figurative modes of expression" *in poetry* (p. 400), and that, arising from his allegedly literalistic view of "accommodation" in Scripture, Milton entertained a pervasive "suspicion of metaphor and the symbolic use of images" in literature, and especially in religious literature (p. 402). The crux of the difficulty with MacCallum's argument is this: how far is it admissible to press, without distinction as to context of application in either the treatise or the poem, an identification between techniques formulated specifically for the strict interpretation of *doctrine*—what Milton is referring to when he speaks of "the public interpretation of Scripture" in *Of Christian Doctrine* I.xxx (*CE*, vol. 16, p. 263)—and, on the other hand, an imaginatively amplified poetic narrative on a sacred subject which includes doctrine but also covers a variety of other matters of serious human importance? MacCallum's statement that Milton entertained a "distrust of metaphor as an instrument of *religious knowledge*" (p. 400, italics mine) begs the question. It does not altogether fit Milton's expressed understanding of the value of figurative language in the Bible, and still less does it fit Milton's use of a wide range of poetic figuration in *Paradise Lost*.

Typological Criticism

This Appendix indicates a number of critical works which have recently espoused a comprehensively "typological" approach to Milton's poetry and notes some others which try to resist extensions of such readings in *Paradise Lost*.

Barbara Lewalski in *Protestant Poetics* gives a comprehensive survey of the background and practice, exegetical and literary, of typological symbolism in the Reformation; see her chapters 3-7 and especially chapter 4, "The Biblical Symbolic Mode", pp. 111-44, and chapter 3, "The Poetic Texture of Scripture", pp. 72-110. She argues that since diverse strata of discourse, mode and metaphor within the Bible were all seen by contemporary Protestant commentators as part of the "literal sense", complex analogies and models—not only of genre, but also including "correlative types"—could therefore be created in Protestant poetry and especially in religious lyric, while the author still in his own eyes served the criteria of "plain truth" (as enunciated for instance by Herbert in "Jordan I"). I think it is correct to say that Lewalski opposes such "correlative types" to the mode of allegory, and that she is dismissive of allegory and inclined to see the mode as by the seventeenth century having been almost entirely dropped—in religious literature, at any rate—in all but the narrowest rhetorical uses (see my chapter 18, n. 1). Although Milton's prose remarks on exegesis form one of Lewalski's starting points in *Protestant Poetics*, Milton's major poems are little mentioned, although in a brief "Afterword", p. 427, she includes some hints as to how to read certain episodes in *Paradise Lost*.

I have argued, conversely to the opinions of Lewalski and other literary historians, that the seventeenth-century disinclination to use the term "allegory" (although Milton in fact *does* use it) does not mean that many of the contents and strategies of serious moral and spiritual allegory were not subsumed into certain aspects of the Protestant exegetical tradition, consequently into its aesthetic, as exhibited in religious verse, in forms which cannot all be satisfactorily identified as "typological". I would argue that a process of tactful assimilation of allegory took place, rather than any full abandonment of it in favour of the more restricted forms of reading represented by typological symbolism, and that it is only in this larger framework that the aesthetic of *Paradise Lost* can be fully apprehended and appreciated.

In "Typology and Poetry" (see p. 43), Lewalski had indeed said something along the above lines: "Protestant exegetes modified the medieval focus upon Christ's life and death as the primary antitype . . . by emphasizing instead the contemporary Christian as antitype. . . . This application of Scripture to the individual is akin to what medieval exegetes called the tropological or moral sense—'so far as the things done in Christ, or so far as the things which signify Christ, are signs of what we ought to do'". Extended "typology" in this view thus becomes a framework which does not exclude St. Thomas' *quid agas*, the "how" of the way men are to behave or the moral "tropological" sense (traditionally closely connected with allegory in the more general understanding of that word). However, in "Typological Symbolism" (p. 81) Lewalski seemingly withdraws recognition of such "kinship": "the third or tropological level of meaning—*quid agas*, moral allegory, in the familiar formula. . . . was discredited by the Reformation clarion call of the 'one sense of Scripture,' the literal meaning".

Arguing against such a total discrediting of allegory in the seventeenth-century reading of Scripture, I earlier pointed to the imaginatively more liberating line of argument pursued by the *Cambridge History of the Bible* in respect of allegory and figuration, and provided, in Milton's *Christian Doctrine* as in works of other Protestant exegetes, by the "one sense to one place" rule, which does not mean the literal sense always, nor imply only predictive figuration. (On this see my chapter 15, section "*Of Christian Doctrine* on Interpreting Scripture".) I also noted the fact that the Protestant view of the "literal sense" as itself a composite sense could be used to admit, quite as much as to exclude, larger figurative applications of the Bible in appropriate contexts (see Appendix D)—as, indeed, the "typological interpreters" have for their part argued. A sensible survey of the problem of sixteenth- and seventeenth-century Protestant uses of typology as those relate to the entire historical development of allegory in exegesis is that of Victor Harris, "Allegory to Analogy in the Interpretation of Scriptures".

A few representative titles of other "typological" studies on Milton are as follows. On "Lycidas" there is, e.g., Michael Lloyd's "The Fatal Bark"; Radzinowicz's views on typology and allegory in "Lycidas" (see my chapter 16, n. 20) stand in contrast. On *Samson Agonistes* there is F. Michael Krouse's *Milton's Samson and the Christian Tradition*; Lynn V. Sadler's *Consolation in Samson Agonistes: Regeneration and Typology*; and Barbara Kiefer

Lewalski's *"Samson Agonistes* and the 'Tragedy' of the Apocalypse". Northrop Frye's work on the "Typology of *Paradise Regained"*, expressing views developed also in Frye's later essays, was followed by Michael Fixler's *Milton and the Kingdoms of God*—this on prophecy in the political context—and by Lewalski's major study, *Milton's Brief Epic: The Genre, Meaning and Art of Paradise Regained.* On *Paradise Lost* there are William Madsen's book, *From Shadowy Types to Truth;* Lewalski's "Structure and Symbolism of Vision in Michael's Prophecy, *Paradise Lost,* Books XI-XII"; and Georgia B. Christopher's *Milton and the Science of the Saints.*

The same vein of typological interpretation has been extended to other seventeenth-century writers, for example Herbert, Vaughan and Marvell, in Lewalski's essays, "Typology and Poetry" and "Typological Symbolism". These views were assimilated into her book, *Protestant Poetics.* Also, C.A. Patrides in *Milton and the Christian Tradition* devotes some attention to typological traditions and elements in Milton's work, along with that of other writers, without totally committing himself to the typological approach. Rosemond Tuve exhibits her customary discrimination in noting the use of "types" in a poet of private devotion such as Herbert—see *A Reading of George Herbert*—whereas in her study of *Comus* in *Images and Themes in Five Poems by Milton* she includes mention of typology but declines to constrain her understanding of Milton's art entirely into such a framework; see her preface, pp. 5-7, where she stresses Milton's figurative and allegorical inheritance in poetry and "the full figurative character of Milton's writing"; also p. 158, where she sees "metaphor, allegory [including typology], and symbolism" as closely "linked in respect to the nature of their relationship to the real".

The typological approach seems to have had two contrasting impacts on criticism, both in their own way narrowing. One is a pressure toward a form of religious literalism in reading. Yet in another sense, typological reading, itself narrowing, has arisen partly as the result of an effort to escape from the narrowly literalistic. Both impulses are evident in the work of, for example, William Madsen. On the one hand Madsen seeks to enlarge typological symbolism into an umbrella which may cover all forms of symbolic representation in *Paradise Lost.* We may observe, on the other hand, the reverse process also, namely, that he, like MacCallum, seeks to interpret Milton's remarks on figuration in *Of Christian Doctrine* literalistically, and then transfers their application from doctrinal exegesis to poetry in a way that exceeds anything demonstrable from Milton's actual remarks in their original context. There seems to be no evidence to support the suggestion that for Milton, figurative language in the Bible and all figuration in *Paradise Lost* are to be interpreted in the light of non-figurative statements and doctrine, as Milton allegedly recommends in *Of Christian Doctrine*—that Milton in *Paradise Lost* means us to "understand figurative expressions in the light of clear, literal statements . . . [and to] interpret obscure passages by the 'analogy of faith' as it were" (p. 82). As far as I can follow them, Madsen's remarks mean that, according to Milton's own thinking on poetry, to be inferred from his prose remarks on scriptural exegesis, all oblique figuration and "obscure passages" in *Paradise Lost* must relate to biblical fact and dogma. In this sense such passages may be construed as "typological". (If such a link existed, such passages might more properly be termed "anagogic".) But in neither case are Madsen's remarks an accurate representation of Milton's stance or practice.

An extreme extension of the above view co-opts even Milton's allegorical personifications in *Paradise Lost* into a literalist reading. Philip Gallagher in "Real or Allegoric" argued that *everything* in Milton's poem, even the allegorical personifications, was regarded by the poet as "inspired" in the sense of having somehow, or in some sense to be understood as having, literally happened. *Paradise Lost* would thus represent a kind of extended personal revelation—a sectarian view which Milton would have repudiated, and a distortion of his actual belief that interpretation of Scripture "according to the spirit" and the "analogy of faith" necessarily involved the discriminating discipline of the whole apparatus of textual and critical scholarship. Still other critics, perhaps as a consequence of the weight of recent typological criticism, seem to have been frightened away from radically figurative readings of *Paradise Lost* altogether. Thus Michael Murrin renounced his valid earlier instinct, expressed in *The Veil of Allegory*, that *Paradise Lost* does somehow belong within the allegorical mode or genre, and in *The Allegorical Epic* deletes Milton's poem from the canon: "Milton *could not* use allegory for his epic"—could not, since the use of allegory was not permissible to a Protestant religious writer, only typology being legitimate. (See *The Allegorical Epic*, p. 170, my italics; cf. also p. 153, "Milton did not allegorize the war of the angels in *Paradise Lost*", and pp. 154-55.)

In contrast to the foregoing critics, we may note that theologians, for example, Roland Frye (see Appendix E), are often able to avoid the contradictions and constrictions imposed by narrowly typological literary readings. "Figurative" is a word which appears frequently in Frye's illuminating exposition of the representation of God and his relationship to man, as seen in Scripture and in *Paradise Lost;* however, the words "type", "typology" and "typical" do not appear in Frye's text or index; the assumption apparently is that this narrower kind of figuration is subsumed in the wider category. In a somewhat different vein, Northrop Frye's book on typological patternings and related matters in the Bible (*The Great Code: The Bible and Literature*, chapters 4 and 5 on "typology") is personal, imaginative, and relates "typology" to rather wide literary contexts, backgrounds and considerations. Gardner (p. 154) objects to exaggeratedly typological readings in criticism of the Gospels and other literature: "as a literary critic, I find it too one-sided, too abstract, intellectual and bookish, too literary and aesthetic an approach to the interpretation of the Gospels. It does not come to terms with the Gospels' proclamation of event, and their appeal through that to the moral imagination". Gardner (p. 143, n.1) cites Jean Daniélou's book as an example of the attempt "to distinguish true typology from its abuse". A recent attempt to correct misinterpretations of Milton's theological and poetic positions concerning "types" is that of John T. Shawcross, "Milton and Covenant: The Christian View of Old Testament Theology", in James H. Sims and Leland Ryken, editors, *Milton and Scriptural Tradition*. MacCallum had earlier argued for Milton's strictness in the matter of "types" and, indeed, had noted Milton's ridicule of the excessive seeking out of "types" by some commentators (p. 409). Finally, Thomas P. Roche, Jr., in "Tasso's Enchanted Woods" in *Literary Uses of Typology from the Late Middle Ages to the Present*, edited by Earl Miner, lodges a protest against the excessive application of typological methods in literary readings. Roche finds that the "Allegoria" to Tasso's *Gerusalemme* contains a wholly valid account of the poem's meaning, expressed in terms both of the Christian endeavour and more broadly of all human experience of moral struggle, humanized through its allegory, but not operating via any imposition of "types" on the central characters or their situations. He protests against "the loss of the distinction between typology and tropology" after the late Renaissance (p. 77); whereas for Tasso, Spenser or Milton such distinctions with their implications for language still remained absolutely clear.

Notes

Chapter 1. Antiquity to the Middle Ages

1. Although there are associated etymologies, *The Shorter OED*, 3rd ed, rev., p. 45, gives the usual derivation for "allegory" as, from Lat. *allegoria*, literally "speaking otherwise than one seems to speak", from Gk. *allos*, "other", + *agoria*, "speaking": signifying *allegoria*, a secondary meaning. See Quintilian, *Institutio Oratoria*, trans. H.E. Butler, vol. 3, Bk VIII.vi.44-59. Quintilian defines *allegoria* as *inversio*, that is, in rhetorical terms (implicitly, as a short metaphor). He notes the relationship of the figure to irony, and to riddle (*aenigma*)—which he considers a "blemish"—and that allegory involves "an element of obscurity", hence may be defined as a "species", since it "always has some property peculiar to itself" ("allegoria vero habet aliquid proprium"); see vol. 3, pp. 327, 331, 333, 334-35.

2. See Edgar de Bruyne, "La Théorie de l'Allégorisme", chap. 7 of Pt. III, in vol. 2 of *Études d'Esthétique Médiévale*, pp. 319-20 and ff. (Further refs. to de Bruyne are to vol. 2.) De Bruyne cites, among others, Aristotle's *Rhetoric* and Quintilian. Cf. Peter Dronke's comments on allegory, *aenigma*, etc., in the classical rhetoricians, pp. 4 and 45 in *Fabula: Explorations into the Uses of Myth in Medieval Platonism*.

3. See Charles S. Singleton, *Commedia: Elements of Structure*, p. 45.

4. Angus Fletcher, in *Allegory: The Theory of a Symbolic Mode*, attempts both such stylistic and also contentual (psychoanalytical) description, whereas, e.g., in *The Allegorical Temper: Vision and Reality in Book II of Spenser's Faerie Queene*, Harry Berger Jr. evaluates Spenser's allegory entirely in terms of bizarre stylistic or aesthetic effects. Rosemond Tuve's theory of *entrelacement* in *Allegorical Imagery: Some Medieval Books and their Posterity* (see esp. pp. 362-69) does relate distinctive allegorical structure (through *entrelacement*, a tantalizing interruption of the narrative) to meaning in Spenser.

5. Torquato Tasso's work in this connection is discussed in my chap. 5, sect. "Lettere Poetiche".

6. An invaluable bibliography and guide to the traditions of classical, post-classical and early medieval epic exegesis (on Homer mainly) is to be found in Robert Lamberton, *Homer the Theologian: Neoplatonist Allegorical Reading and the Growth of the Epic Tradition*. Lamberton's scheme permits only limited space to stylistic analysis.

7. For Macrobius' commentary on Cicero's account of the Dream of Scipio in the last book of *De republica*, see: *The Encyclopaedia Britannica*, 11th ed., gen. ed. Hugh Chisholm, vol. 17, p. 269; Macrobius, *Commentary on the Dream of Scipio*, trans. by William Harris Stahl. Macrobius is discussed by de Bruyne, p. 328, and Lamberton, *Homer the Theologian*, pp. 269-72 and elsewhere.

8. [Porphyry] *Porphyry On the Cave of the Nymphs*, trans. and introd. by Robert Lamber-

ton. See also Lamberton, *Homer The Theologian*, chap. 3, sect. "Porphyry and Homer", pp. 108-33, and App. IV, pp. 319-24; and *The Oxford Classical Dictionary*, ed. N.G.L. Hammond and H.H. Scullard, pp. 864-65.

9. [Fulgentius] On *Mitologiarum libri tres*, see *The Oxford Classical Dictionary*, p. 449. See also Lamberton, *Homer The Theologian*, pp. 279-82.

10. "Piecemeal" allegory, as Lamberton calls it, in *Homer the Theologian*, p. 270. Lamberton does not discuss Jewish or Christian traditions of allegoresis, except for such as relate directly to classical or later exegesis on Homer.

11. As put by Daniel Boyarin, perhaps illustrating that contemporary Jewish exegetes share some of the distrust of the concept of allegory exhibited by so many Christian interpreters and critics: "In order for the Scripture to have an 'inner meaning', there must be an ontological structure that allows for inner meaning. Allegoresis is thus explicitly founded in a Platonic Universe". See "The Song of Songs, Lock or Key?: Intertextuality, Allegory, and the Meaning of Midrash", paper given at the Lechter Institute for Literary Research, 1986, p. 19. This paper has been published in revised form in Boyarin's recent book, *Intertextuality and the Reading of Midrash*, pp. 105-16.

12. Giovanni Boccaccio, [*De genealogiis deorum gentilium*] *Boccaccio on Poetry, Being the Preface and the Fourteenth and Fifteenth Books of Boccaccio's Genealogia Deorum Gentilium*, trans. by Charles G. Osgood. This work is discussed in my chap. 4, sect. "Boccaccio". [Marsilio Ficino] See *Marsilio Ficino's Commentary on Plato's Symposium*, trans. Sears R. Jayne.

13. Félix Buffière, *Les Mythes d'Homère et la pensée grecque*; Jean Pépin (among other works), *Mythe et allégorie: Les origines grecques et les contestations judéo-chrétiennes;* Jean Pépin, "A propos de l'histoire de l'exégèse allégorique: l'absurdité, signe de l'allégorie", and Lamberton, *Homer the Theologian*. I have also benefited from the studies of de Bruyne and the unpubl. Ph.D. dissertation of Danilo L. Aguzzi, *Allegory in the Heroic Poetry of the Renaissance*, which is cited in the earlier parts of my study. Merritt Y. Hughes, *Virgil and Spenser*, has discussed Virgilian influences on Spenser, including that of the Virgilian allegorizations. See also Dronke, as cited in my chap. 1, n. 15. Ernst Curtius in chap. 11 esp., pp. 203-7, and chap. 12 of *European Literature and the Latin Middle Ages*, trans. Willard R. Trask, gives a succinct review of allegorical interpretation in relation to critical theory and to philosophy and religion from Homer to Boccaccio.

14. [Fulgentius] On *Expositio Vergilianae continentiae*, see *Encyclopaedia Britannica*, vol. 11, pp. 292-93; see also Lamberton, *Homer the Theologian*, pp. 279-82.

15. [Bernardus Silvestris] *The Commentary on the First Six Books of the Aeneid of Vergil Commonly Attributed to Bernardus Silvestris: A new critical edition*. Latin ed. by Julian Ward Jones and Elizabeth Frances Jones. On Bernardus, see de Bruyne, p. 328, and Lamberton, *Homer the Theologian*, pp. 284-86. Peter Dronke in *Fabula*, esp. pp. 119-22, and in his article "Bernardo Silvestre" in vol. 1 of *Enciclopedia Virgiliana*, pp. 497-500, discusses Bernardus' contributions to twelfth-century allegorical aesthetics. For Dronke's perceptive survey of the twelfth-century tradition at large, see *Fabula*, introd. and chap. 1.

16. On Boccaccio see Aguzzi, pp. 57-60, and my chap. 4, sect. "Boccaccio"; on Cristoforo Landino see Merritt Hughes and Aguzzi, pp. 124-40.

17. Coluccio Salutati is discussed in my chap. 2.

18. Lamberton, *Homer the Theologian*, p. 286, paraphrasing Winthrop Wetherbee, *Platonism and Poetry in the Twelfth Century: The Literary Influence of the School of Chartres*, p. 126.

19. An interesting representative collection of articles on or inspired by rabbinic commentary is that in Geoffrey H. Hartman and Sanford Budick, eds., *Midrash and Literature*.

20. See *The Cambridge History of the Bible*, vol. 1, *From the Beginnings to Jerome*, ed. P.R. Ackroyd and C.F. Evans, chap. V.13, "Biblical Exegesis in the Early Church" by R.P.C. Hanson, pp. 412-53, and chap. III.8, "Bible and Midrash: Early Old Testament Exegesis" by G. Vermes, pp. 199-231. Vermes' represents a looser view than that presented in *The Cambridge History of the Bible*, vol. 2, *The West, from the Fathers to the Reformation*, ed. G.W.H. Lampe, chap. VI.5, "The Study of the Bible in Medieval Judaism" by Erwin I.J. Rosenthal; of which see p.

253. For a definition of "midrash", see the Glossary in *Midrash and Literature*, ed. Hartman and Budick, p. 365, and, more comprehensively, pp. 91-92 of the same volume.

21. For descriptions of the method see Daniel Boyarin, "Voices in the Text: Midrash and the Inner Tension of Biblical Narrative", pp. 590-96, but esp. pp. 594-95, n.32; and Harold Fisch, "The Hermeneutic Quest in *Robinson Crusoe*", in *Midrash and Literature*, ed. Hartman and Budick, pp. 230-31 in particular.

22. For exemplifications, see Boyarin, "The Song of Songs, Lock or Key?", p. 20 esp.; James L. Kugel, "Two Introductions to Midrash", in *Midrash and Literature*, ed. Hartman and Budick, pp. 77-103; and Fisch, as cited in my chap. 1, n. 21.

23. See the important exposition of Gerald L. Bruns, "Midrash and Allegory: The Beginnings of Scriptural Interpretation", in *The Literary Guide to the Bible*, ed. Robert Alter and Frank Kermode, esp. pp. 639-41.

24. Bruns, pp. 626-27.

25. Ibid., pp. 627-29.

26. See my chap. 19, sect. "Milton's God: Mimesis and Midrash".

27. Milton's interest in Philo is well understood. For a strong affirmation of the importance of Origen to Milton, see Harry Franklin Robins, *If This Be Heresy: A Study of Milton and Origen.*

28. See Lamberton, *Homer the Theologian*, pp. 283-84, for a brief synopsis of scholarly views on this point.

29. [Origen] See *Encyclopaedia Britannica*, vol. 20, pp. 270-73.

30. See Lamberton, *Homer the Theologian*, pp. 80-82, on this point. Lamberton here links Origen with Augustine. It is a probable indication of Milton's awareness of the essential seriousness of the older traditions of religious-allegorical exegesis on Homer that he can, even in his theological treatise, cite *Odyssey* I.7 and I.32 (a pronouncement by Jupiter on free will) as instances of valid allegory. See Bk I, chap. iv, of [*De Doctrina Christiana*] *Of Christian Doctrine*, trans. Charles R. Sumner, ed. James Holly Hanford and Waldo Hilary Dunn, vol. 14 (1933), p. 175, in *The Works of John Milton*, ed. Frank Allen Patterson *et al.* The Columbia ed. is henceforth abbrev. as *CE*. I quote Milton's treatise (henceforth abbrev. *Of CD*) in the Columbia trans. rather than that of the Yale ed. of Milton's prose because Sumner's earlier more literal translation employs an English vocabulary which is often etymologically closer to Milton's Latin. I give significant terms in the original Latin also, when appropriate. Italics in quotations from Milton's prose are my own, except for names and terms.

31. See *The Song of Songs, Commentaries and Homilies*, trans. and annotated by R.P. Lawson. Boyarin, "The Song of Songs: Lock or Key?", pp. 16 ff., notes that the Song of Songs is a late text and itself contains echoes of Exodus and earlier Books; thus it can more clearly be recognised as intended intra-biblical commentary. In the exegetical links of the Song of Songs with Exodus one may see why Dante in his "Epistle to Can Grande" chose two verses on Exodus from Psalm 114 as a model for a similar setpiece of conventional allegorization (see my chap. 1, sect. "Dante", and n. 54). Boyarin draws from Ephraim E. Uhrbach, "The Homiletical Interpretations of the Sages and the Expositions of Origen on Canticles, and the Jewish-Christian Disputation".

32. See *The Cambridge History of the Bible*, vol. 2, chap. VI.3, "The Bible in the Medieval Schools" by Beryl Smalley, pp. 197-220, for a description of C12th scholastic and academic developments in the teaching and interpretation of the Bible. I partly follow this essay in the next section of my text.

33. The historical debate on this matter and its relevance to C17th literature is discussed further in App. D.

34. *Summa Theologica* I. 1, 10, *The Summa Theologica of Saint Thomas Aquinas*, trans. by Fathers of the English Dominican Province, p. 9; as cited also by Singleton in *Commedia*, App. "The Two Kinds of Allegory", p. 88 and p. 96, n.7. On Aquinas (and Augustine), see also my chap. 1, n. 65. For a comprehensive discussion of the aesthetics implicit in the views of Aquinas and esp. Augustine, as articulated by several continental theologian-critics of the

C12th, see Dronke, *Fabula*, Introd. and chap. 1, and "Bernardo Silvestre". Augustine's substantial discussion of the nature and several types of allegory and his embracing definition of allegory (like Quintilian's) as "a trope in which one thing is understood from another" ["Tropus ubi ex alio aliud intelligitur"] is to be found in *De Trinitate*, 15.ix.15, in *Patrologiae Cursus Completus*, series 1, ed. J.-P. Migne, vol. 42, cols. 1068-69. English trans. from *Saint Augustine: The Trinity*, trans. by Stephen McKenna, p. 471.

35. Singleton, p. 28; see also pp. 15, 61.

36. See Erich Auerbach, essay on "Figura" in *Scenes from the Drama of European Literature: Six Essays*, pp. 11-76 (pp. 53-57 esp.); quotations are from pp. 53, 54 and 57. Auerbach minimizes the "historicity" of any of the wider forms of allegorical interpretation. On p. 54, e.g., while he accepts that "figural interpretation is 'allegorical' in the widest sense", noting that "it differs from most of the allegorical forms known to us by the historicity both of the sign and what it signifies", he then proceeds to instance as allegories in the common understanding only those of the most abstract kinds: the *Psychomachia* of Prudentius, the *Roman de la Rose*, and "allegorical interpretations of historical events, which were usually interpreted as obscure illustrations of philosophical doctrines".

37. Cf. de Bruyne, chap. 7, sections 4 and 5. See also Singleton, p. 61, on "God's creation, God's other book". Singleton, p. 25 and p. 43, n. 6, cites Hugh of St.-Victor: "this whole visible world is as a book written by the finger of God". Cf. Thomas Browne, p. 25 of *Religio Medici*, vol. 1 of *The Works of Sir Thomas Browne*, ed. Geoffrey Keynes.

38. Many biblical historians would agree. See chap. VI, "The Exposition and Exegesis of Scripture", sect. 1, "To Gregory the Great", by G.W.H. Lampe, in *The Cambridge History of the Bible*, vol. 2, pp. 155-83, but esp. pp. 177-80. On p. 178: "The historical sense is the foundation for the spiritual, and if the latter subverts the former it is no longer true *theoria* but [fanciful] allegory. . . . Severian of Gabala . . . remarks that it is one thing to preserve the historical sense and add to it the spiritual, and quite another to distort the historical sense into allegory". Cf. Smalley, in *The Cambridge History of the Bible*, vol. 2, p. 214. Cf. Aquinas, as cited in my chap. 1, n. 65. An emphasis on the literal level tends to lead to, as secondary signification, one inclusive *sensus spiritualis* rather than multiple layers of allegorical sub-senses.

39. See my chap. 1, sect. "Dante".

40. Singleton, pp. 14-15, notes this solidity in Milton as in Dante. Singleton speaks of Dante's *Divina commedia* as a unique example of a "literal fiction" (a good phrase). A.C. Hamilton, *The Structure of Allegory in The Faerie Queene*, pp. 29-30, speaks of Spenser's aiming at a biblical-literal effect.

41. Singleton, p. 89.

42. See e.g. de Bruyne, pp. 313 ff., 334 ff. on Hugh, and Richard, of Saint-Victor.

43. On this, see Smalley, in *The Cambridge History of the Bible*, vol. 2, esp. p. 215.

44. Ibid., p. 216.

45. There was, apparently, early precedent for schematic (simultaneous or multiple) readings, without felt contradiction, in late antiquity: e.g., in Porphyry's essay on Homer's "Cave of the Nymphs". See Lamberton, *Homer the Theologian*, pp. 114 ff.

46. See again Smalley, in *The Cambridge History of the Bible*, vol. 2, p. 213-15. In *Convivio* II.1 Dante uses *different* passages from *different* texts (one, non-scriptural) to expound the last three of the traditional four "levels" of meaning—thus showing that the "levels" are neither imposed layers nor in any sense necessary coexisting alternatives, but rather *possible* different types of meaning that might be drawn out in different contexts, depending on the nature of the literal sense in the text involved. See *Dante's Convivio*, trans. and ed. by William Walrond Jackson, pp. 73-74.

47. See de Bruyne, p. 329. See Boyarin, "The Song of Songs: Lock or Key?", for illustrations of midrashic methods applied to the Song of Songs.

48. See Smalley, in *The Cambridge History of the Bible*, vol. 2, p. 213.

49. In this sect. I follow de Bruyne's analysis, pp. 306-12 esp. See further Henri de Lubac,

Exégèse Médiévale; les quatre sens de l'Écriture, vol. 1, p. 23, which gives the famous rhyming verses in Latin on the "four senses".

50. For a more elaborate exposition of the medieval secular scheme, see de Bruyne, chap. 7, sect. 3. On Bacon, see my chap. 3, sect. "Bacon".

51. Singleton, p. 64, cites Augustine on this problem.

52. For comment on Augustine's views on allegorical exegesis and allegorical poetics, see: Pépin, "L'absurdité, signe de l'allégorie", pp. 400-404 (esp. on Augustine's *De Genesi ad litteram* XI.1, 2); Dronke, *Fabula,* pp. 31, 56-57 and n. 2, and elsewhere; and Lamberton, *Homer the Theologian,* pp. 257-61.

53. See my chap. 1, nn. 54 and 46. Cf. de Bruyne, p. 329.

54. Dante expounds the theological "four senses" in two verses on the theme of Exodus from Psalm 114.1-2, in a traditional "setpiece" of theological allegorization in the "Epistle to Can Grande"; see *Literary Criticism of Dante Alighieri,* trans. and ed. Robert S. Haller, p. 99. Even here Dante is thinking primarily in terms of two divisions of meaning, and he goes on to say that "although these mystical senses are called by various names, they may all be called allegorical, since they are all different from the literal or historical. For allegory is derived from the Greek *alleon,* which means in latin *alienus* ['belonging to another'] or *diversus* ['different']". Dante then goes on to develop his own view of the twofold "subject" in the *Commedia* and of "allegory". Similarly, in the *Convivio* II. 1, pp. 74-75, after a longer exposition of the same verses from Psalm 114, Dante again turns to his implicitly "undivided" second theme, and the relatively lesser predominance in his poem of the more arcane subdivided senses: "I . . . when treating of each Canzone, will . . . first discuss the literal meaning, and after that will speak of its allegory, that is, of the hidden truth contained in it, and *sometimes I shall touch incidentally on the other meanings as place and time shall permit*" (italics mine). The authenticity of the "Epistle" has sometimes been questioned; see Peter Dronke, "Excursus (1): the *Epistle* to Cangrande and Latin prose rhythm", in *Dante and Medieval Latin Traditions,* pp. 103-11. However, this problem is not material to the present discussion, since—although the converse has sometimes been alleged to be the case—there seems to be no fundamental incompatibility between Dante's views expressed in the "Epistle" concerning allegory and his statements in the *Convivio.* On the one hand Dante in the *Convivio* and more briefly in the "Epistle" engages in a traditional "setpiece" of fourfold theological exegesis on a text concerning Exodus (which, like the Song of Songs, had long been regarded as particularly attuned to multi-layered interpretation). On the other hand, in both pieces he expresses a more general view in which the "undivided second sense" is paramount—in poetic allegorism, a view which itself has certain connections with formal exegesis on Scripture, and which in a more sustained sense is his main concern in the *Commedia.* Thus Dante's distinction (see Singleton, p. 84) between "the allegory of theologians" and "the allegory of poets" (fictions, in effect) clarifies. Even the "divided" figurative senses inherent in the *Commedia* have the same base in the literal (the factual-verisimilar, the "historical" of the fiction) that scriptural allegory has, and, analogously to the theologians' view of *theoria,* the undivided secondary sense in Scripture, the *Commedia* possesses a predominant, sustained and coherent "hidden truth". On Dante's theory of allegory, see also Robert Hollander, *Allegory in Dante's Commedia.*

55. "Epistle to Can Grande", in *Literary Criticism of Dante,* p. 101. Lat. from *Epistola* XI, in *Il Convito di Dante Alighieri e le Epistole,* in *Opera Minori,* ed. Pietro Fraticelli, vol. 3, p. 518.

56. "Epistle to Can Grande", in *Literary Criticism of Dante,* p. 102. Italics mine.

57. *Convivio* II.1, p. 75.

58. "Epistle to Can Grande", in *Literary Criticism of Dante,* p. 99.

59. Singleton, in his analysis of the *Commedia,* accepts this view as fundamental to Dante's use of allegory.

60. "Epistle to Can Grande", in *Literary Criticism of Dante,* p. 101.

61. Lamberton, *Homer the Theologian* pp. 288-97, stresses Dante's placing of his own

poem in the tradition of continuous moral-allegorical exposition of classical epic, particularly Virgil.

62. Singleton, p. 90.

63. de Bruyne's main point; see e.g. pp. 337, 368.

64. Singleton moves toward this apprehension; contrast his remark that Milton's "action . . . surely [is] given in terms of the literal" (p. 13) with his perception (p. 62) that Milton's poem, like Dante's, is literal *and also* "a vision".

65. On the medieval theological preference for the term *theoria*, indicating an undivided sense firmly grounded in historical fact, as opposed to the term, "allegory", with its implication of hierarchical structure and subdivision of meanings, see Lampe, *The Cambridge History of the Bible*, vol. 2, e.g. pp. 177-78, writing on some early interpreters of St. Paul's words in Galatians: "the apostle treated historical facts as real, while using them as analogies". To Dante's view of the "twofold" nature of his poetic subject ("Epistle to Can Grande", *Literary Criticism of Dante*, p. 99), and of the *inclusive* signification of the word "allegory" in exegesis, cf. de Bruyne, p. 306. Singleton (p. 88) in this context cites Aquinas on the undivided second sense (*Summa Theologica*, I. 1, 10). The passage is as follows: "Therefore that first meaning whereby words signify things belongs to the first sense, the historical or literal. That meaning whereby things signified by words have themselves also a meaning is called the spiritual sense, which is based on the literal, and presupposes it" (*Summa Theologica*, pp. 9-10). Aquinas' discussion attempts to rationalize the various schemes of the four "senses", as applied by St. Augustine and others. Aquinas stresses the inclusiveness of the allegorical sense and, repeatedly, the primacy of the literal sense: "allegory alone stands for the three spiritual senses"; "the parabolical sense is contained in the literal" (p. 10). Singleton also (p. 88) refers to St. Augustine, *De Trinitate* XV.ix.15: "in his first division into two he [Thomas] has made the fundamental distinction, which St. Augustine expressed in terms of one meaning which is *in verbis* and another meaning which is *in facto*".

66. *Allegorical Imagery*, p. 197. On the close relationship of allegory, as understood by the Renaissance, to certain other varieties of metaphorical tropes (metonymy, synecdoche, catachresis), see also Rosemond Tuve, *Elizabethan and Metaphysical Imagery: Renaissance Poetic and Twentieth-Century Critics*, pp. 107 ff.

67. On Dante's exposition of Psalm 114, see my chap. 1, n. 54. The quotations in my text are from Singleton, p. 93.

68. Singleton, p. 5.

Chapter 2. Renaissance Theoretical Developments

1. Three studies in particular, directed toward the English literary tradition of allegory, engage with some of the historical material which I cover in this section: John M. Steadman, *The Lamb and the Elephant: Ideal Imitation and the Context of Renaissance Allegory*; and Michael Murrin's two books, *The Veil of Allegory: Some Notes toward a Theory of Allegorical Rhetoric in the English Renaissance*, and its "continuation" volume, *The Allegorical Epic: Essays in its Rise and Decline*. Murrin's first book, considering theory of typology and mythographical and rhetorical approaches to allegory in the Renaissance, as well as "the poets" (chiefly Spenser), was an effort to isolate an allegorical *methodology* in the Renaissance deriving directly from the classics, one bypassing medieval and biblical exegesis. Recent studies, especially of the medieval and post-classical literary exegetical traditions, increasingly have shown that strong continuities do exist and suggest that to isolate more recent from older allegorical traditions is misleading. Murrin's second and more recent book, adopting a different approach, applies Renaissance (largely Neoplatonic) theories on allegory to the analysis of selected episodes from Landino, Boiardo, Tasso, and Spenser. Murrin now, in contrast to statements in his earlier book, sees *Paradise Lost* as participating in the seventeenth-century "decline" of the allegorical epic—allegory now only residual, in the "language of Milton's Heaven".

2. On the medieval theories concerning *integumentum* and *involucrum*, see Dronke, *Fabula*, pp. 57-67, and chap. 4, "Fables of Destiny", pp. 119-43. I follow Dronke's translations of these terms in *Fabula*, pp. 4-5. Dronke finds also associated with these concepts, as e.g. in the work of writers such as Bernardus Silvestris and others, a more arcane concept of *symbolum* which is distinguishable from "allegory".

3. The Letters of Coluccio Salutati were edited by Francesco Novati in *Epistolario*; vol. 4.1 concerns us here. B.L. Ullman has edited Salutati's augmented allegorizations of the Hercules myths (1405) under the title, *Coluccii Salutati, de laboribus Herculis*. (This title appears to be taken from that of Salutati's unfinished version, written before 1383, while his longer 1405 version had originally been referred to as the *De sensibus allegoricis fabularum Herculis*.) The first version was a short "moralized" treatment of Seneca's play, *Hercules Furens*. The second (1405), which is our concern, is a much extended allegorical treatment of all the Hercules legends, from Hercules' conception and birth (part of Bk II), to his labours (Bk III), to his descent to the lower world, and his wives (Bk IV). Of this ed., Bk I (13 chaps.) represents a compendious defence of poetry. Bk I (chaps. 1, 2 and 13) and Bk II (first 2 chaps.) are at the centre of Salutati's critical discussions. In *The Humanism of Coluccio Salutati*, Berthold L. Ullman surveys the interrelationship and briefly outlines the content of each of these two editions or versions (see pp. 65-68 and 22-27). He also discusses the history of the three letters of Salutati to Giovanni da Samminiato (or San Miniato), of which the third is cited in the present discussion, and the genesis of the subsequent Letter (*tractatus*) to Dominici (see pp. 59-62, 65-68), and indicates something of their concerns.

4. A comprehensive survey of Salutati's ideas on poetry and allegory is that of Aguzzi, pp. 60-107; see pp. 60-90 esp., for the discussion of poetry. Bernard Weinberg in *A History of Literary Criticism in the Italian Renaissance* does not discuss Salutati's Letters, save for a single mention (vol. 1, p. 3). Geoffrey Shepherd, ed., in his Introd. to Sir Philip Sidney, *An Apology for Poetry: or The Defence of Poesy* (1595), p. 29, has a paragraph on Salutati as a humanist critic. The opening of *De laboribus Herculis* (version of *c.* 1383) is briefly cited by Ullman as an indirect defence of poetry via allegory, in *The Humanism of Coluccio Salutati*, p. 68. However, his editor seems to pass over Salutati's critical discussions of poetic theory with almost complete unrecognition of their contemporary relevance; see e.g. the remark (p. 26) that Salutati's approach is "thoroughly medieval". Ullman is not alone; Salutati rates only a passing allusion in Curtius. Aguzzi's illuminating outline is somewhat marred by the fact that he does not provide translations from Salutati's Latin, which is sometimes ambiguous; and Aguzzi's paraphrases (like the marginal synopses in Novati's text of the *Epistolario* of Salutati) do not always seem to follow very closely the passages quoted in the Latin. I have therefore relied on my own translations, given in the text and notes below. I have been generously assisted by Dr. Ilya Gershevitch and Professor Peter Dronke. All italics in quotations from Salutati are mine.

5. Quotations are from the "Letter to Samminiato", *Epistolario*, vol. 4.1, pp. 177-78. In the Lat.: "hic loquendi modus poeticus est, falsitatem corticitus pre se ferens, intrinsecus vero latentem continens veritatem. . . . sit ergo tibi determinare poesis illa locutio, que vel rebus vel verbis aliud intelligit quam ostendat, quem loquendi modum adinvenit necessitas, recepit et ampliavit usus, non solum cum necessitas cogit, sed etiam cum affectat ornatus".

6. *De laboribus Herculis*, Bk I, chap. 13, pp. 69-70. In the Lat.: "Si vero detur aliquid reperiri quod neutri predictorum omnino conveniat, sine cunctatione pronunties id simplex esse carmen et dictamen aliquod, non poema, nec id ad poeticam pertinere. Nam quamvis in diffinitione sequatur metrico imaginarioque sermone, non putes tamen quicquid metro componitur esse poema nisi et id quod coniungitur imaginarius sermo sit, figuris et presertim alieniloquio redimitus. Et intelligo sermonem imaginarium qui per aliquod dictum et aliud intellectum imaginationem et ipsam moveat fantasiam. Quod quidem verbum magis aperte tangit reliqua descriptionis pars, cum dicitur sub alicuius narrationis misterio, id est occulto, vera recondens".

7. See "Letter to Samminiato", *Epistolario*, vol. 4.1, pp. 179-80, 194-95, 198, 200; "Letter to

294 Notes to Pages 20-21

Dominici", *Epistolario*, vol. 4.1, pp. 234, 235, 238, 239; *De laboribus Herculis*, Bk I, chap. 1, pp. 8-13. The *total* value which Salutati accords to allegory or figurative language both in Scripture and in poetry is unusual. (Cf. the passage from "Letter to Samminiato", *Epistolario*, vol. 4.1, pp. 177-78, quoted in my chap. 2, n. 5; also, the second passage in "Letter to Dominici" (*Epistolario*, vol. 4.1, p. 238), quoted in my chap. 2, n. 11.

8. See *De laboribus Herculis*, Bk I, chap. 13, pp. 69-70, as cited in my chap. 2, n. 6. The full context of Salutati's discussion in this chap. needs to be taken into account. Salutati also takes exception to the Aristotelian classification of poetry as "orations of praise or blame"—see "Letter to Samminiato", *Epistolario*, vol. 4.1, p. 177; "Letter to Dominici", *Epistolario*, vol. 4.1, p. 239. In both cases he adds to the older definition of poetry according to metre or genre, the conception of poetry as "translated" discourse (implicitly, with a concealed didactic idea).

9. Aguzzi (p. 68) responds to this aspect in noting Salutati's evolution, in his last writings, toward a "global" theory of allegorical poetry: "he embodied his fondness for allegory in a global conception of the art of poetry".

10. This theory of "translation" may bear some relationship to the principles underlying midrash, as exemplified in, e.g., Philo (who is discussed in my chap. 4, sect. "Philo"). Cf. Bruns, pp. 637-41.

11. The quotations are from *Epistolario*, vol. 4.1, pp. 235 and 238. In the Lat. (p. 235): "*ipsa sit sermocinalis quedam ars atque facultas bilinguis*, unum exterius exhibens, aliud autem intrinseca ratione significans; semper in figura loquens, ac sepenumero versibus alligans si quid refert". And (p. 238): "quid est enim in tota divina Scriptura quod non habeat mysticum intellectum, sive verba sive hystorias sive prohetias sive sapientie precepta consideres? totum est mysticum, totum reducitur ad allegoricum intellectum. *nichil est in illis quod bilingue non sit*, quod non unum in cortice pre se ferat et aliud intrinsecus non intendat". Cf. to the above, Salutati's statement that *even* the beginning of Genesis and the six-day Creation account have been found by some (as in Origen) to have allegorical senses (p. 235). Again (anxious to establish that poetry and Scripture are based on the same poetic-allegorical principles), on p. 240 in the same Letter: "from which, what was to be proved is sufficiently apparent, that the divine page does not always run in prose but sometimes takes on the elegance of songs, so that, since poetry is an art of discourse and a bilingual faculty—that is, always speaking in figures and often binding what it relates in verses—it is certain and most obvious that the fictions [*figmenta*] of poets and the ordering of divine Scripture subsist not through diverse [different] principles but wholly through the same ones". In the Lat. (p. 240): "quibus satis constat quod probandum erat, divinam paginum non semper prosa currere, sed aliquando carminum elegantiam suscepisse; *ut cum poetica sit sermocinalis ars atque facultas bilinguis;* hoc est unum exterius exhibens et aliud autem intrinsecus significans, semper in figura loquens ac sepenumero versibus alligans si quid refert, certum et manifestissimum sit poetarum figmenta et divine Scripture seriem non diversa, sed eadem prorsus subsistere ratione".

12. See "Letter to Dominici", *Epistolario*, vol. 4.1, pp. 235, 240 and 239. In the Lat. (p. 239): "nam cum . . . poesis pene semper intrinsecum occulat intellectum, quid facit aliud poetica quam divina Scriptura? in figura quippe loquitur utraque verbis novatis atque translatis supponentibusque prorsus aliud quam significent".

13. "Letter to Samminiato", *Epistolario*, vol. 4.1, p. 177. In the Lat.: "hic loquendi modus poeticus est, falsitatem corticitus pre se ferens, intrinsecus vero latentem continens veritatem. huius rei peritia, doctrina sive ratio poesis dicitur, poetica vel poetria . . . ex quibus facile videre potes ad hanc facultatem omnes translationes sive metaphoras, schemata, tropos, metaplasmos et allegorias, necnon tropologias et parabolas peculiariter pertinere". Also cf. "Letter to Dominici", *Epistolario*, vol. 4.1, p. 239, as quoted in my chap. 2, n. 12.

14. *De laboribus Herculis*, Bk I, chap. 2, p. 10. In the Lat.: "Alterum autem quod summe iocundum reperias in poetis est illa mirabilis tum verborum, tum rerum, tum etiam gestorum concinna mutatio, quod quidem ad poetam videmus peculiariter pertinere. Omnes enim translationes atque metaphore, comparationes et similitudines, et quicquid verborum aut rerum, orationum et negociorum videmus in aliud commutari poeticum est".

15. See the passage from "Letter to Samminiato", *Epistolario*, vol. 4.1, p. 177, quoted in my chap. 2, n. 13.

16. As in its use in the passage from "Letter to Samminiato", *Epistolario*, vol. 4.1, p. 177.

17. As in its use in the passage from *De laboribus Herculis*, p. 10, quoted in my chap. 2, n. 14. *Translationes* is rendered as "allegory" by Aguzzi, p. 84.

18. See the passage from *De laboribus Herculis*, p. 10, as quoted in my chap. 2, sect. "Coluccio Salutati", and n. 14.

19. Aguzzi, p. 68.

20. Consider *De laboribus Herculis*, p. 10, as quoted in my chap. 2, n. 14; "Letter to Samminiato", *Epistolario*, vol. 4.1, p. 177, as quoted in my chap. 2, n. 13, and further, pp. 177-78—which seem to refer to allegory as a mode of speaking to be kept in use and practice even when "striving after ornament".

21. "Letter to Dominici", *Epistolario*, vol. 4.1, p. 239. In the Lat.: "quoniam poetica, non dico semper, sed, ut superius diffinivi, sepenumero versibus alligat si quid refert, prosam siquidem non recusat sive continuam, ut Apuleius, sive intercisam, ut Marcianus Capella, Alanus". Martianus (spelled Marcianus in Novati's ed. of the *Epistolario*) in the earlier C5th wrote an elaborate prose allegory on Philology and the Liberal Arts.

22. *Convivio*, II.1, p. 73.

23. *Boccaccio on Poetry*, p. 48.

24. "Aguzza qui, lettor, ben gli occhi al vero, / chè il velo è ora ben tanto sottile, / certo, che il trapassar dentro è leggiero" (*Purg.* VIII. 19-21). As quoted from *The Purgatorio of Dante Alighieri* (Temple Classics ed.), p. 94. These lines are quoted by Tasso—seemingly from memory—in his discussion of allegory in Letter 48 (1575); see Torquato Tasso, *Le Lettere*, ed. Cesare Guasti, vol. 1, p. 115.

25. Quotations from Edmund Spenser are taken from *Spenser's Faerie Queene*, ed. J.C. Smith. Italics in Spenser quotations (except with proper names) are mine. For the sonnet to Lord Burleigh, line 10, see vol. 2, p. 492.

26. John Harington, "An Apologie of Poetrie", in *Orlando Furioso in English Heroical Verse* (1591), facs. reprint, fo. iv^v. My quotations from Harington follow this ed. The prefatory folios are not numbered after iii and iv, but I have given numbers to the later folios, as if the series had continued. Italics in quotations, except with names, are mine.

27. Henry Reynolds, *Mythomystes. Wherein a short survay is taken of the nature and value of true Poësie, and depth of the Antients* . . . (1632), introd. by Arthur F. Kinney, facs. rept., pp. 29-30.

28. See Henry Peacham, *The Garden of Eloquence* (1577), facs. reprint, folios Di-Div; George Puttenham, *The Arte of English Poesie* (1589), ed. Gladys Doidge Willcock and Alice Walker, chap. 18; the quotation is from p. 186. Puttenham's exposition continues through 187-90. Italics in quotations from Puttenham and Peacham are (except with the names of rhetorical figures) mine.

29. Peacham, fo. Di.

30. Ibid., fo. Dii. Cf. Tuve, *Elizabethan and Metaphysical Imagery*, pp. 133-38, who cites a longer statement from the 1593 ed. of Peacham (p. 27) to the same effect.

31. For a study of emblematic imagery in *Paradise Lost* (henceforth abbrev. *PL*) and its derivations, see Mindele Anne Treip, " 'Reason is Also Choice': The Emblematics of Free Will in *Paradise Lost*".

32. *Elizabethan and Metaphysical Imagery*, pp. 143-44.

33. Puttenham, p. 186 (from the title to chap. 18).

34. Ibid., pp. 186-87; cf. Peacham, folios Bii-Bii^v.

35. Although Peacham classifies these three figures separately from allegory (sect. beginning on fo. Bii), Puttenham puts all four under the same section (figures of sense, see chap. 17), and lists them along with *metaphora, ironia, sarcasmus*, etc., in chap. 18.

36. *Elizabethan and Metaphysical Imagery*, pp. 99-109 (esp. pp. 105-6); p. 136.

37. Puttenham, p. 188.

38. Peacham, fo. Dii; cf. Puttenham, p. 187.

39. Peacham, fo. Di^v.

40. Puttenham, p. 187.

41. *Elizabethan and Metaphysical Imagery*, pp. 106; 108-9; 219.

42. Peacham, folios Di-Di^v.

43. Puttenham, pp. 186-87.

44. According to Tuve, *Elizabethan and Metaphysical Imagery*, pp. 105-6, allegory is more like a Donne conceit, while metaphor is translative in a looser way. However, a Donne conceit necessarily also is more self-limiting than "continued allegory" of the Spenserian kind.

45. William Nelson in *The Poetry of Edmund Spenser: A Study*, p. 121, disputes the very possibility that the overall framework of Spenser's poem may show any developmental aspect. The knights are "fashion[s]" (images) of the gentleman "of virtuous and gentle discipline" seen at various points in time; but the poem does not show the knight (allegorically or in any other way) as in any process of formation—evolving or *being* "fashioned". This view hinges on the forced interpretation of the single word, "perfec*ted*": Spenser's use of the past tense is said to indicate that the knights are from the outset shown as fully formed. But the total phrase could perfectly well convey the present progressive idea of "*being* perfected"; while the other disputed word, "fashion", is used by Spenser of the knights in a progressive and not a finished sense. "The generall end . . . is *to fashion* a gentleman or noble person in vertuous and gentle discipline". See "A Letter of the Authors to Sir Walter Raleigh" in *Spenser's Faerie Queene*, vol. 2, p. 485.

46. See *Elizabethan and Metaphysical Imagery*, pp. 103, 105, 106-7; 130-33, 136; quotation from p. 219.

Chapter 3. The English Mythographers and Their Tradition

1. Francis Bacon, *The Advancement of Learning* (1605), ed. William Aldis Wright, Bk II.iv.1-5, pp. 101-5.

2. Francis Bacon, [*De sapientia veterum*] *Of the Wisdom of the Ancients* (1609); in vol. 6 of *The Works of Francis Bacon*, ed. James Spedding *et al.*, pp. 695-99. Italics in quotations from Bacon are mine.

3. J.E. Spingarn, *A History of Literary Criticism in the Renaissance*, pt. 3, chap. 2 *passim*, but esp. pp. 268-77; cf. the entirely incorrect statement (p. 276) that "the death-knell of this mode of interpreting literature was sounded by Bacon". Spingarn's extreme bias toward the neo-classical is obvious. Contrast Shepherd in the Introd. to Sidney's *Apology*, p. 29: "Bacon elaborates an allegorical theory of poetry". Shepherd's discussion of allegory in Renaissance poetic theory is illuminating though brief.

4. *Advancement*, Bk II, p. 104.

5. Preface, *De sapientia*, *Works*, vol. 6, p. 695.

6. *Advancement*, Bk II, p. 102. Bacon's term, "parabolical", seems to derive from the fourth and freest of the medieval "levels" as applied to secular poetry.

7. Preface, *De sapientia*, *Works*, vol. 6, p. 696.

8. See Preface, *De sapientia*, *Works*, vol. 6. pp. 697-98.

9. Ibid., pp. 696, 698, 698.

10. Ibid., p. 696.

11. Ibid., p. 698. The first statement is repeated in *Advancement*, Bk II, p. 103.

12. Preface, *De sapientia*, *Works*, vol. 6, p. 698.

13. See preface, *De sapientia*, *Works*, vol. 6, p. 697.

14. *Advancement*, Bk II, p. 104.

15. Ibid. "Inwardness" appears to correspond to Bacon's term *involucrum*, as used in the Latin version of the *Advancement*, *De Augmentis Scientiarum* (1609), Bk II, chap. 13, *Works*, vol. 1, p. 520. The use of *involucrum* at this late date illustrates the essential continuity of medieval to Renaissance thinking on allegory.

16. Preface, *De sapientia*, *Works*, vol. 6, p. 696. Bacon is alluding to both etymological and

narrative allegory. Cf. *Advancement*, Bk II, p. 103: "In heathen poesy we see the exposition of fables doth fall out sometimes with great felicity".

17. Preface, *De sapientia*, *Works*, vol. 6, p. 697.

18. Ibid.

19. See on this Pépin's article, in this context kindly called to my attention by Gordon Teskey: "L'absurdité, signe de l'allégorie". Pépin discusses Augustine on pp. 400-404, quoting (on pp. 400-401) from Augustine's *De Genesi ad litteram* XI.1, 2. After defining the literal character of Scripture, Augustine writes (I give Pépin's Fr. trans.; the italics are mine): "s'il se trouve dans les paroles de Dieu ou de tel interprète élevé à la fonction de prophète une déclaration *qui ne puisse sans absurdité être entendue à la lettre*, il est hors de doute que l'on doit y voir une figure significative". In Eng. trans. (mine): "If there be found, in the word of God or of some interpreter raised to the status of prophet, a statement which cannot be understood literally without absurdity, beyond doubt one must there recognise a figure with a secondary signification".

20. See Preface, *De sapientia*, *Works*, vol. 6, p. 698; *Advancement*, Bk II, p. 103.

21. *Advancement*, Bk II, p. 104.

22. Murrin, *The Veil of Allegory* (see chap. 5 and summary, p. 102), thinks that the Renaissance "levels" have nothing to do with the older scriptural fourfold exegesis, but only with the "classical" (i.e. secular) threefold exegesis. I would suggest that Renaissance allegoresis does have affinities with both the older scriptural and the older secular forms, although these affinities are of a general or loose kind. My feeling is that the old *habit* of tidy hierarchical analysis persists in Renaissance allegoresis, while the preferred content radically shifts, as Murrin says, mainly toward the secular. The Renaissance ambivalence in the use of the term, "allegorie", does not, however (*pace* Murrin, pp. 101-2), imply the inclusion of almost everything else. The term "allegorie", as used by Renaissance editors such as Harington, while suggesting a broad latitude, as did the undivided "second sense" of medieval *theoria*, most often has a moral-psychological application. The "everything else" may indeed be inserted almost anywhere else, under a variety of non-allegorical marginal notations of a scholarly kind, including "historie" (signifying the historical context of the fable) and "allusion" (signifying some ancient historical or political reference); but the main *interpretative* allegorical senses are fairly constant. I must further disagree with the view in this book (later abandoned by Murrin) that all allegory was fundamentally "oral" (p. 74). Renaissance or earlier exegesis was, on the contrary, essentially scholarly and literary in method.

23. I have used the Garland facs. repts., ed. Stephen Orgel, of: Natalis Comes, [*Mythologiae* 1551] *Mythologie*, trans. by Jean Baudouin after the earlier French of I. de Montlyard (1627), and Vicenzo Cartari, [*De imagine gentile deorum*] *Le imagini de i dei de gli antichi* (1571).

24. *Mythologie*, Bk V, in vol. 1, p. 438: "que c'est qu'ils ont entendu par telle deïté".

25. See e.g. *Mythologie*, Bk V, in vol. 1, pp. 435-41.

26. George Sandys, *Ovid's Metamorphoses Englished* (1632), Garland facs. reprint, ed. Stephen Orgel; also publ. in the ed. of Karl K. Hulley and Stanley T. Vandersell, *Ovid's Metamorphosis Englished, Mythologized, and Represented in Figures* (1632).

27. See St. Bernard, Abbot of Clairvaux, *Cantica Canticorum: Eighty-Six Sermons on The Songs of Solomon*, trans. and ed. by Samuel J. Eales.

28. But contrast Bacon, who offers a vigorous defence against the detractors of allegedly "imposed" allegory, in Preface to *De sapientia*, *Works*, vol. 6, p. 698.

29. See Aguzzi, p. 211. John Harington's allegorical systems are discussed, with conclusions somewhat different from my own, by Steadman in *The Lamb and the Elephant*, pp. 100-102, n. 6, and by Murrin in *The Veil of Allegory*, chap. 5, esp. pp. 13-14, 102, 113, 121-22, and elsewhere. The introd. to Robert McNulty's ed. of Harington's *Ludovico Ariosto's Orlando Furioso: Translated into English heroical verse* (1591), pp. xxvii to xxxviii, discusses Harington's views on allegory and his sources, in particular Giuseppe Bononome and Simone Fornari, but McNulty undervalues Harington: he "seems to understand allegory . . . as a series of unrelated arbitrary levels" (p. xxxviii). A full treatment of C16th and C17th allegorizers of Ariosto,

including Bononome, is to be found in Aguzzi, chap. 2. Aguzzi notes (p. 165) that fewer than 7 out of 117 Ital. eds. of Ariosto after 1542 (the date of the first allegorized ed.) were without allegorizations of a similar sort—a fact which has implications not only for Spenser's epic but for Milton's. Earlier studies which also deal with Ital. sources of Harington are those of Townsend Rich, *Harington & Ariosto: A Study in Elizabethan Verse Translation*, in which see on the Italian allegorizers pp. 145-50 esp., and T.G.A. Nelson, "Sir John Harington and the Renaissance Debate over Allegory". Nelson perceives Harington as cautious or even sceptical in his allegorizations on the *Furioso*, as compared with his Italian editorial sources, but not as parodic. There is a sensitive discussion of Harington as allegorist, of Elizabethan allegory and of Fornari in Thomas P. Roche, Jr., *The Kindly Flame: A Study of the Third and Fourth Books of Spenser's Faerie Queene*, pp. 4-10. Roche notes that Harington shows himself aware of the theory of universal allegorical correspondences, of which Roche (pp. 7-8) cites Simone Fornari (via Pico) as exponent. (As I note in n. 39 to my chap. 3, this aspect is perhaps not Harington's primary concern.) The implications for Milton of Fornari's theory of universal correspondences and its sources are discussed in my chap. 16, sect. "Raphael's Theory of Discourse", and n. 9.

30. See *Mythomystes*, pp. 46-50.

31. Ibid., p. 110. Murrin discusses Reynolds' Neoplatonic affiliations in *The Veil of Allegory*, pp. 12-13, in connection with Pico.

32. Orazio Toscanella, *Bellezze del Furioso di M. Lodovico Ariosto . . . con gli argomenti et allegorie dei canti* (1574). For a discussion of this rare work, see Aguzzi, pp. 206-11.

33. "Observation upon the Tale of [N]arcissus" (forward to the Tale), in *Mythomystes*, pp. 105-9.

34. See Preface, *De sapientia, Works*, vol. 6, p. 697, as quoted in my chap. 3, sect. "Bacon".

35. See "A Briefe Apologie", *Orlando Furioso*, folios iv-iv^v.

36. Ibid., fo. iv.

37. Ibid., folios iv-iv^v.

38. "An Advertisement to the Reader before he Reade this Poeme, of Some Things to be Observed", *Orlando Furioso*, fo. A.

39. See again "A Briefe Apologie", *Orlando Furioso*, folios iv-iv^v. This somewhat dismissive exercise in the older styles of largely religious layered allegoresis is rather revealing. Harington refers to "the ancient Poets" and to C12th terminology in his "the utmost barke or ryne" (signifying the "litterall sence", and echoing the earlier term *integumentum*, which meant outer wrapping but also came to imply, "that which is hidden within"). The "Morall sence" in *this* context (as given further on in his next paragraph about Perseus, "a wise man") is clearly a *hidden* sense. But Harington then tries to fit into the old scheme some contemporary secular interests: the "Historicall sence" and "the natural allegory". By the time he gets to the "more high and heavenly Allegorie" and the "Theological Allegorie" of the Perseus legend, the *schema* ceases to work, or perhaps he has lost interest in pursuing the religious applications. He gives up: "the like infinite Allegories I could pike out of other Poeticall fictions, save that I would avoid tediousnes". (This, at least, is my interpretation; Roche, pp. 5-6, takes this passage more seriously as showing a Renaissance insight into the universal nature of allegory.)

40. Murrin agrees on this distinction in Harington; see *The Veil of Allegory*, pp. 13-14. One cannot overemphasize the importance of Harington's distinction. While "allegory" in the Renaissance does sometimes mean just moral example, or the "moral lesson" which we may draw from a didactic story—as Susannah Jane McMurphy argues in *Spenser's Use of Ariosto for Allegory*, p. 15—such "example" does not represent the moral *sensus* or "level". Nelson says that Spenser and Harington use both methods indifferently and do not distinguish between them (p. 130; p. 324, n.24). I shall argue again later that Spenser, like Harington, understood the distinction and used both methods complementarily.

41. See "Letter to Raleigh", *Spenser's Faerie Queene*, vol. 2, p. 485 (later discussed), where Spenser uses this term "ensampled" in apparent contradistinction to other allegorical terms.

42. See "A Briefe Apologie", *Orlando Furioso*, fo. iii; quotations from "A Briefe and Summarie Allegorie of Orlando Furioso", *Orlando Furioso*, p. 410 and pp. 410-13; gloss on Rogero, p. 413 (misnumbered as 113).

43. "A Briefe Apologie", *Orlando Furioso*, fo. iii^v.

44. "An Advertisement to the Reader", *Orlando Furioso*, fo. A.

Chapter 4. "Idea"

1. As Sidney significantly notes, in his discussion of a "second nature" in poetry, *Apology*, p. 101: "these arguments will by few be understood, and by fewer granted".

2. As is commonly assumed of Sidney: on *exempla*, see *Apology*, e.g. pp. 110-13 and 123. But Sidney's discussion is really directed toward a more complex theory of Ideal Imitation. See the ensuing discussion of Sidney's *Apology* in my chap. 4, sect. "Sidney".

3. The Renaissance use of the concept of "Ideal Imitation" is discussed, with focus on the English context, by Shepherd in his Introd. to Sidney's *Apology*, pp. 47-61; "Imitation and Allegory" are discussed briefly on Shepherd's pp. 28ff. Steadman's work on the subject of "Idea" is outlined in my App. B. Steadman cites Erwin Panofsky (see *Idea: A Concept in Art Theory*, trans. Joseph J.S. Peake); but Panofsky's theory is not so much a theory of allegory as of "general representation" or, in the painterly sense, "idealization", as practised e.g. by Joshua Reynolds in the C18th. In my present connection, E.H. Gombrich's work on "Idea" in *Symbolic Images: Studies in the Art of the Renaissance* is more directly relevant. Other critics have converged on the same ground from slightly different directions: see e.g. Annabel Patterson's article, "Tasso and Neoplatonism: The Growth of his Epic Theory". The most comprehensive critical discussion in English of theories of "Imitation" and "Ideal Imitation" in Italian Renaissance theory that I have found is that in Weinberg's two-volume study. However, I find it difficult to correlate Weinberg's largely Aristotelian-directed discussions with my own discussion of allegorical poetics. I attempt a somewhat more complete discussion of "Idea", "Ideal Imitation" and their relation to allegory in my App. B. The second Part of the present study takes up the question again, in relation to Milton's aesthetic; see my chap. 13, and n. 2.

4. See Philo, *On the Account of the World's Creation given by Moses (De Opificio Mundi)*, in vol. 1 of *Philo*, trans. F.H. Colson and G.H. Whitaker. The ensuing quotations are taken from pp. 125 and 17 respectively; paragraphing not shown. Lamberton in his discussion of Philo (see *Homer the Theologian*, esp. pp. 44-54) considers that Philo reconstructs ancient classical approximations of the *quatre sens*, or the "multiple levels of meaning" in Homer and Hesiod (p. 49). Recent Hebrew commentators would not altogether agree; Bruns in "Midrash and Allegory" (pp. 636-40 on Philo) considers that Philo's methods approximate to a theory of "radical translation", or "resituating" of the scriptural text: that is, of allegorical appropriation or making available, in the reading of Scripture, through looking at a single text from a number of different angles. See also my chap. 1, sect. "Rabbinical Interpretation", and Salutati's views on poetry, as discussed in my chap. 2, sect. "Coluccio Salutati".

5. *Boccaccio on Poetry*, Bk XIV, p. 48. The italics are mine.

6. Ibid., pp. 48-49. The "veil" of allegory is an early critical commonplace, reiterated in Harington's "Briefe Apologie", *Orlando Furioso*, fo. iv^v. Cf. Dante, *Purg.* VIII.19-21, on the "truth" hidden beneath the thin "veil": see my chap. 2, n. 24.

7. *Apology*, p. 101. Shepherd (*Apology*, Introd., pp. 54-55), also cites in this connection Pamela's discussion of divine causality in Philip Sidney's *The Countesse of Pembrokes Arcadia*, in *The Prose Works of Philip Sidney*, ed. Albert Feuillerat, vol. 1, pp. 407-10.

8. *Apology*, p. 101.

9. Ibid., p. 124.

10. Consider the flashing clear splendour of Pyrocles' appearance, riding the rough seas on a spar, in our first view of him in Bk I, chap. I, of *The Countesse of Pembrokes Arcadia (Prose Works*, vol. 1, p. 10)—emblem of triumph over and through adversity. Similar significant costume detail in the *New Arcadia* is suggested in an essay of Margaret P. Hannay, " 'My Sheep

are Thoughts': Self-Reflexive Pastoral in *The Faerie Queene*, Book VI, and the *New Arcadia*". A few titles of articles on emblem use in Sidney are given by Jerome S. Dees on p. 415 of "Recent Studies in the English Emblem". A larger study of emblematics in Sidney, by Claire Preston, is in progress.

11. *Apology*, p. 58. The conceptual emblem or image is one manifestation of allegory in poetry. The question of allegory as relating to the problem of poetic language in a wider sense involves, as has been seen from the earlier critics, the nature of poetic language as itself metaphor. Shepherd works toward this idea when he cites John Hoskins, *Directions for Speech and Style* (a Neoplatonic work drawing examples from the *Arcadia*), on "the double speech of man" (sign and interior thing signified)—see *Apology*, pp. 58-59.

12. *Prose Works*, vol. 1, pp. 17-18.

13. Urania as the symbol of wisdom (or vanished wisdom), adapted to the English poetic and epic moral-allegorical tradition, recurs in several of Sidney's poems in *The Countesse of Pembrokes Arcadia*, e.g. "Ye goat-herd gods"; also in Spenser's "The Teares of the Muses" and "Colin Clouts"; and in many other literary contexts, including Dante (*Purg.* xxix.40-43). On the use of the emblematic Urania in Sidney's two *Arcadias*, see Jon S. Lawry, *Sidney's Two Arcadias: Pattern and Proceeding*. On the emblematic Urania as Wisdom in painterly and Miltonic connections, see Mindele Anne Treip, *"Descend from Heav'n Urania": Milton's Paradise Lost and Raphael's Cycle in the Stanza della Segnatura*. John M. Steadman in *Milton's Biblical and Classical Imagery*, chap. 3, "Urania: 'Meaning' and 'Name'", pp. 88-101, discusses some pertinent Renaissance iconographical traditions and significations.

14. *Apology*, p. 124; italics mine. This sentence strongly anticipates certain later neoclassical criticism on the epic: see on René Le Bossu, my chap. 10, sect. "Allegory as the 'Platform' of Truth".

15. See esp. my chaps. 6, sect. "The Mystical Image", and 13.

16. Tasso's published "Allegoria" to the *Gerusalemme liberata* (1581) precedes by fourteen years the publication of Sidney's *Apology* (1595); the latter was written around 1581-83. Publication of Tasso's *Discorsi del poema eroico* (1594), the later version of his *Discorsi*, narrowly precedes that of Sidney's treatise; however, the earlier version, the *Discorsi dell'arte poetica* (1587), dates back to the mid-1570s. Thus the earlier of Tasso's well-known critical writings, including the published "Allegoria", may have been familiar to Sidney, as they were to Spenser and to other English critics of that period and later.

17. Tasso, "Allegoria" (as it will henceforth be referred to, under its Italian title, in my notes), or "The Allegory of the Poem", in *Jerusalem Delivered: A Poem* (1600), trans. by Edward Fairfax, ed. Henry Morley, p. 436. Quotations from Tasso's allegorical preface are taken from this ed. It should be noted that whereas Tasso's "Allegoria" prefaced the 1581 and subsequent eds. of the *Gerusalemme*, including Fairfax's English trans., modern editors from Morley until recently have either relegated the prose allegory to the backs of their volumes or dropped it altogether—an indication of their devaluation of allegory and, generally, of C16th critical prefaces. Tasso's phrases, "lively set before our corporeal eyes" and "the understanders of the nature of things", seem to be paralleled in several places in Sidney's *Apology*; see, e.g., Sidney as quoted in my chap. 4, n. 1.

18. ["The Allegory of the Poem"] "Allegoria", *Jerusalem Delivered*, p. 437.

Chapter 5. Tasso: The Practical Problems of the Allegorical Epic

1. Of Tasso's important critical works, only the *Discorsi del poema eroico* (1594), trans. by Mariella Cavalchini and Irene Samuel, and the "Allegoria" to the *Gerusalemme liberata*, trans. by Fairfax (1600) and recently into prose by Ralph Nash (1987), have thus far been translated in entirety into English. Bernard Weinberg's indispensable two-volume *A History of Literary Criticism in the Italian Renaissance* and Aguzzi's valuable dissertation, *Allegory in the Heroic Poetry of the Renaissance*, give short extracts, sometimes with translations, from a number of Tasso's other prose works. I have quoted from Cavalchini's and Samuel's trans. of the *Discorsi*

del poema eroico, Fairfax's trans. of the "Allegoria" (in Morley's ed.) and, where possible, translations by Aguzzi and Weinberg of passages from other prose writings of Tasso, acknowledgements of the latter two scholars being made in each individual instance. I have quoted Tasso's "Allegoria" to the *Gerusalemme liberata* in the Elizabethan trans. of Fairfax rather than in a modern English version because Fairfax has retained very literally both the sense of Tasso and his characteristic vocabulary, which can be technically important. Other than as indicated above, translations from Tasso are my own, including those of all the passages quoted from the Letters. Where I have closely paraphrased passages of Tasso in my text, I have sometimes given only the Italian originals in my notes, without a running trans. into English. When quoting from the English translations of the *Discorsi del poema eroico* and the "Allegoria", I have not attempted always to give running Italian equivalents, since both the originals and the English are readily accessible in modern eds. Throughout my text and footnotes I refer to Tasso's *Discorsi del poema eroico* and his "Allegoria" always under their Italian titles; however, when I quote in English from these works, the page numbers in my notes refer to the translations in the eds. of Cavalchini and Samuel and of Fairfax. When quoting passages in Ital., in parallel to Eng. translations, from texts of Tasso other than these two, I give parallel references for the English translations (if not my own) and to the Italian originals in Mauro's or other eds. Italics in English and Italian quotations from Tasso's prose normally represent my own emphases.

2. Letter 79, *Lettere,* vol. 1, p. 186: "Dice ben egli ne la Poetica un non so che d'allegoria, ma intende per allegoria la metafora continuata . . . non è quella di cui parliamo". Aristotle, Tasso says, makes no mention at all of allegory in the *Poetics* or other works—unless (he adds enigmatically) one were to understand allegory as being *"in the nature of things"* ("che s'ella non fosse *in rerum natura*"). Aguzzi (p. 511) rightly considers this to be a highly significant remark: "Tasso feels that Aristotle approved of allegory provided that it is conceived as a message of universal value, or as moral philosophy intrinsic to the matter treated by the poet".

3. See [*Discourses on the Heroic Poem*] *Discorsi del poema eroico,* Bk V, pp. 150-54. Tasso here cites Porphyry, Plutarch and older classical allegorizers; his mention of the first two is significant, since each provided a model of continuous moral allegorization on an extended narrative episode. In Letters 48 and 79 (*Lettere,* vol. 1, pp. 116 and 188), Tasso, defending his own epic intentions, cites Proclus and Plutarch, both early allegorizers explicating in a continuous mode; he cites as well Augustine and Ficino. See my chap. 5, n. 27.

4. See Letter 79, *Lettere,* vol. 1, p. 188.

5. *Discorsi del poema eroico,* Bk V, pp. 151-52.

6. Aguzzi's dissertation offers a valuable guide to the entire moral-allegorical tradition in epic in the early and later Renaissance. I have made use of his survey in the first part of the present section.

7. "Heroic Virtue": deriving from Aristotle's "Superhuman Virtue, or goodness on a heroic or divine scale". See *Aristotle: The Nicomachean Ethics,* trans. by H. Rackham, Bk VII.1, p. 375. In the Renaissance commentaries and epics the phrase, "Heroic Virtue", was almost a cliché; iconographically it was often represented by Hercules or the christianized Hercules. Tasso defines "the very highest virtue" and "persons . . . as heroic as virtue is" as the proper matter of epic in the *Discorsi del poema eroico,* Bk II (p. 44). The phrase is constantly used in Spenser's *FQ,* the concept being personified in Prince Arthur and epitomized in Guyon's trials in the Cave of Mammon; and the same phrase echoes (sometimes ironically) throughout *PL* and also *PR.* Tasso wrote a discourse on *Della Virtù Eroica e della Carità.* On the Renaissance tradition of Heroic Virtue, see Frank Kermode, "The Cave of Mammon".

8. *Phronesis* is discussed in Bk VI.v-xiii of *The Nicomachean Ethics. Sophrosyne* as "temperance" is discussed by Plato in the *Charmides.*

9. Tasso intelligently discusses Dante's four "levels" of allegory in *Discorsi del poema eroico,* Bk V, p. 153, perceiving that Dante's third and fourth "levels" are widely defined.

10. *Apology,* p. 101.

11. *Discorsi del poema eroico*, Bk I, pp. 14, 17; p. 10. Cf. Weinberg's summary of these arguments, vol. 1, pp. 339-40.

12. Letter 79, *Lettere*, vol. 1, p. 186: "nel libro de la mente".

13. Murrin points to some of the treatises of Flaminio Nobili as the immediate sources of Tasso's ethical allegory. These were: *De hominis felicitate; De vera et falsa voluptate;* and *De honore;* publ. together (1563). See *The Allegorical Epic*, chap. 4, pp. 112 and 115, and p. 236, nn. 31, 32 and 33 for details. Tasso is on the whole more Platonic than Aristotelian in his ethical *schema*. Murrin cites as evidence of Tasso's Platonism his marginal notations to Nobili's treatises. Tasso's Platonic leaning is also apparent in his remarks in his own letters concerning his anxiety to reconcile Plato with Aristotle, and in the heavily Platonic psychology sketched out in the "Allegoria". Murrin notes (p. 93; p. 235, n.18) that Tasso in 1567-70, well before the second more allegorical stage of composition of the *Gerusalemme*, had himself given academy lectures which were exercises in Neoplatonic ethical allegorization.

14. Letter 76, *Lettere*, vol. 1, p. 179: "Vi vedrete maneggiata, e volta e rivolta gran parte de la moral filosofia così platonica come peripatetica, ed anco de la scienza de l'anima". Letter 79, *Lettere*, vol. 1, pp. 187-88: "la dottrina morale de la quale io mi son servito ne l'allegoria, è tutta sua [Plato's]; ma in guisa è sua, ch'insieme è d'Aristotele: ed io mi sono sforzato d'accoppiare l'uno e l'altro vero, in modo che ne riesca consonanza fra le opinioni. . . . Io crederei accopiando Platone con Aristotele di fare una nuova mistura".

15. On the Platonic hierarchy of powers in the soul, see also *Discorsi del poema eroico*, Bk II, p. 47. On p. 44 Tasso cites the epic hero's "prudence" (*phronesis:* Aristotle's master virtue).

16. Extracts which follow are from "Allegoria", *Jerusalem Delivered*, pp. 436-43.

17. Fairfax's translation is loose in this case, picking up and using again the word "compound" from the line which follows (*Jerusalem Delivered*, pp. 436-37), whereas Tasso had used "double" (*doppia*) the first time, to refer to the two kinds of allegory (contemplative, and moral or practical) mentioned earlier. (See for the Ital. words quoted in my text, the "Allegoria del poema", in *Le Opere*, ed. Giuseppe Mauro, vol. 1, fo. A₂). He also uses "Life" here specifically with reference to man's inward or mental life, not to man's outward circumstances.

18. Cf. also, on Rinaldo's activities, Letter 48, *Lettere*, vol. 1, p. 116.

19. Cf. Murrin, *The Allegorical Epic*, p. 88: "Tasso . . . returns us to the problem of continuous allegory"; he "aligns his poem with works like the *Divina commedia* and the Vulgate *Queste del saint graal*, which demanded from their readers a symbolic interpretation throughout". It may be apposite to add that Tasso aligns his work also with the more contemporary tradition of sustained moral exegesis on classical and Renaissance epic (as cited by himself, along with Dante's poem).

20. Cf. Murrin, *The Allegorical Epic*, p. 88: the idea of an *entire story* as continued allegory is "the other side, the radical nature of Tasso's experiment. It . . . presents the *entire plot* as allegorical". This radical experiment Murrin however declines to explore, taking up instead the complementary question of allegorical "Episodes" in Tasso, in which he finds a different sort of "continued metaphor", a thematic continuity. The example which he chooses is Tasso's magical wood: "I . . . explain a single, magical place: the wood near Jerusalem possessed by demons. . . . Tasso's . . . characters return there again and again, and its signification grows over thirteen Cantos". Tasso's *thematic* treatment of the episode of the Wood thus is said to demonstrate "the differences between continuous and discontinuous allegory". Rather, I would suggest, Tasso's thematic treatment of the Wood offers a demonstration of only one kind of "continued allegory" in the poem.

21. On Prudentius' *Psychomachia* (c. 400 A.D.), see Lamberton, pp. 145-48.

22. C.S. Lewis, *The Allegory of Love: A Study in Medieval Tradition*, p. 334.

23. In *The Allegorical Epic*, chap. 4.

24. Letter 84 indicates that Tasso is, somewhat disingenuously, debating a little with the views of Flaminio Nobili, whose ethical treatise Tasso's correspondent (Luca Scalabrino) had been invoking. To abridge the relevant passage: Tasso (he is being polite) "likes what [F.N.] in

general has to say about Epic allegory"—indeed, it is better than Tasso's own views; still, Tasso *could* have proved his own case with good authority and via "what others have found in Homer or Virgil" (*viz.*, the Landino tradition of the moral growth of an epic character or characters, seen throughout a continued main-plot allegory, and as illustrated,Tasso says, by Maximus of Tyre). Tasso doesn't see "why it is not possible to make [his proposed] allegory more detailed than Nobili's views would permit, and to seek an allegorical sense in the non-fabulous parts also"—since so many interpreters (i.e. the allegorizers) of Homer and Virgil look for allegory in such parts. Tasso had, in this connection, found his own idea of Rinaldo as the concupiscent power very appropriate.

Murrin himself notes, in the table of dates given in *The Allegorical Epic*, pp. 90-91, Tasso's disagreement in this letter with Nobili but seems to pass over it, although the point is crucially involved in Murrin's claim that Tasso fell upon the "solution" of episode allegory for "meta-fora continuata" in his poem from reading Nobili. The Ital. in Letter 84 (*Lettere*, vol. 1, pp. 206-7) reads in full: "più mi piace quel ch'egli [F.N.] dice in generale de l'allegoria del poema epico, che quello ch'io n'avea scritto; sebbene la mia opinione si potea difendere con alcune ragioni, e con l'autorità di Massimo Tirio filosofo platonico nel sermone XVI; ma in somma, quello ch'egli scrive mi par più reale. È ben vero ch'io non veggio perchè non si possa particolareggiare l'allegoria alquanto più che non fa egli, e cercar anche il senso allegorico ne le parti ancora non favolose, poichè ne le parti ancora non favolose molti il vanno cercando in Virgilio ed in Omero; e particolarmente a me pareva che la persona di Rinaldo fosse ben espressa per la potenza concupiscibile".

25. Murrin in *The Allegorical Epic*, chap. 4, pp. 87-107 and associated nn., and the table summarizing Tasso's relevant statements in the Letters of April through July, 1575, takes up in some detail the question of the dates and contents of some of the Tasso Letters which I also discuss in my chap. 5, sect. "Lettere poetiche", in connection with Tasso's formulation of his "Allegoria" for the *Gerusalemme*. Murrin in his text discusses some of the issues raised especially by Letters 75 (22 May, 1576, to Scipione Gonzaga); 79 (June 15, 1576, to Gonzaga); 84 (29 July, 1576, to Luca Scalabrino); and one other to Scalabrino. I had myself noted pertinent material especially in Letter 79, as well as in Letters 48, 56 and 76 (4 October, 1575, to Gonzaga; 5 March, 1576, to Gonzaga; Letter, n.d.: May or June?, 1576, to Scalabrino). My own investiga-tions proceeded independently around the same time as Murrin's; our convergences and differences are indicated in my text and notes. Aguzzi's work (1959) on Tasso's Letters and "Allegoria" precedes both Murrin's work and my own, as far as studies in English are concerned.

26. Letter 76, *Lettere*, vol. 1, p. 179: "ho disteso . . . l'Allegoria non d'una parte ma di tutto il poema . . . non v'è nè azione nè persona principale che, secondo questo nuovo trovato, non contenga maravigliosi misteri. . . . tutte le parti de l'allegoria son in guisa legate fra loro, ed in maniera corrispondono al senso litterale del poema, ed anco a'miei principii poetici". Note that there may be a confusion over Tasso's use of "maravigliosi misteri" here, since he occasionally uses "marvellous mysteries" in the old sense to mean "hidden truths" (as I think he does here); whereas at other times he is thinking specifically of allegory in fabulous episodes.

27. Letter 79, *Lettere*, vol. 1, p. 189: "Io non credo che sia necessario che l'allegoria corrisponda in ogni particella al senso litterale". Cf. Letter 48 when, citing Ficino as his authority, Tasso asserts that not every single part of the woods or of the wanderings of Rinaldo in the *Gerusalemme* need necessarily contain allegory: "Since perhaps it will appear to some persons that every detail of the wood or the wanderings of Rinaldo [necessarily must] contain allegory, I here cite some words of Ficino on the *Convivio*" ("Ma perchè parrà forse ad alcuno di veder che ogni particella del bosco o de gli errori di Rinaldo contenga allegoria, sottoscriverò qui alcune parole del Ficino sovra'l Convivio"). *Lettere*, vol. 1, p. 115. As Gordon Teskey has called to my attention, Ficino is himself citing Augustine, [*De Civitate Dei*] *The City of God*, the end of Bk XVI.ii (elsewhere, Tasso cites the Augustine passage directly; see my chap. 7, n. 38). Augustine says: "Of course one must not assume that all the events narrated

are symbolic, but those that lack such significance are interwoven in the interest of such as do possess it. It is only the ploughshare that furrows the earth, but to enable it to do this you must have the other parts of the plough also. . . . So also in prophetic history ["prophetica historia", i.e. "types"] some details are included that have no significance in themselves but are closely related to significant matters and are, so to speak, bound up with them". *The City of God Against the Pagans*, trans. Eva Matthews Sanford and William McAllen Green, vol. 5, pp. 14-15.

28. Murrin (*The Allegorical Epic*, pp. 96 ff.; see also my chap. 5, nn. 13 and 24) rightly calls attention to the important part played by Nobili in helping Tasso to formulate the Platonic ethical-psychological basis of his allegory. But the further suggestion that Nobili gave Tasso the solution to the structural problems involved seems to me less convincing: "What we still miss was later suggested to Tasso by Flaminio Nobili: *the equation of allegory with the fabulous or nonhistorical parts of a poem*" (p. 96; italics mine). If Murrin means, as his discussion indicates, that allegory is to be confined to marvellous episodes, then it is not the case that even in the Letters Tasso ever accepted such a restricted view of the place of allegory in his epic. His exposition in the "Allegoria" definitely focuses on main-plot allegory, although the marvellous episodes are also woven into his larger allegorical scheme.

29. Letter 84, *Lettere*, vol. 1, p. 207. The relevant statement runs as ff. (see my chap. 5, n. 24, for the full quotation in the Ital.): "I don't see why it is not possible to make the allegory rather more specific than he [Nobili] does, and to devise allegorical meaning in the non-fabulous parts as well—since many [commentators] look for [such allegory] in the non-fabulous parts, too, of Virgil and Homer".

30. Letter 84, *Lettere*, vol. 1, p. 207 (see my chap. 5, n. 24, for the full quotation in Ital.): "it seemed to me particularly that the figure of Rinaldo would be well expressed in terms of the concupiscent faculty". (Does Tasso here mistakenly identify the ireful role of Rinaldo with the concupiscent role of Tancredi, as later described in the "Allegoria"?)

31. Letter 56, *Lettere*, vol. 1, p. 130: "not only have I adjusted, according to my taste, all that pertains to the fiction, but I have also improved many things concerning the allegory. . . . And for this reason I wish to remove the battle of the monster from the fifteenth [Canto] because, in short, this monster had become superfluous in the allegory". In the Ital.: "non solo ho accomodato a mio gusto tutto ciò c'apparteneva a la favola, ma ancora migliorate molte cose che riguardavano l'allegoria. . . . E per questo desidero di rimovere dal decimoquinto la battaglia del mostro, perche'in somma quel mostro era affatto ozioso ne l'allegoria". For more detailed consideration of Tasso's physical alterations to the poem, see Lawrence L. Rhu, "From Aristotle to Allegory: Young Tasso's Evolving Vision of the *Gerusalemme Liberata*", and other literature as cited in App. A, pt. I.

32. Letter 56, *Lettere*, vol. 1, p. 131: "This fountain and this lake are wonderfully useful to me for the allegory" ("questa fonte e questo lago mi servono mirabilmente a l'allegoria").

33. Letter 48, *Lettere*, vol. 1, pp. 114-15: "my marvellous episodes of the wood".

34. Letter 56, *Lettere*, vol. 1, p. 130. After speaking of removing the "battle of the monster", Tasso continues, saying that for "other reasons", and in compliance with the judgement of one of his critics (or readers perhaps), he will diminish or reduce the marvels, presumably, in that Canto; ("iscemare i mirabili"—*iscemare* apparently is an archaic form of *scemare*, to diminish).

35. See Letter 79, *Lettere*, vol. 1, p. 186, where Tasso is critical of random allegorization (as by the fashionable commentators on the *Orlando Furioso*): "each interpreter allegorizes on his own, according to his whim" ("ciascuno de gli interpreti suole dar l'allegoria a suo capriccio").

36. *Del Giudizio sovra la Gerusalemme di Torquato Tasso* (written 1595; 1666), *Opere*, vol. 4, p. 318. This passage is discussed in my chap. 7, sect. "History and Allegory" (see chap. 7, n. 39 for the Ital.).

Chapter 6. Tasso, the *Discorsi*: Aesthetics of the Allegorical Epic

1. "Allegoria", *Jerusalem Delivered*, p. 436.
2. *Discorsi del poema eroico*, Bk II, pp. 31-32. Cf. Sidney, as discussed earlier in my chap. 4, sect. "Sidney". Shepherd conjectures that Sidney's *Apology* (publ. 1595) was written after 1580, perhaps 1581-83 (Introd. to *Apology*, p. 4). Tasso began to revise the earlier into the later *Discorsi* after 1587; however, the famous passage on the poet as "Maker" creating a "little world", similarly the passages on unity-in-variety (Bk III, pp. 77-78), occur also in Tasso's earlier version of the treatise, the *Discorsi dell'arte poetica*; see *Discorsi dell'arte poetica e del poema eroico*, ed. Luigi Poma, "Discorso secondo", pp. 36-37.
3. *Discorsi del poema eroico*, Bk III, p. 78.
4. *Giudizio*, *Opere*, vol. 4, p. 335: "Questo è il fine dell'allegorie, col quale, disvelandosi nell'eterna luce del cielo, l'ombre delle figure, deono tutte cessare, e illustrarsi perpetuamente".
5. *Discorsi del poema eroico*, Bk V, pp. 151-52.
6. Cf. the remarks on medieval theory of *symbolum* in my chap. 2, sect. "Coluccio Salutati"; also see chap. 2, n. 2, for the medieval theories on *symbolum*, as outlined by Dronke.
7. Cf. Aguzzi, as quoted in my chap. 2, n. 9.
8. Aguzzi, p. 490. See Aguzzi's summary (pp. 490-98) of the moral-allegorical values of each of the various cantos of the *Rinaldo*. As he notes, there are not many directly allegorical episodes or personifications in this early epic.
9. "Allegoria del Rinaldo", *Opere*, vol. 4, p. 491; in the Ital.: "in Rinaldo, . . . si scopre, che l'emulazione è un grande stimolo a far che l'animo generoso si muova ad operar virtuosamente. Nell'innamorarsi poi di Clarice, . . . ci scopre, quanto siamo facili ad accenderci nelle fiamme d'Amore, le quali accese ci fanno poi operare virtuosamente, per piacere alla cosa amata".
10. *Discorsi del poema eroico*, Bk I, p. 5. Cf. "Discorso primo", *Discorsi dell'arte poetica*, p. 12: "The epic genre on the other hand requires in its persons . . . the highest pitch of the virtues, which are denominated as heroic, under Heroic Virtue. In Aeneas one finds the excellence of piety, in Achilles of military fortitude, in Ulysses of prudence, or, to come to our own times, of loyalty in Amadigi, of constancy in Bradamante. Indeed, in certain of these [characters one discovers] the sum of all these virtues". In the Ital.: "L'epico all'incontra vuole nelle persone il sommo delle virtù, le quali eroiche dalla virtù eroica sono nominate. Si ritrova in Enea l'eccellenza della pietà, della fortezza militare in Achille, della prudenza in Ulisse, e, per venire a i nostri, della lealtà in Amadigi, della constanza in Bradamante; anzi pure in alcuni di questi il cumulo di tutte queste virtù".
11. *Discorsi del poema eroico*, Bk III, p. 85.
12. Ibid., p. 78.
13. Cf. the passage in *Discorsi del poema eroico*, Bk III, p. 85, as quoted in my chap. 7, n. 3.
14. *Discoursi del poema eroico*. Ibid., Bk II, pp. 31-32.
15. Ibid., Bk V, p. 170.
16. *Giudizio*, *Opere*, vol. 4, p. 335. Aguzzi too (pp. 526-27 and n. 2) cites this passage; but I find that his free paraphrase of the Italian does not bring out the important nuance. The Ital. runs: "Laonde . . . le parole, che si distruggono nella superficie, deono essere intese profondamente: e in questa guisa sovra i fondamenti dell' istoria conviene fabbricar coll' allegoria una fabbrica intellettuale, o della mente, che vogliam dirla".
17. *Discorsi del poema eroico*, Bk III, p. 78. (In place of Samuel's and Cavalchini's "nonetheless" for *nondimeno*, I have translated "no less".)
18. But cf. Rhu, "From Aristotle to Allegory", p. 116, referring to the earlier *Discorsi*: "young Tasso's . . . [Aristotelian-based concept of] universal verisimilitude, which may seem to invite assimilation to allegorical composition and interpretation, [is] to a significant extent developed in terms that resist such a merger". Rhu is drawn toward yet not wholly converted

to the notion of a consistently developing allegorical poetic in Tasso's writings; nevertheless he thinks that Tasso's actual revisions to his poem do support the case for allegory.

19. In *Discorsi del poema eroico*, Bk II, p. 54, Tasso had expressed the conventional view, deriving from Aristotle's view of tragedy in the *Poetics*, chap. 6, that plot is the soul of the epic.

20. "Allegoria", *Jerusalem Delivered*, p. 436.

21. See Letter 48, *Lettere*, vol. 1, p. 115, where Tasso fudges the question, saying that allegory, being "an accessory perfection, cannot outweigh defects of imitation" ("l'allegoria, essendo perfezione accidentale, non possa contrapesare i difetti de la imitazione"). Again, in Letter 56 (*Lettere*, vol. 1, p. 130) the poet says that he has tried to improve many things concerning *both* the fable *and* the allegory (which seems fair enough). A somewhat different inflection occurs in Letter 79 (*Lettere*, vol. 1, p. 187): if the poet has "said anything unconformable with what is right, or with the nature of allegory or of imitation, [he] will gladly be corrected" ("S'avrò detto cosa non conforme a la ragione, o a la natura de l'allegoria e de l'imitazione, volontier son per ridirmi"). Large sections of the *Discorsi del poema eroico*, Bk III, also are concerned with propriety of external representation.

22. The excellent phrase, "a kind of truth", is from Weinberg's synopsis in vol. 1, p. 602. The longer passage is quoted in Weinberg's trans., vol. 2, pp. 1014-15 (italics mine), from the *Discorso sopra il Parere fatto dal Sig. Francesco Patricio [Patrizi]* (1585). In the Ital. (*Opere*, vol. 3, p. 164): "i principi d'Aristotile. . . . sono ancora veri in quel modo, che possono esser veri in un'arte, che insegni il verisimile; perciocchè la poetica [*poetica*: can be rendered also as *poetry*] non è arte, in cui s'apprenda a distinguere il vero dal falso, come nella dialettica: ma da lei impariamo ad imitarlo".

23. See *Discorsi del poema eroico*, Bk I, p. 19.

24. *Apologia* (1585). In the Ital., *Opere*, vol. 2, p. 300: "*For[estiero]* Dunque il poeta non guasta la verità, ma la ricerca perfetta, supponendo in luogo della verità de i particolari quella degli universali; i quali sono idee. *Segr[etario]* Così dobbiamo credere de' filosofi divini. *For[estiero]* E de' poeti parimente, i quali nella considerazione dell'idee sono filosofi".

25. *Discorsi del poema eroico*, Bk III, p. 58.

26. Ibid., p. 61.

27. Cf. the argument throughout *Discorsi del poema eroico*, Bk II, where Tasso, using the touchstones of the *"apparent-probable"* or "credible", is arguing against Mazzoni and seemingly for an Aristotelian type of verisimilitude: "since the poet, in Aristotle's phrase, imitates things either as they are or as they may be or as they are reputed or believed to be, the principal subject of the poet is what is, or may be, or is believed, or is told; or all these together, as Aristotle held. . . . constitute the adequate subject of poetry" (pp. 30-31). But everywhere, Tasso soon circles back to his own peculiar definition of verisimilitude, which is distanced from *external* probability. E.g.: "The probable *insofar as it is verisimilar* belongs to the poet" (p. 29). Tasso's characteristic method of argument is to put an apparently conventional position, using conventional terminology, and then progressively to shift the meaning away from the conventional by changing the content of the terms according to his preferred understanding of them. The Neo-Aristotelian arguments of Castelvetro and the more radically opposed standpoint of Mazzoni, representing respectively the twin extremes in the intricate late C16th debates between which Tasso was caught, are outlined in my chap. 9, sect. "The Late Sixteenth-Century Italian Debates".

28. See again, Tasso's reply to Patrizi, as quoted in my chap. 6, n. 22.

29. See *Giudizio*, *Opere*, vol. 4, p. 318: as quoted in my chap. 7, n. 39.

30. See *Riposta . . . Al . . . Oratio Lombardelli* (1586), p. 18; my trans. is slightly modified from Weinberg's in his vol. 1, p. 629. In the Ital. (using Weinberg's transcription from the original ed. of 1586; see his vol. 1, p. 629, n.116): "Cosi per aventura tutta l'attione non dee esser vera, ma lasciarsi la sua parte al verisimile, il quale è proprio del poema".

Chapter 7. Tasso, the Major Tracts: The Poetics of the Allegorical Epic

1. *Delle differenze poetiche* (1587), in *Le Prose Diverse*, ed. Cesare Guasti, vol. 1, p. 440; the passage is quoted in full in my chap. 7 and n. 4.

2. *Discorsi del poema eroico*, Bk III, p. 78; p. 85.

3. Ibid., p. 85: "We have discussed diversity long enough, showing how it may be increased with episodes, and how they are to be introduced according to either verisimilitude or necessity lest the fable become episodic".

4. *Delle differenze poetiche*, *Prose Diverse*, vol. 1, p. 440. In the Ital.: "E non facendo la natura cosa alcuna per episodio nell'universo; il qual è così grande e così adorno di tutte le specie e di tutte le bellezze, l'arte vorrebbe anch'ella dimostrare a prova le sue ricchezze e gli ornamenti, e ridurre tutte le parti del poema sott'ordine quasi certo, e dare a ciascuna disposizione e dependanza necessaria; ma non potendo pervenir a tanta perfezione, fa verisimilmente alcuna volta quel che non l'è conceduto di fare necessariamente".

5. *Discorsi del poema eroico*, Bk II, p. 36.

6. Letter 87, *Lettere*, vol. 1, p. 214: "Io credetti un tempo che fosse in poema epico l'unità di molti più perfetta che quella d'uno. . . . Questo credo bene più che mai fermamente, che sia quasi impossibile il fare a questi dì poema de l'azion d'un solo cavaliero, che diletti: e credo anco, c'avendosi a tesir l'azion una di molti in uno".

7. Here cf. Weinberg's analysis, vol. 1, pp. 570-71.

8. *Estratti dalla Poetica di Lodovico Castelvetro* (c. 1576; publ. 1875), as trans. by Weinberg, vol. 1, p. 571. In the Ital., *Prose Diverse*, vol. 1, p. 284: "La imitazione richiesta a la poesia . . . si può appellare gareggiamento del poeta e della disposizione della fortuna, o del corso delle mondane cose".

9. *Discorsi del poema eroico*, Bk III, p. 58.

10. Ibid., Bk I. After discussing whether "wonder" is not an effect also of tragedy or other genres, Tasso concludes: "All the same, to move wonder fits no kind of poetry so much as epic" (pp. 15-16).

11. *Discorsi del poema eroico*, Bk I, p. 17, gives Tasso's summary of the epic style and purpose: "We shall say then that the epic poem is an imitation of a noble action, great and perfect, narrated in the loftiest verse, with the purpose of *moving the mind to wonder and thus being useful*".

12. Ibid., Bk II, p. 26.

13. Ibid., pp. 37-38.

14. Murrin's excellent perception in *The Allegorical Epic*, p. 119. Surely Spenser drew his inspiration for the amplified figure of his own Wood of Error in *FQ* I.i and the related figure of the Wandering Isles in II.xii from Tasso? The allegory is of course as old as Dante's "selva oscura" at the opening of the *Commedia* or older, and Tasso invokes it when referring to the early C15th Italian humanist, Francesco Robortello, in *Discorsi del poema eroico*, Bk II, p. 36 (the allusion is to the golden bough of Wisdom, to be brought back from the gloomy grottoes of Proserpina's underworld).

15. *Discorsi del poema eroico*, Bk II, p. 37: "Let us conclude, then, that no poem is to be praised that is excessively full of prodigies, but that sorcerers and necromancers may be introduced with a degree of verisimilitude".

16. *Giudizio, Opere*, vol. 4, p. 306; in the Ital.: "io, nella riforma della mia favola, cercai di farla più simile al vero, che non era prima, conformandomi in molte cose coll'istorie, ed aggiunsi all'istoria l'allegoria, in modo che . . . nel poema non si lascia parte alcuna alla vanità, riempiendo ciascuna di esse, e le piccolissime ancora, e meno apparenti, di sensi occulti, e misteriosi".

17. Ibid., p. 342: "I, having treated it in a poetical manner, and having sought the marvellous through an excess of truth" ("avendole io trattate con maniera poetica, e coll' eccesso della verità ricercata la maraviglia"). Cf. earlier, p. 306: "in certain parts of the fiction I

sought to strengthen the marvellous with an excess of truth" ("in alcune parti della favola cercassi indur la maraviglia coll'eccesso della verità").

18. *Discorsi del poema eroico*, Bk II, p. 38. Cf. *Riposta . . . Al . . . Lombardelli*, pp. 14-15, Weinberg's trans., vol. 1, pp. 629-30: "The poem reaches the highest degree of perfection when these two things [the marvelous and verisimilitude] are joined together, and they may be conjoined in various ways". In the Ital. (Weinberg's transcription from the original, vol. 1, p. 630, n. 118): "all'hora il poema è nella somma perfettione, che queste cose insieme s'accoppiano, e si possono in piu modi congiungere".

19. See the argument in *Discorsi del poema eroico*, Bk II, pp. 36-37 and 37-38.

20. Castelvetro's arguments are discussed in more detail in my chap. 9, sect. "The Late Sixteenth-Century Italian Debates".

21. From Weinberg's synopsis, vol. 1, p. 629.

22. *Risposta . . . Al . . . Lombardelli*, p. 18, in Weinbertg's trans., vol. 1, p. 629. In Ital. (Weinberg's transcription from the original, in his vol. 1, p. 629, n.116): "tutti i poemi habbiano qualche fondamento della verità, chi piu, e chi meno, secondo che piu, e meno participano della perfettione; dee nondimeno haversi avertenza, che si come tutta la fabrica non è fondamento, cosi per aventura tutta l'attione non dee esser vera, ma lasciarsi la sua parte al verisimile, il quale è proprio del poema".

23. *Discorsi del poema eroico*, Bk II, pp. 25-26.

24. Ibid., pp. 43, 51.

25. Ibid., p. 47.

26. Ibid., p. 49.

27. Ibid., pp. 26, 54.

28. Ibid., pp. 34, 39.

29. Ibid., p. 39.

30. Ibid., pp. 54-55.

31. Ibid., pp. 52-53.

32. Ibid., pp. 40-41.

33. Ibid., pp. 26, 27.

34. Ibid., pp. 39-40. The translations, "ecclesiastical" and "spiritual" [*ecclesiastiche* and *spirituale*], are literal: defined as to do with the Church, here possibly to do with doctrines of the Church or perhaps sacerdotal matters.

35. *Giudizio*, speaking of his own poem (*Opere*, vol. 4, p. 341): "As has been already said, the beginning and the end of the fable [should bear] a greater resemblance to truth. And more so, the beginning". ("Già s'è detto, che il principio, ed il fine della favola è più somigliante al vero. E' più somigliante il principio".)

36. Ibid., p. 306. In the Ital.: "Io in quel che appartiene alla mistione del vero col falso, estimo, che il vero debba aver la maggior parte, sì perchè vero dee esser il principio, il quale è il mezzo del tutto; sì per la verità del fine, al quale tutte le cose sono dirizzate: e dove è vero il principio, ed il fine della narrazione, il falso può essere ascoso agevolmente nelle parti di mezzo, e frapposto, ed inserito con gli episodi".

37. *Giudizio*, Weinberg's trans., vol. 2, p. 1056. In the Ital., *Opere*, vol. 4, p. 342: "se le cose vere fossero da me narrate con modo istorico, non meriterei laude alcuna di poeta, ma avendole io trattate con maniera poetica, e coll'eccesso della verità ricercata la maraviglia, in quelle cose, nelle quali ho più conservata l'immagine dell'istoria, e quasi l'aspetto della verità, in quell'istesse ho meritata maggior lode di mirabile artificio poetico".

38. *Giudizio*, *Opere*, vol. 4, p. 306. In the Ital.: "noi abbiam già detto, coll'autorità di S. Agostino nella città di Dio, non esser falso, nè vano quel che significa; laonde l'allegoria co'sensi occulti delle cose significate può difendere il poeta dalla vanità, e dalla falsità similmente. Per questa ragione io, nella riforma della mia favola, cercai di farla più simile al vero, che non era prima, conformandomi in molte cose coll'istorie, ed aggiunsi all'istoria l'allegoria, in modo che siccome nel mondo, e nella natura delle cose non si lascia alcun luogo al vacuo, così nel poema non si lascia parte alcuna alla vanità, riempiendo ciascuna di esse, e le

piccolissime ancora, e meno apparenti, di sensi occulti, e misteriosi; e benchè negli episodi, ed in alcune parti della favola cercassi indur la maraviglia coll'eccesso della verità, in ciò mi parve di adempire quel ch'è proprio offizio del poeta e dell'arte poetica".

39. *Giudizio*, Weinberg's trans., vol. 2, p. 1057. In the Ital., *Opere*, vol. 4, p. 318: "Io mi servo più dell'allegoria in quelle parti del mio poema, ove più mi sono allontanato dall'istoria, estimando, che dove cessa il senso letterale, debba supplire l'allegorico, e gli altri sensi; nondimeno ho avuto risguardo di non usare allegoria, che paia sconvenevole nella figura, e nell'apparenza". Taken on their own, these lines might suggest a diminishment of allegory in the revised *Conquistata*. However, Tasso's enthusiasm for his revisions as *heightening* the allegory and filling the smallest details with allegory (see *Giudizio*, as quoted in my chap. 7, n. 38) makes such an interpretation impossible.

Chapter 8. Spenser as Allegorical Theorist

1. See *Allegorical Imagery*, pp. 126-27.

2. C.S. Lewis, p. 334: "We shall find that it is Spenser's method to have in each book an allegorical core, surrounded by a margin of what is called 'romance of types', and relieved by episodes of pure fantasy".

3. On Harington's uses of earlier allegorizers from the C16th Ital. eds. of Ariosto of 1549 to 1584, see *Ludovico Ariosto's Orlando Furioso*, ed. McNulty, pp. xxv-xli; also my chap. 3, sect. "John Harington", and associated nn. Fornari is quoted in my chap. 16, sect. "Raphael's Theory of Discourse".

4. On continuous moral allegory in Spenser and the Landino tradition, see Merritt Hughes, *Virgil and Spenser* (esp. pp. 399-406), cited also in *The Works of Edmund Spenser: A Variorum Edition*, ed. Edwin Greenlaw *et al.*, vol. [1], *The Faerie Queene*, Appendix I, "The Plan and Conduct of the *Faerie Queene*", pp. 357-59. On this matter and on the relationship of Italian theory and practice, especially Tasso's, to Spenser, see also Aguzzi's study. The importance of Tasso in Elizabethan England and to Spenser is discussed in my App. C.

5. See App. C, pt. II. On the possible influence of Tasso's "Poetical Letters" on Spenser, see also my chap. 8, n. 8.

6. See "Letter to Raleigh", vol. 2, p. 485, of *Spenser's Faerie Queene*.

7. See Kathleen M. Lea and T.M. Gang, eds., *Godfrey of Bulloigne: A Critical Edition of Edward Fairfax's translation of Tasso's Gerusalemme Liberata*, p. 28.

8. Certain of the remarks in Spenser's "Letter to Raleigh" evoke echoes of the problems explored in Tasso's Letters. For instance, both poets confront the question of sustained narrative-allegorical metaphor, which has yet sometimes to be intermitted. Spenser (*Spenser's Faerie Queene*, vol. 2, pp. 487, 485) speaks of "many other adventures . . . intermedled, but rather as Accidents, then intendments" in his "continued Allegory, or darke conceit", while Tasso, having said in Letter 76 that *everything* in his poem is allegorical, qualifies in Letter 79, saying that some incidents must be regarded only as neutral, necessary links in the plot. In Letter 56 Tasso writes at great length of the allegorical suitability of his "Fountain of Mirth", which is the most extensive passage borrowed by Spenser from Tasso. Spenser's allegory upon the borrowed passage as reset in *FQ* II.xii closely resembles Tasso's, and Tasso's Letter on the matter (see my chap. 5, n. 32), if read by Spenser, would have drawn Spenser's attention to the allegorical potential of the passage. Lastly, since we may assume that the *Discorsi del poema eroico* in its earlier version was known in England by the time of *FQ*, then the most important of his Letters may have been known too; for the earlier version of this treatise, the *Discorsi dell'arte poetica*, was printed together with Tasso's "Lettere poetiche" in the ed. publ. in Venice, 1587.

9. Some of the most cogent writing on Renaissance allegory is to be found in books on Spenser's allegory. Steadman in *The Lamb and the Elephant* (pp. 98-99, n.3) gives a list of studies on medieval and Renaissance allegory, including a number of recent books on Spenser, and there have since been a number of important critical allegorical readings which include

Spenser, for example Murrin's two books, *The Veil of Allegory* and *The Allegorical Epic*, and Maureen Quilligan's two books, *The Language of Allegory: Defining the Genre* and *Milton's Spenser: The Politics of Reading*. I am not aware of any study which as specifically as Merritt Hughes' older study brings to the forefront Spenser's affiliation with the Virgil-Landino-Tasso ethical-allegorical tradition.

10. The relationship between Spenser's two principal statements, as illustrative of, respectively, in the "Letter to Raleigh" Spenser's *icastic* approach to art, and in the "Proem" to *FQ* III the *phantastic*, was addressed by Gordon Teskey in his paper, "Information and Disorder: The Proem to *Faerie Queene* III", given at the Modern Language Association of American Convention, 1985. The argument of this paper is also taken up in the article of Teskey discussed in my chap. 11, n. 11.

11. On the Spenser-Harvey letters, see *The Complete Poetical Works of Spenser*, ed. R.E. Neil Dodge, Appendix, pt. III, p. 773 esp. See also *The Works of Edmund Spenser*, vol. [8] *The Prose Works*, Appendix I, pp. 441 ff.

12. *Spenser's Faerie Queene*, vol. 2, p. 485.

13. On Cristofero Landino's *Quaestiones Camaldulenses ad Federicum Urbinatum Principem* (1480), see Aguzzi, pp. 127-39. For Spenser's analyses in the "Letter to Raleigh", see vol. 2 of *Spenser's Faerie Queene*, pp. 485-87. Italics in all quotations from Spenser (except with proper names) are mine.

14. Lodowick Bryskett, *A Discourse of Civill Life* (1606), in *Literary Works*, ed. J.H.P. Pafford, facs. reprint; quotations from pp. 26-27. Bryskett also mentions Giovanni Baptista Giraldi (Giraldi Cintio) on p. 24. Some further details of this work are noted in the Table, my App. C.

15. As could the Toscanella type of allegorization on Ariosto which has been proposed for *FQ*: Arthur *collects* all the virtues into himself, in a static way *displaying* them via the knights, and their opposites via their opponents; see William Nelson, *The Poetry of Edmund Spenser: A Study*, pp. 120-21. This is not exactly what Spenser's Letter says, however. It does not say merely that all the virtues are in Arthur as a "well-rounded man", but that Arthur, as Magnificence, is the transcendent perfected stage of every or any virtue, shown separately in an imperfect, evolving stage in the individual knights: hence arises a separate quality of "Magnificence", approximating to "Heroic Virtue", in Arthur.

16. Bryskett, pp. 26-27; 22. See also the Table, my App. C.

17. *Areopagitica; for the Liberty of Unlicenc'd Printing* (henceforth abbrev. *Areop.*), *CE*, vol. 4, p. 311. Milton's famous inaccurate allusion to the Guyon-Palmer passage is for the present context of discussion irrelevant. Milton's misremembering of the details of Spenser's story does not alter his expressed sympathy with Spenser's view of the human struggle to attain an "heroical degree of virtue".

18. See my chap. 1, sect. 'The Medieval 'Levels' ".

19. The source is Aristotle, *Nicomachean Ethics*, Bk IV.3, and the conception was explored in a dialogue of Tasso entitled *Il forno overro della nobiltà* (1585).

20. *FQ* III, Proem.2. On this differentiation, see Teskey, as cited in my chap. 8, n. 10.

21. Spenser's reference to the paintings of Zeuxis or Praxiteles could be an echo of the opening of Bk II of the *Discorsi del poema eroico*, p. 25, in which Tasso refers to "the art of a Praxiteles or Phidias". Spenser too alludes to Phidias and mere copying, in contradistinction to the sculptor's art, which is true Imitation, in *FQ* IV.x.40.

22. Cf.*Discorsi del poema eroico*, Bk II, p. 5: "their intellect itself becomes a painter who, following its pattern [of poetry], paints in their souls forms of courage, temperance, prudence, justice, faith, piety, religion, and every other virtue that may be acquired by long practice or infused by divine grace".

Chapter 9. Neoclassical Epic Theory: The Debate over Allegory

1. Thomas Rymer's "Preface" to his translation of René Rapin's treatise on Aristotle (1674) is discussed in the final part of my chap. 14, "Historical problems in reading *PL*". In the same place, also, Charles de Saint-Évremond's treatise, "On the Imitation of the Ancients" (1678). Abraham Cowley, "Preface to *Poems*" (1656), is reprinted in *Critical Essays of the Seventeenth Century*, ed. J.E. Spingarn, vol. 2.

2. Probably these are lifted without acknowledgement from Tasso, echoing especially *Discorsi del poema eroico*, Bk II, various places from pp. 25-56. See e.g., Sir William Davenant, "Preface to *Gondibert, an Heroick Poem*" (1650), in *Critical Essays of the Seventeenth Century*, ed. J.E. Spingarn, vol. 2, p. 12: the epic offers "patterns of humane life that are . . . fit to be follow'd"; pp. 10-11, the epic history should be taken from a "former age" or "Century so far remov'd" as not to "fetter [the Poet's] feet in the shackles of an Historian". This un-acknowledged borrowing does not prevent Davenant from censuring Tasso. See also Thomas Hobbes, "Answer to Davenant's Preface to *Gondibert*" (1650), in Spingarn, ed., vol 2, p. 60: the "Heroick Poem . . . is to exhibit a venerable & amiable Image of Heroick vertue"; p. 67: an epic shows the "vertues . . . distribute[d] . . . amongst so many noble Persons", yet repre-sents "in the reading the image but of one mans vertue" (this echoes back as far as Spenser's "Letter to Raleigh" and Toscanella's reading of Ariosto).

3. Davenant: Spenser's "allegoricall Story . . . resembl[es] . . . a continuance of ex-traordinary Dreams, such as excellent Poets and Painters, by being over-studious, may have in the beginning of Feavers". Spingarn, ed., vol. 2, p. 6. Cf. Cowley on "confused antiquated *Dreams* of senseless *Fables* and *Metamorphoses*", in Spingarn, ed., vol. 2, p. 88.

4. Davenant, in Spingarn, ed., vol. 2, p. 5.

5. See Hobbes, in Spingarn, ed., vol. 2, pp. 61- 62.

6. See Hobbes on the defence of "Fancy" in poetry, in Spingarn, ed., vol. 2, pp. 59-60.

7. Davenant, in Spingarn, ed., vol. 2, p. 5.

8. Cowley, in Spingarn, ed., vol. 2, p. 90.

9. See Hobbes' criticism of this lack, in Spingarn, ed., vol. 2, p. 58.

10. See e.g. Davenant, in Spingarn, ed., vol. 2, p. 9: the poet's argument shall concern only "Christian persons" and "such persons as profess'd Christian Religion".

11. See Davenant, in Spingarn, ed., vol. 2, pp. 17ff.; cf. Hobbes, in Spingarn, ed., vol. 2, p. 55: "The Figure . . . of an Epique Poem and of a Tragedy ought to be the same". Dryden's theory and practice concurs; "Love and War" are the fit subjects for his heroic tragedies. Many recent critics have noted the neoclassical approximation of epic form to tragic (there is something of this, of course, in *PL*); the conflation begins with the conservative late sixteenth-century Italian readings of Aristotle's *Poetics*.

12. Davenant, in Spingarn, ed., vol. 2, p. 32, indirectly associates Moses, David and Solomon with epic heroes.

13. Hobbes, in Spingarn, ed., vol. 2, p. 62; cf. Davenant, in Spingarn, ed., vol. 2, p. 11.

14. Davenant, in Spingarn, ed., vol. 2, p. 11.

15. Hobbes, in Spingarn, ed., vol. 2, p. 56; italics mine.

16. Davenant, in Spingarn, ed., vol. 2, p. 11.

17. Cowley, in Spingarn, ed., vol. 2, pp. 81, 90, 87.

18. This view has recently been restated in the general context of Italian sixteenth-century criticism by John M. Steadman, discussing Milton's poetics in *The Wall of Paradise: Essays on Milton's Poetics;* see chaps. 2 and 3, esp. pp. 35-45 and pp. 61-62. Steadman cites Tasso's more general views on history and epic from the *Discorsi del poema eroico* as relevant to Milton, but he opposes Milton's "literal" poetic to Tasso's theories. (Milton, unlike Tasso, did not "need" allegory to "spiritualize" a subject already spiritual.) I do not agree with Stead-man's argument. See further my App. B, pt. II; also nn. to my chap. 13, esp. nn. 8, 15 and 19.

19. See *PL* I.23-25; VII.557; the subject is discussed in my chap. 13.

20. Hobbes, in Spingarn, ed., vol. 2, p. 56.

21. Ibid., pp. 61- 62.

22. See pp. xxii, xxv-xxvii, xli-xlii, of John Hughes' "An Essay on *Allegorical Poetry*". John Hughes edited Spenser; the essay prefaces vol. 1 of *The Works of Spenser*, pp. xix-xli. John Hughes is alluded to by Steven Knapp in *Personification and the Sublime: Milton to Coleridge*, p. 54.

23. See Knapp, chap. 2 on Addison, esp. pp. 52-59, and p. 155, n.2; also his "Epilogue", pp. 133-39. John T. Shawcross in "Allegory, Typology, and Didacticism: *Paradise Lost* in the Eighteenth Century", gives a detailed survey of C18th attitudes, largely negative, to allegory in Milton. But sometimes the critics betray a discernible ambivalence toward literary allegory, as e.g. in the remarks of Thomas Blackwell (drawn to my attention by Shawcross) in his *Letters Concerning Mythology* (1748).

24. See Knapp, pp. 55-56. On p. 156, n. 10 (concerning Addison's individual definition of "fictions" as improbabilities in nature), Knapp points to an important terminological shift as between the late C16th and the 17th to 18th centuries.

25. *Spectator* 315 (March 1, 1712), in Joseph Addison, *The Spectator*, ed. Donald F. Bond, vol. 3, p. 146. Italics in quotations from Addison, except with proper and place names or occasionally substantives, are my own.

26. *Spectator* 297 (Feb. 9, 1712), vol. 3, p. 60; general discussion, pp. 60-61.

27. *Spectator* 315 (March 1, 1712), vol. 3, pp. 144-45.

28. *Spectator* 297 (Feb. 9, 1712), vol. 3, p. 60.

29. *Spectator* 357, vol. 3 (April 19, 1712), pp. 337-38. Knapp (pp. 58-59) points out that this is a false picture of Homer and Virgil.

30. *Spectator* 315 (March 1, 1712), vol. 3, p. 144.

31. See my chap. 14, sect. "Samuel Johnson". The Johnson allusions and quotations are taken from the "Life" of Milton in Samuel Johnson, *Lives of the English Poets*, ed. George Birkbeck Hill, vol. 1, p. 171; Johnson's reference to Le Bossu also is on p. 171.

32. The quotations from Edward Phillips are taken from the Preface to *Theatrum Poetarum* (1675), abridged, in *Literary Criticism: Plato to Dryden*, ed. Allan H. Gilbert. Italics are mine. Gilbert (p. 674, n. 26) notes an echo from the end of the Preface to Bk II of *The Reason of Church-Government urg'd against Prelaty* (henceforth abbrev. *Reason*), CE, vol. 3.1 (1931), p. 241, in the passage from Phillips entitled by the editor, "Epic Poetry requires Learning". Phillips' preference for Italian verse forms as well suited to English poetry, including epic, is expressed in the passage quoted by Gilbert on p. 669. In this as in many other passages there seems little doubt that Phillips is aligning his own views on epic with Milton's views and practices; once Phillips alludes unmistakeably to Milton's poem, and he also echoes Milton's phrase, "Heroic Argument".

33. Phillips, in Gilbert, ed., pp. 672-73.

34. Ibid., p. 673.

35. Gilbert (p. 673, n.19) suggests that Phillips means "that the literal basis of an allegory should be true to life"—which, as regards the larger part of Milton's story, is so.

36. John Toland, "The Life of John Milton" (1698), repr. in *The Early Lives of Milton*, ed. Helen Darbishire. The allusions to Tasso and Manso, and the quotations, are from pp. 94; 182.

37. See *Of Reformation Touching Church-Discipline in England* (henceforth abbrev. *Of Ref.*), CE, 3.1 (1931), pp. 78-79.

38. The relevant dates of major publications are: Castelvetro on Aristotle (1571); Mazzoni on Dante (1572, 1587); Tasso ("Allegoria", 1581; *Discorsi dell'arte poetica*, 1587, revised as *Discorsi del poema eroico*, 1594). The revised *Discorsi* appeared in French translation before the mid-century (1638); they were directly available to Le Bossu, whose treatise appeared in 1675 (trans. into English, 1695).

39. Milton, *Of Education* (henceforth abbrev. *Of Ed.*), CE, vol. 4 (1931), p. 286.

40. See my chap. 7 on Tasso, sect. "History and Fiction in the Epic". Tasso's *Estratti dalla*

Poetica di Lodovico Castelvetro (1576) was not published until 1875. The quotation is from *Prose Diverse*, vol. 1, p. 284.

41. Lodovico Castelvetro, *The Poetics of Aristotle Translated and Annotated* (1570) (selections), trans. and ed. Allan H. Gilbert, in *Literary Criticism: Plato to Dryden*, p. 305. I have used Gilbert's selections together with Andrew Bongiorno's abridged text of Castelvetro.

42. *Castelvetro on the Art of Poetry: An Abridged Translation of Lodovico Castelvetro's Poetica d'Aristotele Vulgarizzata et Sposta*, trans. and ed. Andrew Bongiorno, pp. 255-65.

43. Ibid., pp. 262-63.

44. Ibid., p. 259.

45. Ibid., p. 76; the discussion of Episodes is on pp. 76-79.

46. See the discussion of Johnson in my chap. 14, sect. "Samuel Johnson".

47. *Castelvetro on the Art of Poetry*, pp. 76-79; 141-43.

48. Ibid., p. 109.

49. See *Castelvetro on the Art of Poetry*, pp. 250-55; pp. 110-13. The marvellous is tied to occurrences "out of the ordinary" (surprising or miraculous).

50. Ibid., p. 108.

51. Ibid., p. 259.

52. Ibid., p. 263.

53. See Jacopo Mazzoni, *Della Difesa della Commedia di Dante* (1587, Part I; publ. in an earlier version, 1572; Part II was not publ. until 1688). I have used the translations of Mazzoni's Discourse in Gilbert's more substantial extracts in *Literary Criticism: Plato to Dryden*, from the 1587 version, *On the Defence of the "Comedy"*, supplemented by brief quotations in translation or close paraphrase from Weinberg, vol. 2. For Le Bossu, see my chap. 10, sect. "Allegory as the 'Platform' of Truth".

54. See *On the Defence of the "Comedy"*, in Gilbert, ed., pp. 370-72.

55. Ibid., p. 365.

56. "The credible as credible is the subject of rhetoric and the credible as marvelous is the subject of poetry", from *On the Defence of the "Comedy"*, in Gilbert, ed., p. 370. "Plot" is "an imitation of a human action which did not happen, but which is credible and marvelous, invented and ordered in whole or in part by the poet" (*Difesa*, Weinberg's translation, vol. 2, p. 879). Gilbert (p. 371, n.30) suggests that Milton may have been influenced by Mazzoni in the contrast between rhetoric and poetry quoted above.

57. See *On the Defence of the "Comedy"*, in Gilbert, ed., p. 371.

58. Not Mazzoni, but Weinberg's paraphrase of Mazzoni, vol. 2, p. 879.

59. The phrase is as used by Weinberg, vol. 2, p. 879, in his discussion of Mazzoni.

60. *On the Defence of the "Comedy"*, in Gilbert, ed., pp. 371-72.

61. Ibid., p. 366; p. 365.

62. See my chap. 9, n. 56; I partly adapt Gilbert's insight. The Milton quotation is from *Of Ed., CE*, vol. 4, p. 286.

Chapter 10. Le Bossu on the Epic

1. René Le Bossu, *Treatise of the Epick Poem*, trans. by W. J. (1695), from the French *Traité du Poëme Épique* (1675), in *Le Bossu and Voltaire on the Epic*, ed. Stuart Curran. The editor notes (p. viii) that Le Bossu rivalled Boileau in reputation and that Addison incorporated Le Bossu's codifications into his analysis of *PL* in Spectator 267 (probably in other essays too). Le Bossu's "insistence on the primary focus of an epic as moral", perfectly exemplified in Milton, had, by giving credence to what had become accepted throughout the preceding century, "established the foundation on which an epic purpose such as Milton's could securely rest", and on which the Romantics could also compose their epics proposing "large moral problems, set within an allegorical or symbolic framework" (p. ix). Quotations from Le Bossu in my text are

taken from the English trans. of 1695 in Curran's ed. Italics with proper names and with nouns used as technical terms are as given in this ed.; other italics are normally my own.

The French of Le Bossu may be consulted in the original, the *Traitë du Poëme Épique;* I have used the original ed. of 1675. Le Bossu's terms and their intentions are translated scrupulously by "W.J.", who is particularly anxious to give "Fable" its full sense of "an epic with an antecedent Moral", as intended by Le Bossu. For "allegory" in this general sense Le Bossu uses the French terms, "Fable" (as in Aesop), "Plan", "Morale", or sometimes "Allégorie". For finite allegories (e.g. insets) he uses "allégories" (pl.), "expressions allégoriques", or "machines" (for divine interventions). For subject matter he uses "matière". W.J. translates all of these literally; however, for Le Bossu's "Plan" he gives "Ground-work" or more often "Platform", as in English less ambiguous. W.J.'s "Ground-work" (Le Bossu's "Plan") resembles Sidney's phrase in *Apology*, p. 124: the "imaginative *ground-plot* of a profitable invention". The following extract from the French version ("Livre I", chap. xv, pp. 105-106) illustrates how the English translator has kept faithfully to Le Bossu's intended senses: "Or la Fable Épique n'est point tout cela [ornemens de l'Action]: elle est au-contraire, l'âme du Poëme, & le Plan sur lequel tout le reste doit être bâti". And W.J. (Bk I.xv, p. 43): "Now the *Epick Fable* is none of all this [ornamentation of the action]: 'tis on the contrary the Soul of a Poem, and the *Ground-work* upon which all the rest is built".

2. See Le Bossu, as e.g. Bk I.vi, pp. 14-15; Bk I.xiv, pp. 39-41.

3. See Le Bossu, V.iii, p. 223: An epic has a looser structure than a drama, and many things can be accommodated in it which are unsuitable to a play, in which things are *seen*: "No body cares for seeing Gods or Miracles upon the Stage".

4. See Le Bossu, pp. 53; 14; 53; 16, 15; in Bks I.xv; II.i; I.vi; II.i; and I.vii, vi; respectively.

5. For this use of the term "Fable", see Le Bossu, Bk I.vii, p. 16, and Bk I.xiv, p. 41.

6. On "Moral" and Aesop, see Le Bossu, Bk I.ix, p. 21: "An *Epopéa* is a true *Fable* . . . the Sense is the same, as when we give the Name of *Fables* to the *Fictions* of *Aesop*". The specific association of epic Fable with Aesop's allegories makes Le Bossu's view of epic as essentially allegorical quite plain. Cf. Le Bossu's allegorical treatment of the "Fables" or moral themes of the *Iliad, Odyssey* and *Aeneid,* Bk I.viii, pp. 17-20; Bk I.x, xi, pp. 23- 30; cf. my chap. 10, n. 27.

7. Le Bossu, Bk I.iii, p. 7.

8. Ibid., Bk I.xiv, p. 41.

9. Ibid., Bk I.vi, p. 14.

10. Ibid.

11. Ibid., Bk I.xv, p. 41.

12. See Le Bossu, Bk I.vi, p. 15.

13. Ibid., Bk I.vii, p. 15.

14. Ibid., Bk I.iii, p. 6.

15. Ibid., Bk I.vii, p. 16. Elsewhere (see Bk V.iii, p. 225), Le Bossu uses "Allegories" (pl.) in the C18th sense of "Miracles" or "Machines".

16. Ibid., Bk I.ii, p. 6. In the same way, all the *"Historical Truths* [of the Old Testament] were so many *Fables*, or *Parables* divinely invented, which represent Allegorically to us the Doctrine and the Truths which the Author of them has since discover'd to us" (Bk I.xiv, p. 40). Le Bossu here speaks of allegory in the Old Testament in a typological sense; however, the point of his remark is the analogy between this form of Old Testament allegory and historical allegory in epic.

17. Ibid., Bk I.v, p. 11.

18. Le Bossu discusses "Episodes" in Bks II.v and vi *passim* (but esp. pp. 67-68 of Bk II.vi), and in Bk III.viii, pp. 137-40.

19. Ibid., Bk V.iii, p. 224. In contrast, true Episodes, which are integral, *are* the Action: they are *"necessary Parts of the Action, extended by probable Circumstances"* (Bk II.vi, p. 67).

20. Ibid., Bk I.ii, p. 3. The mention of a "physiological" type of allegory recalls Comes and the Renaissance mythographers.

21. Ibid., Bk V.iii, pp. 223-24.

22. Ibid., p. 224.
23. Ibid., p. 222.
24. Ibid., p. 224.
25. Ibid.
26. Ibid., p. 225.
27. Ibid., Bk III.vii, p. 136. See Le Bossu's more explicit elaborations of the political Morals or "Fables" of Homer and the *Aeneid*, in his Bk I.viii-xi. Cf. Philip R. Hardie's recent revaluation of the *Aeneid* with its theme of *cosmos* and *imperium* (epitomized in the "Giants" motif, taken from Achilles, on Aeneas' shield), and his stress on "the proper, central position" of allegory in the epic: see chaps. 3, 4 and 8 in *Virgil's Aeneid: Cosmos and Imperium*. (The quotation is from the review of Hardie by Nicholas Horsfall, *TLS*.)

Chapter 11. Debts to Renaissance Allegory in *Paradise Lost*

1. See my chaps. 18 and 19.
2. See my chap. 3.
3. See Stephen M. Fallon, "Milton's Sin and Death: The Ontology of Allegory in *Paradise Lost*", pp. 342-50 esp. The use of allegory to convey the particular concept of negativity which Fallon cites does not, however, exclude allegories of other kinds in Milton, either in connection with the infernal trio or other characters in the poem, personified or real, and at other levels than the theological. E.g.: as well as saying in *OfCD*, I.xi, that Sin (or evil) is non-entity ("implies defect"), Milton goes on to say that Sin (or evil) represents "deviation", i.e., it is obliquity or perversity, a tendency to falling-off. "It is called Actual Sin, not that sin is properly an action, for in reality *it implies defect [privatio]*. . . . For every act is in itself good; it is only its irregularity [*obliquitas*], or deviation from the line of right ['anomalia a legis norma proprie'], which, properly speaking, is evil" (*CE*, vol. 15, pp. 198-99). Words or images of deviation or obliquity are to be found associated with Sin and Death, esp. in *PL* Bk X, and also many times with falling or fallen Adam and Eve (see Treip, "'Reason is also Choice': The Emblematics of Free Will in *Paradise Lost*"). In such instances the words and images suggest a moral and psychological value rather than a theological level of allegory. Fallon's further extrapolation that Milton's presentation of Sin or sin as "privation of entity" (p. 344) reflects the alleged "decline of allegory" in Milton and in the C17th (p. 337) seems to me to be unsupported by any consistent evidence and, in the case of Milton, to be contrary to fact. I have not been able to consult Fallon's recent book on Milton, in which he perhaps enlarges on these questions.
4. To Harington's distinction earlier (see my chap. 3, sect. "John Harington"), cf. Le Bossu, p. 41, as quoted in my chap. 10, sect. "Allegory as the 'Platform' of Truth".
5. *FQ* VI.i.6.
6. See esp. my chap. 2, sections "Coloccio Salutati" and "The English Rhetoricians".
7. Cf. Puttenham's figure of "false semblant", p. 186.
8. See my chap. 3, sect. "Bacon", and n. 19 on Pépin.
9. Richard Hurd, as cited by Knapp, p. 55, from *Letters on Chivalry and Romance* (1762), ed. Hoyt Trowbridge, facs. reprint, p. 57.
10. See *The Wall of Paradise*, p. 62. Steadman does not reconcile such statements with his acknowledgements elsewhere of allegorical elements in Milton's usage. See my App. B and chap. 9, n. 18.
11. There is much current misunderstanding of Spenser's and Milton's artistic relationship and their purposes as allegorists. Quilligan has based one book on the thesis that wordplay defines the allegorical "genre" (*The Language of Allegory*) and another (*Milton's Spenser*) on the premise that puns and fictive language in *PL* are, allegedly following Spenser's model, associated exclusively with Sin, Satan and the fallen world. While Quilligan's analyses of linguistic relationships between the two poets is illuminating, her conception of allegory is very restricted, and that of the relation of allegory to "truth" is in my view incorrect. Allegory

is not a *genre*—if anything, it is a *mode*, one of universal application and taking endless literary shapes. Punning in Spenser or Milton forms only a small part of their allegorical rhetoric; and allegory in *Paradise Lost* constitutes a comprehensive vehicle for various forms of discourse, by no means all relating only to the "fallen" aspects of Milton's material. Quilligan follows a convention perhaps established by Blake, and in which Isabel MacCaffrey, Ann Ferry, and others have participated, of considering puns in *PL* as "fallen language". (See e.g. Ann D. Ferry, *Milton's Epic Voice: The Narrator in Paradise Lost*, p. 33.) According to this view metaphor first becomes suspect to Milton, and finally, "fiction" and imaginative language are deliberately shown by him to be erroneous (consider the sentence, "Like Dante, Spenser and Milton must . . . warn their readers about the power of poetry to mislead", *Milton's Spenser*, p. 99). The justification for the argument runs thus: Milton's allegorical figure of Sin is derived from Spenser's figure of Error; "allegory [thus] is a genre of the fallen world" (p. 95); therefore the injection of Spenserian allegory and puns into Milton's *non-allegorical* poem is a warning of its fictiveness (that is to say its untruth), which, by contrast, teaches the reader that the directly historical part is true (*Milton's Spenser*, p. 95; Quilligan's argument runs through chap. 2). This forcefully expressed view, oddly reminiscent of Rymer's bias against Spenserian allegory, unfortunately is a distortion of Milton's text and his allegorical purpose and artistry. Quilligan, like others, also is incorrect in supposing that Milton in *Of CD* "denies the legitimacy of allegorical readings" (p. 109). He does not. This large topic is considered in my final Part, III.

A second avenue of misinterpretation of the Spenser-Milton relationship arises from a recent general tendency to identity rather too closely epic allegory with romance narrative structures. This has led to the line of argument that, since Milton's epic is primarily historical, Milton's artistry therefore cannot be allegorical, or can be so only in a derogatory sense, as, allegedly, in the Sin-Death interpolated "fantastic" episodes. Milton's lesser use than Spenser's of romance *plot* elements does not in itself establish that Milton does not use other vehicles of allegory, or that his allegories are confined to the supernatural personifications and have no relevance to the human side. In a challenging article, "From Allegory to Dialectic: Imagining Error in Spenser and Milton", Gordon Teskey, contrasting Spenser's and Milton's differing subjects, proposes the view that Spenser but not Milton can through allegory "explore nuance and complexity in our ordinary *moral* experience", that Spenser but not Milton associates "error" (romance "error", that is) with *moral* wandering, that the head-on "collision of evil and good [in Milton's subject] . . . leaves no room" for ambiguities, and that *PL* has none of the rich "web work of ethical play, for managing the complexities and tensions of error" (pp. 9, 13, 15; italics mine). I have argued in the present study that Milton through many shadowed devices, including elements of language, allusion, imagery, emblems, and indeed sometimes of romance plot elements, does achieve this kind of rich "web work" (Teskey's excellent phrase), and that it is here exactly that Milton is most richly Spenserian. I would therefore not accept Teskey's claim that Milton because of his Christian plot "had to renounce not only allegory but also the neo-Aristotelian conception of truth [i.e. conceptual truth] in the heroic poem", confining himself to Castelvetro's "similitude of history" (p. 15). Milton in fact followed Tasso's "solution" of combining both kinds of truth, historical and allegorical. Milton never did, even in *Areop.*, envisage truth as more than hopefully one, or indivisible. The argument (by no means uncommon in recent criticism) that Milton "refuses allegory" (p. 16) seems to me to be contrary to all the evidence of *Paradise Lost*—although it is fair to say that Milton does somewhat screen those uses of allegory connected with the human, angelic or deific contexts, in contrast with his more blatant use of allegory in the Sin-Death-Chaos episodes.

12. For a detailed illustration of the Spenserian-Miltonic verbal processes referred to above, see Treip on the "Pythagorean Y" motif, in "The Emblematics of Free Will in *Paradise Lost*". I have tried in this article and the present study to give some sense of analogies in Milton to Spenser's various allegorical schemes, rhetorical practices and emblematic structures.

13. Quotations from *PL* and other poems of Milton follow the ed. of Helen Darbishire, *The Poetical Works of John Milton*, 2 vols.

Chapter 12. Allegorical Poetics in *Paradise Lost*

1. Steadman in *The Wall of Paradise* has comprehensively collated Milton's various prose utterances bearing on his poetics. However (see my chap. 9, n. 18), Steadman directs the Miltonic materials to conclusions different from my own.

2. *Reason, CE*, vol. 3.1, p. 237.

3. Ibid.

4. *Of Ed., CE*, vol. 4, p. 286. These three critics are coupled by Milton with Aristotle and Horace on the "sublime Art" of poetry.

5. *Reason, CE*, vol. 3.1, p. 237.

6. See *An Apology against a Pamphlet call'd A Modest Confutation of the Animadversions upon the Remonstrant against Smectymnuus* (henceforth abbrev. *Smect.*), *CE*, vol. 3.1, p. 304: "I betook me among those lofty Fables and Romances". Milton loved both Spenser and Ariosto, as his numerous allusions to them both testify. He owned a copy of Harington's moralized translation of Ariosto (see William Riley Parker, *Milton: A Biography*, vol. 2, p. 884, n.66), and of course he would have read Ariosto in the original; almost all the Ital. eds. of the period carried allegorical commentaries.

7. *Reason, CE*, vol. 3.1, p. 237.

8. Ibid., pp. 238-40. "Justice, temperance and fortitude": three of the four cardinal virtues traditional to epic, standing first as the objectives of the epic; here an echo of Tasso's *Discorsi del poema eroico*, Bk I, p. 5, and as there, supplemented by reference to the theological virtues.

9. *Reason, CE*, vol. 3.1, p. 240. The short quotations which follow this one in my text are from p. 237. The rather unusual mention of *porches* in the context of the notion of a new form of popular didactic theatre may lead us to speculate a little about the remembered impressions of solemn festivals or celebrations, perhaps witnessed by Milton in the streets of Italy not very long before the date of this tract.

10. I would not agree with Steadman (*Wall of Paradise*, pp. 7-8) that Milton's enthusiastic rhetoric or his citing of "school texts" (i.e., classical treatises on poetry) in the early prose necessarily diminishes the seriousness with which we are to take Milton's statements there as an earnest of future intentions. The very fact that Milton singles out the late Italian critics and models *over* other, classical, theorists taught in the school is significant. He is also well aware of the tensions between the positions of the three major Italian critics whom he cites in *Of Ed.*

11. *Reason, CE*, vol. 3.1, p. 237.

12. "Clime": metaphorically a reference to bad artistic and political conditions, and a pun on the bad English weather—perhaps also a nostalgic reference to the remembered sunny clime and vigorous intellectual climate of Italy, as recorded near the time of his visit there, in Letter 8 to Benedetto Bonmattei (Florence, Sept. 10, 1638); see *The Familiar Letters of John Milton*, trans. David Masson, ed. Donald Lemen Clark, *CE*, vol. 12, p. 37.

13. See *John Milton's Complete Poetical Works: A Critical Text Edition*, ed. Harris Francis Fletcher, vol. 2 (1945), pp. 16, and 26 (for the quotation).

14. See Walter Benjamin, *Ursprung des deutschen Trauerspiels*, trans. as *The Origin of German Tragic Drama*, by J. Osborne.

15. *Areop., CE*, vol. 4, p. 311.

16. The word "accommodated" occurs in *Of CD* I.ii, *CE*, vol. 14, p. 33 (Lat. *accommodans*, p. 32). Its contexts there, its implications for allegorical discourse in *PL*, Milton's uses of the terms "shadows" and "types", his references to the word "allegory", and his own uses of "allegorical expressions" in a number of places in his prose works including *Of CD*, are discussed in detail in the final Part (chaps. 15 to 19) of this study.

17. It is worth noting that Milton owned a copy of *Heraclidis Pontici . . . Allegoriae in Homeri Fabulas de Diis* (1544). See James Holly Hanford and James G. Taaffe, *A Milton Handbook*, p. 318. This ed. has Milton's autograph. See also "Marginalia", *The Uncollected Writings of John Milton*, ed. Thomas Ollive Mabbott and J. Milton French, *CE*, vol. 18, p. 577.

18. Gordon Teskey, on the contrary, in "Milton's Choice of Subject in the Context of Renaissance Critical Theory", suggests that in *PL* Milton made a total break not only with Italian romance epic theory (cf. Teskey, "From Allegory to Dialectic", cited in my chap. 11, n. 11), but also with Italian historical epic: "Only when he had put behind him the theoretical abstraction of an ideal heroic poem could Milton relegate this class of events to the final two books of *Paradise Lost*" (p. 57). Later: "the problem of mixing two species of truth, the truth of fact and of fiction, [was] something that would not sit easily with Milton" (p. 61). Yet such mixing seems to me to have been Milton's deliberate approach throughout the main body of *PL*—although not, as Teskey also notes, in the final Books, which Milton deliberately presents as pure divine history, in contrast to the mixed modes of the earlier Books.

19. Giovanni Battista Manso, dedicatee of Tasso's dialogue, *Il Manso, ovvero dell'Amicizia* [*Manso: on Friendship*], 1586 (see *Opere*, vol. 7, pp. 472-502), is addressed in Milton's "Mansus" as "father Mansus" ("Manse pater", line 25), in language which, as in lines 7-8 and 49-53, reveals Milton's own veneration of Tasso as poet: "Great Tasso and you were once joined by a happy friendship which has written your names on the pages of eternity"; "Wherever in the world the glory and great name of Torquato are honoured . . . you will fly on your way to immortality side by side" ("Te pridem magno felix concordia Tasso / Iunxit, et aeternis inscripsit nomina chartis"; "ergo quacunque per orbem / Torquati decus, et nomen celebrabitur ingens, / . . . Tu quoque . . . / parili carpes iter immortale volatu"). Alastair Fowler's trans., Lat. with Eng., in *The Poems of John Milton*, ed. John Carey and Alastair Fowler, lines 7-8 and 49-53, pp. 260-66.

20. See Toland, p. 94, as cited in my chap. 9, sect. "Edward Phillips and John Toland", and n. 36.

21. See F.T. Prince, *The Italian Element in Milton's Verse*. Mario Praz, "Tasso in England", in *The Flaming Heart: Essays on Crashaw, Machiavelli and Other Studies in the Relations between Italian and English Literature from Chaucer to T.S. Eliot*, esp. pp. 321-30, finds in *PL* (and in Tasso's late drama and last poem) almost better exemplifications of Tasso's metrical prescriptions for *asprezza*, as enumerated in the final Books of the *Discorsi del poema eroico*, than Tasso himself achieved in the *Gerusalemme*.

22. *An Index to the Columbia Edition of the Works of John Milton*, ed. Frank Allen Patterson, records in vol. 2, 19 borrowings by Milton in *PL* from the *Gerusalemme*, plus a few more directly from Fairfax. I have found in *PL* Bks I-VII alone over 60 major borrowings directly from Tasso, many of them extensive and multiple, including many of Milton's most famous similes (far more than the few cited in my text above); and this picture is itself incomplete, since it is based mainly on study of borrowings from only the first four Books of *Gerusalemme*. Nor is the list of Milton's debts confined to the falsely heroic in *PL*, as e.g., in Satan modelled on Pluto-Argantes. Many of Tasso's most fervently religious passages and those concerning Godfrey and the heavenly messengers find echoes in Milton's descriptions of Adam and the archangels. So too, not entirely negatively, is Tasso's Armida (a seductress who repents) echoed in Milton's Eve; so too, in Milton's God are echoes of Tasso's Heavenly Father.

The ff. critics, among others, have noted extensive parallels between *Gerusalemme* and *PL*: Ewald Pommrich, *Miltons Verhältnis zu Torquato Tasso*, publ. diss.; Edward Weismiller, "Materials Dark and Crude: A Partial Genealogy for Milton's Satan"; A. Bartlett Giamatti, chap. 4.2 on Tasso, in *The Earthly Paradise and The Renaissance Epic*, and his article, "Milton and Fairfax's Tasso"; Mario Praz's essay, "Tasso in England", also "The Metamorphoses of Satan", chap. 2 in *The Romantic Agony*; Fowler, in a number of notes in his ed. of *PL*; and Judith A. Kates (more on Tasso and Spenser than on Tasso and Milton) in *Tasso and Milton: The Problem of Christian Epic*. Milton's earlier editors, Thomas Newton and Henry Todd, also noted parallels. However, there is still much work to be done on the full scale and nature of Milton's borrowing from Tasso.

23. Prince in particular, in *The Italian Element in Milton's Verse* (also see F.T. Prince, "Milton e Tasso"), and Lea and Gang, eds., in their Introd. to *Godfrey of Bulloigne*, evaluate the Tasso-Fairfax interaction and Fairfax's distinctive influence on English verse and on Milton (Milton is sparingly treated by Lea and Gang). Kates in *Tasso and Milton* considers the Tasso-Spenser relationship. On Tasso and Fairfax, or on them and Milton, see further Morley's Introd. to *Jerusalem Delivered*; Charles G. Bell in (among other articles) "Fairfax's Tasso"; and Giamatti, "Milton and Fairfax's Tasso".

24. On these aspects see: James William Conley, *Tasso and Milton: I Discorsi, La Gerusalemme Liberata and Paradise Lost*, Ph.D. diss.; Thomas Greene, *The Descent from Heaven: A Study in Epic Continuity*, chap. 8, pp. 180-218 on Tasso; and John M. Steadman, *Epic and Tragic Structure in Paradise Lost*, chap. 3, pp. 29-40. Conley makes the important point that in *PL* as in the *Ger*. the outcome of the epic action depends upon the actions of the tragic hero, who falls because of love (p. 196). Tasso himself (*Discorsi del poema eroico*, Bk II, p. 47) notes that love suits the hero of the modern epic poem: "love is not merely a passion and a movement of the sensitive appetite, but a highly noble habit of the will. . . . we may regard actions performed for the sake of love as beyond all others heroic". While Tasso, as Steadman notes in *Epic and Tragic Structure* (p. 31), does make a formal distinction between the "proper operation" and proper subjects of epic and those of tragedy (*meraviglia* versus "horror and compassion"), Tasso in fact tends to adapt epic practice toward the new combined neoclassical epic-tragic norm—as does Milton to a lesser extent in *PL*. In *Reason*, when Milton speaks of the "refluxes of mans thoughts from within", he is evidently thinking of matter suitable for *either* epic *or* tragic forms: *PL* and *Samson* illustrate, respectively.

25. Annabel Patterson (pp. 106ff.) notes the remarkable congruence of Milton's Heavenly Messenger scenes with Tasso's *Il Messaggiero: Dialogo* (1582). (For the Tasso, see *Opere*, vol. 7, pp. 93-144). In this dialogue Tasso talks to a "gentile Spirito" (p. 93) who, like Milton's Raphael, in "accommodated" speech tells his human interlocutor about the creation of the world and of man, the nature of angels (and demons), the nature of angels' food and love, and draws a distinction between the intuitive reason of spirits and the discursive reason of men. Patterson notes (p. 108) that whereas Milton's angel imparts a biblical ontology to Adam, Tasso's Spirit constructs a Neoplatonic ontology; however she believes (pp. 110-11) that there is a serious possibility of the direct influence of Tasso's dialogue on similar scenes in *PL* and, further, on the impending severance in Book XII of direct relations between heaven and earth. Patterson postulates an influence via Manso. Possibly also Milton was influenced by direct reading of Tasso's prose in the Italian.

26. In broad, the distinction is that made between the more general prescriptions concerning nobility of subject and diction in the *Discorsi del poema eroico* and its recommendations for striking effects of "epic wonder" in the action (as in Bk I, pp. 15, 17), and the more technical arguments in the *Lettere* concerning marvellous or supernatural *Episode*.

27. The word "wonder" or grammatical forms of it used with a Christian association occur in *PL* at III.285, 542, 552, 587, 663, 665, 702; IV.205; VI.754, 790; VII.70, 223; VIII.11, 68; X.482; XI.733, 819; and XII. 200, 468, 471, 500.

28. In Bks I-II and IX-X the "wonders" belong more to Satan's, Sin's and Death's false fabrics or fabrications. See e.g. *PL* I.777; V.54; IX.532, 533, 566, 650, 862; X.312, 348, 487, 510: in most of these "wonder" is used in the specific sense of marvels or the marvellous. Cf. John M. Steadman's remarks on Milton's and Tasso's use of epic wonders in *Epic and Tragic Structure in Paradise Lost*, chap. 8, pp. 105-19, and in "Miracle and the Epic Marvellous in *Paradise Lost*".

29. Cf. *Reason, CE*, vol. 3.1, p. 186: a governor of a state must be one "in whom contemplation and practice, wit, prudence, fortitude . . . must be rarely met".

30. *Discorsi del poema eroico*, Bk I, p. 5.

31. See *Discorsi del poema eroico*, Bk II, pp. 39-41. Phillips probably paraphrased Tasso's passages in his summation of the epic poem.

32. Steadman's discussions of Milton's poetics in *The Wall of Paradise*, pp. 41-48, sometimes read like a paraphrase of Tasso's *Discorsi*; yet Steadman does not suggest that Milton has been echoing Tasso. Surely Milton's very mention of Tasso in this context makes the association specific?

33. *Reason*, preface to Bk II, *CE*, vol. 3.1, p. 237.

34. *Discorsi del poema eroico*, Bk II, p. 39. To Milton's "pattern of a Christian Heroe", cf. also Tasso: "[the poet] paints in their souls forms of courage, temperance, prudence, justice, faith, piety, religion, and every other virtue"; *Discorsi del poema eroico*, Bk I, p. 5.

35. *Smect.*, *CE*, vol. 3.1, p. 303.

36. *Discorsi del poema eroico*, Bk II, pp. 39, 43.

37. See Milton's lines, "to sing the victorious agonies of Martyrs and Saints, the deeds and triumphs of just and pious Nations doing valiantly through faith" (*Reason, CE*, vol. 3.1, p. 238), and "to sing and celebrate thy *divine Mercies*, and *marvelous Judgements*" (*Of Ref., CE*, vol. 3.1, p. 78). Also, to Milton's "gracefull inticements to the love and practice of *justice, temperance* and *fortitude*", expressed in *Reason, CE*, vol. 3.1, p. 240, cf. *Discorsi del poema eroico*, Bk I, p. 5 and Bk II, pp. 39 and 43.

38. *Discorsi del poema eroico*, Bk II, pp. 39-40. See my chap. 7, sect. "History and Fiction in the Epic".

39. See *Of CD* I.xxx, *CE*, vol. 16, pp. 251, 263.

40. *Reason, CE*, vol. 3.1, p. 236.

41. See Rhu, "From Aristotle to Allegory", p. 116.

42. *Discorsi del poema eroico*, Bk III, p. 78. The passage appears in both the early and later *Discorsi*.

43. Knapp, p. 60.

44. For a discussion of the Golden Scales, see Treip, "The Emblematics of Free Will in *Paradise Lost*".

Chapter 13. Allegory and "Idea" in *Paradise Lost*

1. Le Bossu, Bk I.xiv, xv, p. 41.

2. See Irene Samuel, *Plato and Milton*, chap. 6, "The Theory of Ideas", esp. pp. 131-34. Italics under the word "Idea" in the ff. citations are as given by Samuel and normally by Milton; those under the word "exemplar", as given by Samuel. Samuel distinguishes three uses of "Idea" (all deriving from Plato) in Milton: (1) and (2), the doctrines of Ideal Forms or (moral) Essences, either innate or having a kind of independent archetypal existence. In this connection she cites Milton's Prolusions twice; Sonnet 4, lines 6-7 ("sotto nova *idea* / Pellegrina bellezza" ["on a new idea of evanescent loveliness"]); and "De Idea Platonica", line 10 ("*exemplar* Dei" ["the pattern used by God"]—for quotations see *The Poems of John Milton*, p. 94, and pp. 67-68, respectively, for the texts; the first quotation is given in the *CE* trans., the second in Fowler's. She also cites Milton's prose twice: *Tetrachordon, CE*, vol. 4, p. 101, and, with some other examples, *Eikonoklastes, CE*, vol. 5, p. 243 (on the Platonic Forms). We might add to the instances noted by Samuel, these: the perfect shapes (Platonic Ideas) of Faith, Hope and Chastity "see[n] . . . visibly" by the Lady in *Comus*, lines 212-15; a "*patterne* of the best and honourablest things", *Smect., CE*, vol. 3.1, p. 303; and the Jesus of *Paradise Regained*, III.11, who is "of good, wise, just, *the perfet shape*". And (3), most importantly, Samuel distinguishes "the Idea as a pattern in the creative mind, divine or human, according to which a world or treatise or series of events may be shaped" (p. 134.) Samuel cites here Milton's plan for "that voluntary *Idea* . . . of a better Education", *Of Ed., CE*, vol. 4, p. 276; and *Of CD* I.iii twice, in relation to the providential dispositions of God: *CE*, vol. 14, pp. 64-65, "that *idea* of every thing, which he had in his mind" ("ille rerum omnium idea"), and again, pp. 78-79, "the *idea* of that evil event" ("idea certe eventus istius mali"), which God foresees. It is clear, especially

from the instances cited from *Of Ed., Smect.* and the two from *Of CD* (the first of these last two is echoed in *PL* VII. 555-57), that for Milton "idea" signifies an intellectual concept—in relation to God's providence, to be understood as including all the moral and theological implications of the Fall—and that the word in *PL* is not to be understood simply as a reference to God's narrative foresight, or to divine "plot". We may add as further examples, *Reason, CE*, vol. 3.1, p. 197, "those unwritten lawes and *ideas* which nature hath ingraven in us", and also Milton's important statement in Letter 7 (Sept. 23, 1637) to Charles Diodati about pursuing the Idea of the Beautiful: "seek for this *idea* of the beautiful, as for a certain *image* of supreme beauty" (Milton then adds to his lines the word "idea" in its Gk. form; the Lat. equivalent in his original is *imaginem*)—see *Familiar Letters, CE*, vol. 12, pp. 26-27. Italics in the verse quotations from Milton are mine; in the prose, all but those in the quotation from *Of Ed*.

3. Invocation (lines 85-86) to "The First Day of the First Weeke", in vol. 1 of *The Divine Weeks and Works of Guillaume de Saluste, Sieur Du Bartas*, ed. Susan Snyder, p. 113.

4. "Farò comparazione ancora fra la mia Gerusalemme quasi terrena, e questa, che . . . è assai più simile *all'idea della celeste Gerusalemme*". *Giudizio*, Bk I, *Opere*, vol. 4, p. 304.

5. *Discorsi del poema eroico*, Bk II, p. 31.

6. Steadman in *Epic and Tragic Structure*, 9-11, takes a different view of the signification of "Argument" in PL. See my chap. 13, n. 8.

7. *Of CD* I.iii, *CE*, vol. 14, p. 65; as cited also by Samuel, p. 134.

8. Steadman believes that Milton's "Argument" equals his "action" or the events in *PL*, and that the Argument is not equal to "the vindication of 'Eternal Providence' and the justification of God's ways to men". See *Epic and Tragic Structure*, p. 10: "Milton's argument is the fall of man". Although the simple oratorical sense of "Argument" as equivalent to "subject" was indeed used in the Renaissance, and while I agree with Steadman that we should not "confuse Milton's subject with his purpose", I would not agree with his assertion (p. 10) that "the 'essential form' or *idea* of *Paradise Lost* is . . . to be found *primarily in the plot or fable*" (my italics)—that is, that Milton's "Idea" is only a formal concept relating to organizational design. In support of my own view, cf. my citations from Milton's prose and verse in chap. 13, n. 2. Steadman separates Milton's alleged stance from Le Bossu's recognisably allegorical position, just as he separates Milton's from Tasso's position. But I believe that Le Bossu's arguments as to "Moral" or "Ground-work" in the epic were explicit in late seventeenth-century theory, just as they were in earlier theories of allegory in epic and poetry. There seems to be no reason to disregard the evidence of the context of critical theory against which Milton wrote, the statements of Milton's contemporaries, and his own declared sources of inspiration in writers of epic allegory. If the poet's *professed purpose* is indeed to justify the workings of Providence to mankind, any such purpose need not necessarily be achieved only through a purely logical proposition or "thesis" argued out in the poem, something which Milton can "assert" (as we see he often does), or alternatively, at other times exemplify through the action, as Steadman proposes. May not this same purpose also be "figured forth" allegorically, in the time-honoured fashion? The effort to harness Milton's art solely to classical categories seems to me unduly restrictive. So also, I would argue, is the alternative, also proposed by Steadman (p. 160, n. 8), that Milton's "Justification" represents a proposition *so vague* that it is impossible to tie it down to any single moral.

9. Le Bossu, Bk II.v, p. 67.

10. In *Of CD* I.xi, *CE*, vol. 15, pp. 181-83, Milton identifies the eating of the apple as comprising in one act all possible sins.

11. "Allegoria", *Jerusalem Delivered*, p. 436.

12. *Areop., CE*, vol. 4, p. 311.

13. Tasso, in the "Allegoria", *Jerusalem Delivered*, p. 436.

14. *Of CD* I.xi, *CE*, vol. 15, pp. 198-99: "sin . . . in reality . . . implies defect . . . For every act is in itself good; it is only its irregularity, or deviation [*obliquitas*] from the line of right, which, properly speaking, is evil".

15. Steadman cites as typical of such criticism, G.A. Wilkes' *The Thesis of Paradise Lost*,

pp. 4-5 (see *Epic and Tragic Structure*, p. 160, n. 8). Steadman (pp. 10-11) disagrees with Wilkes' assertion that Milton's "Argument" and his "Justification" are one and the same. Steadman's final chapter in *Epic and Tragic Structure* nevertheless moves rather close at certain points to the view of a directing Idea (or ideas) in *PL*, although Steadman clearly wishes to avoid the term "allegory". E.g., consider these statements (italics are mine): (p. 121) *"Logical and ethical patterns* not only *condition the structure* of events within the fable, *but also help to integrate the episodes*—both causally and thematically—*within the design of the main plot"*; (p. 131) *"Milton imitates the concept in action, in dynamic relationship with other ideas"*; (p. 135) "Milton's episodes" (as e.g. with Sin and Death) acquire *"thematic relations with the main plot"*. Nonetheless, Steadman concludes (p. 134) that the poem only "offers us a unified *fable . . .* which involves a wide variety of *themes"*; while "the narrow design of the plot invites comparison with the larger cosmic patterns . . . it does not mirror them. It can portray them only by breaking them up and introducing the fragments as episodes. They enter the formal structure . . . as broken designs" (p. 140). I do not concur with Steadman's preferred conclusion that Milton's unifying allegorical "Idea" cannot incorporate a variety of closely related themes, or in particular, that the tissue of allusive and allegorical language and images with which the main plot is invested and the poet's imitative designs bear no close relationship with the "cosmic patterns" or they with it. I would propose exactly the opposite to be true. *Without* an allegorical verbal artistry and allegorical narrative design, Milton's "themes" *would* remain "broken"; coupled with those, the themes evolve into an allegorical enterprise which taken as a whole does mirror the cosmic providential design.

16. On the iconography of "Urania" in such earlier artists as Raphael (who may have influenced Milton in his conception), see chaps. 2, 3 and 5 and Appendices II and III in Treip, *"Descend from Heav'n Urania"*. In another essay, " 'Celestial Patronage': Allegorical Ceiling Cycles of the 1630s and the Iconography of Milton's Muse", in *Milton in Italy: Contexts, Images, Contradictions,* ed. Mario A. Di Cesare, I discuss similar iconographical connections in Wisdom-Providence figures in ceiling cycles which Milton may have known in Rome and London.

17. *Of CD* I.iii, *CE*, vol. 14, p. 81.

18. Ibid., p. 65.

19. It is essential to bear in mind Milton's distinction, expressed in *Of Ed.*, *CE*, vol. 4, p. 286, that poetry, being the more sophisticated study (since it comes last), persuades in a manner antithetical to that of logic. The *modus operandi* of poetry therefore must be different from or further and above that involved in "convinc[ing] by a probable demonstration" or "mak[ing] the central action seem logical and convincing" (Steadman, *The Wall of Paradise*, pp. 45-46). *Proofs* and *demonstrations* belong rather to the realm of logic than to poetry. Although Milton's epic incorporates dialectic and logic, these are balanced by the poetry and its figurative content. Milton's two procedures of "assertion" and "justification" or persuasion may also have some partial origin in the two contrasted methods of rabbinical exegesis, *mishnah* and *midrash,* or the "apodictic" (assertive, i.e. "fixed law") and the "discursive" or "justificatory" ("arguments and discussions"). See p. 2 of David Weiss Halivni, *Midrash, Mishnah, and Gemara: The Jewish Predilection for Justified Law.*

20. On God's reasonableness and man's free will, see *Of CD* I.iii, *CE*, vol. 14, pp. 73-75 and 83-85. Cutting across all arguments for reprobation, Milton says (to quote more fully from these pages): "Nor do we imagine anything unworthy of God, when we assert that those conditional events depend on the human will, *which God himself has chosen to place at the free disposal of man. . . .* On the contrary, it would be much more unworthy of God, that man should nominally enjoy a liberty of which he was virtually deprived". Further: "the sum of the argument may be thus stated *in strict conformity with reason. God of his wisdom determined to create men and angels reasonable beings, and therefore free agents. . . .* Since therefore . . . there can be no absolute decree of God regarding free agents, undoubtedly the prescience of the Deity . . . can neither impose any necessity of itself, nor can it be considered at all as the cause of free actions. If it be so considered, the very name of liberty must be altogether abolished as an

unmeaning sound; and that not only in matters of religion, but even in questions of morality and indifferent things".

21. *Of CD* I.iv, *CE,* vol. 14, p. 135.

22. See Treip, "The Emblematics of Free Will in *Paradise Lost*".

23. See *PL* IX.709, 723, 752; and Adam's long speech in X.723ff. The paradoxes are echoed by God in XI.85-87.

24. Tasso's "Allegoria", *Jerusalem Delivered,* p. 436.

25. *Areop., CE,* vol. 4, p. 311; again, "How great a vertue is temperance", each man's "owne leading capacity" in "the dyeting and repasting of our minds" (p. 309). Milton's "Temperance", like Spenser's, relates to Aristotle's *phronesis* or the "Mean": a virtue which penetrates all the virtues.

26. See *Areop, CE,* vol. 4, p. 319: "a meer artificiall *Adam,* such an *Adam* as he is in the motions"; also *Of CD* I.iv, Milton's arguments on free will, rehearsed in my chap. 13 and n. 20.

27. Le Bossu, Bk III.vii, p. 136.

28. For reference to an earlier understanding of *symbolum,* see my remarks in chap. 2, sect. "Coluccio Salutati", and chap. 2, n. 2.

Chapter 14. Historical Problems in Reading *Paradise Lost*

1. See, e.g., Philip J. Gallagher, "'Real or Allegoric': The Ontology of Sin and Death in *Paradise Lost*", who argues that Milton in some sense believed in the literal truth of every detail of his own story, as if he were writing an inspired amplification of Scripture in the light of a personal revelation. Milton believed in the "absolute historicity of Sin and Death as creatures begotten by Satan"; Milton's epic is (in the scriptural sense) "inspired elaborations of events" and a "literal record of cosmic history", and, (all of it) is "literal, authoritative history" (pp. 318-19). "The poet of *Paradise Lost* rejected allegoresis" (p. 334). It can be seen that while Gallagher and I both take as starting-point Satan's remarks in *PR,* our arguments proceed in contrary directions.

2. On Addison: see my chap. 9, sect. "Addison and Johnson". The anti-figurative bias of Richard Bentley's *Milton's Paradise Lost: A New Edition* is sufficiently notorious to need no specific citations. If, as Johnson alleges (see "Milton", in *Lives,* vol. 1, p. 181), Bentley really knew that there was no such editorial persona as he was engaged in "confuting", my point about eighteenth-century literalism in the reading of *PL* and antagonism to figuration is established even more clearly.

3. "Waller", in *Lives,* vol. 1, pp. 291-93; paragraphing not shown. Italics in this and ensuing quotations from Johnson are mine.

4. For the quotations which follow in the next four paragraphs, see "Milton", in *Lives,* vol. 1, pp. 171, 174-76, 178, 182-87. Johnson of course has misquoted Milton's "justifie the wayes of God to men" in *PL* Bk I.26.

5. On Le Bossu's distinction between "Fable" and "Episode", see my chap. 10, sect. "Allegory as the 'Platform' of Truth".

6. Johnson's comparison of Milton's poetical "process" to Le Bossu's theories occurs in *Lives,* vol. 1, p. 171.

7. On Phillips' comments, see my chap. 9, sect. "Edward Phillips and John Toland".

8. Several recent critics compile suggestive accounts of anti-figurative bias in Protestant writers of the period. For a list of some of the less immoderate views, see C.A. Patrides, *Milton and the Christian Tradition,* chap. 2. Patrides quotes Calvin (in Arthur Golding's translation of 1574), Henry Bullinger (trans. 1579) and other English or "Englished" scriptural commentators; also Donne, whose views on the legitimate uses of allegory are more traditional (on Donne, see further my App. D). For more severe comments, see some of the names and statements compiled by H.R. MacCallum in "Milton and Figurative Interpretation of the Bible". On the literary front, see the list compiled by Davis P. Harding in *Milton and the Renaissance Ovid,* pp. 25-26. Along with more liberal views, Harding cites Sir Walter Raleigh

(*History of the World*, 1614), William Prynne (*Histriomastix*, 1632), and a number of English early neoclassical critics, some of whom I have quoted earlier, as instances of Protestant restrictiveness concerning the use of figure, metaphor, fable, myth and allegory in poetry and especially in serious epic. It is apparent from such lists that the degree of anti-figurative feeling varies not only with the individual writer and context but also with the selection and use of citations by the particular critic. The same writer (Calvin, e.g.) may at different times appear on opposite sides of the fence, sometimes writing against figuration or alternatively in favour of it. However, it is broadly true that the progress from the sixteenth to the seventeenth century was increasingly in the direction of literalism in the reading of Scripture and reduction of some of the more radical forms of metaphor in poetry—as advocated by theologians and certain literary critics, though not necessarily by all or most poets.

9. [*De servo arbitrio* 1525] *The Bondage of the Will*, in *Erasmus-Luther: Discourse on Free Will*, trans. and ed. by Ernst F. Winter, pp. 128-29. I have further condensed Winter's abridged translation; italics are mine.

10. As trans. by Roland H. Bainton, "The Bible in the Reformation", in *The Cambridge History of the Bible*, chap. I of vol. 3, *The West from the Reformation to the Present Day*, ed. S.L. Greenslade, p. 19. On the "literal level", see further my App. D.

11. As trans. by Bainton, in *The Cambridge History of the Bible*, vol. 3, pp. 21-22.

12. Cf. Bainton's remarks on Luther's literalism in *The Cambridge History of the Bible*, vol. 3, e.g., pp. 32-33.

13. Cowley, "Preface to *Poems*", in Spingarn, ed., vol. 2, pp. 88-90. Greene, pp. 369-70, notes that Cowley's censures here and elsewhere bear little relation to his own heavily classicized epic: Cowley in the *Davideis* "betrays" deep "confusions" over the central "issue [in the Christian epic] of epic truthfulness".

14. Saint-Évremond, "On the Imitation of the Ancients" (1678), in Gilbert, ed., p. 664; italics are mine.

15. Rymer, "Preface to the Translation of Rapin's *Reflections on Aristotle's Treatise of Poesie*" (1674), in Spingarn, ed., vol. 2, pp. 168; 167-68. The first italics are mine.

Chapter 15. Scripture and the Figurative Reading of *Paradise Lost*

1. "Letter to Raleigh", *Spenser's Faerie Queene*, vol. 2, p. 486. Sandys, *Ovid's Metamorphoses*, ed. Stephen Orgel, Bk V, p. 190.

2. *Of CD* I.x, *CE*, vol. 15, pp. 144-45.

3. MacCallum correctly points out (pp. 407-9) that Milton restricts his own use of "types", but he minimizes Milton's uses of allegory. He implies that Milton employs allegory only in his secular prose (as e.g. in *The Doctrine and Discipline of Divorce*, where Milton says that he will "use an allegory somthing different from that in *Philo Judaeus* concerning Amaleck"). This interpretation does not acknowledge the importance given by Milton to allegory in *Of CD* (e.g., in his several citations of biblical allegory in Scripture), and especially, Milton's recognition of a form of allegory in relation to the representation of God there. MacCallum suggests, further, that Milton uses allegory in poetry only "when dealing with subject-matter that is not explicitly scriptural"—i.e., he does not use allegory in *PL*. See MacCallum, pp. 404, 414 n.15, and 411. The allusion in *Divorce*, chap. 3, is found in the 1644 ed. only, as given in *Complete Prose Works of John Milton*, vol. 2, ed. Ernest Sirluck, p. 288, where Milton is actually setting his own allegory in parallel to Philo's on the Book of Moses. Laurence Sterne and Harold H. Kollmeier, gen. eds., in *A Concordance to the English Prose of John Milton*—their references are to the Yale *Complete Prose Works*—list other uses of "allegory" or related forms of the word in Milton's prose as occurring in *Colasterion*, "that *allegorical* precept of *Moses*", vol. 2, p. 751, line 12; twice in *Divorce* (1644), "To persue the Allegory", vol. 2, p. 223, line 12, and "those other allegorick precepts", vol. 2, p. 273, line 4; and *Reason*, "[an] allegory of those seven Angels", vol. 1, p. 778, line 3. It can be seen that Milton rather freely associates allegorical figuration with OT matter. A final instance from *Smect.*, "a Prophetick pitch in types, and Allegories",

vol. 1, p. 714, line 4, may suggest that Milton makes a distinction between typology and allegory (since it is not his habit to double terms, that is, give synonyms). In sum, then, we may observe that Milton's uses of "allegory" are numerous, are set in significant contexts, and *always* appear associated with a wider kind of figuration—as opposed to his personal uses of "type" or "types", which imply strict Christological prediction only. There also seems to be not much difference between the way Milton uses "allegory" (or forms of the word) in his secular prose and the way he uses that word in *Of CD*, except that, writing in Latin in the theological treatise, he more often gives cognate terms—*figura, parabola, metaphora*—these being used interchangeably with the Latin *allegoria*.

    4. *CE*, vol. 14, pp. 30-31; vol. 16, pp. 264-65.

    5. *CE*, vol. 14, pp. 92-93; pp. 174-75.

    6. For further discussion of typological views, see App. F.

    7. *CE*, vol. 16, pp. 262-65; pp. 250-51.

    8. Such as the correct interpretation of "Predestination", to which central doctrine one of the longest expositions in *Of CD* is given: see Bk I.iii-iv, *CE*, vol. 14, pp. 63-175.

    9. *Of CD* I.xxx, *CE*, vol. 16, pp. 261; 259.

    10. See Bainton, quoting Luther, as cited in my chap. 15, n. 22.

    11. *Of CD* I.xxx, *CE*, vol. 16, p. 261. Note that there is no reference to allegory in Milton's list of the logical and metaphysical trivia of "scholastic barbarism". Milton is always precise in his choice of words, and had he intended to include allegorical figure he would have named it here.

    12. Cf. *Of CD* I.i, *CE*, vol. 14, p. 25: "It must be observed, that Faith in this division does not mean the habit of believing, but the things to be habitually believed".

    13. *Of CD* I.xxx, *CE*, vol. 16, p. 263.

    14. For further discussion of the "literal level", see App. D.

    15. *Of CD* I.xxx, vol. 16, pp. 262-63. *Saepe* would be more accurately translated as *many times*, or *often*, rather than as *sometimes*, as it is in *CE*. However, the point is immaterial to my argument here. Milton finds *double* readings only in the Old Testament, not the New; but solely figurative passages are not thereby excluded from either.

    16. *Of CD* I.xxx, *CE*, vol. 16, p. 253.

    17. See the listings as given in the *Concordance* of Sterne and Kollmeier, p. 1378, col.1. The eds. note that 12 out of 18 uses of "type" are from *Reason*; many are satire; and all reveal Milton's habit of not extending the theory of types beyond strict prophecy of Christ.

    18. *Of CD* I.xxx, *CE*, vol. 16, p. 251. Nonetheless, Milton does use the Apocrypha for "wisdom".

    19. See *Of CD* I.x, *CE*, vol. 15, pp. 144-45.

    20. *Of CD* I.xxx, *CE*, vol. 16, p. 264-65.

    21. See my chap. 1, sect. "The Medieval 'Levels'".

    22. I see no reason to think that Milton would not have agreed with the further Protestant distinction (discussed in more detail in my chap. 18, sect. "The 'Experiential' Approach") that there also exists in the Bible much description or narration of a literal or factual kind which, while "inspired" in the sense of having been dictated by revelation, is not of specific doctrinal importance, although it can still have great value for purposes of private devotion, meditation or homiletic use. Cf. Bainton in *The Cambridge History of the Bible*, vol. 3, pp. 20-21: "Luther regarded every iota of Scripture as inspired but nevertheless found in Scripture a graded scale of values. . . . The Bible then is an inspired book in every part but not with uniform inspiration. The kernel is encased in a shell, the baby lies in a manger, the Word of God is contained". Quoting Luther directly (p. 20): "Christ is swaddled in Scripture; the manger is the preaching in which he lies and is contained, and from which one can take food and fodder". Thus is pure doctrine to be distinguished from those other parts of the Bible which may be used for devotion and preaching.

    23. For Neoplatonic analogues to and Augustinian sources of the theory of scriptural "accommodation", see my chaps. 15, n.27, and 16, nn. 1 and 6. E.H. Gombrich discusses

"accommodation" doctrines in Dante and early humanist critics in *Symbolic Images*, pp. 234, n. 123 (Dante); 164 (Girolamo Ruscelli); 153-54 and 192 (Christophoro Giarda). For further discussion of recent literature and various positions on scriptural "accommodation", also their implications for Milton's language, see my App. E.

24. William Madsen, *From Shadowy Types to Truth: Studies in Milton's Symbolism*, pp. 82-83, appears to be saying something along these lines, but subsequently narrows his argument toward his thesis (fuller discussion of which is given in my App. F) that the principal contents and figurative meanings of *PL* are typologically determined. For an example of a brief counter-argument analogous to my own, see James H. Sims, "Milton, Literature as a Bible, and the Bible as Literature", in *Milton and the Art of Sacred Song*, ed. J. Max Patrick and Roger H. Sundell, pp. 3-21, but esp. pp. 3-5 and 20-21. See also John T. Shawcross, "Milton and Covenant: The Christian View of Old Testament Theology", in James H. Sims and Leland Ryken, eds., *Milton and Scriptural Tradition: The Bible into Poetry*. Shawcross presents a detailed argument for Milton's restriction of the use of "types" in *PL* to historical figures in the Old Testament; see esp. pp. 186-90 and n. 43. MacCallum also has argued for Milton's restriction of typological reading, in his essay cited earlier.

25. *Of CD* I.ii, *CE*, vol. 14, pp. 30-33. The further quotations on "accommodation" in this sect. are taken from the same chap., pp. 33 and 37. I have earlier given my reasons for preferring the *CE* Lat.-Eng. translations from *De Doctrina* to those of the Yale *Complete Prose Works*. In the important passage on scriptural "accommodation", I have no doubt that *CE* supplies a more sensitive reading than does Yale. The crucial point is how we are to understand "vel describi vel adumbrari". *Vel . . . vel*, although it often means "either . . . or", is also given by the Oxford *A Latin Dictionary* (p. 1963, meaning 1B2a) as, "with weakened disjunctive force" nearly = *et . . . et*) ("both . . . and"). More important, *adumbrare* is defined in meaning B2, "fig." (p. 47), as *"to represent a thing only in outline*, and, consequently, *imperfectly"*, as of deities; also, as part. adj. *adumbratus*, (meaning B, p. 47), as *"devised in darkness, dark, secret"*. The *Shorter O.E.D.*, p. 27, cites a fig. use of *adumbrate* in 1581 as "to represent by 'shadow' or emblem; to typify; hence, to foreshadow", and cites the use of *adumbration* in 1622 to indicate a "symbolic representation". Hence when *CE* translates that the representation of God in Scripture is both literal and *figurative*, "figurative" embodies from the Lat. *adumbrare* (English *adumbrate*) a variety of important associations relevant to scriptural allegory, including also some meanings in the C16th and C17th explicitly relating to formal allegorical structures. The Yale *Complete Prose Works* translation of the crucial line (vol. 6, ed. Maurice Kelley, p. 133) seems intended to efface these important associations and to suppress any allusion to allegory: "God is always *described or outlined* not as he really is" (italics mine).

26. For the views of MacCallum, James Holly Hanford and others on this subject, see my chap. 15, n. 27, chap. 16, n. 1, and App. E.

27. Nonetheless, MacCallum (p. 402; cf. p. 413, n. 8) construes Milton's "accommodation" passage in *Of CD* as "unusually daring" in, similarly to Luther's and Calvin's views, "upholding anthropomorphism". On the basis largely of this construction, he interprets Milton's art in *PL* also as literalistic. C.A. Patrides, *"Paradise Lost* and the Theory of Accommodation", in *Bright Essence: Studies in Milton's Theology*, by W.B. Hunter *et al.*, pp. 159-63, also without much evidence gives a view of Milton's prose remarks and poetic representation as literalistic and anthropomorphic—or rather, "anthropopathic" (p. 163)—even though Milton specifically *rejects* "anthropopathy" as an absurdity in *Of CD* I.ii (*CE*, vol. 14, p. 33). Patrides (pp. 160-61 and 161, n. 4) locates the origin of the "accommodation" doctrine in Augustine (*City of God*), who says that God is shown in Scriptures as "declining to our low capacities". In a second essay in the same volume, *"Paradise Lost* and the Language of Theology", pp. 165-78, Patrides revises his view of the representation of God in *PL*, but very much derogates what he exaggeratedly considers to be the crude literalism of *Of CD*.

28. On "both . . . and" in *Of CD* I.ii, in the *CE* trans., vol. 14, p. 31, see my chap. 15, n. 25. Roland Mushat Frye, *God, Man, and Satan: Patterns of Christian Thought and Life in Paradise*

Lost, Pilgrim's Progress, and the Great Theologians, pp. 7-17, helps to put the difficult matter of "accommodation" into perspective. For discussion, see my App. E.

Chapter 16. Theory of Metaphor in *Paradise Lost*

1. A Neoplatonic explanation of Milton's "accommodation" doctrine was put forward by Hanford in *A Milton Handbook,* pp. 190-91. Hanford makes the Neoplatonic analogy eloquently, and all critics since have followed him, or else have been at pains to confute him: "This idea, the so-called 'theory of accommodation', fitted well with Milton's Platonism. . . . He had early conceived of himself as a revealer of truth in the Platonic sense. Poetic myth was the only possible way of representing the 'ideas' to human apprehension". But having made this connection, Hanford is at once sensible of its discomforts: "We have . . . in *Paradise Lost* a historical fiction divinely sanctioned, embodying not a fallible philosophy of human origin but the verities of the Christian religion itself". The supposition that allegory, metaphorically "accommodated" truths and oblique forms of figuration in poetry (other than "types") involve the acceptance of the whole main body of Platonic humanist philosophy has caused many critics, and Madsen in particular, much difficulty. Renaissance Idealist aesthetics and their relation to allegory in poetry and epic are discussed in my chap. 4 and in App. B.

2. Samuel, p. 32.

3. See Hanford, my chap. 16, n. 1. On the Raphael passage (V.563 ff.) in this context, see Roland Frye, p. 14.

4. MacCallum's view, p. 413, n.8.

5. A passage which closely recalls the ambiguities in both Raphael's remarks and the passage in *Of CD* on the representation of God is that in *PL* VIII on rival astronomical theories, beginning thus in lines 159-63:

> But whether thus these things, or whether not,
> Whether the Sun predominant in Heav'n
> Rise on the Earth, or Earth rise on the Sun,
> Hee from the East his flaming rode begin,
> Or Shee from West her silent course advance. . . .

These lines seem to reveal the same hesitation between alternative explanations, the same studiously neutral attitude, and to end with the same final apparent suppression of doubts ("Sollicit not thy thoughts with matters hid", 167) that we saw in *Of CD* I.ii. Yet we might be more convinced that "Whether Heav'n move or Earth, / Imports not" (70-71) had Raphael not opened the discussion with "To ask or search *I blame thee not*" (66), and had Milton not gone on to explore the variant astronomical theories, Galileo's especially, at such length and in such rich poetry. Whatever this passage says on the surface, we cannot miss from its tone where Raphael's (or Milton's) sympathies lie: namely, with and not against speculation *in a reserved and proper context.* Raphael is simply concluding his long speculative conversation with Adam with a timely warning against excess. There are more pressing considerations than astronomy at a moment of imminent moral danger.

6. On Augustine, see *Homer the Theologian,* chap. VI.D in particular, where Lamberton explicates Augustine's aesthetic theories in *Civitas Dei* and their early sources: "Augustine uses Plotinus to explicate the Sermon on the Mount (*Civ. Dei* 10.14)" and in "*Civ. Dei* 16.2 and 13.21" uses "the Old Testament as an allegorical representation of Christ and his Church to come" (p. 257, nn. 93 and 94). On "Augustine's theory of signs" and his "basic conception of language and the nature of the linguistic sign" as also linked to his theory of "accommodation" in Scripture, see further pp. 257, 259. Cf. Augustine in *De Trinitate* 15.ix.15; see my chap. 1, n. 34. On the C12th mystics of Saint-Victor see de Bruyne, as cited in my chap. 1, n. 42.

7. See my chap. 3, sect. "John Harington".

8. The passage is quoted in the translation of Lawson, from *The Song of Songs,* Bk III,

sect. 12, p. 223. Another parallel to the Fornari passage would seem to be in Dante, *Paradiso* IV.40-48—although this is directed more specifically to theory of "accommodation" in Scripture, a method seen by Dante as emulated in the way the Church teaches scriptural matters.

9. The passage (italics are mine) is from Simone Fornari's *La Spositione di M. Simon Fornari . . . Sopra L'Orlando Furioso di M.L. Ariosto* (1549-50), vol. 2, fo. b2-b2ᵛ, and it is quoted here in the translation given by McNulty, p. xxxvii, in his Introd. to Harington's English ed. of the *Furioso*. For the Ital., see McNulty, p. xxxvii, n.1. It was widely known, its immediate source being the second preface to Pico's *Heptaplus* (1557). Thomas P. Roche, Jr., in *The Kindly Flame: A Study of the Third and Fourth Books of Spenser's Faerie Queene* (pp. 7-8 and p. 8, n. 7), quotes the Pico passage in a parallel trans. into Eng. by Pierre de la Primaudaye in *The French Academie* (London: 1618), p. 671.

10. *Orlando Furioso* p. 291. The Ital. runs as ff.:

> —Tu dèi saper che non si muove fronda
> là giù, che segno qui non se ne faccia.
> Ogni effetto convien che corrisponda
> in terra e in ciel, ma con diversa faccia.
> Quel vecchio, la cui barba il petto inonda,
> veloce sì che mai nulla l'impaccia,
> gli effetti pari e la medesima opra
> che 'l Tempo fa là giù, fa qui di sopra.

Orlando Furioso (XXXV.18), ed. Lanfranco Caretti, p. 913. The crucial words, in terms of allegory, are "signe" (*segno*), "act" or "action" (implied in line 1 of the Ital., in *muove*), "effects" (*effetti*), and, of course, "correspondence" (*corrisponda*); Harington is alert to the tenor of Victorine allegorism (as is Ariosto), and his translations are exact.

11. See "Marginalia" VIII ("Notes on Ariosto"), in *CE*, vol. 18, *The Uncollected Writings of John Milton*, pp. 330-36.

12. Don M. Wolfe points out in vol. 1 of the Yale *Complete Prose Works* (pp. 810-11, n. 71) that in *Reason* Milton's expressed literary ambitions seem to be echoing Harington's essay on "The Life of Ariosto". There (see Harington's *Orlando Furioso*, pp. 416-17) Harington tells an ancedote in which Ariosto expresses his aim to enrich his own language by writing in his native tongue, saying that he would rather be one of the principal among Tuscan writers than second or third among the Latins. In *Of Ref.* Milton, further, quotes or translates two stanzas from the *Furioso*, XXXIV (72 and 79 in Harington's trans., or 73 and 80), naming Ariosto. (The first stanza is that where Astolfo meets "St. John": this initiates Ariosto's long allegory of true versus false and fleeting poetic fame. The second stanza is satirical, and concerns the corruption of the Church after Constantine.) See Wolfe, *Complete Prose Works*, vol. 1, pp. 559-60, and n. 147, for remarks on this borrowing. For the corresponding locations of the Milton passages in *CE*, see *Reason*, vol. 3.1, p. 236 and *Of Ref.*, vol. 3.1, p. 27.

13. Augustine connects allegory in the Bible with literary allegory. See my chap. 1, sect. "The Church Fathers", and n. 34.

14. See Puttenham, p. 186; Peacham, fo. Di; discussed in my chap. 2, sect. "The English Rhetoricians". Cf. Salutati's theory of poetry as "translation", discussed in my chap. 2, sect. "Coluccio Salutati".

15. My interpretation of the Raphael speech runs counter to that of Madsen, pp. 87-89. Madsen's view is discussed further in my App. F.

16. As e.g. in Tuve, *Elizabethan and Metaphysical Imagery*, p. 105.

17. The contrast indicated here is in general outline not new. See e.g. the remarks of Mary Ann Radzinowicz in *Toward Samson Agonistes: The Growth of Milton's Mind*, pp. 306-9.

18. On this ambiguity see Helen Gardner, "The Historical Sense", in *The Business of Criticism*, p. 137, quoting a sermon of Donne. The passage is given in my App. D.

19. As Madsen, also, notes (pp. 78-79, in the chap. "Lively Image"), the words "shadow" and "lively" both are used in the period not only in connection with typological figuration but in much wider homiletic contexts, and in literary discussions to signify allegorical figures of speech.

20. We may refer to Radzinowicz's discussion (*Toward Samson Agonistes*, pp. 122-24) of "Lycidas". The complex interrelationship between allegory (understood here as allegorical figure embodied in personal fantasy) and "truth" which she perceives in "Lycidas" is analogous to that which I suggest in *PL*. In the earlier poem's development, with each new phase or "movement", "One level of allegory yields to a truer level of allegory in 'a higher mood'. . . . [each of the three movements] positing a fictional allegory and replacing it with a real allegory. . . . In all three, the allegorical seems to be proposed and then withdrawn, but in fact, the new truth itself is a superior form of allegory. The mind discards a false image in favor of a realistic image, which itself contains a true fiction".

21. Gombrich, p. 157, connects Tasso's remarks on symbolism with Dionysius the Areopagite and Neoplatonic aesthetics, citing Tasso's famous passage on poetic images as mystical signs (see *Discorsi del poema eroico*, Bk II, pp. 31-32, earlier discussed). On p. 129 Gombrich comments in general terms on the potency of allegorical art and symbolism to "conjure up the vivid presence of any notion which to the logical mind appears as a 'concept' "—that is, to become the "expressive evocation of a concept"; further, on p. 125: "where there is no clear gulf separating the material, visible world from the sphere of the spirit . . . not only the various meanings of the word 'representation' may become blurred but the whole relationship between image and symbol assumes a different aspect. . . . the human mind [tends] to confuse the sign with the thing signified, the name and its bearers, the literal and metaphorical, the image and its prototype. . . . Our language . . . favours this twilight region between the literal and the metaphorical. Who can always tell where the one begins and the other ends?"

22. An interesting light on Milton's views on symbolism is given in his comment on the sacred writers' treatment of sacramental symbols in the Old Testament (*Of CD* I.xxviii, *CE*, vol. 16, pp. 199-201). While Milton obviously must argue against a doctrine like consubstantiation, and so gives the conventional Protestant interpretation that the physical sacraments are a "seal . . . pledge or symbol", his own language is not that of one who derogates the power of symbolic language in sacred contexts: "The object of the sacred writers, in thus expressing themselves, was probably *to denote the close affinity between the sign and the thing signified*". This hardly seems a "cautious rationalistic approach to metaphor" comparable to that of "Bacon, Hobbes, and the proponents of the Royal Society" (see Madsen, p. 70). Madsen, p. 80, cites other Protestant writers who, similarly to Milton, refer to the sacraments powerfully, as a "lively image" (p. 77).

23. A curious echo of "conspicious" here occurs in Bk VI.298-99 ("to what things / Lik'n on Earth conspicuous"), when Raphael is again discussing the powers of human or angelic metaphor.

24. Dronke (*Fabula*, pp. 32-45) discusses the use of *imago, similitudo* (which also translates as *analogy*) and *simulacrum* in medieval aesthetic theory deriving from Plato and St. Paul, and as represented in the work of William of Conches, "to suggest a far more substantial bond between the divine mind and the human" (p. 36).

25. See "Milton and the Scene of Interpretation: From Typology toward Midrash", in *Midrash and Literature*, ed. Hartman and Budick, pp. 195-212. The reference to *Reason* in my text is from *CE*, vol. 3.1, p. 236.

Chapter 17. Typology and the Figurative Dimension in *Paradise Lost*

1. See my chap. 15 and n. 24.

2. For a list of some representative "typological" readings of Milton's poems and discussion, see App. F.

3. From Barbara Kiefer Lewalski's *Protestant Poetics and the Seventeenth-Century Religious Lyric*, p. 111. Georgia B. Christopher undertakes analogous investigations in *Milton and the Science of the Saints*.

4. See my chap. 18, sect. "The 'Experiential' Approach".

5. Madsen, pp. 88-89.

6. Bainton, in *The Cambridge History of the Bible*, vol. 3, p. 26. See also Barbara Kiefer Lewalski, "Typology and Poetry: A Consideration of Herbert, Vaughan, and Marvell", p. 42 in *Illustrious Evidence: Approaches to English Literature of the Early Seventeenth Century*, ed. Earl Miner, where she speaks of "patterns of prefiguration, recapitulation, and fulfillment by reason of God's providential control of history".

7. Cf. Madsen's remark, p. 111, n.27: Raphael's metaphor is "primarily . . . typological" because it is "oriented toward the future".

8. See Gardner, chap. 3, "The Historical Sense", *passim* (see my chap. 15, n. 3); discussed also in my App. F. Partly, too, as MacCallum has shown, Milton simply did not believe in exaggerated typology.

9. *Of Ed.*: "what glorious and magnificent use might be made of Poetry both in divine and humane things". *CE*, vol. 4, p. 286.

10. See my chap. 15.

11. Jean Daniélou, S.J., [*Sacramentum Futuri: Études sur les Origines de la Typologie biblique*] *From Shadows to Reality: Studies in the Biblical Typology of the Fathers*, trans. Dom Wulstan Hibberd; see esp. Conclusion, pp. 287-88, paras. 2, 3, 5 and 8.

12. "Of the Office of the Mediator and of his Threefold Functions", *Of CD* I.xv; see esp. *CE*, vol. 15, pp. 287-303.

13. Gardner, p. 142.

14. Cf. *Of CD* I.xv, in *CE*, vol. 15, p. 287: "The name and office of mediator is in a certain sense ascribed to Moses, as a type of Christ".

15. Radzinowicz (*Toward Samson Agonistes*, pp. 308-9) clarifies the important correlation between Raphael's discourse and poetic mode in *PL* and Michael's very different kind of discourse and mode. Greene's earlier remark (p. 404) that Michael's lapse into the plain style of "relating" is a sign of imaginative weariness in Milton's poem was surely misconceived: "the vigor of his language flags . . . in just these two concluding books where human history is related". Milton deliberately associates the "plain and perspicuous" manner of Michael's discourse with the content of scriptural history and doctrine conveyed in the last two Books and, linked to history and doctrine in those Books, with his own view of literal prophetic types. The two different narrative approaches in question, Raphael's "accommodated" or fictive art and Michael's plain historical narration embracing historical types, are conjoined in many different places and ways throughout *PL*.

16. Gardner, p. 143.

17. Cf. Fowler's remarks in *The Poems of Milton*, n. to *PL* X.832. Fowler quotes J.B. Broadbent, *Some Graver Subject: An Essay on Paradise Lost*, p. 152, who says that Adam (in *PL* X.832 and elsewhere) repeats "the central *ploce* on 'me'" from Christ's speech at III.236: "This is the spring of self-sacrifice which Adam and Eve draw on after the Fall to recover sanity and love".

18. On the apocryphal provenance of the figure of Abdiel, see Fowler, *The Poems of Milton*, n. to *PL* V.805-7. On Milton's use of uncanonical material from traditional "Wisdom" literature, see my chap. 19, sect. "Milton's Uses of Extra-Canonical Matter".

19. Daniélou notes (p. 288, para. 7) that one form of typology "saw the fulfilment of the types even in the events of the Old Testament". There is no fulfilment in the passages which I have quoted from Milton in this paragraph of my text, only negative reiterations.

20. See Lewalski's discussion of "correlative types", cited in my App. F.

21. Quotations from Gardner, p. 143.

Chapter 18. Protestant Homiletics and Allegory in *Paradise Lost*

1. Madsen, pp. 79 and 82, mentions homily briefly in connection with rhetoric and allegory, finding in preaching techniques a wide mixture of figurative techniques and practices. Lewalski in *Protestant Poetics* (chap. 4, esp. p. 123) identifies some of the more imaginatively extended typological structures which she cites with Protestant homiletics, i.e. with nondoctrinal expositions of Scripture. Yet both critics are reluctant to bring any of the concepts or practices involved in allegory to bear on either Milton or Protestant sermonizing, or on Protestant religious poetry in general. Cf. Lewalski: "allegorical exegesis" was a "limited and literary approach", p. 122. However, Lewalski is much more cautious in her claims for typological symbolism in *PL* than is Madsen.

2. The quotations from Bainton which follow in the next two paragraphs of my text come from *The Cambridge History of the Bible*, vol. 3, pp. 24-25; 23; 27; and 37. Italics in the longer passage (p. 25) are mine.

3. Bainton, in *The Cambridge History of the Bible*, vol. 3, p. 27.

4. See Christopher Hill, *Milton and the English Revolution*, pp. 341-45. Hill has a few paragraphs on *Paradise Lost* as conjunction of history and allegory, "truth and myth at the same time" (p. 344).

5. Bainton, in *The Cambridge History of the Bible*, vol. 3, p. 20, quoting Luther: "We must be shown the place where Christ lies. This is the manger where we may find him. . . . That is to say, that Christ is swaddled in Scripture; the manger is the preaching in which he lies and is contained, and from which one can take food and fodder". The writer of the article comments: "The distinction between the Word and Scripture accounts for the apparent contradiction that Luther regarded every iota of Scripture as inspired but nevertheless found in Scripture a graded scale of values".

6. In writing of the Judgement and the six-day account of the Creation, Milton respects the literal sense of the Bible even though, as he elsewhere observes, "time" is not certain in respect of God's creative acts. See *PL* VII.152-55: "I . . . /*in a moment* will create /Another World". Fowler cites Augustine, *De Genesi*, i.1-3 on this matter; see *The Poems of Milton*, n. to *PL* VII.154.

Chapter 19. "Accommodation" in *Paradise Lost*: The Internal View

1. Cf. Isabel Gamble MacCaffrey's cautious statement in *Paradise Lost as "Myth"*, p. 21: "The claim for the truth of events is absolute: these things happened; for the truth of images— the poem's places and personages—less absolute, but still insistent".

2. The phrase, "according to the spirit", does not in itself imply literalism. In *Of CD* I.vi, *CE*, vol. 14 (see esp. pp. 357-81), Milton notes that in the Bible the word "spirit" is used in a great variety of ways, sometimes indistinguishably from the Son or Father (although Milton stresses that the Holy Spirit is not co-equal with either), and that there is very little written concerning the Spirit as "personality"—that is, as the third Person of the Trinity. It is interesting that Milton should in *PL* similarly use "spirit" or the cognate concept of inspiration in a variety of ways: sometimes representing Urania or the Christian Muse, sometimes as God's creative agent or the dove (contrast *PL* I.6-7 or VII.1-3 with I.19-23), sometimes identified with Light (the Son) or Wisdom (see III.1-8 and 51-55). Milton's allusions to illumination by the Spirit are also frequently attached to a prayer for correctness ("*Instruct me*", I.19). The wish now apparently is that he not misrepresent the Word. Here is the Reformers' effort to read Scripture "only by that spirit in which Scripture was written"—that is, the scholarly attempt to seek out a pure and consistent body of doctrine across the Holy Scriptures through prayer, humility and study. For citation of some of the literature on Milton's uses of "spirit" and further comment, see Treip, *"Descend from Heav'n Urania"*, chap. 5.

3. In *Of CD* I.xxx, *CE*, vol. 16, p. 251, Milton makes the points that the Apocrypha are

not "of equal authority with the canonical" Books; that they may not "be adduced as evidence in matters of faith" (used to prove doctrine); and he adds that they "contain much that is at variance with the acknowledged parts of Scripture, besides some things fabulous, low, trifling, and contrary to true religion and wisdom". The statement superficially belies his actual free use in *PL* of the Apocrypha, or at least of certain "things" in those Books, although not for doctrine but for "wisdom".

4. The allusions linking Milton's Raphael with Tobias in Bks IV.170 and V.222 derive from the apocryphal Tobit iii.17, viii.3, etc. (see Fowler, *The Poems of Milton*, nn. to *PL* IV.166-71 and V.221-23); details in Book V of Raphael's visit, meal, etc., from Genesis 18 and a number of rabbinical glosses on it, as e.g. Rashi's (see Jack Goldman, "Perspectives of Raphael's Meal in *Paradise Lost*, Book V")—although Raphael's name is never mentioned in Genesis. Hanford, p. 203, n. 105, finds the most important analogue to be in Tobit. Gabriel, although occurring in the canonical books, in Milton's development in Bk IV seems to relate more to the pseudepigraphic Book of Enoch xx.7 (see Fowler, n. to *PL* IV.549-50). Uriel in Bk III similarly derives from the apocryphal 2 Esdras and other Jewish cabbalistic traditions (Fowler, n. to *PL* III.648). For other details in the angel scenes drawn by Milton from extra-canonical sources or traditions, see Virginia R. Mollenkott, "The Pervasive Influence of the Apocrypha in Milton's Thought and Art", in *Milton and the Art of Sacred Song*, ed. Patrick and Sundell. She gives a comprehensive survey of the influence of apocryphal writings on Miltonic themes in *PL*, especially of those Books or commentaries traditionally grouped under "Wisdom" literature, with its distinctive Hellenistic-Judaic and humanist blend of thought, so readily incorporated into the Christian tradition. In a related context, Golda Spiera Werman, in "Midrash in *Paradise Lost: Capitula Rabbi Elieser*" analyses similarly plausible but fictive material concerning Adam and Eve in the Garden, taken from Vorstius' Latin trans. (1644) of *Pirkei de-Rabbi Eliezer*.

5. From the Thirty-Nine Articles, as quoted in *The Concise Oxford Dictionary of the Christian Church*, ed. Elizabeth A. Livingstone, p. 28. However, while using some "fabulous" things for edification, Milton presumably excludes those "low, trifling" things of which he speaks with disapproval in *Of CD* I.xxx; see *CE*, vol. 16, p. 251.

6. See App. D.

7. Witness the well-known objections recorded by A.J.A. Waldock, *Paradise Lost and its Critics*, and William Empson, *Milton's God*. "Lack of charity" in Milton's God was a student comment which seems worth recording.

8. Quotation from *Of CD* I.xxx, *CE*, vol. 16, p. 259. On Milton and the Psalms, see Mary Ann Radzinowicz, *Milton's Epics and the Book of Psalms*. On the structuring of the heavenly dialogues, cf. C.A. Patrides' remarks in "The Godhead in *Paradise Lost*: Dogma or Drama?", in *Bright Essence*, pp. 71-77.

9. See my chap. 15, sect. "'Accommodation' in *Of Christian Doctrine*". Barbara Kiefer Lewalski in *Paradise Lost and the Rhetoric of Literary Forms*, p. 113, points to Milton's "radically metaphoric but yet insistently biblical imagination of God", relating this to Milton's understanding of "accommodation". The insistent literalism "gives Milton full warrant as poet to portray God as an epic character who can and does feel a range of emotions". Lewalski also notes: "the fact that for Milton the Bible itself offers only accommodated images of God evidently sanctions for him the use of other literary accommodations that . . . help to expand the biblical images". Such other accommodations in Lewalski's view include "a mix of generic patterns". I would suggest that many other verbal devices and structures besides a mixture of generic patterns similarly perform a function of accommodation, and that the *over*-literalism of Milton's representation itself directs attention to the transcendent aspects of God intimated in other instances or even in the same instances in the poem.

10. On the *mashal*, see Boyarin, "The Song of Songs: Lock or Key?", and "Rhetoric and Interpretation: The Case of the Nimshal". See also David Stern, "Rhetoric and Midrash: the Case of the Mashal".

11. See David Stern, "Midrash and the Language of Exegesis: A Study of Vayikra Rabbah, Chapter 1", in *Midrash and Literature*, ed. Hartman and Budick, pp. 105-24.

12. As Boyarin has dramatically shown in "Voices in the Text". Cf. my chap. 1, sects. "Rabbinical Interpretation" and "The Church Fathers".

13. See *De Opificio Mundi*, LV-LVIII, in *Philo*, vol. 1, pp. 123-29.

14. On the background and uses of such elements in midrashic exposition see, in *Midrash and Literature*, ed. Hartman and Budick, the ff. essays: Kugel, pp. 88-89, 91-92, esp.; Stern, "Midrash and the Language of Exegesis"; Betty Roitman, "Sacred Language and Open Text"; and Budick, pp. 208-11 esp. Budick finds midrashic parallels in the language of the opening lines of *PL* Bk XI.

15. For an analysis of this scene and Milton's figural treatment, see Budick.

16. Budick, p. 207 and p. 212, n. 14, cites Harry Austryn Wolfson, *The Philosophy of the Church Fathers*, vol. 1, *Faith, Trinity, Incarnation*, pp. 40-41. Wolfson says that the "predictive interpretations" of the rabbis (as Budick notes, "a dimension of typology that seems to have been unknown to Auerbach") "are all described by terms borrowed from Philo's vocabulary, namely, allegory, type, shadow, and parable". That is to say, the very arcane forms of midrashic "typology" (Budick uses this word, but he intends a rather different, special form of figure relating to the mediating or "dividing" Word, as instanced in the opening scene of *PL*, Bk XI) are closely linked with other forms of allegory in Philo or the midrashicists.

Chapter 20. Toward an Allegorical Poesis in *Paradise Lost*

1. See *Discorsi del poema eroico*, Bk II, p. 52: "in duels with lances and in sword blows, let [the poet] seek verisimilitude, not going too far beyond what happened, might happen, is believed, or is told". On the episode of the War in Heaven with its conventional Elizabethan weaponry, we may refer to Tasso's caution (Bk II, pp. 51-53) against using too much detail of manners and habits of men taken from too recent and too familiar history and customs. Milton of course is trying by this very means to undercut the episode and to enforce other kinds of reading than the literal.

2. Le Bossu, Bk V.iii, p. 222.

3. Hill, p. 345, makes a parallel point: "God is history, is the world as it really is, not as we would romantically like it to be". The answer to Adam's and Satan's difficulties obliquely lies in the preceding verses in James (1.13-14): "Let no one say when he is tempted, 'I am tempted by God'; for God . . . himself tempts no one; but each person is tempted when he is lured and enticed by his own desire".

4. Steadman, *The Lamb and the Elephant*, p. 95.

5. Greene, p. 386 and n.38, notes a similar phenomenon in others of Milton's similes in *PL*, a hovering between comparison and reality. Satan "as a Tiger" (IV.403) "seems to stray into a simile while still remaining outside it"; likewise Raphael "as that sole Bird" (V.272) is at one and the same time only *like* and yet seems to have taken *the actual form* of a phoenix.

6. *Pace* Hill, p. 342: "We must distinguish between allegory, in which characters have a single and consistent significance, and the method of allusion". The total separation of allegory from allusion is, I would argue, a false distinction.

7. See Bentley, p. 115 (misnumbered as p. 215) n. to *PL* IV.268.

8. The emblem of the Scales, along with other emblem images in *PL* relating to Free Will or Choice, are discussed by Treip in "The Emblematics of Free Will in *Paradise Lost*".

9. Le Bossu, Bk I.v, p. 11.

10. P. 439 of Tasso's "Allegoria": discussed in my chap. 5, sect. "Moral Content: Tasso's 'Allegoria'".

Chapter 21. The "Language of Allegory" and Milton's Allegorical Epic

1. See my chap. 1, n. 4.

2. Cf. Hill, p. 344: "[the poem] is truth and myth at the same time"; "Such an approach
. . . . enables us to respond to the design of *Paradise Lost* as a whole rather than as a collection
of episodes: the epic has a tough intellectual structure". Hill is of course thinking primarily of
a political allegory, but his argument moves in a correct general direction.

3. See the discussion of Phillips and Toland in my chap. 9, sect. "Edward Phillips and
John Toland".

4. Phillips (see my chap. 21, n. 3) and Tasso (see my chap. 7, sect. "History and Fiction
in the Epic") both were emphatic about the necessary brevity or minimalist treatment of
history. For discussion of the familiar Milton quotations in the next two paragraphs, see my
chap. 12, sect. "Structuring the 'Diffuse' Epic".

List of Works Cited

Primary Works

Addison, Joseph, contributor. *The Spectator*. Edited by Donald F. Bond. 5 vols. Oxford: Clarendon Press, 1965.

Aquinas, Saint Thomas. *The Summa Theologica of Saint Thomas Aquinas*. Translated by Fathers of the English Dominican Province. Revised edition by Daniel J. Sullivan. Great Books of the Western World. Chicago: Encyclopaedia Britannica and William Benton, 1952.

Ariosto, Ludovico. *Orlando Furioso*. Edited by Lanfranco Caretti. Milan and Naples: Riccardo Ricciardi, 1954. See also under **Harington,** translator.

Aristotle. *The Nicomachean Ethics*. (1926). Translated by H. Rackham. Rev. ed. Loeb Classical Library. London: William Heinemann, and Cambridge, Mass.: Harvard Univ. Press, 1934.

Augustine, Saint. *The City of God against the Pagans*. Vol. 5 of 7. Translated by Eva Matthews Sanford and William McAllen Green. Loeb Classical Library. Cambridge, Mass: Harvard Univ. Press, 1965.

———. *Saint Augustine: The Trinity*. Translated by Stephen McKenna. The Fathers of the Church, no. 45. Washington, D.C.: Catholic Univ. of America Press, 1963.

———. *De Trinitate*. In vol. 42 of *Patrologiae Cursus Completus*, series 1. Edited by J.-P. Migne. Paris: Gallice, 1841 [1845].

Bacon, Francis. *The Advancement of Learning* (1605). Edited by William Aldis Wright. 5th ed. Oxford: Clarendon Press, 1968.

———. *The Works of Francis Bacon*. Edited by James Spedding *et al*. 14 vols. London: Longman, 1861. Contains in vol. 1 *De augmentis scientiarium* (1623). Contains in vol. 6 [*De sapientia veterum*] *Of the Wisdom of the Ancients* (1609).

du Bartas, Guillaume de Saluste. See under **Sylvester,** translator.

Bentley, Richard. *Milton's Paradise Lost: A New Edition*. London: Jacob Tonson, 1732.

Bernard, Saint, Abbot of Clairvaux. *Cantica Canticorum: Eighty-Six Sermons on the Songs of Solomon*. Translated and edited by Samuel J. Eales. London: Elliot Stock, 1895.

Bernardus Silvestris. See under **Silvestris.**

Bible. *The New Testament*. Revised Standard Version. New York: Thomas Nelson and Sons, 1946.

Boccaccio, Giovanni. [*De genealogiis deorum gentilium*] *Boccaccio on Poetry, Being the*

Preface and the Fourteenth and Fifteenth Books of Boccaccio's Genealogia Deorum Gentilium. Translated by Charles G. Osgood. Princeton: Princeton Univ. Press, 1930. Reprinted Indianapolis and New York: Liberal Arts Press and Bobbs-Merrill, 1956.

Browne, Thomas. *Religio Medici* (1643). Vol. 1 of *The Works of Sir Thomas Browne*. Edited by Geoffrey Keynes. 4 vols. London: Faber and Faber, 1928.

Bryskett, Lodowick. *A Discourse of Civill Life* (1606). In *Literary Works*. Edited by J.H.P. Pafford. Facsimile reprint. Farnborough, Hants.: Gregg International Publishers, 1972.

Calvin, John. *The Institutes of the Christian Religion*. Translated by John Allen. Vol. 1 of 2. Philadelphia: Presbyterian Board of Publications, n.d.

Cartari, Vicenzo. [*De imagine gentile deorum*] *Le imagini de i dei de gli antichi* (1571). The Renaissance and the Gods, no. 12. Edited by Stephen Orgel. Facsimile reprint. New York: Garland Publishing, 1976.

Castelvetro, Lodovico. *Castelvetro on the Art of Poetry: An Abridged Translation of Lodovico Castelvetro's Poetica d'Aristotele Vulgarizzata et Sposta* (1570). Translated and edited by Andrew Bongiorno. Medieval and Renaissance Texts and Studies, no. 29. Binghampton, N.Y.: Medieval and Renaissance Texts and Studies, 1984.

———. [*Poetica d'Aristotele* 1570] *The Poetics of Aristotle Translated and Annotated*. Selections. In *Literary Criticism: Plato to Dryden*. See under **Gilbert,** editor. Pp. 304-57.

Comes, Natalis. [*Mythologiae* 1551] *Mythologie*. Translated by Jean Baudouin after earlier French of I. de Montlyard (1627). Edited by Stephen Orgel. 2 vols. The Renaissance and the Gods, no. 26. Facsimile reprint. New York: Garland Publishing, 1976.

Cowley, Abraham. "Preface to *Poems*" (1656). In vol. 2 of *Critical Essays of the Seventeenth Century*. See under **Spingarn,** editor. Pp. 77-89.

Dante Alighieri. *Il Convito di Dante Alighieri e le Epistole*. Vol. 3 of *Opera Minori*. Edited by Pietro Fraticelli. 3 vols. 4th ed. Florence: G. Barbèra, 1873.

———. [*Divina commedia*] 3 vols. Vol. 1, *The Inferno*. Vol. 2, *The Purgatorio*. Vol. 3, *The Paradiso*. London: J.M. Dent and Sons, 1956.

———. *Dante's Convivio*. Translated and edited by William Walrond Jackson. Oxford: Clarendon Press, 1909.

———. *Literary Criticism of Dante Alighieri*. Translated and edited by Robert S. Haller. Lincoln: Univ. of Nebraska Press, 1973.

Davenant, Sir William. "Preface to *Gondibert, an Heroick Poem*" (1650). In vol. 2 of *Critical Essays of the Seventeenth Century*. See under **Spingarn,** editor. Pp. 1-53.

Donne, John. *John Donne: Devotions Upon Emergent Occasions*. Edited by Anthony Raspa. Montreal and London: McGill-Queen's Univ. Press, 1975.

———. *The Sermons of John Donne*. Edited by George R. Potter and Evelyn M. Simpson. 10 vols. Berkeley: Univ. of California Press, 1953-1962.

Fairfax, Edward, translator. *Jerusalem Delivered: A Poem* (1581). Translated by Edward Fairfax. Edited by Henry Morley. London: George Routledge and Sons, 1890.

———. *Godfrey of Bulloigne: A Critical Edition of Edward Fairfax's translation of Tasso's Gerusalemme Liberata*. Edited by Kathleen M. Lea and T.M. Gang. Oxford: Clarendon Press, 1981.

──────. *Jerusalem Delivered* (1600). Edited by John Charles Nelson. New York: Capricorn Books, n.d.

Ficino, Marsilio. *Marsilio Ficino's Commentary on Plato's Symposium.* Translated by Sears R. Jayne. University of Missouri Studies no. 1. Columbia: Univ. of Missouri Press, 1944.

Fornari, Simone. *La Spositione di M. Simon Fornari . . . Sopra L'Orlando Furioso di M.L. Ariosto.* Vol. 2 (of 2 vols. in 1). Florence, 1549-1550.

Fulgentius. See under **Secondary Works.**

Gilbert, Allan H., editor. *Literary Criticism: Plato to Dryden.* American Book Co., 1940. Reprint ed. Detroit: Wayne State Univ. Press, 1962.

Harington, John, translator. *Orlando Furioso in English Heroical Verse* (1591). The English Experience: its Record in Early Printed Books, no. 259. Facsimile reprint. Amsterdam, N.Y.: Da Capo Press, 1970.

──────. *Ludovico Ariosto's Orlando Furioso: Translated into English heroical verse* (1591). Edited by Robert McNulty. Oxford: Clarendon Press, 1972.

Hobbes, Thomas. "Answer to Davenant's Preface to *Gondibert*" (1650). In vol. 2 of *Critical Essays of the Seventeenth Century.* See under **Spingarn**, editor. Pp. 54-67.

Hughes, John. "An Essay on *Allegorical Poetry*". In vol. 1 of *The Works of Spenser.* Edited by John Hughes. 6 vols. London: R. Tonson and S. Draper, 1750. Pp. xix-xli.

Hurd, Richard, Bishop. *Letters on Chivalry and Romance* (1762). Edited by Hoyt Trowbridge. Facsimile reprint. Los Angeles: William Andrews Clark Memorial Library, 1963.

Johnson, Samuel. *Lives of the English Poets.* Edited by George Birkbeck Hill. 3 vols. Oxford: Clarendon Press, 1905.

Knox, John. *On the Meaning of Christ.* New York: Scribner's Sons, 1947.

Le Bossu, René. *Traité du Poëme Épique* (1675). Paris: Chez Michel Le Petit, 1675.

──────. [*Traité du Poëme Épique* 1675] *Treatise of the Epick Poem.* Translated by W.J. (1695). In *Le Bossu and Voltaire on the Epic.* Introduced and edited by Stuart Curran. Gainesville, Fla.: Scholars' Facsimiles and Reprints, 1970.

Luther, Martin. [*De servo arbitrio* 1525] *The Bondage of the Will.* In *Erasmus-Luther: Discourse on Free Will.* Translated and edited by Ernst F. Winter. New York: Frederick Ungar, 1961.

Macrobius. *Commentary on the Dream of Scipio.* Translated by William Harris Stahl. New York: Columbia Univ. Press, 1952.

Mazzoni, Jacopo. [*Della Difesa della Commedia di Dante* 1572, 1587] *On the Defence of the "Comedy".* Selections. In *Literary Criticism: Plato to Dryden.* See under **Gilbert,** editor. Pp. 358-403.

Milton, John. **Collected Editions.**

──────. *Complete Prose Works of John Milton.* General editor Don M. Wolfe. 8 vols. New Haven: Yale Univ. Press, and London: Oxford Univ. Press, 1953-1982. Includes: Vol. 1 (1953), edited by Don M. Wolfe. Vol. 2 (1969), edited by Ernest Sirluck. Vol. 6 (1973), edited by Maurice Kelley. Vol. 2 includes *The Doctrine and Discipline of Divorce* (1644 edition.)

──────. *John Milton's Complete Poetical Works: A Critical Text Edition.* Reproduced in photographic facsimile. Edited by Harris Francis Fletcher. 4 vols. Urbana: Univ. of Illinois Press, 1943-1948.

————. *The Poems of John Milton*. Edited by John Carey and Alastair Fowler. London: Longmans, 1968.

————. *The Poetical Works of John Milton*. 2 vols. Edited by Helen Darbishire. Oxford: Clarendon Press, 1952, 1955.

————. *The Works of John Milton*. Edited by Frank Allen Patterson *et al*. 18 vols. plus 2 vols. Index. New York: Columbia Univ. Press, 1931-1940. Contains the individual works cited below.

Milton, John. **Individual Works.**

————. *An Apology against a Pamphlet call'd A Modest Confutation of the Animadversions upon the Remonstrant against Smectymnuus*. Edited by Harry Morgan Ayres. In vol. 3.1 of *The Works of John Milton*. 1931.

————. *Areopagitica; for the Liberty of Unlicenc'd Printing*. Edited by William Haller. In vol. 4 of *The Works of John Milton*. 1931.

————. [*De doctrina Christiana*] *Of Christian Doctrine*. Translated by Charles R. Sumner. Edited by James Holly Hanford and Waldo Hilary Dunn. With the Latin text. Vols. 14-17 of *The Works of John Milton*. 1933-1934.

————. *Of Education*. Edited by Allan Abbott. In vol. 4 of *The Works of John Milton*. 1931.

————. *Eikonoklastes*. Edited by William Haller. In vol. 5 of *The Works of John Milton*. 1932.

————. *The Familiar Letters of John Milton*. Translated by David Masson. Edited by Donald Lemen Clark. In vol. 12 of *The Works of John Milton*. 1936.

————. *The Reason of Church-Government urg'd against Prelaty*. Edited by Harry Morgan Ayres. In vol. 3.1 of *The Works of John Milton*. 1931.

————. *Of Reformation Touching Church-Discipline in England*. Edited by Harry Morgan Ayres. In vol. 3.1 of *The Works of John Milton*. 1931.

————. *Tetrachordon: Expositions upon the Foure Chief Places in Scripture, which Treat of Marriage*. Edited by Chilton Latham Powell. In vol. 4 of *The Works of John Milton*. 1931.

————. *The Uncollected Writings of John Milton*. Vol. 18 of *The Works of John Milton*. Edited by Thomas Ollive Mabbott and J. Milton French. 1938.

Origen. *The Songs of Songs, Commentaries and Homilies*. Translated and annotated by R.P. Lawson. Westminster, Md.: Newman Press, and London: Longmans, Green, 1957.

Peacham, Henry. *The Garden of Eloquence* (1577). Facsimile reprint. Menston, Yorks: Scolar Press, 1971.

Phillips, Edward. Preface to *Theatrum Poetarum* (1675). Abridged. In *Literary Criticism: Plato to Dryden*. See under **Gilbert,** editor. Pp. 667-77.

Philo. *On the Account of the World's Creation given by Moses (De Opificio Mundi)*. In vol. 1 of *Philo*. Translated by F.H. Colson and G.H. Whitaker. 10 plus 2 vols. Loeb Classical Library. London: William Heinemann, and Cambridge, Mass.: Harvard Univ. Press, 1929.

Porphyry. *Porphyry On The Cave of the Nymphs*. Translated by Robert Lamberton. Barrytown, N.Y.: Station Hill Press, 1983. (See also under **Secondary Works**).

Puttenham, George. *The Arte of English Poesie* (1589). Edited by Gladys Doidge Willcock and Alice Walker. Cambridge: Cambridge Univ. Press, 1936.

Quintilian. *Institutio Oratoria*. Translated by H.E. Butler. 4 vols. Loeb Classical

Library. London: William Heinemann, and Cambridge, Mass.: Harvard Univ. Press, 1920.

Reynolds, Henry. *Mythomystes. Wherein a short survay is taken of the nature and value of true Poësie, and depth of the Antients* (1632). Introduced by Arthur F. Kinney. Facsimile reprint. Menston, Yorks: Scolar Press, 1972.

Rymer, Thomas. "Preface to the Translation of Rapin's *Reflections on Aristotle's Treatise of Poesie*" (1674). In vol. 2 of *Critical Essays of the Seventeenth Century.* See under **Spingarn**, editor. Pp. 163-81.

de Saint-Évremond, Charles de Saint-Denis. "On the Imitation of the Ancients" (1678). Selections. In *Literary Criticism: Plato to Dryden.* See under **Gilbert**, editor. Pp. 663-65.

Salutati, Coluccio. *Epistolario di Coluccio Salutati.* Edited by Francesco Novati. 4 vols. in 5. Rome: Forzani e C. Tipografi del Senato, 1891-1911. Includes vol. 4.1, 1905.

———. *Coluccii Salutati, de laboribus Herculis.* Edited by B.L. Ullman. 2 vols. in 1. Zurich: In Aedibus Thesauri Mundi, 1951.

Sandys, George, translator. *Ovid's Metamorphoses Englished* (1632). The Renaissance and the Gods, no. 27. Edited by Stephen Orgel. Facsimile reprint. New York: Garland Publishing, 1976.

———. *Ovid's Metamorphosis Englished, Mythologized and Represented in Figures* (1632). Translated by George Sandys. Edited by Karl K. Hulley and Stanley T. Vandersell. Lincoln: Univ. of Nebraska Press, 1970.

Sidney, Sir Philip. *An Apology for Poetry: or The Defence of Poesy* (1595). Edited by Geoffrey Shepherd. London: Nelson, 1965.

———. *The Countesse of Pembrokes Arcadia.* Vol. 1 of 4. In *The Prose Works of Philip Sidney.* Edited by Albert Feuillerat. Cambridge: Cambridge Univ. Press, 1912.

Silvestris, Bernardus. *The Commentary on the First Six Books of the Aeneid of Vergil Commonly Attributed to Bernardus Silvestris: A new critical edition.* Latin edition by Julian Ward Jones and Elizabeth Frances Jones. Lincoln: Univ. of Nebraska Press, 1977.

Spenser, Edmund. *The Complete Poetical Works of Spenser.* Edited by R.E. Neil Dodge. Boston: Houghton Mifflin, 1908. Includes some of the Spenser-Harvey correspondence in Appendix, pt. III, pp. 768-73.

———. *Spenser's Faerie Queene.* Edited by J.C. Smith. 2 vols. Oxford: Clarendon Press, 1909.

———. *The Works of Edmund Spenser: A Variorum Edition.* Edited by Edwin Greenlaw *et al.* 9 vols. plus Index. Baltimore: Johns Hopkins Press, 1932-1938.

Spingarn, J.E., editor. *Critical Essays of the Seventeenth Century.* 2 vols. Oxford: Clarendon Press, 1908.

Sylvester, Joshua, translator. *The Divine Weeks and Works of Guillaume de Saluste, Sieur Du Bartas.* Edited by Susan Snyder. 2 vols. Oxford: Clarendon Press, 1979.

Tasso, Torquato. **Collected Editions.**

———. *Dialoghi.* Edited by Ezio Raimondi. 3 vols. in 4. Florence: G.C. Sansoni editore, 1958.

———. *Discorsi dell'arte poetica e del poema eroico* (1587; 1594). Edited by Luigi Poma. Bari: Gius. Laterza e Figli, 1964.

———. *Le Lettere.* Edited by Cesare Guasti. 5 vols. Corrected ed. Naples: G. Rondinella editore, 1857. Pagination differs slightly from the ed. of 1852-1855.

————. *Le Opere*. Edited by Giuseppe Mauro. 12 vols. Venice: Presso Carlo Buonarrizo, 1722-1742.

————. *Prose*. Edited by Ettore Mazzali. Verona, Milan and Naples: Riccardo Ricciale, editore. 1959.

————. *Le Prose Diverse*. Edited by Cesare Guasti. 2 vols. Florence: Successori Le Monnier, 1875.

Tasso, Torquato. **Individual Works.**

————. "Allegoria del Poema" [to *Gerusalemme liberata]* (1581). In vol. 1 (1722) of *Le Opere*, edited by Giuseppe Mauro. Stands as preface, 6 pp., unnumbered. Appears also in vol. 12 (1742). Pp. 208-12.

————. "Allegoria del *Rinaldo*" (1583). In vol. 4 (1735) of *Le Opere*. Edited by Giuseppe Mauro. Pp. 491-92.

————. "The Allegory of the Poem" [to *Gerusalemme liberata*]. In *Jerusalem Delivered: A Poem* (1600). See under **Fairfax,** translator. Pp. 436-43.

————. *Apologia . . . in difesa della Gerusalemme Liberata* (1585). In vol. 2 (1735) of *Le Opere*. Edited by Giuseppe Mauro. Pp. 285-332.

————. *Delle differenze poetiche per risposta al Signor Orazio Ariosto* (1587). In *Le Prose Diverse*. Edited by Cesare Guasti. Pp. 431-41.

————. *Discorsi dell'Arte Poetica e in particolare sopra il Poema Eroico* (1587). In *Prose*. Edited by Ettore Mazzali. Pp. 349-410.

————. *Discorsi dell'arte poetica* (1587). In *Discorsi dell'arte poetica e del poema eroico*. Edited by Luigi Poma. Pp. 1-55.

————. *Discorsi del poema eroico* (1594). In *Prose*. Edited by Ettore Mazzali. Pp. 487-729.

————. *Discourses on the Heroic Poem* (1594). Translated by Mariella Cavalchini and Irene Samuel. Oxford: Clarendon Press, 1973.

————. *Discorso sopra il Parere fatto dal Signor Francesco Patricio in difesa di Lodovico Ariosto* (1585). In vol. 3 (1735) of *Le Opere*. Edited by Giuseppe Mauro. Pp. 163-72.

————. *Estratti dalla Poetica di Lodovico Castelvetro* (1875). In *Le Prose Diverse*. Edited by Cesare Guasti. Pp. 275-95.

————. *Il Ficino, ovvero dell'Arte. Dialogo*. In vol. 7 (1737) of *Le Opere*. Edited by Giuseppe Mauro. Pp. 3-15.

————. *La Gerusalemme Liberata*. Edited by Scipione Gonzaga. Published by Francesco Osanna. Mantua: 1584.

————. *Gerusalemme liberata: Poema eroico di Torquato Tasso* (1581). Edited by Angelo Solerti *et al*. 3 vols. Florence: G. Barbèra, 1895-96.

————. *Il Goffredo, ovvero la Gerusalemme liberata* (1581). In vol. 1 (1722) of *Le Opere*. Edited by Giuseppe Mauro.

————. *Jerusalem Delivered: an English Prose Version*. Translated and edited by Ralph Nash. Detroit: Wayne State Univ. Press, 1987. The "Allegory of the Poem" is on pp. 468-74.

————. *Jerusalem Delivered* (editions of Fairfax translation). See under **Fairfax,** translator.

————. *Del Giudizio sovra la Gerusalemme di Torquato Tasso, da lui medesimo riformata, libri due* (1666). In vol. 4 (1735) of *Le Opere*. Edited by Giuseppe Mauro. Pp. 299-376.

————. *Lettere Poetiche . . . particolarmente in materia della Gerusalemme Liberata* (1587). In vol. 10 (1739) of *Le Opere*. Edited by Giuseppe Mauro. Pp. 75-232.

————. *Il Manso, ovvero dell'Amicizia. Dialogo* (1586). In vol. 7 (1737) of *Le Opere*. Edited by Giuseppe Mauro. Pp. 472-502.

————. *Il Messaggiero. Dialogo* (1582). In vol. 7 (1737) of *Le Opere*. Edited by Giuseppe Mauro. Pp. 93-144. P. 144 is misnumbered as 128.

————. *Il Porzio, ovvero delle Virtù. Dialogo* (1666). In vol. 7 (1737) of *Le Opere*. Edited by Giuseppe Mauro. Pp. 400-455.

————. *Il Rinaldo* (1562). In vol. 4 (1735) of *Le Opere*. Edited by Giuseppe Mauro.

————. *Risposta Del S. Torq. Tasso, Al Discorso Del Sig. Oratio Lombardelli*. Ferrara: Vittorio Baldini, 1586. 32 pp.

————. *Della Virtù Eroica e della Carità. Discorso* (1583). In vol. 8 (1738) of *Le Opere*. Edited by Giuseppe Mauro. Pp. 210-21.

Toland, John. *The Life of John Milton* (1698). In *The Early Lives of Milton*. Edited by Helen Darbishire. London: Constable, 1932.

Toscanella, Orazio [Oratio]. *Bellezze del Furioso di M. Lodovico Ariosto . . . con gli argomenti et allegorie dei canti*. Venice: Pietro de Franceschi, 1574.

Secondary Works

Aguzzi, Danilo L. *Allegory in the Heroic Poetry of the Renaissance*. Ph.D. dissertation. New York: Columbia University, 1959.

Auerbach, Erich. "Figura". In *Scenes from the Drama of European Literature: Six Essays*. Gloucester, Mass.: Peter Smith, 1973. Pp. 11-76.

Bainton, Roland H. "The Bible in the Reformation". Chapter 1 in vol. 3 of *The Cambridge History of the Bible*. Pp. 1-37.

Bell, Charles G. "Fairfax's Tasso". *Comparative Literature* 6 (1954):26-52.

Benjamin, Walter. [*Ursprung des deutschen Trauerspiels*, Frankfurt a.M., 1963] *The Origin of German Tragic Drama*. Translated by J. Osborne. London: NLB, 1977.

Berger, Harry, Jr. *The Allegorical Temper: Vision and Reality in Book II of Spenser's Faerie Queene*. New Haven: Yale Univ. Press, 1957.

Boyarin, Daniel. *Intertextuality and the Reading of Midrash*. Bloomington and Indianapolis: Indiana Univ. Press, 1990.

————. "Rhetoric and Interpretation: The Case of the Nimshal". *Prooftexts: A Journal of Jewish Literary History* 5 (1985):269-80.

————. "The Song of Songs, Lock or Key?: Intertextuality, Allegory, and the Meaning of Midrash". Paper, Lechter Institute for Literary Research (Bar Ilan University, 1986). Published in revised form in Daniel Boyarin, *Intertextuality and the Reading of Midrash*.

————. "Voices in the Text: Midrash and the Inner Tension of Biblical Narrative". *Revue Biblique* 93 (1986):581-97.

Brand, C.P. *Torquato Tasso: A Study of the Poet and his Contribution to English Literature*. Cambridge: Cambridge Univ. Press, 1965.

Broadbent, J.B. *Some Graver Subject: An Essay on Paradise Lost*. London: Chatto and Windus, 1960.

Bruns, Gerald L. "Midrash and Allegory: The Beginnings of Scriptural Interpretation". In *The Literary Guide to the Bible*. Edited by Robert Alter and Frank Kermode. London: Collins, 1987. Pp. 625-46.

de Bruyne, Edgar. "La Théorie de l'Allégorisme". Chapter 7 of Part III in vol. 2 of *Études d'Esthétique Médiévale*. 3 vols. Recueil de Travaux de La Faculté de Philosophie et Lettres de Gand, vols. 98-99. Bruges: De Tempel, 1946.

Budick, Sanford. "Milton and the Scene of Interpretation: From Typology toward Midrash". In *Midrash and Literature*. See under **Hartman and Budick**, editors. Pp. 195-212.

Buffière, Félix. *Les Mythes d'Homère et la pensée grecque*. Paris: Les Belles Lettres, 1956.

The Cambridge History of the Bible. 3 vols. Vol. 1: *From the Beginnings to Jerome*. Edited by P.R. Ackroyd and C.F. Evans. Cambridge: Cambridge Univ. Press, 1970.

The Cambridge History of the Bible. 3 vols. Vol. 2: *The West from the Fathers to the Reformation*. Edited by G.W.H. Lampe. Cambridge: Cambridge Univ. Press, 1969.

The Cambridge History of the Bible. 3 vols. Vol. 3: *The West from the Reformation to the Present Day*. Edited by S.L. Greenslade. Cambridge: Cambridge Univ. Press, 1963.

Castelli, Alberto. *La Gerusalemme Liberata nella Inghilterra di Spenser*. Pubblicazione della Università Cattolica del Sacro Cuore. Serie 4, *Scienze Filologiche*. Vol. 20. Milan: Società Editrice "Vita e Pensiero", 1936.

Christopher, Georgia B. *Milton and the Science of the Saints*. Princeton: Princeton Univ. Press, 1982.

The Concise Oxford Dictionary of the Christian Church. Edited by Elizabeth A. Livingstone. 2nd ed. abridged. Oxford, London and New York: Oxford Univ. Press, 1977.

Conley, James William. *Tasso and Milton: I Discorsi, La Gerusalemme Liberata and Paradise Lost*. Ph.D. dissertation. University of Wisconsin. 1974. Microfilm no. 1850 in Cambridge University Library.

Curtius, Ernst. *European Literature and the Latin Middle Ages*. Translated by Willard R. Trask. London: Routledge, 1953.

Daniélou, Jean, S.J. [*Sacramentum Futuri: Études sur les Origines de la Typologie biblique*] *From Shadows to Reality: Studies in the Biblical Typology of the Fathers*. Translated by Dom Wulstan Hibberd. London: Burns and Oates, 1960.

Dees, Jerome S. "Recent Studies in the English Emblem". *English Literary Renaissance* 16 (1986):391-420.

Derla, Luigi. "Sull'Allegoria della 'Gerusalemme Liberata'". *Italianistica* 7 (1978): 474-88.

Dronke, Peter. *Dante and Medieval Latin Traditions*. Cambridge: Cambridge Univ. Press, 1985.

———. *Fabula: Explorations into the Uses of Myth in Medieval Platonism*. Leiden and Köln: E.J. Brill, 1974.

———. "Bernardo Silvestre". In vol. 1 of *Enciclopedia Virgiliana*. Rome: Istituto della Enciclopedia Italiana, 1984. Pp. 497-500.

Empson, William. *Milton's God*. London: Chatto and Windus, 1961.

The Encyclopaedia Britannica. 11th ed. General editor Hugh Chisholm. 28 vols. plus index. Cambridge: Cambridge Univ. Press, 1910.

Fallon, Stephen M. "Milton's Sin and Death: The Ontology of Allegory in *Paradise Lost*". *English Literary Renaissance* 17 (1987):329-50.

Ferry, Ann D. *Milton's Epic Voice: The Narrator in Paradise Lost.* Cambridge, Mass: Harvard Univ. Press, 1963.

Fichter, Andrew. *Poets Historical: Dynastic Epic in the Renaissance.* New Haven: Yale Univ. Press, 1982.

Fisch, Harold. "The Hermeneutic Quest in *Robinson Crusoe*". In *Midrash and Literature.* See under **Hartman and Budick**, editors. Pp. 213-35.

Fixler, Michael. *Milton and the Kingdoms of God.* London: Faber and Faber, 1964.

Fletcher, Angus. *Allegory: The Theory of a Symbolic Mode.* Ithaca, N.Y.: Cornell Univ. Press, 1964.

Fowler, Alastair and Leslie, Michael. "Drummond's Copy of *The Faerie Queene*". *Times Literary Supplement.* London: July 17, 1981. Pp. 821-22.

Frye, Northrop. *The Great Code: The Bible and Literature.* Toronto: Academic Press Canada, 1981.

———. "The Typology of *Paradise Regained*". *Modern Philology* 53 (1956):227-38. Reprinted in *Milton: Modern Essays in Criticism.* Edited by Arthur E. Barker. London: Oxford Univ. Press, 1965. Paperback ed. Pp. 429-46.

Frye, Roland Mushat. *God, Man, and Satan: Patterns of Christian Thought and Life in Paradise Lost, Pilgrim's Progress, and the Great Theologians.* Princeton: Princeton Univ. Press, 1960. Reissued New York and London: Kennikat Press, 1972.

[Fulgentius, *Expositio Vergilianae continentiae*]. Entry in vol. 11 of *Encyclopaedia Britannica.* Pp. 292-93.

[Fulgentius, *Mitologiarum libri tres*]. Entry in *The Oxford Classical Dictionary.* P. 449.

Gallagher, Philip J. " 'Real or Allegoric': The Ontology of Sin and Death in *Paradise Lost*". *English Literary Renaissance* 6 (1976):317-35.

Gardner, Helen. "The Historical Sense". In *The Business of Criticism.* Oxford: Clarendon Press, 1959.

Giamatti, A. Bartlett. *The Earthly Paradise and the Renaissance Epic.* Chapter 4.2, on Tasso. Princeton: Princeton Univ. Press, 1966.

———. "Milton and Fairfax's Tasso". *Revue de Littérature Comparée* 40 (1966):613-15.

Gilbert, Allan H., editor. See under **Primary Works.**

Goldman, Jack. "Perspectives of Raphael's Meal in *Paradise Lost*, Book V". *Milton Quarterly* 11 (1977):31-37.

Gombrich, E.H. *Symbolic Images: Studies in the Art of the Renaissance.* 1972. Small format ed. Oxford: Phaidon Press, and New York: E.P. Dutton, 1978.

Greene, Thomas. *The Descent from Heaven: A Study in Epic Continuity.* New Haven: Yale Univ. Press, 1963.

Halivni, David Weiss. *Midrash, Mishnah, and Gemara: The Jewish Predilection for Justified Law.* Cambridge, Mass: Harvard Univ. Press, 1986.

Hamilton, A.C. *The Structure of Allegory in The Faerie Queene.* Oxford: Clarendon Press, 1961.

Hanford, James Holly, and Taaffe, James G. *A Milton Handbook.* 1926. 5th ed. New York: Appleton-Century-Crofts, 1970.

Hannay, Margaret P. " 'My Sheep are Thoughts': Self-Reflexive Pastoral in *The Faerie Queene*, Book VI, and the *New Arcadia*". *Spenser Studies* 9 (1991):137-59.

Hanson, R.P.C. "Biblical Exegesis in the Early Church". Chap. V.13 in vol. 1 of *The Cambridge History of the Bible.* Pp. 412-53.

Hardie, Philip R. *Virgil's Aeneid: Cosmos and Imperium.* Oxford: Clarendon Press, 1986.

Harding, Davis P. *Milton and the Renaissance Ovid*. Illinois Studies in Language and Literature, vol. 30, no. 4. Urbana: Univ. of Illinois Press, 1946. Pp. 3-105.

Harris, Victor. "Allegory to Analogy in the Interpretation of Scriptures". *Philological Quarterly* 45 (1966):1-23.

Hartman, Geoffrey H. and Budick, Sanford, editors. *Midrash and Literature*. New Haven: Yale Univ. Press, 1986.

Helgerson, Richard. "Tasso on Spenser: Or the Politics of Chivalric Romance". Paper given at The University of Reading Conference (July, 1989) on "Politics, Patronage and Literature in England, 1558-1658".

Hill, Christopher. *Milton and the English Revolution*. London: Faber and Faber, 1977.

Hollander, Robert. *Allegory in Dante's Commedia*. Princeton: Princeton Univ. Press, 1969.

Horsfall, Nicholas. Review of *Virgil's Aeneid: Cosmos and Imperium*, by Philip R. Hardie. *Times Literary Supplement*. London: August 29, 1986. P. 943.

Hughes, Merritt Y. *Virgil and Spenser*. University of California Publications in English, vol. 2, no. 3. Berkeley: Univ. of California Press, 1929. Pp. 263-418. Reissued, Port Washington, N.Y.: Kennikat Press, 1969.

Hunter, W.B., Patrides, C.A. and Adamson, J.H. *Bright Essence: Studies in Milton's Theology*. Salt Lake City: Univ. of Utah Press, 1971.

Jusserand, J.J. "Spenser's 'twelve private morall vertues as Aristotle hath devised'". *Modern Philology* 3 (1905–1906):373-83.

Kates, Judith A. *Tasso and Milton: The Problem of Christian Epic*. Lewisburg, Pa.: Bucknell Univ. Press, 1983.

Kennedy, W.J. "The Problem of Allegory in Tasso's *Gerusalemme Liberata*". *Italian Quarterly* 15-16 (1972):27-51.

Kermode, Frank. "The Cave of Mammon". In *Elizabethan Poetry*. Stratford-upon-Avon Studies, no. 2. London: Edward Arnold, 1960. Pp. 151-73. Reprinted in Frank Kermode. *Shakespeare, Spenser, Donne: Renaissance Essays*. London: Routledge and Kegan Paul, 1971.

Knapp, Steven. *Personification and the Sublime: Milton to Coleridge*. Cambridge, Mass. and London: Harvard Univ. Press, 1985.

Krouse, F. Michael. *Milton's Samson and the Christian Tradition*. Princeton: Princeton Univ. Press, 1949.

Kugel, James L. "Two Introductions to Midrash". In *Midrash and Literature*. See under **Hartman and Budick**, editors. Pp. 77-103.

Lamberton, Robert. *Homer the Theologian: Neoplatonist Allegorical Reading and the Growth of the Epic Tradition*. Berkeley and Los Angeles: Univ. of California Press, 1986. See also under **Porphyry.**

Lampe, G.W.H. "To Gregory the Great". Section 1 of chapter VI, "The Exposition and Exegesis of Scripture". In vol. 2 of *The Cambridge History of the Bible*. Pp. 155-83.

A Latin Dictionary; founded on Andrew's Edition of Freund's Latin Dictionary. Revised, enlarged, and in great part rewritten by Charlton T. Lewis and Charles Short. Oxford: Clarendon Press, 1879, repr. 1962.

Lawry, Jon S. *Sidney's Two Arcadias: Pattern and Proceeding*. Ithaca, N.Y.: Cornell Univ. Press, 1972.

Lewalski, Barbara Kiefer. *Milton's Brief Epic: The Genre, Meaning and Art of Paradise Regained*. Providence and London: Brown Univ. Press, 1966.

————. *Paradise Lost and the Rhetoric of Literary Forms.* Princeton: Princeton Univ. Press, 1985.

————. *Protestant Poetics and the Seventeenth-Century Religious Lyric.* Princeton: Princeton Univ. Press, 1979.

————. "Samson Agonistes and the 'Tragedy' of the Apocalypse". *Publications of the Modern Language Society of America* 85 (1970):1050-62.

————. "Structure and Symbolism of Vision in Michael's Prophecy, *Paradise Lost,* Books XI-XII". *Philological Quarterly* 42 (1963):25-35.

————. "Typology and Poetry: A Consideration of Herbert, Vaughan, and Marvell". In *Illustrious Evidence: Approaches to English Literature of the Early Seventeenth Century.* Edited by Earl Miner. Berkeley, Los Angeles and London: Univ. of California Press, 1975. Pp. 41-69.

————. "Typological Symbolism and the 'Progress of the Soul' in Seventeenth-Century Literature". In *Literary Uses of Typology from the Late Middle Ages to the Present.* See under **Miner,** editor. Pp. 79-114.

Lewis, C.S. *The Allegory of Love: A Study in Medieval Tradition.* 1936. Corrected ed. London: Oxford Univ. Press, 1938.

Lloyd, Michael. "The Fatal Bark". *Modern Language Notes* 75 (1960):103-8.

de Lubac, Henri. *Exégèse Médiévale; les quatre sens de l'Écriture.* 2 vols. in 3. Théologie: Études publiées sous la direction de la Faculté de Théologie S.J. de Lyon-Fourvière 41. Aubier, 1959.

MacCaffrey, Isabel Gamble. *Paradise Lost as "Myth".* Cambridge, Mass.: Harvard Univ. Press, 1959.

MacCallum, H.R. "Milton and Figurative Interpretation of the Bible". *University of Toronto Quarterly* 31 (1962):397-415.

McMurphy, Susannah Jane. *Spenser's Use of Ariosto for Allegory.* Washington Publications in Language and Literature, vol. 2. Seattle: Univ. of Washington Press, 1924.

[Macrobius]. Entry in vol. 17 of *Encyclopaedia Britannica.* P. 269.

Madsen, William. *From Shadowy Types to Truth: Studies in Milton's Symbolism.* New Haven and London: Yale Univ. Press, 1968.

Miner, Earl, editor. *Literary Uses of Typology from the Late Middle Ages to the Present.* Princeton: Princeton Univ. Press, 1979.

Mollenkott, Virginia R. "The Pervasive Influence of the Apocrypha in Milton's Thought and Art". In *Milton and the Art of Sacred Song.* See under **Patrick and Sundell,** editors. Pp. 23-43.

Montgomery, Robert L. *The Reader's Eye: Studies in Didactic Literary Theory from Dante to Tasso.* Berkeley, Los Angeles, and London: Univ. of California Press, 1979.

Murrin, Michael. *The Allegorical Epic: Essays in its Rise and Decline.* Chicago: Univ. of Chicago Press, 1980.

————. *The Veil of Allegory: Some Notes toward a Theory of Allegorical Rhetoric in the English Renaissance.* Chicago: Univ. of Chicago Press, 1969.

Nelson, T.G.A. "Sir John Harington and the Renaissance Debate over Allegory". *Studies in Philology* 82 (1985):359-79.

Nelson, William. *The Poetry of Edmund Spenser: A Study.* New York: Columbia Univ. Press, 1963.

Olini, Lucia. "Dalle direzioni di lettura alla revisione del testo: Tasso tra *Allegoria del Poema* e *Giudizio"*. *La rassegna della letteratura italiana,* Anno 89, series 8 (1985):53-68.

[Origen]. Entry in vol. 20 of *Encyclopaedia Britannica.* Pp. 270-73.

The Oxford Classical Dictionary. Edited by N.G.L. Hammond and H.H. Scullard. 2nd ed. Oxford: Clarendon Press, 1970.

Panofsky, Erwin. *Idea: A Concept in Art Theory.* 1968. Translated by Joseph J.S. Peake. Icon Editions. New York: Harper and Row, 1968.

Parker, William Riley. *Milton: A Biography.* 2 vols. Oxford: Clarendon Press, 1968.

Patrick, J. Max and Sundell, Roger H., editors. *Milton and the Art of Sacred Song.* Madison: Univ. of Wisconsin Press, 1979.

Patrides, C.A. *Milton and the Christian Tradition.* Oxford: Clarendon Press, 1966.

———. "The Godhead in *Paradise Lost:* Dogma or Drama?". In *Bright Essence: Studies in Milton's Theology.* See under **Hunter**. Pp. 71-77.

———. "*Paradise Lost* and the Language of Theology". In *Bright Essence: Studies in Milton's Theology.* See under **Hunter**. Pp. 165-78.

———. "*Paradise Lost* and the Theory of Accommodation". In *Bright Essence: Studies in Milton's Theology.* See under **Hunter**. Pp. 159-63.

Patterson, Annabel. "Tasso and Neoplatonism: The Growth of his Epic Theory". *Studies in the Renaissance* 18-19 (1971-72):105-33.

Pépin, Jean. *Mythe et allégorie: Les origines grecques et les contestations judéo-chrétiennes.* 2nd ed. Paris: Études augustiniennes, 1976.

———. "A propos de l'histoire de l'exégèse allégorique: l'absurdité, signe de l'allégorie". In vol. 1, pt.1, of *Studia Patristica.* Edited by Kurt Aland and F.L. Cross. 1957. Issued as vol. 8 of *Texte und Untersuchungen zur Geschichte der altchristlichen Literatur.* Edited by Kurt Aland *et al.* Berlin: Akademie Verlag, 1957. Pp. 395-413.

Pommrich, Ewald. *Miltons Verhältnis zu Torquato Tasso.* Dissertation, University of Leipzig. Halle a.S.: Ehrhardt Karras, 1902.

[Porphyry] Entry in *The Oxford Classical Dictionary.* Pp. 864-65.

Praz, Mario. "The Metamorphoses of Satan". Chap. 2 in *The Romantic Agony.* 1933. 2nd ed., 1951. Reissued with new Introduction. London and New York: Oxford Univ. Press, 1970.

———. "Tasso in England". In *The Flaming Heart: Essays on Crashaw, Machiavelli, and Other Studies in the Relations between Italian and English Literature from Chaucer to T.S. Eliot.* Pp. 308-47. New York: Doubleday, 1958.

Prince, F.T. *The Italian Element in Milton's Verse.* Oxford: Clarendon Press, 1954.

———. "Milton e Tasso". *Rivista di letterature moderne e comparate* 13 (1960):53-60.

Quilligan, Maureen. *The Language of Allegory: Defining the Genre.* Ithaca, N.Y.: Cornell Univ. Press, 1979.

———. *Milton's Spenser: The Politics of Reading.* Ithaca, N.Y. and London: Cornell Univ. Press, 1983.

Radzinowicz, Mary Ann. *Milton's Epics and the Book of Psalms.* Princeton: Princeton Univ. Press, 1989.

———. *Toward Samson Agonistes: The Growth of Milton's Mind.* Princeton: Princeton Univ. Press, 1978.

Renwick, W.L. *Edmund Spenser: An Essay on Renaissance Poetry.* London: Edward Arnold, 1925.

Rhu, Lawrence L. "From Aristotle to Allegory: Young Tasso's Evolving Vision of the *Gerusalemme Liberata*". *Italica* 65 (1988):111-30.

———. "Tasso's First Discourse on the Art of Poetry as a Guide to the *Gerusalemme liberata*". *Journal of the Rocky Mountain Medieval and Renaissance Association* 7 (1986):65-81.

Rich, Townsend. *Harington & Ariosto: A Study in Elizabethan Verse Translation*. Yale Studies in English, no. 92. New Haven: Yale Univ. Press, 1940.

Robins, Harry Franklin. *If This Be Heresy: A Study of Milton and Origen*. Illinois Studies in Language and Literature, no. 51. Urbana: Univ. of Illinois Press, 1963.

Roche, Thomas P., Jr. *The Kindly Flame: A Study of the Third and Fourth Books of Spenser's Faerie Queene*. Princeton: Princeton Univ. Press, 1964.

———. "Tasso's Enchanted Woods". In *Literary Uses of Typology from the Late Middle Ages to the Present*. See under **Miner**, editor. Pp. 49-78.

Roitman, Betty. "Sacred Language and Open Text". In *Midrash and Literature*. See under **Hartman and Budick**, editors. Pp. 159-75.

Rosenthal, Erwin I.J. "The Study of the Bible in Medieval Judaism". Chapter VI.5 in vol. 2 of *The Cambridge History of the Bible*. Pp. 252-79.

Sadler, Lynn V. *Consolation in Samson Agonistes: Regeneration and Typology*. Salzburg: Universität Salzburg, 1979.

Samuel, Irene. *Plato and Milton*. Ithaca, N.Y.: Cornell Univ. Press, 1947. Cornell Paperbacks, 1965.

Shawcross, John T. "Allegory, Typology, and Didacticism: *Paradise Lost* in the Eighteenth Century". In *Enlightening Allegory*. Edited by Kevin L. Cope. New York: AMS Press, 1993.

———. "Milton and Covenant: The Christian View of Old Testament Theology". In *Milton and Scriptural Tradition: The Bible into Poetry*. See under **Sims and Ryken**, editors. Pp. 160-91.

The Shorter Oxford English Dictionary. Revised with addenda by C.T. Onions. 3rd ed. Oxford: Clarendon Press, 1956.

Sims, James H. "Milton, Literature as a Bible, and the Bible as Literature". In *Milton and the Art of Sacred Song*. See under **Patrick and Sundell**, editors. Pp. 3-21.

Sims, James H. and Ryken, Leland, editors. *Milton and Scriptural Tradition: The Bible into Poetry*. Columbia: Univ. of Missouri Press, 1984.

Singleton, Charles. *Commedia: Elements of Structure*. Dante Studies 1. Cambridge, Mass.: Harvard Univ. Press, 1954. Reprinted Baltimore and London: Johns Hopkins Univ. Press, 1977.

Smalley, Beryl. "The Bible in the Medieval Schools". Chapter VI.3 in vol. 2 of *The Cambridge History of the Bible*. Pp. 197-220.

———. *The Study of the Bible in the Middle Ages*. 1941. 2nd ed. Oxford: Basil Blackwell, 1952.

Solerti, Angelo. *Vita di Torquato Tasso*. 2 vols. Turin and Rome: Ermanno Loescher, 1895.

Sozzi, B.T. "La Poetica del Tasso". *Studi Tassiani* 5 (1955):3-58.

Spingarn, J.E. *A History of Literary Criticism in the Renaissance*. 2nd ed. New York: Columbia Univ. Press, 1908.

———., editor. See under **Primary Works**.

Steadman, John M. "Allegory and Verisimilitude in *Paradise Lost*: The Problem of the 'Impossible Credible'". *Publications of the Modern Language Association of America* 78 (1963):36-39.

———. *Epic and Tragic Structure in Paradise Lost*. Chicago and London: Univ. of Chicago Press, 1976.

———. *The Lamb and the Elephant: Ideal Imitation and the Context of Renaissance Allegory*. San Marino: Huntington Library, 1974.

———. *Milton's Biblical and Classical Imagery*. Pittsburgh: Duquesne Univ. Press, 1984.

———. *Milton's Epic Characters: Image and Idol*. Chapel Hill: Univ. of North Carolina Press, 1959.

———. *Milton and the Renaissance Hero*. Oxford: Clarendon Press, 1967.

———. "Miracle and the Epic Marvellous in *Paradise Lost*". *Archiv für das Studium der Neueren Sprachen und Literaturen* 198 (1961–1962):289-303.

———. *The Wall of Paradise: Essays on Milton's Poetics*. Baton Rouge: Louisiana State Univ. Press, 1985.

Stern, David. "Midrash and the Language of Exegesis: A Study of Vayikra Rabbah, Chapter 1". In *Midrash and Literature*. See under **Hartman and Budick**, editors. Pp. 105-24.

———. "Rhetoric and Midrash: The Case of the Mashal". *Prooftexts: A Journal of Jewish Literary History* 1 (1981):261-91.

Sterne, Laurence and Kollmeier, Harold H., general editors. *A Concordance to the English Prose of John Milton*. Binghamton, N.Y.: Medieval and Renaissance Texts and Studies, 1985.

Teskey, Gordon. "From Allegory to Dialectic: Imagining Error in Spenser and Milton". *Publications of the Modern Language Association of America* 101 (1986):9-23.

———. "Information and Disorder: The Proem to *Faerie Queene* III". Paper, Convention of the Modern Language Association of America. Chicago, 1985.

———. "Milton's Choice of Subject in the Context of Renaissance Critical Theory". *English Literary History* 53 (1986):53-72.

Treip, Mindele Anne. "'Celestial Patronage': Allegorical Ceiling Cycles of the 1630s and the Iconography of Milton's Muse". In *Milton in Italy: Contexts, Images, Contradictions*. Edited by Mario A. Di Cesare. Binghamton, N.Y.: Medieval and Renaissance Texts and Studies, 1991. Pp. 237-79.

———. "*Descend from Heav'n Urania*": Milton's Paradise Lost and Raphael's Cycle in the Stanza della Segnatura*. English Literary Studies, no. 35. Victoria, B.C.: University of Victoria, 1985.

———. "'Reason is Also Choice': The Emblematics of Free Will in *Paradise Lost*". *Studies in English Literature* 31 (1991):147-77.

Tuve, Rosemond. *Allegorical Imagery: Some Medieval Books and their Posterity*. Princeton: Princeton Univ. Press, 1966.

———. *Elizabethan and Metaphysical Imagery: Renaissance Poetic and Twentieth-Century Critics*. Chicago: Univ. of Chicago Press, 1947.

———. *Images and Themes in Five Poems by Milton*. Cambridge, Mass.: Harvard Univ. Press, 1957.

———. *A Reading of George Herbert*. London: Faber and Faber, 1952.

Uhrbach, Ephraim E. "The Homiletical Interpretations of the Sages and the Expositions of Origen on Canticles, and the Jewish-Christian Disputation", *Scripta Hierosolymitana* 22 (1971):247-75.

Ullman, Berthold L. *The Humanism of Coluccio Salutati.* Medioevo e Umanesimo, no. 4 (second part). Padua: Editrice Antenore, 1963.

Vermes, G. "Bible and Midrash: Early Old Testament Exegesis". Chapter III.8 in vol. 1 of *The Cambridge History of the Bible.* Pp. 199-231.

Waldock, A.J.A. *Paradise Lost and its Critics.* Cambridge: Cambridge Univ. Press, 1947.

Weinberg, Bernard. *A History of Literary Criticism in the Italian Renaissance.* 2 vols. Chicago: Univ. of Chicago Press, 1961.

Weismiller, Edward. "Materials Dark and Crude: A Partial Genealogy for Milton's Satan". *Huntington Library Quarterly* 31 (1967):75-93.

Werman, Golda Spiera. "Midrash in *Paradise Lost: Capitula Rabbi Elieser". Milton Studies* 18 (1983):145-71.

Wetherbee, Winthrop. *Platonism and Poetry in the Twelfth Century: The Literary Influence of the School of Chartres.* Princeton: Princeton Univ. Press, 1972.

Wilkes, G.A. *The Thesis of Paradise Lost.* Melbourne: Melbourne Univ. Press, 1961.

Wolfson, Harry Austryn. *The Philosophy of the Church Fathers.* Vol. 1: *Faith, Trinity, Incarnation.* 1956. 3rd ed. rev. Cambridge, Mass.: Harvard Univ. Press, 1970.

Index

For the most commonly used titles in the index subheadings, the following abbreviations will appear throughout: Spenser, *FQ* for Spenser, *The Faerie Queene*; Tasso, *Ger. lib.* for Tasso, *Gerusalemme liberata*; and Milton, *PL* for Milton, *Paradise Lost.*

Accommodation, theory of, and literary allegory: Aquinas on, 278; Augustine on, 199, 325-26 n. 23, 326 n. 27, 327 n. 6, 328 nn. 6, 13; Dante on, 325-26 n. 23, 327-28 n. 8; in Milton, *PL*, including Raphael's discourse on, 11, 127, 182-83, 191-203, 215, 227-28, 240, 279-81, 285, 327 n. 5, 328 n. 15, 329 n. 23 (*see also* Milton, *PL*—modes of "accommodation"); possible sources for Raphael's discourse on, 196-200

Accommodation, theory of, and the representation of God in Scripture, 182-90, 255, 285, 325-26 n. 23, 327 n. 3, 332 n. 9; anthropomorphic readings of, 187-89, 205, 234, 278-81, 284-85, 326 n. 27; anthropomorphic readings of, refuted by Milton, 188-90, 326 n. 27; Aquinas on, 278; Augustine on, 326 n. 27; Thomas Browne on, 279; Donne on, 277; Milton on, in *Of Christian Doctrine*, 181-83, 186-90, 192-95, 200, 205, 227-28, 255, 278-81, 317 n. 16, 324 n. 3, 326 n. 25, 327 n. 5, 332 n. 9; Neoplatonic readings of, 187-89, 191-92, 195-96, 279-80, 327 n. 1; in Reformation tradition, 278-81

Addison, Joseph: on Milton and allegory, 109-10, 114, 115, 122, 173, 269, 312 nn. 24, 29, 313 n. 1. *See also* Allegory—personification; Epic—credibility in

Aeneas, *see* Epic—of active life, —of contemplative life; Virgil, *Aeneid*

Aesop, as model for secular allegory: Le Bossu on, 120, 314 nn. 1, 6; Salutati on, 14; Sidney on, 46

Aguzzi, Danilo L., 72, 258, 259-60, 288 nn.

13, 16, 293 nn. 4, 9, 19, 295 n. 17, 297-98 n. 29, 300-1 n. 1, 301 n. 6, 303 n. 25, 305 nn. 7, 8, 16, 309 n. 4, 310 n. 13

Alan of Lille, 22

Allegory, 329 n. 20. *See also* Epic *passim*
—and the absurd (bizarre, "irrelevant"), 3, 41, 133, 288 n. 13; Augustine on, 32, 297 n. 19; Bacon on, 24, 32-33, 35-36, 133; in early Christian use, 32, 133, 297 n. 19; in Milton, *PL*, 126, 127, 134, 166, 239-41, 243, 248-50; in Spenser, *FQ*, 33, 134, 248, 250, 287 n. 4
—and "accommodation", *see* Accommodation, theory of, and literary allegory
—"allegorical" sense in, as technical term for prophetic level of, *see* Typology—"allegorical" (term) in
—"Allegorie", as general term for a secondary meaning in, 130; in Harington, 38-39, 41, 297 n. 22, 298 n. 39
—Allegories (pl.), *see* Allegory—fantastic episode in, —personification
—anagogic or parabolical (as fourth or spiritual) sense in, 13; Aquinas on, 292 n. 65; Luther on, 177; in Milton, *PL*, 110, 130; in Reformation preaching, 223; in Spenser, *FQ*, 104
—in or on Bible, *see* Bible *passim*; Exegesis—on Scripture; Midrash
—civic or political, 34; Bacon on, 32, 34; in Castellio, 224; Harington on ("Allusion", "Historicall sence"), 38, 104, 298 n. 39; in Le Bossu on Virgil, 125, 165, 315 n. 27; in Milton, *PL*, 115, 130-31, 140, 213, 225, 344 n. 2; Spenser on, 101-2, 105, and in *FQ*, 104; Tasso on, 48-49, 56, 59, 61-62, and in

Ger. lib., 260-61; in Toland on Milton, 114-15
—as continuous exposition of extended narrative episode, 4-6, 301 n. 3; in early, medieval and Renaissance mythographers, 4-6; in *Ovide Moralisé*, 5; in Salutati, 6, 22, 293 n. 3, 295 n. 21; Tasso on, 53, 301 n. 3. *See also* Exegesis—on classical myth
—cosmological, *see* Allegory—physical
—as defence of poetry (by analogy to Bible): in Boccaccio, 45; in Dante, 23; in Salutati, 19, 20-21, 293 nn. 3, 4, 294 n. 11
—and dramatic genres: Milton on, 139-40, 317 n. 19. *See also* Comus
—in dream or vision, 3; in Milton, *PL*, 126, 135, 136, 164, 201-3, 218
—and emblem, 299 n. 11, 300 n. 11, 316 n. 12; in Dante, 3-4; in Milton, *PL*, 85, 126, 127, 130, 134, 135-37, 148-49, 155, 165, 247-49, 252, 255, 265, 295 n. 31, 316 n. 12, 320 n. 44, 322 n. 16, 323 n. 22, 333 n. 8; in Sidney, *The Countesse of Pembrokes Arcadia*, 46-47, 299-300 n. 10; in Spenser, *FQ*, 136-37, 316 n. 12
—and enigma or riddle, 3, 12, 33, 71, 133, 255, 287 n. 2; Aristotle on, 287 n. 2; in Bible, 12; in Dante, 3-4; in Delphic riddles, 23; in Milton, *PL*, 136, 166-67, 247-48, 250; Quintilian on, 287 nn. 1, 2; in Reynolds, 23; in Spenser, *FQ*, 4, 24, 103, 247; Tasso on, 54, 71, 154. *See also* Allegory—as hidden truth, in Saint Paul
—etymology of: Dante on, 291 n. 54; Quintilian on, 3, 287 n. 1; Salutati on, 20
—etymological: Bacon on, 31, 296-97 n. 16; in Reynolds, 35, 37; in Sandys, 37; in Spenser, *FQ*, 98
—as *exemplum* or exemplary moral, 94, 147; in Ariosto, 99, 131; Boccaccio on, 45; in eighteenth-century English critics, 109; Harington on ("Morall"), 38-40, 99, 104, 298 n. 40; in Johnson on Milton, 40, 111, 113-14, 121, 122, 156, 158, 176, 270; in Milton, *PL*, 130-32, 136-37, 145, 147-48, 152, 153, 156, 158, 165, 265-66, 315 n. 10; in seventeenth-century English critics, 108; Sidney on, 46, 299 n. 2; in Spenser, *FQ*, 39-40, 99, 102, 104-5, 131, 298 n. 40; in Tasso's two epics, 71-72, 92, 93, 131, 270, 305 n. 8. *See also* Allegory—moral and *exemplum*, distinction between
—"Fable" (sing.), as term for central allegory in epic: Boccaccio on, 45; Le Bossu on, 121, 122, 124, 314 nn. 5, 6, 315 n. 27. *See also* Aesop; Allegory—and Idea
—"Fables" (pl.), *see* Allegory—fantastic episode in
—fantastic episode in, 109; in Addison on

Milton and Spenser ("Allegories", pl.), 109-10, 122; Castelvetro on need to restrict, 116-18; censured by seventeenth-century English critics, 107-8; in John Hughes on Spenser and Milton, 109-10; in Johnson on Milton, 110-11, 175; Le Bossu on ("Allegories" pl., "Fables" pl., "Fictions"), 109, 122-24, 148, 248, 314 nn. 1, 6, 18, 19; Mazzoni on (*see also* Imitation—as theory of "poesia phantastica"), 117-18; in Milton, *PL*, 64, 67-68, 73-74, 82, 84, 113, 117-18, 122-23, 126-27, 134-37, 148-49, 154, 165, 240-43, 247-50, 252, 265, 315-16 n. 11, 322 n. 15; in Rymer on Spenser, 179; Spenser on ("accidents intermedled"), 102, 103, and in *FQ*, 33, 64, 67, 99-100, 123, 135-37, 148, 252, 315-16 n. 11; Tasso on, 33, 55, 60, 63-68, 73, 79, 80-93, 99, 258, and in *Ger. lib.*, 123, 148, 149, 252. *See also* Allegory—personification
—and fantastic episode, thematic unity via: Le Bossu on, 117, 122-23, 154; Mazzoni on, 117; in Milton, *PL*, 73-74, 117, 122-23, 154, 248-50, 265, 322 n. 15, 334 n. 2; in Spenser, *FQ*, 102-3; Tasso on, and in *Ger. lib.*, 64-65, 73-74, 81-85, 93, 99, 102-3, 274, 302 n. 20, 307 n. 3
—figural (or figural prophecy), *see* Typology
—four (or three) senses of, in secular: Le Bossu on, 120; in medieval literary allegorism, 13-14, 33, 221, 291 n. 50, 296 n. 6, 297 n. 22; Spenser on, 104. *See also* Aesop; Allegory—schematic
—four (or three) senses of, in theological, 9-14, 16, 28, 29, 33, 35, 37, 38, 221, 223, 290-91 n. 49, 297 n. 22; Aquinas on, 11, 130, 292 n. 65; Augustine on, 16, 292 n. 65; Dante on, 290 n. 46, 291 n. 54; in medieval allegorism, 12-13; in Milton, *PL*, 130, 131; in Origen, 9, 11. *See also* Allegory—schematic, —undivided secondary sense in
—global, *see* Allegory—total or global
—as hidden truth (mystery, concealment), and vocabulary for, 3, 33, 42, 329 n. 19; Addison on, 110; Bacon on ("*involucrum*", "inwardness", "veils and shadows"), 30-31, 249, 296 n. 15; Boccaccio on ("veil"), 19, 23, 45; Dante on ("cloak", "veil"), 23, 291 n. 54, 295 n. 24, 299 n. 6; Harington and Reynolds on ("barke", "kernel", "ryne"), 23, 298 n. 39, 299 n. 6; in John Hughes on Spenser, 109; Le Bossu on, 120-24, 125; in medieval theory (*integumentum, involucrum*), 19, 293 n. 2, 298 n. 39; in Milton, *PL* ("shadows", "secrets"), 49, 56, 140-41,

Allegory (*cont.*)
 163, 181-82, 193-96, 198-99, 201-2, 207,
 210, 250, 317 n. 16; in Milton, the prose
 writings (allegory, *allegoria, figura, meta-
 phora, parabola*), 181-82, 324-25 n. 3, 326
 n. 25; in Saint Paul (*aenigma*), 49, 154;
 Salutati on (*in cortice, intrinsecus*), 19; in
 Sidney, 45-47, 49; in Silvestris, 293 n. 2;
 Spenser on ("dim vele", "shadow"), 23,
 39, 103-4, 181; Tasso on ("mysteries"),
 and in *Ger. lib.*, 49, 54, 60-61, 65, 70-71,
 84, 89-90, 303 n. 26
—historical continuities of, 1-49 *passim*;
 Bacon on, 29-30
—houses and pageant in, *see* Allegory—
 personification
—and Idea, didactic-anterior, 20, 22, 23,
 42-43, 63-64, 67, 74, 115-16, 263-64, 294 n.
 8, 299 n. 3; in Addison, 109, 110; in du
 Bartas, 150, 151; Boccaccio on, 27, 44-45,
 133; Cowley on, *see* Invention; Harington
 on, 40; John Hughes on ("cover'd mor-
 al", "tacit Parallel"), 109; in Johnson on
 Milton ("Moral"), 176; Le Bossu on
 ("Platform", "Ground-work", "Moral",
 "Fable"), 109, 120-22, 124-25, 150, 151,
 155, 176, 248, 253, 254; in Milton, *see*
 Milton—Idea in; Phillips on ("proper
 allegory"), 112-13, 176, 253; Philo on,
 43-44; Puttenham on ("intendement"),
 24; Salutati on, 20, 22, 133; Sidney on
 ("foreconceit", "ground-plot"), 27,
 45-47, 299 n. 2, 314 n. 1; Spenser on ("the
 whole intention"), 64, 99, 102, 104; Tasso
 on ("Idea"), 47-48, 54, 55-62, 63, 64, 70,
 72, 74, 75, 78-79, 80, 84, 90, 91, 92, 93,
 108, 111-12, 147, 149, 150, 155, 253-54, 261,
 301 n. 2, 321 n. 4; in Toland on Tasso
 and Milton ("peculiar allegory or Mor-
 al"), 175, 253. *See also* Allegory—
 Platonic; Imitation, Ideal
—and "implication", technique of: in
 Milton, *PL*, 243-47; in Spenser, *FQ*, 244.
 See also Allegory—and simile
—"imposed", 4, 5, 290 n. 46; Bacon on,
 29-33, 290 n. 28; in Italian allegorizers of
 Ariosto, 36
—intermittent or episodic, 8, 41; in
 Ariosto, *Orlando Furioso*, 67, 99, 131; in
 Harington, 41, 131; in Italian allegorizers
 of Ariosto, 5, 36, 41, 304 n. 35; in Italian
 Neoplatonist humanists, 5; in Milton,
 PL, 131-32; in Philo, 44; in the Renais-
 sance mythographers, 34, 41, 131;
 Salutati on, 22, 295 n. 21; in Spenser,
 FQ, 99; Tasso critical of, 5, 131, 304 n. 35
—and irony, 133, 244
—juncture of form and meaning in, 5-7,

9-11, 18-22, 129, 133, 266; Bacon on, 31-33,
 35, 296-97 n. 16; in Dante, *Commedia*,
 11-12, 15-17; in medieval allegorism, 11; in
 Milton, *PL*, 11-12, 152-56, 160-67 *passim*,
 266; in patristic allegorism, 9; in Sa-
 lutati's theories, implicit, 22; Tasso on,
 73-74
—in landscape: in Milton, *PL*, 127, 135,
 202-3, 246-47; in Spenser, *FQ*, 135, 247
—levels of, *see* Allegory—four (or three)
 senses of, secular, —four (or three)
 senses of, theological, —literal level in,
 —schematic, —schematic (flexible or
 loose applications of)
—and linguistic texture: in Milton, *PL*, 74,
 127, 135-37, 153-54, 159-67 *passim*, 219-21,
 228, 230, 243-50, 315-16 n. 11, 322 n. 15; in
 Spenser, *FQ*, 74, 99-100, 135-37, 244, 246,
 315-16 n. 11; Tasso on, 74
—literal level (as first sense) in, 14-16, 130,
 275-77, 283; Aquinas on, 292 n. 65
—literal level in, importance of, 10-11, 49,
 75-77, 129, 221; Dante on, 291 n. 54, and
 in the *Commedia*, 11-12, 14, 15-17, 129, 290
 n. 40, 292 n. 64; in medieval allegorism,
 11-12, 223; in Milton, *PL*, 11-12, 17, 129,
 132, 191-92, 221, 228-29, 276, 290 n. 40,
 292 n. 64; Sidney on, 45
—main-plot: in Bunyan, 64; in Milton, *PL*,
 64, 68, 147-48, 165, 249-50, 252-53, 266; in
 Prudentius, 64; in Spenser, *FQ*, 39-40,
 64, 97-103, 105, 249; Tasso on, and in
 Ger. lib., 55-68, 92, 97-98, 147-48, 302 nn.
 19, 20, 302-3 n. 24, 304 nn. 28, 29. *See
 also* Allegory—as "metaphora con-
 tinuata", Tasso on structural problems,
 —as moral progress, —psychological
—main-plot and episode in, conjunction
 of: Le Bossu on, 120; in Milton, *PL*, 64,
 67-68, 73-74, 124, 131, 148-49; in Spenser,
 FQ, 64, 67, 97, 103; Tasso on, and in *Ger.
 lib.*, 55, 59-60, 63-68, 72, 73-74, 85, 92,
 97, 103, 124, 148-49, 308 n. 18 (*see also*
 Allegory—as "metaphora continuata",
 Tasso on structural problems)
—marvels, marvellous, marvellous-ver-
 isimilar (as Tasso's phrases for various
 avenues of narrative allegory) in, 63-67,
 80-85, 89-90, 91, 92, 93, 106, 107, 110, 113,
 116-17, 122, 124, 144, 147, 180, 253-54, 273,
 274, 301 n. 1, 307-8 n. 17, 308 n. 18, 319 n.
 24. *See also* Allegory—fantastic episode,
 —and verisimilar, truth of the, in Tasso;
 Epic—wonder
—medieval schemes of virtues in, 6, 40,
 70; in Bryskett on Spenser, 101-2; in
 Spenser, *FQ*, 95-96, 97-98, 100, 103,
 104-5, 270-71, 310 n. 15

—and metamorphosis: in Milton, *PL*, 247-48. *See also* Allegory—fantastic episode in; Ovid

—and metaphor, fundamental relation, 18, 23, 133, 275, 277, 284, 296 n. 44, 300 n. 11; Bacon on, 30-31, 33; Donne on, 277; in Milton, *PL*, 284; Peacham on, 25-26; Puttenham on, 24-26; Quintilian on, 287 n. 1; Salutati on, 20-22, 23; in Tasso, *Ger. lib.*, 70

—as "metaphora continuata", 23, 25-27, 92, 93, 96, 99, 133, 255, 275, 296 n. 44; Augustine on, 303-4 n. 27; n Milton, *PL*, 26-27, 127; Peacham on, 25-26, 53; Puttenham on, 25-26; Spenser on, 102, 309 n. 8, and in *FQ*, 25, 26, 39-40, 133; in Tasso, *Ger. lib.*, 133, 302 n. 20 (*see also* Allegory—main-plot); Tasso on structural problems of, 53-54, 62, 65-68, 133, 301 n. 2, 302 nn. 19, 20, 302-3 n. 24, 303 n. 25, 303-4 n. 27, 304 nn. 28, 29, 30, 31, 34, 309 n. 8. *See also* Allegory—as rhetorical trope

—and midrash, *see* Midrash

—in Milton, *see* Allegory *passim*; Milton—statements on allegory; Milton, *Paradise Lost passim*

—in the mixed historical-allegorical epic, *see* Epic

—as mode rather than genre, 315-16 n. 11; Puttenham on, 24

—moral (as third or "tropological") sense in, 12-14, 33, 40, 223, 283; Aquinas on, 283; Dante on, and in the *Commedia*, 15; as foremost sense in Milton, *PL*, 130, 131, 132, 208; Harington on (under inclusive term "Allegorie"), 38-40, 104; Le Bossu on, 120, 123-25; Luther on, 177; in Philo, 209; as predominant in the Renaissance, 28, 34, 36, 55-57, 96, 123, 125, 131, 297 n. 22; in Reformation preaching, 223, 283; in Sandys, 37; Salutati on, 21-22; Spenser on, 104, and as foremost sense in *FQ*, 130; Tasso on, 55-67, 150; as universal in epic, in Le Bossu on Virgil, 125. *See also* Allegory—as moral progress; Typology—and moral allegory, distinction

—moral, and *exemplum*, distinction between, 131; Harington on, 38-41, 131, 298 n. 40, 315 n. 3; Le Bossu on, 121, 122, 315 n. 4; in medieval interpretation, 12-13; in Milton, *PL*, 147; Spenser on, 39, 298 n. 40; in Tasso, *Ger. lib.*, 147

—as moral progress, 36, 55-57, 100, 303 n. 24; in Badius, 6; in Boccaccio, 6; in Dante, *Commedia*, 15-17, 129, 178, 291-92 n. 61; in Fulgentius, 6; Harington on, 96; in Landino on Virgil, 6, 98, 101, 132-33;

in Milton, *PL*, 6, 16-17, 102, 129, 132, 164-65; in Salutati, 6; in Silvestris, 6; in Spenser, *FQ*, 6, 16, 95-103, 132, 178, 270, 296 n. 45, 309 n. 4; Tasso on, 16, 17, 55-66, 72, 92-93, 96-99, 132, 270. *See also* Allegory—main-plot

—and mystery, *see* Allegory—as hidden truth

—and mystical theology, 150-51; Bacon on, 30, 31; in Milton, *PL*, 49, 163; Reynolds on, 35; Sidney on, 45-46; Tasso on (also as "the mystical image"), 48-49, 70-71, 74, 75, 117, 150-51, 163, 329 n. 21

—mythographic, 28-41. *See also* Bacon; Cartari; Comes; Ficino; Exegesis—on myth; Fulgentius; Hercules legends; *Ovide Moralisé*; Reynolds; Salutati; Sandys

—natural-scientific, *see* Allegory—physical

—Neoplatonic, 4, 7, 8-9, 16, 18, 36, 45, 49, 58, 207, 292 n. 1, 300 n. 11; and "accommodation" theory, 195-96; in Boccaccio, 5-6; in Ficino, 5; in Landino, 6, 270; in Milton, *PL*, 195-200; in Origen, 8-9; in postclassical allegorizers, 4-6; in Reynolds, 37, 298 n. 31; in Sidney, 45-46, 48; in Silvestris, 6; Spenser on, and in *FQ*, 104-5, 270; Tasso on, 48-49, 71-72, 75, 253, 258, 262, 299 n. 3, 302 n. 13, 319 n. 25. *See also* Allegory—Platonic; Imitation, Ideal

—and obscurity (or dissimulation), 3, 33; Peacham on, 24; Puttenham on, 25, 133, 315 n. 7; Quintilian on, 287 n. 1. *See also* Allegory—as hidden truth

—or *parabola*, *see* Allegory—as hidden truth, vocabulary for, in Milton

—parable in, *see* Allegory—"parabolic"

—"parabolic", as general name for allegorical poetry: in Bacon ("poetry allusive", "poetry parabolic", "parable"), 14, 29-31, 33, 36, 37, 296 n. 3

—parabolic (as fourth or figurative) sense in secular, 13-14, 229

—parabolical (as fourth or spiritual) sense in theological, *see* Allegory—anagogic sense

—personification: in Addison on Spenser and Milton ("Allegories", pl.), 110; in Ariosto, 84; in John Hughes on Spenser and Milton, 109; in Johnson on Milton, 111, 175-76; Le Bossu on, 121-22; in Martianus Capella, 295 n. 21; in Milton, *PL*, 26-27, 84, 126-27, 134-37, 165, 234, 240-42, 247-50, 252, 265, 285, 315-16 n. 11; Phillips on, 112; in Prudentius, 64; in *Roman de la Rose*, 290 n. 36; in Spenser, *FQ*, 26-27, 64, 84, 95, 98-99, 135-37. *See also* Allegory—fantastic episode

Allegory (cont.)
—physical and natural-scientific, 4-5, 28,
34, 130; Bacon on, 4, 29-30; in Comes
and Sandys, 4, 35, 37; Harington on, 298
n. 39; Le Bossu on, 123, 314 n. 20; in
Macrobius, 4; in Milton, *PL*, 130, 154,
243; in Spenser, *FQ*, 104, 130
—Platonic (the "Forms" or "Ideas" in), 4,
5, 40, 288 n. 11; in Boccaccio, 44-45;
Milton on, and in *PL*, 145, 150-51, 263-64,
320-21 n. 2, 327 n. 1; in Philo, 43-44; in
Sidney on, 45-47, 57, 58, 78; Spenser on,
and in *FQ*, 95, 105, 264, 270, 274; Tasso
on, 72, 74, 76, 78, 90, 93, 145, 263, 265,
270, 310 n. 22. *See also* Allegory—and
Idea, —Neoplatonic; Imitation, Ideal
—political, *see* Allegory, civic or political
—in preaching, *see* Homiletics
—prophetic or predictive of Christ, *see*
Typology—"allegorical" (term) in
—in prose: Salutati on, 19-20, 22, 24, 25,
295 n. 21
—psychological (psychic fragmentation),
56, 281 n. 4; in Harington, 96; Le Bossu
on, 123; Milton on, 139, 154, and in *PL*,
64, 127, 131-32, 143, 249-50; in Philo, 44;
Spenser on, 269, 270, 271, 274, and in
FQ, 64, 96-100, 102, 105, 132, 139, 143,
249; Tasso on, 48, 58-66, 72, 75, 92, 93,
96-99, 139, 154, 249, and in *Ger. lib.*, 132,
143
—as psychomachia: in Milton, *PL*, War in
Heaven, 130. *See also* Prudentius
—and puns: in Milton, *PL*, 161, 315-16 n. 11;
in Spenser, *FQ*, 99, 161, 315-16 n. 11. *See
also* Allegory—and linguistic texture
—rabbinic, *see* Midrash
—and reader-response: in Milton, *PL*,
249-50, 255; Puttenham on, 25
—relation of, to other figures, 3, 24-27, 33,
133, 292 n. 66, 296 n. 44; Puttenham and
Peacham on, 24, 25, 133, 295 n. 35;
Quintilian on, 287 n. 1. *See also* Alle-
gory—and enigma, —and irony, —and
metaphor, —as rhetorical trope
—as rhetorical trope, 18, 20, 23-27, 94, 95,
255; Addison on ("short expressions"),
110, 114, 312 n. 19; Aristotle on, 3-4;
Donne on, 276; in Johnson on Milton,
110; Peacham and Puttenham on, 24-26,
53; Phillips on, 114; Quintilian on, 3, 287
n. 1; Salutati on, 21, 295 n. 20; Spenser
on, 95, 103; Tasso dismissive of, 4, 5,
53-54, 75, 91, 93
—schematic (flexible or loose applications
of): in Bacon, 32; in Cartari, 34; in
Comes, 34-35; in Dante, 14-17, 290 n. 46,
291 n. 54; in Harington, 37-40, 104, 237,
297 nn. 22, 29; in medieval exegesis,

13-14, 15-16; in Reformation homiletics,
224; in Renaissance exegesis, 28, 104,
130, 297 n. 22; in Sandys and Reynolds,
35, 37; Spenser on, 104; in Tasso on
Dante, 301 n. 9
—schematic (multiple or simultaneous in-
terpretation), 12-14, 15, 29, 33, 39, 213; in
Aquinas, 130; in Saint Bernard (on Song
of Songs), 13, 35, 38; in Dante (on theme
of Exodus), 14, 15-16, 17, 35, 38, 130, 289
n. 31, 291 n. 54; Donne on, 276; in
Harington (on Perseus legend), 38, 298
n. 39; in Italian allegorizers of Ariosto,
36, 37; in midrash (on Songs of Songs
and Exodus), 9, 17, 289 nn. 22, 31; in
Milton, *PL*, suggestions of, 124, 130-31,
221, 243; in Origen (on Song of Songs),
9, 11, 13, 289 n. 31; in Philo, 44, 237, 299
n. 4; in Porphyry (on Homer's Cave of
the Nymphs), 9, 290 n. 45; in Reforma-
tion exegesis, disapproved of, 276; in
Reynolds (on Ovid's Tale of Narcissus),
35. *See also* Allegory—four (or three)
senses of; Bible—allegorization as suited
to certain Books
—"sensus spiritualis" in, *see* Allegory—
undivided secondary sense in
—and simile: with negative comparison, in
Milton, *PL*, 245-46; proleptic, in Milton,
PL, 148-49, 243-47, 249, 250. *See also*
Allegory—and "implication"
—in Spenser, *see* Allegory *passim*; Spenser,
FQ passim
—spiritual, *see* Allegory—anagogic or par-
abolical sense in
—Stoic, *see* Allegory—physical
—and supernatural machinery: Le Bossu
on ("Machines"), 123-24, 148, 175, 314 n.
15; in Milton, *PL*, 123, 127, 130-31, 134,
142-44, 148, 175-76, 202, 203, 232-33,
239-40, 247, 263; in Tasso, *Ger. lib.*,
142-44, 148
—suspicion of: in Calvin, 323-24 n. 8; in
Cowley, 178-79; in contemporary Milton
criticism, 172-73, 280-81, 282, 285, 315-16
n. 11, 323 n. 1, 333 n. 1; in Davenant,
107-8, 311 n. 3; in eighteenth-century
English criticism (including of Milton),
109-10, 243, 265, 312 n. 23, 323 n. 2; in
Luther, 177; post-Romantic, 29, 300 n.
17; in Reformation tradition, 8-9, 171-73,
177-78, 193, 224, 283, 285, 323-24 n. 8; in
Rymer on Ariosto and Spenser, 179-80;
in Saint-Évremond, 179; in sixteenth
century criticism, 91; in Tasso criticism,
history of, 261 (*see also* Tasso—under
Counter-Reformation). *See also* Bible—
literalism in the reading of, and anti-
figurative bias

—and symbol or *symbolum*, 323 n. 28, 329 n. 21; in medieval theory, 19, 166, 293 n. 2; in Milton, *PL*, 166, 329 n. 22; Reynolds on, 37; Salutati on, 19; in Silvestris, 293 n. 2; Tasso on, 71, 329 n. 21

—in Tasso, *see* Allegory *passim*; Tasso—critical theory, influences, —evolution of theories on allegory; Tasso, *Ger. lib. passim*

—theological: in Dante, 130; Harington on, 298 n. 39; in Milton, *PL*, 124, 130, 215, 235-38; 240-42, 249, 250, 255 (*see also* Accommodation, theory of, and literary allegory; Milton, *PL*—modes of "accommodation"); in *Ovide Moralisé*, 5; in Spenser, *FQ*, 130; in Tasso, *Gerusalemme conquistata*, 259, 260. *See also* Allegory—anagogic or parabolical sense

—*theoria* in, *see* Allegory—undivided secondary sense

—total or global, 18, 71-74, 133; in Milton, *PL*, 74, 153, 160, 204, 221, 315-16 n. 11; in Origen, 10; in Philo, 10, 20; Salutati on, 19-22, 71, 74, 133, 293-94 n. 7, 294 n. 9; in Spenser, *FQ*, 74, 99; Tasso on, 54, 303 n. 26, and in *Ger. lib.*, 22, 63, 69, 71, 74, 79, 89-90; in the Victorine mystics (*see* Allegory—and universal correspondences, theory of)

—as "translation" or transferred meaning, 3, 18, 33, 43, 71, 103, 239, 133; Augustine on, 290 n. 34; Harington on, 38; in Milton, *PL*, 129, 199; Peacham and Puttenham on ("translation", "alteration of sence"), 24-26; Quintilian on (*inversio, permutatio*), 287 n. 1; Salutati on ("translation", *commutatio*, poetry is "bilingual"), 19-22, 23, 25, 27, 42, 63, 294 nn. 8, 10, 11, 295 n. 17

—tropological (as third or moral) sense in, *see* Allegory—moral sense in

—"typick" or "type" (as third or typical-generic) sense in secular: in Reynolds, 37; in Sandys ("the type of Ambition"), 181

—typological (as second) sense in theological, *see* Typology—"allegorical" (term) in

—undivided secondary sense in, 13, 14, 42, 130, 213; Aquinas on ("sensus spiritualis"), 292 n. 65; Augustine on, 292 n. 65; Bacon on ("parabolic"), 14; Dante on ("twofold subject"), 11, 15-17, 21, 42, 291 n. 54, 292 n. 65, and in the *Commedia*, 12, 15, 21, 291 n. 54; Harington on ("Allegorie"), 38-39, 41, 104; in patristic theological allegory (*theoria*), 13-14, 290 n. 38, 292 n. 65, 297 n. 22; Salutati on (poetry is "bilingual"), 21; Spenser on ("generall end" of *FQ*), 104

—and universal correspondences, theory of: in Ariosto, *Orlando Furioso*, 196-99; in Augustine, 196; Fornari on, 196-99, 298 n. 29; 327 n. 10; Harington on, 297-98 n. 29, 328 n. 9; in Milton, *PL*, Raphael on, 196-200; Origen on, 196-99; in Pico, 196-97; Victorine systems of, 10, 12, 196-200, 290 n. 37, 328 n. 10

—usefulness of: Bacon on, 30-31. *See also* Homiletics

—and verisimilar, truth of the: in Tasso (as special term for the truth of allegory in epic), 67-68, 72-73, 75-79, 80-86, 89-90, 91, 93, 107-8, 112-13, 124, 146-49, 273-74, 305-6 n. 18, 306 nn. 22, 27, 307 n. 15, 308 n. 18. *See also* Epic—verisimilitude and inner truth in

—Victorine, *see* Allegory—and universal correspondences, theory of

—vocabulary for, *see* Allegory—as hidden truth, vocabulary for

Apuleius, 22, 295 n. 21

Aquinas, Saint Thomas, 10, 11, 130, 278; Milton on, 140; *Summa Theologica* of, 10, 292 n. 65; theories of allegory in, 283, 289-90 n. 34, 292 n. 65. *See also* Accommodation, theory of, and literary allegory; Accommodation, theory of, and the representation of God in Scripture; Bible—allegory in, as model for poetic figuration

Ariosto, Ludovico, *Orlando Furioso* of, 5, 35-41, 55, 72, 118, 130, 131, 138, 196-99, 269, 273, 299 n. 42, 328 nn. 9, 12; Addison on, 110; English allegorizers of, *see* Harington; intended allegory in, 67, 84, 99, 131, 198, 258, 328 n. 12; Italian allegorizers of, 5, 36, 37, 41, 96, 100, 196-98, 304 n. 35, 309 n. 3, 310 n. 15, 311 n. 2, 317 n. 6 (*see also* Bononome; Fornari; de'Franceschi; Toscanella); Milton's use of, 140, 196-98, 317 n. 6, 328 n. 12; Spenser on, 274, and as Spenser's model, 96, 99, 100, 101, 103, 179, 272; statements on allegory in, 196-99, 328 n. 10. *See also* Allegory—intermittent; Epic—romance variety

Aristotle, 3, 4, 30, 43, 178, 252, 273, 301 n. 2; as cited by Milton, 138, 317 n. 4; as cited by Spenser, 274; as ethical source for Milton, 164, 250; as ethical source for Tasso's "Allegoria del Poema" (to *Ger. lib.*), 56-62, 302 n. 15; influence of, on medieval allegorism, 95, 271; influence of, on seventeenth-century criticism, 93, 106-7, 115-16, 119-20, 311 n. 11; influence of, on sixteenth-century poetic theory, including Tasso's and Spenser's, 53-54, 72, 73, 75, 76-79, 80-81, 84, 88, 93, 103,

Aristotle (*cont.*)
116, 259, 273, 274, 287 n. 2, 294 n. 8, 306
  nn. 19, 22, 27, 316 n. 11; *Nicomachean
  Ethics* of, 58, 103, 164, 301 nn. 7, 8, 302 n.
  15, 310 n. 19, 323 n. 25; *Poetics* of, 72-73,
  78, 301 n. 2, 306 n. 19, 311 n. 11, 324 n. 15;
  Rhetoric of, 287 n. 2. *See also* Castelvetro
Aristotle, synthesis of thought with Pla-
  to's: in the Renaissance, 39, 56-59, 65; in
  Spenser's thought, 103; Tasso on, 56-62,
  103, 302 nn. 13, 15
Augustine, Saint, 7, 9, 18, 66, 196, 199, 260,
  326 n. 27; *The City of God* of, 89, 303-4 n.
  27, 326 n. 27, 327 n. 6; *De Genesi* of, 331
  n. 6; Tasso on, 89, 301 n. 3; theories of
  allegory in, 9, 14, 16, 32, 289 n. 30,
  289-90 n. 34, 291 n. 52, 292 n. 65, 297 n.
  19, 303-4 n. 27, 325-26 n. 23, 327 n. 6, 328
  n. 13; *De Trinitate* of, 289 n. 34, 292 n. 65,
  327 n. 6; view of evil in, 130. *See also*
  Accommodation, theory of, and literary
  allegory; Accommodation, theory of,
  and the representation of God in Scrip-
  ture; Allegory—and the absurd; Bible—
  allegory in, as model for poetic figura-
  tion
Auerbach, Erich, 10, 12, 290 n. 36, 333 n. 16

Bacon, Francis, 4, 14, 35; *Advancement of
  Learning* of, 29-31, 33; *De sapientia veterum*
  of, 29-33; theory of allegorical poetry in,
  24, 29-33, 34, 37, 133, 249, 296 nn. 3, 15.
  See also Allegory *passim*
Badius, Jodocus, 6
Bainton, Roland H., 207, 223-25, 283, 324
  n. 12, 325 nn. 10, 22, 330 n. 6, 331 nn. 2,
  3, 5
du Bartas, Guillaume de Saluste, 150-51,
  321 n. 3. *See also* Sylvester
Baudouin, Jean, translator of Tasso, 112,
  119
Bell, Charles G., 319 n. 23
Benjamin, Walter, 140
Bentley, Richard, 173, 246, 323 n. 2
Berger, Harry, Jr., 287 n. 4
Bernard, Saint, Abbot of Clairvaux, 13, 35,
  38. *See also* Bible—allegorization as
  suited to certain Books
Bernardus Silvestris, *see* Silvestris
Bible, 49, 162, 222-30, 299 n. 4. *See also*
  Allegory—as defence of poetry by anal-
  ogy to Bible; Epic—religion and doctrine
  in, treatment of; Exegesis—on Scripture;
  Homiletics—experiential approach to
  Bible in; Midrash; Typology
—allegorization as suited to certain Books
  of, 13-14; on Exodus, 13, 17, 35, 38, 209 n.
  31, 289 n. 31; on Revelation, 9; on Song
  of Songs (Song of Solomon), 9, 13-14, 17,

24, 35, 38, 289 n. 31, 290 n. 47, 291 n. 54,
  333 n. 12. *See also* Allegory—schematic
—allegory in, as model for poetic figura-
  tion, 9, 13-14, 24, 49, 129, 221; Augustine
  on, 9, 14, 289-90 n. 34, 291 n. 52, 303-4 n.
  27, 327 n. 6, 328 n. 13; Aquinas on,
  289-90 n. 34; Bacon on, 30; Boccaccio on,
  45; Dante on, 291 n. 54; Le Bossu on,
  120, 314 n. 16; and Milton, *PL* (*see*
  Accommodation, theory of, and literary
  allegory; Milton, *PL*—modes of "accom-
  modation"); Salutati on, 19, 20-21, 294 n.
  11
—allegory, intended, in, 186, 229, 277. *See
  also* Allegory—as defence of poetry by
  analogy to Bible; Milton—statements on
  allegory, in *Of Christian Doctrine*
—analogy of faith in reading, 285. *See also*
  Bible—rules for interpretation
—Apocrypha of: Milton's uses of in *PL*,
  184, 186, 228-29, 232-34, 325 n. 18, 330 n.
  18, 332 nn. 4, 5; proper uses for
  "Wisdom", Milton on, 184, 228, 232,
  331-32 n. 3, 332 n. 5; Reformation uses of
  in homiletics and moral allegory, 233
—Apocrypha and Pseudepigrapha of,
  Books: Enoch, 332 n. 4; 2 Esdras, 332 n.
  4; Tobit 233, 332 n. 4
—Books of, New Testament, including
  Milton's uses of: four Gospels of, 146,
  153; I James, 242, 333 n. 3; Matthew, 185
—Books of, Old Testament, including
  Milton's uses of: Exodus, 13, 17, 35, 38,
  209, 232, 289 n. 31, 291 n. 54; Ezekiel,
  181-82; Genesis, 20, 43-44, 88, 129, 132,
  145-46, 148-49, 152, 158, 163, 166, 192, 207,
  211, 215, 224-27, 232, 237, 253, 254,
  278-80, 294 n. 11, 332 n. 4 (*see also* Philo
  on Genesis); Hosea, 185; Isaiah, 194, 199;
  Job, 12, 138, 266; 2 Kings, 144; Psalms,
  17, 208, 235, 276, 289 n. 31, 291 n. 54, 292
  n. 67, 332 n. 8; Revelation, 9; Song of
  Songs (Song of Solomon), 9, 13-14, 17,
  24, 35, 38, 196, 237, 289 nn. 22, 31, 290 n.
  47, 291 n. 54, 333 n. 12
—Holy Spirit in: in Milton, *Of Christian
  Doctrine*, 331-32 n. 3; as represented in
  Urania in Milton, *PL*, 232. *See also*
  Bible—"inspiration" in reading of
—"inspiration" in reading of, 13, 227;
  Luther on, 177, 331 n. 5; Milton on, 185,
  323 n. 1, 325 n. 22; 331 n. 2 (chap. 19),
  and as reflected in *PL*, 224-27, 232, 285;
  in Reformation exegesis, 223-27
—interpretation of, *see* Bible—rules for
  interpretation; Exegesis—on Scripture
—literal historical level, importance of in
  reading, 8-9, 10-12, 129, 172, 191-92, 227,
  286; in Donne, 276-77; in medieval scho-

lastic reading, 10; reflected in Milton, *PL*, 132, 226-27, 331 n. 6 (chap. 18); in Reformation tradition, 10. *See also* Allegory—literal level in, importance
—literal sense in, inclusiveness of, 177, 186-87, 229, 282, 283; Donne on, 276-77; in medieval interpretation, 12-13, 275
—literalism in the reading of, 278; Thomas Browne on, 238, 279; Donne on, 234
—literalism in the reading of, and antifigurative bias, 177-78, 183, 324 n. 8, 326 n. 27, 331 n. 2 (chap. 19); in Johnson on Milton, 173-77, 183; in Luther, 177-78, 292 n. 1, 315-16 n. 11, 324 n. 12, 326 n. 27; in Milton criticism, and imputed to Milton, 77, 135, 171-73, 183, 188, 204, 206, 231-38 *passim*, 266, 279-81, 284-85, 323 n. 1; in seventeenth-century English criticism, 107-8, 179-80
—representation of God in, *see* Accommodation, theory of, and literary allegory; Accommodation, theory of, and the representation of God in Scripture
—rules for interpretation of, 5-6, 7-8, 230; Donne on, 276-77; Luther on, 177; in midrashic reading, 7-8; in Milton, *Of Christian Doctrine*, 171, 183-87, 228, 251, 253, 281, 283, 284-85; in Reformation tradition, 171-72, 177; in scholastic reading, 9-10, 12-13, 289 n. 32
—spectrum of modes of discourse and figuration in, 9, 12-14, 32, 146, 221, 228, 282; Luther on, 226; Milton on, 183-87, 205, 227, 229-30, 325 n. 15
—spectrum of modes of discourse and figuration in, and aesthetic implications for the literary representation of Scripture, 146, 171, 183-87, 190, 221, 229-30, 280-81, 282; for the representation of Scripture in Milton, *PL*, 208, 210, 226-30, 235-38, 280-81 (*see also* Milton, *PL*—biblical stylistic influences on, —modes of "accommodation")
Blackwell, Thomas, 312 n. 23
Blake, William, 316 n. 11
Boccaccio, Giovanni, 5, 6, 19, 23, 27, 44-45, 133, 150, 265, 288 n. 16
Boiardo, Matteo, 178, 292 n. 1
Boileau, Nicholas, 112, 115
Bonmattei, Benedetto, Italian correspondent of Milton, 317 n. 12
Bononome, Giuseppe, allegorizer of Ariosto, 96, 297-98 n. 29
Boyarin, Daniel, 288 n. 11, 289 nn. 21, 22, 31, 290 n. 47, 333 n. 10
Brand, C.P., 261, 268
Broadbent, J.B., 330 n. 17
Browne, Sir Thomas, 238, 279, 290 n. 37

Bruns, Gerald L., 7-8, 289 nn. 23, 24, 294 n. 10, 299 n. 4
de Bruyne, Edgar, 15, 275, 287 nn. 2, 7, 288 n. 13, 290 nn. 37, 42, 47, 49, 291 nn. 50, 53, 292 nn. 63, 65
Bryskett, Lodowick, 101-2, 103, 273, 310 n. 14. *See also* Spenser, *FQ*—early plans for
Budick, Sanford, 203, 289 n. 20, 333 nn. 14, 15, 16
Buffière, Félix, 6
Bunyan, John, 64

Calvin, John, 156, 184, 224-25, 278, 325 n. 27, 326 n. 27
Camões, Luis de, *Os Lusiadas* of, 101, 178. *See also* Epic—the historical
Cartari, Vicenzo, mythographer: allegorical apparatus of, 34
Castelli, Alberto, 268
Castellio, Sebastian, 224-25. *See also* Homiletics
Castelvetro, Ludovico, 175; Milton on, 115, 138, 254, 317 n. 4; *Poetica d'Aristotele* of, 86, 312 n. 38; and Tasso, 115-17, 262, 274, 306 n. 27, 313 n. 40 (*see also* Tasso, Works—*Estratti dalla Poetica di . . . Castelvetro*); theory of epic, 75, 86, 115-17, 120, 175, 265, 274, 313 nn. 45, 49, 315-16 n. 11. *See also* Allegory—fantastic episode; Epic—credibility in, —the historical
Christopher, Georgia B., 206, 284
Cicero, 4, 287 n. 7
Cintio, Giraldi, 103, 273, 310 n. 14
Comes, Natalis, 4, 37, 38, 39, 40, 41, 314 n. 20; allegorical apparatus of, 33-36
The Concise Oxford Dictionary of the Christian Church, 325 n. 5
A Concordance to the English Prose of John Milton, 324 nn. 3, 17, 325 n. 17
Conley, James William, 319 n. 24
Corneille, Pierre, 112
Counter-Reformation, *see* Tasso—under Counter-Reformation
Cowley, Abraham, 85, 106-8, 109, 115, 144, 178-79, 269, 307 n. 8, 311 nn. 3, 8, 324 n. 13; *Davideis* of, 108, 268, 324 n. 13. *See also* Allegory—suspicion of; Epic—Christian history in, —Christian miracles in, —hero, the scriptural-historical, in
Creation accounts: in du Bartas, 150-51; in Milton, *PL*, 125, 226-27, 331 n. 6 (*see also* Bible—Books of, Old Testament, Genesis); in Origen, on allegory on Genesis, 294 n. 11; in Philo, allegory on Genesis, 43-44; in Salutati, on allegory on Genesis, 20, 294 n. 11; in Tasso, *Le sette giornate del Mondo Creato,* 142

Curran, Stuart, 313 n. 1
Curtius, Ernst, 288 n. 13, 293 n. 4

Daniélou, Jean, 208-9, 286, 330 nn. 11, 19
Dante Alighieri, 44, 55, 115, 178; *Convivio*
  of, 15-17, 38, 290 n. 46, 291 n. 54, 303 n.
  27; *Divina commedia* of, 3-4, 6, 11-12,
  15-17, 23, 26, 32, 48, 100, 129, 130, 290 n.
  40, 291 n. 54, 295 n. 24, 299 n. 6, 300 n.
  13, 307 n. 14, 328 n. 8; "Epistle to Can
  Grande" of, 15-17, 289 n. 31, 291 n. 54,
  292 n. 65; Mazzoni on, 117; and Milton,
  importance to, 15; Tasso on, 54, 302 n.
  19, 303 n. 27; theories on allegory, and
  allegory in the *Commedia*, 14, 15-17, 21,
  27, 31, 32, 35, 38, 42, 54, 56, 61, 130, 265,
  289 n. 31, 290 n. 46, 291 n. 54, 291-92 n.
  61, 292 n. 65, 295 n. 24, 299 n. 6. *See also*
  Accommodation, theory of, and literary
  allegory; Allegory—schematic, —un-
  divided secondary sense
Davenant, Sir William, 107-8, 109, 115, 178,
  269, 311 nn. 2, 3, 7, 12. *See also* Epic—
  Christian history in, —hero, the scrip-
  tural-historical, in
Decorum: in epic, Phillips on, 112, 113
Dees, Jerome S., 300 n. 10
Derla, Luigi, 259
Diodati, Charles, correspondent of Milton,
  321 n. 2
Dionysius the pseudo-Areopagite: Tasso
  on, 70, 329 n. 21
Dodge, R.E. Neil, 270, 271
Donne, John, 234; *Devotions* of, 277; *Ser-
  mons* of, 276-77
Dronke, Peter, 287 n. 2, 288 nn. 13, 15, 290
  n. 34, 291 nn. 52, 54, 293 n. 2, 305 n. 6,
  329 n. 24
Drummond, William, of Hawthornden,
  267, 274
Dryden, John, 164, 268, 269

Eliot, John, 265, 274
Elizabeth I of England, 268; in Spenser, *FQ*
  (also as "Gloriana"), 39, 98, 104-5, 181
Empson, William, 332 n. 7
The Encyclopaedia Britannica: on Fulgentius,
  288 n. 14; on Macrobius, 287 n. 7; on
  Origen, 289 n. 29
Entrelacement in romance, *see* Epic
Epic. *See also* Allegory *passim*
—"Action" or plot in: Le Bossu on (the
  "fictive" plot), 120, 121, 152, 314 n. 19;
  Mazzoni on, 313 n. 56; in Milton, *PL*,
  152-53
—of active or morally effortful life: in
  Milton, *PL*, 56; in Spenser on Homer
  (*Iliad*), Tasso and Virgil, 101-3, 269; Tasso

on, 48-49, 56, 61-62, 302 n. 17. *See also*
  Allegory—as moral progress
—allegory as central to, 132; Le Bossu on,
  120-21, 123, 124, 125, 167, 313-14 n. 1, 315
  n. 27; in Milton, *PL*, 124, 132, 167, 251-56;
  Sidney on, 57; Tasso on, 47-49, 54,
  57-58, 91, 253, and in *Ger. lib.*, 259,
  260-61. *See also* Allegory—and Idea
—alternation of allegory with verisimilar
  narration in: in Milton, *PL*, Spenser, *FQ*
  and Tasso, *Ger. lib.*, 251-52
—"Argument" in: as oratorical concept, *see*
  Imitation, Ideal—as theory of formal
  design; in Milton, *PL*, conceived as
  abstract centre to poem, *see* Allegory—
  and Idea
—balance of history and fiction in, 69, 75;
  Bacon on, 32; disputed between Cas-
  telvetro, Tasso and Mazzoni, 115-18; Le
  Bossu on, 120-22, 124; in Milton, *PL*, 88,
  126-28, 141, 144-49, 151-52, 230, 251-54,
  315-16 n. 11, 333 n. 1; Phillips on, 112-13,
  144-45, 334 n. 4; in Spenser, *FQ*, 315-16
  n. 11; Tasso on, 32, 67, 76, 81-94, 101, 144,
  147, 230, 274, 307 n. 15, 315-16 n. 11, 333
  n. 1, 334 n. 4, and in *Gerusalemme
  conquistata* and *Ger. lib.*, 89, 148, 252-54
—the brief: Milton on, 138-39
—cardinal and theological virtues in:
  Milton and Tasso on, 317 n. 8
—Christian history in: Cowley on, 107-8,
  179; Davenant on, 107-8, 311 nn. 7, 10;
  Milton on, 139, and in *PL*, 107-8, 137,
  233. *See also* Epic—hero, the scriptural-
  historical
—Christian miracles in: Cowley on, 85,
  107, 144, 179, 307 n. 8; in Johnson on
  Milton, 109, 111, 174-75; Le Bossu on, 123;
  in Milton, *PL*, 85, 127, 144, 319 n. 27;
  Tasso on, 60, 85, 92-93, 111
—of contemplative life: in Spenser on
  Homer (*Odyssey*), 101-3; in Tasso on
  Dante, Homer (*Odyssey*) and Virgil,
  48-49, 56, 61, 302 n. 17
—credibility in, 33, 109; Addison on
  ("probability"), 110; Castelvetro on ("the
  possible"), 116; in *Dante, Commedia*, 129;
  Davenant on ("probability"), 107-8;
  Hobbes on ("possibility"), 107-8; in
  Johnson on Milton ("probability"), 111,
  174-75; Le Bossu on ("human", "Divine"
  and "poetical" "probability"), 120, 121,
  123-24, 314 n. 19; in Mazzoni on Dante
  ("the credible marvelous"), 117, 313 n.
  56; in Milton, *PL*, *see* Milton, *PL*—
  credibility in; Phillips on ("verisimility",
  "probable circumstances"), 112, 113, 253;
  Rymer on ("probability"), 179; Tasso on
  ("necessity", "apparent-probable"), 147,

233, 239, 258, 306 n. 27, 333 n. 1. *See also* Imitation—as theory of external representation
—didactic end of, *see* Allegory—and Idea; Epic—allegory, as central to
—encyclopaedic emphasis in: in Milton, *PL*, 153
—*entrelacement* in: in medieval romance epic, 252, 287 n. 4; in Milton, *PL*, Spenser, *FQ* and Tasso, *Ger. lib.*, 251-52
—episode, fantastic, in, *see* Allegory
—episode, true (as differentiated from fantastic episode), in: in Castelvetro ("Digressions"), 116-18; in Johnson on Milton, *PL*, 111, 116, 122, 153, 175; Le Bossu on ("proper episode"), 122-23, 124, 153, 175, 314 nn. 18, 19, 323 n. 5; in Milton, *PL*, 153; Tasso on, 81
—Fable (sing.) or Fables (pl.) in, *see* Allegory
—hero, the Christian and moral, in, 132; in Landino on Aeneas, 55; Milton on, 87, 101, 102, 139-40, 144-45, 164-65, 319 n. 29, 320 nn. 34, 36; in Salutati on Hercules, 55; Spenser on, and in *FQ*, 56, 87, 101-3, 223, 274; Tasso on, 87, 92, 101, 145, 320 nn. 34, 36
—hero, the scriptural-historical, in: seventeenth-century English critics on, 107, 179, 311 n. 12
—Heroic Virtue in, 55-56, 301 n. 7; Hobbes on, 311 n. 2; in Landino on Virgil, 100; in Milton, *PL*, 56, 132, 144, 164, 301 n. 7; in Milton on Spenser's Guyon, 103, 310 n. 17; origins of concept in Aristotle, 301 n. 7, 310 n. 19; in Spenser, *FQ*, represented in Prince Arthur, 56, 100-101, 104, 270, 301 n. 7, 310 nn. 15, 17; in Spenser on Virgil's Aeneas, 101, 103; Tasso on, 144, 270, 301 n. 7, 305 n. 10, 310 nn. 19, 22, 319 n. 30
—the historical, and history in the: in Camões, 101, 178; Castelvetro on, 86, 115-17, 315-16 n. 11; Hobbes on, 107-8; in Le Bossu on Virgil, 125; in Milton, *PL*, 141, 145, 253-54, 315-16 n. 11, 318 n. 18; Phillips on, 111; Spenser on, 100-102; Tasso on, 86, 89, 178, 233, 254, 258, 260, 311 n. 18; in Trissino, 108, 178. *See also* Epic—balance of history and fiction, — Christian history, —hero, the scriptural-historical, —the mixed allegorical-historical
—Invocation in: Davenant on, 107; in du Bartas, 321 n. 3; Hobbes on, 311 n. 9; in Milton, *PL*, 108, 145, 151-55, 164, 183
—love in: Dryden on, 269; in Milton, *PL*, 143, 241, 319 n. 24; Tasso on, 62, 72, 86, 107, 269, and in *Ger. lib.*, 143, 269, 319 n. 24

—the mixed historical-allegorical, 69; Milton on (the "diffuse"), 100-101, 254, and as seen in *PL*, 67-68, 106, 111, 117-18, 128, 134-41, 151-56, 165-67, 239-43, 251-54, 266, 315-16 n. 11, 318 n. 18, 331 n. 4 (chap. 18); Sidney on, 46-47; Spenser on, 100-101, and as seen in *FQ*, 67, 251-53; Tasso on, and as seen in *Ger. lib.*, 47-49, 63, 67-68, 91-92, 106, 115-18, 135, 144, 146-49, 252-54, 315-16 n. 11
—national and patriotic: Milton and Tasso on, 145. *See also* Allegory—civic or political
—plot, *see* Epic—"Action"
—of private life: in Spenser on Tasso's Rinaldo and Virgil's Aeneas, 101-102, 269
—religion and doctrine in, treatment of: Cowley on, 107-8, 178-79, 324 n. 13; Davenant on, 107-8, 178; in Johnson on Milton, 110-11, 173-76, and on Waller, 173-74; Milton on, 139-40, 145-46, and in *PL*, 87-88, 129, 145-46, 149, 153, 222-30, 235, 253-54 (*see also* Accommodation, theory of, and literary allegory; Milton, *PL*—biblical stylistic influences, —modes of "accommodation"); in Saint-Évremond, 179; Tasso on, 85, 86, 87-88, 145-46, 308 n. 34, and in *Ger. lib.*, 149
—romance variety in, 37, 41, 68, 138, 178, 179, 251-52, 309 n. 2, 315-16 n. 11; in Ariosto, *Orlando Furioso*, 100, 130, 138, 178, 179, 273; Milton on, 138-39, 317 n. 6, 318 n. 18, and in *PL*, 315-16 n. 11; in Rymer on Ariosto and Spenser, 179; in Spenser, *FQ*, 26-27, 95, 100, 131; Tasso on, 63, 72-74, 80-82, 83, 91, 92, 106, 138-39, 147, 149, 254, 260, 305 n. 2
—supernatural machinery in, *see* Allegory—and supernatural machinery
—and tragedy: Le Bossu on, 120, 124, 314 n. 3; in Milton, *PL*, 108, 124-25, 139, 143, 162; seventeenth-century English critics on, 107-8, 311 n. 11; in Tasso, *Ger. lib.*, 143
—verisimilitude in, *see* Epic—credibility in
—verisimilitude and inner truth in, 14, 69, 113, 230; Le Bossu on, 120, 121, 122, 124, 165; Mazzoni on, 117, 306 nn. 22, 27, 313 n. 56; in Milton, *PL*, 73-74, 134, 146-49, 151-54, 165-67, 225-26, 230, 251, 253; Phillips on, 112-14, 253; Tasso on, see Allegory—and verisimilar, truth of the
—wonder: Castelvetro on, 116, 313 n. 49; eighteenth-century English critics on ("sublimity", "astonishment"), 109-10; Le Bossu on (the "surprizing"), 122; in Milton, *PL*, 84, 144, 266, 319 nn. 27, 28; Tasso on, 57, 90, 144, 307 nn. 10, 11, 319 nn. 26, 28. *See also* Allegory—fantastic episode, —marvels, marvellous, mar-

Epic (*cont.*)
   vellous-verisimilar (as Tasso's phrases);
   Epic—Christian miracles
Euhemerism: in Milton, *PL*, restricted, 212
Exegesis
—on classical epic, 4-9 *passim*; 18, 29-33,
   36, 43, 53-56, 65-66, 98-103, 105, 107, 128,
   132, 167, 252-53, 255, 269, 270, 274, 287
   n. 6, 288 n. 10, 289 n. 30, 290 n. 45,
   291-92 n. 61, 302 n. 19, 303 n. 24, 310 nn.
   9, 13, 314 n. 6. *See also* Homer; Landino;
   Virgil
—on classical myth, 4-6, 19-22, 28-41, 43,
   45, 53, 55, 95, 212; as reflected in Milton,
   PL, 212, 292 n. 1, 293 n. 3, 297 n. 22, 298
   n. 39, 301 n. 7. *See also* Bacon; Cartari;
   Comes; Hercules myths; Ovid
—on medieval epic, 15-17, 291 n. 54, 292 n.
   1, 302 n. 19. *See also* Dante
—on Renaissance epic, 5-6, 35, 36-41,
   47-49, 55, 63, 92-93, 96-98, 100-105,
   114-15, 253, 269, 270, 274, 302 n. 19, 310
   n. 15. *See also* Ariosto *passim*; Tasso,
   Works—"Allegoria del Poema" (to *Ger.
   lib.*), —"Allegoria del *Rinaldo*"
—on Scripture, 4, 7-14, 16-18, 43-44, 49,
   129, 166-67, 181-90, 192-93, 200, 204-31
   passim, 236-38, 252, 255, 275-79, 282-86,
   288-89 n. 20, 289 nn. 21, 31, 32, 290 n. 38,
   291 n. 54, 292 n. 1, 297 n. 19, 299 n. 4,
   322 n. 19, 331 n. 1, 332 nn. 4, 10, 14. *See
   also* Bible *passim*; Homiletics; Midrash;
   Typology

Fairfax, Edward, translator of Tasso, 261,
   268, 300 n. 17, 300-301 n. 1, 302 n. 17, 318
   n. 22; influence of verse on Milton's,
   143, 146, 319 n. 23
Fallon, Stephen M., 315 n. 3
Ferry, Ann D., 316 n. 11
Fichter, Andrew, 260-61
Ficino, Marsilio, 5, 262, 263, 288 n. 12, 298
   n. 31, 301 n. 3, 303 n. 27; Tasso on, 66
Fisch, Harold, 289 nn. 21, 22
Fixler, Michael, 284
Fletcher, Angus, 287 n. 4
Fornari, Simone, allegorizer of Ariosto, 96,
   297-98 n. 29, 298 n. 29, 327 n. 10, 328 n.
   9; and Milton's sources for Raphael's
   discourse in *PL*, 196-99. *See also* Accom-
   modation, theory of, and literary
   allegory
Fowler, Alastair, 267, 318 n. 22, 330 n. 17,
   332 n. 4
de'Franceschi, Pietro, allegorizer of
   Ariosto, 36
Fraunce, Abraham, 268
Frye, Northrop, 284, 285

Frye, Roland Mushat, 278-79, 285, 326-27
   n. 28, 327 n. 3
Fulgentius, Fabius, 5-6, 288 nn. 9, 14

Galileo Galilei, 327 n. 5
Gallagher, Philip J., 285, 323 n. 1
Gang, T.M., 268-69
Gardner, Helen, 209, 211, 218, 276, 277,
   285-86, 328 n. 18, 330 n. 8
Giamatti, A. Bartlett, 318 n. 22
Gilbert, Allan H., 312 nn. 32, 35, 313 nn.
   56, 62
Goldman, Jack, 332 n. 4
Gombrich, E.H., 202, 299 n. 3, 325-26 n. 23
Gonzaga, Scipione, correspondent and ed-
   itor of Tasso, 257-58, 259, 261, 272, 273,
   303 n. 25
Greene, Thomas, 263, 319 n. 24, 324 n. 13,
   333 n. 5
Grey, Arthur, Lord Grey de Wilton, 104

Halivni, David Weiss, 322 n. 19
Hamilton, A.C., 290 n. 40
Hanford, James Holly, 189, 192, 279-80, 327
   n. 1, 332 n. 4
Hannay, Margaret P., 299 n. 10
Hanson, R.P.C., 288 n. 20
Hardie, Philip R., 315 n. 27
Harding, Davis P., 323-24 n. 8
Harington, John, translator and allegorizer
   of Ariosto: allegorical systems of, 36-41;
   and Milton's sources for Raphael's dis-
   course in *PL*, 196-98; theories on
   allegory, 19, 23, 35, 37, 38-41, 72, 96, 98,
   99, 100, 104, 131, 166, 237, 265, 268-69,
   295 n. 26, 297 n. 22, 297-98 n. 29, 298 nn.
   39, 40, 299 n. 6, 309 n. 3, 315 nn. 3, 4,
   317 n. 6, 328 nn. 9, 10, 12. *See also*
   Allegory *passim*
Harris, Victor, 283
Hartman, Geoffrey H., 289 n. 20
Harvey, Gabriel, 100, 270, 271, 272. *See also*
   Spenser, *FQ*—early plans for
Helgerson, Richard, 260-61
Heraclidis Pontici, 318 n. 17
Herbert, George, 207, 235, 282, 284
Hercules myths, as subject of early alle-
   goresis, 6, 19-23, 55, 301 n. 7; Salutati on,
   19-22, 293 nn. 3, 4. *See also* Salutati, *De
   laboribus Herculis*; Seneca.
Hill, Christopher, 225, 331 n. 4, 333 nn. 3,
   6, 334 n. 2
Hobbes, Thomas, 107-8, 109, 115, 311 nn. 2,
   9, 11
Hollander, Robert, 291 n. 54
Homer, epics of, 86, 108, 128, 240, 243; as
   Milton's model, 138, 140, 146, 152
Homer, epics of, as subject of early alle-

goresis, 4-5, 6, 8, 9, 41, 100, 102, 107, 287
n. 6, 288 nn. 8, 10, 13, 290 n. 45, 299 n. 4,
312 n. 29, 315 n. 27; Addison on, 110;
Bacon on, 29-32, 34; Castelvetro on, 116;
Le Bossu on, 314 n. 6, 315 n. 27; and
Milton, 182, 289 n. 30, 318 n. 17; Spenser
on, 101-2, 269, 274; Tasso on, 48, 53-54,
66, 303 n. 24; Toland on, 114
Homiletics, 222-27, 255, 329 n. 19, 331 n. 1.
See also Bible—Apocrypha, Reformation
uses
—in Donne's sermons, 276-77
—experiential approach to Bible in: analo-
gies in midrash, 236-37; reflected in
Milton, PL, 129, 163, 199-200, 224-27, 253;
in Reformation preaching, 222-27,
236-37, 253
—free use of Old Testament types in,
222-25
—Luther on, 325 n. 22
—and moral allegory, close connections
of, 7-8, 12-13, 27, 331 n. 1 (chap. 18); as
seen in Milton, PL, 199-200, 222, 224-28,
230; Raphael on, in Milton, PL, 293; in
Reformation use, 7-8, 222-28 passim, 283
Horace, 25, 317 n. 4
Horsfall, Nicholas, 315 n. 27
Hugh of Saint-Victor, mystic, 290 n. 37. See
also Allegory—and universal correspon-
dences, theory of
Hughes, John, early editor of Spenser,
109-10, 115, 312 n. 22
Hughes, Merritt Y., 270-71, 288 nn. 13, 16,
309 n. 4, 310 n. 9
Hurd, Richard, Bishop, 115, 135, 269

Imitation
—Ideal, see Imitation, Ideal
—as theory of external representation, 69,
75; Mazzoni on (the "icastic"), 117; and
Milton, PL, 265-66 (see also Johnson—on
Milton); Sidney on, 57; Spenser on, 105,
310 n. 10, 21; Tasso on, 47-48, 54, 76-77,
91, 150, 153-54, 258, 306 nn. 21, 27, 310 n.
21. See also Bible—literalism in reading
and anti-figurative bias; Castelvetro;
Epic—credibility in
—as theory of "poesia phantastica":
Mazzoni on, 117-18; Spenser on, 310 n. 10
Imitation, Ideal, 163-64, 191, 265. See also
Allegory—Neoplatonic, —Platonic
—as theory of formal design, or unified
plot: Castelvetro on, 116-17; Le Bossu on,
120; as applied to Milton, PL, 264-65, 321
nn. 6, 8, 321-22 n. 15; in neoclassical
criticism, 107; in sixteenth-century poetic
theory, 43, 75, 80-81, 263-65; Tasso on,
72-73, 92, 263-64. See also Aristotle

—as theory of generalized representation,
43, 299 n. 3
—as theory of moral-ideal representation,
42-43, 263-65, 270, 299 n. 3; Davenant
on, 311 n. 2; Milton on, and as reflected
in poetry of, 243, 263-64, 320-21 n. 2;
Sidney on, 45-48, 57, 77, 78, 79, 299 nn.
1, 2, 3; Spenser on, and as reflected in
FQ, 310 n. 21, 311 n. 2; Tasso on (see
Allegory—Neoplatonic, —Platonic);
Toscanella on, 311 n. 2
—as theory of moral-ideal representation,
overlap of, with allegory, 43, 264-66, 299
n. 3; in Sidney, 45-47, 299 n. 2; Spenser
on, 105; Tasso on, 69, 75-79, 91
Invention, in poetry, 45, 78; Cowley on,
108; Phillips on, 112
Italian allegorizers of Ariosto, see Ariosto

Jerome, Saint, 20
Johnson, Samuel, 40, 156, 178; on Milton,
109-11, 113-16, 117, 119, 121, 122, 153, 156,
158; 173-76, 231, 239, 265, 270, 323 nn. 4,
6. See also Allegory—as exemplum, —and
Idea; Epic—credibility in, —true episode
in
Jusserand, J.J., 273

Kabbalah, see Midrash
Kates, Judith A., 261, 267, 318 n. 22, 319 n.
23
Kennedy, W.J., 259, 260
Kermode, Frank, 301 n. 7
Knapp, Steven, 148, 312 nn. 23, 24, 29, 320
n. 43
Knox, John, 278
Krouse, F. Michael, 283
Kugel, James L., 289 n. 22, 333 n. 14
Kyd, Thomas, 268

Lamberton, Robert, 6-7, 196, 287 nn. 6, 7,
288 nn. 8, 9, 10, 14, 15, 18, 289 nn. 28, 30,
290 n. 45, 291 n. 52, 291-92 n. 61, 299 n.
4, 302 n. 21, 327 n. 6
Lampe, G.W.H., 290 n. 38, 292 n. 65
Landino, Cristoforo, allegorizer of Virgil,
6, 55, 65, 66, 98, 100, 101, 132-33, 262,
270, 288 n. 16, 292 n. 1, 303 n. 24, 309 n.
4, 310 nn. 9, 13. See also Allegory—as
moral progress
Lawry, Jon S., 300 n. 13
Lea, Kathleen M., 268-69
Le Bossu, René: theories on epic and
allegory, 109, 111-12, 114, 115, 117, 119-25,
128, 148, 150, 151, 152, 153, 154, 155, 165,
167, 175-76, 240, 248, 253, 254, 300 nn.
14, 19, 312 n. 38, 313-14 n. 1, 314 nn. 1, 3,
5, 6, 15, 16, 18, 19, 20, 315 nn. 4, 27, 321

Le Bossu, René (*cont.*)
    n. 8, 323 nn. 5, 6. *See also* Allegory
    passim; Epic *passim*
Leslie, Michael, 267
Lewalski, Barbara Kiefer, 206, 276, 277,
    282-83, 284, 330 nn. 6, 20, 331 n. 1, 332 n. 9
Lewis, C.S., 64, 95, 99, 309 n. 2
Lloyd, Michael, 283
de Lubac, Henri, 290 n. 49
Luther, Martin, 7, 177-78, 184, 223-26, 253,
    325 n. 22, 326 n. 27, 331 n. 5

MacCaffrey, Isabel Gamble, 316 n. 11, 331
    n. 1
MacCallum, H.R., 189, 280-81, 284, 286,
    323 n. 8, 324 n. 3, 326 nn. 24, 27, 327 n.
    4, 330 n. 8
McMurphy, Susannah Jane, 298 n. 40
McNulty, Robert, 297 n. 29, 309 n. 3
Macrobius, 4, 287 n. 7
Madsen, William, 207, 284-85, 326 n. 24,
    328 n. 15, 329 nn. 19, 22, 330 n. 7, 331
    n. 1
Manso, Cardinal Giovanni Battista, patron
    of Tasso, 114, 262; and Milton, 141, 146,
    318 n. 19, 319 n. 25. *See also* Milton—and
    Italian literary connections, —Works:
    "Mansus"; Toland
Martianus Capella, Alanus, 22, 295 n. 21
Mashal, *see* Midrash
Mazzoni, Jacopo, 175; on Dante, 117; *Della
    Difesa della Comedia di Dante* of, 312 n. 38,
    313 n. 53; and Milton, 115, 117, 138, 254,
    313 n. 56, 317 n. 4; and Tasso, 117-18, 175,
    260, 274, 306 n. 27; theory of poetry and
    allegory in, 115-18. *See also* Allegory—
    fantastic episode; Imitation—as theory
    of "poesia phantastica"
Midrash, 288 n. 19, 288-89 n. 20, 289 n. 21,
    294 n. 10, 299 n. 4, 333 nn. 14, 16. *See also*
    Accommodation, theory of, and literary
    allegory; Accommodation, theory of,
    and the representation of God in Scrip-
    ture; Allegory—schematic; Bible—
    allegorization as suited to certain Books,
    —rules for interpretation
—definition of, 289 n. 20
—and homiletics, close connection of, 7-8,
    234-38, 289 n. 23
—and Kabbalah, 10
—Milton's uses of, 332 n. 4
—paraliterary genres in, 7-8, 236-38, 289
    nn. 21, 22, 332 n. 10
—radical linguistic methods of, 7-8, 213,
    234-38, 255, 299 n. 4, 333 n. 16; origins in
    Philo, 237, 299 n. 4, 333 n. 16; reflected
    in Milton, *PL, see* Milton, *PL*—modes of
    "accommodation"
Milton, John. *See also* Addison; Creation

accounts; Imitation, Ideal; Midrash; Phi-
    lo; Plato
—and Bible, *see* Bible *passim*
—defences of free will in, 115, 156-65, 182,
    240-42, 248, 289 n. 30, 322-23 n. 20, 323
    n. 26, 333 nn. 3, 8
—defences of providence in, 73, 108,
    151-66, 182, 240-41, 252-53, 255, 320-21 n.
    2, 321 n. 8
—early interest in allegory, 139-40, 317 n.
    9, 318 n. 17
—epic ambitions of, 138-40, 145, 254, 328
    n. 12
—evil, view of, 130, 152, 154-63, 213, 242,
    315 n. 3, 321 nn. 10, 14, 323 n. 23. *See also*
    Augustine
—Idea in: as used in *Of Christian Doctrine*,
    pertaining to God's foresight, 151,
    155-57, 320-21 n . 2 (*see also* Milton, *PL*—
    Justification of God); seen as abstract
    allegorical centre of *PL* (also its "Argu-
    ment"), 49, 64, 73-74, 128, 129, 132, 135,
    138, 140, 141, 145, 147-49, 150-67, 171, 176,
    252-55, 264, 311 n. 32, 320-21 n. 2, 321 n.
    8, 321-22 n. 15; various uses of the word,
    150-51, 320-21 n. 2
—and Italian literary connections, 119, 128,
    138-40, 141, 146, 317 nn. 10, 12, 318 nn. 18,
    19. *See also* Diodati; Manso; Toland
—oeuvre of, in parallel with Tasso's,
    141-44
—statements on allegory in (including
    allegory in Bible), 128, 317 n. 6; in *Of
    Christian Doctrine*, 171, 181-82, 184, 186-90,
    205, 229, 289 n. 30, 324-25 n. 3, 325 n. 11,
    326 n. 25; in the English prose writings,
    182, 324-25 n. 3; in *Paradise Regained*, by
    Satan, 171-72, 181-82; by Raphael in *PL*,
    see Accommodation, theory of, and liter-
    ary allegory. *See also* Allegory—as
    hidden truth, in Milton
—theory of epic in, 115-18, 144-49. *See also*
    Allegory—and Idea; Castelvetro; Epic
    passim; Mazzoni; Milton, Works—*The
    Reason of Church-Government*; Phillips;
    Tasso—critical theory, influences
—theory of poetry in, 159-60, 163, 313 n.
    56, 317 nn. 1, 4, 322 n. 19, 330 n. 9. *See
    also* Allegory *passim*; Mazzoni; Milton,
    Works—*Of Education*
—typology in, *see* Typology *passim*
Milton, *Paradise Lost. See also* Allegory
    passim
—Abdiel, figure of, in, 165, 215, 232, 239,
    263, 330 n. 18. *See also* Allegory—theo-
    logical
—allegorical "levels" in, 129-31. *See also*
    Allegory—four (or three) senses of,
    —literal level in, —schematic

—allegorical rôle of Satan in, 84, 137, 148-49, 247, 248-49, 318 n. 22. *See also* Allegory—and emblem

—allegorical rôles of Adam and Eve in, 263-64, 266. *See also* Allegory—main-plot, —as moral progress, —psychological

—allegorical rôles of the angels in, *see* Allegory—and supernatural machinery

—allegorical rôles of Sin and Death in, 26-27, 82, 110-11, 117, 123, 124, 126, 130-32, 134, 136-37, 173, 175-76, 216, 229, 234, 240-43, 248-49, 315 n. 3, 315-16 n. 11, 322 n. 15, 323 n. 1. *See also* Allegory—personification, —theological

—allegorized moral themes in, 159-60, 164-65, 213, 219-20, 248-50, 323 n. 25, 333 n. 8. *See also* Allegory—and emblem

—Apocrypha, uses in, *see* Bible—Apocrypha of

—the Bard in, figure of, 231-32

—biblical stylistic influences on: and the apodictic and justificatory modes, juxtaposition of, 151-67, 253, 255, 322 n. 19, 330 n. 15; and the apodictic and justificatory modes in narrations of Michael and Raphael, 200, 210, 280, 330 n. 15; and biblical genres, 208, 213, 229, 235; and plain style, 146, 149, 153, 185, 200, 208, 210, 211, 214-15, 226-27, 233, 235, 241. *See also* Epic—religion and doctrine in, treatment of; Milton, *PL*—modes of "accommodation"

—borrowings in: from Ariosto, *see* Ariosto, *Orlando Furioso*; from Spenser, *see* Spenser, *FQ*; from Tasso, *see* Tasso, *Ger. lib.*

—Chaos allegory in, 126, 130-31, 137, 148, 216, 242, 243, 248, 316 n. 11. *See also* Allegory—fantastic episode, —physical

—convergence of multiple avenues of allegory in, 126-35, 251-56

—credibility in, 265-66; Johnson on, *see* Johnson; in main lines of poem, 126-28, 129, 152-54, 174-75, 224-26, 234; prevailing air of, 232-33; and shifting levels of realism and non-realism in poem, 233-34, 239-43, 248, 333 n. 1; undercutting of, *see* Milton, *PL*—modes of "accommodation"

—deliberate allegory in, 126-29

—epic features and structure in, *see* Epic *passim*

—Garden of Eden in, 243-47. *See also* Allegory—in landscape

—God in, 127, 151, 154-65, 173, 201, 203, 240, 242, 255, 318 n. 22. *See also* Accommodation, theory of, and the representation of God in Scripture; Milton, *PL*—modes of "accommodation"

—homiletic techniques in, *see* Homiletics *passim*

—Invocations in, *see* Epic

—Limbo of Fools in, 110, 126, 134, 137, 149, 196, 198. *See also* Ariosto, *Orlando Furioso*

—Justification of God in, 150-65, 252-53. *See also* Milton—defences of free will, —defences of providence, —Idea in

—modes of "accommodation" in, as radical allegory, 127, 141, 254, 330 n. 15, 332 n. 9; and Eve's dream, 202-3; and figurative or literal, blurring of boundaries, 134, 143, 148-49, 200-203, 228-29, 241-43, 245-46, 333 n. 5; and God and the Son, merged identities, 234-35, 236; and human and divine time, 236; and human-divine relationships, 201, 203; and midrashic linguistic methods in representation of the Word, 8, 213, 236-38, 255, 333 nn. 14, 16; and pseudoliteralism, 148, 173, 234-36, 238, 239-40, 332 n. 9, 333 n. 1; and the representation of God's person, 190, 227-28, 234-38, 240-41, 255, 279, 332 n. 9, 333 n. 16; in the War in Heaven, 192-95, 202-3, 236, 239-40, 243

—Paradise of Fools in, *see* Milton, *PL*—Limbo of Fools

—Raphael, figure of, in, *see* Accommodation, theory of, and literary allegory; Milton, *PL*—War in Heaven

—similes in, 142-44, 148-49, 174, 212, 233, 243-47, 249, 250, 318 n. 22, 333 n. 5

—the Son in, 201, 203, 234-35, 236. *See also* Milton, *PL*—modes of "accommodation"

—Spenserian echo as a form of allegorical allusion in, 246-47

—supernatural machinery in, *see* Allegory—and supernatural machinery

—theoretical critical influences on, *see* Accommodation, theory of, and literary allegory, possible sources for Raphael's discourse; Augustine; Origen; Tasso—critical theory, influences

—typology in, *see* Typology *passim*

—Urania in, *see* Urania

—War in Heaven in, 127, 130, 160, 173, 175-76, 192-95, 198-200, 202-3, 236, 239-40, 243, 333 n. 1. *See also* Milton, *PL*—modes of "accommodation"

Milton, Works
"Adam unparadiz'd" (Trinity MS), 140, 175

An Apology [for] Smectymnuus, 145, 317 n. 6, 320-21 n. 2, 324-25 n. 3

Areopagitica, 103, 140, 153, 156, 164, 310 n. 17, 316 n. 11, 317 n. 15

Of Christian Doctrine, 146, 150-51, 154, 156-57, 159, 171, 181-200 *passim*, 205-10, 218, 222, 227-29, 232, 233, 235, 253,

Milton, Works (*cont.*)
  278-85, 289 n. 30, 315 n. 3, 320 n. 39,
    320-21 n. 2, 321 nn. 10, 14, 322-23 n. 20,
    324-25 n. 3, 325 nn. 8, 11, 12, 15, 329 n.
    22, 330 n. 14, 331-32 n. 3, 332 nn. 2, 5
  Colasterion, 324-25 n. 3
  Comus, 139, 140, 191, 264, 284, 320 n. 2
  The Doctrine and Discipline of Divorce,
    324-25 n. 3
  Of Education, 77, 115, 138, 158, 208, 254,
    317 nn. 4, 10, 320-21 n. 2, 330 n. 8
  Eikonoklastes, 320 n. 2
  Familiar Letters, 317 n. 12, 321 n. 2
  "De Idea Platonica", 320 n. 2
  "Lycidas", 140, 206, 329 n. 20
  "Mansus", 141, 318 n. 19
  Marginalia, 318 n. 17, 328 n. 11
  "Nativity Ode", 212
  Paradise Lost, see Milton, *Paradise Lost*
  Paradise Regained, 135, 171-72, 181-82, 206,
    211, 213, 214, 264, 320 n 2
  "Il Penseroso", 140
  Prolusions, 320 n. 2
  The Reason of Church-Government, 138-40,
    145-46, 154, 183, 198, 203, 254, 312 n.
    32, 319 n. 24, 320 nn. 33, 37, 321 n. 2,
    324-25 n. 3, 325 n. 17, 328 n. 12
  Of Reformation, 114-15, 145, 320 n. 37, 328
    n. 12
  Samson Agonistes, 139, 140, 142, 183, 206,
    319 n. 24
  Sonnets, 142, 206, 320 n. 2
  Tetrachordon, 320 n. 2
Mollenkott, Virginia R., 332 n. 4
Montgomery, Robert L., 260
Morley, Henry, editor of Tasso, 319 n. 23
Murrin, Michael, 64-65, 258-59, 260, 271,
  285, 292 n. 1, 297 nn. 22, 29, 298 nn. 31,
  40, 302 nn. 13, 19, 20, 303 nn. 24, 25, 304
  n. 28, 307 n. 14, 309-10 n. 9

Nash, Ralph, 300 n. 1
Nelson, T.G.A., 298 nn. 29, 40
Nelson, William, 264, 296 n. 45, 310 n. 15
Newton, Thomas, editor of Milton, 318 n. 22
Nimshal, see Midrash
Nobili, Flaminio, correspondent of Tasso,
  65, 66, 302 n. 13, 302-3 n. 24, 304 nn. 28,
  29

Odysseus, *see* Epic—of active life, —of
  contemplative life; Homer, epics of
Olini, Lucia, 259
Origen, 8-9, 10, 11, 13, 14, 18, 20, 178,
  196-99, 289 n. 31, 294 n. 11; as indirect
  source for Raphael's discourse in *PL*,
  196-98, 289 n. 29. *See also* Bible—alle-
  gorization on certain Books

Osanna, Francesco, early publisher of
  Tasso, 259, 273
Ovid, *Metamorphoses* of: as subject of Ren-
  aissance allegoresis, 4, 35, 36, 37, 131,
  181. *See also* Reynolds; Sandys
Ovide Moralisé, 5, 38
The Oxford Classical Dictionary, 288 n. 9

Panofsky, Erwin, 299 n. 3
Parable, *see* Allegory—parabolic (as fourth
  or figurative) sense in secular
Parker, William Riley, 317 n. 6
Patrides, C.A., 284, 323 n. 8, 326 n. 27, 332
  n. 8
Patterson, Annabel, 257-58, 263-64, 299 n.
  3, 319 n. 25
Paul, Saint, "Apostle of the Gentiles", 48,
  49, 154, 223, 329 n. 24
Peacham, Henry: theories of allegory in,
  24-27, 38, 53, 295 nn. 29, 30, 34, 35, 328
  n. 14. *See also* Allegory *passim*
Pépin, Jean, 6, 14, 32, 291 n. 52, 297 n. 19
Phillips, Edward, biographer and nephew
  of Milton, 115, 119, 120, 183, 230; and
  Milton, 183, 312 n. 32; on theory of epic
  and allegory, 111-14, 144-45, 176, 253, 320
  n. 31, 334 nn. 3, 4
Philo: (on Genesis), 9, 10, 20, 43-44, 45,
  209, 237, 294 n. 10, 299 n. 4; importance
  to Milton, 9, 44, 289 n. 27; midrashic
  parallels to 44, 237, 294 n. 10, 299 n. 4,
  333 n. 16; Milton on, 324 n. 3. *See also*
  Midrash—radical linguistic methods
Pico della Mirandola, 196-97, 298 n. 29, 328
  n. 9
Plato: *Charmides* of, 301 n. 8; different
  concepts of "Idea" in, 263-64, 320-21 n.
  2; as ethical source for Renaissance
  allegorizers, 5, 56-62, 273, 329 n. 24; as
  ethical source for Tasso's "Allegoria del
  Poema" (to *Ger. lib.*), 56-62; importance
  in Milton's thought, 191-92, 195-96, 320
  n. 2, 327 n. 1; and medieval aesthetic
  theory, 329 n. 24; *Republic* of, 58-59, 61;
  Tasso on, 72, 302 nn. 13, 15. *See also*
  Allegory—and Idea, —Platonic; Aris-
  totle, synthesis of thought with Plato's;
  Imitation, Ideal; Tasso, Works—*Lettere*
Plotinus, 196, 327 n. 6
Plutarch: Tasso on, 53, 301 n. 3
Pommrich, Ewald, 318 n. 22
Pope, Alexander, 119, 269
Porphyry, 4-5, 9, 55, 196, 287-88 n. 8, 290
  n. 45; Tasso on, 53, 301 n. 3. *See also*
  Allegory—Neoplatonic
Praz, Mario, 268, 318 n. 22
Preaching, *see* Homiletics
Preston, Claire, 300 n. 10
Prince, F.T., 318 n. 21, 319 n. 23

Proclus, 196; Tasso on, 53, 301 n. 3
Prudentius: *Psychomachia* of, 64, 290 n. 36,
  302 n. 21
Puttenham, George: theories of allegory
  in, 24-27, 38, 133, 295 nn. 28, 33, 34, 35,
  315 n. 7, 328 n. 14. *See also* Allegory
  passim

Quilligan, Maureen, 310 n. 9, 315-16 n. 11
Quintilian, 3, 133, 287 nn. 1, 3, 290 n. 34

Racine, François, 112, 178
Radzinowicz, Mary Ann, 280, 283, 328 n.
  17, 329 n. 20, 330 n. 15, 332 n. 8
Raleigh, Sir Walter, 104. *See also* Spenser,
  Works—"Letter to Raleigh"
Raphael, Sanzio (Rafaello d'Urbino),
  painter, 300 n. 13, 322 n. 16, 331 n. 2
  (chap. 19)
Reformation, 8-10, 13, 171-73, 185, 207,
  222-30 *passim*, 255-56, 276, 278-81. *See
  also* Accommodation *passim*; Allegory
  passim; Bible *passim*; Homiletics *passim*;
  Typology *passim*
Renwick, W.L., 270, 274
Reynolds, Henry, 19, 23, 35, 37, 269, 298 n.
  31. *See also* Allegory *passim*
Rhu, Lawrence L., 258-59, 271, 304 n. 31,
  305-6 n. 18, 320 n. 41
Rich, Townsend, 298 n. 29
Robins, Harry Franklin, 289 n. 27
Robortello, Francesco, 307 n. 14
Roche, Thomas P., Jr., 286, 298 n. 39, 328
  n. 9
Roitman, Betty, 333 n. 14
Roman de la Rose, 290 n. 36
Rosenthal, Erwin I.J., 288-89 n. 20
Rymer, Thomas, 107, 109, 178-80, 316 n. 11.
  See also Allegory—suspicion of

Sadler, Lynn V., 283
de Saint-Évremond, Charles de Saint-
  Denis, 106-7, 179
Salutati, Coluccio, 6, 30, 42, 44, 55, 293 nn.
  3, 4, 294 nn. 8, 13, 295 nn. 15, 16, 17, 20,
  299 n. 4; *De laboribus Herculis* of, 19-22,
  293 nn. 3, 4, 6, 294 nn. 7, 8, 11, 295 nn.
  17, 18, 20; *Epistolario* of, 19-22, 293 n. 3,
  293-94 n. 7, 294 nn. 8, 13, 295 nn. 15, 16,
  20; theories on allegory of, 19-22, 23, 24,
  71, 74, 133, 293-94 n. 7, 294 nn. 8, 9, 11,
  295 nn. 20, 21, 323 n. 8. *See also* Allegory
  passim
Samuel, Irene, 150, 191
Sandys, George, translator and allegorizer
  of Ovid, 4, 35, 37, 131, 181
Scalabrino, Luca, correspondent of Tasso,
  65, 66, 302 n. 24, 303 n. 25

Seneca, *Hercules Furens* of, 293 n. 3. *See also*
  Salutati, *De laboribus Herculis*
Shawcross, John T., 286, 312 n. 23, 326 n.
  24
Shepherd, Geoffrey, 46-47, 293 n. 4, 296 n.
  3, 299 nn. 3, 7, 305 n. 2
The Shorter Oxford English Dictionary, 3
Sidney, Sir Philip, 48, 180, 191, 268; *An
  Apology for Poetry* of, 45-47, 70-71, 299
  nn. 1, 2, 3, 7, 300 nn. 16, 17, 305 n. 2, 314
  n. 1; *The Countesse of Pembrokes Arcadia*
  of, 46-47, 57, 58, 299 n. 7, 299-300 n. 10,
  300 n. 13; theories on poetry and alle-
  gory of, 27, 45-48, 49, 57, 58, 77, 78, 79,
  150, 265, 293 n. 4, 296 n. 3, 299 nn. 1, 2,
  3, 314 n. 1. *See also* Allegory *passim*;
  Imitation; Imitation, Ideal; Tasso—crit-
  ical theory, influences
Silvestris, Bernardus: theories on allegory,
  6, 288 n. 15, 293 n. 2
Sims, James H., 326 n. 24
Singleton, Charles, 10, 12, 13-17, 287 n. 3,
  289 n. 34, 290 nn. 37, 40, 291 nn. 51, 59,
  292 nn. 64, 65
Smalley, Beryl, 9-10, 12, 275, 289 n. 32, 290
  nn. 37, 43, 46, 48
Smith, J.C., 267
Solerti, Angelo, editor of Tasso, 259, 261
Sozzi, B.T., 260
Spenser, Edmund, 292 n. 1; comparative
  dates of Tasso/Spenser publications,
  272-74. *See also* Ariosto; Aristotle; Ho-
  mer; Imitation, Ideal; Plato; Virgil
Spenser, *The Faerie Queene. See also* Alle-
  gory *passim*
—allegorical rôles of Arthur, Duessa, Ar-
  chimago and other principal characters
  in, 97-99, 101-2, 139, 140, 246, 248, 249,
  264, 270, 310 n. 15
—borrowings from Tasso in, *see* Tasso,
  Ger. lib.
—denigration of by neoclassical English
  critics, 107-8, 109, 110, 179, 311 n. 3
—early plans for, 101-2, 270, 272-73
—epic structure and features in, *see* Epic
  passim
—evolution of theories of allegory for,
  95-105, 267-74. *See also* Spenser, Works—
  "Letter to Raleigh"; Tasso—critical the-
  ory, influences
—figure of Error in, as source for Milton's
  Sin, 136-37, 316 n. 11
—influences, and borrowings from: in
  Milton, *PL*, 100, 103, 105, 108, 128, 134-37,
  140, 149, 161, 246-48, 251-52, 254, 315-16
  n. 11, 316 n. 12, 317 n. 6
—influence of Tasso upon, *see* Tasso, *Ger.
  lib.*—borrowings from
—Milton on, 103, 140, 310 n. 17

Spenser (*cont.*)
—Phillips on, 112
—*Wood of Error* in, 84, 136-37, 164
Spenser, Works:
  Amoretti, 271
  The Faerie Queene, see Spenser, *The Faerie Queene*
  Fowre Hymnes, 271
  "Letter to Raleigh", 39, 97, 100-105, 181, 223, 269-71, 273-74, 296 n. 45, 298 n. 41, 309 n. 8, 310 nn. 10, 15, 311 n. 2
  Mutabilitie Cantos, 271
  The Shepheardes Calender, 271
  Sonnet to Lord Burleigh, 23, 295 n. 10
Spingarn, J.E., 29, 296 n. 3
Steadman, John M., 135, 140, 264-66, 292 n. 1, 297 n. 29, 300 n. 13, 309 n. 9, 311 n. 18, 315 n. 10, 317 n. 10, 319 n. 24, 320 n. 32, 321 nn. 6, 8, 321-22 n. 15, 332 n. 19
Stern, David, 332 n. 10, 333 n. 11
Sumner, Charles, Bishop, translator of Milton's *Of Christian Doctrine*, 289 n. 30
Sylvester, Joshua, translator of du Bartas, 150

Tasso, Bernardo, father of Torquato Tasso, 273
Tasso, Torquato, 4, 5, 6, 41, 120, 295 n. 24. *See also* Allegory *passim*; Aristotle; Imitation—as theory of external representation; Imitation, Ideal; Manso; Nobili; Plato; Scalabrino
—allegorical vocabulary special to, *see* Allegory—marvels, marvellous, marvellous-verisimilar; Epic—verisimilar, truth of the
—annotated list of some earlier editions of, 261-62
—and Castelvetro and Mazzoni, 115-18, 175, 254, 260, 262, 274, 306 n. 27, 312-13 n. 40. *See also* Tasso, Works—*Estratti dalla Poetica di . . . Castelvetro*
—comparative dates of Tasso/Spenser publications, 272-74
—under Counter-Reformation, 257, 258
—critical literature on, in English, 257-61
—critical theory of, influences: on eighteenth-century English critics, 110; on Milton, 94, 95, 106, 108, 111-18, 128, 138-40, 141, 143-49, 253-54, 260-61, 262, 267-68, 317 n. 8; on seventeenth-century English critics, 107-8, 111-15, 311 n. 2, 320 n. 31; (possible) on Sidney, 300 nn. 16, 17; on Spenser, 54, 95, 96-103, 144, 254, 260-61, 269-74, 300 n. 16, 309 n. 8, 310 n. 21
—evolution of theories on allegory, 53-94, 97, 257-61, 263-64, 270-74, 302 n. 13. *See also* Tasso, *Ger. lib.*—allegorical development

—and Milton connection, *see* Toland
—Milton on, 138, 139, 141, 146, 318 n. 19, 320 n. 32. *See also* Milton, Works—"Mansus"
—Milton's oeuvre in parallel with, *see* Milton
—reputation of in England, 97, 261, 267-69, 273, 309 n. 8
—Spenser on, 269. *See also* Spenser, Works—"Letter to Raleigh"
Tasso, *Gerusalemme liberata. See also* Allegory *passim*; Tasso—evolution of theories on allegory; Tasso, Works—"Allegoria del Poema" (to *Ger. lib.*)
—allegorical development of and revisions to, 66-67, 69, 76, 91, 147, 257-59, 261, 271-73, 302 n. 13, 303-4 n. 24, 304 nn. 31, 34, 306 n. 21. *See also* Allegory—as "metaphora continuata", Tasso on structural problems; Tasso, Works—*Gerusalemme conquistata*; Tasso, *Ger. lib.*, as revised in *Gerusalemme conquistata*
—allegorical rôles of Godfrey, Rinaldo, Tancredi, Ismen, Armida and others in, 84, 92-93, 98, 101, 132, 139, 148, 267, 269, 303 n. 24, 303-4 n. 27, 304 n. 30, 305-6 n. 18, 318 n. 22
—borrowings from: in Milton, *PL*, 108, 141-44, 149, 260-61, 267, 268, 318-19 n. 22, 319 n. 23; in Spenser, *FQ*, 66, 97, 99, 139, 14, 143, 260-61, 267-68, 273, 274, 307 n. 142, 309 n. 8, 318 n. 22, 319 n. 23
—denigration of by seventeenth-century English critics, 104, 107-8
—early publishing history of, 261, 262, 271-73
—epic structure and features in, *see* Epic *passim*; Milton—oeuvre of, in parallel with Tasso's
—garden of Armida in, 142, 143, 267, 273
—influence of on Milton's verse, 142, 318 n. 21
—Italian allegorizers of, 262
—as revised in the *Gerusalemme conquistata*, 88-90, 309 n. 39
—similes in, 142
—structural parallels to, in Milton, *PL*, 143-44, 149, 319 nn. 24, 25
—translations of, 268, 300-301 n. 1
Tasso, Works
  "Allegoria del Poema" (to *Ger. lib.*), 47-49, 54-67, 69-70, 71, 75, 76, 78, 85, 90, 92-93, 96-98, 100-101, 105, 114, 124, 139, 144, 146, 153, 154, 163, 257-62, 268, 269, 271-72, 273-74, 286, 300 nn. 16, 17, 300-301 n. 1, 303 n. 25, 304 nn. 28, 30, 321 nn. 11, 13; 323 n. 24; compositional and publication history of, 258-60, 261, 262

"Allegoria del *Rinaldo*", 71-72, 258, 262, 273
Aminta, 141, 271; cited by Spenser, 269
Apologia, 55, 77-78, 273
Della differenze poetiche, 81, 274
Discorsi dell'arte poetica, 53, 72, 73, 75, 76, 83, 97, 101, 146, 257-60, 263, 270, 271, 272, 273-74, 300 n. 17, 305 nn. 2, 18, 309 n. 8, 312 n. 8, 320 n. 42; compositional relationship of, to *Discorsi del poema eroico*, 257-58; potential for allegory in, 258
Discorsi del poema eroico, 53-55, 57-58, 63, 67, 69-90, 91-93, 97, 100-101, 105, 107, 112-13, 119, 120, 139, 144-49, 150-51, 257-60, 263, 269, 270, 272, 274, 300 n. 16, 300-301 n. 1, 301 n. 3, 302 n. 15, 305 nn. 2, 13, 306 nn. 21, 27, 307 nn. 2, 3, 14, 15, 309 n. 8, 310 n. 21, 311 nn. 2, 18, 312 n. 38, 318 n. 21, 320 nn. 31, 32, 34, 37, 38, 329 n. 21, 333 n. 1; compositional relationship of, to *Discorsi dell'arte poetica*, 257-58
Discorso sopra . . . Patricio, 77, 306 n. 22
Estratti dalla Poetica di . . . Castelvetro, 82, 86, 116, 307 n. 8, 312-13 n. 40
Il Ficino, 263
Il forno overro della nobiltà, 310 n. 19
Gerusalemme conquistata, 84, 88-90, 141-42, 259, 309 n. 39
Gerusalemme liberata, see Tasso, *Gerusalemme liberata*
Del Giudizio sovra la Gerusalemme, 55, 57, 63, 67, 69, 70-71, 74, 75, 78, 83, 84, 85, 88-90, 92, 150, 260, 305 n. 16, 307 n. 17, 308 n. 35, 309 n. 39
Lettere, 53-55, 58, 59, 63-68, 69, 75, 76, 77, 82, 83, 85, 89, 91, 96, 97, 101, 146, 147, 257-60, 262, 267, 271-74, 287 n. 5, 295 n. 24, 301 nn. 2, 3, 4, 302 nn. 13, 18, 303 nn. 24, 25, 304 nn. 28, 34, 35, 306 n. 21, 309 n. 8, 319 n. 26
"Lettere poetiche", see *Lettere*
Il Manso, ovvero dell'Amicizia, 318 n. 19
Il Messaggiero, 143, 263, 319 n. 25
Il Re Torrismondo, 142, 318 n. 21
Rime, 141, 271
Il Rinaldo, 71-72, 101, 258, 267, 270, 271, 272, 274, 305 n 8; cited by Spenser, 269, 273. See also Tasso, Works— "Allegoria del *Rinaldo*"
Risposta . . . Al . . . Lombardelli, 78, 85-86, 88, 273, 306 n. 30, 308 n. 18
Le sette giornate del Mondo Creato, 142, 269, 271, 318 n. 21
Della Virtù Eroica, 301 n. 7
Teskey, Gordon, 310 nn. 10, 20, 316 n. 11, 318 n. 18
Todd, Henry, editor of Milton, 318-19 n. 22

Toland, John, biographer of Milton, 119, 120, 176, 225; on Milton, *PL*, 113-15, 175, 253, 334 n. 3; on Tasso-Manso-Milton connection, 114, 141. See also Allegory— and Idea
Toscanella, Orazio, allegorizer of Ariosto, 37, 264, 298 n. 32, 310 n. 15, 311 n. 2
Treip, Mindele Anne, 295 n. 31, 300 n. 13, 315 n. 3, 316 n. 12, 320 n. 44, 322 n. 16, 323 n. 22, 331 n. 2 (chap. 19), 333 n. 8
Trissino, Giangiorgio, *Italia liberata dai Goti* of, 108, 178, 258
Tuve, Rosemond, 16, 24-27, 95, 98, 105, 200, 252, 275, 284, 287 n. 4, 292 n. 66, 295 n. 30, 296 n. 44
Typology (or typological reading of Bible), 8, 10-12, 45, 129, 130, 146, 173, 195, 199, 204-21, 280, 290 n. 36, 292 n. 1, 329 n. 19, 333 n. 16
—"abuses" of, 285-86
—"allegorical" (term) in, understood as second or prophetic sense in allegory, 13, 223, 290 n. 36; Satan on, in *Paradise Regained*, 171-72
—Aquinas on, 10
—Augustine on, 303-4 n. 27, 327 n. 6
—correlative types in, see Typology—expanded forms of
—expanded forms of: Milton dismissive of, 286; and moral allegory, close relation to, 283, 286 (see also Homiletics— free use of Old Testament types in); problems raised in reading into Milton, *PL*, 206-8, 211-20 passim, 228, 282, 284-86; in recent readings of Milton, *PL*, 183, 200-201, 204-7, 213-17, 282-86, 326 n. 24; in Reformation exegesis, 207, 222-25, 228, 282-83, 321 n. 1; restricted in Milton, *PL*, 181, 185-86, 207-8, 210-18, 284, 324-25 n. 3, 326 n. 24; in seventeenth-century devotional verse, 206-7, 282, 284
—"figure" (or figural prophecy) in, as term for true historical type in, 10, 209, 290 n. 36; in Donne, 277; in Milton, *PL*, 209
—fundamental historical types (figures or events) in, 209; Milton on, in *Of Christian Doctrine*, 209, 228; as used in Milton, *PL*, 209-10, 228
—historical allegory in literature seen as analogy to, see Allegory—in Bible, as model for poetic figuration
—historical avenues of: Alexandrine or New Testament kind, 208-9, 216-18, 219-20; as employed in Milton, *PL*, 211, 217-18, 220-21; patristic (messianic or Old Testament kind), of two sorts, 208-9, 216-18
—literal historical "types" in: in Donne, 277; Milton on, in *Of Christian Doctrine*,

Typology (*cont.*)
181, 185-87, 205, 207-8, 218, 220, 305 n.
39, 324-25 n. 3, 325 n. 17; in Milton, *PL*,
130, 181, 186, 207-8, 210, 214-15, 218, 220,
221, 229, 255, 275, 326 n. 24; in Milton,
Paradise Regained, 206, 214
—literal level, importance in, 172
—and midrash, 333 n. 16
—Milton on correct practice of, in *Of
Christian Doctrine*, 185-87, 325 n. 15
—and moral allegory (tropology), to be
distinguished, 208-9, 286
—and the reading of Milton, *PL*, 282-86.
See also Typology—expanded forms of
—and the reading of Tasso, *Ger. lib.*, 259,
286
—and rôles of Adam, Eve and Michael in
Milton, *PL*, 209, 210, 214, 215
—type-antitype relation in, 172, 205-6; in
Milton, *PL*, 209-12, 214-18; in Reforma-
tion exegesis, 283 (*see also* Typology—
expanded forms of)
—and typologically suggestive patternings
in Milton, *PL*, as forms of allegory, 208,
212-21
—word "type" in Milton, use of, 188, 205,
208, 209-10
—words "type" or "typical" in, referring
to theological sense in allegory, *see* Ty-
pology—"allegorical" (term) in. *See also*
Allegory—"type" or "typick" sense in
secular

Uhrbach, Ephraim E., 289 n. 31
Ullman, Berthold L., 293 nn. 3, 4
Urania, muse of Christian poetry: in

Dante, 300 n. 13; in Milton, *PL*, 154, 232,
300 n. 13, 322 n. 16, 331 n. 2; in Raphael,
painter, 300 n. 13, 322 n. 16; in Sidney,
The Countesse of Pembrokes Arcadia, 47,
300 n. 13; in Spenser's poetry, 300 n. 13

Vermes, G., 288 n. 20
Victorine mystics, 10, 12, 196-200. *See also*
Allegory—and universal correspon-
dences, theory of; Hugh of Saint-Victor;
Richard of Saint-Victor
Victorinus, Marius, 196
Virgil, 86, 108, 140, 141, 146, 175, 268, 312 n.
29; as character in Dante, *Commedia* of,
17; Milton on, 138
Virgil, *Aeneid* of, as subject of earlier
allegoresis, 6, 8, 9, 41, 48-49, 61, 65, 102,
103, 107, 128, 132, 165, 263, 270-71, 288 n.
13, 291-92 n. 6, 310 n. 9; Addison on, 110;
Castelvetro on, 116; Le Bossu on, 125, 314
n. 6, 315 n. 27; Milton on, 140; Spenser
on, 98, 100-102, 269, 274, 288 n. 13; Tasso
on, 66, 72-73, 86, 303 n. 24. *See also*
Landino

Waldock, A.J.A., 332 n. 7
Waller, Edmund, 173-74, 323 n. 3
Weinberg, Bernard, 260, 262, 293 n. 4, 299
n. 3, 300-301 n. 1, 302 n. 11, 306 n. 22,
307 n. 7, 313 nn. 56, 59
Weismiller, Edward, 318 n. 22
Werman, Golda Spier, 332 n. 4
Wetherbee, Winthrop, 6-7, 287 n. 18
Wilkes, G.A., 321-22 n. 15
Wolfe, Don M., 328 n. 12
Wolfson, Harry Austryn, 333 n. 16